Hablot Knight Browne, Augustus Septimus Mayhew

Paved with Gold

The Romance and Reality of the Streets of London

Hablot Knight Browne, Augustus Septimus Mayhew

Paved with Gold
The Romance and Reality of the Streets of London

ISBN/EAN: 9783744674195

Printed in Europe, USA, Canada, Australia, Japan

Cover: Foto ©Thomas Meinert / pixelio.de

More available books at **www.hansebooks.com**

Paved with Gold

OR

THE ROMANCE AND REALITY OF THE

STREETS OF LONDON

BY

AUGUSTUS MAYHEW

TWENTY-SIX ETCHINGS BY PHIZ

DOWNEY & CO., Limited

12 YORK STREET, COVENT GARDEN, LONDON

1899

CONTENTS.

Book the Third.

THE ROAD TO RUIN.

CONTENTS

LIST OF ILLUSTRATIONS.

———◆———

PAVED WITH GOLD.

———◆———

CHAPTER I.

A CROWD.

A KENSINGTON 'bus first pulled up, then a hansom, then a parcels delivery cart, then a Chaplin and Horne's van, then a "Royal Blue," an "Atlas," and two perambulators.

Her Majesty's police-van was the only vehicle that drove by, and the gentleman in uniform who daily takes the air in the open cupboard at the end, continued to read his penny "Morning Star" undisturbed by the stoppage and the crowd.

The black windowless omnibus divided for a few seconds the attention of the throng in the road and on the pavement.

The Kensington driver asked the police coachman, "What's yer fare all the way, my proosshun blue?"

The Atlas cad shouted out to the police conductor, "Won't any of your inside gents be so good as to ride outside to oblige a lady?"

Not only was the roadway blocked, but the pavement was covered by a mob, huddled together as closely as rats in a corner. It was a bitter, frosty winter's day, with an easterly wind blowing, that, as you faced it, filled the eyes with water, and made them smart like hartshorn; but, despite the cold, the black circle of the crowd seemed every moment to acquire an additional circumference of curious passengers. Where the people came from was a marvel. They seemed to leak in from all sides. Yet hardly any out of the scores that had collected together knew why they were stopping, or could even get a peep at the principal object of attraction.

"What's up, Jim?" said one of the 'bus drivers to his conductor, as the latter was returning to his bracket after diving into the mob. "Is it cream o' the walley or fits as has overcome the lady?"

It was the dusk of the evening, and though the streets were thinned of their work-a-day traffic, the policeman had no sooner said to a woman seated on the door-step, "Now then, this won't do; you must move on, you know," than instantly every person who was passing the spot was brought to a dead halt. There were City gentlemen going home to dinner, and nurses wheeling the children home to tea; clerks and linendrapers' assistants going back to business; bricklayers with empty hods, ticket porters with their hands in their pockets, men about town, street boys, private soldiers, bill-stickers, return postmen, "roughs," and costers, and, indeed, the same incongruous mass that is always to be found in a London crowd; for, as each person came drifting up the street, he seemed to be turned suddenly round by his curiosity, like a cork in a pent stream, so that ere long the mob appeared to consist of the same curious collection of odds and ends—human chips, straws, and rags, as it were—as is seen jumbled together in front of a miller's dam.

The most important business gave way to the excitement. There was a confectioner's man with an ice pudding in the green box on his head, and that pudding, so slowly thawing into liquor in the heated atmosphere of the mob, had been ordered for a neighbouring dinner party, which had already eaten its way down to the game. There was an electric telegraph boy with his despatch-box at his side, containing a most important commercial message, which had just arrived by the submarine telegraph. There was a doctor's boy, with his little double-flapped market-basket, and he in a peevish voice was calling on the crowd to take care and "not go smashing his aperients." There was a milliner's lad, too, with his oil-silk covered basket, in which was carefully packed an elaborate head-dress for a lady, who, attired for the theatre, was anxiously watching for the arrival of the messenger, and yet there he was, jammed in the crowd, calling out every minute, "Where are you a shoving to, stoopid?" and "Now then, keep back there, can't you, or you'll be a squashing this here turband and feathers." And there was a host of other people besides upon equally pressing errands. But every kind of business and work appeared to have come to a standstill until each looker-on had been able to satisfy himself as to the cause why he, among a hundred others, was loitering there.

A milkman who was near the centre of the crowd remarked to an elderly dame, as the policeman shook the wretched creature on the door-step, "She don't seem like an impostor, do she?"

"Well, there's no telling, I'm sure," replied the lady; "but, if you ask me my private opinion, I should say she's been foolish enough to allow herself to be overtook by liquor."

"Come, you mustn't be sitting here in the cold, do you hear? Where do you live?" cried the officer, as he took the woman roughly by the arm.

She looked up with a vacant, sleepy expression, and muttered, "Nowhere."

A carpenter, with a nut-basket of tools over his shoulder, here stepped forward, and asked, in a kindly tone, "Ain't you got no lodgings, my good woman?"

"I was turned out of them two days ago," was the almost inaudible reply, for she spoke in so low a tone that her interrogator had to put his ear down to her bonnet to catch her words.

"But haven't you got any friends, who'll take you in?" continued the workman.

"No, no; I'm a stranger here." And her chin and under lip began to work with the rising sobs.

A man in the mob said coarsely to his companion, "Oh, come on Bill, it's only a dodge." And the doctor's boy, seeing somebody quitting the crowd, suddenly thought of the powder he had in his basket for the baby in convulsions, and darted off at full speed.

"Well, you know," said the policeman, "if you persist in stopping here, I must take you to the station."

"Oh, thank you—anywhere," was the woman's reply.

The policeman stood still, uncertain how to act, and the crowd began to discuss among themselves the merits of the case; some declared that she was "fairly starved down," others, "that she was only trying to excite compassion so as to get some drink out of it." A few of the more sensible, however, said she was ill, and that she ought to be taken to the doctor's directly.

"If that young woman," exclaimed one, "were well fed and decently dressed, she'd be as tidy a looking girl as you could meet with in these parts."

"You should take her to the workhouse," observed the carpenter; upon which a man, with a pair of boot-fronts under his arm, burst out vehemently, saying, "It's the right of every true-born Briton to have food and shelter give 'em, and I mean to say as it's a cussed shame that any poor creature should be left to starve like a dog in the streets, as this here party is."

Then there was a cry among the mob of "Ah! so it is indeed," as if the thought had only just struck them all.

"I tell you they won't take her in at the Union," expostulated the policeman, in answer to a hundred and one directions, "and I can't charge her at the station. Here, come along with me, young woman; the only place for you is the 'sylum for the houseless in Playhouse Yard."

As she did not attempt to move, but was settling down as if going to sleep again, the officer took hold of her arm to help her to rise; but the miserable woman was so weak and faint with the cold and starvation, that she was unable to stand, and staggered back on to the step.

"Shame! shame!" cried the mob, growing indignant with the thought that she was to be dragged as a criminal through the streets. "Why don't you go and fetch a doctor, Bobby?" shouted a coster; "you see the poor thing can't step it."

One of the neighbours, who, with her shawl turned over her head, had been standing on the next door-step, patiently watching the whole of the proceedings, now made her appearance with a cup of steaming tea in her hand.

"Here, my dear," she said, as she stooped down and held a saucerful to the lips of the poor soul, "drink this; it'll do you more good than listening to a pack of men's talk."

The wretched, fainting creature sipped at the hot drink, and, though she seemed to swallow with difficulty at first, she said, in a short time, "Oh, thank you! thank you! that warms me a bit." And then, after a few more sips, she passed her hand over her forehead like one waking up from stupor, and, as she pushed the hair back, murmured, "I've had enough, I'm obliged to you; I can go now."

The policeman led her off, grasping her firmly under the arm, and half pushing her along, as though he were taking a "drunk and disorderly" to the station-house. The woman staggered in her gait, and seemed so helpless, that many among the crowd, gazing after her, were still divided in their opinion as to whether she were in liquor or in want. A host of little boys and straggling men and women followed in her wake along the pavement, like the sympathizing crowd at the tail of an Irish funeral.

"Ah! she's seen better days, she has," said the kind-hearted dame who had brought out the tea, and who, with the cup still in her hand, was looking after her. "Her talk warn't like that of a common person; and them hands of hern ain't done much work."

A crowd of female neighbours began to collect round the last speaker, and one observed, "I really think, do you know, Mrs. Perks, she had nothing on but that black stuff petticoat, and that she'd made away with the very gownd off her back. Why, it's enough to freeze all her blood to ice in such weather as this here."

A thin woman, with a dry cough, observed, with a contemptuous toss of her cap, "Well, all I've got to say is this one remark: If she's so very genteel as you ladies would wish to implicate, why don't she go to her friends? Surely they might help her at least to emigrand. But this I will say, if a piece of goods like her is to meet with rewards for miscondick—for every mother of a family among you must have noticed the situation she was in, and not so much as a wedding-ring to be seen on her finger—why, where'd be the use of females remaining virtuous and being circumspicious in their behaviour, like ourselves?"

"Shame on yer, Mrs. Sparrar!" ejaculated the dame with the tea-cup; "I hope it may never be your lot to be so sittewated yourself and have a person to sit in judgment, jury and witnesses, on you, as you've been a doing to her, poor soul."

It was, however, too cold to continue the discussion; so Mrs. Sparrow and the neighbours retired to their respective homes to talk the matter over with their husbands and fellow-lodgers.

CHAPTER II.

FROZEN OUT.

It was a bitter winter's day. The snow had fallen thickly during the night, whilst all London was asleep, and the early waker in the suburbs, as he lay in his bed wondering what made the road so still and the morning light so bright, heard the song of the market carter, that without the rumble of a wheel he had traced creeping from the distance, cease suddenly, and followed by a cry of " Here, police! come along, lock sharp!" Then, as his curiosity sent him shivering to the window, he saw in the dawn the black, steaming horse stretched at full length upon the white roadway, kicking up the powdery snow like foam, with the carter leaning on its neck, and the piles of green cabbages in the cart all dabbed with flakes of snow.

On the other hand, the heavier sleeper in the town was roused out of his last nap by the sound of shovels scraping harshly on the pavement, as if a hundred knife-grinders were at work in the street ; and others, who dozed still later, had their dreams abruptly cut in two by some dozen cadgers from the nearest low lodging-house, who, with a frost-tipped bit of green stuff raised on a pole, were all shouting together, at the top of their voices, " Poor froze-out gard'ners ! poor froze-out gard'ners !"

Truly there is hardly a more startling sight than to wake up and find the town, which yesterday was black with its winter's coat of soot and dirt, suddenly changed to a city of silver, seeming as if it were some monster capital at the Polar regions, glittering with its glacial architecture, and bristling with its monuments, pinnacles, and towers, like so many palaces and temples hewn out of ice. Every house-top seems to be newly thatched with the virgin flocks, and every cornice striped as if with a trimming of the fairest down. All the verandahs are as white as a tent-top, and the railings look as if made out of pith rather than ironwork; every window-sill, and, indeed, the least ledge on which the foamy powder can lie, is thick and bulging with its layer of alabaster-like particles. On each door-step is spread the whitest possible mat, and each street-lamp is crowned with a nightcap of the purest fleece, whilst the huge coloured lamps over the chemist's seem gaudier than ever, and their blue and red bull's-eyes look like huge gems set massively amid lumps of frosted silver.

The various signs over the tradesmen's shops are nearly blotted out by the drift that has clung to them. The monster golden boot above the shoemaker's is silvered over on the side next the wind; the "little dustpans" are filled with a pile of white fluff; the golden fleece, hanging over the hosiers' shops, seems to have changed its metallic coat for one of the purest wool; the three balls at the pawnbroker's appear to have been converted into a triad of gelder-roses; and the great carved lions and unicorns between the first-floor windows of the royal tradesmen, have huge dabs of snow resting on their necks, like thick, white, matted manes.

The surface of the earth itself is white as a wedding-cake. In the roadway, in the early morning, you can count the traffic by the ruts the wheels have made, for every one leaves behind it a glistening trail as if some monster snail had crawled along the way. What a change, too, has taken place in the tumult of the busiest thoroughfares! The streets that formerly deafened you with their noise are now hushed as night, and everything that moves past is silent as an apparition. Even the big clots of snow that keep on falling from the copings and the lamps and trees, startle you, from the utter absence of all sound, as they strike the earth. The wheels of the heaviest carts seem to be muffled, and roll on as if they were passing over the softest moss. The horses go along with their hoofs spluttering where the trodden ground has been caked into slipperiness, and the drivers walk at their head, with their hand upon the rein, while the nervous, timid brutes steam with the unusual labour, and their breath gushes down from their nostrils in absolute rays of mist.

It is at this period, too, that the ice-cart makes its appearance in the streets. The costermonger, who can no longer drive his trade at the green-markets, now looks to the pond for a living, and comes to town with a load of transparent splintery fragments, that seem like jagged pieces of broken plate-glass windows. The omnibuses have an extra horse put on when they reach the metropolitan hills, for the snow in the roads has long before mid-day been rolled into ice, and the highways are like a long, broad slide. To accommodate the outsiders hay has been wound round the stepping-irons, and the gents on the "knife-board," along the roof of the first 'buses, appear with thick railway-rugs tucked round their knees, whilst, at the different halting-places, the conductor jumps down and stamps on the pavement, as he does a double-shuffle to warm himself, flinging his arms across his chest, and striking the breast of his top-coat with the same energy as if he were beating a carpet.

Snow or sunshine, work must be done; but now the mechanics and clerks that you meet in the streets go along with their heads down and their hands in their pockets, at a half-trotting pace. Their necks are bound round with thick wisps of comforters, and the tips of their noses, that overhang the worsted network, are red, as if tinselled, and all sniff and cough, as they carefully dodge by the round iron plates over the coal holes of the metropolis. The pave-

ment in front of the bakers' shops is the only place from which the
snow had entirely disappeared, and where the pedestrian can tread
with safety. The whole town seems to swarm with boy and men
sweepers, who go about from house to house, knocking at the doors,
and offering to clear the pavement before the dwelling, according to
Act of Parliament, for twopence. Everybody you meet has the
breast of his great-coat and hat-rim dredged with white; and the
policeman's shiny cape is, with its fur of snow, more like a nobleman's
ermine tippet than the ordinary hard-weather costume of the force.

How bright the air, too, seems with the light reflected from the
snow. You can see to the end of the longest streets. There is a
white cold look about the scene; and everything is so black from the
contrast of the intense glare of the ground, that even at noonday you
might fancy that a silver harvest moon was shining in the skies, and
that the snow itself, lying on one side of each object, was but the
reflection of the pale brilliance of the white beams falling on them.

The sky looks almost like a dome of slate, and the parks and
squares like large new plaster models of countries without a single
path or bed to be traced, except where the few passengers have worn
a narrow dirty streak across them. The trees, too, are all ashy grey,
and the objects in the distance seem to be twice as near as usual,
while the dark specks of the people moving over the great snowy
waste appear like blots on a sheet of paper.

The statues throughout the metropolis have lost all artistic model-
ling in their form, and strike one as being as rudely fashioned as
if they were so many figures moulded by schoolboys out of snow.
Some, however, are merely speckled with the flakes, and have their
Grecian draperies splashed over with white, like a plasterer's clothes.
Sir Robert Peel, gazing down Cheapside, looks as if some miller had
rubbed violently up against him. Old Major Cartwright, seated in
his arm-chair in Burton Crescent, has at least a couple of pounds of
snow resting on the top of his skull and dabbed over his face, and
giving him the appearance of having been newly lathered previous to
having his head and cheeks shaved. The periwig of George III.,
at Charing Cross, has turned white in a night, like the hair of Marie
Antoinette. The mounted effigy of F. M. the Duke of Wellington, at
Hyde Park Corner, continues, despite a spadeful of snow at the nape
of his neck, to point with his baton—which is now white as a wax-
candle—majestically in the direction of the White Horse Cellar, his
patient steed having its hind-quarters covered with so heavy a deposit
that his Grace seems to be sitting, like a life-guardsman, on a mat of
bleached sheepskin.

Now the water-supply of the metropolis begins to be almost as
scarce as in Paris; while the water-pipes of the more prudent of the
householders are seen bandaged round with straw, like the wheel-
spokes of a new carriage. The turncocks, with their shiny leathern
epaulets, go along with their immense keys, like those of some monster
beer-barrel, and erect tall wooden plugs for the temporary supply of

the neighbours, who flock there with pails and pitchers, and wait in a crowd to take their turn at the tap, while the waste water gutters and hardens over the snow like so much grease.

But if there be a scarcity of water the public-houses, at least, have determined to make up for it, for in the windows are printed placards announcing that " HOT ELDER WINE " and " HOT SPICED ALE " may be had within.　Taking advantage, too, of the " inclemency " of the weather, all kinds of warm comestibles suddenly appear on the street-stalls.　The fish kettles, full of "hot eels " and " pea-soup," have a cloud of steam issuing from them, and the baked potato-cans are spirting out jets of a high-pressure vapour, like the escape-pipe of some miniature steam-factory.　As you walk along the street, too, the nostrils are regaled by pleasant odours of baked apples and roasted chestnuts from the neighbouring stalls, at which sit old women in coachmen's many-caped coats, with their feet in an apple-basket, and a rushlight shade, full of red-hot charcoal, at their side—the fire shining in bright orange spots through the holes.

The pert London sparrows seem almost to have disappeared with the frost, and the few that remain have a wretched half-torpid look, and have gone all fluffy and turned to a mere brown ball of feathers. In the suburbs, the robins are seen for the first time leaving little trident impressions of their feet on the garden snow, and their scarlet bosoms looking red as Christmas berries against the white earth. Then as the dusk of evening sets in, and you see in the squares and crescents the crimson flickering of the flames from the cosy sea-coal fire in the parlours, lighting up the windows like flashes of sheet-lightning, the cold, cheerless aspect of the streets without sets you thinking of the exquisite comfort of our English homes.

But if grateful thoughts of comfort are suggested by the contrast of the snow, the same cause leads the more imaginative to think of the sharp, biting misery gnawing into the very bones of the luckless portion of London society.　To those who can put on warm flannel, and encase their bodies in a thick great-coat, a sharp frost means only " healthy, bracing weather," and to such people the long evenings are welcome, from a sense of the happy family circle gathered round the bright cherry-coloured fire.　To the well-born young silver-spoonbills of the West End, Christmas is a season of mirth and holiday games, of feasting, pantomimes, and parties.　By the elder gentlefolks it is regarded as a time of good cheer, with its cattle-shows and " guinea-hampers," and presents of fat turkeys from the country ; for such as these, the butchers' shops are piled with prize-meat, coated with thick fat, and decorated with huge cockades—for such as these, the grocers' windows are dressed out with dried fruits and spices, and studded with lumps of candied peel; and Covent Garden is littered with holly, laurel, and mistletoe, and fragrant with the odours of bright-coloured fruits.

But how, think you, must the cold be welcomed by those whose means of living cease directly the earth becomes like cast-iron with the frost. How merry must Christmas appear to those whose tattered clothes afford no more protection than broken windows against the bleak, stinging breeze. How pleasant and cosy must the long evenings be to such as have to spend them crouching under the dry arches; and how delicious the sight of the teeming markets to poor wretches who, to stay their hunger, must devour the refuse orange-peel lying about the stones there.

Some readers, maybe, will fancy that such winter's misery is far from being common among our people; but they should remember that in the lottery of life the prizes, as in other lotteries, are but the exception, and that the greater proportion of the chances are dead against those entering the lists, so that where one adventurer gets a lucky cast, thousands are doomed to end the game as badly as they began it. Readers should bear in mind, too, that with the luckless, the winter is especially the season when the wants are not only greater, but employment is scarcer, and, therefore, life harder than ever.

Not to speak of the really destitute and the outcast, the well-to-do in London are surrounded by thousands whose labour lasts only for the summer—such as bricklayers, market-gardeners, harvest-men, and the like; besides multitudes of others, such as navigators and ground-labourers, who can ply their trade only so long as the earth can be made to yield to the spade and the pick; and others again, as the dock labourers and 'long-shore men, who depend upon the very winds for the food and fuel of themselves and families.

The geography of the Asylum for the Houseless is somewhat difficult to make out to those whose knowledge of London extends no farther eastwards than the Royal Italian Opera House, or even Exeter Hall. There are some streets that even the most experienced cabmen have to descend from their box half a dozen times, in order to ferret out the road to; and Playhouse Yard—the locality of the refuge—is one of these.

The way lies up a long, narrow street, rendered still narrower by a double flank of stalls trestled along the kerb. At the corner of every turning hereabouts is a gin-palace, with a monster lamp suspended over the entrance, and a long shell-fish stall in front of the door, set out with a trefoil arrangement of pen'orths of oysters, as big as muffins. Outside the bakers' shop-windows are stuck large bills, always announcing the grateful intelligence that bread is "DOWN AGAIN TO EVEN MONEY"; and at the tea-dealers' there are comic placards, designed and coloured by ticket-writers, setting forth either the advantages of joining their "pudding club," or the dangerous strength of their "gunpowder tea." Pawnbrokers, too, abound in the neighbourhood; and at their door hang blankets and patchwork counterpanes, suspended from one corner, as in auction-rooms, while the watches, ranged in the windows, are as big and thick as the bull's-eye to a dark lantern. Nor is there any lack of coal and potato sheds; and at these the current price of fuel is always

quoted in chalk on a board at so much " per cwt." Here, too, on
every Sunday in the summer season, the light spring van, which at
other times is used for enabling the neighbours to indulge in that
exciting lunatic sport known as "shooting the moon," puts on
curtains, and starts with a party of pleasure and a beer barrel for
Hampton Court.

The yard christened Playhouse is a lane that it is ridiculous to
dream of entering in a cab. Accordingly, two or three street-stalls
have to be disarranged, in order to allow your vehicle standing-room,
and never was such commotion among the coster trucks and apple-
stalls as when your hansom endeavours to draw up to the kerb. As
you turn the corner, you enter even a poorer district than before.
Here pawnbrokers will not flourish, and " dolly-shops " are found to
prevail instead, where even the pledges which have been refused by
the " cruel uncle " are not rejected by those ebony " babes in the
wood " that swing over the door as signs of the Black Doll. The
baker's shop, the grocer's, and the coal warehouse have severally
disappeared, and been rolled into one omnium-gatherum store in
"the general line."

The old Fortune Theatre stood in this same Playhouse Yard some
two centuries and a half ago, and never was more pathetic drama
performed there, under the auspices of the blind goddess, than that
which is nightly represented at the Asylum for the Houseless; for
rightly viewed, the scenes and changes enacted there are but a
portion of the great play of fortune, and the ragged crowd within the
walls but the wretched mummers to whom Fate has cast the sorriest
parts.

It is impossible to mistake the Asylum if you go there at dark, just
as the lamp in the wire cage over the entrance door is being lighted :
for this is the hour for opening, and ranged along the kerb is a kind
of ragged regiment, drawn up four deep, and stretching far up and
down the narrow lane, until the crowd is like a hedge to the roadway.

It is a terrible thing to look down upon that squalid crowd from
one of the upper windows. There they stand shivering in the snow
with their thin cobwebby garments hanging in tatters about them.
Many are without shirts; with their bare skin showing through the
rents and gaps, like the hide of a dog with the mange. Some have
their greasy garments tied round their wrists and ankles with string
to prevent the piercing wind from blowing up them. A few are
without shoes, and these keep one foot only to the ground, while the
bare flesh that has had to tramp through the snow is blue and livid-
looking as half-cooked meat.

You can pick out the different foreigners and countrymen in that
wretched throng by the different colours of their costume. There
you see the black sailor in his faded red woollen shirt; the Lascar in
his dirty-white calico tunic ; the Frenchman in his short blue smock;
the countryman in his clay-stained frock, with the bosom worked all

over like a dirty sampler; and the Irish market-woman with her faded straw bonnet, flattened by the heavy loads she has borne on her head.

It was to this refuge that the policeman referred when he said to the woman whom he found half-frozen on the door-step, " The Asylum for the Houseless is the only place for you." It was to this refuge that the officer and the faint and weary creature were on their way— so faint and weary, indeed, that Heaven only knows what wretched fate would befall her if the bare hospitality of the place should be denied to her.

CHAPTER III.

THE REFUGE.

SOME gentlemen had called at the Asylum that day to see the place, and the class of persons usually admitted there. The superintendent was busy, before the opening of the doors, explaining to them, in the office at the side of the passage, the rules and customs of the institution.

The bare whitewashed entrance was so like that to the stage of some minor theatre, and the little office, with its wicket window giving into the passage, reminded one so forcibly of the room occupied by the stage-door keeper, that you might almost have fancied it had formed part of the old Fortune Playhouse.

In a corner of the office itself stood several square bread baskets, as big as sea chests, piled with little blocks of cut-up loaves, resembling both in size and colour so many fire-bricks.

"We give each person, on coming in at night," said the superintendent to the visitors, "half a pound of the best bread, and a like quantity on going out in the morning; and children, even if they be at the breast, have the same, which goes to swell the mother's allowance. That gentleman," continued the officer, pointing to the clerk who was standing at the high desk beside the wicket window, "enters in this ledger" (it was as thick as a banker's) "the name, age, trade or profession—for we've all classes here, I can assure you —and place of birth of the applicants, as well as where they slept the previous night."

The strangers glanced their eyes down the several columns of this striking catalogue of destitution. The entries under the first three divisions showed, as we have said, that the asylum was the refuge for the outcasts of all ages, callings, and countries, but the last division was that which told the saddest tale of all; for as the eye ranged down the column indicating where each applicant had passed the previous night, it was startled to find how often the clerk had had to write down, "in the streets"; so that "ditto," "ditto," continually repeated under the same head, sounded as an ideal chorus of terrible want in the mind's ear.

As the superintendent and the visitors walked round the wards a messenger from the outer office approached the official, and said, partly aside to him, "There's a policeman, sir, at the gate, has brought a woman along, whom he says he found half frozen on a door-step. She seems a better kind of person."

"Very well," answered the head officer; "take her name down, as usual, and let her go upstairs to the chapel ward, and I'll see her directly."

"The policeman says, sir, he thinks she wants food," continued the messenger.

"Indeed," replied the officer; "then you had better tell the matron to give her a basin of gruel directly, and not wait for the doctor's seeing her."

"Now there's an instance of the good we effect, gentlemen," he added, turning to the visitors. "What would a poor creature like that have done if it hadn't been for some such charity as this?"

The chapel ward is the place whither all fresh applicants are sent to be examined by the doctor, previous to admission for the night. This ward was a long, bare, and binned-off apartment which, owing to the pile of forms used for divine service on the Sunday, as well as the academy-like tall desk near the stove in the centre of the room, had much the look of an empty day-school. The only evidence, however, of the ecclesiastical character of the place was a clumsy brown pulpit, as rude as if it had been made by a packing-case maker.

Here, on forms, sat the fresh cases of that evening, the males on one side of the room and the females on the other, whilst the doctor stood at the desk with his minute-book open before him. "Now then, the male cases," he said; and the men advanced in single file. His assistant at his side cried, "Come along, show the back of your hands and open your fingers well;" and immediately afterwards he held a lighted candle close to the skin of each, as they stretched out their arms for examination.

"Now then, the women, come along!" called out the assistant. And instantly the long line of wretched outcasts rose as suddenly as if a hymn had been given out.

At the end of the form the woman who had been brought there by the policeman had been sitting—as far apart from the others as the limits of the bench would admit of. When the signal was given for them to come forward, she rose a minute or two after the rest, for she had been roused from brooding over her misery only by the noise of her neighbours' feet. And when she stood up she hung her head so that none could see her face.

Presently it reached her turn to approach the desk. She held out her hands methodically as the others had done. The quick eye of the doctor noticed how thin and spare they were, for the whole mechanism of the fingers seemed to be visible under the transparent skin. He took her by the wrist, and as he kept his fingers on her pulse, looked first at her face, then glanced at her figure, and said, " My good woman, this is no place for you—are you married ? "

He had asked the question rather abruptly—in the ordinary way of business—and he was somewhat surprised to see the colour mount to the poor thing's cheeks with shame at the question. She, however, replied plaintively, as she sighed and shook her head, " I wish I was not."

" I didn't mean to wound your feelings," continued the doctor, in a kindly tone, " but I saw no wedding-ring on your finger."

She shrugged her shoulders, and replied, " I was forced to part with that long ago."

The doctor called the superintendent, and drew him aside to talk with him in private. After a time the official returned to the woman, and said, " My good soul, it's against the rules of this institution to receive anybody in your condition. I'll tell you what we must do with you. We shall give you a shilling, as we do others like you, so that you may obtain a night's lodging somewhere, and then you will have a settlement and a claim on the parish where you slept."

The woman grew blanched as she heard the words, and she staggered back in utter despair. Poor thing! she had already applied at one Union, and they had told her that she must go back to where she had been born, for her settlement was there; and she had heard that at the Asylum for the Houseless cases were received which the workhouse refused, and now she learnt that the last refuge was denied her, and she felt that nothing was left her but to die in the streets.

" If your case was very urgent we should send you to the hospital," added the official, soothingly; " but as it is, you had better rest here awhile and have another ration of bread and some more warm gruel, and then you'll be able to find a lodging for yourself."

The wretched creature thought what was to become of her when that little shilling was gone, and she hid her face in her hands as she sobbed convulsively.

The strangers, who had been watching the woman for some little time, now stepped forward, and inquired the cause of her grief.

" Have you no friends or relatives living ? " asked one of them. But the woman made no answer, and looked proudly at the speaker, as if questioning his right to pry into her misery. Then she buried her face in her hands once more.

" We would serve you if possible, my good woman," continued the stranger; " so pray tell me, since you are married, where is your husband ? "

She answered bitterly, as if stung by the remembrance of the illtreatment she had suffered, " He has deserted me after robbing me of all I had." And then, as if fancying she had committed herself, she added, " Ask me no more—ask me no more, I beg of you ! "

The superintendent here interposed, saying, " We had a case much like this last year—a very nice girl, who had run away and got married against her family's consent, but we wrote to her friends and got them to take her back again."

The woman shook her head as she heard this, and smiled at the wrong guess they had made as to the cause of her misery.

" But you've quarrelled with them at home, I know," said the official. " Come, now, give me your parents' address, and let me write them a nice, dutiful, and penitent letter for you."

" And let them know that their daughter is in rags, and begging for a night's shelter at the Asylum for the Houseless ! " And her lips worked convulsively in scorn at the proposal.

" Are your friends in a position to assist you if they choose ? " asked one of the strangers.

The woman grew impatient at the continued questionings, and looking at her interrogator said, reproachfully, " Oh ! can't you understand that when decent persons are driven here they wish to keep their misery as secret as they can ? If I had wanted to publish mine, I could have gone round the town, from door to door, with a petition filled with the whole particulars."

The gentleman was taken aback by the answer. He stammered out some excuses, such as, " Really, you mistake me. Indeed, I am the last man to—"

Here the doctor and the superintendent drew near, and the latter observed, " She stated at the door that she has passed three entire nights in the streets—that she belongs to no trade or occupation—that she's twenty-three years old, and that her name is Katherine Merton."

" I gave my mother's name," she cried, looking up as she heard the last words.

The officials and visitors retired a short distance from her, and consulted together.

It was at last agreed, at the doctor's suggestion, that the poor woman should be placed under the care of the house-matron, who should make her a cup of tea, whilst the doctor prepared for her a stimulating draught to recruit her sinking powers.

In a few hours afterwards the noise and chattering of the boys below, and the gossip of the women above, as well as the squealing of the beggar-children in the nursery, had all ceased. The more tidy of the women, who had remained darning their gowns after they had taken them off for the night, had put their work away, and stowed their letters and other humble treasures in the locker under the wooden pillow at the head of their " bunks." The men had quitted the warm fire and crept one after another to their berths, where, rolled round in the leather coverlids provided in place of blankets as being strong and durable and not retaining vermin, they were sleeping as sound as squirrels in the winter. The buckets of chloride of lime had already been placed at intervals in the gangways to fumigate the wards; the fires had been banked up for the night, and the gas-lights had been lowered, so that in the half light, as you moved about the silent, solemn place, and saw the rows of tightly-bound figures, brown and stiff as mummies, it seemed like wandering amidst some large catacomb. The stillness was broken only by the snoring of the sounder sleepers and the coughing of the more restless.

It was a marvellously pathetic scene to contemplate. Here was a herd of the most wretched and friendless people in the world, lying down close to the earth as sheep; here were some eight score of outcasts, whose days are an unvarying round 'of suffering, enjoying the only moments when they are free from pain and care—life being to them but one long, painful ,operation, as it were, and sleep the chloroform which, for the time being, renders them insensible.

The sight set the mind speculating on the beggars and the outcasts' dreams. The ship's company, starving at the North Pole, dreamt, every man of them, each night, of feasting; and was this miserable frozen-out crew now regaling themselves with visions of imaginary banquets?—were they smacking their mental lips over ethereal beef and pudding? Was that poor wretch, whose rheumatic limbs rack him each step he takes—was he tripping over green fields with an elastic and joyous bound, that in his waking moments he can never know again? Did that man's restlessness and heavy moaning come from nightmare terrors of policemen and treadwheels?—and which among those runaway boys was fancying that he was back home again, with his mother and sisters weeping on his neck?

The next moment the thoughts shifted, and the heart was overcome with a sense of the heap of social refuse—the mere human street-sweepings—this great living mixen, that was destined, as soon as the spring returned, to be strewn far and near over the land, and serve as manure to the future crime crops of the country.

Then came the self-congratulations and the self-questionings; and as a man, sound in health and limb, walking through an hospital, thanks God that he has been spared the bodily ailments, the mere sight of which sickens him, so in this refuge for the starving and the homeless, the first instinct of the well-to-do visitor is to breathe a thanksgiving, like the Pharisee in the parable, that " he is not as one of these." But the vain conceit has scarcely risen to the tongue before the better nature whispers in the mind's ear, " By what special virtue of your own are you different from them? How comes it that you are well clothed and well fed, whilst so many go naked and hungry? " And if you, in your arrogance, ignoring all the accidents that have helped to build up your worldly prosperity, assert that you have been the " architect of your own fortune," who, let us ask, gave you the genius or energy for the work? Then get down from your moral stilts, and confess it honestly to yourself that you are what you are by that inscrutable grace which decreed your birthplace to be a mansion rather than a " padding-ken," or which granted you brains and strength, instead of sending you into the world a cripple or an idiot.

It is hard for smug-faced respectability to acknowledge these dirt-caked, erring wretches as brothers, and yet, if from those to whom little is given little is expected, surely, after the atonement of their long suffering, they will make as good angels as the best of us.

That night the superintendent, whilst going round the wards for the last time, said to the matron, "By-the-bye! about that young woman whom the policeman brought here; how was she when she left? Better—eh?"

"Oh, yes, she was much better—getting on very nicely, I may say," was the answer. "She had a comfortable hot cup of tea and a good warm beside the fire in my room—for I took her there, poor thing, she seemed so decent like. I gave her the shilling to get her bed with; but she's as helpless as a child, and knows nothing about London ways."

"Did she tell you anything more about who she was?" asked the superintendent.

"Yes, poor simple thing, she did," answered the dame; "when she got well warm, she had a good cry at being in such a place; and as I told her not to take on so, and that this world was only one of trial, she began to talk away as if her heart was full to bursting, and she was glad to find some one that she could tell her troubles to."

"Well, and are her parents well off?" asked the male official.

"Oh dear, yes," replied the dame; "from all I could make out they seem to be very rich and very proud—a good deal like that black-haired girl's case that was here last winter—you know, the one that had gone off with the play-actor fellow. But she didn't seem to like to speak much about her home; and do what I would I couldn't get the address out of her. All the time she was talking about her father's pride, I was saying to myself, 'You don't know it, poor thing, but you're every bit as proud yourself'—a chip of the old block, as the saying goes—for she kept on protesting she'd rather die of starvation in the streets than ever go home again."

"It's very shocking to think of the pride of some people," observed the superintendent.

"Ah!" sighed the dame, "we can none of us see the beam in our own eye." Then she went on, "I only got her story from her by bits, and all of a jumble like; but what I gather is this: She was married when she was very young to an Indian officer, and when he died she came home a young widow thing, and had a good pension—enough, indeed, to keep her quite independent like of her friends, though she went to live among 'em."

"Well, what has she done with it?" asked the superintendent.

"Wait a bit!" expostulated the dame; "you see this is how it came about, as far as I can guess. After she had been home some little while, she got to find the time hang heavy with her, and so began to take lessons in French of one of those refugee fellows who had come and settled in her neighbourhood; and then she got listening to the Frenchman's palavering when she ought to have been minding her learning, and the end of it was, there was a secret marriage between 'em, quite unbeknown to her friends."

"Ah, I see!" cried the superintendent. "He was beneath her station, and she was afraid to let her family know the imprudent match she had made."

"No, no! you're too quick by half," said the matron. "That was only a small part of the reason, let me tell you, for her saying nothing about the wedding. You see the pension she was entitled to as an officer's widow would have ceased directly it became known that she had married again; so, naturally wishing to preserve her independence—for she knew her husband was too poor to maintain them both—she would not let even her most intimate bosom friend know of the marriage, lest it should creep out, and her pay be stopped at the India House."

"And I suppose somebody found it out and went and informed the authorities?" speculated the superintendent.

"No; nothing of the kind," expostulated the dame. "Now you really must allow me to tell the story my own way. Well," continued the lady, sucking her mouth dry as if making ready for a long oration, and crossing her forefingers, "things went on as I have told you without anyone so much as dreaming of what had took place, until the poor dear found she was likely to become a mother, and at last it got to be beyond the power of cloaks and shawls to hide her condition. Then there was a tremendous to do!"

"Dear me! dear me! I see it all!" cried the superintendent. "They turned her into the streets and shut their doors against her. Wasn't that it—eh?"

"Do have a little patience—pray!" interrupted the dame, annoyed at having the story "taken out of her mouth." "You shall know all in good time. Her father seems to have been as hasty as he was proud, and took up rash notions without inquiring whether they were true or not. Seeing her in the situation she was, and of course knowing nothing of the marriage, he began abusing her, and then and there called her a shameless hussy, and threatened to turn his back upon her."

"But what a silly girl!" exclaimed the officer. "Why didn't she show the certificate of her marriage, and set it all straight at once?"

"How you talk! Didn't I tell you she was afraid of losing her pension if her marriage got abroad? Besides, she was as proud every bit as her father was," answered the dame; "and, what is more, she seems to have been quite as hasty, too; for when he called her harsh names, her spirit was up. So, as she knew she had been properly married at the altar, and had a feeling that she was independent of her family so long as her pension wasn't stopped, she packed up her things, and off she went, and lived with her husband, leaving her relations to think just what they chose."

C

"Bless my soul!" exclaimed the superintendent, "what mad things a person's silly spirit will lead one to do! And she might have cleared it all up by one little word. And just see what it has come to, now. Of course the French fellow ill-treated her after all? for such matches seldom turn out well."

"Ah! poor dear, she's been punished enough for her headstrong doings," sighed the pitying matron. "What strange romances do turn up in this place, to be sure! Well, as I was saying, she lived with her husband away from home, putting up with the jibes and taunts of the world for the sake of the man and the money that was to keep them from starvation; for when I tell you she had been his only scholar, you may fancy his teaching business didn't bring in much to the home."

"I should think not!" exclaimed the officer. "Why, we've had plenty of foreigners here who would have been glad to give lessons in their language for a meal."

"Well, it soon came out, poor thing! what the Frenchman had married her for," mournfully added the matron. "Of course Mr. Mounseer had heard my lady had got a pension at her back, before ever he thought of making love to her; and though, before the marriage, she had explained to him that she would lose every ha'penny she had if it ever came out that she was no longer a widow, yet they hadn't been man and wife a week before she got to see plainly enough that the fellow didn't believe a word of what she had said to him, and fancied she had made up the story just to keep the money in her own hands. Even before she left her father's house, this man kept on worrying her to let him go down and draw some of the money; and he told her right out that he knew that as her husband he was entitled to whatever property she possessed. However, so long as she was at her father's he was a bit afraid to appear in his true character, and he was kept quiet by a sovereign now and then; but no sooner had the noise took place and she gone to live with him entirely, than he threw off the double-faced mask of caring for anything but her money, and plainly said to her, in French, 'I ain't going to be bamboozled, my lady!' So what do you think? why, he takes all the money there is in the house at the time, and comes up to London, and walks straight to the India House, and there, showing the marriage lines as proof of his being her husband, demands that the pension should be paid only to him in future."

"The mean hound!" the superintendent could not refrain from exclaiming. "But the fellow bit his fingers nicely, of course; for such a step naturally put a stop to all money from that quarter."

"Think, though, of what a blow it must have been to her, poor thing!" said the matron. "I'm sure I thought her heart would have broke before me, as she told me how she had given up father, home, and friends, for that man's sake, and how for him, too, she had put up with taunts and suspicions that are the hardest of all for a woman to bear; and then for him to go away from her and leave her directly he

found that his selfish blunderings had made a beggar of her! I dare
say, too, he was a good bit ashamed of himself, and didn't like to face
her after what he had done."

"Ah! not only that," interrupted the officer, "but it is clear
enough he married her only for her money, so as soon as he found
that there was none, why, of course my gentleman went off."

"If you had only heard her tell it all to me, it would have made
your eyes smart to see how she took on about the vagabond," said the
kind-hearted matron. "The silly thing must have loved him, of
course, or she wouldn't have made the sacrifices she had done on his
account. Well, when she found he didn't return home, she began to
think all sorts of things, and to get half crazy with his neglect of
her, especially in the situation she was. Still she wouldn't allow
herself to think bad of him, though she could hardly keep down the
suspicions that came up in her mind. Well, she waited and waited,
watching day and night for him to come back, and writing to him all
manner of imploring things to get him home again, until at last she
was fairly worn out; and, as it was just upon the time for her to
draw her pension, she borrowed a few shillings, and came to London
herself."

"And found out how she had been used by the fellow," guessed
the superintendent.

"Yes, indeed!" continued the dame, tossing her head. "She
hunted for him everywhere she could think of; she went to all the
places she had heard him talk about; but he was nowhere to be
found. Then when quarter-day arrived, she set off to the India House
to receive her pension! and then, poor soul! what a thunderclap the
clerks had got to hurl at her. They taxed her with being married,
and said they were surprised at her boldness in coming there when
she knew that her pension was forfeited."

"Bless me, it must have been a blow to her to lose both money
and husband the same afternoon, as it were," soliloquized the superintendent. "But at least it had the effect of opening her eyes to
the true character of the man."

"When a woman takes to a man, it's wonderful how slow she is
to think badly of him," moralized the matron. "This poor thing
stayed in town, still hoping to meet with him somewhere, for she
couldn't bring her mind to believe he had abandoned her. She lived
on her things, one going after another, as we well know is the case
with half the poor creatures who comes to us here, until at last all
was gone, and she was turned out of her lodgings for rent."

"Oh! I've no patience with such folly," the officer exclaimed;
"why didn't she write home?"

"How can you say that, when you know we have had scores and
scores here, who would sooner suffer all the agony of the sharpest
hunger and cold, rather than humble themselves by confessing the
degradation their folly and self-will had brought them to? It's the
fear of being taunted that does it."

"And their own stupid, worldly pride, too," added the officer.

"But if you come to think of it," remonstrated the dame, "it must be a dreadful struggle for those who have been well to do, to bring themselves to write home to their friends and confess they are starving in the streets. To have to put an address to a letter is a terrible trial to stiff-necked people, even though they be in rags. Do all I could—though I'm sure I talked, and begged till my tongue was sore—I could not get that young woman to promise me she'd write as much as a dozen words to her friends. 'No, that she wouldn't,' she said, 'not even if it cost her her life!' I never set eyes on such stubbornness of spirit in all my born days."

"Well, such people must pay the penalty of their own obstinacy," exclaimed the superintendent. "But did she say anything about calling again in the morning? for those gentlemen that were here to-day seemed to take great interest in her case, and wished to know what could be done for her."

"Indeed, I couldn't get her to make any regular promise," was the answer; "for though she didn't say she wouldn't come, still I'm sure she is too much afraid of our finding out who she is ever to show her face inside this asylum again."

CHAPTER IV.

ADRIFT.

WHAT a silent, dismal, deserted place is the City of London on a Sunday! It reminds one of Defoe's description of the metropolis during the plague, when every shop and house was closed and barred and the citizens had fled to the suburbs. You can tell now how few of the large blocks of houses are used as dwelling-places by the citizens, for there is scarcely a wreath of smoke issuing from the crowded stacks of chimneys, and the air is clear and unfogged with the sooty fumes, so that you are startled to be able to see from one end of Cheapside to the other, and wonderstruck to find that the roadway—which the day before was so blocked up with cabs, omnibuses, and vans, that you could almost have run along their roofs like a line of housetops—is now nearly as open to the view as a railway cutting. The pavements, too, that were yesterday black with their jostling, hurrying crowds, are now scarcely speckled by the few stragglers that saunter along them, whilst the one omnibus that creeps lazily on its journey has hardly a passenger in it, and has the whole street to itself as clear as a race-course.

At the Old Bailey, where, on other days, the carts of the suburban carriers stand opposite the inn-yard, drawn up like a row of bathing-machines, the cocks and hens are out in the roadway scratching up

the litter as in a farm-yard; and farther down, in front of the
Criminal Court, where, at other times, the entrance-door and the
neighbouring public-houses are thronged with troops of witnesses and
suspicious-looking prisoners' friends waiting the results of the trials
within, now the pigeons walk unscared along the causeway, pecking
the dust as they strut along; neither is there any longer here a smell
of hot boiled beef, nor a cloud of steam issuing through the area-rails
of the adjoining eating-house, for the shutters are up there, and the
linen-jacketed man that, in a state of perpetual perspiration, carves
the ruddy rounds—big as butchers' blocks—behind the window, is
now away airing himself, maybe, in the river's breeze upon the halfpenny boat.

Where are the colonies of clerks that yesterday you noted filling
the dining-rooms in Bucklersbury, or feasting on their "half steak"
at Joe's, Ned's, Sam's, or any other of the familiar tribe of Christian-
named chophouse-keepers?—where the army of porters and ware-
housemen that worked at each block of buildings round about St.
Paul's, peopling every floor as thickly as sailors do the decks of a
merchantman?—where the colony of bankers, merchants, factors, and
brokers that gobbled their soup at Birch's, or took their sandwiches
and sherry at the South American, or teased their stomachs with the
cream-tufted tarts at Purcell's? The Bay-tree, too, is closed, and not
a City man stands eating his shilling snack "hot with vegetables" at
the counter; the Lombard Street taverns, moreover, with their portions of pink pickled salmon spotting their pewter bars, have put up
the chain and locked their doors, whilst the proprietors have driven
out in their light "shay" traps to drink tea at Hampstead, Kew, or
Harrow.

It is almost impossible to recognize Thames Street again, for the
wharves along the river-side have the gates all closed, except where
the little wicket is left ajar; and down the yards of some of these
you can see the huge empty waggons, with their thick shafts
turned back and pointing high in the air. Here, too, the cranes,
that on a week-day project like iron gibbets from every floor,
are turned on one side, in the same manner as the crutch for
the bottle-jack is bent back to the chimney-piece when the roast-
ing has ceased. The carts no longer block the road, nor are there
huge bales dangling, like monster money-spiders from a thread,
and swinging in the air. At the Coal Exchange, the only thing
stirring is the weathercock, and the office desks, seen through the
windows of the floors above, look as deserted as those in a schoolroom
during the holidays. On the other side of the way, Billingsgate is
lonely and empty, and has a dreary, cloister-like stillness about it;
and where but lately the air rang with a positive Babel of voices, you
can now hear a whistle echo against the metallic roofing of the broad,
expansive shed. The benches and stalls are packed on top of one
another, like old discarded tables in a lumber-room; and as you look
down into the basement through the square opening in the paving,

that seems like the hatchway to a ship, you see the huge empty shell-fish tubs, giving the place the look of a large laundry out of work, rather than being the periwinkle and whelk portion of the market.

Now step down to the floating-pier and see what a change the day of rest has made in the traffic of the river, as well as the shore. So doubly silent is "the silent highway," that the birds chirping among the Old Exchange statues at Nicholson's wharf sound as noisy as the aviary at the Pantheon. There is not the flutter of a paddle-wheel, nor the roar of the escape-pipe to a newly-arrived steamer to be heard; but the rushing of the tide chafing against the bridge piers gurgles in the ears, broken only by the barking of the curs—noisy as alarums—that are left alone on board the lighters to guard such as are moored close to the shore. There is "no admission for visitors," at the docks on Sunday, and the big gates are closed, so that the little side door alone is left ajar for the ingress and egress of seamen, whilst the alphabetic warehouses seem still, moody, and closely barred as hulks; and in the unfrequented roadway outside the walls, a gang of young thieves from the purlieus of Rosemary Lane are playing "chuck ha'penny" with the chance of a passing waggon to interrupt their game.

Even money, too, seems idle on the day of rest. The Bank of England, squat as a cash-box, looks positively as if it were "to let," and you expect to see bills posted up at the various corners announcing the forthcoming sale of "the valuable effects." The coffers of the world now seem to be closed as a worked-out mine, and you wonder whether the great draining engine of five per cent. has ceased working or not. Who passes his Sunday within this citadel of wealth? If you were to pull the bell, would anybody answer it? Who ever saw the Bank of England servant taking in the milk? or a butcher's cart or baker's truck waiting at the area gate, even on a week day? Is the man who guards the building on the Sunday twin-brother to the keeper of Eddystone Lighthouse? and is he, too, left there for four weeks at a time to wander alone about the desolate place? Where have the silver-haired, prim-looking bankers of the deserted Lombard Street flown to? and where are the Exchange men that but yesterday crowded the quadrangle? Look through the iron gates and you will see the poor statue of Queen Victoria as lonely as a scarecrow in a corn-field, and the whole place as desolate as ruins after a fire.

Then London Bridge, the main duct of all the metropolitan traffic, where policemen, like dyke inspectors in Holland, are stationed to see that the great commercial tides setting in from Middlesex and Surrey flow on quietly without breaking down the restrictions of the City; this immense thoroughfare is now so clear of vehicles that fathers walk with their children in the roadway; and on the other side of the water, so completely has the business of the week ceased, that a street-seller has erected her stall on the entrance-steps of "HIBERNIA CHAMBERS," and the piled-up oranges, ranged in little pyramids, like golden cannon-balls, rest against the closed massive doors; for the hop-merchants that rent the offices of the palatial building have forgotten all about their " pockets " for a time, and left the chances of " cent. per cent." to the fruit-woman.

As you enter the narrow passages of Leadenhall Market, you startle maybe some bone-grubber, carrying a rush hand-basket, and who seems to have been taking advantage of the solitude of the Sabbath to purloin a slice of meat from the two or three carcases that are left hanging in the open space. Here, too, the long rows of unoccupied butchers' hooks seem like the hat-pegs at a bankrupt railway hotel, and the narrow arcades of shops, with their shutters up, have the appearance of some deserted Indian bazaar. Not a footfall is heard upon the pavement, and the piano at the licensed game-dealer's, jingling forth the 100th Psalm, fills the place, like an empty room, with its sounds.

Indeed, go where you will—to Whitechapel shambles, or the Temple—walk down Cannon Street, Barbican, or Bishopsgate—or visit the busiest of the public offices, such as the Post Office or the India House—all is as quiet and deserted as if it were some two or three hours after midnight, rather than only an hour or two after noon; so that you might fancy you were wandering through the sleeping city of the fairy tale, and that all the bankers, merchants, and brokers, as well as their attendant army of clerks, shopmen, and porters, were slumbering in their chambers, as if spell-bound with the magic trance.

But if the streets appear thus desolate to those who welcome the Sabbath as a day of rest and home retirement—how fearfully lonely and sad must the City seem to the poor creatures who, without a shelter to hide in, are forced to wander out the day, waiting impatiently for the night to come and screen their wretchedness with its darkness. On this day, when even the humble manage to put on clean linen, and unshorn beards have entirely disappeared, how shame-stricken and heart-broken do those wretched beings seem who have to shuffle along the pavements in their every-day rags, wearing the one dust-coloured suit of tatters that even on the week day made the passers-by shrink from them with the fear of contact.

There was one miserable soul who crept along the forsaken pathway, seeking only those streets where the warehouses lay the thickest, and glancing down each turning before she entered it, to make certain that she would meet with none better clad than herself. Occasionally she rested for awhile in the corners of gateways or crouched on steps with her head on her knees, remaining motionless as if in a deep slumber.

After paying for her night's lodging she had eked out what was left of the shilling she had received at the Asylum, eating only when her hunger grew painful, and allowing herself scarcely more than the rations dealt out to a shipwrecked crew. She felt hourly that her strength was failing her, and that both reason and body were giving way with her pangs.

In the early morning—for the night had been passed dozing in a coffee-shop—she had crawled about the West End; but as the day advanced, and the cleanly-dressed people began to stir abroad, she had gradually crept away before them, and so reached the lonely City. Whilst the crowds were flocking to church she hid herself down mews, and when the bells had ceased ringing she slunk forth again, and stole cautiously into one of those odd, out-of-the-way City churches, with a burial-ground like a back garden up a court, and whose congregation is always about as numerous as the audience to a scientific lecture at a mechanics' institution. Here she slided to the least conspicuous of the free seats and tried to pray, but the place was warm to drowsiness, and tired and faint as she was, the hum of the organ lulled her to sleep.

It had thawed during the day, but as the night came on, the sky grew clear and starry and the air keen and frosty, so that in a few hours the pavements were a sheet of glass, and the lumps of mud as hard and sharp as the slag of a foundry. The street slush had during her Sunday's pilgrimage oozed through the gaps and holes in her burst boots, and as the cold of the night returned, her wet stockings froze to her chilled feet and wounded them at each step she took.

Now she had not even a penny left to pay for the cup of coffee that would have entitled her to a short slumber at the night-houses with her head upon the table. She counted each hour through the night, as does a sick person restless with a fever, and heard the hundred steeples of the City chiming the time, in the darkness and chill of the early morning, until she thought the sunlight would never come again.

As the air seemed to grow colder than ever at the fag-end of the night, and the streets had long been rid of the few remaining brawlers, leaving her the only wanderer through them, she grew more wretched and desperate than ever. Driven by the policeman from door-step to door-step, and finding that she was not allowed to sit, much less sleep, in the thoroughfares, she began to think it better to end such a life as hers, and sauntered on, shuddering, towards the river. But when there, the water was like a sheet of steel, and looked so witheringly cold as her mantle flew open in the nipping breeze, that her timid resolves took flight, and she felt she lacked the courage, even though heart-broken and half-frozen as she was, for such a death as that.

So on she wandered again, half sleeping as she walked, and trying to find some hidden corner where, unseen by the policeman, she might doze against the wall, until at length the reviving bustle of the market carts roused her from her stupor, and she was filled with hopes, almost as faint and comfortless as the cold morning light, that some lucky accident might happen to her in the coming day.

How that day was lived through it is difficult to tell. The poor soul had already been thirty odd hours adrift in the streets without food or sleep, or even rest. Still, while the daylight lasted, and

London was alive with the rattle of its traffic, she staggered along, borne faintly up by the continual excitement of the passing throngs, and feeling still a half presentiment that she would meet with her husband somewhere among the crowd.

But when she saw another night beginning to dusk the air, and the lines of street-lamps starting one after another into strings of light, she felt no longer faint and torpid, but grew positively furious with the frenzy of the thought of passing another such a time in the streets. Moreover, the sky was overcast, and the half-melted snow-flakes fell now in a shower of sleet, that, as it beat against the face, stung the skin with the sharp splinters of ice mixed with the rain.

Then, more terrible than all, she began to feel that another life besides her own was at stake, and to be roused with all the madness of maternal instinct lest any danger should befall her child.

Whither could she crawl to hide her head at such an hour? What place would open its doors to receive her? She had been turned from the workhouse, and dismissed with a shilling from the last haven of all—the Asylum for the Houseless.

It was no time for seeking shelter as a charity; she must have it, even though it be adjudged to her as a punishment. It had been refused her as an act of mercy to herself; it should now be forced upon her as an act of justice to others.

The first thought was to do as she had read of women doing when rendered as desperate as herself; and, stung by the anguish of the moment, she seized a stone from the newly-macadamized road, and was about to fling it at the first street lamp. But then came the thought that perhaps the authorities might take pity on her for so trifling an offence; so, turning round, she flung the stone with all her remaining strength at the first brilliantly-lighted window that caught her sight, and shattered a huge sheet of plate glass—as big as a masquerade posting-bill—that adorned the showy front of a neigh-bouring shawl and mantle warehouse.

At the sound of the crash and rattle of the glassy fragments, a crowd of shopmen rushed into the street; and on the woman confess-ing herself the offender it was but the work of a moment to hand her over to the police, whilst the enraged proprietor vowed "that if it cost him a hundred pounds, she should have three months of it."

And the tradesman was true to his word.

CHAPTER V.

THE RELEASE.

"What, Simcox, my boy, who'd have thought of seeing you?"

"Bless my heart! why, it's Mr. Nathan, as I live!"

These gentlemen met outside Tothill Fields Prison. Mr. Simcox, of the firm of Simcox, Son, and Nicholls, had his hand on the prison knocker, ready to lift the two hundred-weight of metal, when the approaching figure of Mr. Nathan, of Lyon's Inn, startled him from his purpose.

"This is the very last place where I should have thought of meeting you!" exclaimed that ornament to his profession, Simcox.

"And I certainly never expected to see you here," returned the buckish Israelite.

"If it ain't impertinent, may I ask what brings you to these parts?"

"Well, do you know, I was just going to put the same question to you."

"Oh, I've come about a poor woman who has got into trouble."

"Ha, ha! and my case is with a female too."

"The girl I've come about is here in the name of Katherine—Katherine—let me see—what's her other name?"

"It isn't Merton, is it? For that's the one I want."

"Dear me! this is strange. That's the very party I'm after, sure enough."

"How remarkably odd! If it's a fair question, who are you concerned for?"

"Oh, certainly—without prejudice, you know! I come here on the part of the husband."

"The husband! He's a Frenchman, isn't he? Used to teach languages, I think? Well, I'm instructed by the family—very old clients of mine, and highly respectable people."

"And what do they want to do with the girl?"

"I really don't think I should like to go so far as to answer that question."

"I don't see that it can prejudice your case at all, for I am quite decided as to the course I shall pursue."

"I tell you what," proposed Simcox, "you tell me, and I'll tell you—that's fair."

"Without prejudice, of course?"

"Certainly! Well, I have come here to pay the fine, and release her."

"You surely must be joking—that's just my errand."

"Bless my heart, you don't say so! And what do you propose to do with her when you get her out?"

"Well, as we are to be frank, the husband wishes to have her sent over to France to him. He has taken a singing coffee-house—a 'cafe shontong,' as they call it—and—"

"Ah, I see; and he thinks, as Katherine is a pretty girl, she'd look well sitting behind those portions of lump sugar, and taking the money for him."

"And what does the father mean to do with her, eh?"

"Why, I am to send her down to an aunt of hers in the country, and I believe she is to be despatched to Australia."

"You speak as if you were sure to have her. You forget the husband has a prior claim."

"We deny the marriage!"

"And we are in a position to prove it. I have a copy of the certificate among the papers that my client has sent me."

"Nonsense! that fellow was villain enough to forge any document."

"I tell you it was a bona fide marriage."

"Pooh! pooh!"

"I intend to claim the woman on behalf of the husband."

"And I shall go in with you and serve the prison authorities with notice, that if they deliver her up to you, they'll do so at their peril."

"Well, well, we needn't quarrel about it here." And so saying Mr. Nathan gave a heavy knock at the door.

In a moment the ponderous gateway was open, and the two solicitors were ushered into the clerk's office at the side.

Both, in their impatience, began shouting at the same time, "I've called to pay the fine—"

"One at a time, gentlemen," interfered the steady-going clerk.

"In the case of Katherine Merton," said Mr. Simcox, "I give you notice that you do not hand over the body to Mr. Nathan here—"

"And I have come to give you similar notice not to part with her to this gentleman; I claim her on behalf of the husband."

"And I deny that there is any husband at all, and come here on the part of the father."

"Come, gentlemen, you needn't quarrel about it," said the clerk, solemnly; "neither husband nor father can claim her now."

"She hasn't been released?" asked the lawyers in one breath.

The clerk answered gravely, "She was buried this morning."

"Good Heavens!" cried Mr. Simcox, starting back.

"Dear me! what an awful thing!" said Nathan, turning pale. "We have no power now, Simcox, so we had better go and have a glass of sherry together, for the shock has made me feel quite faint."

They were about to quit the office, when the clerk called after them : " By-the-bye, gentlemen, there's a baby—a little boy—that Katherine Merton has left behind her. What are we to do with him ? "

" Boy ! " they both exclaimed, as they stared at one another.

Then Simcox said : " Oh, he belongs to the husband, clearly ! "

" Husband ! " exclaimed Nathan. " Why, you denied the marriage just now. He had better be sent home to his mother's family. Couldn't be in better hands, I'm sure."

" Well, gentlemen," said the clerk, " settle it amicably between you ; which shall we hand the infant over to ? "

" Oh, I've no instructions on the matter."

" And I'm sure I've none."

" I am certain my clients are of too high standing in the world to countenance any child of sin born under such disgraceful circumstances ! " exclaimed the moral Simcox.

" And I expect my client," tittered the wily Nathan, " will be only too glad to get rid of the burden."

" But will you leave the addresses of your clients, gentlemen," asked the clerk, " so that we may communicate with them ? "

Both the lawyers seemed to consider such a proceeding perfectly unnecessary, and precipitately left the prison.

Now what fate, reader, think you, would be likely to await a being born under such circumstances, and in such a place ? To what end is such a beginning likely to lead ? Is such a one likely to find the streets of London ." paved with gold " ?

Book the First.

YOUNG WORKHOUSE AND FATHER PARISH.

CHAPTER I.

DRAGGED UP.

An individual, costumed in a fashion which partook of the conjoint characters of the police-inspector, the railway-guard, and the half-pay officer, jerked at the long dangling bell pull beside the gate of a large building, the architecture of which was of that non-ornate, government-establishment, contract style peculiar to hospitals, prisons, mad-houses, factories, and barracks.

That individual was a prison-warder, and that building a workhouse—the workhouse of "St. Lazarus Without."

"The House"—as all the poor in the neighbourhood called it, speaking of it as if there was no other house in the entire parish worthy of consideration, and always prefixing the definite article to it, as merchants talk of "the bank" when referring to any of the places of business belonging to Messrs. Coutts, Drummond, Hoare, Twining, Rogers, and Co.—the House, we repeat, was of the true parochial pattern, such as may be seen in almost any quarter of the metropolis. Had it not been for its high outer wall, it might have been mistaken for an hospital; but for its want of bars before the windows, it might have been supposed to be a prison; if it had only had a tall chimney-shaft, the stranger in London might have come to the conclusion that it was an extensive factory; or a couple of sentries pacing in front of it, and a few pairs of regimental trousers drying outside the windows, would have convinced the visitor from a garrison town in the country that it was some barracks.

The little square wicket in the gate was opened, and a round, red face appeared behind the gridiron-like bars. The eyes of the face twinkled again as they glanced at the prison arms on the warder's stand-up collar, and the mouth was seen to expand into a grin as its owner said,—

"Now, then, what's up? You a'n't come after any of our chaps, have you?"

The prison officer felt somewhat piqued that the "parish" should presume to address the "county" in so trifling a tone, and answered as sharply as if he had been on drill—"Letter from the guv'nor."

The gate was unlocked, and, when the warder had passed through, a woman carrying a child was about to follow, whereupon the workhouse porter thrust her back, saying:

"Now, young 'ooman, where's your order?"

"A' right!" cried the turnkey, with true official elision. "One of our female warders. You're to receive the body of this here baby," he added, as he nodded at a long roll of clothes that the woman was carrying under her mantle.

Now, if the male official had been roused at the porter's want of proper respect for his superiors, the female one—who wore the full uniform of blue-trimmed bonnet and green-plaid cloak distinctive of a prison-matron—grew positively crimson with indignation at the idea of being mistaken for an applicant for relief. She felt, however, that it was beneath her as an "officer," who had been "many years in the service," to bandy words with a workhouse porter, much as she might have been inclined to tell him "a bit of her mind."

Inside the workhouse gate the Union character of the place was as unmistakable as the Union Jack itself. Close beside the gateway was the little square cottage of a porter's lodge, placed there like a huge dog-kennel to guard the entrance. The big, brawny old soldier who did duty as gate-keeper, had evidently been chosen with a view to the overawing of "sturdy vagrants;" and though displaying but little softness in his nature, exhibited an odd fancy for pigeons and singing birds; for against his door-post a lark hopped about upon a few square inches of turf, and the room inside the lodge was as chirrupy as a barber's shop with its cages of linnets and goldfinches, whilst the pigeons strutting about the large, bare, gravelled court-yard—as pompous and gorgeous as beadles—belonged also to the official.

Across the yard was the big entrance-hall, where rows of black leathern fire-buckets dangled from the ceiling, as at an insurance office; and once within this, the true character of the building was made apparent to every sense. The nose could sniff pauperism in the smell of bread and gruel which pervaded the air. The eye read helplessness and poverty-stricken dependence in the crook-backed old figures, tottering about, as if palsied with weakness, in their suits of iron-grey; whilst the ear recognized the same tale in the mumbling, wheezy voices, the asthmatic coughs, and the occasional shouting of the hale officials into the ears of the half-fatuous inmates —for all about the place were "so hard of hearing" that they had to use their hand as an ear-trumpet when spoken to.

To cross that workhouse threshold was to step, as it were, into another country, peopled only by beings in their second childhood;

and the sight of such a multitude of old creatures, toddling along with all the ricketiness of babyhood, set the mind wondering how so many shaky greybeards—for all were far older and weaker than any seen abroad in the streets—could ever have been collected together. It was, indeed, a perfect museum of old age, where every variety of decrepitude might be noted and studied. A few of the inmates went staggering across the sanded floors, propped on two sticks, others sat out on the yard benches in the spots where the sun fell, hoping to add a little heat to their expiring fires; and many of these had white night-caps showing under their hats, as though they were always ready for sleep, and fully prepared for the last long nap of all.

The prison officials were ushered by a trembling old pauper "messenger"—who, by virtue of his office, had been promoted to the dignity of an entire suit of cords, and looked not unlike a superannuated charity boy—into the deserted board-room, where they were left for a while to scan the "regulations concerning disorderly and refractory paupers," or to study the "dietary tables," or else to pore over the maps that hung round the room as thickly as show-boards at a railway station. They had also time to contemplate the portrait of "Margaret Fleming," who, as the inscription said, "died in this workhouse, aged 103;" as well as to reckon, by the number of mahogany chairs drawn up in single file along the walls, how many guardians were in the habit of sitting, on full board days, round that ample green-baize-covered, horse-shoe table, which, with the high-backed chair standing alone at the upper end of it, seemed to fill the entire place.

In a few minutes the master entered with the governor's letter open in his hand. He looked at the baby, whose little chin the female warder was now busy tickling, in the hopes of coaxing it into a smile, and said,—

"Oh, that's the child, is it? It seems healthy enough! No skin disease, eh?"

"It's as beautiful a baby as ever was born, bless its little heart!" answered the female officer, as she continued to fondle the infant; "and has all its limbs straight, thank goodness."

"The governor tells me here that its name is Philip Merton," proceeded the master, glancing at the note.

"Yes; Merton was the name the mother was in by," replied the woman; "and an exceedingly well-conducted person she was."

The master went on reading the letter, speaking aloud as he did so,—

"'The mother died in prison of puerperal fever,'—ah!—very good—'four days after the birth of the child,'—dear me! sad case—very good—'can't say whether married or not,'—hem—ah! very good—'reason to suppose the relations of the mother are well off,'—so—so, indeed—very good—'but no clue as to their name, or whereabouts,'—tut! tut! how unfortunate; well, we must see whether we can find 'em out, and make them pay for the maintenance of the child."

Then opening the door, he cried out,—

"Here Hogsflesh, ask the matron to be good enough to step this way."

When that lady made her appearance, a conversation took place as to whether any of the mothers then in the Union could be found willing to nurse the child in addition to her own.

The matron ran over the names of several, and at last said,—

"There's Mary Hazlewood! I'm sure her little Bertha is no drag upon such a strong, healthy woman as she is; and she'd be glad enough to take the boy, I dare say, for the allowance of beer and meat she'd get by it."

The conversation was suddenly brought to a close by Hogsflesh again appearing at the door, and saying, as he thrust his head in,—

"Please, there's three ounces of wine wanted for the infirmary—and quick, please."

It was, therefore, rapidly settled that the proposition should be made to the before-mentioned strong and healthy woman, and the female warder took her parting kiss at the plump cheeks of the unconscious little outcast, prattling to it in childish language the while; and even though it was fast asleep, telling it that they would all come and see it, and bring it some nice playthings as soon as it was old enough to use them.

In a short while afterwards the hungry little Philip was butting his head like a young lamb against the side of Mary Hazlewood, whilst his pauper foster-sister was put to suck her fist and sprawl in the workhouse cradle at the foot of the woman. His prison baby-clothes had been exchanged for the blue-and-white-striped frock and the duster-like checked pinafore composing the workhouse infant suit.

The life of a workhouse infant has as little variety connected with it as that of a lighthouse keeper. The days of little Philip Merton came one after another, and were as similar in appearance as those in a new diary, without an event worth noting to fill up the blank. Even the old mill-horse is said to have enjoyed the pleasing relaxation of turning the other way on the Sabbath, but to the Union babies Sunday brought no difference to the week's monotony of periodical pap and gruel. True, Sunday was white pinafore day, and there were no clothes then hanging to dry in the exercising yard; and the workhouse chapel organ, too, might be heard droning across the yard, about as loud as the hum of a bumble-bee among the flowers; but although the mothers told the children to "listen to the music," they none of them, poor things! knew what music was—for not even an itinerant hurdy-gurdy was ever heard within the walls of St. Lazarus Without; nor had they ever seen a bumble-bee; nor, indeed, a flower (as nothing grew in that small Sahara of a gravelled

yard); neither was any living animal seen within the Union gates, beyond the tabby cat out of the "old women's ward."

But the workhouse babes could not even enjoy the sports peculiar to infancy, such as thrusting in their dolls' eyes or sucking the tail of a sucking-pig; for in St. Lazarus's Union the dolls' eyes were stitched in black thread upon the rag faces; and such delicacies as sucking-pigs have never been heard of as forming part of the workhouse rations—even within the memory of Margaret Fleming herself, who died, as we have said, aged 103.

Mary Hazlewood, with her two infants, had so much to do, that the days passed anything but slowly with her. By the time night came round, and she had the children cleanly dressed for bed—for the washings were as regular as the meal hours—and cuddling one another in their cradle, she was glad to sit down quietly beside them, and darn their tiny workhouse clothes; and then, as she saw their hair mixing together on the pillow, she would declare that she was getting to like that dear Phil almost as much as her Bertie, though it wasn't doing right to her own flesh and blood.

The woman, indeed, belonged to a better class. Her husband had been a seafaring man, and had gone out one morning—after a few words, when rather the worse for liquor—to look for a ship, but had never returned; and whether he had deserted her, or stumbled over the dock's side, she had been unable to learn. The birth of her child had forced her into the workhouse; but here she had conducted herself so much to the satisfaction of the matron that, on the death of the old woman who looked after the children in the upper nursery, she was installed as nurse to the family of little two-year-old outcasts.

By the time Philip had reached his second year, and had been transferred to the upper nursery, he had, thanks to his foster-mother, grown into a plump, healthy-looking child, and so fat, too, that he had mere creases for joints and dimples for knuckles. His hair was light-brown, while his skin was pinky and transparent, so that it had often been a debate with the mothers in the ward as to whether he would grow up fair or dark. He was still too young for his features to have any distinct mark about them; nor did they bear as yet any trace of his father having been a foreigner; though, perhaps, he was quicker in his temper and more sudden in his affections than any of his little playmates. He was a great favourite among the women, from his pretty fresh colour; and the matron, in her rounds, often pinched his cheeks as she went by, and called him her little pet, with the long, dark eyelashes.

The occasional visits, too, of the female warders from the prison served to throw, not only an importance, but a sympathy, about the little fellow; for it soon got bruited about that his mother had once been "a lady," and had died in prison after days of destitution in the streets. Thus he got to be the most petted of all the pauper children; and if ever he toddled to the other side of the yard, and paid a visit to the old women's ward, there was almost a quarrel among the aged crones there as to who should have him on her knee, or hold the cat for him to stroke and pull about. And even when he went over there with "sister Bertie," as he was taught to call her, the ounce papers of brown sugar allowed to the poor old creatures were brought out more as a grand feast for " Phil " than to please the little girl.

There were some fifteen wretched little pauper children in the nursery. There was little Annie Inwards, who had neither father nor mother—and there was Susey Collins, whose father had been killed at the railway—and Billy Thompson, whose three little brothers were in the Union also, but had been sent to the infirmary for ill-health—and Tommy Liddle, whose aunt wouldn't keep him any longer—and ten or eleven others, all with some wretched story, which affected everybody but themselves almost to tears.

But among the number there were two for whom little Phil had very different feelings. The one was Emma Dixon, a big girl of eight, whose mother wasn't "right in her head," and wouldn't let her go to school; and her the little fellow was almost as much afraid of as he was taken with poor blind Willie, who had come out of "Pancridge Union," as the women called it, and who had no other name that they knew of. But this one, after sister Bertha, he loved better than all the rest—though he hardly knew why. When a mere baby, Phil had been attracted towards the blind boy by the strange, wandering, upturned look of his dead opaque eyes, and next to the cat, Willie's eyes were the most curious sight for him in the place; so he would sit and watch the restless, useless eyeballs, and as they seemed to turn back into the head, ask a thousand childish questions of the afflicted little orphan.

For three years Phil stopped in the workhouse, till in his little mind it was not only a home but an entire world to him. Seldom did his walks extend beyond the limits of the exercising-ground, so that he had no knowledge of nature, or hardly of mankind. So entirely had his little life, indeed, been hemmed in by the Union walls, that he grew up with a notion that there were only two classes of people in the world—paupers and guardians; and, consequently, when he and the other little ones were allowed, as a great treat, to o out for a walk with Nurse Hazlewood, he would call every well-dressed man that passed "a guardy," whilst every respectable dame he pointed at as a "matey"—the nursery name for matron.

Nor had the little fellow any more vivid idea as to the necessity of working in order to live. He had seen day after day go by and some three or four hundred people regularly supplied with food without the least exertion on their part; and he had got to fancy that nature sent breakfasts and suppers in the same way as she did light and darkness. The only work of which he had any notion was washing and cooking; for he had often been into the laundry on one side of the yard, and it was a favourite amusement of his to peep down into the kitchen and watch the big cauldrons of gruel being stirred. Accordingly, the men he had seen working when out on his walks he had fancied to be playing. Though, too, he had never asked himself or any one else where bread or gruel came from, it is almost certain that if he had been hard pushed on the subject, the boy would have shown there was some vague idea lingering in his mind that quartern loaves were obtained in the same manner as the paving stones he had seen dug up out of the roads; whilst gruel, no doubt, he thought to be as easily collected in tubfuls as the rain-water they caught for the washing.

As for money, he had never even heard the chink of it, and had a shilling been shown to him, he would probably have taken it for one of the Union metal buttons.

When little Philip had turned his third year, it came to the time when he must quit the Union for the pauper farm-schools in the suburbs. Little Bertha was to go with him, but blind Willie and Nurse Hazlewood, or "mother," as he called her—his only other friends in the world—were to stay behind. The two children were hardly aware that they were about to be taken away "for good;" and as they were being dressed for their departure, they were full of glee, under the idea that they were going for a short time outside of the old brick walls; so they laughed and clapped their hands, whilst Nurse Hazlewood was sobbing so that she could hardly see to tie their clothes for the tears that were in her eyes. She knew that she could stop the leaving of her daughter, but over her foster-boy she had no power; and then came the idea that even if Bertha did remain with her there inside those four high walls, she would grow up half silly, like Emma Dixon, the crazy woman's child. The poor thing sobbed and moaned as if her heart were breaking, but still she was determined, for the child's sake, to bear up against the agony of the parting.

And when the time came for leaving, and she saw the two unconscious children eager to quit her, she flung her arms round them and pressed them to her till all the clean clothes she had been so busy arranging were crumpled and soiled with her affection.

They had at last to tear the children away by force, and as they did so, she cried aloud, "I can never let them go, matron; oh! don't take them from me."

In kindness the little ones were hurried away from her, and as the door closed, the poor pauper mother flung herself on the table, and, bursting into a convulsion of grief, called God to help her, crying aloud, "All's gone from me! all's gone from me now! I'm a lone woman—lone—lone!"

CHAPTER II.

THE PAUPER BOY'S NEW HOME.

YOUR true Londoner seems to have as little affection as a bird for the place of his birth—the prevailing desire among Cockneys being to get away from their parent metropolis, and settle down in some civic country-cousin of a suburb. A statistical quidnunc has laid it down as an ethnological law that scarcely a Londoner can trace a pure Cockney descent for three generations, urging that if the great-grandfather of a family had been born within sound of Bow Bells, the great-grandson seldom remains in the capital to inhale smuts with his air, but retires to end his days in the land of pure milk and fresh-cut vegetables.

We cannot say whether there be any general truth in the statist's views of Cockney genealogy, but certain it is that London is becoming more and more a city of warehouses, chambers, wharves, offices, and shops, rather than dwelling-houses and lodgings. Now that the metropolis has been transformed into a huge spider's web, with railway fibres radiating from its centre, the citizen, like the round-bellied insect itself, builds up a little retreat on one side of the great web, and is only seen to dart along the lines when there is anything "alive and stirring" that promises a "good catch" for him.

It is this yearning for a mouthful of country air that sends the Londoner—yellow and smoke-dried as a Finnie haddock—gasping down to the sea-side every autumn, and it is a like craving to see more of the earth and its vegetation than the disc of mangy turf within the railings of a square that has caused the mushroom towns, with their colonies of lath-and-plaster villas and tiny stucco mansions, to spring into existence around every suburban railway station.

By means of fast "business trains," Brighton is now scarcely farther from the capital "by rail" than is Hampstead "by 'bus;" and the longitude of Windsor, measured by time, is hardly greater than that of St. John's Wood computed by the "City Atlas." And so it comes that morning and evening trains, as long as sea-serpents, rush up and down the line with each joint of their monster tail closely packed with season-ticket-bearing merchants.

Near one of these small and new out-of-town towns was situated the pauper school to which our hero was consigned. The town itself was as yet only in the bud, for many of the carcases of the houses had hardly had time to blossom into villas. Every patch of ground had a board up, announcing, "THIS ELIGIBLE SITE TO BE LET ON A BUILDING LEASE." Of the residences already erected, the larger majority were still unfinished, the works having been brought to a sudden stoppage by the evident bankruptcy of the speculating builder,

and of these the " DESIRABLE CARCASES " were advertised for sale;
whilst the few tenements that had been completed and rendered fit
for habitation were in the excruciatingly genteel style of compo-
grandeur, and in the " florid Cockney order " of architecture. They
had all palatial porticoes, and a double importance had been given to
them by the cunning of the architect, who, by building them in pairs,
had succeeded in imparting to two small houses the dignity of one
large one. Each couple of villas, too, had a carriage-drive, big enough
for a pony-chaise between them, and the little shrubs and delicate
trees in the strips of gardens were evidently only just out of the
nursery. Dotted all about was a thick sprinkling of public-houses,
showing that the place was a favourite resort for Sunday excur-
sionists from London; and every one of the taverns had a grand
balcony, fitted with benches, at the first floor, besides a flat roof,
furnished with tables and a flag-staff for the accommodation of
Cockney smokers.

The St. Lazarus Industrial School was a long building, as plain in
its architecture and set with as many windows as a contracting
builder's factory. It was of red brick, with white trimmings, and
cocked-hat like pediments to the wings, that gave it a thorough
British regimental look; and it stood on the top of a hill, surrounded
by its own grounds, and with an enormous central shaft rising above
its roof like a lanky lighthouse. It had nothing of the look of a
school, for there were no rows of white-curtained beds to be seen at
the windows; so that you expected, as you went by, to hear the whir
of wheels and the clatter of hammers rather than the hubbub of
children at play.

On approaching the walls of the play-ground, however, the hum of
hundreds of voices burst on the ear like the roar of the sea heard
inland, and you saw hovering over the huge quadrangle behind the
building a multitude of paper kites of all shapes and sizes, that seemed
like so many birds poised in the air. The branches of the trees, too,
around the wall were garlanded with the tattered remains of kite
tails and bodies that had got entangled among the twigs, and made
them look, with the bits of paper and string clinging to them, as
untidy as old brooms.

In this building were housed some seven hundred children, who,
like young Phil, had been thrown upon the parish for support.
They were of all ages; some so young that they could hardly walk
steadily, and others almost strong and expert enough to get a living
for themselves; and they were of all casts, too. A few had fathers
and friends; though such parents were hardly worth the mentioning for
the assistance they could afford their offspring in the world, for they
were mostly paupers, like the children, whom poverty had stripped of
home and cut off from the claims and ties of kindred. Fewer still
had relations who were in a position to visit them, and bring them
small tokens of remembrance—petty offerings that had been squeezed
out of the out-door relief, and yet were prized and envied as much

as any hamper of good things ever received at the most "select" academy for young gentlemen. The majority of the pauper pupils, indeed, were the mere waifs and strays of the world—social driftwood and salvage, cast upon the shores of London from the many wrecks of the stormy city. Some of these were foundlings, wretched little beings picked up on a door-step, for whom even parochial vigilance could not trace a pedigree. Others were orphans in the profoundest sense of the word, with only parish guardians for a stepfather, and who could never remember any home, nor, indeed, the inside of any house but that of the Union. A large proportion, moreover, bore the ironical stigma of being "love children," though these had known so little of love in the world that once got rid of by their "unfortunate" mother, they had never seen her face or heard her voice afterwards.

The pauper school was the rag-fair of life, whither was brought the refuse of society—the "things" that had been discarded as so much lumber; and, as in the old-clothes' market the mind wonders what is the history of the left-off coats, trousers, bonnets, and gowns collected there, as well as what possible use they can be hereafter put to, so, in this assemblage of infant cast-offs, one cannot help speculating as to the origin and ultimate destiny of the poor living rags and tatters that others have flung aside as being utterly worthless to them.

Of course, little Phil, mere babe as he was, was no more aware of the misery and degradation of his position in the world than a lordling in long clothes is conscious of the peculiar good fortune that has befallen him. Young Phil sipped his gruel from the iron spoon with an appetite as keen as that with which the sprig of nobility sucks his "soojee," from his silver pap-boat; for such undeveloped palates have not yet learned to discriminate between the vulgar and refined flavour of the different metals in the mouth. Neither had the little lad the faintest sense that the house he lived in was in any way different from that of other people; for, could he have expressed his ideas on the subject, and generalized upon the rules of life, he would as surely have laid it down that all children are born in workhouses, as a savage would that blankets and rum are the perfection of human luxury. Consequently, had Phil been made to understand, while on his way to the St. Lazarus Industrial School, that he was going to spend the next ten years of his life at a pauper academy, he might have burst into tears at the tidings; still, his sorrow would have been caused by the thought that he was leaving "home" and Mammy Hazlewood for good; for the Union was linked in his little mind with all that made life dear, while the workhouse women, who had shared their ounce packets of sugar with him, seemed to his purblind vision the most admirable and favoured of human beings.

The old pauper who drove the workhouse covered cart in which Phil and Bertha were being taken to the school was an object of no slight envy and importance in the little community of St. Lazarus, getting, as he did, extra rations of meat and beer for the duty. He was remarkable for the peevishness of old age, and, from a half-idea that he was earning his living, had grown to have a contempt for his fellow-paupers, as well as to treat them with all the tyranny of petty authority. He seemed disgusted with the playfulness and restlessness of the children on the journey, for when they came near him, and shouted "Gee, gee!" to the horse, and touched the reins, or wanted to handle the whip, he grew as growly as as old lapdog at the tricks of a kitten, and cried out, "Lie down, or I'll give you a crack." Nor was he more inclined to listen to their wonderings and prattle by the way; for when they beheld a fashionable footman for the first time in their lives, and—taken with the bright colours of the livery, as the man strutted, cane in hand, after his mistress—inquired if he was not a beadle, the old pauper grew more surly than ever at the mere mention of that despotic functionary, and, shaking the children's hands off his shoulders, said, "Cuss all beadles!—don't bother me."

On reaching the suburbs, and seeing the cows grazing in the fields, little Bertie, whose knowledge of natural history did not extend beyond the cat in the old women's ward, clapped her hands and jumped about, as she called out, "Puss! puss!"

"Go back'ards, will you!" snarled the old driver, angry at being roused out of his half-doze over his pipe.

Then came a young ladies' school, with the little girls walking two-and-two, and the tall mistress behind, whereupon both the children seemed to fancy that the governess occupied the same position as Mary Hazlewood had to them, for they exclaimed, at the top of their little voices, "Nursey! nursey!"

"Confound yer, keep quiet!" snapped the tetchy old fellow, as he knit his shaggy eyebrows at the little ones, till he looked as grim as a Skye terrier.

At the St. Lazarus Industrial School, the new comers were shown into no handsome reception-room, nor was any cake or wine had up to stop the tears of the fresh pupils; neither was Phil taken between the knees of the master and patted on the head, nor told he would one day become as distinguished a gentleman as his father. Not that the children were ill-treated on their arrival at the pauper schools, but rather they were received in the regular way of business, and little or no heed given as to whether they cared about coming there.

Poor Phil and Bertie, indeed, were handed from the workhouse cart as unceremoniously as parcels from a railway van, and the same ticket given with them in acknowledgment of their receipt. Phil heard the superintendent read the piece of paper, beginning, "Please to receive the following children," and saw him stare first at himself and then at Bertie, as he muttered, "An orphan, and one other child;" but the poor boy could hardly tell what it all meant. He felt frightened at the sight of the new faces and the big building, but still he had no definite idea that the place was to be his home for many a year to come, or that he was about to be separated from his foster-mother.

When, however, the grumbling old driver had mounted into the workhouse van again, and the children heard the wheels crunch over the gravel drive on its way back to the Union, both the little things understood for the first time that they were to be left behind, and struggled to get to the door, screaming the while, " Mamma, come to me! Mamma, come to me!"

A child's fears are always excessive, and seem to grown people, from their intensity, like the caricatures of emotion, for with the very young there is no judgment to check the imagination, and fright once raised outruns all probability where there is no experience to check it. Little Phil and Bertha trembled and sobbed as if they had a confused notion that they were about to be killed. Every face they saw seemed to be of the ugliest possible character to their minds, for no matter whether it came smiling or frowning to them, they screamed and roared as if it belonged to that ideal enemy of all children, "Old Bogie" himself. If they had ever heard of fairy tales—and among the illiterate paupers such nursery-book lore is unknown—the little things would assuredly have fancied they had got into the castle of the Ogre in Hop-o'-my-Thumb, or into the stronghold of the Giant in Jack and the Bean-stalk, and that all the children whom they saw were intended to be eaten up alive.

First of all, they were half frightened to death by a tall woman, who dragged them through long passages and up steep stone stairs to a room, where their workhouse clothes were taken off, as if they were really going to be murdered on the spot! and they made certain that such was to be the case, when, despite their screaming and cries for Nurse Hazlewood, they were plunged into a bath full of hot water, and there scrubbed till their skins and eyes smarted again with the friction and the soap.

Nor was their confidence in any way restored when, dressed in the school costume, they were taken into the infant play-ground, where a hundred little things were playing about; for as soon as the new comers entered, the others left off their games, and drew round them in a circle, staring at them like so many sheep at a dog. Phil and Bertha did nothing but cling together and cry, for they were too young even to say a word of consolation to each other; their little minds indeed being filled with a dull blank of grief. At supper they left their slice of bread-and-butter and mug of milk-and-water untouched, for then they were scared by the sight of the fifty little ones gathered together in the nursery for the meal, and they had never seen so many children assembled in one room before. Everything they saw and heard, too, was so strange and different from the workhouse nursery, that they sat with their fingers in their mouths, looking timidly and wildly about them.

When the bell rang for bedtime, and they were taken up into the infants' dormitory, where, instead of Nurse Hazlewood, a strange woman came to undress them, their little senses once more noted the difference of their situation, and their tears showed that they felt they were never to see "dear mother" again. Then as they cuddled together in one of the dumpy little iron bedsteads that crowded the large sleeping-room, they twined their arms about each other's necks as if they had really laid themselves down to die, like the babes in the wood; and there they sobbed away till their tears formed a wet patch about their heads, so that the black lines of the tick could be seen through the moistened pillow-case.

Before a week had passed, however, Phil had forgotten all the miseries that had so nearly broken his little heart on entering the school; and ere long he had grown as attached to the place as he had been to his former home, so that had anybody attempted to remove him from his new one, he would most likely have felt the separation as keenly as he did his departure from the Union. He soon became, indeed, one of the merriest of the children there, for he made friends among his little toddling companions, and slowly grew to be as fond of his new nurse as he had been of his old one. His first year was spent in the babies' room, and here he was the biggest of the boys, for some of the others scarcely reached above the nurse's knee, whilst he was just tall enough to look over the iron bars of the nursery fender.

His life in this part of the establishment had little to distinguish it from that in the workhouse, with the exception that at the industrial school the child's days were not utterly toyless—playthings not being wholly unknown to the infants there. Over the mantelpiece in the dormitory was kept the humble stock of pauper playthings—a curious collection of broken penny articles and bits of gilt paper, which, poor as it was, was yet more than the workhouse itself could boast. There was a Noah's Ark hardly bigger than a baby's shoe, and a wooden money-box, like a miniature trunk, but containing a few beads instead of coins : and there was a cardboard cottage, decorated with pith, and a cat without a head, besides a few lids of old soap boxes, embellished with varnished pictures and gilt borders, together with a little tin grate and a baby dustpan. But the grandest toy of all was the wooden horse, about as big as a pet spaniel, which the chaplain had given the little things. To ride on this was the great treat of the infants' room, and one which none but those who had been "as good as gold" were allowed to enjoy.

A year's playing with the tin plate, stamped with the alphabet round the rim—a year's rattling the beads in the money-box, with a few rides on the chaplain's wooden horse, and Phil had become old enough to be moved down into the "infant boys' room," to take his first lessons in the infants' school, as well as to share in the games in the infants' play-ground. His seat during school hours was on the lowest stair of the broad flight of wooden steps that constituted a

kind of gallery for the little pupils to be ranged upon during their
lessons. The play-ground, too, was a fine place to jump about in,
and it had no clothes hanging to dry in it, like the exercising-yard at
the workhouse, so that he and Bertha could run and gambol in it
without having the wet linen flapping in their faces. The superintendent's wife, too, had given Philip a penny battledoor and shuttlecock,
and this was so precious a treasure that the little fellow, on first
receiving it, wanted to carry it to bed with him at night, and nearly
had it taken away because he screamed and kicked on not being
allowed to do so.

Wretched little pauper schoolboys! We who can remember the
sums that were spent in the toys of our youth—the Christmas-boxes,
and school money, and birthday gifts that were laid out with the old
cake-woman of the school, or at the counters of that fairyland of our
holidays, the bazaar—such as we may, perhaps, wonder how so poor
a plaything could cause such great happiness as Phil's penny present
yielded him. But to those whose babyhood is comparatively toyless,
who hardly ever know even the childish luxury of a sweetmeat, and
who are content to amuse themselves with a piece of paper fluttering
at the end of a thread; to them—lower as they are in the scale even
than they who get an occasional "farthing to spend"—the present
of a penny toy is an event in their young pauper lives to be remembered and dated from.

CHAPTER III.

THE PAUPER SCHOOL.

TIME was when your pauper schools were little better than pauper
pens for pauper cattle to be kept in until they were old enough—
according to law—to work their way, slowly but surely, from the
workhouse to the prison, and thus shift the burden from the parish
to the county. In such days the maintenance of the young pauper
herd was put up to competition, and he who bid the lowest figure had
the job. Nor was it until some violent fever had broken out and
threatened a pestilence among the ratepayers, or until the expenses of
the parish funerals had amounted to unwieldy sums which no nicety
of finance could conceal, that guardians began to trouble their heads
about the fate of the miserable wretches to whom they had consented
to act as deputy fathers.

Luckily for Phil, he had begun his career in life at a time when the
outcast children of the land were no longer fed and trained by contract. It had already been discovered that the best means of putting
a stop to the habitual pauperism which infested our workhouses as
thickly as rats do a sewer, was by training the young parish outcasts

to some calling which would enable them to keep clear of the Union for the future; and it is this discovery which has called into existence a class of institutions which are at once the noblest and most useful in the land—the Pauper Industrial Schools.

The school at which Phil had been placed differed but little from those now scattered about the suburbs of London. It was a little self-supporting community, the children being taught to do almost every office that was needed for themselves and their fellows. The boys worked upon the farm and the farm-yard, growing the fodder for the cattle that yielded the milk, which the girls made into butter and cheese for the parish scholars. Again, the linen on their backs, as well as their clothes and shoes, were all made in the parish-girls' needle-room or the parish-boys' workshops. The school steam-engine, moreover, was stoked and tended by young pauper engineers, and even the repairs of it wrought by young pauper smiths, whilst the mangles and washing-machines which the steam set in motion were managed by young pauper laundresses, who did all the washing for the little colony. Thus some seven hundred childish creatures were taught to live with all the economy, regularity, and beauty of a hive. The bread they ate was kneaded and baked by their own young hands, the meat cooked by them, and the place cleaned; whilst even the gas which lighted the building young paupers had helped to manufacture. Indeed, there was hardly a want in the place that was not supplied by the same young labourers. There were boy carpenters to build or repair, as well as boy painters and glaziers to colour the woodwork and mend the windows, together with boy bricklayers to whitewash. And yet, while the hands were being taught the mind was not left untrained; and so sound was the teaching, that some of the more apt of the pauper pupils were being educated to become the future masters of that or some similar institution.

It was a sad day for Phil when his time came to be removed from the "infants'" side to the "boys'" portion of the school buildings. The change was like going into a new world again, for he had to leave all his little friends with whom he had been associated for so long a time. Moreover, the boys in the upper play-ground were all strangers to him, and so much bigger than himself, that he felt the same fear of going among them as he had done on first coming to the school itself. But though he was now old enough to be ashamed of showing such a feeling, still the thought of being separated from Bertie, whom he had got to love as a real sister, caused him more grief than he had artifice to conceal. The little girl, however, had no check upon her sorrow, and, as they sat apart under the shed in the play-ground, she whimpered and rubbed her eyes with her knuckles until her tears were coloured with the dirt off her hands, so that she seemed to have been weeping Indian ink. But Philip was just little man enough to know that the big boys he was going among would laugh at him if they saw his eyes were red with crying; so he swallowed his sobs, and endeavoured to persuade her (and himself at the same time) that "there was no good in fretting, for it wasn't as if they were going to be shut up away from one another, as he would still be able to see her at meal-times and at chapel on Sundays, and he would take care and nod to her every day even if he couldn't speak."

One marked difference that existed between the infants and the boys at the Industrial School was that the younger children had not yet sense enough to speculate as to their origin or the condition of their parents; whereas the elder boys were continually puzzling their brains with the mystery of their existence. No less than two hundred out of the three hundred lads who thronged the upper play-ground were orphans in the fullest sense of the word, and even the parents of the less destitute children were either in the Union or in the receipt of out-door relief. It was reckoned among the boys at that school as extraordinary a circumstance for a lad to have a father living, as it is at other seminaries remarkable for a youth to be without one. At the generality of academies for young gentlemen, there is some one pupil, whose parents being out in India, or who, having only a guardian to look after him, is left at the school during the vacation, and such a one is always an object of pity among his companions, and sympathized with even by the servants of the establishment. At the pauper school, however, there were no holidays at all, simply from the fact that there were no homes to go to, nor even with the larger proportion of the seven hundred little outcasts were there any mothers or fathers to receive them.

When Phil, in his skeleton suit of corduroy, was turned into the big play-ground, the "new boy" was soon spied out; and as the news spread round, the games were stopped, and the lads at the farther end of the ground left off swinging round the gymnastic pole, whilst those who had been making kites, or indulging in "fly the garter," came streaming out of the "play-room" to have a peep at the fresh comer. They stared at him at first as strange animals gaze at each other, until at last began the round of boyish questions touching his private history and condition.

"What's your parish?" was the first question, and which came as naturally to the orphan scholars as the inquiry concerning the parentage of a new pupil is common among other schoolboys. The speaker was the big boy of the school, who, by virtue of his size, had been promoted to a cord jacket, vice a skeleton suit resigned.

Phil gave no answer, for he felt that if he said a word he must burst into tears.

"Are you an orphan?" asked another, who was not, and was always glad to show off a bit before his less lucky schoolfellows.

Phil nodded his head, on which he was told to "speak up, and say at once whether he had got a father and mother, or not."

"Nurse Hazlewood, please, is the only mother I've got," stammered Phil.

At this there was a shout from several boys who belonged to St. Lazarus Without, and who instantly exclaimed, "Why, she's the Union nurse, spooney!"

A lad with a crutch, anxious to befriend little Philip, here observed: "He means perhaps she's his foster-mother"—for all the boys at that school understood the most minute relations of orphanage, so that terms that would have been as Greek to more favoured children were naturally comprehensible to them.

The speaker, however, was set upon by the united boys belonging to St. Lazarus, all of whom shouted, "What can you know about it? you came from St. Job the Martyr; so just shut up!"

It was curious how the boys at the Industrial School were divided into little cliques, the lads from the different parishes making cronies of their fellow-parishioners just as those from the same county become friends at other seminaries.

"Are you a foundling?" inquired another lad. "Come, young'un, you needn't be timorsome over it, for there's a jolly lot of us here."

Almost the only thing that young Phil remembered concerning his origin was having heard Nurse Hazlewood once tell one of the guardians, while going his rounds of inspection through the workhouse, "that he was the boy whose mother had been a lady, and died in prison;" he remembered it well, because the gentleman had patted him on the head, and given him his first halfpenny at the time. So Philip paid no heed to the question, but turned away from the speaker.

"Come, don't sulk," cried one of the boys; and, pointing to another, he continued: "This chap, here, was tied in a fish-basket to the relieving officer's knocker."

"No, I wasn't," retorted the other, in the midst of the laughter. "My mother's a washerwoman, and has two-and-sixpence a week and two loaves, out-door relief, on account of her rheumatiz."

The examination-in-chief was then taken up by the lad with the crutch, who said: "Cheer up, don't be afraid to tell us chaps here. You were deserted, I suppose, and haven't got any friends?"

"I've got Nurse Hazlewood," Philip answered, simply, as if he thought that was everything in the world.

"She ain't the sort of friend we mean. Ain't you got no relations, such as will give you a red comforter like we've got?"

The comforter here referred to was the great mark of distinction between those boys who could boast of some kindred and those who were utterly friendless in the world. The parish allowance, by way of neck-tie for the scholars, consisted merely of a piece of black shoe-ribbon, to fasten the shirt-collar; and the bright-coloured worsted cravat, to keep the chest and throat from the cold had come to be a regular sign in the school that the wearer had somebody to care about him: so that, as the eye glanced over the play-ground, it could pick out the children who were not utterly destitute as easily as corporals can be distinguised from privates by their stripes.

" Don't you know where you were born, and how you came to have a settlement in St. Lazarus ? " was the next inquiry.

Philip shook his head ; for though he had often heard the word " settlement " used in the Union, and knew that it was looked upon by the inmates as a kind of indisputable claim or birthright to the place, still he had not yet got to understand what it meant so clearly as his questioners.

" Well, tell us how you became chargeable ? Was your father an able-bodied or in-doors man ? "

" Please, I've heard mother Hazlewood say my real mother was a lady."

A shout of laughter burst from the boys at the reply. " Ho, ho ! " roared one, " here's another gentleman's son come ! " as if it was usual for the foundlings to fancy they were born of distinguished parents. One lad, called Billy Fortune, had evidently been indulging in such a dream, for somebody cried out, " I say, Bill, here's one of your sort ; you say your father was butler in a nobleman's family, and I shouldn't wonder now if this young un' had bounce enough to tell us his mother had been cook in the same place."

Philip could restrain his tears no longer, but turned his head round to the wall, and, as he hid his face against his arm, wished to himself that he had never been taken away from the infant side of the school, but allowed to pass his life near sister Bertie.

At this moment, the newly-finished large kite, that had been the talk of the school for weeks, was brought out of the play-room, and as it was known to have exhausted the pocket-money of six of the richest boys, who had " gone partners " to buy the fourpenny ball of string for it—even though the engineer had made them a present of an old twopenny newspaper to cover it with—all the boys instantly quitted Phil, and ran off to the new toy, the same as if a Punch and Judy's call had been heard chirruping them away.

The only one who stopped behind was the boy with the crutch. He said nothing, but remained quietly listening for a while to Phil's whimpering. Presently he tapped the little fellow on the shoulder, and said, " Don't take on like that, for if the chaps see you they are sure to call you ' cry-baby.' "

There was another pause, and when at last Phil brightened up sufficiently to turn round, the lame boy added, " If you'll be my crony I'll be yours. I haven't got any fellow I care much about, for I can't join in their games on account of my leg." As he mentioned the affliction, the boy stuck out a mere stump of a limb, which had been taken off so close to the hip that the poor fellow seemed all lop-sided, and made one fancy that he couldn't even stand, much more walk, if it wasn't for his crutch.

Phil was so taken with the sight that he could hardly remove his eyes from the mutilated limb, whilst the cripple, taking advantage of the silence, ran on with a kind of introduction of himself as the best beginning to their friendship.

"My name is Ned Purchase. My mother died in the hospital, and I belong to St. Vitus-in-the-Fields. I don't remember my father, but he kept a beer-shop in Newcastle-on-Twine, and paid rates for ever so many years. I'm called Goosey here 'cause I've only one leg."

"Were you born like that?" asked Phil, pointing to the stump.

"No, it was took off for a white swelling at the Free Hospital by Surgeon Sharp. Who was your parents?"

"Did it hurt?"

"I can't remember it now, for I wasn't above four year old. Do you recollect your father?"

"You can't do anything without a leg, can you?"

"Oh, can't I though!" answered Ned Purchase, who, like all afflicted persons, was rather vexed than pleased with the continual iteration of pity to which his misfortune daily subjected him. "Why, I ain't half as bad as Tom Lott here—he's lost his right arm—for I can work at a trade, and he can't do nothink but run errands if he don't get to be a pupil teacher, which he won't, for he ain't half quick enough. Then there's Mike Saunders, poor chap, his backbone is injured, and there he has to go about bent double as if he was down at leap-frog. He'll never be able to do nothink at all, but will have to remain in the Union till he dies. Ah! we've got a lot of chaps here like that—heaps!"

The two new friends then made the round of the play-ground. It was a large gravelled court-yard, two acres in extent, set with gymnastic poles at the end by the long shed, under which the boys played in wet weather. On one side was a series of cottage-like buildings; and these were the shops where the various trades were taught to the pauper pupils. Thither Phil was led by his lame companion, and told to look through the wirework protecting the windows. He saw a lad busy planing at a bench, and the long curling shavings twisting about his hands, whilst another was busy knocking together with his mallet the framework of a door. Phil, as he gazed at the result of the boys' handiwork, looking so clean and smooth, could not help exclaiming with delight,—

"I'll ask them to let me be a carpenter."

"You'd better leave it alone," answered Ned Purchase, "and make up your mind to go to farm-work, for that's what you'll have to do, 'cause you're strong."

The next window they peeped through was at the tailors' shop, and there Phil saw some twenty boys seated cross-legged on the shop-board, with their coats and jackets off, and stitching away at the stiff, new corduroy suits of the school.

"How would you like to be a tailor?" asked Ned, with a look of glee.

"It would not suit me at all to sit like that all day long," replied Phil.

"It's going to be my trade," said Ned, proudly; "you see my leg won't be missed when I'm sitting down in that way."

Then they glanced at the shoemakers' miniature factory, and saw the little fellows in their leathern pinafore-like aprons, jerking out their arms as they pulled the waxen thread through the shoe-leather or hammering big, square-headed nails into the soles. Phil cried,—

"Well, I'd rather go to farm-work and be out in the fields than be stuck down to that sort of thing."

"Ah! would you?" responded Ned, with a sneer; "you'll tell a different tale when you've been here a few years. All the shoemaker chaps get into a place and begin doing something for themselves in no time, but the farm-boys stick on hand, and can't be got off no-how; many of them, too, after all, have to be sent back to their parishes, to be bound to a chimley-sweep or a butcher, maybe."

From this they passed to the boiler-house, and watched the great engine flinging its brazen arms up and down, whilst a little fellow, scarcely bigger than Phil, passed his hand between the network of moving mechanism, as he poured oil into the joints as calmly as if he were feeding a lamp. Philip felt his heart swell as he thought how he should like to be able to manage such an enormous machine as that; but his dream was interrupted by Ned Purchase saying to him, "Ah! there's lots of boys would give anything if they could get put into the engine-room, but there's no chance, for there's only two ever wanted there."

By this time the kite had been raised high into the air, and nearly all the boys were collected in a circle round the happy lad who held the string, so Ned Purchase thought it a good opportunity for taking Phil into the play-room.

This was a long, empty outhouse, and against the walls hung the skeletons and bodies of kites, in every stage and style of manufacture. Some were only bits of brown paper cut into the shape of a heart, with a thread and tadpoley tail hanging to them. Others were mere frameworks, ranged against the wall like an armoury of infantine cross-bows; and others again were half covered and like a patchwork counterpane with the various bits of paper out of which they had been formed, and among which the eye recognized now a page of a penny London journal, and now a leaf of an old copy-book, with a round-hand lesson upon it, and line after line repeating, "ENGLAND WAS ORIGINALLY PEOPLED BY—"

Thus it was that Philip and the lame boy made friends; and that evening was passed in telling stories one to another of all they could remember of their early history, and all that they knew of the work-house where they had been brought up. They compared the dietaries, too, of their different Unions, and asked innumerable questions as to whether they had ever heard of this and that pauper (for the boys seemed to fancy all the poor must be acquainted with each other, in the same manner as even educated people imagine that anybody who has been to India must have been intimate with every Englishman out there). They chatted, moreover, about the guardians who had taken notice of them, or—more memorable than all—that had ever given them a penny.

Long before the bell rang for bedtime, the two boys were sitting together with their arms twined round each other's neck, talking the wildest romance that, like hope and dreams, is the heritage of even pauper youths in common with all others. It was then duly arranged that Ned Purchase was to marry sister Bertie; and when Phil's father —who it was at last settled must have been some grand gentleman— was found, they were all three to live together, and do nothing but ride on ponies all day, and have pudding for dinner every day in the week.

"Ah, don't I wish I was as rich as a guardian—that's all!" said Phil. "How much money do you think a guardian has got—a hundred pounds?"

"Much more than that, you silly," answered Ned, "or how could they pay for the keep of such a lot of people as they do—more like five hundred pounds."

"Five hundred pounds!" exclaimed the thunderstruck Phil, lost in the immensity of the sum. "I wonder how much that makes in farthings? I only wish we had got it, we wouldn't wait for father's coming back then!"

"But God won't let all be rich," answered Ned, moralizing. "Though, as the chaplain says, there's the same God for the rich as the poor."

Phil looked down thoughtfully on the ground, and murmured: "Why should God like the rich better than the likes of us, I wonder, and give them such a lot, and leave hardly anything for the poor!"

"I can't tell, I'm sure," said the simple Ned; "but the chaplain says we are to have our reward by-and-by when we die, and that a rich man might as well try to squeeze himself through the eye of a needle as to get into the kingdom of Heaven."

"Well, but," inquired Phil, "if only the poor are to go to Heaven, what a number there will be up there; and if there ain't to be any guardians, who will take care of us then?"

"Why, don't you know that God is the great guardian of all?" said Ned, who, workhouse orphan as he was, had learnt to regard the Deity in that character rather than as the great Father of all. "And didn't He make the world and all the money that is in it, thousands and thousands of years ago?"

"Thousands and thousands of years ago!" murmured Phil, half to himself, "why, that was when I was nothing."

CHAPTER IV.

FOUR YEARS AND THEIR CHANGES.

THE history of one day at the pauper school was so like that of another, that to describe the daily routine was to record the events of the last four years that Phil passed at the place. The changes in the week days were hardly known to the boys by the names they bore, but rather by the alteration they brought in the diet; for what are ordinarily called Tuesday and Thursday were spoken of at the Industrial School as "meat-pudding days," whilst Sunday, Wednesday, and Friday were "suet-pudding days," and Saturday "soup-day," instead of being styled after the usual nomenclature of the almanac.

To those under eleven years of age the school itself presented little or no variety, whilst to those above that age it afforded the relief of working in the shops or on the farm every alternate day in the week.

With these slight exceptions, the life of the pauper seminary was as much a matter of drill, order, and regularity, as if the establishment had been some infantry rather than infantine barracks.

Every morning at six the bell in the courtyard rang with the same clatter as for a departing steam-boat, and instantly all the dormitories, which a few seconds before had been almost as quiet as hospital wards, were alive and bustling as a ship's company in a sudden squall.

The dormitories themselves were long, bare, but cleanly wards, with a row of iron bedsteads ranged down either side of them, whilst in one corner was a compartment partitioned off as a separate berth for the pupil teacher. The only things that broke the monotony of the white walls were the large placards of Bible texts placed over the doors, some impressing the precept, "SPEAK NOT EVIL ONE OF ANOTHER," and others bearing the words, "SET A WATCH, O LORD, BEFORE MY MOUTH, KEEP THE DOOR OF MY LIPS."

A minute or two after the bell ceased ringing the lads were up and partly dressed, with their bedclothes turned back, and ready waiting for the order of the pupil teacher to "face their beds." Then came the command "Kneel down," and in an instant all was silent again, with the youths bent in prayer at the foot of the iron bedsteads, and inwardly breathing their supplications to Heaven.

At such times even the most callous might have been touched by the solemn sight of the wretched fatherless creatures appealing to their spiritual Father for care and protection throughout the day.

The next minute the boys had taken their jackets from under their pillows, and, drawn up in file before the dormitory door, were awaiting the signal of "forward," to pass from the room and get their shoes from the nest of pigeon-holes in the lobby outside.

Then came the calling over names, and the washing in the lavatories at the side of the play-ground; and this done, the whistle of the drill-master was heard, and the boys were drawn up in rank and file for inspection.

All was now ready for breakfast and family prayer, but long before the meal the boys and girls who helped in the kitchen had been busy ranging along the tall, narrow benches that served for tables, and made the dining-hall look like a huge writing academy, the seven hundred cans of milk-and-water, and the seven hundred thick lumps of bread and butter, that formed the provision for the morning's repast. And when the large hall, big as an assembly-room, was filled for morning prayers with every soul in the place, except the youngest of the infants—officers and servants, as well as boys and girls—the eye was enabled to comprehend the extent of the bounty feeding such a host of mouths that must otherwise have gone without a crust. Nor could the visitor help contrasting the cleanly and tidy look of the destitute little throng with the filth and raggedness of other poor children, who are thought to be better off in the world than those who are driven to the parish for support.

When, in answer to the three taps on the table, the entire multitude stood up to say "grace," the clatter of their sudden rising was like the shooting of a load of stones, and as they remained with their eyes shut, half-intoning the supplication for a blessing on their food, they seemed like a legion of blind mendicants, all uttering the same petition for charity.

The boys were delighted with the drill that formed part of the summer exercises; for it was not only like playing at soldiers, but, from its half gymnastic character, had all the excitement of an athletic game. The old drill-master, too, who had served at Waterloo, was as pleased with the work as the lads themselves, and evidently felt the same enjoyment at the mimic military evolutions as veterans are said to experience when teaching their grandchildren to shoulder their crutch.

Phil liked the drill much better than the schooling, and, indeed, had already made up his mind to be a soldier directly he was tall enough to "'list;" and when he heard that one of the boys had taught himself to play the flute so well that the superintendent had got him to be taken into the Guards as a fife-player, he thought it the greatest good luck that could possibly befall a human being, and every night made it a special request in his prayers that Heaven would be equally kind to him.

With the "pupil-teachers" Phil bore the character of being a dunce, but with his companions in the play-ground he was considered to be one of the sharpest among them. He was generally at the bottom of his class, though at gymnastics he could mount to the top of the pole quicker than any other; at arithmetic even the smallest boys on his form could jump over him, but at fly-the-garter he could take the " five foot leap," and clear a back, without even "toeing the line," far easier than boys double his size.

Immediately the summons was given for assembling for school, his animal spirits seemed to leave him ; and no sooner did he enter the big schoolroom, with the different classes divided off by red baize curtains, and the lecture-hall-like seats, ranged gallery fashion, one above another, than his heart sank within him, and he sat lumpishly in his place, staring at the maps hung round the walls— first glancing, half-vacantly, at the chart of " The travels of the Apostle Paul," then wandering away to the "Land of Promise after its conquest by the Israelites."   Nor did he wake up from his reveries even when the big blackboard, hung like a cheval-glass, was wheeled in front of the class, and the pupil-teacher chalked the simple addition sum upon it ; for when the boy-master asked the lads how many 6 and 8 made, Phil thrust out his hand mechanically with the others as a sign that he could tell, though, on being bidden to do so, the guess of twenty-two showed that his little mind was far away, wondering what Asia was like from the map, and how long it would take him to walk there.

At reading aloud from the " daily lesson book " he made as sad a mess as at figures ; and even though the twenty boys before him had all repeated the exercise of " The Bird's Nest," drawling out the little verse,

> God taught the bird to build its nest
> Of wool, and hay, and moss ;
> God taught her how to weave it best,
> And lay the twigs across.

Nevertheless, when it came to his turn, he stammered over nearly every word, and had to spell half the syllables, so that it was utterly impossible to get any sense out of the simple rhyme.

But what Phil hated worse than all, and what he firmly believed was nothing but an ingenious torture devised by some demon peda-gogue, for the express purpose of worrying little boys, was the exer-cise called " Dictation "—especially that upon " words spelt differently but having similar sounds," so that he was fairly driven out of his wits when he had to write down such a sentence as the following :

" You are right in saying that rite means a ceremony and wright a maker, as the marriage rite and a wheelwright, but it is difficult to write them all rightly, so pray write this sentence, ' Mr. Wright's marriage rites gave the wheelright's daughter—so she writes—all the rights of a married woman.' "

A stranger visiting the Industrial School with the knowledge that at least two-thirds of the little pauper boys were orphans, would doubtless have been startled to find them playing about the gravelled quadrangle as merrily as if they had the kindest and best of parents to take care of them ; such a one would have come to the conclusion that others felt their destitute condition more keenly than the boys themselves. Nevertheless, there were moments when even the most thoughtless of the orphan lads were roused to a sense of their terrible loneliness in the world, and these occurred principally when any of the more lucky boys were visited by their friends; for then a kind of wretched envy seemed to seize upon the most destitute, as the conviction forced itself upon them that they might stop there for years and years without the chance of any friend ever coming to see them.

Sometimes, when all the little fellows were playing together, laughing and jumping about, the cry of " Hodge wanted," or " Cumber visited," would echo through the play-ground; then all the games ceased, and as the happy Cumber or Hodge was seen scampering towards the combing-room, where the friends visited the boys, the others would creep up to the door and try to catch a glimpse of that great rarity—a friend—and afterwards slink away to talk moodily together, about either what they remembered as to their own father or mother, or else what they had merely heard about them.

But what seemed to lacerate their little hearts more sharply than all was when the self-same fortunate youths, some half-hour afterwards, reappeared among them, their faces red and glowing with delight, and carrying in their hands the peg-top or the orange that had been brought them. Then all would gather round, and twenty voices ask at once, " Who had been to see them, and what they had given them;" while the sight of the halfpenny or even the farthing they had received, would cause many and many a sigh, and wish they had such rich friends to visit them. Some, too, would follow the lucky lad about the ground, and watch him as he rolled his orange round and round in his hands " to make it juicy," and beg, as he ate it, for even a bit of the peel. For the remainder of that day, too, there was a general depression throughout the school, and nothing else was talked of but Hodge or Cumber and his grand friends, and numbers wished they were only like him.

Phil had two friends who sometimes came to see him—the one Nurse Hazlewood, and the other the principal matron of the prison in which he had been born; but though the latter, when she called, gave her true name of Miss Perriman, still, for the boy's sake, she was anxious that neither he nor any one else should know who she was. The visits of Nurse Hazlewood, however, were but little thought of among the schoolboys; for as she was known to be in St. Lazarus Union, and she generally asked, when she came, to see many of the other boys who had been under her care, scarcely any excitement was produced by her presence at the school. Moreover, the poor old woman hadn't the means to give such costly tokens of her love as halfpence or oranges to each of her nurselings : and the half-pint of nuts which she usually brought with her appeared so little when it came to be doled out among them all at the rate of six to each, that Phil was rather taunted than envied during the two days in the year on which his foster-mother came. But to do the little fellow justice, he cared far more to see his workhouse mother than the grand lady with her velvet mantle and parasol, who gave him sixpence every time she called.

The old nurse, when he entered the visiting-room and ran to throw his arms about her neck, would seize hold of "her own Phil," as she always called him, and hug and kiss him as much as she did sister Bertie at her side. And there they would sit for more than an hour together talking about the "house," and she would tell him of the changes that had taken place in it since he left, while they would listen with the same interest that others do to the tales of home.

She would chat to him, too, about blind Willie, and when she had brought the little fellow vividly back to Phil's mind again, he would ask all kinds of questions about the poor lad, and what he and Will used to do when they were in the Union together.

There was one question, however, that was always uppermost in Philip's mind. He had heard the orphan boys so often sit speculating by the hour as to their parentage, and others telling tales of what they had known of their family, that a craving had come upon him to learn something about his own—more particularly about his mother, of whom he had heard so little, and yet that little implied so much.

Accordingly, whenever Nurse Hazlewood made her appearance at the school, he was sure to ask her how she knew that his mother had died in prison.

The answer was invariably the same, " You mustn't ask me, child. I can't tell you anything more than I have."

"But Ned Purchase says it's only wicked people who are sent to prison," continued Phil.   "Was mother, then, wicked ? "

Poor Nurse Hazlewood was shocked at the words, and exclaimed, as she threw up her hands, "Heaven forbid, boy, that I should ever live to say such a thing to a child of its poor dead parent ! "

" Ned Purchase declares she couldn't have been a lady if she died in prison," continued Phil, sorrowfully.   " But she was a lady— wasn't she ? "

"Tell Ned Purchase not to go bothering his head about other people's mothers," the nurse would reply.

" But, nursey," coaxed Phil, creeping up to the old woman, " who was it told you she was a lady ? There, don't shake your head, but try and recollect—do, please—for me, nursey. You'll learn all about it, won't you, now, by the next time you come ? "

And every time she came the same questionings and answerings went on.

Phil's other visitor produced a far greater commotion among the boys : for whenever she paid her yearly visit, it was instantly buzzed over the school that the grand lady had come to see Merton again ; and as she always gave him a silver sixpence on leaving, she was classed by the poor pauper lads as being among the most wealthy in the land.

No sooner, too, was the visit at an end, and Phil among his companions again, than all crowded enviously round him, to hear what the lady had said.

"She says she knew mother," Phil would exclaim, boastingly, and not a little proud that his mother should have had such a friend.

"Did she though? Then I shouldn't wonder if your mother was a real lady, after all!" one of the boys would reply.

"Yes, she says mother stopped at her house some time," the elated Phil would go on.

"It's no use trying to cram us," one of the less credulous would exclaim. "If she was a friend of your mother, why did she let you become chargeable, eh?"

There was a laugh of derision among the boys, and Phil, in dudgeon, turned upon his heel, and retired to talk with Ned Purchase alone.

"It's all true that I said just now, Ned—it is, upon my word and honour!" he would proceed, for he was as excited with what he had heard during the visit as he was angry at having the story doubted. "She told me what mother was like; and I'm sure she's seen her, and knows a lot about her too. She says she had dark hair and eyes, like me; and that she has some letters of hers. She saw my mother, Ned, just before she died."

"And is it true, then, she died in prison?" inquired Ned Purchase, who knew all Phil's secrets. "Why didn't you ask her what she was in for?" he added; for the workhouse is so close to the gaol, that lads reared in the one are mostly acquainted with all the details of the other.

"So I did," answered Phil, full of what he heard, and gasping out the words in his excitement; "but all she would tell me was that mother had been treated dreadful, and that she had been drove to do what she did."

Phil became more of a dunce than ever, for, though when out in the play-ground the excitement of the games roused his boyish spirits, no sooner was he seated on the form of his class than his mind was away speculating as to what "the lady" had told him, and building up hopes upon the flimsy foundation of his father being still alive; so that when it came to his turn to answer the sum that the master had chalked on the blackboard, "If a boy had sixty plums to eat in ten minutes, how many must he eat per minute?" Phil, who was dreaming of his mother, replied, "Just five-and-twenty when she died."

Then as all the class burst out laughing, and the master thought Phil had meant the reply for a joke, he had to stop in school that afternoon for the blunder.

When it came to Phil's time to be put to a trade, it was agreed that farm labour was the only thing suited to him, for he was naturally loutish, they said, and therefore the work couldn't have the same blunting effect upon his intellect as it was found to produce upon quicker lads.

The out-door work did Phil some little good, for he had less time to brood over his dreams, and the exertion of turning up the earth served to put an end to all his romantic fancies; for digging-in manure and cleaning out pigsties are occupations which contribute but little to the development of the imagination.

The agricultural portion of the Industrial School covered an estate some sixty acres in extent, and reminded one of a model farm, for the grounds were tilled with the greatest care, and the fields laid out almost with the same regularity as garden-beds. All trees had been cleared from the ground, and hedges replaced by invisible fences, so that the estate had more of a foreign than an English look about it, for the pasture-land seemed to be undivided from the arable, and even the kitchen-garden and the sprouting orchard were hardly distinguishable from the farm itself.

Far down at the bottom of the sloping land ran the channel of the railway, hidden by the depth of the cutting, so that the rattle of the carriages, and the gusts of white steam that seemed to issue from the earth, as well as the working of the arms of the tall signal-posts hard by, were the only evidences of the passing trains.

The boys, in gangs of some half-dozen, with the bailiff at their head, tilled the earth by manual labour; and often as a train rushed past, Phil would rest upon his fork to gaze after the engine as he saw it appear in the distance and lose itself among the hills; and he would wonder to himself whither it went, and what the earth was like there, and whether he should ever be carried over the land by one of those quick darting things.

This occurred day after day, and a craving at length fastened upon him to get out into the world and see the country and the towns of which he knew so little; for as yet his travels had never extended beyond his ride in the cart from the workhouse, and an occasional walk out with the school to have a game of cricket on the neighbouring common.

Working in the same gang with Phil was Billy Fortune, one of the biggest boys in the school, who had been at farm labour so long that he had grown weary of waiting to be put out in the world, and was always grumbling at seeing those who had been taught trades easily provided with situations, whilst he remained on hand to dig and dig day after day as he had done for years before.

"I wish a cove could only get away to sea," he'd say, sulkily, to Phil, when the bailiff was not near, "wouldn't I precious soon hook it. Where's the good of a fellow stopping at this work and never getting a halfpenny for hisself? I want to be earning something, and if they won't help me to it, why, I shall save them the trouble some of these fine days."

Then Billy Fortune would proceed to tell Phil about ships, and

Philip at the Pauper School

how jolly the life of a sailor was, and give him such accounts of foreign lands as he had been enabled to gather from the school geography, until his little companion thought if it wasn't for Bertie and Ned Purchase, he, too, would like to go seafaring.

The tie, however, which held Philip to the school, and which made it seem like a home to him, was destined shortly to be broken.

Sister Bertie, who had grown to be a big girl, had risen so high in the estimation of the schoolmistress, that she had been promoted to the post of waiting-maid to the superintendent's wife. She had become, too, such a favourite with the chaplain, that he had promised to place her out in the world as soon as possible, and to get her a good situation. Phil, when he first heard of the promise, had half prayed that it might never be realized; so when he was told that the situation had really been obtained, and that the day was even fixed for his sister's departure, he hardly slept that night for crying; for though it was seldom that he could speak to the girl, yet every day at meal times he could nod his head to her and see her smile in return. Sometimes, too, he was allowed to have half an hour's interview with her in the passage between the girls' and boys' play-grounds; consequently, he had never felt utterly alone in the place.

When the time, however, arrived for the parting, and Bertie, dressed for her journey, had come to the play-ground door to say good-bye to her foster-brother, Phil was half surly in the selfishness of his grief at losing her.

"Why, Phil, isn't it better, now?" said sister Bertie, consolingly to him. "I am to get £5 a year, after the first year, and only think what a help that will be to mother and you."

"Well, I don't know what you want to go at all for," grumbled Phil, "and leave a fellow all alone here. I wouldn't have done it to you."

"I am going, Phil, to a sick old lady's," continued Bertie, playing with his hands, "who wants a girl to read to her; and only suppose if any of her friends should have a place for a boy, why, I should speak up for you of course, and then, perhaps, we might be near one another again."

Phil pretended to treat the notion with contempt, but still he smiled with inward pleasure at the care of his sister for him.

"Come, don't be angry, dear Phil," pleaded Bertie; "you know the chaplain visits once every three months all those who have got situations, and you can always hear of me from him."

Philip could not bear to look at the girl, so he turned his shoulder round, and she, thinking he was still angry, clung to him as she cried,—

"Oh, Phil, don't be cruel now! you'll never let me go from you in such a way."

The appeal was more than the boy could bear, and half-choked with his sobs, he stammered out,—

"It isn't that, Bertie; but you can't tell how hard it is for a chap to lose his only friend in such a big place as this."

For some time after sister Bertie's departure, Phil bore up with the hope that perhaps her words might come true, and he be sent for to come and live at some friend of her mistress's; but when week after week went by and no such happy message arrived, the only consolation left the boy was to waylay the chaplain on his rounds and ask him whether he had seen or heard of Bertie lately. At such times the minister would tell him either that "she was going on very satisfactorily indeed," and that he had "every reason to be gratified with her conduct;" or else he would kindly take him into his room and read him the remarks he had written in his report-book, after his last visit to the girl.

"There, Merton, you see, Bertha Hazlewood has one of the best characters in my reports," he would say, patting Phil on the head, as he spread the book out before him. "Her conduct, you perceive, is exemplary—rises early—obeys cheerfully—works hard and willingly —is regular at her devotions, and, altogether, her moral and religious deportment of a very pleasing and consoling character."

The effect of Bertie's absence, however, soon began to show itself on Phil, by the daily increasing impatience that he felt to be out in the world like his sister, doing something for himself; and whenever he heard that some of the boys in the tailors' or shoemakers' shop, who had entered the school after himself, had been apprenticed and "put out," he and Billy Fortune would grumble together, and vow that they wouldn't stop there farm-labouring much longer.

About this time, too, it so happened that the guardians of St. Vitus-in-the-Fields discovered that Ned Purchase had no legal settlement in their parish—that indeed he belonged to some union in the north of England, and that they had been keeping him unlawfully for the last eight years. In a few hours everybody in the school knew that Ned Purchase had been found to have another parish, whereupon the young paupers were all busy, like so many little parochial authorities, discussing the niceties of settlement, and arranging how he was to be "passed" to his new union.

When Phil and Billy Fortune returned from farm labour in the afternoon they found a crowd of lads round the cripple boy, who was half crazy at the idea of being torn away from what had grown to be a home to him, as well as terrified at the doubtful character of the new place he was to be sent to.

And, indeed, it must be hard to such as him to find, when long associations have twined the affections round the haunts of their boyhood, that the ardent friendships of youth are to be severed with the signing of a discharge-paper; and that they themselves are so utterly powerless and unheeded in the world, that directly it is discovered the burden of their keep can be legally shifted, they are moved from one "farm" to another as rapidly as cattle sold at a fair.

The day after the news had been made known that Ned Purchase was to be passed to his legal settlement, he and Phil were seated in

one corner of the play-ground shed talking earnestly with Billy
Fortune, and with their heads so close together that they had
evidently some profound secret among them.

"I tell you," said Billy, "there it is printed, and I read it myself—
it's in the old newspaper we had give to us to cover the big kite with,
and it says he was a poor cabin boy, that got aboard a ship at Portsmouth, and he went over to the Ingies, and now he's come home
with whole shiploads of money, and has got made a member of
Parliament in consequence. If you like you can see it all yourselves—
just at the bottom near the tail of the kite; there's the very speech as
the gentleman made at a slap-up dinner he was asked to."

"Whereabouts is Portsmouth?" asked Phil, for he had not the
least idea whether it was in Europe, Asia, Africa, or America.

"Oh! it ain't far off," answered Billy, who had a vague notion that
it was somewhere near London Bridge; "we could easily walk it and
get a ship there, in less time than you can catch a tittlebat."

"I should like to get out to India," observed Phil, "and go riding
in castles on elephants' backs, and shooting tigers, like it says in the
history of 'Warren 'Astings' that's in the library."

"But they wouldn't take me as a cabin-boy, would they?"
nervously asked the poor cripple.

"Why not, Goosey?" inquired Billy Fortune; though presently a
sudden thought seemed to strike him, and he exclaimed, "Oh, you
mean 'cause of your leg! Pooh! lots of fellows have told me that
half the old sailors at Greenwich have got no legs at all, and Lord
Nelson, in his portraits, I know is always drawed with only one arm."

Whereupon the youngsters settled among themselves, and proved
to each other's satisfaction, that a seafaring life was just the business
for a cripple like Ned Purchase, as all that a sailor had to do was to
pull ropes and steer the boat. Besides, as they very cogently urged,
there couldn't be much walking about to be done on board such a
small place as a ship. "And once out in India," continued Billy
Fortune, "you'll be quite at home, Goosey; for in every picture I've
seen, there the kings and princes is sitting cross-legged like tailors,
and you've been brought up to that business here, you know."

The rest of the day the boys passed in the most out-of-the-way
places about the building, plotting how their escape was to be
managed. If anybody stopped near them, they instantly moved off
to some more deserted spot.

"You see," said Phil, "Saturday's half-holiday, and that's our
time to be off, just after the names have been called over; for then,
you know, we're allowed to go about the grounds where we like.
Besides, we shall have a clear start all Sunday, for they can't well
come and look after us during church-time."

"I vote," said the cripple, "that we walk out into the farm-fields,
just as if we were going to fly our kite, and then we can sneak off
round by the stables, and be through the hedge into the wood, at the
back here, in a jiffy."

"But when we're in the wood, how are we to get anything to eat?" asked Billy, who was of rather a hungry disposition. "We can't sell our clothes to get any money, you know, for, as they belong to the parish, they might have us took up for stealing."

"Well, that is good! How do you think Robinson Crusoe lived, that we were reading about only the other night in the bedroom?" cried Phil. "And if he could do it on an uninhabited island, surely we can manage it in a wood, where there's plenty of prime black-berries. What's nicer than them I should like to know?" And at the thoughts of the fruit Phil uttered the boyish exclamation of "Golly!" and rubbed his waistcoat up and down as expressive of intense delight.

It was then ultimately arranged by the young runaways, after long deliberation, that they were to save as much bread as they could from their meals, and immediately after the Saturday's dinner they were to take their last farewell of the school, and then, making the best of their way to the Thames, walk along the banks of the river till they came to Portsmouth—which Bill Fortune assured them he knew was somewhere in that neighbourhood.

CHAPTER V.

THE RUNAWAYS.

THE little pauper rebels, having made up their urchin minds to decamp from the Industrial School, became inseparable companions, and passed every moment of their playtime in maturing their boyish plans. They had their secret meetings in the most out-of-the-way places and obscurest corners, where they held solemn debates in mysterious whispers, at the same time keeping a sharp look-out on the monitors and the drill-sergeant. If their privacy were disturbed by any stray school-fellow, the whole character of the assembly was instantly changed; and so as to remove all suspicion of its unlawful object, the moment the signal of "somebody coming" was given, one of the conspirators would begin to whistle loud and boldly, whilst the others broke out into noisy conversation, or commenced romping together.

So totally were the poor boys absorbed in their plottings, that, like true conspirators, they were nervous and uneasy unless in one another's society. Feeling rather timid as to the success of their plans, nothing appeared to give them so much courage as treating the possibility of a failure as an absurdity. Whenever Philip felt that his fears were overcoming him, he invariably made a point of accusing Billy Fortune with "being afraid and wanting to back out of it," and the indignant denials and energetic manner of that bold young pauper never failed to inspirit the meeting and restore confidence.

Before two days had passed, the little rebels had, by their altered manner, attracted the notice of the whole school, and but for the speedy execution of their plans they would certainly have been found out before a week had elapsed. Had they been three Roman patriots arranging the overthrow of Tyranny and Ambition, their general behaviour could not have been more marked and singular. Did any lad invite the stern Philippus Mertonus to join in the giddy delights of "hop-scotch," or "leap-frog," he answered with a haughty sneer, such as would have become a Brutus spurning the offers of a Cæsar. Twice on the Friday was Billy Fortune discovered drawing ships on his slate instead of "doing his arithmetic," and when threatened with punishment he tried to look as defiant as he could, for he was saying to himself, "To-morrow at twelve I shall be miles away."

Each of the three boys, whenever they met for consultation, always managed to bring with him some article or other which he had pilfered during the day, thinking it would be likely to prove useful during their stay in the wood.

"I've got some lucifer matches," said Ned Purchase, at one of their rendezvous. "I collared them out of the tailor's shop. Won't they be jolly useful making fires?"

"Ay," cried Billy Fortune; "and I think I knows where there's a potato-field, and if one thing is primer than another it's baked 'murphies.'"

"Here's my bread; I didn't eat a bit at dinner on purpose," said Phil, pulling out a big slice from his jacket pocket. "Have you saved anything, Billy?"

"No, I eat my bread," answered the fat conspirator, "but I've prigged this string from Tom Close's kite. It will do first-rate for tying branches together when we make our cave."

When Friday night came, and the three boys were sleeping in their school beds for the last time, as they thought, they could none of them close an eye for thinking of the step they were about to take on the morrow. Phil felt almost ready to cry with depression, for however "jolly" he may have called the scheme when chatting it over with the others, yet something within himself warned him that he was about to take a foolish step in life, which would plunge him into the uncertainty of the world's struggles before he was fitted to encounter them.

Billy Fortune was of too brutal and coarse a nature to bestow two thoughts upon anything that he did. He only thought that he desired a change of scene, and running away was the easiest mode of gratifying himself.

With Ned Purchase, however, the case was very different. The poor cripple knew that he had only to choose between being sent away from the place which he had grown to love as a home, and leaving it of his own accord.

School hours were over, and the Saturday's half-holiday had begun. The three boys, with their pockets bulging out with the pieces of crust they had saved, crept round by the kitchen-garden, crouching against the wall, until they reached the hedge that divided off the wood; when, dashing through an opening in the fence, they plunged into the thicket, and ran off like frightened hares into the darkest part of it.

Now all their boyish dreams of a merry forest life were soon to be dispelled. Now they were to learn that Robin Hood had not been the most favoured of mortals, and that most likely, if the offer had been made him, he would willingly have quitted the romantic delights of the "greenwood shade" for the more solid enjoyments of a well-roofed dwelling. For the first time they were to learn by experience that Robinson Crusoe on his desert island led a life of privation, compared with which a workhouse existence was one of luxury and enjoyment.

After running for at least an hour, and darting through briers and underwood till their hands and faces were torn with thorns, the three young scamps came to a halt. The first thing they did was to hunt for a place to pass the night in, and great was their surprise to find the ground wet and soddened with the past rains, so that even the pressure of the foot brought the water up to the surface like squeezing a sponge.

"I say, I don't half like this," said Phil, with a disappointed look, and turning to Billy Fortune, he added, "I thought you said there was lots of dry moss here?"

"So there is, you silly, when you've dried it," retorted Master Fortune.

Ned Purchase stammered out something about going back again, but was soon silenced by the redoubtable Billy.

"You may go if you like," he said, "only it's all found out before this; and won't you get a licking—rather! You'll have to take our share and your own too, I can tell you."

The runaways tried to light a fire, and one by one the lucifers were held to the decayed leaves, but without success. To console themselves, they sat down on a bent bough, and tried to raise their drooping spirits by planning the delicious future that awaited them as soon as they dare leave the wood and start for Portsmouth. Already they were on shipboard, pulling at ropes, and letting out sails; or else they were catching flying-fish, or watching the changing colours of the dying dolphin. Now they were landing on some island where they were all received with the greatest kindness by the black inhabitants, and even welcomed by the king himself. After feasting on sugar-cane and delicious fruits, they were to return to their own country laden with presents consisting chiefly of diamonds the size of eggs, and lumps of gold as big as quartern loaves.

"Catch me giving that old drill-master any, that's all," cried

Billy Fortune, as earnestly as though his dreams had been realized.

When the twilight came, the truants ate the bread they had brought with them, but it had grown so hard with being kept in the pocket that it broke like biscuit. Neither was there enough even to take the "edges" off their appetites.

"Oh, I've got such a pain here," said Billy Fortune, pressing his stomach; "I never felt so hungry in all my life. It's the running's done it!"

"Chew some leaves, they're just like spinach," suggested Ned Purchase to the disgusted William.

"You said we should find blackberries and birds' eggs," exclaimed Phil, reproachfully.

They found some amusement in imagining to themselves the sensation their absence had created in the school when the name list was called over at night. From the place where they were sitting they could hear the big school-bell ring for supper, and afterwards for bedtime. They watched all the lights in the different windows of the building, trying to find out by them which was their dormitory. Then came wonderings as to what "So-and-so was doing," or "what the head-master had said," and whether any search would be made for them that night.

At last Billy Fortune declared he could stand his "awful hunger" no longer. He vowed he was starving, and that as he had often read that was the worst death possible, he was determined to do something desperate rather than dwindle slowly to a skeleton. When his companions saw him jump up from the ground as if he meant to leave them, they both began to charge him with being the cause of their present suffering, and the first to "turn tail."

"That's all you know about it," shouted Bill, brutishly. "I shall be back again in an hour, only I can't stand this beastly hunger. I've got a plan for freeing us all, I tell you. I'm only going back to the school to get some grub. I know the place where it's kept, and there's a window quite handy in the wall. All a feller's got to do is just to put in his arm and help hisself. So just keep your hearts up and never say die, and I'll be back in less than no time with some jolly new bread, which is the primest eating in the world, to my fancy."

And, despite their entreaties that he would not run so great a risk, off went the stubborn lad.

"Do you think he'll blab if he's caught?" said Phil, nervously, as if he half suspected the answer.

"Yes," replied Ned.

Now that they dare neither of them go to sleep for fear that the marauder should be detected and their hiding-place hunted after, it was as much as they could do to keep their eyes open. They knew it was far in the night by the long time since it had been dark. They grew nervous, too, thinking of robbers—poor workhouse lads!

Neither of them had spoken a word for more than an hour—and, indeed, each had imagined the other to be asleep—when Ned suddenly cried out,—

"What's that, Phil? Did you hear anything?"

Phil answered "No;" but he spoke in a whisper, for he had heard the whistle plainly enough.

Before another second had passed, Ned Purchase, breathless with fear, pointed to some lights moving in the wood not a hundred yards off.

Phil was on his feet in a moment.

"That sneak, Fortune!" he muttered; "he has gone and blabbed where we are. Come on, Ned; let's cut as hard as we can."

Ned Purchase was nearly frozen, and the stump of his leg was aching with the cold.

"I can't stir, Phil," he said. "You go! Good-bye. We shall meet again some time."

Phil gave the cripple his crutch, and seized hold of him to help him up.

"Do you think I'd leave you?" he cried. "Quick! Jump up like a man. I'll help you on."

"No, let me be, Phil," said Ned, with the tears streaming down his cheeks. "How could a one-legged chap like me get clear off? Hark! they've got dogs with them. Cut! cut! Do, Phil; I should only die if I followed you. Run, run! here they are."

Phil looked round, and among the dark trees he saw the lights moving about like monster fire-flies. He could hear the rustling of the bushes being pushed aside, and off he darted, shouting out a "Good-bye, dear Ned," as he bounded in the black wood.

The street-lamps had just been lighted when a boy wet through with the rain, and dragging his feet after him as if he had hardly strength to raise their weight, crept along the pathway leading to the Elephant and Castle. Then coming suddenly to a halt, he stood staring about him as if dismayed at the sight of the several roads branching off in front.

It was such a night that no one who had a home to go to would think of loitering about. Even those who had umbrellas ran along the pavement to escape as fast as possible from the rough weather. But though the rain came down with a force that made it splash up again from the stones, there the lad stood, looking down the long vista of bright lamps, and staring before him almost as intently as a sailor on the look-out at sea.

Poor Phil! he was his own master at last! He was free to go where he liked and do what he pleased, and yet, with all the world before him, he dared not trust himself to advance a foot lest it should lead him into evil and suffering.

And now what is to become of him ?

The streets of London make, at the best, but a stony-hearted parent, the gutter forming but a sorry cradle for foundling babes to be reared in. The " back slums " of the metropolis are poor academies for youth, and moral philosophy is hardly to be picked up under " dry arches " and in " padding kens."

Book the Second.

CHILDHOOD IN THE STREETS.

————◆————

CHAPTER I.

THE START IN LIFE.

"HERE, my coveys," cried a suspicious-looking youth, as he entered the kitchen of one of the low lodging-houses near the Mint, "I've caught a young flat what's been and hooked it from the House at Nor'ud. He didn't know where to stall to in the huey. I found him out in the main toper, and told him to step it along with me, for I was going into a ken in the back drum. Just twig his bunch of fives, Conkey" (this was said to a gentleman with a peculiar bottle-nose). "S'elp me! if a mauley like that there ain't worth a jemmy a day to a kenobe at wiring. Why, they're just made for hooking a fogle out of a clye."

Poor Phil Merton, to whom the above unintelligible jargon referred, stood in the centre of the wretched room trembling with fright at the strange and dismal character of the place, as well as the savage-looking people he had just been introduced to.

The purport of the above communication, though incomprehensible to most people, was not so to one who was known among the gang as Van Diemen Bill, and who sat by the fire, swathing his bare ulcerous feet in a long roll of rags. He, however, was sufficiently well versed in "cant" to know that it meant to say that the strange boy couldn't tell where to get a lodging in town, and that "Buck" (the name of the lad who had brought Phil to the house) had found him in the high road, and told him to come with him, as he was going to a lodging-house in one of the by-streets. He knew, moreover, that Buck had drawn his friend Conkey's attention to the delicacy of the boy's hand, declaring that such a one was worth a sovereign a day to a thief at picking pockets, and adding that Phil's fingers were made expressly for hooking out handkerchiefs.

The speech, however, had hardly been finished before Van Diemen Bill had suddenly slipped on the old shoes at his side, and, going

towards Buck, said, as he folded his arms and looked at him surlily
in the face,—

"Shut up, will you—shut up, now! I tell you, you ain't a-going to
make a gun (thief) of this here young flat; it's a bad game, you
know as well as I do, and I won't stand by and see a mere kid like
this here put in the way of being lagged or scragged (transported or
hanged), as he is sure to be at last if he goes on the cross like us.
You knows, Buck, as well as I do, that we leads the life of dogs.
Arn't we all on us spotted here? and ain't the Bobbies at our heels
directly we stirs a foot, so that we can't even do a kingsman (silk
handkerchief) in a day, let alone a skin or a soup (a purse or watch)?
Stand back!" he shouted, as Buck appeared to make an advance
towards the lad, "and leave the kid alone, or I'll put out my Chalk
Farm (my arm) and give you a wrap with my Oliver Twist (fist) over
your I suppose (nose) that'll flatten your chevy chase (face) for you!"
he added, menacingly, between his teeth, as he shook his clenched
hand in the air.

Then stooping down to the scared lad, he said, in as tender tones
as he was capable of,—

"Come with me, young 'un, this ain't no place for you; they're all
on the cross here; and you must keep square, my lad—keep square,
whatever you do!" And so saying, the old thief seized Phil by the
arm and led him out of the house—much to the astonishment of the
younger and less squeamish rogues infesting the place.

Nor was there anything very extraordinary in such an act; for let
us say, for the honour of such characters, who are generally considered to be utterly dead to every kindly feeling, that we ourselves
have had honest boys brought to us by old returned convicts, and
that solely from a disposition to save the lads from leading the same
life as their own, for none but the very basest of thieves seem to
wish others to be like themselves; and it is by no means uncommon
for a person to hear, when some one of the fraternity says he has
made up his mind, and is "going to square it" (live honestly for the
future), the others, one and all, exclaim, "Well, I'm glad on it; I only
wish I could do the same!"

To say the truth, Van Diemen Bill had led such a life of suffering
and crime that now, in his advanced age, when he found himself
no longer capable of the more daring exploits by which heavy "swag"
could be obtained, and too closely watched by the police to be capable
of any of the minor thefts, he felt angry at the thought of any
young lad being trained to a life like his. It was impossible, as he
said, for such as him to get work, and neither could he steal—indeed,
it was only by continued "friendly leads" among his old pals,
and the gathering of the few bits of rag and bones from the
muck-heaps in the streets, that he was enabled to eke out a living
at all.

Phil was no sooner in the street than the man led him hurriedly
away to a low public-house in the neighbourhood; and there, entering

the little tap, that was so dark that the gas was always kept burning during the day-time, he said,—

"Come, lad, have a bit o' scran, and I'll stand a shant o' gatter, I've got a teviss here;" and then, suddenly remembering that he was no longer talking to one of his own fraternity, he added, "I meant to say, have a bit of this here vitals, and I'll pay for a pot of beer, I've got a sixpence. A party as is kind to me on my rounds gave me some broken bits and an old jacket this morning, and I sold the jacket to the dolly-man for a bob. So come, eat now, boy, you needn't be afraid of me; for, though I'm a thief, I wouldn't harm the hair of your head—that I wouldn't."

Phil looked up in the old convict's face, and in the corner of his eye he could see a bright tear drop shimmering against the swarthy skin. Had the boy been more knowing as to the lives and characters of such people, he might have guessed that some recollection of his early home, or a dead parent's advice, had suddenly flashed across his mind; but the soft thief's hand was rubbed hastily over the brow, and the ugly memory shaken out of the brain with a half shudder and toss of the head.

The sight of the tear, however, inspired Phil with some little faith in the humanity of his companion, and assured him more than any words could do that the man really had some feeling for him.

In a few minutes the handkerchief of broken victuals was spread upon the table, and Phil was eating heartily, for the first time that day, and sipping occasionally at the half-pint of threepenny ale that his kindly, if not honest, friend had supplied to him. Nor was it long before the convict had learnt from the runaway workhouse lad his whole story, and more especially how, as he stood loitering about the Elephant and Castle, the lad Buck had accosted him, and finding him without a lodging, had promised to provide him with one if he would follow him to his home.

The story ended, Phil could hardly help giving way to his feelings, and sobbed aloud in his alarm at the danger he had been in.

"There, there, boy," said Van Diemen Bill, "you must keep your pluck up whatever you do. Come, now, I'll tell you what I mean you to try. All I can give you, my good lad, is a sixpence; and if it hadn't been for the old coat I got this morning I couldn't have done that. Howsomever, the sixpence you're welcome to, and thank God it was honestly come by for your sake. Well, you see, twopence of it will find your bed to-night, and with the other fourpence you must begin a-trading upon. You may stare, but at the place where I'm going to send you to, there's many a poor soul whose stock money is only a penny, and yet they can manage to keep themselves out of the workhouse, or the gaol too, by turning that small sum over and over again. Ah! in that place twopence is enough to keep a lad like you for a year or two, and there's many an old couple has lived on even less for a much longer time. Well, I'll tell you," said the man, "for I see you're all eyes to know what it is,—it's the water-crease market

I means to send you to. I'll get you an old tin tray at the 'Dolly,' Tuses, and start you fair with this here sixpence; and mind you, if ever you touches your stock money, if you eats a farden of it, you're a lost mutton you are. Take my tip, lad—the advice of a man who has seen more trouble, perhaps, than any other cross-chap in London —and starve on and on rather than make your fourpence a farden less; for remember it's only by making it more that such as you can ever hope to keep out of a prison that has even now got its jaws ready wide open to receive you."

A few moments after the above scene had taken place the boy had been furnished with his tin tray, and was launched fairly into the wide world of London, with sixpence to trade upon in his pocket and an old thief's blessing on his head.

CHAPTER II.

THE WATER-CRESS MARKET.

THE retail trade in water-cresses is followed by the very poorest of the poor, as the stock-money for this calling need consist only of a few halfpence. This class of street-sellers are generally honest, industrious, striving people, and consist of young children who have been deserted by their parents, and whose strength is hardly equal to any great labour, or old men and women crippled by disease or accident, who, in their dread of a workhouse, linger on with the few pence they earn by street selling. The children are mostly sent out by their parents "to get a loaf of bread somehow," and the very old take to it because they are unable to carry heavy loads, and anxious to avoid becoming positive paupers in their old age.

At the lodging-house to which Van Diemen Bill had taken young Phil to get him a bed for the night, the boy met with an old woman who told him all about the trade he was in the future to live by.

She was sitting before the kitchen fire, toasting a herring for her supper, and seeing that Phil carried a little tin tray under his arm, she at once recognized the symbol of the water-cress trade, and said to him,—

"I suppose you're at creases, young un? Done pretty well to-day? I'm in the line myself."

"I've never sold in the streets yet," answered Phil; and then he told her the story of the great peril he had just run, and how the old convict had behaved to him.

"Well, that Van Diemen Bill is a kind cretur, and bless him for it, though I ain't the pleasure o' knowing him," said the old crone. "And how much do you say he guv you? Fourpence! You ought to do uncommon well on that, for there's very few on us got more than twopence or threepence, and lots on 'em only a penny. Why, let me see, for a penny you ought to have a full market hand, or as much as I can take hold of at one time without spilling; for threepence you should have a lap full enough to earn about a shilling off: and for fourpence you gets as many as I can cram into my basket."

"Then I shall make a lot of money," smiled Phil.

"Well, my dear," she continued, "it ain't so easy to earn a mouthful of bread. Many a time I've walked through the streets, and when I've seed a bit of old crust, as the servant has chucked out of the door—maybe for the birds—thinks I to myself, 'I can enjoy that as much as the sparrers.' Besides, it takes a deal of larning to buy your goods properly. Ha! ha!" she chuckled, "the dealers can't take me in, though. When one on 'em tries to give me a small hand of creases, I says, 'I ain't a-going to have that for a penn'orth,' and I moves to the next basket, and so on all round; and that's what you must do, I can tell you."

"Oh! they shan't cheat me," said Phil, knowingly.

"Are you fond of getting up early?" asked the old woman; but without waiting for a reply, she went on: "It don't matter if you do or no if you wants to live by selling creases. I gets up in the dark by the light of the lamp in the court, and ain't it cold in winter! It pains my poor hands dreadful to take hold on the creases, specially after we've pumped on 'em to wash 'em. You're a strong boy, and won't mind the cold so much as us old folk. Ah, it's the poor children, too, I pities in the winter time. Poor babes, they make my heart ache to see 'em without shoes, and their pretty feet quite blue with the frost, so that many on 'em don't know how to set one foot afore the other, but stands still and cries with the cold, poor dears!"

Phil was beginning to get rather alarmed at the picture the old woman was drawing of the privations and sufferings connected with the business he was about to adopt.

"But I thought there was very few selling creases in the streets?" he interposed.

"Very few!" exclaimed the old thing—"very few! Why, where's the lad lived all his days? I tell you, the market's crammed with 'em of a morning buying their stock. In summer time I've seed 'em so thick that you might a'most bowl balls along their heads, and there they are all a-fighting for the creases, making a reg'lar scramble to get at 'em, so as to turn a halfpenny out of 'em. Why, I should think at this time o' the year, there's as many as four or five hundred on 'em down at Farringdon Market all at one time, between four and five in the morning, and as fast as they keep going out others keep coming in. Ah! if I was to say there's a thousand young and old folks in the street crease-trade, I should be under the mark."

"A thousand!" exclaimed Phil, with a downcast look. "I shall never be able to do nothing if there's such a lot as that."

"Nothin' like trying, my lad," continued the crone, quite delighted to have some one to listen to her. "You must push along as all of us does. Now, I finds places where big buildings is going on very good for selling at, and you must hunt for them. When the carpenter and bricklayer goes to breakfast at eight o'clock, they enjoys a relish with their bread. Then again, courts and little streets is very tidy selling, but mews is the places. They're first-rate. Why coachmen's families should be so very partial to creases, I can't say, but they is. Perhaps it's the smell of the horses does it."

"I thought everybody liked creases," ventured Phil, who, from having lived at a workhouse school all his life, had never tasted them, and, indeed, had rather a confused notion of what the vegetable was like.

"Thank Hevin!" answered the woman, "creases has their attractions. They're reckoned good for sweetening the blood in the springtime, you see; though, for my own eating, I'd sooner have the crease in the winter than I would at any other time of the year."

Next morning Phil and the old woman were up and out in the streets while the stars were shining coldly in the silver-grey sky. As they passed on their way the streets were all deserted, and the policeman, in his long great-coat, busy throwing the light of his bull's-eye on the doors and parlour-windows as he passed on his rounds, making the panes flicker with the glare as if a jack-a-dandy had been cast on them. On the cab-stands, as they went shivering along, they found but one or two crazy cabs left—the horses dozing, with their heads down to their knees, and the drawn-up windows of the vehicle covered with the breath of the driver sleeping inside. Then they encountered the early coffee-stall keeper, with his large coffee-cans dangling from either end of the yoke across his shoulders, and the red fire shining through the holes in the fire-pan beneath, like spots of crimson foil. Next a butcher's light chaise-cart rattled past, on its way to the early meat markets, with the men huddled in the bottom of the vehicle, behind the driver, all with their coat collars turned up, dozing as they drove along. Then some tall and stalwart brewer's drayman walked by (for these men are among the first in the streets), in his dirty, drab, flushing jacket, red nightcap, and leathern leggings, hastening towards the brewery; whilst here and there they came to a bone-grubber, in his shiny grimy tatters, with a lantern in his hand, "routing" among the precious mud-heaps for rich rags and valuable refuse, before the scavengers were abroad to disturb them.

On reaching the market, the shops all round about are shut. The gaslights over the iron gates burn brightly, and every now and then is heard the half-smothered crow of some cock caged in a neighbouring shed or bird-fancier's back parlour.

By slow degrees the street-sellers come creeping up in every style of rags, one after another, towards the gates. They shuffle up and down in front of the railings, stamping to warm their feet, and rubbing their hands together till they grate like hearth-stoning. Some of the boys have brought large hand-baskets, and carry them with the handles round their neck, so that the basket covers their head as with a wicker hood. Others have their "shallows" fastened to their back with a strap, the holes at the bottom of some of the baskets having been darned with rope or string, and others being lined with oilcloth or old pieces of sheet tin. One little girl, with the bottom of her gown tattered into a fringe like a blacksmith's apron, stands shivering in a large pair of old drab cloth boots, holding in her blue hands a bent and rusty tea-tray. A few poor creatures make friends with the coffee-man, and are allowed to warm their fingers at the burning charcoal under the can; as the heat strikes into them they grow sleepy, and yawn.

Phil and the old crone, with her rags and thin shawl drawn tightly about her, join in the crowd, the boy staring and being stared at by all around.

As the church clocks are striking five, a stout saleswoman, well wrapped in her shawl and cloak, enters the gates, and instantly a man in a waggoner's cap and smock sets to work arranging the baskets he has brought up to London. One dealer has taken his seat, and remains with his hands in the pockets of his grey driving-coat. Before him in an open hamper, with a candle fixed in the middle of the bright green cresses, and as the light shines through the wicker sides of the basket it casts curious patterns on the ground.

Now the business commences; the customers come in by twos or threes, and walk about looking at the cresses, or bending over the hampers, the light tinting their swarthy faces, while they jingle their halfpence and speak coaxingly to the dealer, to wheedle him into giving them good bargains. The saleswomen sit with their hands under their apron and their feet in an apple-sieve, talking to the loungers, whom they call by their names as if they had long known them.

After the street-sellers have bought the cresses, they generally take them to some neighbouring pump to wet them. This is done to make them look fresh all the morning, and so that the wind shouldn't cause them to "flag," for having been packed in a hamper all night they get dry; moreover, the "hand," or quantity in which they are bought, has to be parcelled out into six halfpenny bunches. Some do this as they walk along, while others sit in one corner of the market upon the bare stones, with their legs curled up under them, and the ground round about green with the leaves they have thrown away. In the summer one may see hundreds of poor things, young and old, sitting, thick as crows in a corn-field, tying their bunches up in the market. Many, however, go and sit on the steps of St. Andrew's Church, in Holborn, and there make up their stock of green meat into "ha'porths." There are crowds of poor little souls to be seen there of a morning between five and six.

It was to this spot that young Phil and the old dame, who had undertaken to instruct him in the mysteries of the business, had betaken themselves. There they were, seated amid a bevy of old and young, all busy tying up their water-cresses, and chatting the while to one another over the gossip of the market and the trade.

"I didn't see little Mary M'Donald this morning," said one; "I suppose her father's gone back to ' brick-laying ' again. Poor feller ! it's a load upon a man having eight small children to feed, and out of work half his time. Mary's the oldest on 'em, and a very good girl she is to pick up ha'pence."

"And I ain't for a long time set eyes on Louisa as goes along with her," chimed in an old man, who had one side of his face paralyzed ; "perhaps her feet's burst out agin. Let's see, she ain't got ne'er a father, have she ? She's as fine a gal for twelve as ever I met with."

"I remember Louisa's father well," said an old seafaring man; "he was a carpenter by trade. It was he as put me up to this werry crease-selling when times was bad, and he was obligated to turn to it hisself."

"Did you notice poor Mrs. Saunders a-crying this morning ? " inquired a sickly-looking girl, who had evidently been a maid-servant, of the woman next her; "the parish only buried her husband yesterday, and last night she was turned out of her lodging. Ah ! it's hard upon a 'oman near seventy."

And so they went on chatting, the only subject they cared to talk about being their miseries. Many complained of their ailments, and described their pains and sores as minutely as if they were being cross-examined by a doctor. Sickness was a favourite theme with the aged, and they were evidently trying to outvie each other in picturing the acuteness of their sufferings. One declared he had been told at the dispensary that his case was the worst ever known, and he was quite proud of it. Another made herself famous by stating that she had been sent from the hospital as incurable. Others, determined to take some share in the general conversation, detailed their coughs, or the operations they had undergone, or the medicines they had taken for this or that disease. With the hale the discourse took a different turn, and was generally about "the days when they were better off." Mechanics, too old for work, moaned and sighed over the times when they could earn "their six shillings easy." Ruined dressmakers bragged of the number of hands they had once employed, and of the rich ladies for whom they had worked. The eyes of one crook-backed creature brightened again as he boasted of having "always lived as footman in the fust of families," and a reduced laundress, throwing up her head with pride, talked of the time when "she kept her cart, and bought creases 'stead of selling them."

The little children were the only ones who talked about water-cresses. With them "good bargains" and getting pennies for ha'porths, were what they best liked to chat over. If ever the theme was changed it was to gossip about eating, and then adventures were told of how "a big bit of pudding with gravy over it" had been procured through a very ingenious method of making somebody buy the stock of cresses at double their price.

When Phil, by dint of watching how the little girls twisted the rushes round each farthing bunch, had "dressed up" his tray as well as he could, he started off on his rounds to make his first attempt at street selling.

The lad, who was strong and healthy, startled the old people by the vigorous way in which he went to work, crying, "four bunches a penny, water-creases."

"He's got a woice, ain't he?" said a broken-down coster, who had lost his own.

"Ah! creases 'ill soon take it out on him," replied a wretched old crone, whose trembling hands were as transparent as smelts.

For the first day or two Phil only just managed to pick up sufficient halfpence to buy mere bread. At night he slept along with a number of other lads in a half-finished house. Many a time as he lay on the hard ground did he long for his soft bed at his old school, and wish that he had never listened to the wild dreams of Billy Fortune.

It was a little girl of eight who first taught Phil the knack of street selling, and how, if he would succeed, he must force people to buy his green-meat. She was herself as clever a little saleswoman as ever made up a farthing bunch, but she was so small and weak that often the boys in the streets, half jealous of her success, would try to drive her from their quarter of the town—indeed, it was in protecting her that Phil first made her acquaintance. She had asked him whether she might stop by him or even walk after him, for he seemed to her to be the kindest and bravest boy she had ever met with. She was a thin, stunted child, with a face white for want of food, and wrinkled where the dimples ought to have been, and she sighed continually, as if overwhelmed with trouble. She half-frightened Philip by the calm earnestness with which she talked of the bitterest struggles of life, for she made him fancy that he, in his turn, would also have to endure them. This child-woman of the world soon saw that Phil was no adept at cress selling.

"I say," she cried, when Phil turned away from the shops at the first denial,—"I say, you musn't do that! You see I'll go and sell 'em a bunch!" And to work she went, begging and curtseying, so that at last the coin was given more in pity, or to get rid of her, than for the sake of her goods.

"Hard work to sell any, ain't it?" said Phil to her one day.

"Ah! it's nothing to what it is in the middle of winter," was the quick reply of the street baby; "then people says, 'Take your creases away, they'll freeze our bellies.' I've had then to go so long without eating that I was ill one day in the puddin shop from the smell of the meat."

Phil felt horrified, and cried out: "You're always talking in that way, Ellen! It's enough to make a chap quite afreard of you." Then, in a reproachful voice, he added: "I never yet seed you laughing; why don't you?"

"Where's the good of laughing?" she replied.

"But don't you never play, nor nothink?" asked the lad.

"Yes, sometimes of an evening we has a game of 'honey-pots' with the gals in our court; but it don't make me laugh, cos going out with the creases tires me."

"Then, why don't you go to bed if you're tired?" remonstrated Phil.

"Well, there's mother's room to put to rights," was the answer. "I cleans the two chairs, and I takes a flannel and scrubbing brush, and does the floor."

"But you're killing yourself," insisted the boy.

"Oh, no, I ain't," was the calm reply. "It was much wuss in the winter and that ain't killed me, you see."

Struggle as Phil would, he could never manage to put anything out of his daily earnings. It is true, he had grown quite an adept at his work, and instead of sleeping under dry arches, could now afford to return to his twopenny bed at the lodging-house, but he found it difficult to pay for his day's scanty food, and yet not draw upon his little stock money.

By dint of entering shops and following old ladies, as tea-time drew near, he could always get rid of the contents of his tray, and so double his fourpence. But two-pennyworth of bread doesn't go far with a growing boy, and many a night he had gone to rest as early as the lodging-house-keeper would let him, so as to sleep his hunger off, and avoid the temptation of spending the money that Van Diemen Bill had given him. Indeed, it was only fear of the old convict that kept him from "breaking into" his little bank, and ending his watercress life with a good gorge of hot food.

But at last the day did come.

It rained when poor Phil trudged early to market, with his tray over his head in lieu of an umbrella. The wet seemed to have cast a chill upon all water-cress eaters, for though he walked about the entire morning, he had only sold four bunches, and that was to a man at a public-house who had drunk himself into a fever. He tried all his old "rounds," but everywhere he met with the same answer of "No, it's too cold to-day, my boy."

When, in the evening, he sat down in a gateway to count his "takings," he found that he had only fourpence in his pocket, the same as when he went to market in the morning.

Poor Phil's legs were aching with fatigue so severely, that he almost fancied the shin-bones had given way, and were bulging out with the weight of his body. Still, he went to work again, hobbling and shouting out with all his might, and grew so energetic in his endeavours to get rid of his stock, that he made tempting offers to all faces looking over parlour blinds, or full-length figures standing at drawing-room windows, or heads seen down areas. He even went so far as to attempt a sale with a footman cleaning some third-floor windows, but the man declined to purchase, shooting back in answer that he " always bought his creases wholesale—by the ton."

Determined not to give in until he was positively forced, Phil crept towards the mews at the back of the squares, hoping that he might be able to tempt the coachmen's wives with large pennyworths. He caught two or three women taking in for the night the linen that had been drying on the pole over the hayloft door, but, though he increased his lots to five bunches a halfpenny, still they wouldn't listen to him. One, indeed, did look down to examine the contents of his tin tray, but it was only to abuse them by saying, " They were turned as black as tea-leaves, and he ought to be given in charge for trying to pisen people."

For the moment the idea crossed Phil's head that everybody had taken a sudden dislike to him, and was determined to crush him; but he wouldn't allow his courage to give way, and once more crawled back to the streets. He thought he would try what he could do by entering the shops, and selecting one where an old lady was stitching behind the counter, he pushed back the door and nearly startled the dame out of her life by the suddenness with which he offered to let her have all his tray contained for the small sum of threepence.

" Drat the boy," cried the lady, still panting with her fright, " and what do you think I'm to do with all that green stuff; I ain't a rabbit—am I ? "

The lad, as it grew late, felt quite spirit-broken. He sat down on a doorstep to rest himself and moan over his ill-luck. " Everybody can't have given up eating water-creases all of a sudden," he remarked to himself. " No, it's luck that's agin me, and is breaking a chap down ; " and as he, like most street-vendors, had grown to be a firm believer in the omnipotence of " luck," he felt convinced that he had better " give in at once, instead of tiring himself to bits and doing no good after all ! " To make sure that his luck was really so resolutely opposed to his welfare, he took his fourpence out of his pocket and began tossing. He determined that if he won twice out of three throws, he would make one more attempt, but if he lost he would eat the water-cresses himself and give over for the day. The trial ended in Phil jumping up with fresh hope in his bosom, and away he trotted, shouting, " Wa-a-ater-cre-e-eases, fine wa-a-ter-cre-e-ases ! " as lustily as if he was making his first morning round.

He trudged down Tottenham Court Road, and straight through St. Giles, up Drury Lane, as far as Long Acre, and yet his tray was not a bunch the lighter. He stopped at every pump to moisten the hanging leaves of his cresses into the semblance of freshness, but nobody would have anything to do with him or his goods. A kind of disgust for the world, and all the water-cress eaters in it, made Phil come to a sudden stand-still at a corner lamp-post, and, as he leaned against it, mutter out, "I wish I had never been born, nor nobody else either."

He remained in this position some time, picking off the dead leaves from his little bunches, and ruminating on the enormous drawbacks there were against the chances of earning a comfortable independence by selling water-cresses, when on raising his eyes and looking about him, he observed a crowd gathered round a shop-window on the other side of the way. The window-panes were covered with a mist that almost made them seem like ground glass; but the mob appeared to be very much interested in something that was going on within, and Phil, like a boy, in a moment forgot his sorrows in his curiosity, and crossing over made one of the lookers-on.

It was a cook-shop—not a fashionable eating-house, where there are separate rooms for ladies; where dead game and magnificent un-cooked joints of the finest meat are tastefully arranged before the wire-blind in the window; nor was there a bill of fare framed and glazed at the door-post, with the dishes of the day written in a bold, round hand; no! it was a cook-shop with the long window-board lined with pewter, in which wells had been sunk like small baths to receive the puddles of gravy in which joints of meat were perpetually steaming. There anybody who had twopence in his pocket could boldly purchase cooked flesh, only, instead of receiving it in a plate, it was handed to him in a piece of old newspaper, thereby combining intellectual enjoyments with animal indulgences, for the possessor, having eaten his dinner, might afterwards peruse a few of the events that happened the week before last. Behind the counter of this shop stood the cook himself, a sodden-looking man, with a face like a washerwoman's hand. Philip gazed on him with admiration, as in his suit of white linen he turned from joint to joint, brandishing a carving-knife, long and elastic as a harlequin's wand, and whipping off a half-moon slice from this leg, or whisking out a clever morsel from that shoulder.

There was a pagoda of boiled beef, composed of some twenty pieces pegged into a pile with a metal skewer, till it reminded one of a file of receipted bills. There were legs of pork, from which the crackling was slowly barking off, peeling away with long steaming like the jacket of an over-boiled potato; and there were legs of mutton with the sides scooped out like the shape of a lady's collar, and from them all rose a dense steam like that of a fire made with green wood, which condensed on the windows, ceiling, and walls of the shop, and then trickled in snake-like rivulets towards the floor again.

Such sights as a cook-shop window may seem very sickening to those who have dinner always ready for them at six o'clock, but to poor Phil, who was so hungry with his sixteen hours' fast that he had been forced to drink cold water to allay the cramps in the stomach, the reeking steam that came up through the area railings and curled out at the entrance door, carried with it an odour which was perfume in his nostrils. The worst of it was that this smell of meat brought back again the longing for food which he thought he had drowned at the pumps, and the terrible hunger cramps again began to lay hold of his stomach, grasping it like a hand.

He felt in his pocket, and commenced turning over mechanically the fourpence, which was all he possessed in the world.

"I mustn't have anythink," he said to himself; "but I'll look at the meat, and perhaps the smell will make me fill sick, and then I shall be all right."

He watched everybody that entered. He saw one man buy a plate full of scraps of meat, which, after they were shot into his handkerchief, he commenced eating whilst his change was being counted out. Another, a boy, bought some fried potatoes and held them in the hollow of his hands, which he shaped like a basin, and ate from as a horse would. Then poor Phil examined all the hot joints one after another.

"There are some people eat meat like this every day," he couldn't help thinking, with envy.

Presently one of the women servants in the shop hurried from the back, carrying before her an immense iron tray filled with smoking pudding, which she placed on the window-board. This pudding Phil instantly recognized as being what lads call "plum-duff." The appearance of this favourite delicacy created an immense sensation among the crowd outside. It was brown as varnished oak, and divided into large squares like a sample of tile-work. Several of the youths near Phil were struck with the size of the pieces, and openly expressed their approbation of the proprietor's liberality.

"Ain't they big 'uns," observed one boy; "and thick 'uns, too," he added, after taking another look.

"With gravy it is just prime," remarked another, "and wonderful filling at the price."

The rush which was made for this tempting pudding swept away all Phil's resolves to be prudent. He could not resist the temptation, but gently yielding himself a prisoner to plum-duff, he was soon struggling among the mob at the counter, calling out as loud as the others, "Me, master, I was first, please."

What are six inches square of savoury pudding to a lad who was up at four, and did not breakfast? A pair of gloves in a carpet-bag, a baby in a railway carriage, a horse on a common! When Phil had devoured his portion, he stood still for a while, and watched those who were still munching. The sight was too much for him, and cost him another penny. When he had eaten that to the last crumb, it had almost the same effect upon him as drink, and made him feel merry, and think what a silly fellow he had been to feel so cut up at his bad day's work, and nearly break his heart with disappointment, when, after all, his only misery was that he wanted something to eat. It struck him that the best friend he had met with that day was "plum-duff," and, determined not to part with so encouraging a companion until he was forced, he continued crossing the threshold of the cook-shop until his fourpence was spent.

When the boy had finished his feast, he gave up his place on the steaming railings to those pushing behind him, and retired once more to the lamp-post over the way to digest his food and think upon what he was to do. His stock-money was gone, and it was useless to think any more about water-cress-selling. He had run through his little fortune, got rid of all his property, like a nobleman, by feasting, and now he must begin the world again. By the way in which he continued repeating inwardly to himself, "It can't be helped, it was no fault of mine," it would almost seem that Phil's mind was divided against itself, and that while one half was accusing him of extravagance, the other had undertaken his defence.

He looked at the few water-cresses that remained on his tray. They had swollen and turned soft, so he leisurely tossed them bunch after bunch into the gutter. His greatest fear was lest Van Diemen Bill should by any means become acquainted with his banqueting excesses.

"He said he'd break my neck if I played him false, and I know he'd do it too," thought Phil. "Of course he'd never believe it was no fault of mine!"

To avoid the possibility of ever meeting with his eccentric patron, he determined upon retiring for a short time from all kinds of street life that would be likely to bring him in contact with the old convict's powerful arm.

Where was he to sleep that night? He couldn't pay for a night's lodging, and he knew nobody who could shelter him till morning. But lads turned loose in the street are seldom, when the nights are warm, at a loss for some corner in which to double themselves up and sleep. Like a dog that had strayed from its master, Phil, when it grew late, sauntered along, examining every place that he thought would make a convenient temporary bedstead. By good fortune he wandered into a stable-yard, and found a cart half filled with hay. He soon jumped into it, and placing his old water-cress tray under his head by way of pillow, he was in a few minutes sleeping as soundly as if he rested on the softest feathers ever made into a bed, and dreaming that he was back again at his old school, walking round the play-ground arm-in-arm with Ned Purchase.

CHAPTER III.

CATEN-WHEELING AND HEAD-OVER-HEELS.

THE next morning Phil was roused from his sleep by a severe
jolting, and on rubbing his eyes he found to his alarm that his bedstead was moving. He had so completely covered himself with hay
that when the men had put the horse to they had not perceived the
youngster.

Like a stupid fellow, Phil in his surprise gave a cry, which made
the man at the horse's head turn round.

"What are you doing there?" inquired the driver, throwing in
such a big oath at the end of the sentence, that the boy instantly
tried to scramble over the cart's side and be off. But the man seized
him by the arm before he could reach the ground.

"I thought there was no harm sleeping on the hay," stammered
Phil.

"And how do you think cows is to eat hay after you've been a
flattening of it? Do you think they likes their wittals warmed
up?"

Phil thought it better, instead of answering, to begin to whimper;
but it didn't help him much, for the carter, before he released his
hold, gave him a couple of smart whacks with his whip-handle, which
made his shoulders burn as if they had been branded.

As the lad was scampering off, he suddenly remembered that he
had left his tray behind him. "It was worth tuppence," he said to
himself; and then he began to calculate which was better—to try
and recover his property, and run the risk of another thrashing, or
to keep his body sound and lose the money. As his shoulders were
still smarting, he preferred letting his pocket suffer instead of his
back.

For four hours Phil wandered about the streets, scarcely knowing
what to do to pass the time, for all the shops were closed, and there
was nobody stirring. He leant against the posts, one after another,
and whistled all the tunes he knew.

When the shop-boys began to take the shutters down, he found a
great relief in examining the interior of the various establishments,
and by his steady staring greatly annoyed some ladies at an outfitting
warehouse, who all the time they were "dressing up" the window
felt persuaded that he was a young thief watching for an opportunity
to burst into the shop and carry off a good armful of the best fancy
articles of wearing apparel.

By-and-by, he earned a slice of bread and butter by assisting a
sleepy-looking lad to polish the name-plates and ornaments that
embellished the front of a chemist's establishment.

The sleepy boy made the first advances, by calling out, "I say, you there, do you want a job?"

It being entirely a matter of business, Phil answered, "What will you give us?"

The heavy-eyed employer suggested that some of his master's rose drops would be a fair price for a fair morning's work, but Phil, having his suspicions of doctors' sweetstuff, suggested a more solid kind of food as his remuneration, and, the terms being accepted, he in a very short time frictioned up the dull brass till it shone like ormolu.

It struck Phil that Trafalgar Square would be a nice airy spot for him to rest in whilst taking his morning's meal. It was close at hand, too, so that he needn't keep his breakfast waiting long.

Observing one or two gentlemen in difficulties, who were performing their morning's ablutions at the fountains, Phil determined upon imitating them, and having cleared away with his hand the film of soot and grease floating on the surface of the water, he made a clear place and ducked his head in and out till he was out of breath. After wiping his face in his cap, the boy chose for himself a granite post which the sun had warmed, and jumping on to its broad, round top, attacked his bread and butter with determination, biting out pieces as big as pigeon-holes.

When breakfast was over, finding his seat rather hard, he shifted his position to the railings round the statue of Charles the First at Charing Cross, and with the sun shining full upon him he gazed upon the world as calmly as if he had been in an arm-chair at a first-floor window.

There was an old crossing-sweeper working at the mud, and clearing a path across the broad road by the statue; and, as there were very few persons to stare at, Phil amused himself by watching him.

He was a fat-nosed man, with a forehead so filled with dirty wrinkles that the dark waved lines resembled the grain of oak. His costume was of what might be called "the all sorts" kind, and from constant wear it had lost its original colour and had turned into a species of dirty green-grey hue. He seemed to have a passion for buttons, for his waistcoat was held together by a variety in glass, metal, and bone. He wore a turn-down collar over his coat, which was a dress one, long past its evening-party days, and faded into an iron-mould colour. It fitted so marvellously tight that the stitches were stretching open like wickerwork.

But the most singular portion of his toilet were his boots. They were so much too long for him that the portion beyond the toes had flattened down and turned up like a Turkish slipper, whilst the heel was worn into a wedge shape which made the foot rest sideways, like a boat upon the shore.

When the sweeper saw that Phil was watching him he seemed to grow uneasy, for he several times stopped in his work to wipe his

G

face with a piece of old flannel and stare back again. At last he advanced towards the boy.

"You must have a werry 'andsome hindependence, my lively young cock salmon," he said, "for to spend the bloom of your days observing human natur."

Phil didn't answer him, for he was busy watching the old fellow's exposed throat. It was brick-red, and the flesh, from age, had contracted over the muscles and windpipe, so that each time he swallowed, the whole of the throat seemed to move as the tight skin was drawn over the dents and ridges of the cartilage beneath.

The crossing-sweeper, angry at meeting with no reply, continued,—

"You seems to have growed sarcy since you come into your property. I can tell yer what, my little spring radish, you was bound 'prentice to laziness, and now you're out of your time, do-nuffin is your trade, you lazy young warmint."

"I ain't lazy," mildly answered Phil. "I ain't got no work, worse luck. I'll help you, if you like."

This offer so startled the old crossing-sweeper that he rubbed his unshorn chin, on which the bristles stood up like the brass pegs on the barrel of a musical box. It made a noise like stroking a hairbrush, and the sound appeared to soothe him.

"Here, let's see what you're made on," he said, after a time— "whether you're real solid flesh and blood, or mere spurious imitashun and counterfeits. Take this broom and let's see how you can polish off this side the stattey;" and he pointed to the unswept portion of the road.

Phil set to work in a minute, thinking he was to have a penny for the job. The old man leant against the railings and criticised his labours, at the same time instructing the youth whenever he saw occasion.

"Take your sweeps longer and firmer, and give more play to yer helbows—that's it! Send the mud off yer broom with a jerk! The mud's as stiff and sticky as batter-pudding, and requires hartfulness —very pretty! Don't grind the broom down so uncommon wicious, or you'll have all them twigs wore down to stumps as quick as haircutten. Never mind getting hot, it saves firen, and a moist skin is wholesomest. What are you about? Can't you see where you're a goen. Keep the line, my lad, as straight and regular as wirtue's path, that's the way to be happy and get ha'pence."

When Phil had made the crossing as "smooth and regular as a hoilcloth passage"—to use his professional friend's words—he was summoned back to the statue, and both sat down against the railings.

"I'm agreeably disappointed in you," said the old fellow. "I'm uncommon pleased with your condict. My name is Stumpy."

Phil exclaimed "Oh!" and now he knew what to call him, once more examined Mr. Stumpy minutely, as if he were a curiosity. Feeling that a similar confidence was expected of him, he also told his name.

"Philup ain't such a nice name as Thummus," said Mr. Stumpy, thoughtfully. "I once knowed a Philup as was borned without toes to his feet. I wish you'd been a Thummus."

Phil tried to look as if he also was aware of the invaluable blessing he had lost.

"Yes," continued Stumpy, "Thummus is more of a poetry name than yourn, and betterer to rhyme with, and, consekently, a sweeterer name. But never mind, Philup, we all has our trials, and werry lucky is those as is acquitted not guilty, discharge the prisoner."

This little moral reflection cast a gloom on the conversation, to dispel which Phil asked whether Mr. Stumpy thought there was just then an opening in life for a youth who had set his heart upon becoming a crossing-sweeper.

"Well, Philup, you certainly 'ave got gifts and qualities, and the way you handled your broom just now gives hopes of werry flattering promise," began Mr. Stumpy, in an affected voice; "but, bless you, sweeping ain't nothing to what it were. The only advantage it have, as I can call to mention, is the remarkable small amount as is required to set up shop. How much money have you got, Philup?"

Poor Phil, half ashamed of himself, confessed he hadn't a farthing.

Mr. Stumpy seemed quite startled at the reply. For a few seconds his speech failed him. At last, with an effort, he said, in saddened tones, "Either your imperrence or your pluck is wonderful frothy, Philup. If you've no money, where's your broom to come from? How do yer expex to sweep? Aire you to do it with a duster, or with your hand, scoopways? or does you expex brooms grows from seed, like cabbage and other stalky wegetables?"

"But if I had a broom?" ventured Phil.

"Philup, your notions is over-exacted!" continued Stumpy. "You're a good boy, with clean dispositions, which I saw you sluicing yourself like a pidgeon in the fountings not an hour sins, though you didn't use my washing-basin. That there is my dressing apartment," he added, pointing to one of the fountains, "and if the board of wurks was to pervide jack-towels and the loan of a hair-brush, it 'ud be the most convenientest in the uniwerse."

Seeing Mr. Stumpy had wandered away from the subject, Philip gently led him back again to crossing-sweeping.

"It's a hard life, and not much of a living for anybody," answered the old man. "As yer ain't a hincome-tax collector, I don't mind tellin' you I tuk one and eightpence yesterday, and that's an uncommon good take, too. I feel in a ways obligated to help yer for your morning's job, so I'll give you a trial. Yer shall have my crossing whilst I'm at dinner, which is an hour, and I'll lend yer my broom, and all you can yarn you may keep."

"Oh, thank you," cried Phil.

"And mind this here, Philup," continued Mr. Stumpy, "if you don't press the people you won't get nothing. They'll all say they ain't got no coppers, but don't believe it, and stick to 'em. If you can cry easy, it's a werry good help. The women is the shabbiest; they always uses the best of places and gives the least; but stick to 'em all the same, and say your mother's took bad, or something affecting. The only place you has women on is the feelings. Say mother's queer and the baby dying o' thirst, and that may fetch a ha'penny."

Mr. Stumpy continued to give his pupil all the advice he could, until the business of the day commenced, and called the professional gentleman away to his labours. Having cautioned Philip to watch him narrowly, he took up his station on the other side of the road.

Philip watched Mr. Stumpy's conduct minutely, but, for the life of him, he could discover no very great display of art in the manner in which he obtained his money. The old man took up his stand on the other side of the road, and all he appeared to do was to touch his hat whenever anybody passed. It struck the lad that it was one of the easiest methods of earning a living that he had ever witnessed.

Mr. Stumpy, when the time came for him to go to dinner, made, as he handed up his broom, a point of asking Phil whether he had observed the art with which he had coaxed this old gentleman or wheedled that old lady, or frowned at the young children; but although Phil expressed great admiration of the sweeper's tact, yet he could not remember witnessing it.

Just as Mr. Stumpy was about to hobble off to the public-house where he took his meals, a boy came running up, shouting out, " I say, old Stumpy, I'll give a penny for your crossen whilst you're feeding." But, despite the offer, the old man remained true to his word, and answering, "You're too late, Jim," left Phil as his true and lawful representative during his absence. When Jim found his bid was refused, he eyed Phil savagely.

" How much did you pay him ? " he asked.

" I didn't pay him nothink; he give it me," replied Phil.

But Jim evidently had a poor opinion of old Stumpy's generosity, for he exclaimed, "None of yer lies; don't try to come cramming of me;" and sat down to nurse between his legs an old broom with a worn-out stump, which had been worked as round as a ball.

Jim was a good-looking lad, with large eyes, whose whites shone out with extra brilliance on account of his face being a light slate colour with dirt. His hands were so black from want of washing, that anybody might with reason have imagined that he had been walnut-peeling, and stained them brown with the juice. His costume was light and easy, consisting of a blackened shirt with so many rents in it, that the only wonder was how he knew which one his head was to go through, and a pair of trousers as full of slits as a fly-catcher, so that they formed a kind of network, through which the flesh was seen.

This young gentleman, with his legs curled up under him like a cat's, sat watching Phil, who, imitating Stumpy, had taken up his stand near the pavement, and was touching his cap to everybody. But the passengers passed by without giving anything, and Jim rolled about like a plaster tumbler, laughing with delight at the failure his rival Phil had made. At last he seemed to take pity on the misfortunes of the novice, for he crossed over the road, and, tapping him on the shoulder, said,—

"It's easy to see you ain't been up to this game long. Why, you ain't no good at all!"

"I don't know why they won't give me anythink," stammered the downcast Phil.

"If you likes to go halves, I'll help you," offered Jim.

Phil was only too pleased to accept the proposal, for it struck him he might learn a few of the tricks of the calling more easily from one of his own age.

Directly Jim had fetched his broom he went to work. His whole nature seemed to have altered in a moment. As soon as anybody set foot on the crossing, Jim was at them, grinning and looking up in the face as he ran before the passenger, sweeping away with savage industry, as if he took especial care in the person's boots. He moaned, and begged, and prayed, and rolled his big eyes about, too, in so extraordinary a style, that if they had been worked by clockwork, and made on purpose, they could not have shown more of the whites. Then sometimes he held out the dirty stuff bag he called a cap, and exposed to view a crop of hair that had matted itself into so many tufts, as if they were paint-brushes; or else he ran on, pulling at his forelock, as if pecking at it with his hand, as a bird does at a hard crust. And all the time, too, that he was doing these things, he was whining out, half coaxingly, "Give poor little Jack a copper, your honour—a little copper for poor little Jack!"

Phil watched his companion for a few moments, and then, imitating him as well as he could, he commenced the same kind of play.

His success was astonishing. He was a pretty boy, and the excitement gave him a fresh colour, which had a wonderful effect upon the ladies. His being decently clothed was also rather in his favour, for one old lady even went so far as to say "he was a good boy to keep himself so decent, and make so good an appearance as he did."

By the time Stumpy came back the boys had done excessively well. They sat down to share the proceeds.

"I've taken fippence," said Phil; "and here's your tuppence-ha'penny. How much did you get?"

"Only tuppence, on my oath," said Jim, coolly, though he knew very well that every farthing of the fourpence in his pocket had been earned on that very crossing.

"I thought I saw you take more than that," said Phil; for it struck him that Mr. Jim's offering to "take his oath," even before he was accused, sounded very suspicious.

"Search me, if you like," cried Mr. Jim, at the same time slipping the other twopence into a hole in his sleeve.

When Mr. Stumpy heard of the success of his protege, he felt a little envious, but was nevertheless highly pleased.

"You and Jim had better stick together," suggested the old man; "he is a pushing lad, and full of derwices. He know so many dodges, that if the Bank of England was to buy 'em at four a penny, it 'ud be smashed up before he sold 'em half."

Phil and Jim walked away together.

"You want a broom, don't you?" asked Jim, cunningly. "I'll sell you mine for three 'arpence." It was a worn-out stump, only worth burning, but stupid Phil paid the money.

"I say," said Jim, when they had walked a little further on, "I wish you'd lend me your waistcut. I'm so jolly cold, and you've got a coat."

Simple Phil thought the request very reasonable, and granted it, but he never got the garment back again.

When they had reached St. Martin's Church they sat down on the steps, and the new friend began to advise Phil as to what he would in future be expected to do.

"I works in a gang," said Jim, "and we has all the crossings from here right up to Waterloo Place. Jack Drake—as we calls 'the Duck' —is our Captain, and we've made Teddy Flight our king, because he's the best tumbler of the lot of us. When I takes you on to the crossing, they'll try to pitch into you, but you mustn't mind that, and I'll stick up for you. Hit 'em hard. You don't mind being larrupped, do you?"

"Not that I know of," answered Phil, so readily that he gave Jim the impression that, on the contrary, he was rather partial to the amusement.

"And, I say, there's something else," added Jim.

"What's that?" asked Phil, trembling lest the difficulty should be insurmountable, for he had set his heart upon crossing-sweeping.

"You know you must give me third of all you takes, or I shan't have nothink to do with you," stipulated the blackguard little usurer.

All preliminaries being agreed to, the couple moved forward to join the gang. It so happened that they were just then working the crossing between the Lowther Arcade and the passage by the side of St. Martin's Churchyard.

The moment Phil, carrying his broom, was seen by the young rogues, a shout was raised of "Here's a fresh 'un! here's a Greek!" and they all gathered round him, holding their handles as if they meant a fight.

"Are you going to sweep here?" asked a very little fellow in a very pert tone.

"All right, Teddy," put in Jim, "he's one of the right sort—a friend of mine."

Teddy didn't seem to think it was all right, for he answered,—

"There's too many of us by a long sight, and it won't do;" and as if to show that he meant what he said, he hit poor Phil over the head with his broom and ran off.

All the boys called out, "Where's the Duck—where's Jack Drake?"

A kind of fight had commenced when Jack made his appearance. A mob, too, had begun to collect, and a policeman was seen approaching in the distance. Under these circumstances, the first thing Mr. Drake did was to shout out, "What are you making a row for?" the next was to order an adjournment to the "Jury House," by which important name the steps of St. Martin's Church were distinguished by the band.

On the way to the Jury House, Jim whispered in the Captain's ear that the new comer was willing to pay his footing to the amount of twopence, a statement which seemed to please the Duck, for he smiled and winked.

The King, as Master Teddy Flight was called by his companions, was a small-featured boy about as tall as a mantel-piece, and with a pair of grey eyes that were as bright and twinkling as chandelier-drops, and moved about suddenly and quickly as mice. He was clothed in a style of comparative magnificence befitting his title, having on a kind of dirt-coloured shooting-jacket of tweed, the edges of which were quickly fraying into a kind of cobweb trimming at the edges. His royal highness's trousers were rather faulty, for at both the knees there was a pink wrinkled dot of flesh, and the length of the pants was too great for his majesty's short legs, so that they had been rolled up like a washerwoman's sleeves, making a thick roll about the feet, which, though wonderfully small, required a good deal of washing to render them attractive, and set off their beauty of formation.

In the course of that day Philip had many opportunities of witnessing his majesty's wondrous tumbling powers. He would bend his little legs as round as the long German sausages in the ham-and-beef shops, and when he turned head-over-heels, he curled up his tiny and august body as closely as a wood-louse, and then rolled along, wabbling over like an egg.

On the other hand, the Duck, or to give him his proper rank, Captain Jack Drake, was a big boy, with a face devoid of the slightest expression, until he laughed, when the cheeks, mouth, and forehead instantly became crumpled up with a wonderful quantity of lines and dimples. His hair was cut short, and stood up in all directions, like the bristles of a hearth-broom, and was of a light dust tint, matching with the hue of his complexion, which also, from neglecting to wash himself, had turned to a decided drab, or what house-painters term a stone colour. He had lost two of his big front teeth, which caused his speech to be rather thick, though it enabled him to be an expert whistler, and which also allowed the tongue, as he talked, to appear through the opening, in a round nob like a raspberry.

Captain Drake's regimentals were in a shocking condition; he had

no coat, and his blue-striped shirt was as dirty as a French polisher's
rags, and so tattered that the shoulder was completely bare, and the
sleeve hung down over the hand like a big bag. Of course he had no
shoes on, and his black trousers, which were, with grease, gradually
assuming a dull, leathery look, were fastened over one shoulder by
means of a brace composed of bits of string.

The solemn conclave at the Jury House ended in an uproar which
required all the influence of the Duck to quell, and nearly ended in
the King himself throwing up the broom of office, and resigning his
throne. But Jim, by mortgaging Phil's future earnings to the
amount of ninepence, at length succeeded in satisfying all parties.

The knowing Jim having already had some experience in Phil's
success, took him with him to a crossing by themselves; and he was
right, too, for they both did so well that by nine o'clock they had
made 1s. 3d. each. They might have earned more, only it came on to
rain, so Jim said he should knock off for the night.

"We in general goes up to the Haymarket, and tumbles and begs
about there until two or three in the morning," said Jim, "but it
would be no go to-night in the rain, so I shan't bother with it. I'l
take you to-morrow instead."

Whilst going home, Jim showed Phil the shops where he usually
bought his eatables.

"I shall buy a pound of bread," said Jim, "because I've done
pretty tidy, that's tuppence-farden—best seconds; and a farden's
worth of dripping—that's enough for a pound of bread—and a
ha'porth of tea, and a ha'porth of brown sugar. We've got cups and
saucers where we lodge."

"Don't you ever eat meat?" asked Phil, who was fond of it.

"Yes, once or twice a week we get meat," answered Jim. We
club together and go into Newgate Market and get some prime
pieces cheap, and boils them at home. We tosses up who shall have
the biggest bit, and we divide the broth, a cupful each, until it's lasted
out."

"I say, where shall I sleep? I haven't got e'er a place," said Phil,
whom these pleasing visions of Jim's home had roused to a sense of
his destitution.

"Haven't got a crib!" answered the crossing-sweeper. "You'd
better come along with us. It's only thruppence a night, and there's
a stunning nice flock-bed where four on us can sleep easy and comfortable, and the covering is so warm it makes a cove steam in no
time. Besides, it's betterer than a regular lodging-house, for if you
want a knife or a cup, you don't have to leave nothink on it till it's
returned."

The two boys started off for Drury Lane, and entered one of the
narrow streets which branch off from that long thoroughfare like the
side-bones of a fish's spine.

It was one of those streets which, were it not for the paved cartway, would be called a court. On the night in question the drizzling

rain had driven all the inmates in-doors; but its appearance in the daytime, when the sun is shining, is very different. Then at each side of the entrance in Drury Lane is seated a coster-woman with her basket before her, and her legs tucked up mysteriously under her gown into a round ball. They both remain as inanimate as if they were a couple of carved trade-signs placed there to show that coster-mongers dwell in the street, and it is only when a passenger passes that they give any signs of life, by calling out in a low voice, like talking to themselves, ' Two for three-harpence, herrens," and " Foine honneyens."

This street is like one of the thoroughfares in the East. Opposite neighbours cannot exactly shake hands out of the windows, but they can chat together very comfortably; and indeed, all day long, women are seen with their arms folded up like cats' paws, leaning from the casements and conversing with their friends over the way. Nearly all the inhabitants are costermongers, and the narrow cartway seems to have been made just wide enough for a truck to wheel down it. The owners of a beer-shop and a general store, with a couple of sweeps, whose residences are distinguished by a broom over the door, seem to form the only exceptions from the street-vendors who inhabit the court.

On entering the place, it gives you the notion of belonging to a distinct colony, or as if it formed one large home, or private resi-dence; for everybody seems to be doing just what he or she likes, and the way in which any stranger who passes is stared at proves that he is considered in the light of an intruder. Women squat on the pavement, knitting and repairing their linen; the door-ways are blocked up with bonnetless girls who wear their shawls over their heads, as Spanish women do their mantillas; and the coster youths, in their suits of corduroy, ornamented with brass buttons, are chatting with the maidens, and loll against the house walls as they smoke their pipes, blocking up the pavement with no more ado than if they were in a private garden. Little children find that the kerbstone makes a convenient seat; and parties of men seat them-selves on the footway and play with cards which have been thumbed to the colour of brown paper, making the points they gain with chalk upon the flag-stones. The parlour windows which look into the street have all of them wooden shutters as thick and clumsy as the flaps to a kitchen table, and the paint is turned to the dull colour of a greased slate. Some of these shutters are evidently never used as a security for the dwelling, but only as a table upon which to chalk the accounts of the day's street sale.

Before some of the doors are costermongers' trucks—some standing ready to be wheeled off, others just brought home, stained and muddy with the morning's work. A few costers are seen dressing up their barrows, arranging the sieves of waxy-looking potatoes; others taking the stiff herrings—browned like a meerschaum with the smoke they were dried in—from the barrels that look as clean as a captain's biscuit, and spacing the fish out in penn'orths on their trays.

You can almost tell what each costermonger is out selling that day by the heap of refuse swept into the road before the door. At one place is a mound of blue mussel-shells—at another a pile of the outer leaves of brocoli and cabbages, turning yellow and slimy with bruises and moisture.

Hanging up besides some of the doors are bundles of strawberry pottles, stained red with the fruit, and their pointed ends sticking out in all directions, like the rays of a monster compass. Over the trap-doors to the cellars are piles of market-gardeners' sieve-baskets, all ruddled like a sheep's back with big red and blue letters. In fact, everything that meets the eye seems to be in some way connected with the coster's trade.

From the upper windows poles stretch out across the court, on which blankets, petticoats, and linen are drying; and so numerous are these poles that they remind one of the flags hung out at a Paris fete. Many of the sheets have patches as big as trap-doors let into their centres, and the blankets are—some of them—as full of holes as a pigeon-house.

"Rows" are very frequent in such a court. The first day Phil passed at his new residence he had the opportunity of witnessing one. He couldn't tell how it began. All he saw was a lady, whose hair wanted brushing, leaning out of a first-floor window, and haranguing a crowd beneath, throwing her arms about her as if she was struggling in the water, and in her excitement nearly pitching her body half-way out of her temporary rostrum, with the same energy as that with which Punch is made to jerk himself over his theatre.

"He dragged her," she shouted, "by the hair of her head for at least ten yards into the court—the villun! and then he kicked her, and I see the blood on his boot! Oh, you murdering hound, you! you villun!"

She shook her fist at a sweep—as black as a fly—who had been behaving in this cowardly way to some poor creature. Still the man had his defenders in the women around him. One with very shiny hair, and an Indian handkerchief round her neck, answered the lady in the window, calling her "a d—d old cat," whilst the sweep's wife rushed about, clapping her hands together as if she were applauding at a theatre, and calling somebody "an old vagabond as she wouldn't dirty her hands to fight."

This row had the effect of drawing all the dwellers in the court to their windows, many of whom inquired, "What's up with old Parkers?" Their heads popped out as suddenly as dogs from their kennels in a fancier's yard.

When the two lads reached the door of the house where the gang lived, Jim stopped suddenly to say to Phil,—

"Don't mind what old Mother O'Donovan says to you. We calls her Mother Doo-nuffin. She's not a bad sort, when she isn't drunk."

And, I say, don't pay her if she's lushy, 'cos she's sure to forget all about it in the morning, and want you to pay again."

With this admonition, Phil stumbled after his companion up some stairs, which, in the dark, seemed to him to be all wedge-shaped, and to be continually twisting round.

At last Jim stopped and opened a door. As he entered the room he cried out, "Mother, I'm always doing you a good turn. Here, I've brought you a new lodger."

"If he's got threepence he's intirely welcome," answered a shaky voice from inside. So Phil, having that sum, stepped boldly forward and presented himself to his landlady. She was dressed in a linen jacket, which joined on to a short petticoat, and as her naked feet and a considerable portion of the legs were visible, she had something the appearance of a bathing-woman. She wore a frilled night-cap, which, from her having no hair, fitted her head as tight as a bladder.

"You're a nice-looking boy enough," she said, eyeing Phil; "I hope you'll behave yourself and pay your rent regular, and not follow the example of the Duck, who niver has a penny in his dirty pocket."

If she was pleased with Phil's looks, he was rather startled by hers, for one of her eyes was slowly recovering from a blow, and her lip, too, was cut and swollen.

"Is it my eye you're looking at, child?" she said, noticing his surprise. "It was a dirty blackgeyrd gave it me, and turned it as blue as a mussel."

The room was scarcely larger than a larder, and the ceiling was so low that a fly-paper, suspended from a clothes-line, was on a level with the head, and had to be carefully avoided when moving about. One corner was completely filled up with a big four-post bedstead, which fitted into a kind of recess as perfectly as if it had been built to order. There were two forms lying asleep in this bed, and by a round, fair arm, put out to pull up the coverlid, they were evidently women. The old landlady had endeavoured to give the dwelling a homely look of comfort by hanging about the walls little black-framed pictures, scarcely bigger than pocket-books. Most of them were sacred subjects, principally of saints, with large yellow glories round their heads as big as straw hats; though between the drawings of two Apostles, undergoing their martyrdom, was an illustration of a red-waistcoated "Jolly Sailor," smoking his pipe, and the Adoration of the Shepherds, ingeniously coloured in red, blue, and yellow, was matched on the other side of the fireplace by a portrait of Daniel O'Connell in a gorgeous cloak. The chest of drawers was covered over with a green baize cloth, on which books, shells, and clean glasses were tidily set out.

The first thing Jim did on entering was to wash his muddy feet. Whilst he was doing this, Phil whispered to him, "We don't all sleep in that bed, do we?"

"Of course not," answered Jim, "our place is in the next room, a fust-rate turn-out!"

They had scarcely been home ten minutes before another of the boys made his appearance. It was one that Phil had never seen before.

Mike was a short, stout-set youth, with a face like an old man's, for the features were hard and defined, and the hollows had got filled up with dirt, like a wood carving. This youth wore a man's coat, which made him look all body, for the waist reached to his knees. His hair, too, was very peculiar, for it spread out from the crown like a tuft of grass where a rabbit has been squatting.

The boy's countenance was so dirty that Mother Doo-nuffin roared out in horror when she saw him. The rain had beat in his face, and he had rubbed it with his muddy hands until it was marbled like a copybook cover, with circles, streaks, and dots.

"You ought to be ashamed of yourself, Mike—and that's Gospel truth—not to go and sluice the muck off yourself. Instead of washing like a Christian, you've been larking with them girls over the way."

A voice under the bedclothes cried out, "Yes, I seed him along with them, going on with their pranks."

Mike laughed feebly, and replied, "I can't get this here off without a drop of hot water." But the old lady indignantly silenced him by screaming out, "And haven't you had time to heat gallins by this time?"

About eleven o'clock the remainder of the gang returned home, wet through, and tired out. The moment the old woman saw the Duck she began to attack him.

"Where's the rent you owe me, Mr. Drake? I know you've got money, so cash up."

"Ah, you are hard upon a chap," pleaded the Duck. "It's the candid truth I'm telling, when I say I can't tell you the last shilling I handled."

"For shame on ye, Drake—for shame on ye!" cried the landlady; "now didn't you make six shilling last week—now, spake Bible truth—didn't you?"

"What! six shillings!" cried the Duck, "six shillings!—it would make a bright youth of me." And he looked up to the ceiling, and shook his hands. "Why I never heard of such a sum. I did once see half-a-crown; but I don't know as I ever touched one."

"Thin," roared the old lady, "it's because you're idle, Drake, and don't study when you're on the crossing, but lits the people go by without ever a word. That's what it is!"

The Duck, who made more money than any one else in the gang, pretended to feel the truth of the reproach, and said, with a sigh,—

"I knows I am fickle-minded."

"Look at Teddy Flight," continued the dame, "he's not quarther your size, Drake, and yet he brings home his eighteenpence reg'lar.

I blush for yer, Drake; you're disgracing the world by living in it, and never paying a penny of the rint all the time."

To escape being scolded, the Duck retired to rest and was speedily followed by the others.

The bedroom was merely an empty apartment, with a big mattress on the floor.

They remained talking for some time before they went to sleep, and the conversation—for the sake of Phil—turned upon the science of throwing cart-wheels or caten-wheeling, as they termed it, coupled with the art of turning head over heels.

" I was the first as ever did caten-wheeling on a crossing," said the Duck, proudly, " and I learnt the others to do it. That's why I was made Capten, because I was the best tumbler."

" Ah, Teddy Flight is the one to tumble, though!" cried Jim, "go along the streets like any think, he can! Ah, to see him and the Duck have a race, it is just beautiful! Away they goes, but Teddy leaves him a mile behind in less than no time."

The Duck said humbly, " I called Teddy the King of Tumblers— the king, and I'm Capten—yet I learned him. Ah! I'd give all my health and strength to that little fellow if I could, I'm that proud of him."

" Does it hurt, tumbling ? " asked Phil.

Mike, who was taking lessons in the art, broke in, " Hurt! I be- lieve you. It makes the blood come to the head and sets all the things about a-turning. And don't it tire you, too, that's all. Only try it."

Phil had already made up his mind to do so.

CHAPTER IV.

ON THE CROSSING.

PHILIP MERTON is a crossing-sweeper—a most accomplished and successful crossing-sweeper.

He has ended his apprenticeship, and thoroughly learned his business. He no longer pays blackmail to the usurious Jim, nor lends halfpence, that are never to be returned, to Captain Drake; neither does he trouble himself about discharging the taxes so whimsically imposed by that most free-and-easy monarch, King Teddy Flight the First. If he chose, he could depose that upstart sovereign, or cause the gallant Duck to be degraded to the ranks; for Phil has such " luck on the crossing," that the half-dozen little rips who compose this muddy band are envious of his success, and treat him with the greatest respect. Phil has only to raise the broom of rebellion, and the dynasty of the Flights would be puffed out as easily as a rush-light in a gale of wind.

And here it may, perhaps, be as well to remark that the great commercial principle of superior wealth has the same influence over little dirt-stained crossing-sweepers as over great and glorious City gentlemen. The day Phil cleared four shillings he was complimented and carnied by his ragged companions as thoroughly as was Mr. Stearine, of the firm of Margerine and Co., when he appeared on 'Change, after realizing a cool thirty thousand by the rise in tallow.

In the arts of throwing "cart-wheels" and turning head over heels, Phil has become so efficient that even the Duck himself stands entranced and fascinated when watching his graceful tumbling. The compliments paid by the Duck are quaintly vulgar, but unmistakably sincere. "The first time I see him," remarks the ragged Captain, "I could see he were all there, and a rare bit of stuff."

With his limbs outspread like opened scissors, Phil trundles along the pavement, looking one mass of revolving legs; so that had a Manx man happened to pass, he might have fancied the arms of his native island had wandered from their escutcheon and come to London, where necessity had compelled them to sell their casings of steel and put up with tattered corduroy. Even that acknowledged bounding favourite, King Flight, whose acrobatic feats had sent him head over heels on to the throne, dares not contest with Phil for gymnastic superiority; and the great match made some fortnight since "to caten-wheel" along the north side of Trafalgar Square for a wager of threepence has not yet come off, nor is it ever likely to be decided, for his royal highness is very doubtful of the result.

But Phil has learned to do other things besides tumbling and begging. He has won the admiration of this band of lawless mud-sweepers by the fulness and fire of his big oaths. If he had worn a beard a foot long, or if he had been a drill-sergeant, or the stage manager of a theatre, he could not have sworn rounder curses than came from his boyish pouting lips. When he is angry he will roar out his blistering oaths, jumbling them up together in senseless confusion, for he has picked up the silly words without understanding their meaning, and he throws them at his antagonists in the same way as he would stones. In his quiet, pleasant, friendly converse, he garnished his remarks with swearing, spacing out his words with fiery exclamations, and rougeing up his sentences with powerful adjectives; but he does so, stupid lad, more because it makes his companions laugh than from what he knows of their purport or the use they may be to the phrase. When any oath stronger than usual is made use of, Mike, who is a great admirer of Phil, has been heard to remark, "He do like a bit of scarlet;" and Jim has more than once observed that "You might a'most see to go to bed by Phil's swearing, it's so blazing powerful."

To hear these terrible words rise fuming from a child's dimpled mouth causes many well-disposed persons, as they pass along, to draw in their breath with horror, for they experience the same shock as if they had seen a babe playing with a sharp knife. Should any kind enthusiast be bold enough to stop and counsel the silly boy, he soon discovers how useless his admonitions are, for oath after oath detonates in his face as if the lad were defending himself with a revolver loaded with blasphemy, and all the gang, like so many village curs, come yelping around the poor moralist, barking out their volleys of curses until he is driven away.

The poor child, too, has acquired a dexterous knack of petty pilfering. To show his skill at purloining, he snatches up cabbages from outside greengrocers' shops and throws them away again when he is out of sight. The old man who sells sheep's trotters outside the public-house in the Haymarket fears Phil more than a policeman, for whenever the young rip passes, either the mustard spoon is whipped up, and all covered as it is with the yellow condiment, rammed down the vendor's neck, or else the bottom of the basket receives a vigorous tap, which sends the dust-coloured articles of food jumping into the air like parched peas on a drum. When a dairy girl goes past, swinging her body to and fro with the weight of her milk-pails, Phil lifts up the lids of the cans and drops stones inside, which splash down into the white liquid, and then rattle about inside the tin vessel with a noise like theatrical thunder. He chalks the backs of highly-dressed gentlemen; he stuffs orange peel into the hoods of ladies' cloaks, and he pricks the quivering calves of fashionable footmen. At the general dealers' where the boys buy their bread and dripping, nothing is safe from Phil's quick fingers. A slice of bacon is hidden in the sleeve with the same dexterity as a conjuror passes a card, and though the general dealer herself keeps her eye upon him, he manages to rob like a clown in a pantomime, and apparently for the same result, for all the pilfered onions, potatoes, and herrings are afterwards flung about as in the "pelting" scene on the stage. Many a time has an apple woman, whilst dozing on the kerb-stone, been startled out of her life by the cries of "Hi! hi!" the scamp has—as if a cab were close behind her—shouted in her ear, in order that he might, during her flutter, purloin the penny pyramids of fruit.

The innocent look that once gave interest to Phil's face, and made wayfarers generous through pity, has now changed to an impudent, roguish air, which from its archness amuses sufficiently to be profitable. He can twist his flexible features in twenty expressions in less than a minute; at one time appearing exhausted and suffering, then stretching his lips into a smile as readily as a circus rider, or assuming a sly raven's glance as he peeps up sideways into a lady's bonnet. The monkey manners and buffoon tricks he has picked up give a gloss to his begging, so that when the people look into his pretty face and see it bright and restless as a jack-a-dandy, they are forced to laugh, and then Phil knows he is sure to get a penny.

The silly boy looks upon his present life as a holiday; he laughs at the time when he had masters over him, and grows extravagant and uproarious with his freedom. Already has he become habituated to the courses of his companions, and, in endeavouring to imitate, he surpasses them.

There is but one who could save Phil from the destiny that seems to await him. Could Sister Bertie meet with him, could he but hear her coaxing voice, he would run rejoicingly to her as a dog that has strayed bounds to the call of its master, for he bears her an earnest love which would make her reproaches sting him like whips, and force him to obey her good counsels. Sister Bertie is his conscience. She is the only one he dreads to meet as he stands in his rags on the crossing. He thinks of her by day and night, she fills his bosom like his breath. When he is tossing on his flock bed, awake though his eyes are closed, it is Bertie that will not let him sleep, for she is at his ear, whispering recollections of the peaceful days gone by, and bringing back memories that make him feel faint as they pass through his brain. "Mother often wonders where you are," whispers conscience Bertie; and the boy's temples grow hot, and he lies so still that he feels his heart beat with a dull weight that shakes all his body.

In the darkness of the night when he shuts his eyes, Phil can, by thinking intently, call up the image of any person that he resolutely fixes his thoughts upon, and many a time has he summoned to him the form of that tender-hearted woman, Nurse Hazlewood; and then she stands before him, vivid as the image on a stained-glass window, with her eyes downcast, as he has so often seen them when gazing up in her face. Then Phil can scarcely draw in his breath, and, choking with fear, he tosses about, and tries to drive the shadowy form away. As if he dreaded that those phantom lips might reproach him, he sobs out excuses to his "dear mother," and pleads so earnestly for pardon that sometimes his companions are awakened, and, fancying he has been dreaming, shake him violently. These regrets and sorrows are the emotions that humanize the boy, and help to preserve him from total ruin of soul. Whilst his fellows are laughing at his impotent oaths, or, in their rough manner, praising his last larceny, Sister Bertie has her hand on his heart, tightening it with remorse, or he feels a chill pass over his forehead, as if "mother" had breathed upon him; and then he answers the flattery with a forced laugh, that does not rise from the chest with a joyous ring in it, but is dead and toneless as a moan.

The laws by which the little community of associated crossing-sweepers was governed were of so simple a nature, that, after studying them for a matter of twenty minutes, Phil was sufficiently versed in jurisprudence to commence his muddy profession without fear of offending any member of the body. There was a rough notion of honour preserved among these lads which condemned any attempt at cheating among themselves, although, as a kind of compensation for this privation, it was enacted that every other member of the human family should be considered as a fair object of plunder, whom it was perfectly right to cheat, defraud, trick, or otherwise impose upon. The only system of punishment enforced under this muddy code was of a summary nature, somewhat resembling in speediness of execution the celebrated Lynch law, although no instance has yet been recorded of death having followed its infliction, the culprit being usually permitted to escape when the torture measured out to him had reached to "within an inch of his life."

According to an act which was made and passed in the second year of the reign of His Majesty King Teddy Flight, it was enacted that any boy attempting "to crab," i.e. cheat, another, should then and there, and without warning, "have a broom broke about him," or, indeed, receive such other bodily injury as any member of the little community might feel inclined to inflict, such as kicking, hitting, or pulling of hair.

By another clause of this same act it was further ordained, in order to put an end to the constant quarrels which arose during business hours as to the rightful owner of the halfpence given by the foot passengers, that a system of "naming" should be adopted, by which the boy who was the first to call out that he saw anybody coming, should lawfully and of his own right be entitled to take, receive, pocket, and apply to his own use, any money or moneys that might be handed, thrown, or otherwise given by the wayfarers aforesaid.

In order to conceal their language as much as possible from their arch-enemy the policeman, a kind of slang was adopted by the sweeping crew, which was supposed to render their proceedings mysterious and unintelligible to any but themselves. For this purpose the rather degrading appellation of "toff" was given to all persons of the male gender, whilst the insulting epithet of "doll" was applied to every aged female, the younger members of the gentler sex being known by the peculiar title of "doxy." If, while they were begging, a policeman was seen to approach the crossing, the signal of "tow-row" was instantly given, so that the gang might have time to take to their dirty little heels and escape from the Berlin-gloved grasp of the law, which they all well knew highly disapproved of alms-seeking in the streets. As a better precaution against any sudden surprise from the constables stationed near their haunts, each "active officer" of Scotland Yard had a nickname given to him, which was generally of an insulting character. There was "Old Bandy," a highly intelligent member of the force, so called from the peculiar construction of his legs, which allowed an opening shaped somewhat like a horse collar to be seen between his limbs. Another was called "Black Diamond," from his having singularly brilliant eyes, which shone out from his pale, cream-laid countenance like blots. A third was known as "Bull's Head," owing to the apoplectic appearance of his neck, and the tight, crisp curls which

H

covered his forehead. Besides these there were Messrs. "Cherry-legs" and "Dot-and-carry-One," and "Shivery-shanks," all of whom had earned their sobriquets by their offensive vigilance and strict supervision of this more or less honourable Company of Crossing-sweepers.

A system of compulsory fines had, shortly before Phil's introduction to the society, been instituted by the Captain, who, being the first to put it in force, had styled the measure "smugging," and its operation was something like the following: we will suppose that Mr. Mike has dishonourably endeavoured to appropriate to himself Mr. Jem's "naming" of some approaching foot passenger; for this want of courtesy the injured Mike would be justified in "smugging" the offender's broom, or—if he wore one—his cap, and he would even be held harmless should the confiscated property be thrown down the nearest area or into the most convenient water-butt. While explaining to Phil the working of this law, King Flight, to impress it thoroughly on the novice's mind, made use of these remarkable words,—

"I'm the littlest chap among our lot, but if a feller as big as the Duck was to behave unhandsome, I'd smug something, and get his ha'pence, even if he smashed me like a winder."

This sentiment pleasingly illustrates the strong determination ever felt by his ragged majesty to see the laws of his dynasty properly respected and carried out.

Owing to the late hours the gang were in the habit of keeping—through their business engagements in the Haymarket, where they were usually professionally employed until three in the morning—the boys seldom made their appearance upon their crossings before midday.

"I never stops out all night," said one of the band, a promising youth of eleven, to Phil, who was inquiring into their habits; "it kills me for the next day. The Duck is dreadful for late hours—he likes it; but I can't manage nohow without my rest, for I bees so sleepy that I ain't fit to handle a broom."

When Phil had become accustomed to his new life, he entered into all the peculiarities of it as earnestly and noisily as the oldest hand in the troop. If the weather was dry and the roads dusty, he generally preferred "tumbling" and "caten-wheeling" along the passage by St. Martin's Church. Three or four of the young gentlemen would take up their stand at the end near the Lowther Arcade, and with their eyes intently fixed upon the bazaar-like thoroughfare, await the approach of any "likely-looking" persons. Presently an old lady and her child are seen advancing.

"A doll and a kiddy!" shout two of the lads in one voice; and immediately afterwards—to prevent disputes from their having "named" them simultaneously—one of them adds, "Go you halves," and the terms being accepted, they both commence twirling and twisting like imps in a pantomime round the dame and her progeny,

who, startled at finding the muddy feet dart past her eyes rapidly as
the sails of a windmill, draws back in horror and disgust.

"Shy us a copper, mum," pleads one.

"Poor little Jack, miss," whines another; and then they both
writhe and pull their hair supplicatingly to the unprotected couple.

"A toff and a doxy," roars Phil, in his turn, as a fashionably-attired
youth, in earnest flirtation with an elegant damsel resting on his arm,
nears the "school."

But Phil has not noticed the little child that, laden with toys, is
trotting by the maiden's side, and the sharp-eyed Jem shouts out—
quick as the report of a pistol—"And a kiddy," and so claims the
"call," for it had been wisely enacted by King Flight that accuracy
in these matters is the sole method of business.

The lovers are checked in their sweet converse by the supple Jem
placing his broom behind him and assuming a "honey-pot" position,
in which attitude he rolls before them wobbling like a nine-gallon
cask, and at the same time imploring, in a voice rendered thick by
his head being held down, that the "Captain will give poor Jacky a
little sixpence."

Phil, by constant practising on the flock bed in the sleeping apartment of his lodgings, has arrived at that state of gymnastic perfection
that he can turn over head and heels about thirty times consecutively.
This talent has procured him a great deal of custom, even among
his companions, for, should one of them, who is unable to "tumble,"
make a "call," he will depute Phil to perform for him, and share the
proceeds—if any. With gentlemen of sporting dispositions Phil is
invariably appointed to provide the acrobatic entertainment. As
soon as anybody wearing the natty tight trousers and flat-brimmed
hat peculiar to frequenters of betting rooms is seen lounging afar
off, the boys know that nobody can coax so many halfpence from
him as Master Phil, and he is always requested to give his performance. On such occasions the lad generally styles himself "The little
Winner of the Derby." After he has wabbled over some ten times, he
stops to see if the "sporting toff" is laughing, and even the faintest
smile is sufficient to send him trundling on again like a hat before
the wind. It is not an unfrequent occurrence for the sport-loving
gent to give the young monkey that peculiar allowance known as
"more kicks than halfpence," for he has been known to run at the
curled-up boy, and saying "Get out of that," administer a vigorous
thrust with his boot, which has sent Phil rolling like a foot-
ball.

During their meal hours, which were by no means regular, the boys
would talk in a professional manner of the day's exploits. If the
earnings had been small, the conversation usually took a melancholy
turn.

"They're a-gettin' pretty nigh sick of caten-wheeling," said the
King, sorrowfully, as, seated on a doorstep, he munched his bread
and dripping. "It's enough to make a chap's 'art turn sour, it is,"

he went on, his cheeks puffed out with the last mouthful until they were as tight and round as a horn-player's.

Another of the Associated Sweepers, who was known by the nickname of the "Stuttering Baboon," spluttered out—"And 'ead and 'eels ain't 'arf a living for a feller, for if you only does it four or five goes, they says, ' Oh, hany body could do that there,' and they won't give nuffen."

" Dear, dear ! " sighed the Duck, " money is tight; it's like pulling a tooth out getting ha'pence now. People's feelings has reg'lar froze up to what they was."

" Ah ! " chimed in Jem, " we works hard for what we gets; nobody more so. And then there's the perlice always a-birching us so spiteful."

Phil, too, would add his groan to the rest. " And such crammers as I've heard people tell. One old chap says, ' I hasn't any coppers,' when I could hear him a-playing with 'em in his pocket, a-rattling on 'em like a tambourine."

If, on the other hand, the morning's receipts had been equal to their expectations, the gang would laugh and make as much noise over their twopenny entertainment as if they were so many gentlemen at a Blackwall dinner.

" Did you see how I forced that chap in the shooting-jacket ? " boasts Jem on such occasions. " Says he, ' I ain't got no ha'pence,' and, says I, ' I ain't perticular if it's silver ; ' and he laughed and chucked me a fourpenny."

The Duck, too, is in excellent spirits, and, contrary to his usual habit, admits that he has done " pretty well." Referring to one exploit, he says, " She gave me threepence ; " and a sweet smile burst over his grimy face; " and it were done up in paper, like a young gal's curl on a Sunday morning."

At this point King Flight joins in joyously, " I seed a feller a-courting a gal, and he gave me a 'hole handful of coppers just to show off he were tender-hearted afore her."

" The most I got," chirps Phil, " was by following a 'oman with a baby, and says I, keeping close to the young un, ' Spare a trifle, kind lady, for there's five on us at home, and all took awful with the small-pox ;' and says she, ' Keep off!' And she scrunches up the child into a lump, and so I got sixpence."

When the ground was muddy, so that a number of persons were forced to make use of Phil's crossing, his pocket would fill rapidly with halfpence. On one such day—it had been raining " beautifully " all night, and the roads were dirty as the path round a piggery—he had as much as a crown given to him, " and all in coppers, without one bit of silver among it." As soon as he had collected a shilling, the little fellow would run off to the general dealer's and deposit it with " old Mother Savings-bank," as they nicknamed the woman. This prudent step was taken through fear of getting into trouble with the police from begging; for all in this sweeping community well knew

that, if when taken into custody money was found on them, not only
would the magistrate punish them severely for asking charity when
they were not in positive want, but worse than all the little fortune
tied up in a rag and stowed away in pockets and corners of linings
was forfeited and taken from them for that most terrible of all fates—
to be spent by somebody else.

Whilst Phil was, one day, having this terrible point of the law
explained to him by Captain Duck, he could not refrain from asking,
" And who gets the money they collars from the chaps ? "

The gallant Mr. Drake, whose opinion of the uprightness of a police
magistrate was but a poor one, replied with a wink, " Ah ! that's the
game ! He makes out the Crown have it; but if the Crown don't get
more than he lets slip through his fingers, why the Crown must be
wery hard up, I should say."

Young Phil held a share, as joint proprietor, in three crossings ; for
although the ground from the Lowther Arcade down to the Haymarket belonged nominally to the entire gang, yet, to avoid disputes
and ruinous opposition during business hours, they had divided the
different roads among them. Of a morning before starting for the
day's labours, they would talk of their crossings as noblemen do of
their estates.

" I think I shall take a run down to Charing Cross," Jem would say,
" I ain't been there ever such a time; it's one of the best stands
I has."

What'll you sell us your crossing for ? " would ask the speculative
Duck, who was fond of " dabbling " in muddy ventures. " Owe you a
bob and a broom for it."

" I likes opposite to the Arcade best," Phil would observe, " it's as
good a bit o' ground as any in London."

There was a crossing near Spring Gardens, in which Phil also had
an interest, though he used to underlet it to a little girl, who at night
would give him part of her earnings. This property was known
among the gang as Grub Street, it being chiefly valuable for the
" broken victuals " it brought in ; for the servants in the neighbourhood would employ the young scavengers to run errands for them,
and in return give them " the bits " that came from the table of
Dives, their master. Teddy Flight used often to moan over the slight
revenue that his property returned him. " It ain't sixpence a week
to a chap," he would lament, " for all the gentlemens as lives there
has such a lot of carriages—that catch 'em a walking, that's all."
Sometimes the food—or scran as they called it—given to the urchins
consisted of the plate-scrapings, collected from yesterday's dinner-
party, and included many scraps of the " greatest delicacies of the
season." On such occasions the feast was usually held on the stone
steps leading to St. James's Park. As soon as the cap which did
duty as dish was emptied of its contents and the banquet exposed
to view, an equal partition of the dainty viands took place, though
not without a good deal of quarrelling among the al fresco party.

The Duck seeing a morsel of "mayonnaise de volaille," would instantly implore that the "chicken with the shaving soap" might fall to his lot. On such occasions, bits of jelly were termed "size," and "fricandeau de veau" was familiarly spoken of as "hedgehog." Bargains, too, would be made after the following fashion : " Give us some of your smashed taters for these here fish 'eads ; " or, " I'll give you that there big bit of fat for some of your cold carrots."

The criticisms on the cooking, too, were peculiar and original; curry being declared to "beat peppermint at warming a chap," and pieces of almond-flavoured custard considered to be a kind of perfumery manufactured on the same principle as scented hair-oil.

When evening came on, the boys left their crossings and made for the Haymarket, which they looked upon as the great hunting-ground for "coppers," and so much more profitable did they find their nocturnal exploits, that, even when they had taken nothing during the day, they seldom felt depressed if the night turned out to be fine, for then they were certain that there would be plenty of people " out on the loose," and pennies as plentiful as buttons.

Neither were the boys so much afraid of the constables when they could carry on their tricks by gas-light. The nimble young rogues could fly away from the stout-limbed guardian of peace as easily as sparrows from a lap-dog. Besides, if ever a hunt were attempted, the bare-footed urchins had their "harbours of refuge " and "strong places." They would dart across the road, dodging safely among the cabs which were hurrying to and fro—driven so recklessly that, had the officer attempted to follow, he would assuredly have been minced among the wheels—and when once the band had reached the stone balustrade round Trafalgar Square, they soon dropped the deep wall and were safe below, where they usually remained for a time talking pleasantly to the constable, who, not daring to follow them, rested his elbows on the parapet, and looked down upon the grinning culprits, and harangued them threateningly on their bad conduct. The boys firmly believed that the policeman was not yet born who would have courage to jump that high wall. They referred with delight to the great victory they had once gained over a "red lioner "—as the officers of the Mendicity Society were termed. The rash but intrepid constable, in endeavouring to jump that very balustrade, had so seriously injured his trousers that they were " split to ribbons," and from that day, warned by his example, none who had any regard for appearances had ever repeated the expensive experiment.

CHAPTER V.

A NIGHT ON TOWN.

WHEN all London is at rest—when bedroom blinds are drawn down and street doors locked and chained—when lights are rarely seen but in the windows of the sick wards of hospitals, which seem the only places where any are awake—then the Haymarket is in its glory, gay and lively as a ball-room, with the gaudily-dressed multitude sauntering along its broad pavements, crowding them as on an illumination night. The gas is flaring from the shop windows, and throwing out its brilliant rays until the entire street is lit up as a stage.

The dissolute and the idle are pouring down to this great playground of folly, like moths attracted by the glare that must sooner or later destroy them. On they come, some in silks and satins, dressed out for the fete, and others with the money in their pockets that is to pay for the banqueting and revelry. The cabs that rattle down Regent Street have all been told to stop at the corner of the Haymarket. Men that have taken their fill of wine at the dinner-table have come thither to finish up the night. Officers with heavy moustaches have come up from the garrison towns, travelling many a mile on purpose to enjoy this one night on town. Bearded foreigners, who have heard of these midnight revels, are strolling about, smoking their white cigarettes and gesticulating violently as they criticize the vice of England and denounce the scene they have nevertheless determined on visiting every night during their stay in the metropolis. Husbands are there too, who, when they reach home, will pass off their insobriety as exhaustion, as they tell their wives how business detained them at chambers; and brothers loiter about, caring little for the hour, though sisters are waiting up for them to open the street door silently, so that the strict father, sleeping above, may know nothing of their son's excesses.

Groups of men and women block up the pavement, laughing and joking roughly together; every corner has its little assembly of gossips, who presently go off in couples to the nearest oyster-shop or public-house.

This same Haymarket is the great republic of vice, where all who enter are hail fellow well met, for every one knows why the other has come there, and virtue being cast off for the time, all rank and station cease. Outside the tavern doors are gathered clusters of "gentlemen of the land" talking to the poor souls who, disguised by some "magasin de modes," have hidden the servant-maid under the toilette of the lady. The public-house door swings back to let pass the "hope of a family," who is about to sip gin at the counter with the chip bonnet at his side. Seated at a supper-table is a pink-faced boy, fresh from his country home, helping with delicate attention the rouged-up form beside him. She laughs noisily as a man, flinging her arms about, and as the champagne foams in her glass she tosses her head like a Bacchanal. But what by daylight would disgust seems charming in the blaze of the Haymarket gas, and the lad looks with admiration upon the companion whom on the morrow he would pass without even a nod of recognition.

Every street in the vicinity of this Haymarket partakes more or less of its debauched character. In some there are mysterious, closed-up houses, into the back parlours of which none may enter but the initiated, there to empty tumblers of such drink that in a wiser hour they would push from them as unfit even to allay the pain of thirst. Seated on soft-cushioned sofas that are as yielding as they—poor simpletons—have been, are women decked out like shop windows, clothed in the rich gloom of velvet or the brilliance of satin, with costly laces—richly worked as a Gothic tracery, such as few virtuous women could afford—filagreeing about their arms and necks. But how little of the woman do these foolish maidens retain beyond the clothes they wear! They are bolder and wilder than the men who have come there to court them; they answer gentle speeches with the slang of a cab-driver, and even in their merriment they jerk out oaths with their laughter. And this is called seeing life!—yes, it may be so, but it is such life as that which exists in the drop of putrid water—the life of the ditch and sewer.

They say there is no rest for the wicked, and certainly there is none for the Haymarket; it is the owl of London, that wakes up at dusk lively and fresh for the night, and hoots and screeches till morning comes again.

Those who dwell and trade in this thoroughfare have pale faces, countenances blanched from the lack of sunlight, that in the day look used and "seedy" as a masquerade dress, but at night are fevered up into seeming health when the warmth of the gas strikes upon the cheek. They sleep away the morn with closed shutters and drawn curtains, and the healthful breezes of the sun-warmed day never blow against their sickly skin. They seek for health from the doctor and for cheerfulness from the wine bottle; and when, after a few years, they have heaped together the round sums they so longed for, the body that was to have enjoyed them is withered and rotten, and they envy the hunger of the beggar and the strength of the ploughman.

Each member of the associated beggar-boys was as well versed in the Haymarket as the district postman himself, and knew the different shops and the names of the proprietors as thoroughly as if he had learnt them off from the "London Directory." The lads had also studied with much attention Waterloo Place, and had even managed to pick up an acquaintance with some of the gentlemen who lounged about there smoking their cigars. The magnificent pave-

ment of this latter thoroughfare, and its half desertion, afforded the
" school" many excellent opportunities for tumbling, an exercise which
was utterly impossible in the crowded Haymarket, from the fact of
most persons objecting to have either their face slapped by the cold
muddy foot of the young caten-wheeler, or to be tripped up by the
rolling human bundle coming head over heels against their unsuspecting legs.

" It's not a bit o' good a-getting to the Haymarket afore nine," the
Duck would say. " There's only the swells a-going to the Opera, and
they're too clean to laugh. Just wait till they've crumpled their
waistkits a bit, and then they unbends theirselves more to a chap."

The Haymarket, considered as a street, may be said to have two
natures: one moral, and the other immoral; for on one side of the
roadway the shops give every indication of being virtuous and well-
behaved dwellings, for they work at their trades during the day, and
put up their shutters at dusk, as if they had closed their eyelids to
prepare for sleep. Of these two sides our young band invariably
chose the immoral one as the scene of their night exploits. They
cared little about promenading before the closed windows of upright
trunkmakers, chemists, and print publishers. They liked the glare
of the gas as much as a cat likes the warmth of the fire, and it was
before the full blaze of oyster-shops, supper-rooms, and taverns, that
these lads carried on their professional labours.

Until the busy time of the evening arrived, the boys would loiter
about Windmill Street, watching the crowd flock to the Casino, hoping
that good luck might throw them a penny for opening some cab-door,
and putting their ragged coat-tails against the muddy wheels to
protect the dresses of those alighting. They stood looking down the
narrow street, gazing listlessly at the red and blue lamps placed like
illuminated posters over the supper-room doors, until any vehicle
drove up, when all of them would dart forward in a body, more as
if they were going to attack and rifle the cab than act as ragged
lacqueys.

To vary the monotony of door-opening, the young gentlemen would
sometimes amuse themselves by peeping over the red silk curtains of
the " Cafe de la Regence " at the corner, either making faces at the
coffee-drinkers within, or flattening their noses against the plate-glass
until they were as white as button mushrooms, much to the horror of
the lady with the accroche-cœurs flourished upon her cheeks who was
seated in state behind the comptoir. Determined not to lose a
chance for legitimate begging, the boys carried paper with them to
accommodate gentlemen whose cigars had gone out ; and if any such
luckless person chanced to approach, instantly the " spills " were
lighted at the convenient jets at the cafe door, and thrust up to the
smoker's countenance, more as though they were about to singe him
like a chicken than tender a civility.

So as not to interfere with each other in their begging expeditions,
the gang would separate, and whilst some crossed the road to that

side of Piccadilly which is a medley of hotels, betting-rooms, and restaurants, to act as self-appointed door-openers to the crowds entering the tavern known as "the noted house for Brighton tipper," others would make for the Opera Colonnade to fascinate the French gentlemen with their bounding exercises, whilst the remainder of the gang prowled about generally, either energetically sweeping the flagstones before some well-dressed idler, or officiously dusting the boots or scraping off the splashes from the trousers of the first person who happened to be standing still. In fact, they elected themselves to numerous offices, all of a more or less useless character, and in the greater number of instances it would have been more agreeable to the favoured individual if they had not shown him such delicate attentions.

The boys had very knowingly arranged a number of plaintive requests that were peculiarly suitable to the occasion. It was the invariable custom of the Duck, when he chanced to be outside a tavern door, to ask, gigglingly, for "half a pint o' beer to drink his honour's health." If, whilst gazing in at a baker's window, admiring the pale red tarts, or longing for the hard-crusted Scotch buns, so temptingly slashed with the snuff-coloured preserve, Mike caught the eye of any passer-by, he would instantly hint that he was on the point of starvation, and beg a penny "to buy a poor orphan boy a mossel of bread." With that genius which usually characterized all his actions, King Teddy Flight had framed a petition intended to move the hearts of those frequenting tobacconists' shops, for he would ask them, in his most winning tones, "to stand a farden's worth of snuff to a poor boy out of work." But perhaps the most impudent of all these requests was the one that Phil had adopted; for whatever the time of year might be—whether Christmas or midsummer—he always tendered an oyster-shell to any one he met, begging with an innocent face that they would "please to remember the grotto," adding—although it was a nightly request—"that it only came once a year."

A favourite rendezvous for the tattered rips was in Coventry Street, in front of the fish-shop where the barrel-shaped lamps hang from the first-floor balcony. They delighted to watch the row of aproned men who passed the evening of their lives opening oysters. To attract attention, King Flight was in the habit of requesting any customer who might be sipping his bivalves to "chuck him one,"—a demand which was seldom responded to. These impertinent urchins were also fond of criticizing the feasters and their mode of eating, making rude observations which caused many of the customers to feel very uncomfortable and nervous.

Phil used to like gazing at these fish-shops, with the window dressed out with fresh green salads and crimson lobsters, until it was as gay as a bed of geraniums. He delighted in touching the quires of dried haddock that looked stiff as untanned leather, and he wondered why the lobsters should always have the end of their cactus-looking claws bound round with string, as if they had been clumsily repaired like the leg of a table. The big crabs, buff as hard-baked pies, and some of them lying on their backs and showing their hairy legs parted down the middle, were especial favourites of his. And so were the brick-red crayfish, with their nutmeg-grater backs, and their feelers sticking out like riding-whips; and so strong was the boy's curiosity concerning this "lobster's big brother," that nothing but the presence of the men in the shop prevented him from taking one out of the window for the mere pleasure of opening its springy tail, that was always tucked under like that of a frightened dog.

When the London season is on and the Opera open, then, as the night advances the Haymarket becomes choked up with carriages ordered to "fetch" at eleven the red, white, and blue cashmere cloaks that have been flirting and chatting out the evening, thoroughly in-different as to whether Amina should fall off that terrible nine-inch plank or not, or the roguish Rosina ultimately marry her tenor lover. Now the street gains additional importance and profit. The night broughams, the lofty chariots, the genteel fly, all crowd together, hiding from view the centre line of vulgar cabs as completely as a spaniel in the tall grass. The footmen take their ease at their public-house until the howl of the link-boy shall summon them to duty. The powdered retainer from Belgrave Square graciously drinks from the full pot that the greasy-hatted attendant from Barnsbury Park, Islington, has admiringly offered him, for the humanizing effects of porter soften his proud aristocratic soul. The silk-stockinged coach-man lolls on his hammer-cloth as on a couch, chatting condescend-ingly with the check-trousered fly-driver who has paid for the hot gin-and-water. By-and-by the mob of drab-coated servitors advance to the colonnade, some to stand inside the grand entrance which commands a view of stairs covered with crimson drugget, while others, to kill the time and get rid of the smell of tobacco, air them-selves by hanging about the stage door in the hope of catching a glance at some Madlle. Pettito, or captivating with a love at first sight those delights of the ballet, Mesdames Tootsi and Pootsi.

Presently, gentlemen looking unnaturally fashionable emerge from the eight-and-sixpenny entrance, all humming the grand finale as they pack up their binocular glasses. Then the footmen, knowing that the opera is over, become agitated. In a few moments mighty names are shouted out by husky-voiced men, and my lord's carriage comes swinging to the kerb-stone, and my lady's brougham darts up as if it were trying to smash itself against the columns. Now, the street-loungers form a double row like a human palisade, to see the "company" come out. Ladies with carefully dressed hair skip across the pavement, holding up their dresses as on a rainy day, and jump into little bandbox vehicles which they fill like a chair. Steps are clattered down, and old gentlemen with pink heads are hoisted up by straining lacqueys. Now slowly advances the big clarence from the livery stable, the gaunt horse shrinking from the pressure of the collar, despite the whip that whistles like a breeze 'about his big hips. Those who have hired the vehicle plunge head first into its drab interior, and the crowd, startled at the number, count them with increasing amazement as yet another dress bounds past.

Nobody could have enjoyed the Opera nights with a greater gusto than did Phil and his companions. Had they been consulted on the subject of the Lyric Drama, they would have expressed themselves in terms of unqualified approbation upon the great good it effected, for they not unfrequently picked up more money in the half-hour after the performance was over than they had made by the entire day's hard begging and tumbling. Their peculiar business was either to run for cabs, or else to open the doors of such as had been fetched. The boys, to avoid disputes with the police, always politely tendered their services to those ladies and gentlemen who, in their hurry to get home, had wandered a short distance from the theatre, and were helplessly staring about them in the hope of hailing a stray vehicle.

On these occasions all the boys separated, that none might interfere with another's scramble.

One very wet night, when the rain had been falling all day long, and had converted the streets to level plains of liquid slush, into which the lamps were reflected as into a canal, Phil, who had only made twopence—and that was for turning a mad cat out of a single lady's coal-cellar—trotted down to the Opera House, offering up supplications to "luck" that he might earn the threepence necessary for a night's lodging at Mrs. O'Donovan's.

Just as the music-loving public were rising from their intellectual feast, the rain came down in streams of water as if the clouds above were being wrung like wet blankets. "Here's a soaker!" thought the young Bohemian, looking about him with delight, as he paddled ankle-deep in the mud; "they'll be drowned as safe as caught fleas if they tries to swim home in their Opera kicksies."

Presently a gentleman, "carrying milk-pails," as the boys called it —that is, with a lady on each arm—advanced up the colonnade, gazing mournfully at the rain that came down straight as iron wires. Three or four times did the attentive beau shout out "Hi!" to the passing cabs. Phil had seen this group in the distance, and was galloping towards them, his naked feet slapping the pavement like fish on a marble slab.

"If we have to stay here all night, William, I'm not going through that," said one of the ladies, pointing to the shower-bath without.

"I should spoil everything I've got on!" added the other damsel, who wore a light-blue tissue dress, that in two seconds would have pulped like silver paper. The gentleman, who was strong and manly, muttered something about "coming out with women who were afraid of a drop of water," when Phil, bounding up to them, exclaimed, as he pulled at his hair like a check-string, "Shall I fetch a cab, yer honour?" He only heard one of the ladies direct him to "go directly, like a good boy," and off he flew among the vehicles, shouting out, as he passed, "Who wants an out-and-out job?"

He ducked under horses' necks, he sidled between wheels that went within an inch of his naked feet, but every conveyance he ran up to seemed engaged. He saw Mike go by, seated like a nobleman on a box, and in vain he offered him a penny for his "find." Some of the cabmen, although taken, asked him "where to?" and seemed inclined to play their retaining fares false, but Phil's answer of "ever such a way" was evidently not distinct inducement enough to warrant their being dishonourable. At length, as the rain fell heavier and heavier, the boy thought the best method was to mount beside the first driver he passed; so up he clambered, saying,—

"Why, where've you been to? I was a-lookin' for you ever such a whiles, all over."

"Oh, were it you as was the boy wot engaged me?" asked the man.

"Why, in course it was," answered Phil, with assumed indignation,. "and a fust-rate fare it is, too, with a glass of spirits at the end of it."

He had been absent some twenty minutes, hunting for the vehicle, but "his people" had not moved from where he left them, which proved to Phil that cabs were very scarce indeed that night, and made him think a shilling would not be too much for his trouble.

Nothing could exceed the gallantry displayed by the young sweeper, as he offered his hand, dirty as a cheese-rind, to assist the ladies into the vehicle, or twisted his body round so that his tattered skirt might cover the dirty wheel; and when at last the door was closed, and the time had come to receive his payment—if any—he stood, wet through as a dog at the Serpentine, grinning like a hurdy-gurdy boy, and saying, in supplicating accents,—

"Remember a poor boy, miss! Very wet, sir! It's the last cab left on the rank, mum! Took me half an hour, sir!"

"Mind you pay the poor boy well, William," said one of the ladies, whilst the other added, " He must have caught his death, poor child."

"Here's more than you ever had in your life before," cried the gentleman, slipping, as the vehicle drove off, what Phil thought was. sixpence into his hand.

Master Merton had got into the habit of mistrusting his fellow-man; so, disregarding the elegant appearance of the gentleman, he bit at the coin to see if it were a good one. He had his doubts about its genuineness, for it felt very heavy, and nervously he advanced to a lamp to examine it.

It was half a sovereign! Directly he beheld it he clenched it up in his hand as suddenly as if he had been catching a fly, for fear anybody stronger than himself had been watching him. Then he sneaked off, still looking around him in mistrust, until he came to a deserted court, and there, raining as it was, he sat down on a step to-feast his eyes on his treasure. He turned it over and over as a monkey does a bit of biscuit; he read by the gas-lamp the inscription on both sides of the coin, and he weighed it on the tips of his fingers, and made it ring upon the muddy stones, wiping it carefully on his coat when he was tired of the music.

How often he had seen these golden coins behind the bars of public-houses, and wondered if he should ever have one of his own. He had seen little wooden bowls full of them at the money-changers', and he had stood there by the half-hour thinking over the number of things he could buy with only one of the little bright discs.

Then he grew grateful to the donors, and suddenly remembered how beautiful the two ladies were; and his heart also inclined very much towards the gentleman, and he regretted that he had not heard where the cabman had been told to drive to, that he might have done his benefactor some service in return for his generosity, if it were only to sweep a crossing before his door or caten-wheel in front of the parlour window for the ladies to see him.

As it was, Phil thrust the half-sovereign into his cheek, that being the safest purse he knew of, and, determining to say nothing about his wealth to his brothers in mud, he scampered off to find them.

On a fine night, what is called "the fun" of the Haymarket seldom begins before one o'clock, for by that time gentlemen of lively dispositions have imbibed enough strong drink to render them reckless of consequences.

The men and women who have come there to sell fruit and flowers have doubled their prices, and are plying their trade with the greatest industry, displaying their bouquets whenever they see a gentleman talking to any one, in the hope that he may be made to buy the extravagant nosegay, or thrusting baskets of expensive but tempting plums into the centre of conversing groups, and placing the male portion of them in the uncomfortable position of having to appear mean if they refuse to purchase, however earnestly they may wish to escape the outlay.

It is about this time, too, that "rows" begin to take place. Should the police attempt the capture of any illegal practical joker, rescues are attempted by his friends, and a crowd soon collected, which sways about the roadway, the shiny top of the officer's hat always forming the centre of the riot.

The young crossing-sweepers enjoy this time immensely. Should any gentleman who has been too thirsty at his supper, evince any inclination to joke with our muddy community, the boys, far from checking these attempts at familiarity, rather use their utmost endeavours to encourage the acquaintance. On one occasion, the "school" having discovered a couple of gentlemen limp with liquor, and bending backwards and forwards with the elasticity of foils made from the best steel, instantly surrounded them and commenced tumbling. As these unsteady revellers were in that condition when lamp-posts and houses revolve and spin around, their giddiness found no relief from having half a dozen pairs of legs twisting like wheel-spokes before their eyes.

It was about this time that the Duck, finding that some novelty was sadly wanted to give a spirt to street-begging, introduced into the Haymarket his celebrated feat of "standing on his nose." It has been much doubted whether Captain Drake was really the first to think of this eccentric gymnastic exercise. One Judy Jack, who was intimate with the Duck—being in the same profession, though he carried on business in Camden Town—has since brought forward evidence of a rather strong nature to prove that it was he who had taught the Duck the knack of performing the trick, and had even showed him how he must "bear on his hands to take the weight off the nose, or he'd dent it in as easy as a trod thimble."

The Captain's method of proceeding was to accost wild-looking young men, and after asking for a copper for poor little Jack, to add, "I'll stand on my nose for a penny, your honour;" and if the tempting offer were accepted, up went the Duck's nimble legs, and there he rested with his face flat to the ground, at the same time drawing the attention of his patrons, in a voice resembling that of a person afflicted with a severe head cold, to the fact that his "dose was slap agin the bavebelt."

After each night's labours, the gang were accustomed to adjourn to the Jury-house, as they termed the steps around the portico of St. Martin's Church, there to reckon up what they had made during the day. It was usually about three o'clock in the morning when this business meeting took place, but the young rogues, far from feeling sleepy, were generally as fresh as bees, and in the best of spirits, especially if the "takings" had been equal to their expectations. Lolling against the massive iron railings, the counting up of halfpence would proceed in clerk-like silence.

"Fourteenpence!" Mike would cry out when his reckoning was over. "None so dusty, neither!"

"Elevenpence harpenny," would call out in his turn the King; "that's better than smashing your leg."

"One-and-seven," Phil would say; and, imitating his companions' style of expression, he would add, "and nobody's eye put out."

On hearing this amount, the Duck, who for some unknown reason always pretended to be the least fortunate of the party, would beseech Phil to give him twopence for luck. If Phil saw no just reason for granting this request, Mr. Drake would decrease the amount asked for to one halfpenny, and if that gift was also refused, he would beg pathetically that his wealthy young friend would, when he took his morning's pen'orth of coffee at the street stall, spare him a little of it in the saucer. There was no pride about the Duck, and he always took things as they came, and, indeed, not unfrequently when they didn't.

During the fag end of the season, when the gay idlers of London had gone to the sea-side to pick up the health they had thrown away

in the Haymarket, the troop did not make such excellent incomes as
they could have wished; indeed, their expenditure not unfrequently
exceeded their gains by exactly the threepence which Mrs. O'Donovan
required for the night's lodging, and much to that lady's disgust
she would be forced to give her young gentlemen credit. The
establishment of Mrs. O'Donovan being avowedly conducted on the
ready-money principle, and the wardrobes of the youths, consisting
only of the few rags they, by great ingenuity, managed, with the aid
of pins and strings, to carry on their backs, the landlady grew
nervous when the amount due to her amounted to sixpence a head.

At such a time, this severely punctual woman, knowing the habits
of the boys, would rise from her pillow, and in the blue light of dawn
suddenly appear before the assembled younkers as they sat at their
accounts on the Jury-house steps. The Duck, who was always the
heaviest defaulter, would instantly endeavour to escape from the
cold, determined gaze of his creditor's grey eye; but her voice would
pull him back like a hand.

"Misther Drake!" she would say, shaking her head as if prepared
to quarrel—"Misther Drake, oi want mee monee. I'm a harrud-
worrucking woman, Misther Drake."

"Why, I never seed you working yet!" would equivocate the
Duck.

"You owe me sixpence, Mr. Drake," she would continue, without
heeding the reply, "and I'll thank you kindly for that same."

She waited in silence for a few seconds, gazing with dreadful
sternness at the other debtors; but on the Duck beginning to
whistle, she lost her temper, and broke out wildly.

"Why don't you distrain?" asked the Duck.

"Is it distrain, ye say?" roared the lady, "yer bundle o' filth, ye!
It's at the rag-shop I must carry yer thin, yer villin, and its onlee
brown paper they'ud make o' yer at the best o' times. Pay mee sixpence, Misther Drake."

"Why, it's months since I've seed a sixpence," said the Duck in
persecuted accents. "I wish I had, and I'd have eaten somethin'
instead of never tasting nothen all the blessed day."

"That's a loie, Mister Drake," screamed the landlady; "you've
had onions, for I can smell them here, and enough to knock me
down. I want mee sixpence."

"Why don't you ask the other chaps, 'stead of only bullying me?"
complained the debtor.

The fiery Mrs. O'Donovan was trembling with rage, shaking like
the hand of a drinker. She was about to follow the Duck's advice,
and had commenced her attack upon the gang by howling out, "Ye
herd o' plundering locusts" . . . when the whole of the troop took
to their legs and darted away from her, leaving her to shake her
fists and scream after their retreating forms.

As they knew it would be useless to return home in the absurd
hopes of being allowed to sleep there, the entire party made the best

of their way to St. James's Park, and, having climbed the railings, they silently sought out some convenient spot that would serve them for a bedstead.

At length they discovered what Teddy Flight termed a place that had been "made o' purpose, knowing they were coming." The overhanging boughs of some valuable shrubs, the names of which were carefully painted on the labels near their roots, formed a kind of gipsy's tent, and the withered leaves that had fallen covered the ground with a soft, dry mattress, almost equal, they declared, to a truss of straw.

Into this branch-curtained retreat the lads crept on all fours, one after another, to enjoy their "doss," as, in their slang, they called sleep.

"Of all beds these here flower-beds is the primest for a doss," said Mike, "it's as soft as feathers!"

"If we pulls our coats over our ears, and then scrunches together in a lump, we shall do prime," was the advice of the experienced Duck.

"The last in bed blows out the glim," jocosely remarked Master Jim.

Then, huddling together like a litter of kittens, the boys fell asleep; some with their head resting on the stumps of trees as a pillow, others with their legs and arms sprawling about, so that the limbs were crossed together like wicker-work.

Such was the kind of life these miserable lads were accustomed to lead—an existence that had no pleasure in it beyond its daring and its lawlessness; where liberty was purchased at the expense of rags and hunger; and which was gradually training them for the gaol, by teaching the boys that the least laborious method of earning their bread was by transgressing the laws of society, instead of conforming to them. Already they were ranked among the outcasts of the world, those for whose safe keeping policemen had been appointed and prisons built.

Phil, from living among these boys, had picked up their slang, and forgotten the "good words" taught him at his school as completely as a child sent to a foreign land loses its native language. His mind, too, had taken their stamp—the one that often seals a destiny—and his morality had become as muddy as his rags. When well-to-do people passed near him in the streets, they often placed their hands in their pockets, mistaking him for a thief, for there was a cunning side-look in his eyes; and when he sneaked after them to beg, his step was more like that of one ready to decamp than bent on following.

He had been one year at this sad work. He had passed through the winter, treading the snow with frost-bitten feet, and cuddling together the rags that fluttered about him like a storm-rent sail. The only time he had known warmth was when he was scraping the snow from before the houses, and the only variety to his miserable life was when the boys pelted each other with snow-balls for the halfpence that were thrown to them, or swept open spaces on the ice for skaters at the Serpentine.

I

But when the warm spring returned, when the chilblained feet had healed, and the rags, holey as a worm-eaten leaf, once more felt warm enough, then Phil forgot the wise resolutions he had made in his time of suffering, and returned, as a matter of course, to his old habits.

But for a mere accident he might to his dying day have remained a member of the Associated Crossing Sweepers.

Late one night, when all the gang were prowling about the Haymarket like cats on a flower-bed, they saw two gentlemen lolling against the post at the corner of Windmill Street, and evidently wishing they could hit upon some amusement to relieve them from the hard work of having nothing to do. By their long moustaches and the hair close cut behind, the quick-eyed and experienced young beggars instantly recognized them as belonging to her Majesty's Service, though whether foot or cavalry they neither knew nor cared.

As pigeons to peas, the boys flew to the perfumed sons of Mars.

The Duck instantly volunteered to stand on his nose and beat time with the soles of his feet to the tune of " Is the Battle over, Mother P " for the trumpery equivalent of one penny.

The King, Edward Flight, ever willing to meet the times and distance competitors, offered to turn head over heels as rapidly as a pith ball rotates on a fountain, for the totally insufficient remuneration of one halfpenny.

Phil, whose business principles were small profits and quick returns, endeavoured to undersell his rivals by proposing to catenwheel until he was black in the face for the small charge of one farthing.

" Well, then, the whole lot of you go to work," said one of the officers; and a second afterwards the solo with the foot accompaniment had commenced, and the other lads were twisting about as rapidly as the paddles of a steamer; but just as the entertainment was half over it was unfortunately interrupted by the approach of a policeman, who, taking off his belt, dealt the performers such lusty blows with the buckle that they were glad to spring to their feet and scamper away.

As the dogs driven from a tripe-shop return to gaze again at the wet washleather-looking dainty, so did these beggar boys once more appear before the officers as soon as they had given the policeman what they called the " lucky dodge."

The officers laughed to see the young scamps, as they came up grinning and whining to ask for "the little bit of silver," and they were kind enough to make several inquiries as to whether the castigation they had received had hurt them or not. But as to the payment of the money the boys thought they had earned, the gentlemen complained that the performances they had bartered for had not been given, and vowed they would not " cash up " until they had witnessed something more for their money.

Then they set the boys a variety of comic tasks. One of the gentlemen had a box of dinner pills in his pocket, and four of them were placed in Mike's hand, and he was ordered to swallow them instantly. The boy shuddered with the disgust all lads feel for medicine, and he made a face which drew up all his features into a variety of wrinkles, but as there was scarcely any enormity he would not have committed for one penny, he hastened to the pails by the cabstand, and ducking his head like a horse, filled his mouth with water, and swallowed the pills as pleasantly as if they had been four black currants.

The next boy ordered to stand forth was King Teddy, and he was led, by the eccentric gentlemen on town, into a pastrycook's shop, and there, being mounted on one of the marble-topped tables, he was ordered, like a monkey on a drum-head, to begin his exercises. The young lady in the shop behind the pewter hot-water apparatus where the veal-and-ham pies are kept tepid, screamed out, as the cobwebby Flight entered, "Turn that dirty boy out! I won't have him here!" But those who promised him sixpence ordered him to advance, and although he plainly heard the fearful words, "Run for the police!" the naughty child commenced his gymnastics.

When Master Teddy, growing nervous, asked whether "Please, sir, he might go now," instead of the "Yes" he hoped for, he was commanded to caten-wheel the whole length of the shop, despite the crowd of customers, and in he plunged, as into water, making the tart-eaters fly before him. His legs revolved within an inch of trays of cracknels, and nearly brought down dishes of custards, or sent yellow jellies quivering over the oilcloth, and all the time parasols and canes beat at him as he trundled along. Even now these officers would not give the "little sixpence" that was once more implored for. A task of a decidedly cruel nature was given to the whole band, but nevertheless it was one from which these inhuman ragamuffins did not shrink.

"Go and pull that tipsy man over," was the order; and like dogs at a weak cat the pack flew at the staggering drunkard, and upset him as easily as a ninepin. Their work completed, they once more asked for their money; but no! the gentlemen were enjoying themselves too much with the sport to put so speedy an end to the fun. Thinking over what mischief they could next invent, they happened to catch sight of a woman going by, and Captain Drake, as the biggest boy of the troop, was directed to "go and sweep mud over her."

With a vigorous dig of his broom the Duck sent a broad sheet of liquid dirt against the poor soul's dress, covering it as with a patch of brown paper. She turned round in wonder to see what had struck her, pulling her cotton skirt about her with a look of disgust and astonishment that made the troop and their fashionable abettors shout with laughter.

Why does not Phil roar and dance with the enjoyment of the mischief, like his companions? His face has turned as white as if a sickness had suddenly smitten him. As he saw the woman's features, his hair was lifted from his head, as when a gust of wind blows against the temples.

He thanked Heaven that she did not see him among her insulters —that poor nurse that used to call him her "own pretty boy;" the kind, patient creature that, even when he richly deserved it, would not hurt her Phil, but would rather kiss the pouting lips of the sulking boy, and coax him to laugh away his ill-humours.

Time was when Phil was innocent, and he had impulses which gave him no time for thought, but would have sent him bounding forward at the joy of seeing that face again. But now he is one of the foxes of the street, and as he would not be seen in bad company, he sneaks round the corner, and runs along back courts, to reappear again higher up in the same street; and there he stops till his Nurse Hazlewood shall advance towards him. Whilst he is impatiently waiting her approach, he runs into the road to watch what she is doing, and when he catches glimpses of her through the openings in the moving crowd, he perceives her pointing to her dress, and appealing indignantly to the lookers-on. The muscles of his face twitch again, and his fingers work like a beetle's claws, as he thinks to himself, "If she only knew that I was one of them that did it!"

Presently she advances, and, panting and trembling with anxiety, he creeps after her. Twice he calls out "Mother!" but in so low a voice that he is not heard; and he is glad of it, too, for he dreads the look he knows she must give him when she sees her Phil a ragged street boy. More than once the thought of "runaway" has entered his mind, but the wish to hear of Bertie is stronger than the fear of any scoldings he may receive. At last the nervous boy pulls at her shawl, and, as his nurse looks round, his head falls on his bosom, and he says, "It's me, mother."

She knows the voice in a moment, and, taking that head with the dust-coloured hair between her hands, she raises it to the full glare of the gas, and mutters, as if to herself, "Good God! it's Phil."

The poor soul is silent with grief, but the boy thinks the scolding is coming, and he stammers out, "It's no good a-rowing a chap, it can't be altered now."

"Are those the only clothes you've got?" she asked.

As Phil played with his fingers, he answered, "Yes; and the best's uncommon bad, ain't it?" And then he peeped up to see if she was laughing.

But her countenance was full of grief. "And what are you doing to earn a living?" she inquired.

"Oh, knocking and rowing about, mother; doing a job at any-think."

"Oh dear! oh dear!" she sighed, "that my own Phil should come to this!" And she took up his hand, but dropped it again when she saw how black and dirty it was. "Oh that I should live to see my boy in this state. Dear! dear! I almost wish I hadn't met

you, for I used to think of you as you once were, with your pretty
pink face and child's talk, and now, when you come into my mind, I
must always see you dirty and in tatters, and with the words and
ways of bad people in the streets. Oh, I wish I hadn't lived to see
you, Phil."

"Where's the use of crying, mother? That won't do no good,"
the boy stammered out.

"It is hard, after bringing you up and nursing you as if you were
one of my own, to see you turn bad like this, with only rags to your
back, and perhaps dying of hunger."

"Well, if a chap is, I don't see that telling him on it is much
help."

"God help you!" she faltered, wiping her eyes on her shawl.

One or two errand boys had stopped to look at Phil and his nurse,
and others, as they passed by, turned round to stare at the weeping
woman and the abashed boy by her side, who was trying to take the
edge off his despondency by picking to pieces the twigs on his
broom.

Observing that they were noticed, the pair strolled towards
Leicester Square. For some time they walked by the railings around
the enclosure, neither of them saying a word, the woman sighing
and weeping, and the boy with his heart like a lump of lead in his
bosom, although he tried to look as if he "did not care," and kicked
at the stones that were in his way or tossed halfpence with apparently
the greatest indifference.

Sometimes he would look up at her slyly to see if she were still
crying, and then finding that her grief was not allayed, he grew impatient and jerked his head on one side, as much as to say, "I can't
stand this much longer."

At last he summoned courage to speak. "Mother, where's
Bertie?" he asked, but in a meek tone, half-expecting the information would be refused.

Turning round suddenly, so that her tearful face was looking full
at him, she cried out in fear, "You shan't go there!"

"Why not? What have I done to her, I should like to know?"
he grumbled out.

"No, Phil," the woman said, excitedly, "you shan't go tempting
her into your ways and courses. If you've gone wrong, at least I'll
keep her honest and good. You shan't go near her, I tell you."

"You are a-laying it on," he answered impertinently; "one would
think I was everything bad to hear you talk."

"God only knows what you are, Phil," the poor thing moaned out;
"but I know what Bertie is, and how good and pure is the heart
within her. No, you shan't go there from any telling of mine, so
don't ask me."

"Now look here, mother," began the boy, after swallowing two or
three times, as if his throat were dry, "you seem to think I ain't all
right. But I am all right—none righter. What have I done I should

like to know? Of course I begs; but that ain't stealing. A feller must live."

"I knew you couldn't steal, Phil," was her mild reply, and it cut him the more because he knew himself better than she did.

"Well, then, what do you mean? Don't you think I love Bertie? Now, look here, if a chap was to try and do her any harm, I'd go in at him if he was as big as a house. I tell you that you and her is the only two I like in the world—except Jim a little bit. I've been waiting to see you this year gone, for something told me we should meet. Many a time I've run afore people to see if it was you, and this is the way you serves a fellow when you do run up agin him."

He was crying and rubbing the knuckles into his eyes, so that he could not see the kind look with which she turned towards him. He felt her hand rest upon his shoulder, but he shook it off like an angry child.

"Now I'll just tell you, mother, and it's Gospel truth, too," the boy continued, sobbing, "when I've been on the crossing, or a caten-wheeling after 'busses I've often wished tremendous I might catch sight of Bertie. I do like her really; so you might as well tell me where she lives." As no answer was given, he began to taunt his old nurse. "Ah! it's because I've got rags on you won't notice a chap now."

"No, no, my Philip," she cried out quickly; "it isn't the rags and mud on your back that grieve me. I was shocked, to be sure, to see the boy I loved and reared as one of my own, looking like a street-beggar, but it's the mud in you that hurts me so deeply. You talk mud and think mud, Phil, and you mustn't see Bertie."

This made the lad angry.

"Mind what you're about, mother, or you'll make me reg'lar wild. If you don't tell me where Bertie lives, may my arm never come straight if I don't get locked up to-night, and have three months of it." He stretched out his little arm to the clouds, and as she, in horror, seized his hand, he continued: "Now mark my words—and I ain't joking—if I have gone wrong, you and Bertie is the only ones as could put me straight again. I'd mind what you might say, but you won't help a feller. If Bertie were to say 'you shan't caten-wheel again,' I'd give it over as quick as that"—and he snapped his fingers. "There! that'll show you how fond I am of her. Now, do tell me where she is; or, if you doubt a feller, take me yourself to see her, and I'll do any mortal thing you choose, as a quits."

Like all boys, Phil, now that he had given vent to his anger, became very depressed, and his former excitement changed into a passionate flood of tears. All the time he was crying he continued to talk, entreating, with the greatest earnestness, to be told the girl's address, and throwing his arms about him, or hitting the iron railings with his broom, as if he was venting his spleen upon the metal. If he could only have performed one tithe of the noble actions he in his rude manner of speech promised his foster-mother should dignify his future career in life, in case she acceded to his entreaties, poor Phil would in himself have furnished virtuous illustrations sufficient for another volume of the Percy Anecdotes. At length the old nurse, seeing what influence his foster-sister possessed over him, and knowing that whatever counsel the gentle-minded girl gave would be as pure and good as innocence and affection could prompt, acceded to his request.

But she affixed these conditions :—

"You must be there," said she, beginning with stipulation No. 1, " long before seven o'clock in the morning, for it would be as much as Bertie's place is worth if the lady of the house, who has a deal of plate, was to bear of you coming after her in those rags, Phil."

"All right," answered Phil, without feeling the least insulted at the remark in his toilette; "I'll go and sleep all night on the doorstep, with my head on the scraper to wake me early."

"And you must ring the area bell, mind," was clause No. 2.

"Yes, and I am a first-rate hand at ringing bells; I'll make it sing out like church time."

"No, no, you mustn't make a noise, you silly fellow, or else you'll get Bertie turned away."

"No! no! I forgot. What a flat I am! I'll scarce touch it loud enough to wake a weasel."

"And you'll promise," was the third condition, "to do as she tells you?"

"Of course I will, upon my sacred civey. Why, if Bertie was to tell me to chuck a stone at the Lord Mayor of London hisself, I'd have a shy at him, if I had to get into his gold coach to take aim."

CHAPTER VI.

THE INTERVIEW.

THE next morning, long before five o'clock, Phil was leaning against the railings of the house where Bertie lived. He had not been to bed for fear that he might oversleep himself, and miss seeing his foster-sister, so the moment he could get away from the conversation at the Jury-house he had set out for the place of meeting.

For nearly two hours the boy had to amuse himself as well as he could in front of those railings, and to endure the annoyance of having arrived too soon at the rendezvous. To help the time along he picked up stones in the road, and had a game by himself at pitch-in-the-hole, looking up anxiously at the house, between the throws, to see if anybody was stirring within. But all the blinds were down, and not a sound could he hear, listen as attentively as he would. The silence made him feel sleepy, and to shake off the drowsiness he attempted to establish an acquaintanceship with an old black cat that was resting motionless as a miniature sphinx in a corner of the area. First he called out "Puss! puss!" in his most captivating tones; but the animal, having opened its amber eyes to take a rapid glance at his costume, seemed to recognize him as belonging to the class it most dreaded, and wisely refused to stir; upon which the boy, to resent the want of confidence, changed his tactics, and jerked pebbles at it, more to the danger of the kitchen windows than the poor beast, who philosophically retired to the dusthole to finish its doze.

At last he heard a great ringing of bells inside the house, and a few moments afterwards the kitchen shutters were opened, and on peeping cautiously down the area he beheld a man in a striped jacket, who was evidently the bed-loving footman the bells had been intended to rouse; and never did he enjoy any pastime more than watching this servant, as he shaved himself at a glass, no larger than a saucepan lid, suspended in the window. Without being aware of it, that footman was watched attentively, from the moment when he first lathered a chin as black as a crape band on a white hat, to that satisfactory period when he was passing his hand over the flesh and enjoying its satin-like smoothness.

When Phil heard the clock strike six he thought he would take his first pull at the area bell. He felt excessively nervous as the jingle sounded below, scarcely louder than a clock striking, for he knew the barbered footman would come out to speak to him in a contemptuous manner, and Phil, who was a "child of liberty," felt that he really could not stand any "bounce" from a footman.

Much to the boy's astonishment, he found that no notice was taken of him or his summons. The menial merely advanced to the window, and having examined him for a minute, by waving his body about with a parrot-like movement, retired again into the dark recesses of his apartment. After the sixth time of ringing, the kitchen door was opened to make way for a woman's head, with a dull, stale look about it, caused by her having omitted to wash her face.

"What are you worriting for, boy?" the maid inquired; "can't you stand still and leave that bell alone for a moment, and not go rousing the house? She'll be here directly."

Naturally enough Phil concluded that the "she" referred to Bertie, so he answered,—

"Oh, thank you, miss," and felt considerably easier in his mind, though it struck him as being very strange that this young woman should have been acquainted with the object of his visit.

It was not long after this that a woman so fat that all her features hung down in pouches which shook as she walked, made her appearance, carrying a heavy market-basket, which dragged her sideways like a pail of water. She toiled up the stone-steps, smiling at Phil, as she said half-coquettishly,—

"Ah, your legs is younger than mine." An observation to which the lad mentally responded,—

"And a jolly sight thinner too, I'll bet, missus."

As the cook hoisted the pilferings over the area railings to the boy, she said,—

"Give this to your mother, my dear, and tell her it's my day out next Sunday, and I shall come round early to dress, and she's to mind and have my pink muslin starched; and ask her to be so good as borrow them tongs agin, for I don't know as I shan't curl my hair."

At first Phil stared, and looked into the basket to learn what it meant. When he saw the slices of meat and the half-finished joint mixed up with cold potatoes and remnants of loaves, he burst out laughing, and said,—

"You've regular took the wrong turning, mum, and lost your way entirely. I ain't the party as is waiting for this here breakfast." And as he saw the pilfering cook stare with amazement, he added, "If you'll tell a young woman what lives here, of the name of Bertha Hazlewood, that she is wanted, I'll take it as a obligation."

"How dare yer come a-ringing at this time in the morning?" shouted the cook in a passion. "I shall do nothing of the kind, for your imperence."

The knowing street-boy was too well aware that he had the servant in his power to care much for her threats, so he leaned against the railings, and remembering the meat in the basket, said calmly, "Very well, mum, you can do as you like, only mind this here: the family had roast pork for dinner yesterday; and by-and-by I shall pay my respex to your missus, and jist ask her if she'd like to know where the cold jint is gone to."

The result of this threat was, that when Bertie came to speak to Phil, she found him eating a thick slice of bread and meat.

The boy was hurt at the look of surprise and disappointment with which his foster-sister greeted him.

The last time she had seen him was when they parted at the Norwood school, and he was then a bright-faced, promising boy. She had often called to mind the picture of that separation, and how in his sorrow at losing his Bertie he had surlily quarrelled with her, almost as if she had been leaving him of her own free will.

Then had come the news that Phil had run away, and she had heard with aching heart the many speculations that had been made as to what would become of him. Whilst others croaked out their evil prophecies, and augured, from the flight of this workhouse bird, the sinful future that awaited him, Bertha, who judged of everything through her love rather than her reason, alone stood up in her Phil's defence. Many a battle of words did she fight with stubborn talkers, arguing, poor girl, till the tears came into her eyes, that her dear brother would push his way honourably through life, and would come back to them again—when many years had passed, perhaps—if not a rich, at least a just and upright man. And so often had Bertie in this way argued, even to quarrelling, in Phil's defence, that at last she had, by constant repetition, forced herself to believe that what she hoped for so devoutly was really truth.

And now the reality was before her, and her courage and hopes drew back snail-like into her heart at this one touch of truth. There sat the boy she had nightly prayed for, dirty as a dust-heap, and draped in rags that hung from him like the fleece of a muddy sheep. Phil saw her stare, and her gaze cut him to the heart.

"Don't look like that, Bertie," he said; "it's enough to make a feller turn desperate."

She did not answer him, but her large eyes were stretched wide open, and her mouth apart. For some time she could not speak; but at last she gave a sigh, as if the pain of surprise had left her, and her rigid limbs, that had been fixed with wonder, relaxed suddenly as if tired out by the emotion.

"I have been waiting for you a long time, Phil, but—" She could not finish the sentence, for there was an unkind thought in it.

"I know what you mean by that ' but,'" said Phil; "you mean all this here." And he pushed his hands among his rags, making them flutter like feathers.

Bertie could not answer him, for he had guessed her meaning.

"Ah, Bertie, you can't love me half as much as I do you," he whined out, crumbling up the bread he had but a moment before been biting at so hungrily. "I knew you'd be shocked to see me, but, though I was afraid, I came. If it had been the safe death of me, I should have come all the same. You're not altered a bit," he added, looking at her; "it's only me as is altered."

He hoped his sister would have spoken to him, but not a word did she utter.

"Come, Bertie," he implored, "give a feller one little word. I've stopped up all night just to hear your voice, and now you won't speak anything. I don't ask you to kiss a feller, or anythink of that sort, but I did think you wouldn't be downright unkind. It takes the life out of one, it do."

"And Phil, it has taken the life out of me, too," said Bertie sadly, "for you were part of what I lived for, and I was waiting so impatiently for the day when I should see you once more, that now it has come it kills me."

Poor girl, her eyes were running over with tears, though her face was calm and her voice steady. Phil, as he sat on the doorstep, shuffled along until he was close to her, and then he felt the hot tears fall upon his upturned face. Now he, too, could not speak. There was a working in his throat and a tightness in his chest. She saw that the flood-gates of his sorrow were open, and, kneeling close to the crouching boy, she drew his head to hers and kissed him as a token that the prodigal was loved and forgiven.

She could not talk about the past, so they chatted over the future.

"You must leave this life, Phil," she said; "it will be ruin to you."

"Well, it ain't much better now," he answered. "I only made ninepence yesterday."

"I don't mean ruined for want of money, Phil; I mean you would grow up a bad man," said the little woman of fifteen. "Just think how mother and me would fret if anything was to happen to you, and we were afraid to talk of you before people."

"But what am I to do?" said Phil. "Nobody'll give me work with such clothes as these. I might just as well try to get took on at a bank."

After they had been talking together for some time, and he had given her a rough outline of the life he had been leading, Bertie commenced her good counsels by hinting that washing the face and hands not unfrequently added to the personal appearance. She also suggested that stopping up all night was not the natural life that had been ordained for striplings; and she further continued her admonitions by stating that, in order to obtain decent clothing, the first step was to save up some of the daily earnings, and not expend every penny that was given to him, either in purchasing pudding at the cook-shop, or paying gambling debts for lessons at pitch-farthing.

But Bertie's moralizing lost nearly all its effect from Phil's attention being just then occupied by watching a man who, mounted on the extreme end of a donkey, was coming up the street, leading another of the patient animals by a rope round the neck. This man, to his astonishment, stopped before the very door where he and Bertie were chatting. He saw him dismount, and kneeling down rest his head against the donkey's ribs and begin milking it into a small measure he drew from his pocket.

"Who drinks that stuff?" asked Phil, turning up his nose in disgust.

"Stuff, indeed!" cried Bertie; "it's very dear stuff, and Miss Tomsey, the lady I read to, takes it as medicine—a pint every day."

Phil still kept his eyes fixed on the donkey-man, and, attracted as all lads are by animals, he could not help going up to them and playing with their ears.

"Ah," said he, "if I could only get a job as a stable-boy or something, I should be made for life. That's what I'm most fittest for."

Bertie, on mere speculation, ventured to ask the vendor of donkey's milk whether he happened to know of any place vacant just then, where an active, and she added "honest," boy might get employment.

"Any charackter?" asked Mr. Sparkler.

"Oh, I know him well," said Bertie, as Phil scratched his head, not knowing what to answer.

"Well, boys is asked for pretty plentiful just now at Hampstead," answered the man. "Can the young man run?"

"I'll lick any 'bus on the road," said Phil, boastingly.

"And has the young man any clothes besides them there things?" continued Mr. Sparkler, evidently not very pleased with Phil's costume.

"Yes," said Bertie, firmly, which made Phil stare at her with surprise.

"Well," said the donkey proprietor, "he can go see my missus, and talk it over with her. Ask for Mrs. Sparkler, donkey keeper, the Drying Ground, Hampstead, Hollyhock Cottage."

"Which is the nearest way there?" asked Phil with delight.

"Well," said Mr. Sparkler, "keep up the road till you come to the William the Fourth, then turn round as far as the Hare and Hounds, and anybody 'll tell you which is the Trusty Friend, and my place is close by, four doors from the Jolly Sailor."

CHAPTER VII.

HAMPSTEAD.

CALL the world into school, and when the millions are seated in their classes, let the schoolmaster walk among the forms, and ask, "What is happiness?" How many guesses will be made at the riddle?

"Glory," roars the soldier. And yet those who have burned cities into dust-heaps, have—when they came to sift the cinders—found little happiness among the ruins. Alexander died of delirium tremens, aged thirty-three; Miltiades expired in prison; Siccius Dentatus, the hero of one hundred and forty battles, was assassinated; Hannibal poisoned himself; Belisarius had his eyes put out; Cæsar was murdered; and Napoleon—everybody knows his fate.

"Titles," suggests the politician. But if a short name cannot bring happiness, how can a long one?—will extending a man's cognomen, like the lengthening of a ship, add to his qualities? A firmament of stars may decorate a bosom, but—according to Louis XVI. —there are clouds that will overcast even such a heaven.

"Riches," cries the poor man, forgetting that to have more than we can enjoy is the same as not having it at all. Demidoff owned gold mines, but he ate and drank himself a cripple, and what benefit was his treasure to him? He died worth millions, and passed the better half of his life in a chair on wheels. The only privilege of his wealth was to prevent others from possessing it.

"Health," groans the rich man, turning his back on the labourer, who, although he never knew a day's sickness, sighs heavily over his misery in having to support the most salubrious of families on seven shillings a week.

"Beauty," simpers the woman of fashion. A five years' glory and a life's misery; for even when the beauty is gone, it leaves behind it the insolent remembrance of its possession. Where did lovely Helen of Troy die? Did she expire with the serpent of remorse gnawing at her heart, with as sharp a tooth as when the asp of the Nile fastened upon the arm of the splendid Cleopatra?

What is happiness? For how many hundred years have stoics and epicureans made themselves miserable, and pummelled and cudgelled each other in argument, without being able to settle the point? A house might be built with the volumes that metaphysicians have written on the subject. Does happiness consist in sensual or mental delights, or is it a state of continual agreeable feeling, or the gratification of some desire which enables us to enjoy the blessings already in our possession? Let wiser and better heads than ours grow grey and bald in settling the matter. We have a youth near at hand who will speedily reveal to us how his happiness was brought about, and of what it was composed. Come here, Philip Merton. What's perfect happiness, sir?

" A strong boy's corduroy suit, with a double row of pearl buttons down the breast, and a coat cut like a groom's."

Philip is happy and chirping with delight, because his clothes are as sound as the skin of an orange. He walks along, upright with pride, as if he had a family tree at his back to straighten it.

A drawer had been unlocked and a little treasure taken out, and Bertha, with a half-sigh, had counted the silver pieces into Philip's hand.

He seemed to be abashed at taking the girl's earnings, for, as if his conscience troubled him, he said, " I have no right to take this from you, Bertie, and mother, too, a-wanting it all along." But he closed his fingers on the coin nevertheless.

With his hands in his pockets, he strutted up Tottenham Court Road, delighted with himself as a footman in a new livery. At nearly every step he cast a complacent glance at his clothes, either brushing away any dust that may have fallen on them, or admiring the neat manner in which his trousers fell over his thick highlows. The reflection of his tout ensemble in the shop windows afforded him singular satisfaction. He seemed to be greatly pleased with his general effect, and took an essential delight in making his nether garments " whistle," as the noise produced by the friction of corduroy is musically styled by the vulgar.

In those times the route to Hampstead was very different in appearance from what it is now. The road of Tottenham, which in our day looks like a poor relation of Regent Street, had then no furniture shops to block up the pavement with sofas, chairs, and tables; neither had American photographists discovered the economic process of taking correct likenesses for sixpence; nor had Italian pastrycooks hit upon the original notion of giving a wine-glassful of strawberry cream or lemon ice for a penny.

Down the Hampstead Road the spirit of commerce had not then converted the gardens before the houses into shops, but every tenement had its railed-in patch of gravelly-looking mould and mouldy-looking gravel, where nothing seemed green but the weeds, and no plant flourished but the Michaelmas daisy, amid whose luxuriant stems the stray cats of the neighbourhood found excellent sleeping accommodation, curling themselves up in the middle of the rank herb as securely as a slug in a box border. In the hopes of getting a flower for his button-hole, Phil entered several of these unthriving plots, but he only found lilac bushes with twigs as black as crayons and leaves as dusty as a top shelf.

When you call back the recollections of your youth, is it not wonderful to think how this big London of ours has grown and stretched itself out within the last few years? Squares and crescents have crept out like the suckers of a tree, the jagged edges of the town fill up the fields where, in Philip's time, cows were feeding and boys flying their kites. Mother Redcap's had waggons and carriers' carts in front of it instead of yellow omnibuses, and where a row of shops are now built Philip laid himself down in the tall grass and chewed buttercups.

On trudged Phil, with his coat on his arm and a holly leaf in his mouth, wishing that the hills were not so steep nor the day so hot and dusty. He passed the then country-looking roadside inn, "The Load of Hay," and, thirsty as he was, he felt as if he could have snatched the mug of beer from the drover—who, whilst his flock of sheep were lying panting about the road, was drinking at the bar.

To prove the superiority of man over the brute creation, our youth made a point of passing every omnibus upon the roads, leaving them and their three horses to creep up the hills after him; and he even entered into a spirited competition with a washerwoman's cart, and could have easily distanced the hopping mop-tailed cob, but he felt himself turning to a lobster tint with the heat, and his legs growing stiff as stilts. He never rested unless it was to take a peep over the oak palings and square-clipped hedges that enclosed some of the grounds by the way. The sight of the old Queen Anne Mansions, looking as red as a strawberry in the midst of the huge green trees, with their frowning roofs surmounted with a wedding-cake ornament of a belfry, seemed to fascinate him to the spot, and he could not help thinking to himself what a "jolly easy time of it" the young ladies must have whom he saw working at the bow-windows that opened into the lawn. "Ah!" thought Phil, "if I had a house like that, what a first-rate chap I should be all of a sudden;" and he gazed at the flower-beds piled up with bloom and spotted with colours as a mound of wafers, and he stared at the square paddocks of rippling grass divided by the neatest of iron hurdles, and imagined to himself what delightful fun those same young ladies would have when the hay-making time arrived, romping among the new-mown crop, and how they would enjoy sleeping in its perfume by night.

The Belsize estate also met with our young gentleman's warmest approval, and he stood at the iron gates staring down the long avenue of trees that covered in the carriage-drive like a green hood, until somebody came out of the lodge to ask him "what he wanted," and his desires being at that moment of an impossible nature (being, indeed, no less than a wish to possess the estate), he did not think fit to enter into any explanation, but moved away.

He had reached Downshire Hill before he caught sight of any evidence of the donkey business being in a thriving condition. Standing at a garden-gate was a Bath chair, with one of the patient dust-coloured animals harnessed in front of it. The boy was so much pleased with this ingenious vehicle for invalids, that he endeavoured to enter into conversation with its owner, informing him that he considered the turn-out to be a kind of young cabriolet before its wheels were properly grown; but the proprietor, not being in a conversational mood, gave grunts in reply, and eventually made a remark about the advantage to be gained by some one " stepping it." After Phil had seen an old lady on crutches deposited inside the chair, where she bore a strong family likeness to the prompter at the Opera, he went on his way again, staring about him with the greatest industry. He even became interested in the welfare of the inhabitants, and wondered to himself whether Neale, the carrier, who announced that he visited " all parts of London daily," made a pretty good thing of it.

At the coach-office he made inquiries as to the whereabouts of Hollyhock Cottage, the residence of Mrs. Sparkler. It was some time before he could get anybody to attend to him, and the delay afforded him ample opportunities for studying the habits of omnibus drivers. He heard one lady who was seeking for information about the " time of starting," receive the unintelligible reply of " a quarter a'ter, half a'ter, quarter to, and at ; " he witnessed a dispute between a conductor and his coachman, who was upbraiding him for " never looking about him nor nothen ; " and he heard inquiries made as to " whether Jim had greased that off mare's fetlock," or had " had that bay osse's collar took in a bit."

He was told to climb up a steep embankment that stood like a cliff by the roadside, and then turn down long narrow lanes as steep as staircases, and round by stable-yards, where fierce dogs rushed about and barked behind the gates and endeavoured to force their wet noses through impossible openings. He asked everybody he met which way he should go, and it was only after he had turned to the right at least twenty times that he at length arrived at the residence of the Sparkler family.

There was a little colony of some dozen cottages, and washing and donkey-letting were the trades the inhabitants lived by. Over every door hung a board with either " Mangling done here," or " Donkeys for hire; " and, as if to avoid too great a monotony in repeating these announcements, every style and size of writing had been employed, though the thin white spider letter on the black ground appeared to be the favourite type. The day being propitious for drying, the gardens and hedges about were covered with linen ; lace collars and nightcaps were spread upon bushes, pocket-handkerchiefs and stockings were fastened down with stones on grass-

plats, and shirts and petticoats, distended to their utmost tightness
by the wind, fluttered from the lines, their proportions looking so
terribly unfit for human use, that a notion crossed the mind that all
the owners must be in the last stage of dropsy.

Mr. Sparkler was evidently a refined man, who, although to the
world he might seem to devote himself to the letting out of donkeys,
was at heart a florist. His cottage—which was about as large as a
hayrick, and had a straw thatch cut close over the windows—was
ornamented in front by a small one-two-three-and-jump garden,
intersected with gravel paths not broader than deal boards, which
entailed balancing on those who tight-roped its walks. The beds
were not larger than mattresses, but no lodging-house couch was ever
more crowded. The flowers were packed as closely as nosegays, and
how the mould could support such a crop—unless concentrated like
portable soup—was a great, unanswerable mystery. Standard roses,
with their blooming tops, stood gay as new bonnets perched up in
a milliner's window; pansies as large as butterflies, hollyhocks like
rosette-adorned fishing-rods, and pinks big as shaving-brushes,
decorated this essence of a garden. In one corner stood the summer-
house, where of an evening Sparkler smoked his pipe; and even here
the consummate taste of the man had exhibited itself. Adorning its
summit was an arm-crossed statuette of Bonaparte, and china dogs
and plaster images decked the roof like a mantelpiece.

Philip stood at the gate of this Eden, not daring to pass the
palings of butter staves, which shut him out from its delights. He
might have doubted if such splendour could belong to any being who
supported himself by sixpenny donkey rides, if it had not been for
the board over the door, announcing that Tobias Sparkler was in
that line of business.

All the Sparkler family were away from home, the care of the
house being for the time entrusted to a ginger-edged cur, with a tail
that might have been used as a crumb brush, who went into a
paroxysm of barking, and showed all his front teeth in an uncivil
manner. This dog was evidently kept as a kind of "knock and ring"
to the Sparkler family, and no double rat-tat or bell-pull could have
more effectually announced a visitor. Four stout women issued
from a neighbouring cottage to see what the noise was about, and
Philip, picking out the one whose hands seemed least like a washerwoman's, instantly addressed her as "Mrs. Sparkler, mum."

"So he said you was to talk it over with me," said that lady, after
the cause of the visit had been explained. "What do I know about
'boys'? There's nothen but boys now-a-times; I never see such a
lot of boys. They swarm—literal swarm!"

Phil tried to look as if, despite the present glut, there were very
few who could come up to him.

"Where the boys spring from," continued Mrs. Sparkler, addressing her friends, "is more than in me lies to say. If they was
imported by barrelfuls they couldn't be more abounding. And they

come to you as cool as imaginable, and says, 'Do you want a boy?'"

"I had two come to me last Thusday," said one of the washer-women, in corroboration—"both nice boys enough; but what use is boys to me?"

"Mrs. Millins's boy, too, is out of work," added another lady, "and, as it might be yesterday, she ask me if I wanted a boy. 'What for?' says I."

"Why can't Sparkler see to his own boys, 'stead of worreting my life with 'em?" was the wife's complaint. "One can't sit down to a cup of tea but, before you've raised your saucer to your lips, there's boys must be attended to. They're wuss teasers than flies. Dear me! these boys is wearing me to shreds."

She was a stout woman of thirty, in form somewhat resembling a cottage loaf, and Phil felt perfectly convinced that she would last her time, despite her troubles. To try and conciliate her, he ventured to say that if he were engaged, the only reason he should have for living would be to comfort and assist his mistress.

"It's too bad of Sparkler to leave everything to me," continued the woman. "It's slaving from first thing when you get up till it's time to go to bed again. First there's saddles to look to, then there's donkeys to be sent out, then there's accounts to keep, and 'undreds of other things."

"I don't mind what I do, and I am very fond of gardening, or working anyhow that's useful," said Phil, beginning to enumerate his good qualities.

"Then there's seeing that them other boys don't cheat the very eyes out of your head," she grumbled.

"I'm sure I wouldn't do anybody out of—no! not so much as half a farthing, mum," murmured the lad.

"Don't tell me, boy!" growled Mrs. Sparkler. "It's like your impudence to say so. All boys is alike. You're human natur', ain't you? Then hold your tongue."

This interview ended in an appeal to the feelings of the women, made by Master Merton in a fit of desperation at the slight prospect he saw of an engagement. He commenced by saying that it was very odd, but people seemed to take an especial pleasure in perse-cuting him, detailing with great excitement and feeling the struggles he had gone through, and wound up with a half threat that if his good intentions were this time thwarted he saw no help for earning a living but by leading a most abandoned and vicious existence.

"It's hawful to hear him talk," cried one of the washerwomen; "where's your parents, you wicked boy?"

"I am an orphan, and that's what's agin' me," he muttered. "If I'd got some one to help a fellow, do you think I'd be like this? Ah, I only wish you was orphans, you'd find it out then."

They were preparing to answer him, when he broke out again,—

K

"It ain't as if I came here without a good word to back me, but Mr. Sparkler knows our people well enough."

"Who's your people?" asked Mrs. S.

"Why, Tomsey's people," he replied, "as takes in their pint of ass's milk regular."

Mrs. Sparkler suddenly entered her cottage. She had gone to see if Tomsey's account had been settled. The examination of the memorandum book was evidently satisfactory, for Philip was told to proceed to the Heath, and ask for one Fred Jackson, and announce to him that for the future he was to be employed among the long-eared stud.

Fred Jackson, or, as his companions called him, Swinging Fred, was a tall, gipsy-looking fellow, with a sunburnt face and a couple of black ringlets hanging down each cheek. He was celebrated among donkey-drivers both for the length of his locks and the admirable manner in which he managed the steeds, for, whilst he could tie his curls under his chin, he, on the other hand, was so clever with his stick, that, with one blow struck somewhere under the ear, he could most surely bring any rebellious animal to the ground. Dressed in his dirty flannel-jacket and leaning over a saddle, he did not look such a terrible fellow; but the donkeys knew him well enough, and even when he coughed up went the ears, as if they were on their guard against their strong-armed foe.

The first thing Swinging Fred did was to make the new boy pay his footing, which he fixed at sixpence, for a pot (his drink was ale with gin in it, of which he could swallow immense quantities), and the next was to roar out, "Sam Curt" in so loud a voice that all the donkeys on the Heath heard him and grew restless. "Here, Sam Curt! Where is yer?"

"Gone to Frognell Rise"—"No he ain't"—"Why I see him there a minute since"—"Got a job to the Spaniards," shouted so many at once, that replies seemed to come from all quarters. Eventually, a lad came shuffling up, who turned out to be the same Curt who was in such great demand.

"Been touting on the hill, Fred," he said, in a frightened voice.

"And who told you to do it?—What do you do it for, then?" growled the Swinger. "I'll break every bone in your skin, you young rat."

And Sam looked frightened, and all the donkeys that had been lying down rose up very rapidly and fidgeted about.

Phil thought to himself, "He's a nice sort of a master to have to spend your days with."

"Here, take that young 'un along with you," said Swinging Fred, pointing to Merton, "and put him up to what he's got to do. Do you hear?—then do it."

There wasn't much work on hand for the first week or so that Phil was at Hampstead, and he had plenty of time to study the details of the business. His greatest delight was to lie down on the grass, or sit on the chains that keep the flag-post steady, and look at the landscape. The broad Heath stretched out before him, covered with dots of furze-bushes that seemed to freckle the ground like a country-man's sunburnt face. What a glorious fringe of trees surround this London's play-ground! If it were not for the lamp-posts in the road beyond, who could imagine so lovely a spot was so near to the monster city?

Sometimes the lad would wonder who lived in the grand houses on the skirts of the Heath. They lie concealed in the verdure of their surrounding trees, as if, after having crept up so close to the public ground, they were afraid of being sent back again, and had hidden themselves from sight. The round, tall chestnut-trees were in bloom, with their white pagodas of flowers standing up at the tips of the boughs like candles on a Christmas tree. Philip could, from where he lay stretched on the turf, see into the gardens belonging to some of these mansions and catch sight of the fruit-trees in the orchards, big mounds of blossom with all the ground about them speckled with the falling bloom, as if a thousand love-letters had been torn into small pieces and thrown there.

Sometimes a donkey, enjoying himself in the distance, would begin to bray, and then other donkeys scattered about would answer as cocks do, and eventually, after the music had been taken up in all corners of the Heath, the whole body of those on the top would join in chorus, and throw out their music with deafening effect.

On one side of the Heath—the West-end side—there is an avenue of old elms, where the young ladies' schools walk up and down, treading among the sundrops that have fallen through the leaves and made golden rings on the ground, and it was our boy's delight to sit down on one of the benches and listen to these little scholars chatting with their French governess. "What on earth," he would think to himself, "does she mean by saying, after looking at me, 'Regard, mam'selle, ce sal petit garsong-la'?" If ever these little ladies extended their promenade into the Heath itself, he followed the petticoated regiment as it appeared and disappeared among the risings and hollows of the ground, and wondered in his mind whether Bertha would ever have such nice clothes as they wore, and be able to talk about the "Sal garsong-la" as they had done.

Round the pond with the rusty iron pipe sticking up in it are ranged the donkey-gigs and one-horse flys, and further on are clustered together the saddled asses, all with their heads together, as if they were whispering like jurymen considering their verdict. How those gigs can "pay" we never could imagine. They are curious, shattered-looking turn-outs, as clumsily put together as a schoolboy's paste-board model—overgrown children's carts, with wheels not larger than a wheelbarrow's, and lined with limp chintz, or patched with worn-out japanned cloth that had once formed part of a table-cover. The donkeys that pull them are all pot-bellied, and have under their round, drooping stomachs a fringe of hair so long that the wind blows it about. The poor brutes, with their long ears lopping down, look like big rabbits. Nor are the one-horse flys much better than the gigs, for their linings all look tumbled, as if they had been slept in, and the big gaunt steeds have long· heads, with a drooping, sulky-looking under-lip. One has been fired in the fetlock, and the bulging flesh is scored like a melon with the scars. Another—a white horse with a black nose and a dirty draggle tail, stuck together at the tips—is blind of both eyes, and his ribs ripple up the carcase, each one as distinct as the folds of an accordion.

Aided by his friend Sam Curt—or Snorting Sam, as he was called from an unfortunate habit of breathing loudly—Philip soon got to know every donkey on the Heath as perfectly as a shepherd distinguishes every sheep in his flock.

The stud of donkeys then exposed for hire by the ten or eleven proprietors who "worked" Hampstead formed a most various and eccentric collection, for they were of all ages and colour, some so small that Swinging Fred could straddle them like a colossus, and others so large, that, with their bulging saddles on, they might almost have passed for stunted camels. Their harness was neither first nor second-rate, but of the lowest possible rate, fastened together by string instead of buckles, with the leathern tongues sticking out in every direction. The greater number of the animals were so thin that the backbone stood up almost like the keel of a boat. To prevent any rubbing from the saddle, pieces of drugget or sacking, and even whisps of hay, were tucked as a pad under the seat, so that, everything considered, the poor brutes had an untidy, sluttish appearance, as if they had dressed themselves with the hurry of a maid-of-all-work at a lodging-house. Perhaps those destined for the especial service of ladies were the most remarkable for slovenly neglige, their costume being something after the grandeur of a circus palfrey, with the slight mixture of the Roman toga, for over the wide-seated saddles were placed linen coverings, decorated with red braid edgings, which, when clean and not too much torn, no doubt had a very smart appearance. These "ladies' donkeys" were also distinguished by being nearly cut in two by the girths, which were pulled up so tightly that their waists seemed to rival in smallness the formation of the frog—a species of tight-lacing which did not improve the appearance of the long-eared quadrupeds.

Whenever Sam Curt took the new boy among the donkeys for the purposes of instruction, it was his practice to direct the attention of his pupil to any particular animal worthy of his notice, by flicking it adroitly on the part which he considered to be the tenderest of the body.

"There, that's a nice 'un," said the youth, pointing to one of the brutes with the inside of its ears as full of hair as a lady's slipper; "we calls her Everlasting Teakettle. Get up you there, Everlasting Teakettle! Mothers of fam'lies and nusses allers ask for her of a morning. They're very fond of her, 'cos she carries two;" and he

pointed to a child's swing of a chair, which was strapped to Everlasting Teakettle's back.

"Where's the one you call the winner of the Derby?" asked Phil.

"We've got such a lot of 'em," answered Sam. "They've all been winners, only every year we changes 'em. Now this little chap as is at present called Lady Snuffers, has been Eclipse, and the winner of the Two Thousand Guinea Stakes, and Flying Dutchman, and ever so many more. He's as fat as a little pig and get his own living—don't want nothing to eat of us. Here's Crab-apple Betsy, too," he continued, advancing a few paces; "she has been the winner of the Oaks and the Chester Cup, and a heap of others. She's so gentle, you can a'most do anything with her." And to prove his words he administered a smart cut with his whip, which made poor Crab-apple Betsy hop vigorously. She took it gently enough.

A big donkey, with rough, curling hair, whose hind legs had been clipped to allow the stick to have a better effect, attracted Phil's notice.

"He is a beauty if you like," cried Snorting Sam, leaning against it. "He's Elm-tree Joe, and the quickest that ever runs. Just you see." And he set to work beating the clipped portion of the animal's body, whilst in a guttural voice he growled out, "Go along with yer, Joe," so that the brute, finding that serious work was intended, darted off at a full gallop, the boy following and trailing his stick in the road to make a noise.

It was astonishing to hear how well Master Curt was acquainted with the good qualities of the different donkeys he patronized with his notice, and yet surprising to witness the cruelty with which he accompanied his praise. He passed a row of them, standing as quiet as if they had been toys on a shelf, but he could not refrain from rousing them out of their sleep with his knocks.

"Come up, there, Crazy Jane!—hi! hi! you White Alice!—stir up, you Old One Eye—I'll give you something, you Bobtail—now then, you Old Dook of Brunswick."

The hollow sound of the stick on the ribs made the mass move uneasily, and run together like a drove of sheep.

"That's such a one as you don't see often," said Snorting Sam, stopping before a donkey with a vicious eye, shaped like the slit in a violin. It had a thick mop of fur on its forehead, which afforded Master Curt a firm grip whilst he said, "Every hair in its 'ead is worth pounds, and all over alike. You might go one thousand miles and not meet with such a one-er as this here Ingia-rubbia is. Stir up, there, Old Ingia-rubbia. It can do a'most everythink but speak," added the driver, lashing at its ears as if he was trying to cut them off like tall weeds, and certainly one of the things that India-rubber could do was to kick, and very near to Snorting Samuel, too.

It happened that some of the asses, being, perhaps, soured with life, and rendered quarrelsome by persecution, began to fight and bite each other. Like a hawk darting at a hedge-sparrow, Snorting

Curt dashed into the midst of the fray, and layed about him vigorously, shouting to the music of his blows,—

"Hulloa, you Prince o' Wales!—would you, Laura Smith!—what are you about there, Bonny Black Bess?—I'm after you, Lady Milkmaid—and you too, Gentleman Jerry!"

When the battle had ended and quiet was restored, Sam, in answer to the question as to which was the best donkey of the lot, thus delivered his opinion:—

"We calls Hearts of Gold the pride of the world, 'cos she's the fastest, and biggest, and prettiest—a piebald, very handsome, and a curiosity, which is in her favour, which was offered four pound for. But I'd as soon have Lightheart. You'll say why? Well, for this here: I fancies him more, and he'd go till he bustes hisself."

After a pause, he added,—

"But, after all, what's donkeys to ponies for fastness? Mr. Lamfret, him as owns the white and roan ponies, he wouldn't take a ten pound note for either of them. There they stand with their nosebags on, and one of them's got eyes as blue as plums. Only the worst of ponies is this: a gentleman says I want a half-crown ride, and off he goes for an hour and don't come back again, and the next thing we hears of is, that the pony is in the pound or at the green-yard, and they come down on you for ten bob."

The duty assigned to Phil was that of touting for custom, Mr. Sparkler considering that the newness of the boy's clothes should be duly taken advantage of, as an evidence of the respectable manner in which he conducted his business.

The instructions given to the lad were to take up his stand by the Coach and Horses public-house, and, whenever, he saw anybody coming, to rush up to them, and, no matter what their age or size might be, to ask them perseveringly, "Do you want a nice saddle-donkey?"

With an honest enthusiasm Phil carried out these instructions to the quick, and in a few days he became the terror of every old lady in the neighbourhood; indeed, many most respectable persons have asserted that "he did it on purpose."

"Do you want a nice donkey, mum?" he would half confidentially ask of these aged matrons; and when they turned round to say "No, my boy; how ridiculous!" he would add, "Nice comfortable soft saddle, mum, uncommon easy!"

"Go about your business, sir," would be the reply.

Then Phil would walk by their side, whispering, "Have a nice cheer, mum, or a nice easy shay, mum?"

"No, no, no, I tell you!"

"Got some very nice saddle-ponies, mum—carry you like a feather!"

Then the elderly matrons lost all patience, and they stood still and looked about them for a policeman, as they muttered between their gums, "I'll give you in charge, you bad boy! How dare you ask me to ride on a pony?

When giving Philip his instructions, Mr. Sparkler had laid down this important axiom: "Say everything's nice—nice donkeys, nice saddles, nice shays, nice everything. It's time enough for them to find out if the things is nasty after they've paid their money."

Philip didn't enjoy this "touting" much, for he was longing to have his share of the fun on the Heath; and every night, when Sam Curt related to him the adventures of the day, he would inveigh bitterly against old Sparkler for "keeping a fellow sticking down in the beastly village."

No doubt to Phil the town of Hampstead did seem a melancholy place enough. There wasn't a shop he cared to look into, for even at the library they never changed the prints exposed for sale. He hated those chemists' shops with the small greenhouse windows, where pickles, sauces, and cigars were vended as well as medicine; and he looked with contempt upon the draper's establishment, where hats, shirts, boots, and cotton prints were exposed for sale in a compartment scarcely larger than a one-horse stall. The boy said it was like being in a country town a thousand miles from town. The farrier's shop opened on to the road, and the tea-dealer, the butcher and the tailor all announced that they were from London in so pompous a manner, it was impossible to fancy you were only five miles away from it.

It does indeed seem like some old-fashioned town. In some parts of the road there are high embankments, with tall elms, in which the rooks have built, leaning over the highway as if they were top-heavy from their round, full branches. All the place is so silent that the livery stable cocks at one end of the street crow out and defy those crowing at the greengrocer's at the other extremity of the town. The only excitement the place knows is when some travelling circus pitches its tent on the Heath, or when some horse, coming down the steep hill, grows frightened with the pressure of the vehicle, and runs away, in which case the carriage and its contents are—at the sudden turning of the road—sure to dash into the coffee-house next the Black Boy and Still, smashing the windows and scattering the customers.

If you cross the road and seek out West End Square, you will find it the most rustic-looking place, with a tree growing in the centre of the pavement, whilst the houses have a William and Mary look about them, being built of red brick, with heavy white casements, as clumsily made as the stage-coach windows of old, and over the street doors are old-fashioned carved porticos. They don't make such stout leaden water-pipes nowadays as those against these houses, neither do we forge such iron lamp-holders and gates, with twisting watch-spring curls, and scrolls and foliage.

It was near this square that Philip lived, down a court by the side of a rag-shop, kept by the mother of Redpole Jack, another of Sparkler's boys. Mrs. Burt gave the best price for white linen rags, and a high price for kitchen fat, and the full value for copper and brass, besides letting out lodgings at threepence a night.

Slowly but surely did Philip advance to the highest honours that can befall a donkey-driver. His first promotion was being allowed to drive a chaise, which conveyed four ladies to the foot of Havistock Hill. Next, he was entrusted with the care of those donkeys which were hired for children, and so well did he behave himself on these occasions, that eventually he was raised to the dignity of accompanying young ladies in a delicate state of health. The tenderness with which he checked all desire to trot on the part of the animals soon gained for him a name among the invalids of Flask Walk and the Vale of Health. Still this was not what Philip longed for. He wanted to join in the exciting chase of following up some twenty young damsels galloping along the road, and it was only when his grumbling was slightly tinged with the abusive that Mr. Sparkler yielded to his entreaties.

The night before this great advancement took place, the following conversation was held between Redpole Jack and our young friend. They had gone into the churchyard, not for serious contemplation, but because the graves afforded a comfortable seat. And with an immense yew-tree spreading out like a wing above them, the converse began.

"Shall I tell you why Sparkler wouldn't let you come on the 'eath?" asked Jack. "Why, because you're so well clothed, and those new things of yours gets him a name for having respectable boys. Why, there's nothing pays so well as sick people, and they won't have any driver but is decent-looking."

"Well, I shall be up there to-morrow, so I don't mind," answered Phil.

"And a nice messing you'd a made of it, if I hadn't seen you first," continued the Redpole. "Now, look here! S'pose you was a driving Old One-Eye, and you wanted him to gallop, what would be your little game?"

"Why, shout at him, and hit him as hard as I could—give him with all my might a good feed of 'long oats' and 'ash beans,'" answered Phil.

This made Mr. Jack Burt sneer with disgust.

"O' coorse you would," he said. "I knowed it. That's like you and your proudness, thinking you know everything. And what would you get? Why, Old One-Eye would stand still and kick at you. I had my hand swolled dreadful through him."

"What should you do?" asked Phil.

"Now you're coming to it," answered Master Burt. "Why, first of all I should give him three or four over his 'ead to let him know who I was."

"Well," asked Phil, "and after that, when he did know who you was?"

"Why, then I'd give him two or three sharp 'uns on the top o' the hock to show him who he was."

"Go on," said Phil—"what then?"

"Why, then he'd git one o' my lefthanders, as should knock him on one side, and another as should knock him back again, and send him hopping for two or three yards."

"And what's the end of it?" asked Phil.

"Well, for the minute," added the lecturer, "Old One-Eye wouldn't know whether he was afoot or a-horseback, but off he'd go, regular spanking, first-rate."

Philip's reply to his instructor consisted in reading from one of the tombstones near him the following epitaph:

At morn in cheerful health he rose,
At noon and eve the same,
At night, retir'd to calm repose,
The awful summons came.

CHAPTER VIII.

ON THE HEATH.

ONE night, as Mr. Sparkler was enjoying his pipe in his summer-house, and smoking the spiders into a restless condition, his wife called out to him.

"I forgot to tell you, Tobias, there's a job for to-morrow night. The same party as had the picnic by moonlight last year called to-day about hiring some donkeys for another jollification."

"Do you mean that lot o' servants as stopped out all night on the Heath? Oh they're going on the loose again, are they?" And after laughing, he added, "And when does the spree come off?"

"To-morrow; and they wants the loan of a kettle, and three nice donkeys for the girls to ride when so inclined. It was Mr. Boxer, the footman from Tomsey, that came about it, and he says there'll be a good dozen of 'em."

"To think of that now!" exclaimed Mr. S.

"It appears their families is out of town," continued the woman, "so they can manage it without being the slightest uncommodated. Teddy Cuttler, Captain Crosier's groom, is to be one of the party, and he's thought a deal of. They've got fiddles and all a-coming."

On the following evening, just as the shades of night were stealing over the Heath, a cab drew up in the road near the pond, and a stout male form, fashionably attired in pumps and Berlin gloves, stepped from the interior, and gazed anxiously down the road. On the roof of that cab there was a hamper, and on the box beside the driver there were paper parcels with grease showing through.

After the gentleman had peered about in every direction, he returned to the vehicle, and addressing a lady inside, said, "Nothing wisible of them yet, Wortey: but where's the hurry?"

"I know'd that Mary h'Anne of ours would be late," answered the so-called Wortey; "she's always such a time cleaning herself, and figging up with her gewgaws and fallals."

The gentleman seemed inclined to bear the delay with patience. He strutted up and down, cleaning his nails, and humming airs known only to himself; and whenever the voice in the cab inquired, "Do you see them yet, Boxer?" he answered in the most cheerful of voices, "Not yet, Wortey."

At length a group of ladies and gentlemen were seen creeping up the hill, and instantly Mr. Boxer became excited, and commenced waving his pocket-handkerchief with the utmost gallantry.

Some of the young damsels, seeing the signal, ran laughing towards the cab, the full skirts of their light dresses swinging in the wind as they scampered along.

"What a uncommon fine-growed gal that Susannah is," observed Mr. Boxer. "She's a remarkable showy dresser to be sure."

"Then she's been at missus's drawers again," snarled Mrs. Wortey.

When the cab was surrounded, the introductions, reproaches, and excuses began.

"Here we are, Wortey, dear," cried Mary Anne. "This is Fanny from No. 12, and here's Susannah and Caroline from No. 16."

"What on h'earth's kept you so long, Mary h'Anne?" answered the surly Mrs. Wortey. "If you'd been dressing for a h'evening party you couldn't have been more time."

"It was that horrid shoemaker never sent Susannah's high-'eeled home; and she is such a fiddle," playfully observed the fair accused.

"Oh! how can you, Mary Anne?" cried Susannah. "It was all along of her a-doing out her ringlets, and then cleaning her white kid gloves with Indey-rubber."

"Have you brought the shrimps?" asked Mrs. Wortey, in a half whisper, "and the cowcumber?—there's a good girl. Where've you put 'em? Oh, in your pocket. Mind you don't get sitting on them, there's a dear, for they're not worth a thank'ee if they're scruntched."

Every one in the party was dressed with such scrupulous cleanliness that the stiffness of the linen seemed to impart a corresponding rigidity to the behaviour. The coachman from No. 27, with his face firmly fixed in his unbending shirt-collar, seemed to have lost the use of his neck. Indeed, Mrs. Wortey, observing that when he wished to turn his head round his body moved also, inquired of Mary Anne if the man "had a carbuncle on his nape—or what?"

You might have mistaken the gentlemen for noblemen's sons, for their boots creaked when they walked, and their hats were shiney. In the bow of their satin ties some had stuck double breast-pins, whilst a big brooch ornamented the centre plait of Mr. Boxer's shirt-front. Whenever they stood still, it was with an imposing attitude, the hand either resting on the hip, or being thrust into the coat-tail.

The ladies, in their light starched dresses and black silk mantillas, looked divinely aerial. Those who had on shoes and open-worked stockings, coquettishly raised their skirts to allow their boots to be seen. With the hair done in ringlets—with the parasol firmly grasped in one white-gloved hand, whilst the other held the pocket-handkerchief ready to relieve the warm countenance—those who beheld these damsels must have imagined them to be so many duchesses of the land.

When Mr. Sparkler first saw the company, he mistook them for a wedding-party that had dressed overnight so as not to be late in the morning.

Even the cabman was dazzled by the gorgeous display of raiment; and though Mr. Boxer paid less than his fare, yet the imperious manner in which that gentleman answered his grumblings, by saying, " I live in 'Arley Street, No. 23, and if you don't like it, summons me," completely awed the vulgar fellow into respect.

The place fixed upon for holding the picnic was at the lower extremity of the Heath, and, the gentlemen carrying the hampers, they all adjourned there.

Now came the delights of the evening. Shawls were spread over the furze-bushes, so as to form tents, and some dry wood having been collected, a fire was lighted to boil the kettle and supply hot water for tea and grog.

The unpacking of the hampers was witnessed by all with great interest. Nothing had been broken but a bottle of gin, which had given rather an intoxicating flavour to the veal and ham pie.

" Now, who on earth brought this here bit of cold lamb ? " asked Mrs. Wortey in disgust, as she drew forth the remainder of a shoulder.

" Hush ! " whispered Mary Anne. " It was Caroline ; and she says she's very sorry, but it was the only thing in their larder, so she made up with a pot of pickles, some lump sugar, and half a bottle of ginger wine."

" And don't No. 16 keep their butcher ? Couldn't she order something, I should like to know ? " murmured the cook. " I've no patience with such timidity. If we could run the risk for a veal and 'am pie, what was to prevent her ? "

Mr. Sparkler and the donkeys, on one of which Phil was mounted, were received with a cheer of delight from the entire party, and, flattered by their reception, they in return rendered every possible assistance in spreading the cloth and arranging the glasses. The moment Phil saw Mrs. Worte and Mary Anne, he recognized them.

" Why, there's the cook from where Bertha lives," he thought to himself ; " and blessed if that ain't the girl and the man too."

But as they did not remember his face, he was but too glad to escape detection.

Whilst they were eating, no behaviour could, for elegance or gentility, have surpassed that which dignified the actions and conversation of these picnicers.

"Allow me the honour of a glass of ale with you, Mrs. Wortey, ma'am ?" asked Teddy Cuttler. "Please pass the stone jug, Mr. Boxer. Your good 'ealth, ma'am, and prosperity ekal to my best wishes, ma'am."

"Try another bit of this custard-pudding, my dear," said Mr. Boxer, looking skittishly towards Miss Caroline ; "it won't hurt you, my gal ; and the dancing will shake it down. What ! haven't got room for it ! Well, I'm glad you've eat hearty."

Healths were even proposed, Mr. Boxer speaking in the highest terms of Mrs. Wortey, and saying, "It was an honour to live in the same establishment with her, for her behaviour was, he might and would say, at once conciliating, virtuous, and complesarnt."

But the health which Miss Mary Anne undertook to give met with the greatest success. It would seem that Bertha Hazlewood was not a favourite with Miss Tomsey's domestics, for when Mary Anne, after sarcastically stating that she was about to speak of " one whom they h'all adored," added, " need I mention that my allushun is to Miss Bertha ? " her speech was received with shouts of laughter, in the midst of which Mrs. Wortey was heard distinctly to say,—

"Drat the stuck-up minx, I'd Bertha her out of the house if I had my way."

Philip was so startled at this singular incident, that—by mere accident—he let fall a glass of ale right over Miss Mary Anne's bonnet, an act for which he was pursued some considerable distance by the enraged Teddy Cuttler, and narrowly escaped a severe drubbing.

Nothing could persuade Mr. Boxer to join in the dances that subsequently took place. He had eaten so much, dear man, that he preferred lying down with his head resting on Mrs. Wortey's lap ; and in this position he quietly smoked his pickwick, whilst she, kind soul, plied him with hot gin-and water, lifting the liquid by spoonfuls to his lips.

The moon was up, and shining brightly, and from under their shawl-covered resting-place they could hear the music of the vigorous violins, and see their companions stepping it like fashionable fairies on the green sward.

"That Caroline's a sweet dancer," murmured Boxer ; "and for a hupper housemaid, her foot and ankle are above her station. I've seen many a worse stepping into a carriage."

"It haught to be a nice one," answered the spiteful Wortey, "for there's enough of it ; but if you call that a leg—I don't—posts is their right name. Hopinions differ, Boxer, and I know what a leg is as well as any woman who has one."

"That there Fanny, from No. 12," continued the gay unabashed Boxer, "is a well-formed gal, but I'm afraid she pulls her figure in a bit, and her hands is uncommon hot and rough."

"Lord, do ha done, Boxer," again remonstrated Mrs. Wortey, hitting him on the nose with the spoon. "If you was the Grand Serag of Turkey himself, you couldn't be more after the girls."

But Boxer heeded her not.

"What a luptious eye that gal. Susannah have!" he muttered, in an exhausted tone. "But her nose for a woman's is perposterious, and at meals she's a gluttonous feeder."

The indignant Mrs. Wortey made no reply to this, but suddenly rose from her seat and allowed the head of Boxer to fall with a dull sound on the ground. It took him a quarter of an hour before he could pacify the outraged lady and coax her to rest him once more in her lap, and ladle gin-and-water into his mouth.

As it grew late—after many dances, when the fiddlers were tired, and the donkeys had been galloped to death—the whole party assembled in a circle to partake of further refreshment, and Bertha being the person they most disliked, they once more commenced to talk of her.

"What Miss Tomsey can see in her," cried Mary Anne, "a supercillious, high-flown squit, with her ' Please do this,' and ' Be so kind do that '—oh, it's most comicable."

"And, after all, who is she? " added Mrs. Wortey. "Is her pretentions beyond her humble spear? Has she any fortune? I never in my life see such a small box as she brought. Has she any birth? I myself hear her call a common beggar-boy 'her brother!'"

"I'm sure, she has no beauty," added Mary Anne, with a sneer. "If you was to take away her hair and mouth, she'd be a nice object, poor thing."

"But there's some persons, perhaps, thinks she's a perfect Weners de Mediciny," slyly remarked Mr. Cuttler.

"La!" cried all the young ladies, "you do not mean to say that you—"

"Thin gals is not my choice," answered Mr. Cuttler, looking fondly at the plump Mary Ann by his side. "If I liked, I could tell something that would make you all laugh fit to burst your laces."

"Oh, do now, won't you?" shouted the ladies in chorus; and some of the party thought they heard the donkey boy call out, "Oh, do," like the rest of them. But, on looking round, they found that Phil was fast asleep.

"Well, you're very hard on me, but I must give way," fascinatingly replied Mr. Cuttler. "One day Captain Merton Crosier—my young chap—was a standing at our window, and talking to Mr. Tattenham and another gent, the Hon. Chanticleer Sutton, by name—friends of ours—and they see your Bertha. They was down on her in a minute."

"You don't say so!" cried the ladies.

"Ah, they was, though. The captain says, 'Tat, I must look after my neighbours a little ' and, says Mr. Sutton, 'She's as nice a little toddles as ever I see.'"

"And what then?" they asked.

"Well, I left the room then, you see," replied Mr. Cuttler; "but he's always at the window looking over your way, and if you keep a spy on her, there'll be some fun."

In such pleasant sport did the night pass, and by the time the grey morn showed in the east everybody was thoroughly tired out. The plump Boxer, fuddled with gin-and-water, was carried on a donkey to the nearest cab-stand, his head reclining on the shoulder of the compassionate Wortey, who walked by his side, whilst ever and anon he in gratitude tried to look up in her face, as he murmured forth "Dear cookey."

Susannah and the coachman from No. 27; Fanny and the young man at the baker's; Mary Ann and Teddy Cuttler, all sauntered across the fields in the direction of town, their personal appearance bearing strong testimony to their having been out all night.

The next day, when the twelve o'clock postman called at Miss Tomsey's with a letter, he had to knock three times, and eventually the parlour window was opened, and the epistle was taken in by a pair of tongs, at the end of which was a plump arm with a red elbow, a limb much resembling one to this day in the possession of Mrs. Wortey.

CHAPTER IX.

EVERY MAN HAS HIS FANCY.

In one of the back streets near the Haymarket there existed, in the days whereof we write, a small, humble-looking public-house, well known to all sporting gents and members of the prize-ring, for its proprietor was no less a person than the celebrated Alf Cox, the champion of the "light weights." So long as England is a sporting nation, the name of Cox must be remembered with admiration, as belonging to one of the most gentlemanly boxers in the profession. Those who had the pleasure of being present on the occasion when he fought and beat Ned Box, have never failed to declare that he was the prettiest sparrer ever out, and that when he sent one of his right handers "home," it was the severest punishment ever witnessed.

The renowned Alf Cox had been prudent enough to retire from the ring and all "active sporting life" while he was in the height of his fame, and now he devoted the entire of his attentions to his public-house, exerting all his "strenuous endeavours to please," and holding out innumerable inducements to attract lovers of the fancy to his tavern, for, like the rest of the world, Alf Cox's fondest desire of his heart was to make his fortune.

The entertainments given at the "Jolly Trainer" were of the most varied description. On Monday evenings there was a galaxy of sport in the shape of sparring, at which such glories of the pugilistic world as the Clapham Smasher and the Hackney Crasher assisted. The great match between the Southwark Pounder and Tripey Faggits was got up at his house, and the men showed there publicly the night before the battle. It was well known to his friends that Alf Cox was a great advocate for reviving "old times" —indeed, his circular says as much. He would, too, in his printed cards invite the lovers of song to meet their "social brethren" at his house, on Thursday, Friday, and Saturday, and on such occasions that public favourite, Mr. Thomas Timms, presided, assisted by a host of talented friends. These musical treats were, as Alf Cox said, "open to all, he ever catering," the only return expected from the visitors being, that they would drink as rapidly and as largely as they could. To make use of the noble lines printed in large type over the bills wafered up in the tavern window, the especial mission that Alf Cox had marked out for himself was the Reunion of old Friends and the Fancy generally; Harmony! Conviviality!! and Good-fellowship!!!—Refreshments moderate, and of the best quality.

A favourite hobby with Alf Cox was the improvement of the breed of dogs, and he was reckoned among the dealers to be as good a judge of what a dog was, or ought to be, as any man in the metropolis. Moreover, he was the founder and chairman of the West End Spaniel, Terrier, small Bull-dog, Bull-terrier, and Toy-dog Club, and a meeting of the members was held every Wednesday in his public parlour, when any other fancier was also invited to attend and exhibit. On such occasions the glass circulated merrily, and the waiter was ever in the room to receive the gentlemen's orders, whilst the most interesting discussions were held as to the excellence of this terrier's strain, or the points in that bull's build.

But of sports, that for which Alf Cox was more especially renowned was his public ratting, which came off every Tuesday evening at his "public hostelrie." He said that the reason why he gave away silver snuff boxes as prizes, "to be killed for by novice dogs of any weight," was because he was determined to encourage the useful and good sport of destroying that destructive vermin, the rat; but we fancy he must have had some other motive, for such excessive devotion to the public welfare would, in the end, have entailed certain ruin; and no publican, however enthusiastic, could have afforded to indulge in such expensive antipathies.

Mr. Alf Cox had caused two hundred handbills to be printed and distributed amongst his friends and patrons, and they caused the greatest excitement among all earnest supporters of the fancy. In these handbills he announced that a "great hundred rat match" was to come off, and all the grocers, barbers, and tailors in the neighbourhood were already discussing the chances the different dogs had of winning the silver collar that was to be "killed for." This great match, too, was, according to the handbill, by "distinguished desire," and many were the pots of beer emptied at the bar of "The Jolly Trainer," in the hopes of discovering who was to be the patron of the evening.

"It's no good asking me, Mr. Noakes," replied Mrs. Cox to her constant customer, the cab proprietor; "but I'll tell you this much, Viscount Ascot and Lord Oakes are as fond of sport as any man I ever see of their weight and size."

When the important evening arrived, the open space before the long bar of "The Jolly Trainer" was, long before the performances were to take place, crowded with customers, who were all drinking, smoking, and talking about the match. Most of them had brought dogs with them, so that a kind of canine exhibition was going on. Some carried under their arm small bulldogs, whose flat, pink noses rubbed against the arm as you passed; others had skye-terriers, curled up into balls of hair, and sleeping like children, as they were nursed by their owners. The only animals that seemed awake, and under continual excitement, were the little brown English terriers, which, despite the dandy brass-ringed leather collars by which they were held, struggled to get loose, as if they smelt the rats in the room above, and were impatient to begin biting their foes.

There was a business-like look about this tavern which at once let you into the character of the person who owned it. In establishing it, the drinking seemed to have been only a secondary notion, for it was without any of those adornments which are generally considered so necessary to render a public-house attractive.

The ceiling was low and bulging, and the flies had speckled it into a granite colour, whilst the tubs in which the spirits were kept were as dirty as water-butts, and blistered with the heat of the gas—even the once gilt hoops had turned black as shoe-ribbon. Sleeping on an old hall-chair reclined an enormous white bulldog, "a great beauty," as many of the drinkers observed, with a head as round and smooth as a clenched boxing-glove, and seemingly too large for the body. Its forehead seemed to protrude in a manner significant of water on the brain, and almost overhung the small nose, from which it breathed heavily. It was a white dog, with a sore look, from its being peculiarly pink about the eyes, nose, and indeed, at all the edges of its body.

On the other side of the bar was a bull-terrier dog, with a black patch over the eye, which gave him rather a disreputable look. This gentleman was watching the movements of the customers in front, and, occasionally, when the entrance-door swung back, would give a growl of inquiry as to what the fresh-comer wanted. Mr. Alf Cox was kind enough to inform a particular friend of his, who was patting the fork-like ribs of the brute, that he considered there had been a little of the greyhound in some of his ancestors.

As the hour advanced, the visitors arrived in such numbers that Mrs. Cox, finding that her appeals to the gentlemen not to block up the bar were of no use, was obliged to get her husband to address the multitude in a neat speech.

"My good friends," he cried, mounting a chair, "there's as nice and comfortable a parlour as ever was used, if you'd only step that way. Though I'm fond of seeing handsome faces about me, yet I'm too busy now for such enjoyment."

Then did the laughing crowd make for the green-baize door of the parlour, headed by a waiter shouting out, "Give your orders, gentlemen!"

No pains had been taken to render this parlour attractive to the customers, for, beyond the sporting pictures hung against the dingy paper, it was devoid of adornment. Over the fireplace were square pigeon-hole boxes, containing the stuffed heads of dogs famous in their day. Pre-eminent among the prints was that representing that wonder among rat-killing dogs, Mr. Cox's Tiny, five pounds and a half in weight, "as he appeared killing two hundred rats."

"He was the 'andsomest little thing as ever entered a pit," Mr. Alf would say, "and in honour of his performance—which is unekalled in annals—I had that engraving printed on white silk, which you see before you. Poor Tiny! they don't make 'em like him now. He wore my missus's gold bracelet as a collar, such was his proportions."

Among the stuffed heads was one of a white bulldog, with tremendous glass eyes sticking out as if it had died of strangulation. Young Mr. Cox—Alf's eldest—was kind enough, whenever he saw any stranger examining the canine mausoleum, to offer up a tribute to the memory of the departed favourites. "They've spoilt her in stuffing—made her so short in the head—but she was the greatest beauty of her day. There wasn't a dog in England as dared look her in the face. There's her daughter," he would add, pointing to another head, something like that of a seal, "but she wasn't reckoned half as handsome as her mother, though very few could show agin her, especially for form. That is a dog," he would continue, directing his finger to one represented with a rat in its mouth, "that was the best in England, though it was so small a quart pot might be its kennel. I've seen her kill a dozen rats almost as big as herself, though they killed her at last, for sewer rats are dreadful for giving a dog canker in the mouth, however much you may rinse the mouth out with peppermint-and-water."

The room seemed full of dogs. They were standing on the different tables, or tied to the legs of chairs, or crouching under forms, or sleeping in their owners' arms. Each animal in its turn was minutely criticized, the limbs being stretched out as if feeling for fractures, and their mouths looked into as if a dentist were examining their teeth. Nearly all the dogs were marked with scars from bites. "Pity to bring him up to rat-killing," said one who had been admiring a fierce-looking bull-terrier; and although he did not indicate what line in life the' brute ought to pursue, still everybody understood that "fighting" was the occupation referred to.

Mr. Cox had taken "the chair," and installed himself as head man of the meeting.

"Now, gentlemen," he cried after he had lighted his pipe, "give your minds up to drinking. Do just as you would at home, and get drunk as soon as you like."

The laughter which followed this neat address set all the dogs barking.

"Silence, dogs! order, little dogs!" shouted Mr. Alf; "I'm ashamed of you!" After a time he asked, "Has anybody got a Skye pup he's tired of?"

"Don't believe him," answered one of the men; "he's only a kidding of us. If you says you have, he'll tell you to go and eat it for your supper or somethink."

Mr. Alf Cox, far from feeling displeased at this attack upon his character, began to titter, and merely said, "Well, you are a good 'un for a tale, uncommon."

"I say, Alf, when are you going to begin?" asked somebody in the room.

"I'm only waiting, my dear friend, for these here swells. Can't be long now." And, ringing the bell, he made inquiries of his first-born, which ended by Mr. Cox suddenly vacating the chair; for, as he told the company, with a wink, "his distinguished patronage was in the bar-parlour, and his missus making love to them."

In the dingy little back parlour, which was the ex-prize-fighter's sanctum, sat the noble patrons of the ratting-match. They had come there more out of curiosity than any love of the sport; indeed, it was Captain Merton Crosier who had tempted them to witness the performance. There was Viscount Ascot lolling on the horsehair sofa, smoking a cigar as big as a desk ruler, and watching Mrs. Cox, who was preparing some brandy and water for his cousin, Lord Oaks.

They had brought with them a French officer (he had lately arrived in England with letters of introduction to Captain Merton Crosier, in which le Colonel Victor Baudin Rattaplan, du 11e Leger, was spoken of as one of the braves of Algeria), and at that moment the foreigner and the captain were engaged in a discussion on dogs, to which Fred Tattenham, Tom Oxendon, and the Hon. Chanticleer Sutton—the remainder of the distinguished patronage—were listening with considerable delight.

The colonel, who spoke English almost fluently, had related an anecdote of a friend of his who had endeavoured to give a fashionable appearance to his "bouledog anglais" by having it shaved like a poodle.

The sports of the evening were naturally enough made to await the leisure of such noble guests. It was in vain that the company in the parlour stamped on the floor and rang the bell. Even when Jack Pike, the celebrated rat catcher, was sent to the bar to make

inquiries, it did not advance matters, for the ambassador, being recognized by Captain Merton Crosier, was instantly had into the room,
and ordered to assist Alf Cox in emptying a quart pot of champagne,
as well as to amuse the noble company by some of his vermin-
destroying experiences.

Before such honourable society Alf Cox put on his best behaviour.
He saw in a moment that the "cap'en" was only asking him questions, that he might show off before his friends.

When Jack Pike was seated, the conversation was taken up at the
point where it had been interrupted.

"Well, cap'en," said Alf, in answer to a question put by that
gallant officer, "I should think I buy in the course of the year, on an
average, from three hundred to seven hundred rats a week. I've had
as many as two thousand rats in this very house—ah, that I have!—
at one time. Eat a sack of barley meal a week they would."

"I suppose they fight each other like fury?" suggested the captain.

"Well, my esteemed friend, if I didn't feed 'em they'd get uncommon ill-behaved," answered Mr. Cox. "They'll eat each other like
rabbits—so vicious is their propensities—for I've watched 'em; and
when they've done devouring their companions, they turns the dead
'uns' skins inside out as neat as purses, and polish the flesh off
beautiful clean."

"Where the devil do you get them from?" asked the Honourable
Chanticleer Sutton.

"Get them from, my good friend? It's a regular trade, bless you,"
cried Mr. Cox. "I should think I have twenty farmmerlies depend-
ing on me, and I suppose I have hundreds of thousands of rats sent
me in iron cages fitted into baskets. They don't make a bad thing of
it neither. I paid a man five guineas only yesterday for thirty-five
dozen, at threepence a head. Catching them is dangerous work, take
my word for it."

"Do you mean the bites?" nervously suggested Viscount Ascot.

"You see, my esteemed friends, there's a wonderful deal of difference in the specie of rat," explained the landlord. "The bite of
the sewer and water-ditch rat is, I can assure you, very nasty, for
they live on filth. Now Mr. Barn-rat is a plump fellow, and live on
the best of everythink, and he ain't so poisonous. Sewer rats is
shocking for dogs."

"You may say that, and for men too," cried Jack Pike. "I was
once, gentlemen, bit on the muscle of the arm, and I shall never
forget it if I live twenty thousand year. It turned me queer all of
a sudden, and made me feel upheaving, and there I was kept in bed
for two months, and my arm swole, and went as heavy as a ton
weight pretty well."

"Curse 'em, it's true," cried Captain Merton Crosier, looking at
Lord Oaks, who was beginning to feel uncomfortable, lest any accident should happen to him during the match. "What dithguthting
beaths," lisped his lordship.

"Oh, I've been bit by 'em hundreds o' times," continued Jack Pike; "it's a three-cornered bite, like a leech's, only deeper, of course, for it goes right to the bone, just as if you had been stuck with a pen-knife. And the quantity of blood that comes away, dear! dear! The best thing I ever found for a bite was the bottoms of a porter-cask as a poultice."

"It's all gammon," exclaimed Tom Oxendon. "I've seen fellows handle them as coolly as possible."

"Ay, and I've handled many a hundred," said Jack Pike, calmly; "but they don't bite the less for all that. Look here, and here," he added, showing some scars on his hands. "Right through this thumb-nail, too, yet Alf Cox has seen me handle 'em; hav'n't you, Alf?"

"That I have, my noble friends," replied the landlord, "and much do I admire your nerve, Jack. Why, I've seen him put rats inside his shirt next his bosom, and into his coat, and breeches-pockets, and on his shoulder—in fact, anywhere. He let 'em run up his arm while he was stroking their backs and playing with 'em. Would you like to see him do it, my esteemed friends?"

"No, hang it, not here. Make a fellow sick," cried the patrons; on which le Colonel Rattaplan, seeing that there was a fair opportunity for showing off, pretended to be much grieved at the timidity of his companion, and said something about un brave not being alarmed by une pauvre bete.

"The most dreadfullest, spitefullest rat I know of is the snake-headed rat, as we calls it, gents," observed Jack Pike, who, during the silence, had been taking a long pull at the champagne-pot.

"So it is, my friend, a very ugly customer," said Mr. Alf Cox, in corroboration.

"They are what we calls the blood rat, gentlemen," continued Jack; "and I give you my word, I've known 'em attack children asleep in their cot, and gnaw their little hands and feet."

"How could you tell that rats did it?" asked Viscount Ascot.

"Because, your honour," he replied, "I traced the blood which their tails had trailed through the openings in the lath and plaster. Ah, what two pretty little children them was—uncommon handsome. Whenever they see me now, they says, 'Oh, here's Ratty, ma!'"

"I can't sthand thith any longer," said Lord Oaks. "Itth enough to make you ill."

And, despite the assertions of le Colonel Victor Baudin Rattaplan that it "woss meare shild's play talk," the whole body of the patrons rose from their seats, and whilst Mr. Cox returned to the parlour to make his peace with the crowd, the "distinguished desire" was conducted to the room above, where the pit had been erected for the purposes of the match.

To avoid all reproaches, Mr. Cox, as he entered, cried out, as if addressing somebody, "Let me know directly the shutters is closed in the room above, and the pit lighted up." This announcement seemed to raise the spirits of the impatient assembly, and even the dogs tied to the legs of the tables ran out to the length of their leathern thongs, and their tails curled like eels, as if they understood the meaning of the words.

But although pacified, the customers were surly at the delay. So the cunning Mr. Cox had to win their esteem once more, by noticing their dogs. " Why, that's the little champion," said he, patting a bull-terrier with thighs like a grasshopper, whose mouth opened back to its ears. " Well, it is a beauty ! I wish I could gammon you to take a fiver for it." Then, looking round the room, he added : " Well, gentlemen, I'm glad to see you do look so comfortable."

At last word was brought that all was ready, and instantly a rush was made to the door, which caused dogs to yell and growl, and men to swear and curse. In a few moments all the customers were mounting the broad wooden staircase, which led to what was once the drawing-rooms, and having dropped their shillings into the hand of the doorkeeper, entered the rat-killing apartment.

What was called the pit looked like a small circus, some six feet in diameter, about as large as a centre flower-bed, with strong wooden sides, reaching to elbow height. Over it the branches of a gas-lamp were arranged, which lit up the white painted floor and every part of the little arena. On one side was a recess in the room, which the proprietor calls his " private box," and this apartment the noble patrons had taken possession of, whilst the audience clambered into convenient places upon the tables and forms, or hung over the sides of the pit. All the little dogs which the visitors had brought up with them, the moment they saw the pit, began to squeal and bark, struggling in their masters' arms as if they were thoroughly acquainted with the programme of the evening's sport ; and when a rusty wire cage of rats, filled with the grey moving mass, was brought forward, the noise of the dogs was so great that Mr. Cox was obliged to shout out, " Now, you that have dogs, do make 'em shut up, or take 'em out of the room."

The captain was the first to jump into the pit. A man wanted to sell him a bull-terrier, spotted like a fancy rabbit, and a dozen rats was the consequent order. The captain, to show off before his friends, insisted upon pulling the rats out of the cage himself, laying hold of them by their tails and jerking them into the arena. He was cautioned by Mr. Cox, with great tenderness of manner, to desist, lest any of the brutes should bite him, for, " Believe me," were the words, " you'll never forget it ; these here rats are none of the cleanest."

Whilst the rats were being counted out, those that had been jerked into the arena innocently amused themselves by sniffing about the white-painted floor, little knowing the fate that awaited them. Sometimes one of the poor doomed brutes would cause great merriment by running up the captain's trousers, making that gallant officer shake his leg vigorously as he exclaimed, "Get out, you varmint!" Miserable little wretches! some of them were even sitting on their hind paws cleaning their faces.

When the dog that was to massacre this dozen was brought into the room and saw the rats, he grew excited, and stretched himself out straight in his owner's arms like a Gothic water-spout, whilst all the other animals in the apartment burst into a full chorus of whining. "Chuck him in," cried the captain; and over went the dog, and in a second the rats were running round the circus, or trying to hide themselves between the small openings in the side-boards.

Although Mr. Alf Cox, who was very intimate with the owner of the spotted terrier, endeavoured to speak up for the dog, by declaring "it was a good 'un, and a very pretty performer," still it was evidently not much worth in a rat-killing sense. If it had not been for his "backer," as the youth who accompanied the terrier into the arena was called—if this boy had not beaten the sides of the pit with his hand, and shouted "Hi! hi! at 'em!" in a most bewildering manner, it was very doubtful if the terrier would not, as far as he was concerned, have preferred leaving his antagonists to themselves to enjoy their lives. Some of the rats, when he advanced towards them, sprang up like balls in his face, making him draw back with astonishment. Others as he bit them, curled round in his mouth and fastened on his nose, as that he had to carry them as a cat does its kittens. It also required many shouts of "Drop it—dead 'un," before he would leave those he had killed.

We have never been able to ascertain from Captain Merton Crosier whether he eventually bought the dog; but from its owner's saying, in a kind of apologizing tone, "Why, he never saw a rat before in all his life," we fancy no dealings took place.

The captain seemed very anxious to afford his friends as much sport as he could before the grand match came off, for he frequently asked those who carried dogs in their arms whether "his little 'un would kill," and seemed angry when such answers were given as "His mouth's a little out of order," or "I've only tried him at very small 'uns."

"Here, let my young 'un have a sniff at the dead 'uns," said a coachman, who had a rough-haired little terrier under his arm. As soon as the animal was in the pit, it seized hold of a carcase almost as big as itself, shaking it furiously, till it thumped the floor like beating a tambourine. A shout of laughter burst from the audience, and Alf Cox, looking at the coachman, said patronizingly,

"I say, Mews, he's a good 'un at heads and tails, ain't he?"

Preparations now began for the grand match of the evening. The bodies of the rats slaughtered in the last match were gathered up by their tails like so many candles, and flung into a corner. The arena was swept clean, and a boy sent downstairs with orders to tell Tom to bring up "that basket which had the rats picked for the match —the one that came from Enfield ditches."

During this delay in the performance, the following dialogue took place between Viscount Ascot and Fred Tattenham.

"Who the devil's that French fellow?" asked the nobleman, nodding with his head in the direction of le Colonel Victor Baudin Rattaplan, du 11ᵉ Leger.

"I don't know," answered Tattenham; "he's a friend of Crosier's. I never saw him before."

"Hang me if I like the fellow's face at all. It has a kind of hang-dog look about it. Don't you think so?"

"It strikes me I've seen him before, but I don't know where," replied Fred Tattenham. "He speaks English very well for a Frenchman. Didn't you hear him saying, 'Go it, you cripple?' That doesn't sound as if it was his first visit to England, does it?"

"I don't like him at all," continued the Viscount. "Has Merton spoken about him?"

"Why, Crosier's as much puzzled as we are," was the reply. "I'm told he brought excellent introductions with him, and, what is stranger than all, he seems to have known a good deal about Merton's family affairs—at least, so he told me."

This conversation was put an end to by the entrance of men carrying a big flat basket, like those in which chickens are brought to market, but it had a wirework top, under which were moving mounds of closely packed rats.

An attempt was made among the lookers-on to do a little betting, but nobody seeming inclined to "make a book," the pugilistic landlord cried out that, for the sake of sport, he would make a wager, and straightway offered to lay his eldest son a bottle of lemonade on the match, stipulating, however, that he should have first drink; and he added, "As your mother says you take after me in a'most everything, you shall take after me in lemonade. You won't drownd in what I leave, I can tell you."

Of all the sights of the evening, the one which most seemed to astonish the noble patrons was the daring manner in which Mr. Alf Cox's first-born introduced his hand into the basket of rats, sometimes keeping it there for more than a minute at a time as he fumbled about and stirred up with his fingers the living mass, picking out, as he had been requested, "only the big 'uns."

When one hundred animals had been flung into the pit, they gathered themselves together into a mound, which reached one-third up the sides, and reminded one of the heap of hair-sweepings in a barber's shop after a heavy day's cutting. They were all sewer and water-ditch rats, and the smell that rose from them resembled in offensiveness that from a hot drain.

Captain Merton Crosier was immensely excited by these preparations. He amused himself by flicking at the rats with his scented pocket handkerchief. For the fun of the thing he offered the little brutes the lighted end of his cigar, which they ran up to and tamely sniffed at, and then convulsed the company by the droll manner in which they drew back after singeing their noses. It was also a favourite amusement of the captain—who was allowed to do anything he chose—to blow on the grey pyramid of rats, and so much did they dislike the cold wind, that it completely broke up their gatherings, and sent them fluttering about like so many feathers; indeed, whilst the match was going on, whenever the little animals collected together and formed a round mass, into which the dog dare not force its nose, the cry of "Blow on 'em! blow on 'em!" was given by the spectators, and the dog's backer puffed at the rats as vigorously as if he were extinguishing a fire, and away they darted like so many sparks.

The company was kept waiting so long for the match to begin that the impatient captain at last threatened to leave the house, and was only quieted by the proprietor's reply of "My dear friend, be easy, the lad's on the stairs with the dog."

True enough, a noise of wheezing and screaming was heard in the passage without, as if some strong-winded animal were being strangled, and presently a boy entered, carrying in his arms a bull-terrier in a perfect fit of excitement, foaming at the mouth, and stretching its neck forward, so that the collar which held it back seemed to be cutting its throat in two. It was nearly mad with rage, scratching and struggling to get loose.

"Lay hold a little closer up to the head, or he'll turn round and nip yer," cried Alf Cox, in tenderness, to his son.

Whilst the gasping dog was fastened up in a corner to writhe its impatience away, inquiries were made for a stop-watch, and also for an umpire to decide, as it was comically observed by Mr. Cox, "whether the rats were dead or alive when they're killed, as Paddy says."

When all the arrangements had been made, the second and the dog jumped into the pit, and after allowing the terrier to "see 'em a bit," he was let loose.

The moment he was free, he became quiet, and in a most business-like manner rushed at the rats, burying his nose in the mound of fur, snapping and snuffling until he brought out one in his mouth. In a short time a dozen rats, with necks wetted by the terrier's mouth, were lying bleeding on the floor, and the white paint of the pit became grained with blood, as if hens had been scratching about on a wet red flooring, or a painter had been imitating some crimson-veined wood.

Everything was proceeding very pleasantly for the dog, when a rat, more bold than the rest, fastened on to its nose, and, despite his tossing, still held on dangling there. In vain the terrier dashed the pendant rat against the sides, for though it left a patch of blood, as if a strawberry had been stuck there, still it clung to the snout.

"He doesn't squeal, that's one good thing, but he looks rare and silly over it," said one of the lookers-on.

"He's lost forty-two seconds by that ornament on his snout," cried the time-keeper when this brave rat had at last been shaken off and killed.

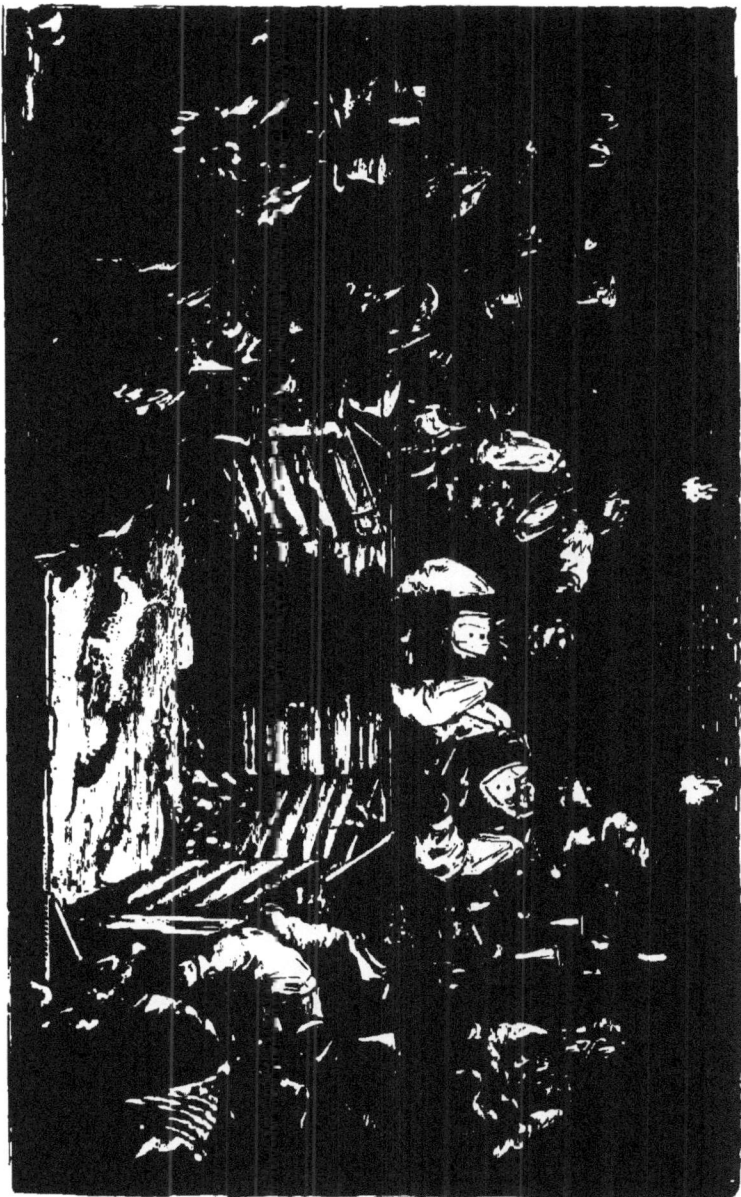

When any of the hundred fell on their sides after a bite, they were collected together in the centre, where they lay quivering in their death gasps.

"Hi, Butcher! hi, Butcher!" shouted the second. "Good dog! Hurr-r-r-r-h!" and he beat the sides of the pit, like a drum, till the dog flew about with new life.

"Dead 'un—drop it!" he howled, when the terrier "nosed" a rat kicking on the floor, as it slowly expired of its broken back.

When four out of the eight minutes allowed for the match had expired, "Time!" was called out, and the dog was seized by the backer, and forced to repose itself.

Panting, as if it had been running miles, with its neck stretched out like a serpent's, it remained staring intently at the wounded rats which crawled about the floor.

The poor little wretches that had as yet escaped, as if forgetting their danger now their enemy was held back, again commenced cleaning themselves, some nibbling the ends of their tails, others hopping about, going close up to the legs of the lad in the pit, smelling at his trousers, or advancing, sniffing, to within a few paces of their executioner, the dog.

After all his panting and screaming the dog lost the match by half a minute. Mr. Cox most honourably paid the bottle of lemonade to his son; but he was evidently displeased with the dog's behaviour, for he said, "He won't do for me—he's not one of my sort! Here, Jim, tell the first costermonger that passes he may have him if he likes, for I won't give him house-room."

The conduct of le Colonel Victor Baudin Rattaplan, du 11e Leger, was, whilst this match was going on, in the highest degree remarkable. With every rat the dog killed he seemed to grow more and more excited, beating the pit sides with the backer, and laughing louder than anyone in the room.

Strange to say, too, he suddenly began to speak English with almost a pure accent; indeed, if he had been born in the metropolis itself, the pronunciation could not have been much better or clearer.

"Good dog! at 'em! pitch into 'em! hi, hi! bite their d—d heads off! hah! hah! hah!" cried le Colonel Victor Baudin Rattaplan, urging on the terrier.

Even Mr. Cox was startled by the Frenchman's sudden improvement, for he urbanely remarked to him,—

"Very good, mounseer—you tree bong. Learn very well here, good lesson—see kill rat." And, turning to his other noble patrons, he added: "You must bring the mounseer here again, my esteemed friends, and by ——, after three ratting matches, he'll speak like a Member of Parliament."

The French officer, who at first had seemed slightly agitated by Mr. Alf Cox's remarks, soon recovered himself, and, indeed, joined with great good-humour in the laugh which had been raised against him.

"Qu'il est drole, ce Corx," he remarked to Viscount Ascot; but the

nobleman either paid no attention to the observation, or else was rather deaf.

During the pause which now took place in the proceedings, the gentlemen were again requested by the landlord to "give their minds up to drinking."

"You know the love I have for everybody here, and that I don't care a cus for any of you," jocosely remarked Alf Cox, though there was more truth in the observation than many fancied.

"Any other gentleman like to have a few rats?" asked the first-born, whilst he was gathering up the halfpence which had been thrown into the pit as a reward for his exertions in backing the dog.

"Let's have a dozen," cried a man, who spoke as if he had been struggling to resist the temptation, but could not. Another batch of rats and another bull-terrier were thrown into the pit. This dog did his work so well—cracking the necks of the rats like so many walnuts—that the admiration of the spectators was focussed upon him.

"Ah," said the owner, "he'd do better at a hundred than twelve, I know;" whilst another, hanging over the pit, observed, "Rat killing's his little game, I can see;" and Mr. Cox himself, in his admiration, cried out, "She's a very pretty performer, and though not my own dog, and no ways interested, I'd back her to kill against anybody's at eight and a half, or nine."

It was nearly twelve o'clock when the noble patrons rose to depart. There were a good many persons on the staircase as they went down, and a little pushing took place, despite all that Mr. Cox could do to prevent his esteemed friends being in any way annoyed.

They parted outside the door, the Viscount and Fred Tattenham going one way, and the remainder of the party directing their steps towards the Haymarket, it being their intention to treat le Colonel Victor Baudin Rattaplan to a night on town.

When Viscount Ascot reached his club, he found, on searching for his purse to pay the cab, that his money was gone.

"It's a good haul, too, for the fellow that's got it," he said, "for there were thirty odd pounds in it, and I never bother myself about the number of notes. It's a nuisance to lose so much though, isn't it? There was a blank unsigned cheque in one of the pockets, but that doesn't matter so much."

"I'd give notice to the Bank about it, all the same," suggested Fred Tattenham. "It might be filled up for you."

As they were going up the steps the Viscount stopped suddenly, and taking hold of his companion's arm, said, earnestly, "Do you know, I half suspect that French colonel of the robbery. I can't be certain, on account of the pushing on the stairs, but I remember he kept very close to me as we came down."

"Confound him!" replied Tattenham. "I have my suspicions too."

What these ended in remains to be told.

CHAPTER X.

FRIENDS ARRIVE.

ONE day, whilst the boys were waiting for a turn to go out with a job, Mr. Sparkler, casting his eye over the Heath, saw a young woman, whom he instantly recognized as the maid-servant from Madame de Blanchard's establishment for young ladies, advancing in the direction of the donkey-stands. Being a thorough business man, and knowing that such orders were generally very excellent and extensive, Mr. Sparkler did not think it beneath his dignity to play the part of touter, but hurried forward to meet the young woman with a rapidity which showed that he was rather nervous lest anybody else should snatch the chance from him.

The reason of Mr. Sparkler's sudden departure was soon discovered by his brother proprietors, and as they were all well acquainted with the girl from the school, a pang of jealousy passed through all their hearts, and the quiet of the Heath was disturbed by angry voices. In the heat of the moment, masters began to strike their boys for not being on the look-out, and boys to squeal and abuse their masters for taking the law into their own hands. All Mr. Sparkler's movements were watched with the greatest interest. He was seen to touch his hat with great politeness to the girl, and it was concluded, from his respectful demeanour, that the expense of a first-rate job formed the subject of conversation.

" It's a good thirty donkeys at least," cried one owner, shaking his whip at his boy, who had retired to a safe distance.

It was in vain that preparations were set on foot to try and cut the ground from under Mr. Sparkler, for the herd of animals hurried off towards the servant had scarcely been roused into a trot, before Mr. Sparkler was seen returning, his countenance so beaming with inward satisfaction, that the four-legged deputation was ordered back again, it being evident that every arrangement had been concluded, and the job secured.

The Hampstead donkey-masters, although they will fight amongst themselves for a sixpenny ride, and seem influenced by feelings of the deepest hatred when any business is on foot, are, nevertheless, an amiable and accommodating race of men, assisting each other on half-profits with the greatest cheerfulness when an order of any magnitude has to be executed. Hence, when Mr. Sparkler rejoined his friends with the announcement that eighteen donkeys were wanted at the ladies' school by one o'clock, he found no difficulty in securing long-eared steeds to that number.

" Here, you Phil, you'll have to be one to go along with this lot,"

said Mr. Sparkler, beginning his preparations; "and mind old Indy
Rubber is for the governess, for she's a mortal fine woman, and takes
a deal of carrying, so the girl telled me."

For at least half an hour every hand in Mr. Sparkler's employment
was hard at work, tidying up and arranging saddles, so as to make
the cavalcade look as respectable as possible. The patronage of the
ladies' schools in the neighbourhood was very much sought after,
for although the prices given were not high, still the orders were
extensive, and came at a time in the day when business was extremely slack. All the time that Mr. Sparkler was adorning his
steeds, by hiding the ends of straps, stuffing straw under the saddles,
or arranging the linen covering so as to hide, as much as possible,
the faulty condition of his harness, he continued giving his directions
to Phil.

"Put one o' the young 'uns on Laura Smith," he said, "she's very
tender on the back; and keep your eye on Bobtail, or he'll be up to
kicking, and breaking some of their necks, if he have a chance. And,
Phil, mind you be particular civil to the girl's missus, and don't let's
hear of your being up to your larks, getting any of the young 'uns
chucked off. You'd better let old One Eye go alongside of Crazy
Jane, or she'll be a lying down in the road, or some other wicious-
ness." And as he spoke of the bad-hearted One Eye, he tapped her
smartly on the shoulder with his stick, to show that he disapproved
of her general behaviour. "Mind, too, Phil," he continued, "they're
only out for two hours, and don't you go running their legs off, and
knocking them up for their afternoon's work."

Eighteen handsome donkeys, accompanied by five sluiced and
combed boys, drew up, as the clock struck one, before the iron gates
of Madame de Blanchard's establishment. The effect was very imposing, and everybody who passed stopped to admire the gaily attired
stud, and to glance at the windows, where the young ladies, with
their bonnets on, were impatiently peeping over the blinds, and
gazing wistfully on the donkeys. The establishment gained great
glory that day, and many were the praises uttered about the great
affection Madame felt for her pupils, and her motherly treatment of
them.

Presently the doors of the academy opened, and out marched the
young damsels, trying, by screwing up their little lips to the size of
cherries, to look as serious as they could in the presence of their
governess, but every part of the face was laughing except the mouth.
These attempts at solemnity were nearly choking some of the little
misses, and making their faces as pink as rose-leaves. All the young
ladies were dressed in their best clothes, and looked very prim and
pretty, with their smooth hair so neatly dressed and tucked behind
the ears that it seemed a sad pity to derange it with galloping. Their
little collars and cuffs, too, were so brilliantly white it was sorrowful
to think how soon the dust would soil them.

As they stood in the front garden—the prettiest flowers there, be it understood—the governess said there was a great deal too much chattering; and we are sorry to have to relate that a little pushing and quarrelling occurred whilst the young ladies were being placed in their saddles. One Miss Wagbird—a terrible, wicked girl, as the mistress called her—was ordered to write out "Do not push!" one hundred times, in play hours, for disorderly conduct. Then one Miss Clara Marsh had to be severely reprimanded, and threatened with being sent back, for taking a violent prejudice against the Duke of Brunswick, whom she declared to be a dusty thing, with a sore on its back. Another young lady—Miss Twining, who wore her hair down her back, and had dimples under her eyes—was rated for her affectation in pretending to be nervous when Sam Curt was helping her on to the saddle; and, worse than all, she showed some temper, asserting that she couldn't help it, for it tickled. Yet the governess preferred believing Master Curt's explanation of " It's her skin's so creepy, ma'am. It itches in a moment."

The governess—a fine, tall thin woman, but inclined to wither—endeavoured to govern the young ladies in a half-military fashion, calling out their names in succession when it came to their turn to mount. There was a great deal of confusion caused by some of the little misses putting the wrong foot in the stirrup, and a great deal of time was wasted in fidgeting about in the saddle to get comfortable, and in altering straps which were either too long or too short. If the mistress had not been a woman of great nerve she would never have been able to preserve order among her pupils. Cries of " Adone, Mary ! " or, " Let me alone, Tilda ! " evinced the unsettled condition of some of the scholars' minds. Others would grumble because their donkey was the worst of the lot, or because its knees were broken : and one even took a strong prejudice against her steed because she said its eyes were full of flies.

" Miss Smith, I'm ashamed of you ! What are you about, Miss Collis ? Pull the other rein directly—where are you to going to ? Arrange your dress, for goodness' sake, Miss Trelawny ; and take your parasol out of that donkey's ear, Miss Simpson."

There was one young lady—she could not have been older than fourteen—who caused more disturbance than all the school put together. Somehow or other, whenever Philip was about to lift her on the saddle, the donkey was sure to hop out of the way ; and as all the other young ladies laughed, it certainly did appear as if it was no accident.

" Kick that patient animal again, Miss Crosier, and you shall be sent back," at last called out the governess.

What made the pupil's conduct look very black indeed, was, that the very next attempt after this threat the young damsel was jumped on to the back with as little trouble as a circus-rider.

When the cavalcade was mounted, the governess, with much dignity took her seat on India Rubber ; and whilst she was doing so, it was painful to hear the tittering which crackled among the pupils. She must have heard it, poor lady, for she blushed a deep cinnamon colour.

Philip could not take his eyes off this Miss Crosier, for he had recognized in her the little girl who one day, when he was seated under the avenue by the Heath side, had called him " ce sal petit garsong-la." He did not know what the words meant, but he had a half-notion that they were slightly complimentary, and had been spoken in pity. Once he asked Swinging Fred what " ce sal petit garsong-la " meant, but Mr. Jackson, being unacquainted with the French language, had replied that he could not " tumble to it," and that it was a " regular jawbreaker." So, as he was unable to obtain a translation, Phil contented himself with his own notions on the subject, and felt convinced that the little lady was commiserating with his forlorn lot, and very thankful he felt for her sympathy.

She had a wicked, pretty little face, that would have made anybody like her. It is very difficult to say whether her eyes left off laughing even when she was asleep, and how she ever managed to close them, with all those lashes about the lid, must be guessed at. She had the strange power, too, of working her eyebrows about as a horse does its ears ; and if a fly happened to settle on her forehead, or her hair got out of its place, she would frown like the Saracen's Head on Ludgate Hill, though the next moment the semi-circles were back on her forehead again, and very lovely to look at. The last time she returned home from the holidays her mamma wrote a letter to Madame de Blanchard requesting that Helen might never be permitted to go out in the sun without some covering to protect her skin; and nobody who has seen the pretty child could object to such a precaution, for her complexion is so clear that you can see the blue veins on her temples as distinctly as if she had traced them with cobalt, and even now there are some half-dozen golden spangles of freckles, where the sun had caught her, on the top of her little nose, where the skin is extremely delicate and sparkles like a lily-leaf.

The cavalcade moved along so slowly that this Miss Crosier did nothing but grumble at the pace, and ask Emma Twining, who was next her, " When that old thing "—meaning, we are sorry to say, the governess—" was going to let them gallop ? " She was evidently a very rebellious young damsel, and far from settled in her mind. Whenever the mistress called out, " Throw your shoulders back, Miss Crosier, you're stooping dreadfully," the wicked child, far from feeling grateful for the kind reproof, as we should, only shook herself, and pouted, and her eyebrows moved about so rapidly with frowning, that it seemed as if they would never become round again.

The cavalcade was going along very prettily, all the pupils holding themselves delightfully upright, and looking very solemn and lady-like, with the mistress in the rear, keeping a strict eye over them to see that there was no talking whilst they were passing through the town. But what did Miss Crosier care for the governess ? She was determined not to hold her tongue for anybody, but would speak as much as she liked, and to whom she liked. Now, Emma Twining was a much better-behaved young lady, and when the insurrectionary Helen whispered any question, the only reply she received was, "Don't—she's looking," or, "Don't—she'll hear us," or some such nervous repulse.

So Helen called Emma "a disagreeable thing," and determined, as there was nobody else to chat with, she would talk to the donkey-boy, Phil. But first of all, with a cunning far beyond her years, she warned the lad not to look at her when he answered her questions, but to keep his head straight in front of him, so that the mistress might suspect nothing.

"What's your name, boy?" she asked.

"Philip Merton, miss," was the reply.

On hearing this she gave a laugh, which made the governess call out, "Pray be more steady, Miss Crosier!" but she didn't seem to attend in the slightest degree to the warning, but continued the conversation.

"Merton!" she said, in an astonished tone; "la! what a curious thing! my brother's name is Merton. I wonder if you're a relation?" and as she felt she must laugh, she pushed her bonnet strings into her mouth. After a moment, she added: "Where do your parents live, boy?"

"My mother's dead—the heavens be her bed!" was the sad reply. "I never saw my father, and I don't know where he is."

The pretty maid was sorrowful when she heard this answer. As if she was comparing the happiness of her lot with the misery of his, she said,—

"Both my papa and mamma are alive. I have a brother, beside, who is an officer in the army."

Another cry of, "No talking, Miss Crosier," came from the governess.

After a moment, when she thought the governess's suspicions were allayed, the simple child asked, "Shouldn't you like to see your father?"

The boy, forgetting the warning she had given him, looked up in her face, and answered sorrowfully, "I would walk miles even to see where he was buried, if I knowed the spot. I have been told he was a gentleman, but even if he was the poorest man living, I'd crawl on my hands and knees—ay, hundreds of miles—if I knowed where to see his face."

Here the conversation dropped, for Helen, who was a gentle-hearted girl for all her laughing, seeing with what earnestness Philip had spoken, began to upbraid herself for having unconsciously wounded his feelings. When she heard Emma Twining sigh and mutter, in her rich, soft voice, "Poor boy!" Helen took it as a rebuke for her thoughtlessness, and whispered back, excusingly, "I did not mean to hurt him, dear."

The dreams and fancies that used to fill the lad's mind even when he was a mere infant at the pauper school—the strange ideas to which he had often, as he lay on the grass with his face turned up to the clouds, sought to give shape and truthfulness, again came rising to his brain. He seemed to have forgotten that anybody was near him, and walked along in a kind of somnambulistic condition, talking to himself aloud: "They never would tell me anything about her; no, not even nurse wouldn't. If she was a lady, as that Miss Perriman said she was, where was the harm of my knowing it? Of course I ought to know. They ought to tell me everything. I can't even see her when I want to, because they wouldn't tell me what she was like. I dream of Sam Curt and a lot of others, but I can't dream of her, and all through them."

For the next few moments not a fault had the mistress to find with Miss Merton's behaviour, for the little donkey-boy's soliloquy had frightened her into silence. The first to renew the conversation was Philip. One of the animals stumbled, and called him back to himself again. He was a singular, fitful youth; in tears one second, and laughing the next. Directly he saw the little ladies' faces, he seemed to wake up from his dreams; he even thought it was an excellent opportunity for obtaining a translation of the French words the little lady had spoken about him, so, half turning round, he said, "I've seen you before, and you called me a 'sal petit garsong-la.' What does that mean?"

At first Miss Helen blushed as scarlet as her brother's brightest regimentals, and then she began to shake with laughter, so that Emma was obliged to think of the mistress, and say to her, "Oh! don't, there's a dear!"

When she had partially recovered from her excitement, she felt embarrassed as to what answer to give. She did not dare to tell Philip to his face that she had called him a dirty little boy; it would be much kinder, she thought, to deceive him by telling a fib, and, looking him full in the face, she replied, with the greatest sang-froid, "It means, 'What a handsome young man that is.'"

Now it was Philip's turn to look silly, and feel uncomfortable, whilst Emma Twining was so astounded at her friend's duplicity, that she began to splutter with giggling, whilst her cheeks puffed out, and her eyes puckered up, in endeavouring to restrain her mirth.

Then came the terrible voice of the governess again, "Miss Twining, copy out 'I must not laugh,' fifty times, when you get home, and as for you, Miss Crosier, I shall report you."

Poor Emma began to tremble like a mariner's compass, and once again did the other wicked child shake herself as if she was trying to slip out of her clothes, and the eyebrows bobbed up and down into all manner of shapes.

"The nasty old thing!" said the bad girl, "I wish that donkey would kick up behind and throw her off, that I do."

Being close to her side, Philip heard her wish, and so anxious was he to do something in return for the complimentary "ce sal petit garsong-la," that he turned round and said, "I could make old Indy Rubber, wot she's riding of, kick in a minute, if I choosed."

"Can you?" was the quick reply; "mind she doesn't see you talking to us. I'll give you a penny if you'll make old India Rubber kick."

"I don't want your pennies," said Phil, indignantly. "I'll do it for nothing, for you."

"Well, look here, boy," continued the little tempter; "my pa's coming to see me on Thursday next, and I'll make him hire you to give me a ride; only mind and bump her well."

This was enough for Philip, and pleased him better than all the pennies in the Bank of England. So he dropped behind, and allowed the cavalcade to pass until he was near the mistress, and under the pretence of asking which way they were to go, he kept by her side waiting for his opportunity to torment her. He well knew that one of India Rubber's peculiarities was extreme irritability whenever anybody placed the hand on her backbone. She could bear a good deal of flogging without evincing much restlessness, but the moment she felt a pressure behind the saddle, she became frisky and gay, and spitefully lively in her demeanour.

The poor governess could not imagine what had come to her hitherto docile steed. She felt herself raised up behind as suddenly as if she had been lifted by a wave, and bumped forward several times in succession—a sensation somewhat resembling that of being churned. India Rubber was lashing her tail about, and throwing her legs vigorously in all directions.

"Go away, boy, it's you frightening her," cried the lady, in alarm; but Phil remained, protesting his innocence, and at the same time pinching India Rubber harder and harder, until at length the enraged animal threw up its heels with as much violence as if it were going to turn a somersault, and the lady, being totally unprepared for this evolution, was propelled forward with the velocity of a champagne cork, although her progress through the air was fortunately checked by the stirrup, which forced her back again to her seat with the jerk of a lasso. The dignified, upright position which had hitherto distinguished her deportment in the saddle vanished entirely, for her body fell down like a lid over the animal's neck, and for a few seconds she remained in an attitude similar to that which Johnny Gilpin is supposed to have assumed when passing through Edmonton.

All the young ladies heard their mistress call out, "Oh, take me off this donkey! take me off! oh, oh, oh!" And as they turned round, and saw her clinging to the pommel, the mirth and enjoyment they were trying to conceal came gurgling up to their little mouths. It is a painful portion of our duty to be obliged to state that Miss Crosier so enjoyed the scene, that her head fell back on her shoulders, and the only sound that came from her open mouth was one which resembled that produced by a person whilst using a gargle. At length

M

her full throat began to work like that of a canary in song, making her bonnet-strings tremble as her laughter streamed up, and then such a flood of rich, melodious chuckles gushed forth, that she must have been heard a mile off, and made everybody within that distance cachinnate from sympathy.

The expression of the countenance of the governess, as she heard the wicked Helen's bursts of delight, was sublime from contempt and fearful with anger, and the remarkable vigour which she threw into the words, " Miss Crosier, write out one hundred times, ' I should not laugh at the misfortunes of others,' " ought to have made that young lady sink to the ground with shame and contrition.

The most melancholy result of this revengeful proceeding was that the governess insisted upon quitting the back of India Rubber, and as she was forced to proceed at a walking pace, she issued an order that all the young ladies should follow her example. So, much to Miss Helen's disappointment, all hopes of a gallop were dispelled.

"Never mind, miss," said Phil, consoling her, " wait till Thursday, and then I'll give you such a run as shall make you stiff for months to come."

For two or three days after this memorable academic expedition, Philip was so wrapt in thought that his bearing towards his companions seemed haughty and distant, and in retaliation it was resolved the nickname of " My nobs " should henceforth be conferred upon him. Whenever he appeared on the Heath the boys used to grin at him, and shout out " My nobs " in full chorus. He did all he could to try and convince his friends that he was not proud, but pensive ; yet he met with no success. He tried to silence their evil tongues by lending them money, but though they were civil enough until the monetary transaction was completed, yet no sooner had the coin changed hands than once more he became " My nobs." Even sharing his food with his enemies did not soften their hearts.

If Phil was thoughtful and abstracted, and did not talk and mingle with the other boys as he had formerly done, it was not, as they thought, because he had suddenly given way to pride, but for a far deeper reason. What on earth was a poor donkey-boy to be proud of ?

He was continually thinking over the words little Helen Crosier had spoken. He would say to himself, " What a curious thing that her brother's name should be Merton as well as mine ! She said she wondered if I was a relation, but she was only laughing at me. Yet everybody used to say my mother had been a lady. Only fancy if we was actually relations ! " And this idea would torment him until it monopolized all his time and thought.

He and the other boys were one afternoon bathing in the pond by the Kilburn Fields, when a direct set upon Phil was made by the satirical young rogues. Nothing was addressed directly to him, but it was evident that he was intended to hear all that was said. He clenched his teeth together very tightly as he heard one ask " Whether

it was true that ' nobs'' father had once been King of England before
he took to keeping an oyster-stall?" and his muscles tightened
when another replied, as soon as the laughter had subsided, "I've
heard ' My nobs'' mother was a heiress, and married the dandy dogs'-
meat man."

In despair of being able to put an end to these annoyances by any
pacific means, Philip uttered the tremendous threat that "The very
next person who insulted him should receive such a drubbing as
should ensure civility for years to come." Now donkey-boys are
notoriously brave, and will never allow anything like intimidation.
The consequence was, that Phil had scarcely spoken his big words
before Bill Kurney, one of Slopman's boys, shouted back in defiance,
"If you want to fight, ' My nobs,' here's for you," and into the water
he leapt.

Now began the horrors of war. First they skirmished about,
splashing each other with water, until at last the savage Merton
waded towards his opponent with clenched fists, whilst the determined Kurney, daring to the last, hissed and shouted out, "My
nobs!" as if he was singing his war-song. They ducked each other
unmercifully, wrestling as well as their wet arms would let them.
Sometimes they held each other's heads under water until the bubbles of their breath came to the surface as rapidly as the gas in soda
water. Then, black in the face, and panting, they would rise to wipe
the moisture from their eyes, and prepare for another tussle.
Philip's rage made him stubborn, and gained him the victory, for
though he was sometimes nearly suffocated, he would give no signs
of his discomfiture, whilst Kurney no sooner found himself overwhelmed by difficulties than he roared out at the top of his voice,
"Murder, murder, help! I'm getting drownded!"

At last it was determined by the lookers-on that the scene of the
combat should be changed from the water to the dry land, and both
combatants, who had apparently had enough of the nautical engagement, willingly assented to the proposal. Whilst the boys were
slipping on their clothes, Jack Burt remarked to a friend of his, "I
never saw two such hard ones; Phil's as tough as cow beef."

"Yes," joined in Snorting Sam, "but if Kurney holds his head up
I don't believe he'll get the worst of it now." Sam Curt never did
like Phil much. Perhaps he was a little jealous of him.

Whilst the boys were dressing, they continued crowing at each
other like a couple of game cocks, threatening to inflict all sorts of
injuries. Whilst menacing each other, they adopted the slang in
fashion among donkey-boys, so that their threats, though very
fearful to their understanding, had rather a comic meaning to the
uninitiated.

Philip intimating that, as soon as he had put on his trousers, he
would blacken Bill's eyes, roared out, "Wait till I've togged my
' round-the-houses,' and then I'll cook your ' mince-pies ' for you."

To this Kurney retorted, "I'll have yer down on ' the last card of your pack' as soon as I've laced my 'German flutes'"—meaning thereby that when his boots were arranged he would throw Philip on his back.

"You won't know your 'lump o' lead' when I've finished with you," cried Merton, referring to his antagonist's head.

"I'll smash your 'glass case,' and damage your 'north and south,'" roared Bill, referring to the face and mouth of his opponent.

In this curious language did they defy each other, speaking of the jaw as a "jackdaw," calling an arm a "five-acre farm," and terming a nose an "I suppose," and, in fact, never making use of the word they intended, but employing in its stead some expression which rhymed with it.

When the young urchins did begin to fight they had a very terrible set-to, and hurt each other as much as ever they could, but it happened most providentially that their limbs were not so powerful as their rage, or they must have knocked each other to atoms. Whilst they were sparring up to each other, Phil would cry out, passionately, "My mother married a dandy dogs'-meat man, did she?" or, "My father was King of England, was he?" and then rush head first at his enemy, who, determined not be intimidated, would growl back in defiance, "Yes, 'My nobs,' that's the exact state of things."

They fought long enough, however, for each of them to discover that they were very well matched, and for the future it would be more prudent to remain friends instead of foes. So Phil allowed Mr. Kurney from that day to call him, behind his back, "My nobs," and never afterwards was Bill heard to threaten young Merton either with "punching his lump of lead," or "throwing out his five-acre farm," or "stopping Phil's jackdaw with a crack on his north and south."

You may be sure that Phil never forgot the promise the little school-girl made him. When Thursday came, he seated himself on the wooden railings near Jack Straw's Castle, and he passed the morning as contentedly as a parrot on its perch. He listened for the roll of carriage wheels, and kept his eyes moving in every direction so as to be the first to discover when a certain pink muslin dress should come fluttering down the road. He was in a dreadful state of anxiety lest any other boy should speak to her before him.

Many times when a carriage passed did he rush into the road and, at the peril of getting run over, peep into the comfortable interior, hoping to catch sight of the little lady's bright face. He had made up his mind that her papa must keep an equipage, for he had noticed that Miss Helen was the only girl in the school who had a gold watch and chain. His greatest fear was, that he should be ordered out with any donkeys, and so miss the damsel. He let Sam Curt go out three times running, and although it was a good sixpence out of his pocket, yet he never thought of that, but was only glad to shuffle the job off to some one else.

"I don't know why I should like her," he thought. "She ain't half so pretty as Bertha, for her eyes is always laughing and making fun, but sister's has such a fond look in them, they wouldn't frighten a bird away. I suppose it's because she said something about my being a relation, though she was only larking."

The afternoon was passing rapidly, and yet he was still on the look-out, though he was getting rather tired and impatient at being made a fool of, as he called it. Several times he had complained to a brick wall close by, asking the solid masonry, "Why did she say she was coming if she wasn't?" Often and often he would run to have a look at the hotel clock, making up his mind he would give her a quarter of an hour longer, and if she didn't come by that time there was an end of the matter. He was, indeed, so doubtful about seeing her, that he had even tossed up some halfpence to see how his luck stood, but the hope was so strong within him that, although he lost five times out of six, he philosophically refused to believe in that method of divination.

At length, just as he was on the verge of despair, and had raised his closed fists preparatory to uttering some dreadful imprecation on the bonnet of the unconscious school-girl, he heard a voice close to him which made him jump off his rail with the vigour of a grass-hopper.

"This is the little boy with the same name as yours, Merton," cried Helen, the owner of the voice. "How do you do, little Merton? I've brought big Merton to see you." And then she began to laugh and nod her head alternately to Phil and a tall young gentle-man, with a dropping moustache, who had fixed his glass in his eye and was examining his namesake. He did not seem pleased with the inspection, for he said nothing, but let his glass fall, and then moved his brows about as if he was getting them right again after frowning.

It was evident that the old gentleman with the tawny, unbleached face, that seemed hard as if it had been carved in bees'-wax, was Miss Helen's papa, for she held his long thin hand in hers, and seemed very happy to be by his side. This old gentleman, although he was trying to smile, looked very severe, for his features were not flexible, but seemed tough and hard as saddle leather, and his expression was more as if he had a nasty taste in his mouth than anything else. His cold eyes, with wrinkles starting in every direction like the cracks in starred glass, made Phil feel uncomfortable when they looked at him. The boy, too, could not help noticing the gentleman seemed to have lost his lips, for there was no red edging to the mouth, but it closed as a slit in an orange would. He was dressed in black, and was solemn and heavy as a hulk, with just one dub of white, like a port-hole, where the shirt showed above the waistcoat. Indeed, Phil half wished that this old gentleman had not come with his little daughter.

"So this is the little fellow, is it?" said papa. "Come, sir, you must be kind enough to let us have your best donkey, to give this young lady a ride."

"Then, if you'll take my word for it, have Light Heart, the best as ever carried a saddle," answered Phil, starting off to fetch the vaunted animal.

The big Merton laughed affectedly at the little Merton's earnest manner. He was a very handsome young fellow, despite a certain languid expression, which gave you an idea that he was ready for bed-time. The keys of a piano were not more regular than his teeth, and his nose was as aquiline as a ratchet cut. As for whiskers, his were so bushy birds might have built in them, and on his chin was a tuft nearly as big as a rabbit's tail. He was not dressed in black, but wore a shawl-patterned waistcoat, and his blue coat was thrown back over his shoulders as open as folding-doors. He seemed very mildly happy, and proud of being able to keep his eye-glass fastened under his eyebrow, though it gave him somewhat the appearance of an owl blind of one eye.

There was a third gentleman present, who was evidently a Frenchman, for whenever he addressed the big Merton he called him "Mon cher Mareton," and gesticulated like a preacher. He had shaved off his whiskers, but you could still trace their shape by a bluish granular stain. His heavy moustache had been clipped over his mouth as regularly as thatch over a cottage window, and he had the faculty of laughing instantaneously and stopping as quickly. One or two donkey-boys, who were watching him, were astounded at the size of his ears, which stood out like handles on each side of his cleanly-shaved face. In his moments of polite merriment, his round, smooth countenance became dimpled and nobbed by the forcing up of the cheeks. Whoever his tailor was, he understood the art of cutting trousers, though his coat fitted his plump body too much like a pudding-bag, and Phil at one time thought he wore stays.

This foreign gentleman also seemed to be very good-natured, for when Redpoll Jack recommended him to have a donkey as well as the young lady, he laughed till he had to wipe his forehead, and told Helen that her friends the boys were "des gamins and tres droles, and wanted to make a donkey of him, he should think, ha! ha!"

He made one observation, which was very curious. He pointed out to his friends that Phil's face was not at all like that of an English boy's, for the features were too round and formed, and in fact, resembled those of the children in his own country. He even went so far as to ask the lad whether either of his parents was an etranger.

There is no sensation more annoying than feeling certain you have seen a face before, and yet being unable to call to mind the when and the where. Philip was turning over all the leaves in his memory endeavouring to satisfy himself where he had seen the big Merton before. He remembered the face as distinctly as he did the statue at

Charing Cross. Later in the day the mystery was cleared up, and in the languid youth Phil recognized one of the officers who one night in the Haymarket, when he (Phil) was a crossing-sweeper, had ordered the Duck to throw mud at Nurse Hazlewood.

"I wish I dare send a stone at him," thought little Merton.

They strolled along as far as Highgate, chatting and talking together, papa never addressing the French gentleman without a great show of courtesy, and pompously calling him Monsieur le Colonel (only he pronounced it Mussu). The foreign officer also behaved with excessive politeness, and whenever he spoke to the languid youth, called him "mon ami Mareton," or "mon cher capitaine." Indeed, it was truly delightful to witness the glossy elegance of manner all the gentlemen displayed. Even laughing little Helen herself felt awed by their imposing conduct, for as she afterwards told Emma Twining, it was like being in school again. It did not make much impression on Phil though, but he walked quietly along, leading the donkey, and never opened his mouth unless it was to check symptoms of frivolity on the part of Light Heart by such exclamations as "No, you don't, you hussey!" or "Steady, you warmint!" to bring her back to a sense of her servitude.

Presently the old gentleman, who was apparently fond of inquiring into the condition of the lower orders, asked Phil, in a condescendingly kind tone of voice, such questions as "How many donkeys his master had, and how much the boys made at the business?" He also called the boy "his young friend."

He listened with the greatest attention as Phil replied,—

"Well, there's eleven masters altogether, and mine—which is Sparkler by name—has got six donkeys, and one on 'em he wouldn't take £4 for. He had another first-rater as we called Lord Cocktail, but she was drowned last winter in the Vale of Health—got on the ice under the hedge for warmth, and the thaw came, and in she went, and then the frost came again, and regular potted her. He gave over £3 for her, for donkeys is wonderful scarce. You can't look at one under fifty shillings. As for what he earns," he continued, remembering the second portion of the question, "that's according to what we brings home. If it's a good day, we get maybe three shillings, or if it's a bad one, only eighteenpence, per'aps; but we depends most upon what gentlefolks give us," he added, giving the old gentleman a strong hint.

"And I hope you're a good boy, and don't use bad language, but go to church regularly, eh?" continued Mr. Crosier, senior.

Philip, who every Sunday had to fetch an old lady home in a Bath-chair when divine service was over, answered without hesitation that he never missed attending church unless it was very wet, which, of course, was perfectly true. The quarrels he had lately had with his companions seemed to have greatly influenced the description he gave of the deplorable and benighted condition of the other donkey-boys. He was evidently avenging himself by slandering them.

"They never goes near a church," said Phil, " unless it's to play at 'chuck and toss' on the tombstones ; and there's one boy, of the name of Bill Kurney, he's got the awfullest foul mouth for swearing you ever came near. You'd wonder his teeth wasn't blighted.and turned black in his head with the words he uses. You shall hear him when we get back."

If Captain Merton Crosier had been by himself, he would have been sure to burst out laughing at this last speech, but the stern-looking father evidently was a great restraint on the son's conduct, and as Mr. Merton, senior, was muttering, "This is sad, very sad," Mr. Merton, junior, thought it more prudent to appear deeply afflicted by the terrible account.

"Never use bad language, my young friend," said the papa, exhortingly.

"I never do, sir, only to the donkeys," answered Phil, putting on a look of innocence.

"But why swear at all?" urged the kind gentleman. "You will tell me that it gives force to your language. You will say that it ensures obedience through fear ; but since it is only the sound of your voice, and not the words, that these animals obey, what need is there for you to blaspheme when a shout would answer as well? Do you understand, my young friend?"

Here the little lady, coming to Phil's defence, said,—

"You mustn't scold him, papa. Remember, I told you he never had any parents to watch over him."

Everybody stared at Phil with curiosity. The French officer appeared quite overcome with sympathy and cried out, "Pauvre moutard!" and the English one looked knowing, as if he suspected that the boy had been gammoning his sister. The solemn Mr. Crosier, senior, shook his head, and asked,—

"Are both your parents dead?"

"My mother's dead," replied Phil. "She went away before I can remember her ; but perhaps my father's alive—though it wouldn't matter, as far as I am concerned, for he never seems to have cared much about me, or else, why did he leave a fellar?"

"Did he desert your mother?" inquired Captain Merton Crosier.

"I don't know if he deserted her, because she died," continued Phil; "but he seems to have left me to take pot-luck."

"Quel scelerat!" exclaimed the French colonel, looking the picture of indignation—as if he would like to punish the villain. "Now, with us in France, such a similar thing is impossible. Our system of passports, however you Anglais grumble at them, prevent such affairs."

"And was your father called Merton?" inquired the old gentleman.

Phil answered, "I don't know about that. I'm called Philip Merton, and Katherine Merton was the name my mother went by—so Nurse Hazlewood told me."

"Katherine Merton!" he cried, with a tone of surprise. Then, in a more quiet voice he added, "And who is Nurse Hazlewood, my little man?"

For a moment the boy hesitated, as if ashamed to reply; but at length, as if he had conquered any feeling of pride, he answered,—

"I ought to call her mother; and I used to when I was young, for she was as good and kind to me as she was to her own child. But if you want to know who she was, she was nurse at the workhouse where I was sent, and it was she as told me my mother was a lady."

There was no reason on earth why the solemn old gentleman should have suddenly become so excited, and anxious to learn more of the history of this boy. Over and over again did he ask, "And are you sure, my young friend, you cannot remember your father's name?" And although Philip answered, "I tell you I never knowed him," until he was tired by the monotony of the reply, yet Mr. Crosier, senior, seemed unwilling to drop the subject, so often begging of the boy to try and remember, that at last little Helen, not understanding what such questionings could lead to, turned round laughing to her father to tease him for his curiosity. Then she saw that his face was pale and his eye unnaturally brilliant with excitement, and involuntarily she cried out,—

"What is the matter, papa? Are you ill? You are so dreadfully pale! Merton, dear, make him sit down."

The solemn papa did not like to be stared at and pitied. He said it was all nonsense, and, forcing up a laugh, asked how they imagined that one of his age could walk so great a distance without feeling distressed? But that was only an excuse, for he was suffering from excitement, and not fatigue, as was evident by his manner.

There was a dead silence among the party when the next question was put, and even Phil was frightened at finding so much interest taken about him.

"Did you ever, my boy—now try and remember—don't be afraid to take your time—did you ever hear anybody mention a person named Vautrin?"

He waited almost breathlessly, until Phil replied,—

"No, I can't say I ever did hear of such a name; but there's a boy on the Heath as is called Volby, if you think he'd suit you."

What should have made the French colonel start and fall back, as if somebody had suddenly called out his name? On the cards he carried in his pocket was engraved "Le Colonel Victor Baudin Rattaplan, du 11e Leger." Then what should he care for such a person as Vautrin? And when the papa took out his pocket-book to write down the name of the workhouse where Philip had passed his infancy, why did this French officer keep on repeating to himself, "St. Lazarus Union," as if he was afraid of forgetting the address?

What will not people do for a few hours' pleasure? There were two maid-servants living in a big white house on the right-hand side-

of the Heath—where the ivy on the walls stands out like a portico, so
that when it rains the cows will go there for shelter—and these
two poor girls would get up at four o'clock in the morning for what?
—to have a donkey ride. They had got their long day's work before
them, and anybody would fancy that every moment of sleep would
be of consequence to give them strength for the day's labour, but
merely for the pleasure of sitting upon a donkey's back, and feeling
it move along with them, they did not mind rising betimes, before
any of the family were stirring. They would go to Phil overnight,
and coax him to be waiting round the corner, and as the clock struck
four they would come out of the back garden gate, and be off on the
romp. It was not a bad job for Philip, although it did come rather
too early in the morning, for when they returned back again at six,
they would give the boy such a big bundle of bread and meat that he
had no occasion to buy any more food for that day at least. They
never met with anybody during such rides, unless it was old Tom
Pugh, the water-carrier, who, striding his tub on wheels like a
temperance Bacchus, sat looking at his white horse, whose wabbling
ears dangled about almost as loosely as the pails swinging behind
the vehicle.

" Good morning, Tom," the girls would cry out. " Don't you tell
you saw us, or we'll beat you as black as a cinder."

While Philip was galloping these girls across the Heath, he saw
something lying on the ground, and as the donkey-boys are always
on the look-out for treasure, the moment Phil saw this something, he
dropped his stick as if accidentally, as an excuse for lagging behind,
and returning to fetch it, picked up a purse.

Judging from human nature, and having closely watched the manners and habits of infants of a tender age, we have come to the conclusion that honesty is entirely a matter of education, and is no more
an instinct born in us than forgiving your enemy, or eating with a
fork. Now, as the education of donkey-driving boys may be safely
quoted at nil, much honesty cannot be expected of them, and even if
it was, the expectation would most certainly be disappointed. When
Sam Curt one day picked up a gold snuff-box, he never for one
moment thought it might possibly belong to somebody, but jerking it
hastily among some ferns, he marked the spot well, and fetched the
treasure at night.

As there was not a soul to be seen stirring on the Heath, Philip did
not think it worth while to take any such precaution with his god-
send, but with a clown's rapidity slipped it into his pocket, thinking
to himself " the early bird catches the early worm," and a very pretty
worm too. He was all impatience until the two servant girls had returned home again, for his fingers were itching to open the clasp and
peep into the interior. He was quite astonished at his good fortune,
for it was along that very road that he had passed on the previous
evening when he was escorting the little school-girl. He felt sure
the purse was not there then, or he must have seen it. When the

ride was over he did not wait to take the donkeys back to the stand, but sought out some very secluded spot and took out the treasure.

"It's a first-rate looking thing," he thought to himself, "and must have gold in it. If there are only a few shillings, however, I shan't mind."

When he opened it, the features of his face relaxed with astonishment, and he flung the purse away with disappointment. There was not a single coin in any of its pockets. The only thing he could find was an old doubled-up card, with "Viscount Ascot" printed in minute letters in the centre and surmounted by an imposing crest.

He could not help exclaiming in disgust, "A viscount, and not a farthing! Why I'm as good a viscount as he is! Call hisself a nobleman, and not carry even such a thing as a pint of beer about him. If that's your aristocracy, why a donkey-boy's a king—that's all."

There was a certain stout foreigner with a thick moustache who would have given Phil a golden sovereign to have regained that purse, although there was not even a farthing in the pockets: but how was the boy to know that?

CHAPTER XI.

CAPTAIN MERTON CROSIER AT HOME.

WITH a handsome allowance from his father, and sick leave of absence from his regiment, Captain Crosier leads the happiest life of any man in London. He has capital rooms in Harley Street. He has bargained for a latch-key, and every morning of his life his breakfast is brought up to him in bed.

If the stern papa, who has just come up from Swanborough to settle some business in town, had the least idea that his son was such a dissipated young dog, it would have caused him not only to feel great parental grief, but also to diminish, by at least one half, the cheques that every three months were paid in to Captain Merton's account. But whilst the "governor" is stopping at Biddle's Hotel in Brook Street, the son is on his best behaviour, and conducts himself with the decorum of a bishop. He bewails in private, to a few intimate friends, what a dreadful bore it is to him to be always bothering about with the old gentleman, and complains of the slow hotel dinners, and being doomed to drink glass for glass from the one bottle of port. But, as he says, "one must be civil to one's own father, you know."

When Captain Crosier dines and spends the evening with his parent, he rings for his hat and gloves as the clock strikes half-past ten, apologizing for his early departure by saying, "I'm sorry to leave you so soon, sir; but I'm on sick leave, and eleven o'clock is my time for bed." Then the father, delighted to see such prudence in his boy, mutters to himself, "I'm glad to see Merton so steady and careful," and shakes his hand almost with gratitude for such exemplary conduct. But, instead of bending his steps towards Harley Street, Captain Crosier lights his cigar and saunters towards the Haymarket, there to mingle with choice spirits like himself, and pass the night in visiting the saloons and night-houses, until he has spent all the money in his pocket but just sufficient to pay for his cab home. It is his boast that he was never yet so "cut" but what he could, after a little fencing with the keyhole, open the street-door for himself.

The captain has been fortunate in finding such excellent apartments, for they have all the convenience of chambers, without their solitude. He seems to do just as he likes in the house. Sometimes, when he comes home at four o'clock in the morning, he will begin to play the piano, but no complaints are ever made about the unreasonable hour of the performance, although the captain, at such times, generally presses down the pedal, and his touch, if not musically correct, is, however, both brilliant and powerful. The handsomest piece of furniture in the room is decidedly a tulip-wood cabinet for holding cigars. There are only one or two chairs, which it is not safe to sit down upon, and the carpet, which was once very handsome, would have a cheerful effect still if the captain and his friends did not spill beer on the white parts and tread cigar-ashes in the dark ones. The walls had a more furnished look when the dissipated lodger first came, but he insisted upon having the three-quarter portrait of the late Mr. Bullunty, by Tomeston, removed from the chamber, giving as a reason, that whenever he returned home at night the head used to stare at him. He threatened that if it was not taken away he should be forced to smash the masterpiece.

About twelve o'clock in the day, Captain Crosier, with his dressing-gown on, throws himself upon the sofa, ready to receive any friends that may drop in upon him. In they come, one after another, Fred Tattenham and Tom Oxendon, both calling out lustily for bitter ale, then Charley Sutton to borrow a clean collar and a razor, and after a time le Colonel Victor Baudin Rattaplan, who makes himself so thoroughly at home that, without being invited, he helps himself to a cigar, and sends clouds of smoke down his nose, as he exclaims, "Dese cigar is capital, mon cher, but dey wants to be kep."

"How did you manage Oakes, last night, after I went away?" asks the captain.

"We put him in a cab, and sent him home," answers Fred Tattenham; "I never saw a fellow so utterly done up."

"I wonder what's become of Tom Garden?" inquires Charley Sutton.

"Oh, he's gone to Boulogne, or the Bench," suggested his friend

Tattenham. "Where did you disappear, colonel?" he adds, after a time, turning to the Frenchman.

"We play at ecarte till breakfast-time," is the answer.

"Then you haven't been to bed?" inquires the captain.

"Ma foi, non. I never care to sleep;" and he smiles as if he thought everybody was saying, "What an extraordinary man he is!" He is asked if he won, and he shrugs his shoulders in reply, that being a kind of answer which can be taken either way, although if the truth must be told, the colonel seldom loses at cards, although he generally plays high.

Whilst Captain Crosier is lighting his cigar, a sudden thought strikes him. He says between the whiffs, "Oh, I've had such a jolly letter from Viscount Ascot, saying that he can't go to the prize-fight on Monday." As he is rather proud of his aristocratic friend, he takes this letter from his pocket and reads it aloud :—

"'DEAR CROSIER,—A hundred thanks, but I'm engaged, though I'd give pounds to be with you. You must be the bearer of my apologies to our different friends. Yours, &c.,

"'ASCOT.'"

When he has finished reading he throws the letter down on the table, adding, "Isn't that like the old fellow—short and jolly?"

Le Colonel Victor Baudin Rattaplan, du 11ᵉ Leger, says, "The style is quite Anglais," and picks up the note. Whilst the others are chatting, he appears to be making quite a study of the handwriting. The words which seem to interest him most are "hundred," "pounds," and "bearer." The signature of the noble lord he apparently admires excessively, for he twists the paper about, and peers into it with extraordinary curiosity. When he puts the note down again, he gives a hasty glance round the room, as if to see if his actions have been noticed, and then, finding nobody had paid the least attention to what he was doing, he slips the epistle under a book, and assuming his most careless manner, walks up and down the room with his hands in his pockets. He is in such excellent spirits, and laughs and jokes with so much vivacity, that it is impossible to believe that he has been up all night. All the fellows agree that the French are a wonderful people and never seem to be tired of amusing themselves, but as the colonel says, "He has passed too many sleepless nights encamped in de plains of Algeria to feel 'epuised' with a little card-playing." When he is asked to tell some of the French stories, he makes the young fellows shout again with his wit, and, indeed, we regret deeply that we cannot introduce some of his capital anecdotes into these pages, only sometimes gentlemen in the army meet with adventures that are not exactly fitted for the ears of civilians.

When le Colonel Victor Baudin has concluded his little performance, the chatting again commences.

"Any of you fellows going to Cressy's party?" asks Charley Sutton.

"I can't stand their sherry," mutters Tom Oxendon.

"The Cressy girls are pretty," remarks another, affectedly.

"I like Julia, the youngest—she is the best of the batch," murmurs the captain; and then, looking up at the ceiling, he adds, "The little devil squeezed my hand whilst I was dancing with her."

The windows were open, and Fred Tattenham had been smoking a cigar on the balcony. He seemed very busily engaged watching the house opposite, staring up at one of the upper windows so earnestly, that Charley Sutton calls out, "What the deuce is Fred up to?" This made everybody else want to know what has so interested their friend, and in a body they darted towards the balcony.

The apartments of the gallant Captain Crosier were exactly in front of the excellent brick-built tenement of which Miss Tomsey held the lease. Following the direction of Mr. Tattenham's up-turned face, everybody discovered the reason why the sly Fred preferred lounging on the balcony. At one of the upper windows sat Bertha, doing needlework, and looking so innocent and beautiful it made you think better of the world to look at her.

Charley Sutton gave Tattenham a tremendous slap on the back, and cried, "You dog! I thought there was a woman somewhere!" All the other fellows had something to say to the detected delinquent, and in rapid succession he was either poked in the side, or jocularly termed "a scoundrel" or "a villain," but which terms, although they have a harsh sound, had really a complimentary meaning, and were intended to refer to the gay Lothario's usual gallantry and great affection for the female sex.

The little girl was stitching away quite unconscious of the commotion she had caused on the other side of the way. If she could have had the least idea that five men were staring at her, and watching all her actions, you must not imagine that she would have remained by the open window. "No: in less than a minute she would have jumped off her chair, and, blushing as red as the cherry riband round her neck, have retired into the dark recess of the room, where most likely she would have muttered something about impudent fellows, and began working again. There was not a more modest or better-hearted girl in Harley Street than Bertha, but nothing annoyed her more than being stared at.

Thousands of times had Captain Crosier seen her working at that window before, and he knew as well as possible how easily the girl was driven away, because one morning he had ventured to give a "hem!" in the hopes of making her look at him, and captivating her with his good looks. But as the only effect his "hem!" had was to drive the girl away, he had never repeated the experiment. Of an afternoon, whenever Bertha took her seat by the window, the captain's usual practice was to half conceal himself behind the chintz drawing-room curtains, and watch the girl through his opera glass.

He would remain for hours enjoying himself in this manner. He had confessed to Lord Oakes that there was "a little devil of a witch in his street on whom he was quite spooney." He became quite angry when Charley Sutton, in the exuberance of his high enjoyment, expressed his intention of whistling to "the little thing" so as to see what kind of a face she had.

It happened most conveniently that Captain Crosier was the possessor of three opera glasses, which, on the impulse of the moment, he produced. Whenever his friends came to see him, he did all he could to amuse them. The telescope which it was his custom to take to the sea-side with him was offered to and accepted by Tom Oxendon, and then did these wild young gentlemen proceed to examine the unconscious Bertha as deliberately as if she had been a dancer at the opera.

How pretty the innocent child looked with her head bent down over her work, and her white face shining with a soft, pearly lustre against the dark interior of the room. Her hair was of a rich autumnal brown, and her neck being arched forward, exposed to view the thick coil circling at the back of the head, which, if it had been undone, must have reached down to her knees at least. How many ladies would have given the last ten years of their lives to have had such hair as that! But Bertha wore her glory without any attempt at display, the rich glossy bands being plainly smoothed down over her temples, and, crossing to the back, hiding all of the ear but the little cherry end.

" These beauties did the gentlemen discover in less time than it has taken us to relate them. They declared Bertha to be so pretty that she amply repaid the exertion of looking at her. Each one endeavoured to be the first to point out some new charm, and a kind of race of discoveries commenced.

" These are capital glasses, Merton," said Fred Tattenham, peering so intently that his face was screwed up as if he had the sun in his eyes. "I can actually see the creases in her plump, creamy little throat."

After everybody had noticed these creases, Charley Sutton exclaimed, "The little darling! I wish I could see her eyes. Ain't they rather goggly, Merton ? "

" If you mean large—yes," answered the captain; "as large as a fawn's, and as gentle."

" If she had ten thousand pounds I'd marry her," volunteered Mr. Sutton; and after a second he added, "Ah! I'd do it for eight thousand—down!"

The Frenchman, who had been having a peep at the girl, determined, as everybody seemed to admire her so much, to be original, and differ from the general opinion. So he said, with indifference, " Yase, she is varry well, my dear fellows, but in Paris I could show you tousands like her, and with plus d'esprit in the face."

This so enraged Fred Tattenham, that his patriotism was roused, and he answered, very rudely, "Then I wish I'd known you when I was in Paris, colonel, for I never saw a pretty woman all the time I was there."

But Victor Baudin merely shrugged his shoulders in reply, as if it were a loss of time to argue with one so blind.

Everything that poor Bertha did was noticed with great exactness. A lock of hair shorter than the rest was seen to flutter on her forehead, and everybody watched the rebellious curl with absorbing interest.

"I wish she'd give it to me," sighed Oxendon; "I'd have a pocket-handkerchief marked with it."

By-and-by Bertha raised her hand and scratched the end of her arm, which was obviously tickling.

"Let me do that for you, dear," muttered Fred Tattenham, speaking at the girl.

How long these gentlemen would have remained looking through their opera-glasses and telescope was uncertain, but when Bertha suddenly rose from her chair and disappeared there was a cry of regret from them all, and a discussion was commenced as to whether she would come back again.

The Frenchman burst out laughing. "My dear enfants," he remarked, shaking his head, "do you fancy she not know that you looking at her? I tell you she know. That is the way with your froides Anglaises. It is prudery, not what you call modesty."

If ladies could occasionally overhear the conversations that take place at these bachelor meetings, no doubt their opinions of man's character would be greatly altered. In the same way, if it were possible to gain admission to any of those friendly chats that take place between young ladies, what a flood of light it would let in upon the mysteries of the female heart!

As Bertha did not return to her chair, the gentlemen grew tired of staring up at the window for nothing, and again adjourned to the room to smoke and drink bitter ale. The first thing Fred Tattenham said, as he threw himself into an easy-chair, was, "I shall look after that little darling, she's too pretty to be lost."

This speech roused the captain, who, lifting his eyebrows in astonishment, cried, "Well, that is cool! No poaching here, Fred."

"Poaching!" answered Tattenham. "I discovered her first, my good sir, five weeks ago. I take possession of her by right of discovery."

"You discovered her—you?" roared Merton, in disgust. "Why, I have known her these six months. No! honour amongst thieves! Don't rob a poor man of his girl!"

They quarrelled for a little time longer as to whose property Bertha really was, and at one time the words grew very high. You would almost have imagined that they were a party of American planters talking about their slaves, for they made use of such phrases as, "The girl's mine"—"I won't part with her"—and "You have no right to her." If Bertha could have known how quietly she had been disposed of, she would have been rather startled.

" You are only wasting your time running after the girl," sneered Tattenham at Merton; "you had better give her up to me. You'll never succeed. You haven't the industry."

To have his reputation as a successful man among women attacked, and in his own house, and before so many people too, made the captain feel very savage.

"What will you bet ?" he cried out. "Make it fifty."

" But how on earth are you to settle it ? " asked Charley Sutton.

" The best method," suggested le Colonel Rattaplan, " is to ask us all to a dinner at Richmonds dis day six month, and she shall be de queen of de festin—if Crosier can bring her."

"Done !" said Crosier, "and the fellow who loses pays for the dinner as well."

It was nearly six o'clock when the smoking party broke up. When they were gone, Crosier had occasion to refer to the note he had received from Viscount Ascot, but though he and Mr. Cutler, his man, searched for nearly a quarter of an hour, the note could not be found.

"Let me see, who was reading it last ?" said the captain, searching in his memory. "I think it was the French colonel. I suppose he must have lit his cigar with it." And consoling himself with the philosophy that "if it was lost that ended the matter," he dismissed the subject from his mind.

CHAPTER XII.

THE FIGHT FOR THE CHAMPIONSHIP.

WE are going to a prize-fight with Captain Crosier and his friends. We are obliged to go, because the captain is supporting Jack Hammer, one of the combatants—indeed, the last deposit of £15 which was made for this important and interesting affair at Alf Cox's "Jolly Trainer" came out of the gallant officer's pocket.

But, before starting, we can promise those who accompany us on this valorous trip that the combat will not be nearly so terrible as they imagine it to be.

How is it that they have never been enabled to put down prize-fights in England ? They could stop bull-baiting and cock-fighting, but it seems as if pugilism defied every attempt at its suppression.

The most curious circumstance is, that this propensity to fisti-cuffing seems born in the British subject. Little boys of seven and eight, who, if they know anything of the use of the fist, must do so by instinct, will square up to each other and begin to pummel their poor little round faces, and all the time they seem to be acquainted with the rules of the ring, and no matter how blinded they may be by rage, they subscribe to the professional etiquette. Look at an English boy in a French school, and see what deference [is paid to the boxeur by his companions, and how carefully they avoid bringing themselves under the penalty of his fist. How to goodness can anybody fancy that it is possible to do away with prize-fighting in England? It's born in us, and is not the cause, but the result of, our bravery. We are a hard-muscled race, and as long as we consider it our right to eat meat at our meals, just so long will our deltoid muscles be as hard as those of a gladiator, and our courage as reckless and impulsive as that of a bull-dog.

The only good resulting from racing is the improvement of the breed of English horses. You have only to travel twenty miles out of England to understand the difference between the round-nosed, big-headed steed of the foreigner, and the high-spirited, exquisitely proportioned animal of our own country. This training of horses is as much English as the art of boxing, and whether it be on the Champ-de-Mars, or the Petroveski plains outside Moscow, you will find your English trainers great persons in authority.

Pugilism has done for Englishmen the same as high breeding has done for British horses. The mere men who fight are of themselves low and useless. The result of their lives may be put down at a two hours' fighting match. But these mere sloggers and bruisers have a great influence over the courage of the nation, and in judging them, we have no more right to look only to the brutalities of the combat than we have to object to the dressing of a field because the manure has a disagreeable odour. The men who marched up the steep accli-vities of the Alma owed their courage to the influence of pugilism. The sailors who, to prevent the escape of the enemy's ship, will lash the vessels together, owe their daring to the influence of the prize-ring. As long as we are Englishmen, so long will pugilism endure; and when we cease to enjoy that brave character which influences the entire world, then the fist will be superseded by the dagger, and the "fair" fight give place to the midnight assassination.

We admit it is a low kind of warfare, but still it is not a mere brutal display of strength. It is a science of great difficulty, and governed by laws wonderful for their generosity to the conquered, and their restraint upon the conqueror. These scenes are the last remnants of the days of the tournament, and if they have not all the trappings and display of the mediæval combat, they have in its stead more generous chivalry.

The day when the celebrated Ned Tongs, through the medium of a well-known sporting paper, challenged the renowned Jack Hammer to fight him in five or six months for any sum from £100 a side up to £500, the pugilistic world was quite taken aback by the temerity of

the man. Every night the parlour of the " Jolly Trainer " was noisy
with the discussions upon Ned's foolhardiness. It seemed to be the
general opinion that Mr. Tongs had overrated his capabilities, as he
would find out by the " thumping damages " when the cause came to
be heard. Jack Hammer was the champion of England,—a man
standing over six feet, with a paving-stone of a fist, a chest like a
dray-horse, and weighing almost as much as a prize ox. He fought
his first battle when he was seventeen, and was then considered the
most promising little big one of the day. He kept on fighting steadily
up the road to glory until, when his face was dented in like an old
hat, he attained the highest honours the boxing profession can award,
and became champion of England. He was celebrated for being a
terrific hitter with his right, and if any of his blows got home, a
coroner's inquest was sure to follow. Now, on the other hand, Ned
Tongs was both a middle height and a middle weight, and it was a
matter of wonderment why he took so strong a fancy to try conclu-
sions with Jack Hammer. He was known by his brother pugs to be
one of the gamest hands in the ring, but as for having a chance for
the victory, that was absurd and silly. It is true that Ned Tongs
had done some work in his time, and was rather looked up to as an
enterprising bruiser; but, as Alf Cox remarked, " It was backing a
fly against a bird. What chance," he asked, " can ten stone eight
have against fourteen stone six? Why, no more than a pane of
glass against a sledge hammer. And," added Mr. Cox, prophetically,
" if Ned gets one of Jack's ' hot 'uns,' he must say good-bye to daylight! "

The place of meeting for all those who wished to witness this great
championship fight was the railway station, and as the clock struck
seven, Captain Crosier and his friends drove up to the terminus, and
being well-known " Corinthians," as the patrons of the ring are
called, were received with much respect by the different members of
the " milling " profession.

The crowd assembled must have numbered some five hundred men,
all dressed in the fancy fashion, wearing shooting jackets and cloth
caps of every colour. They were all pushing very savagely to reach
the ticket-box, and the uproar was increased by those in the back-
ground shouting out to their friends who were getting their passes
such directions as, " Bill, get three for me—Tom Mitchett; " or,
" Just collar mine, will you, Fred ? "

Having secured their seats, our Corinthians passed the time in
looking at the boxing celebrities walking about the platform. In
rapid succession Captain Crosier pointed them out to his friends :
"There's the ' Clapham Smasher ' and his crew, and there's the
' Southwark Pounder,' who gave Tom Fig such a licking the other
day."

" Where are our men ? " asked Tom Oxendon; and he was informed that in order to keep clear of the police, they had been " for-
warded " overnight.

It was an ordinary train by which they were travelling, and among the passengers were a few women, who could not for the life of them imagine why all the carriages should be full of ugly-faced men with broken noses. They were afraid to trust themselves among such a savage-looking crew, and seemed as much alarmed as if they had suddenly tumbled among a band of brigands.

During the journey, the captain, who knew the country well, endeavoured to chat away the monotony of a three hours' run. "It's a nasty country for hunting—so full of rabbit-holes," he would say at one time; and if any one asked whose pack was there, and if there were any foxes, he seemed able to give the required information. He would point out farmers' houses where he had many a time taken a glass of brandy, or, coming to some little secluded woody spot, he would describe a picnic he once had there, and detail a very curious adventure, in which a very lovely young lady acted very imprudently.

It had been arranged by those in power that, to avoid the rabble who always flock to such sights, the train should travel out some seventy miles towards the coast, where a steamer would be in waiting to convey the select party to the place of combat. At every station it was noticed that policemen had been sent down to seize the combatants if they showed themselves. At one stopping-place a crowd was seen to hurry along the platform, following a brown-faced man.

"There's Jack Hammer!" cried Captain Crosier, springing to the window. "What a man he is! If Ned has a taste of his right, he'll be done for."

"Ay, that's Jack, true enough," said a stranger in the carriage, "and as good-hearted a man as any in England. You might throw a glass of ale in his face, and he wouldn't hurt you."

Presently another man, equally brown but not so tall as Jack Hammer, passed along, and this time everybody recognized Ned Tongs.

"How well he looks," cried Crosier. "Confound him! who's his trainer, I wonder?"

Great excitement was produced at this station by a man running from carriage to carriage, offering to bet five to four on Tongs.

After everybody had many times inquired how much farther they had to go, the terminus was reached, and the crowd rushed towards the steamer. The two combatants had already been taken out, and were seen trudging along far ahead, surrounded by their backers and seconds, concealing them as much as possible, for fear of the police.

Now boats of every kind came rushing up to the water's edge to carry the passengers to the steamer lying in wait at a slight distance from the shore. Cockle-shells intended to carry four were crammed with twelve, and so tossed about by the waves every moment, that you expected to see them sink: but none of the small craft, from the

"Lively Jane," scarcely bigger than a sofa, to the "Saucy Ann," a large fishing-smack, met with any accident. There was a dreadful scuffle before any one was received on board the steamer, for the admission was by a two-guinea ticket—an expense which many were desirous of escaping. "Where's your ticket?" shouted the man at the gangway; "can't come up here without a ticket. Pay the two sovereigns, then. Here, take money from this gentleman, sir." This reads very quietly, but it was spoken with foaming of mouth and shaking of fists. Some, who endeavoured to push their way into the vessel, were hurled back again at the risk of death by drowning, for an order had been given to call some fighting men to keep order, and such gentlemen do not stand on trifles.

When the man with the ropes for forming the ring and an interesting cargo of hampers had been taken on board, the steamer began to paddle away. Then, from the cabin beneath, up stepped a man wearing a blue velvet cap. He was brown as a Spaniard, and his close-shorn face and short hair—where gripping was impossible—told you that he was one of the heroes of the day. He looked as hard as iron, and there was great strength in his thick neck, and carelessness in his bulldog air. He lay down on the ground, with a horsecloth over him, supporting his head on the big brown hand that was soon to do such execution. When people asked Ned Tongs whether he felt "up to the mark," he smiled and showed his white teeth, but would not bother himself to answer. On the other side of the boat was another man with a blue velvet cap, lying down with his head in the backer's lap. He, too, was as brown and silent as an Indian, and only roused himself when he was brought some food. Then the lion stood erect—a heavy man, taller than any about him, with a flat, battered face, on which the scars showed like white streaks.

The Corinthians were very numerous, and Captain Crosier met with many majors and lieutenants from such and such a regiment, who talked alternately of the opera last night and the fight to come. Sandwiches were offered, and pocket-flasks passed round. In the fore-cabin the contents of the hampers had been laid out, and half-cold ribs of beef, chickens that had been roasted into only a pink state, veal, and lettuces, were spread upon the table in picnic confusion. Bottled ale had risen to three shillings a bottle, and wine had reached a fabulous price. Men with stone jugs under their arms paraded the deck, calling out, "Who's for a go of brandy?" It was not like the ordinary cognac, but an opaque liquid, brown as strong tea.

How could they have known on the other side of the river that the fight was to take place there? yet the shores were crowded with men, and as the steamer approached the shore a regatta of little boats came off to keep her company, and follow her as a flock of swallows chase a hawk.

Tired with the length of the journey, the fighting community began to gamble on the deck. They had brought dice with them, and sat down to play at hazard. Men in dirty clothes pulled out sovereigns from their pockets, and when they were lost borrowed more from their friends.

There were other gentlemen who had got, somehow or other, on board, who were also fond of gambling; but they only played a very safe game with three cards, out of which they wager that nobody will discover the jack.

At length the place of disembarkation was reached. An embankment of big stones, a dyke half-covered with sea-weeds, formed a kind of screen, hiding the fields on the other side from any one passing on the river. It was a capital snug place; and the little fleet of sailing-boats circled round the steamer in miraculous numbers, and carried to the shore as many as could be crammed on to their benches. The river was covered with craft. Another steamer, which had come from London at cheap fares, came panting up, and poured out its rough, noisy passengers. There were barges, and fishing-smacks, and little sailing-skiffs, and they crept up one after another until the water was crowded as at a regatta. The passengers were landed in the water, and had to scramble up the steep embankment, slipping over the sea-weed or wrenching their feet between the stones. The field of rich grass was soon trampled down by the crowds rushing in the direction of the men who were already measuring off the ring, inside which the fight was to take place. Whilst the stakes were being driven into the ground, those who had bought tickets for the inner ring stuck the blue paper in their hatband, and took up their places near the ropes. The card-sharpers, too, commenced business with their three-card trick, and picked up the sovereigns as fast as the Corinthians chose to stake them. They spread a little green baize upon the grass, and as they shifted the cards about pattered in the old style—"These two you lose; this one you win. I bet anybody fifty sovereigns that they cannot discover the jack." Then up would come the accomplice, and instantly win five pounds. But Jack Anderson, who was "working" the trick, seemed to take such losses very easily, and cried out, "I never mind losing, gentlemen; if I didn't lose sometimes everybody would win always, and then there would be an end to sport. I'd sooner wager fifty sovereigns than ten, and ten than five."

Now the preparations for the fight were proceeding with rapidity. Some three thousand persons had gathered round the ropes, and formed a sloping amphitheatre of heads, the nearest to the ring lying down, those further beyond standing up, and the mob behind raised up on platforms. Bundles of straw were distributed to the different Corinthians to soften their seats on the ground. Boys with dinner-knives were busy clearing away the grass in the ring, and the fighting-men who were appointed ring-keepers, to keep order, were provided with gutta percha whips to beat back the crowd. But suddenly all heads were turned towards the fields, and a cry of disgust was raised as a farm labourer on horseback was seen galloping towards them. For a moment the proceedings were stayed, until Captain Crosier could square the man with half a sovereign. The yokel remained to see the sight.

There was a cheer as the two combatants appeared, their seconds conveying the carpet-bags which contained their professional costume. They had taken off their coats, when another cry of despair was raised, and climbing over the ditches were seen the five dark forms of policemen. "The peelers!" shout the mob; and the umpire, springing to his feet, cried, "Take the men on board;" and before the constables had neared the spot, the boat which carried the heroes of the day was alongside the steamer.

There were at least three thousand men, and yet five policemen were sufficient to disperse them. It is true that a little joking took place, and the sergeant was asked, "Now you've come, what have you got?" Those who were pulling up the stakes inquired of the police "How they enjoyed their walk, and when they had ordered their carriages to fetch 'em?"

Back went the boats to the steamers, the river was dotted with the craft going and returning, and the black specks of passengers were seen climbing the vessel's side. Before he entered his boat, Captain Crosier called out, "Mind, none of you watermen help the police;" and by the unanimous "All right!" shouted in answer, there was no mistaking which side the watermen took.

Off went the steamer again, followed by the fleet of small craft, leaving the five policemen standing on the embankment. A shout of laughter was raised in derision against them, but it soon ceased when a pigeon was seen to fly up into the air, for everybody knew that an express had been sent off to warn the station higher up. Now came the hunt after another and safer fighting-place, and at length the order was given to "stop her" opposite some fields, in the centre of which was a quiet farm, from which a sheep-dog rushed out and barked violently. This time, at any rate, there was no chance of interruption, for the farmer longed to see the combat himself, and offered to lend a meadow at the back of some sheds for the battle to be fought in. Once more the stakes were driven into the earth, and the spectators took their places. Even the tops of the sheds were seized upon by some as a kind of gallery from which to see the fight.

The two men stripped to the waist, and clothed only in the lightest of drawers and the neatest of ankle-jacks, entered the ropes, smiling in the most amiable manner. When time was cried they shook hands heartily, and then stood facing each other as if to allow the crowd an opportunity of examining the build and condition of their bodies. But although each man looked the picture of good temper, and was smiling until his teeth looked white as almonds against the raisin-coloured skin, yet each countenance had a different kind of expression. The big man seemed to despise his diminutive rival,

and looked on him with pity and half contempt; he had told his
seconds that he would soon bring the drop scene down. But the
bold Ned Tongs appeared so impudently brave and so full of confidence, that many who were against him in the morning now began
to change their opinions.

There was great excitement about this contest, because it was
deemed to be a decisive trial between the old and the new styles of
boxing, whether the skill and activity of Ned were a match for the
weight and strength of Jack. It was remarked that the giant was
looking pulpy about the chest, and his back was pronounced to be
too fleshy, but the little 'un seemed like a model in wax, so firm and
hard did he look. But, after all, how was a rat of a man like Ned to
overcome such a bull-dog as Hammer? Betting began at four to five
on the "big 'un."

At length the men, still smiling as jollily as if black eyes and
broken noses were the best fun in the world, fell into their attitudes,
and the contest commenced.

The spectators were divided into two factions, and each, when
their man gained the least advantage, shrieked and howled with delight. The groans and abuse with which they visited the fighting of
the man they bet against—the coarse praise with which they urged
on their favourite, was the music to which the battle was fought.
The combatants themselves paid no attention to the riot, but continued to fight and smile, never appearing so thoroughly delighted
and amiable as when a blow told and left undeniable evidence of its
severity on the face or body of the receiver.

Each of the men had, previous to the fight, done a little profitable
business by selling pocket-handkerchiefs, which they called their
colours. The supporters of Hammer wore their white spotted silk
tied loosely round the neck, whilst Ned's friends sported a similar
ornament, but of an orange colour.

The first round was soon terminated, for Jack got a "cracker on his
nut" which knocked his "rammers" from under him, and the only
wonder was that he did not lose his head instead of his feet. A shout
of delight rose up from the white spots. Some cried, "Ah! where
was you then, Jack?" and one or two offers were made of five to six on
Tongs. The mob pressed forward and were beaten back by the ring-
keepers, who lashed the hats with their gutta percha whips, and
shouted, "Yah! yah! move back'ards, you roughs! what are you
bursting the ropes for?"

At the second round, the men seemed to have made up their minds
what their play was to be. Ned saw that his only chance of victory
was in tiring the giant out, so whenever the huge machine advanced
towards him, he retreated, skipping like a harlequin. In vain did the
white spots howl out, "He's like a d—d lambkin, that ain't fighting." After some sparring, Jack threw out his "pile-drivers" and
caught Ned on the "sniffer," but the nose didn't suffer much, and
the return blow came quick as a racer's kick, and "dabbed the

paint" about the giant's "meat-mincer," making the lip rise like
balm.

"How did that taste?" roared the yellows.

The betting, despite some who still cry out, "The old 'un for a
hundred," is now in favour of Tongs. Although he smiled most
blandly, Jack rushed like a Blunderbore up to the little 'un, but Ned
waltzed out of the way, administering a "full stop" on Jack's "head-
lamps," which changed the colour about the eye to a bright puce.
But the giant only laughed and shook his head, whilst the yellows
cried out, "An eye! an eye!" in a paroxysm of delight. Next came
some more dancing, which roused the indignation of the white spots
to such a fury that some yelled with rage, and others called it "a
game of touch;" but the yellows were in high glee, and asked
Hammer how the last blow tasted. They soon went to work again,
and then Ned sent his "hard dumplings" against Jack's "organ-
pipes," and upset the "port wine," the blood squirting from the nose
in such quantities that some shouted out in delight, "By God, he's
sick! he's sick!" But no such thing, Hammer was not sick, but
foaming with rage. He shook his head, and whilst the mob shrieked
out "He's lumpy!" he rushed in like a bull, and if his right had told,
where would Ned Tongs have been? But the giant is too slow with
his blows. When he struck he frowned with the strength he put into
his thrusts, and the active Tongs had plenty of time to ward them off,
though the immense force of the lunge was shown by the red and blue
marks that appeared on that part of the arm where the blow was
stopped. The little 'un again took to his legs and stepped away
grinning, but when he found Hammer hunting him he turned round
and administered a "chipper," which dented the snuffer-tray, opening
the nose like a ripe pea-pod. How the cheering burst forth from the
yellows as the blood fell drop by drop, fast as the dripping of melting
snow! The giant shook his head and gazed after the nimble Ned;
then he smiled and shook his head in despair, as much as to say, "He
runs away from me."

But before long he again went to business, banging out heavily as a
cart-horse, and Ned got a biter on his "day-opener" which made him
wink the eye violently, whilst the return compliment was on Jack's
"heaver," putting a dab of rouge on the breast. Being both of them
tired, they began to spar, so as to recover their breath. Standing
face to face, they began working their arms about, and with wonderful dexterity did they stop each other's thrust, the arms, when they
met, smacking together with the crack of a whip. After a time, Jack
jerked his drumsticks against Ned's "bone-box" with a force that
must have loosened every tooth, but, although the blood gushed out,
he continued to smile, and nodded approvingly to the leviathan,
caring little for the shout of "There's a doser!" raised by the white
spots. Watching his opportunity, he most amiably returned the
compliment on Jack's cheek, "peeling the bark," setting the "red
ink" running. and the blood streaming from the wound so covered

the face that the man was obliged to retire to his seconds, and get his face wiped with a wet sponge. Sniffing and working his tongue about he returned to the fight, but his eye looked so vicious that Ned took to hopping, and shuffled off, leaving the elephantine Hammer to wear out, his " shufflers " chasing him. Many were the howls of " Stand still, you running flunkey," and "He thinks it's a foot-race." But Ned paid no attention to the criticism, but followed his own tactics, dodging under the giant's arm when the latter had pinned him up in a corner, and wriggling like an eel until he had cleared himself from the perils of close quarters. The active skirmisher, watching his chances, made Hammer's pursuit one of difficulties, by administering another " clipper " into Jack's cheek, opening the old wound afresh, and completely " smashing his panels," and " knocking off the veneer." The giant tried to return the favour, but the little 'un was quadrilling on the light fantastic. So Hammer took advantage of the pause in the performance to go up to his corner, and once more get the " liquid rouge " wiped off his " wig-block." Up to this time, Ned's countenance was almost without a scratch, and presented a strong contrast to that of his wounded antagonist—as the white spots called it.

When Hammer's face had been washed, he returned to his work and the game of touch was renewed, Tongs skipping actively round the ring, and the big 'un so intent on the chase that he gave Ned time to administer a stinger on the wounded cheek, which this time quite upset the bottle, and drenched Jack in a plentiful supply of " his own training-oil." Some sparring and neat stopping followed, winding up with a chipper on the giant's " snuff-box," on the old sore. Then they went to work slogging, Jack delivering a " head-acher " on the " wool-grower," and Ned one not to be winked at on the " peepers," both loud double knocks. Before this round was concluded, Jack took a heavy instalment on his " turret," which must have damaged his " weathercock; " and then he once more retired to do his toilet and get his " red ink " blotted up, after which followed a little more chevy chase, ending in Ned touching up for the third time the giant's " snorer," in return for which Jack tapped with his fives on the little 'un's lid, and completely knocked him off his castors.

Before the fight was finished there were nine such rounds, but it would be monotonous to detail them at full length, for the description would too closely resemble what we have already attempted to picture. Captain Crosier and his friends were seated near the umpire, and although the combat ended in the defeat of the man he had backed, still he always speaks of this fight as being one of the most interesting sights he ever witnessed. "I wouldn't have missed it for thousands," he says, rather pompously, for he is known to be up to his eyes in debt.

Some of the blows were truly terrific. By continually hitting on the wound in Jack Hammer's cheek, it at last opened so that the

quarter of an orange might have been placed in the cut, and the blood flowing from it trickled on to his breast, until his whole body was red, as if he wore a huntsman's coat.. Then the mob yelled with delight, and the fellows vied with one another which should say the most insulting things to the wounded man, the most successful of which was, " S'help me, I should like to have your photograph."

When a round was ended, the men were seized by their seconds, and carried, as in a chair, to their corners, where they were made to rinse their mouths, and water was spurted into their faces to freshen them. From loss of blood and fatigue in chasing his rival, Jack Hammer at last grew so distressed that his head began to reel, but he still struck out vigorously, doing himself great harm by the useless energy of his wild thrusts. Whenever the moments of rest arrived, the seconds would rub his legs vigorously, endeavouring to remove their stiffness, and the yellows never failed to notice this, screaming out with joy, " Look what they're doing ! " or, " Go it, Ned, he hasn't got sixpenn'orth in him." It was certain that the giant would be conquered. His friends, in alarm, tried to assist him with advice, and his backers asked him " Why he didn't throw out his left ? " They endeavoured to inspirit him by hooting at the dancing Ned such remarks as, " Dear, dear, what a pity to fight such a foot-race ! " But it was evident that Hammer would have to yield up his title of champion of England before many rounds were fought.

It was terrible to look on when the men were fighting what proved to be their last round. The excited mob were pressing forward, caring nothing for the whips and orders of the ring-keepers. The worn-out giant seemed now more intent on defending himself than attacking his adversary. " At him, Ned," screamed the yellows. " Make him run about ! " " Break his heart ! " Whilst the only thing the white spots could, in their despair, think of, was to call out hopelessly, " Keep up, old man ! " If the staggering Jack received a blow, there was a yell of, " You went up for something that time ! " Whenever any of his vigorous lunges failed, a laugh of " Ha ! ha ! " burst out on every side. The man was fearful to look at. His face was like a ripe plum with the bruises, and the gash on his cheek was still streaming with blood. At length the final blow was given. It came with a crash upon his lip, tearing it like paper, and making the jaw swell out like the muzzle of an ape. Almost fainting, the big man was carried to his corner.

The brave fellow would have come forward again, but a shout of sympathy arose among the people, and Tongs was told not to touch the old man. The gallant Ned, folding his arms, and looking like a gladiator, stared at his brave foe, and then shrugged his shoulders, as much as to say, " What am I to do if he doesn't know when he's beaten ? " Some shouted, " Get a cradle for the old 'un ! " Others roared, " Send him home ! " until at last those who had been backing Jack Hammer, seeing that the mob were opposed to anything like brutality, declared that their man should fight no more. So the combatants shook hands, and smiled blandly on each other again. A sponge was thrown up as a signal that the combat was over, and Ned Tongs, amid the cheers of those who had been betting on him, was declared champion of England.

The crowd got back to their boats just as another bevy of police were seen advancing in the distance. Such an uproar of laughter greeted these constables that they heard it in the far off and stood still, as if aware that they had come too late. On board the steamer, the conqueror of the fight collected subscriptions among the passengers for the benefit of the conquered, and after he had handed over the twenty-five sovereigns to the dejected Hammer, he generously proceeded to plaister up the wounds that an hour before he had taken such trouble to inflict.

CHAPTER XIII.

ALL WORK AND NO PLAY.

THERE must have been a dash of the vagabond in Phil's disposition, for he hadn't been on the Heath a fortnight before he was perfectly disgusted with donkeys and driving. He repeated so often to himself that "it was the worst day's work he ever did when he first made the acquaintance of Mr. Tobias Sparkler," that at last he convinced himself the remark was true. He was restless and impatient; angry if anything was given him to do, and jealous if the job was handed over to another. The authoritative manner in which Swinging Fred ordered him about was especially displeasing to his pride, and many a time he had been on the verge of rebellion, and of telling the overseer to do it himself, and not to "come the bully over him."

Good Friday had invariably been an immense day for letting. Mr. Sparkler, with his six donkeys, took fifteen pounds, and one man, who had only two animals, earned nearly five sovereigns. So anybody can easily conceive how busy the Hampstead proprietors must have been, and how hard Phil and the other boys were obliged to work.

The holiday people were pouring on to the Heath, all very warm from climbing the hills, but all very good-tempered, and laughing with delight now they had "got there at last." You could tell by the girls' giggling faces that they had come out determined on a romp among the tall ferns and round the furze-bushes. The clean muslin dresses were to be soiled and tumbled till they were not fit to be seen. Most probably gathers would be torn out, and repairs made with pins, before night came. The young men, who now looked so genteel and spruce, would march back to town with their coats off and waistcoats undone, singing in chorus, and carrying boughs of trees or big bundles of buttercups.

Directly the donkey-stands were visible, everybody began to laugh afresh and talk of having rides. The little children became unmanageable, pointing at the poor beasts and crying out that they "wanted them;" big girls, with manly limbs, hinted unmistakably at being treated. Even elderly matrons, stout enough to test the strength of gig springs did not seem averse to a sixpenny jolt, though, it is true, they simpered modestly when the proposition was made, and said, "Go along!" and "To think, now!"

The crowd around the donkeys increased every moment, until at last the animals themselves were hidden by the ring fence of petticoats encircling the stand. Even those who did not intend to be customers felt a pleasure in witnessing the modest strugglings of mounting or the accidents of the start. The road becomes little better than a donkey race-course. The people on the paths seem almost as much amused with the sight as the riders with the exercise. So long as the troop is proceeding in an outward direction, the pace of the animals—except when just started—is easy enough, and there is no difficulty in keeping on. It is at this period of the trip that young ladies endeavour to give the bystanders an idea they are accomplished horsewomen. They rise in the saddle, and hold themselves in an upright attitude. Some of them will whisper to their friends that they find donkey-riding so different to going on horseback, and hint that, if they were mounted on a fiery, prancing steed, they would be in their glory. And all this time the donkeys, half-concealed under the flowing muslin skirts of the maidens, are ambling along at a shuffling, dust-making pace. But how different is it when the heads are turned homewards! How soon all the harmless bragging is put to the proof! Three or four smart blows send the squadron tearing down the road. The girls scream, and hold on by the pommels; back hairs come undone, and curls are soon jolted out of place. Bonnets are blown on to the back of the heads, and mantles nearly torn from the neck by the wind. One frightened maiden calls out as well as the bumping will let her, "Oh! don't, boy, don't!" and another implores the lad to "make him walk," and yet, between each supplication, comes a burst of laughter; and they roll about upon the saddle so that the lookers-on are expecting every moment to see them fall off. Many rude observations, too, are made by the young gentlemen strolling on the paths. They are particularly delighted if the wind should blow aside the petticoat sufficiently to discover the foot and ankle, for on such occasions they most indelicately shout out, "There's a leg!" Imaginary Christian names, too, are made use of by these rude fellows, and they exclaim, "Oh, Sarah! ain't it nice?"

Never had Mr. Sparkler been seen in better spirits. He was

stuffing the sixpences and shillings into his pocket so fast that he began to doubt if it were in the power of calico to bear such a weight of coin. The young ladies that surrounded him were all grumbling about whose turn it was to have the next ride. No sooner did one party return than, even before the saddles were emptied of their flushed and tumbled occupants, the animals were seized upon and almost fought for.

On such a day as this prices rose. The ride which, on ordinary occasions, cost sixpence, was in great request at ninepence. The donkey market, like all others, follows the law of demand and supply. The boys, too, were ordered to forget their moral trainings, and instructed to cheat the distance as much as they could; and many an imprudent party that, before starting, had paid their two shillings a head for a trip to Highgate, were disgusted to find that, before they had gone one-third the distance, the order was given to return. "Why, you're not going to call this Highgate?" one young damsel would, with great indignation, exclaim. "It's been Highgate as long as I ever knowed it," Master Curt would reply. What did he care when all the young women screamed out, in every tone of voice, "We insist upon going further"? He did not even pay the slightest attention to their commands, but turned the donkeys round, and sent them galloping homewards at such a pace that the maidens were obliged to give over the dispute, and devote their entire attention to preventing themselves from being tossed off the saddle.

How many dreadful accidents did Phil have to witness in the course of these holiday experiences! And with how many sixpences was he bribed not to say anything about these fearful occurrences! Some young ladies would be so overcome with laughter that they became completely helpless and limp, and would fall backwards as if they had been on a sofa instead of a saddle. Others would have their gowns torn to pieces by the hoofs of their steeds, and be forced to return to their friends in petticoats of remarkable shortness, which set off to great advantage the black sandal crossing over the open work stocking.

Sometimes gentlemen of such lax morality that they had permitted themselves to indulge too largely in ardent drinks, would undertake to escort ladies on their sixpenny excursions. Their grotesque behaviour in the saddle, their wild shoutings, and unsteadiness of jockeyship, added considerably to the hilarity of the multitude.

Perhaps Mr. Sparkler was wrong in letting out his donkeys to such disorderly persons, but his excuse was, that, although they illused the animals shamefully, yet they paid him like princes—very often in the obliquity of their senses giving twice the sum they had bargained for. The way of the world—the donkeys receive the blows and the Sparklers take the salve.

And so these jolly days passed, the whole Heath ringing with laughter, and everybody almost wild with enjoyment, as if people came to Hampstead not merely to taste pleasure, but to gorge and gluttonize

on it. What would become of London without this large play-ground
for its children to sport in and scamper over? Would they, do you
think, remain quietly at their lessons of daily toil, and patiently get
through their tasks of hard industry, unless there were some such
place as this big Heath to remind them that they may sometimes be
happy and at liberty? It does the heart good to hear their noisy
mirth; their playfulness is that of a colt turned out to grass; they are
as wild with the freedom as a house-dog when its chain is unfastened.
The pure air is stimulating as wine, and, whilst drinking it in, they
giggle and royster like topers. Those who object to the jovial uproar
should be put upon the same short-commons of pleasure as that which
destiny has portioned out to these holiday revellers, and they would
soon discover that when only one day is allowed to gather in the
crop of enjoyment which is, perhaps, to serve for months, such a
harvest-home must be wild and noisy.

When evening came, and the big city in the distance was speckled
with lights—when the men had spent their money, and the women
had tired out their animal spirits—the crowd began to quit the Heath.
Then the saddles were taken off, and the worn-out donkeys turned
loose to see if they could find enough untrodden grass to serve for
their suppers.

Although so fatigued that he could scarcely keep his eyes open,
Philip would still have strength enough left to sit up in his bed, and
count the money that had been given to him for his day's work.
Out of the six or seven shillings he might have earned he would put
aside the greater portion for the repayment of the amount he owed
Bertha. He still had some notions of honour in him, although
how they remained in his heart, after the life he had led, it is impossible to tell.

CHAPTER XIV.

SHOWING THAT CAPTAIN CROSIER HAD NO IDEA OF THE VALUE OF MONEY.

OF all things that are expensive there is nothing which costs more
to keep than late hours. For the same money which the wild youth
squanders for the luxury of walking the streets until the gasman
makes his rounds to put out the lamps, he might revel in many of
those fashionable delights which the opinion of the world has long
since declared to be the end and perfection of happiness.

How many good sovereigns had Captain Crosier, in two short years,
squandered by keeping these late hours! If he had laid down a guinea

for every paving-stone in the Haymarket footway he would still have been in pocket. Short as the journey is down that mad thorough-fare, it is more expensive to the traveller than if he posted to York and back. Many a time, when the captain, on reaching home, emptied his pockets of the few shillings that remained from the round sum he had provided himself with before starting on his mid-night adventures—many a time did he feel some remorse at the largeness of his expenditure, and the inadequacy of the amusement. He would look wistfully at the few shillings left, and some such regrets as these would pass through his mind : " What the deuce can I have done with my money ? I am certain I took out four pounds with me, and yet here are but eight shillings left ! " Then he would begin his accounts, adding up what it had cost him for supper, how much he had given away in shillings for cabs or spent in bouquets for gifts, or laid out in treating to drinks at public-houses. Then he would grow repentant, and, regretting his extravagance, think what he might have bought with the same sum had he laid it out virtuously.

" It is too bad," he would mutter. "There are many poor fellows who have to keep a family on a pound a week, and here am I fooling away four or five pounds every night of my life—and what for ? what for ? How on earth do those poor clerks in the City manage to live on eighty pounds a year ? Why, many fellows reckon themselves to be well off who do not get more in a week than I throw away in a night ! " After such meditations as these, the repentant captain would vow " to cut such d—d stupid work," and for the future renounce his midnight extravagances. As he had made this vow regularly every night for the past two years, it is but fair to presume that he was very earnest in what he said.

The only drawback to these resolves was that they were taken at a time when the gallant youth was depressed with his excesses. After he had been refreshed with sleep, he found his animal spirits and strength restored him, and invariably forgot to follow the good advice with which he had physicked his morals overnight. He had grown so accustomed to his debauched mode of living, that to miss the sport of the Haymarket would have cost him as much pain as for an opium-eater to forego the intoxication of his drug. Even up to his dinner-hour he might remain true to his good intention of stopping at home ; but when his pint of sherry was empty, and he was yielding himself up to the pleasant consequences of a good dinner, his notions of right would lose their virtuous stiffness, and eventually disappear before the philosophical arguments which he conjured up in favour of one night more on town. He would discover that an entire evening passed in that dismal room of his, with no other company than his own, was more than his nerves could endure. He had a mean opinion of his own company. He would say to himself, "Where is the difference between walking in the streets abroad, or sitting in your chair at home ? If I don't spend any money it comes to the same thing. I'll just stroll about for an hour or two, and then creep home quietly to bed." But with strolling about came chatting with friends and visiting taverns. The stiffest buckram virtue grows limp when full tumblers are emptied over it. In a little time, the captain, loosening his moral stays, and throwing off his top-coat of virtue, became reckless. As he grew more and more full of drink, his laughter came floating up on the top of it. He would become the gayest of all the gay young dogs that were jingling their coin on the counters of the night-houses.

They are, indeed, expensive to keep, these late hours. The captain one day made a calculation that, up to twelve o'clock, late hours might be done well for a sovereign, but every hour beyond cost, at a moderate calculation, an additional twenty shillings. For the same sum what might he not have done? He might have gained the affection of his friends by giving a dinner party at least twice a week. Two noble-legged footmen, with canary thighs, glittering like gold foil, might have imparted a lustre to his establishment. He might have had his opera-box, his shooting-box, his money-box, and every other kind of box. Instead of jobbing a cab, a mail phaeton, with his crest as big as a kitchen plate, might be standing in his own coach-house. We will not mention spanking greys with streaming comet tails, nor the natty brougham with electrical lamps to fetch him home from the evening parties to which he would be most certainly invited. Even the luxury of a French cook was within his grasp. With such advantages as these, who could limit the good fortune that would be in store for him? The saloons and casinos would give place to banquet halls, ball-rooms, and dancing teas. He might have his pick among the evening party heiresses. Every low-neck dress would adore him. Perhaps he might make so brilliant a match that his wife's income would permit him even to quarrel with his own father, and, without caring for the paternal allowance, still to live in the utmost extravagance and profusion.

We say he might have done this, though there was this drawback to our speculations. If his father had heard of any such grandeur of living, there would have been much commotion among the Crosier family, and letters with the Swanborough post-mark upon them would frequently be laid upon the breakfast-table—"Your affectionate father, Nathaniel Crosier," would descant upon "my dear Merton's" unwarrantable expenditure. This would considerably have diminished the satisfaction produced by the different kinds of boxes, the canary breeches, and day and night vehicles.

The income of the gallant captain might be some £500 a year, including quarterly allowances of £100 each, and the presents with which a rich aunt and a prosperous uncle chose to celebrate his birthday and cheer his Christmas.

Whenever we hear anybody abusing the world, and calling it such names as a hard-hearted and cruel world, an ungrateful world, we always think of the gallant Merton, and the kindly mundane treatment he met with. Although his income was a small one, yet with

O

it he was enabled to live at a rate of three times its amount. There are certain generous-hearted creatures ever willing to take pity on the gay necessities of the frisky young. If this son had written to his father, beseeching the advance of a hundred or so, his prayers would have been listened to with no more success than if he had petitioned for a couple of the paternal front teeth. So, instead of disturbing papa's quiet, Merton, whenever the sovereigns were scarce, put on his hat, and paid a visit to a friend of his in Holborn. There, by merely signing a simple strip of paper—he wrote very rapidly—he could touch almost any sum he required.

The name of this open-hearted and open-pursed Christian was Edward Dancer, and, if easing the afflicted mind, or assuaging the griefs of our fellow-creatures be a merit, this worthy man must be entitled to infinite respect. All he asked for was security, and all he took was interest.

Between the shops kept by one Bumprel, a hosier, and one Brown, a stationer, there is a small iron wicket leading into a court or blind alley, of a most dismal and deserted appearance. It is a mere fissure in the bricken mass of closely-packed houses, and does not contain above a dozen dwellings—a wretched rat-hole of a place, with a look of old-building materials about it. It is decidedly a bad letting property, and the landlord, if he lives on the rents, must be a needy man, for none of the dwellings—except Dancer's—appears to be occupied. Apparently no exertions are made to find tenants, for, as if it were looked upon as a useless expense, no bills or boards are up. Supposing that some misanthrope, charmed with the seclusion of the place, wished "to take on lease," he would not know where to apply and get cards to view. It is a spot where a distempered dog would hide itself to shiver in peace till it died. The window-panes are whitey-brown with dust and the knockers red and crumbling with oxide, for no hand ever rat-tats there and preserves the metal with its friction. The bricks are dirty and smooth with the soot that has settled on their rough surfaces, and the white lines of the mortar have been smudged out. Many a time did the captain wonder to himself whether any other than Dancer dared to live in this court. He has seen the same big whitewashed "TO LET" on the same window at No. 4 during the two years he has had occasion to visit the spot. The milky purity of the letters has turned to a rich neutral tint, and prove the great age of the inscription. On one door, with the paint blistered as the top of a pie, there is a brass-plate. It is not seen at first, because the once glittering surface is now rusted of a deep pink brown. In that house the fortunes of "Fergusson and Co., Agents and Coal Merchants," were wrecked. The firm undoubtedly bolted. Further on, No. 6 has been afflicted with weakness, and shoring-up has been applied to its front. The rotten bandbox of a house bulges out, and wide cracks meander among the bricks, in some parts so open that a city sparrow has built itself a most conveniently situated nest.

Ragged, yellow bits of blind hang slantways in some of the windows, and for years they have never been either pulled up or drawn down, but have remained as they were when Captain Crosier first saw them. Even the flag-stones to this bad alley are cracked, and in some places so uneven that with every shower the hollows are filled up with puddles, in which bits of paper are trapped like flies on a "catch-'em-alive." Some of the flag-stones are what street boys call "squirters," that is, they secrete under them a considerable quantity of dirty water, which, on the pressure of a foot, they yield up, by squirting it over the owner of the foot. Squirters are dreadful things. Indeed, it was a very dirty walk up this court, and all Mr. Dancer's friends thought so; but gentlemen in want of money do not mind a little mud in their path, so they put up with the annoyance.

About every two months the captain would find himself swinging back the iron gate at the entrance of the alley. His face, when he entered, had a meek, downcast expression, owing, probably, to the doubts in his mind as to whether he should be able "to get anything out of old Dancer." His bearing on these occasions had lost its independence and boldness. He seemed afraid of doing anything that would be likely to offend Dancer. He shut the iron gate very carefully, for fear its clatter should disturb Dancer. Even when he knocked at the bill-discounter's door, instead of giving a vigorous treble rattle, he modulated the knock to a gentleness, almost as if Dancer had been ill.

To look at this rich man nobody would have judged him capable of the kindness and humanity his necessitous visitors never ceased to extol during their interviews. He was a thin, diminutive creature, with a face of the colour of a dried fig; and, but for the quick expression of his eyes, his countenance had an idiotic blankness. He was so thin that his clothes puffed him out as feathers do a bird. At a watering place, such a man would never have dared to bathe in public. As there were always medicine bottles on his mantelshelf, it was evident that Dancer's health was not good. When such big fellows as Captain Merton called to see him, the little man had to look up at them, and squirt his thin voice up to their ears. Or if, as he usually did, he skipped on to a high stool, his little legs swung about, and he seemed like a parrot on its stand. Not unfrequently Crosier thought to himself what a capital jockey Dancer would have made, but he did not like to say as much, for fear the small man should dislike the observation, and the interest be "stuck on" in consequence.

This diminutive money-lender did an excellent business, and was intimate with a great many noble persons whom nobody would have suspected of ever requiring to be accommodated. Whilst the captain was waiting in the parlour for his interview, he would often hear Dancer's small pipe above stairs squalling out excuses to a gruff voice which he recognized as that of a friend he should never have imagined "to be hard up." He had seen Lord Oaks pass by the window as that noble lord left the ready money sanctum, and had frequently noticed Charley Sutton's cab waiting outside Furnival's Inn, though the gay spark, far from having any business with the residents of that legal colony, had crossed the road, and trotted slyly up to Dancer's doorway.

One morning, Captain Crosier, on sending a cheque to his bankers for ten pounds, had received the distressing answer that he had overdrawn his account; whenever this sad event occurred, it was his custom to pay a visit to his accommodating little friend in Holborn.

He found the little man as affable and chatty as ever. They had some delightful conversation about the great scarcity of money, and the enormous rate to which interest had gone up. In a most familiar manner, Dancer asked him to sit down for a few moments, and gave some directions to his clerk, while Merton, who was very affable, read the paper and did as he was told.

For the office of so rich a man as Mr. Dancer, it was decidedly the most miserable hole of a place imaginable. There was not in the entire house a patch of French polish, or varnish, as big as even its owner's dwarfed hand. The desk ruler and the leathern top of the clerk's stool were the brightest things to be seen. To a nervous man sadly in want of money the dismal look of the dwelling was enough to crush and pound to dust the smallest pebble of hope.

The staircase leading up to the "cheque" room was dark and rotten, and those ascending had to be cautioned to "mind their heads," and warned that "there was another step there." The diminutive Dancer could go up and down as easily as a rat through a drain, but anyone above four feet had to stoop and crouch, in dread of knocks, bumps, and crushed hats. The sanctum itself had but little furniture in it, and looked as wretched as if the wealthy Mr. Dancer was the most incorrigible insolvent in the kingdom. One farthing a yard was the price he had paid for the paper on the walls. The red-lead roses festooned into the design had a poisonous, deadly look, and smelt of mould instead of attar. It was a relief to turn one's eyes from these flowers to the Law Almanac hanging over the fireplace, and to stare at the legal notices relating to Judges' Chambers and term times. Even men who had come there to ask for grace preferred the law papers to the roses, despite the ideas they evoked of writs and White-cross Street. With such a multiplicity of business a man like Mr. Dancer had to write numberless letters, and files of them, alphabeti-cally arranged, were hung round the room. Merton knew that his own important correspondence was among the C's. There was a tall desk in one corner where the clerk wrote out renewals of bills and filled up judgments and post-obits. Before the grate was Mr. Dancer's own table, with the big, brass-bound writing-desk, under whose green-baize top reposed the delicious cheque-book, a leaf of which every visitor hoped to take away with him. The most unmistakable object in the room was an iron chest, almost large enough to have served as a prison for Mr. Dancer himself. Even the terrible Queen's Bench did not contain more captives than that strong box. Whenever its iron gates were opened, it was either to admit a fresh captive, or move one to safer custody than that of gaoler Dancer.

It was a very fortunate circumstance that the money-lender's health was failing, because it afforded his visitors an excellent subject of conversation. No man was ever more commiserated than the little money-lender. Some of his clients—especially those doubtful of success—would go into paroxysms of pity as the discounter particularized his ailments; indeed, anyone would have fancied that they, and not Mr. Dancer, were the afflicted beings.

"You really should take care of yourself," said Captain Crosier, on this particular occasion. "Now, do promise me, like a good fellow, that you'll go to some first-rate doctor. You ought to; in fact, for our sakes, you must."

"I've tried them all, every man in London," squeaked the money-lender. "I've spent pounds on pounds, and they tell me I'm incurable. If I hadn't a cast-iron constitution, I couldn't stand against it." As a proof of this, he began a minute account of some particular phase of his malady, which had such an effect upon the sympathetic Merton, that he seemed in an agony of sorrow. But the real truth was that Merton was only trying to soften the discounter's heart, and cared no more what became of him, provided he could get his cheque, than you do for the shells of an oyster after you have eaten the peppered and vinegared bivalve.

In all the visits paid to this little man, every client had to go through a set scene before he could touch his cheque. The moment the little bit of paper was mentioned, Mr. Dancer, although he lived by, and made an excellent income out of such transactions, appeared to be annoyed by the proposition. He would throw up his eyebrows and say, "Money! I wish you'd tell me where I could get some! I don't believe there's any money left in the world." To prepare the way for asking a thumping discount, he would tell anecdotes of how he himself took a batch of bills to the celebrated City firm of Coin, Bullion, and Co., and how they would not even look at them. "I saw Orr myself, and pressed him deuced hard. It was only a bill for two hundred, and, says he, 'Has she got the name of the Bank of England on her? Why, then, take her away, for I won't touch her.' There, that will show you how scarce money is."

When the captain still pressed him, and called him "good fellow" and "dear friend," or condescended to other familiar expressions which he considered should—coming from a man of his position—be irresistible, the diminutive Edward whined as if his heart were breaking at being obliged to refuse, although he still managed to be stubborn. He went to the iron chest, and, unlocking it, drew out a bundle. Then he commenced this sermon:—"Look here, captain!

do you see this? There's four thousand pounds' worth of paper here, and I'll sell it you for twenty shillings. Now, will you believe I've no money?"

It was his habit then to fling this bundle indignantly back to its pigeon-hole, and sigh deeply as he locked the doors of its prison.

"Any of mine among 'em?" asked Captain Crosier, sarcastically. "What have I got to do with other people's debts?"

"Why don't you go to Robins?" pleaded Mr. Dancer. "He'd only charge you sixty per cent., and I'm sure it ain't too much, as times go."

"Robins be hanged!" growled the captain, who was now on the indignant tack.

"If you can get me the name of a good firm on the back of this bill I don't mind seeing what I can do," groaned the little man.

"My good fellow! under those circumstances I should pay it into my banker's," snappishly answered the captain. "It's a good bill as it is, and, if you don't like to do it, you may let it alone."

So well did Captain Crosier, understand Mr. Dancer's policy that even the most decided refusals did not put an end to the negotiation. It was a fight of diplomacy between them, the captain pleading hardest when the money-lender most seemed to draw back, and the latter throwing out some words of hope, and appearing to relent whenever Merton evinced a disposition to give the matter up as a bad job. During the acting of this scene, Mr. Dancer was so greatly affected that it brought back a return of his illness, and he had to take a dose from a bottle containing a dark-brown fluid— evidently a tincture, for it smelt strongly of alcohol. This appeared to relieve him, for presently he exclaimed, "How much have you had from me?" though he knew the amount well enough, and merely as a matter of form turned over the leaves of a ledger at his elbow. "Three thousand four hundred pounds! That's a large sum of money. And what security have I got for it? None!"

There is never more necessity for a man to be upon his guard than when his companion says, whilst discussing, "Now let us speak plainly, and understand one another." It is an acknowledgment that hitherto the latter has acted with duplicity. As he has done so with a show of straightforward conduct, it is certain that the words to come will not be less doubtful than those that have already been spoken. So, when Captain Crosier made this exclamation, Mr. Dancer, who knew the world thoroughly, was not one whit the more inclined to place implicit confidence in his client. He nevertheless assumed an air indicative of the most entire trust.

"I owe you three thousand four hundred pounds, don't I?" said the captain, in his frankest tones, "and you've got, besides my bills for the amount, post-obits on my father. You know my old man is as rich as he can be. You've made inquiries about that. Now, I want five hundred more, and, if you don't like to do it, say so. Let's have no beating about the bush. D—n it! I like plain dealing. Will you, or won't you?"

The money-lender, who had all along made up his mind to entertain this transaction, nevertheless blew out a thin whistle of surprise
when he heard five hundred pounds mentioned. He had made
inquiries about Mr. Crosier, senior, and his agent at Swanborough
had sent back a most excellent account of that banker's wealth and
stability, adding, in answer to one of the inquiries, " He is sixty-seven
years old, and under medical treatment."

When he heard the whistle, Captain Crosier took up his hat, as if
with the intention to depart, saying, although it was a mere invention
of his, " Then, if you won't, I know somebody that will."

" Now, don't be in a hurry. You fellows in the army are so
impetuous," interfered Mr. Dancer. A fresh negotiation was opened,
in which the one sought to decrease the amount required to three
hundred pounds, while the other as strenuously insisted on the sum
first demanded. At last the matter ended by the clerk being sent to
the bank to inquire what balance there remained to the account of
Edward Dancer. This was only an excuse to delay proceedings, and
to afford the little gentleman an opportunity of turning over another
honest penny. So well did the clerk understand the business, that,
instead of going to the bank, he went to the King's Head, close by,
and regaled himself with a glass of mild ale. As the street door
slammed to, Mr. Dancer smiled upon Merton, and in a kind voice said,
" If you are fond of pictures, I'll give you a treat. I've got a Rubens
upstairs—one of the loveliest things you ever saw."

This was an old trick, and the captain knew it well—indeed,
expected it. Nevertheless, he pretended great astonishment and
delight, and hinted that the greatest enjoyment of his life was to see
a good picture. " You don't mean to say you've got a Rubens ? " he
said, opening his eyes with assumed wonder. " Why don't you take
it to the National Gallery ? How that man Rubens must have
painted ! Why, his pictures are everywhere. Let's have a look at it."

An old canvas, which in Wardour Street would have been labelled,
" A genuine Rubens, 30s.," was brought down from a room above,
and the little fox, wiping it with his silk pocket-handkerchief, and
saying, " It's a beautiful thing—very first-rate indeed," held it close
to the window. The big fox looked at it for some time admiringly,
and then, as if he could no longer contain his enthusiasm, cried out,
" By G—d! it's lovely." The little fox laughed, and, in a confidential whisper, said, " And the fellow who owns it doesn't know its real
value—that's the beauty of the thing! He only wants thirty pounds."
The big fox thought the proprietor not only knew the real value, but
had the impudence of Old Harry himself in fixing such a fictitious
one.

" There's flesh ! " cried the money-lender. " You might slap that
arm, I declare you might! I wouldn't sell it if I wasn't a married
man, but Mrs. Dancer is so particular about academic studies. A
surgeon could almost cut those legs off!—couldn't he ? Just look at
this Venus. Isn't she Rubens all over ? "

The captain thought to himself she was not only Rubens all over, but somebody else into the bargain, but he did not say so.

When the clerk had finished his ale, he left the King's Head and returned to his master to whisper something in his ear. All this the captain watched most anxiously, and when he saw the little fox open his desk and take out his cheque-book, he felt as if an iron hoop had been removed from his chest, so great was the relief.

"It appears I've just got money enough," said Mr. Dancer, sighing. Then, in a livelier tone, he added, "Would you like to have that picture, captain?" Now they again began to fence, the soldier saying, "It was a sweet thing, but—" and the civilian endeavouring to convince him into buying it by relating an anecdote of a certain lucky individual, who, having purchased a Correggio for 8s., afterwards sold it to the nation for £20,000. But all this was perfectly understood by the big fox. Before giving a decided answer, he inquired, "What are you going to charge me for interest?"

"Well, I shall take a hundred for the three months, and I don't care much about doing it at that," replied the little man.

"If you like to take £15 for the d—d painting, I'll buy it," offered the borrower.

"Fifteen pounds!" exclaimed the lender, pushing his cheque-book away. "With that flesh! Fifteen pounds! Why it would fetch more in a slave-market. No! no! captain. Say five-and-twenty, if you like." And the cheque was drawn.

Now, although the captain had entered the court meekly enough, his head was remarkably high as he left it. Whenever his pocket was full of money he had courage enough to stare an eagle to blindness. He swore at the puddles he had before modestly stepped over, and swung-to the gate after him with the clatter of a regiment rattling ramrods down their musket-barrels.

CHAPTER XV.

INTO THE FIRE.

WE have said that Phil still had some notions of honour left in him, and we will prove it. He knew very well that Bertha never expected to see again the seventeen shillings she had lent him to buy decent clothing before he entered the service of Mr. Tobias Sparkler. He knew very well, too, that she—timid little girl—would never mention the subject to him. The debt was, therefore, so far as being bothered about it, as good as paid. She looked upon it as a gift, but not so he. Perhaps he wanted to regain her esteem, and to coax her to forget his crossing-sweeping life. Perhaps the fact of knowing she never dreamt of seeing her money again made him stubbornly honest.

But whatever the reason may have been, Phil's resolves of repayment were virtuous and good, and he is entitled to the full benefit of them; indeed, we hope that everyone will applaud his excellent determinations.

He made Mrs. Burt his banker, and whenever he could scrape together sixpence, he paid it into her very large hands. Had he tried to keep it himself, he knew he must spend it, for he was a reckless, young scamp with his wealth; a strong yearning for fruit pies and a passion for pitch and toss were his ruin. When he had accumulated the seventeen shillings he begged a day of Mr. Sparkler, and before seven o'clock in the morning he was ringing at Miss Tomsey's area bell, already enjoying in advance the look of astonishment he felt certain Bertha would give when he handed back the loan.

The chin of that faithful domestic, Mr. Boxer, was every morning remarkable for its blackness. Being of a fat, oily temperament, his beard grew with a mustard-and-cress rapidity. It was a stubborn bristle of metallic toughness. When he lounged out into the area to inquire what the "young man" wanted, his shirt collar was open, and exhibited a throat and jaw which, had he been a rabbit, would have rendered him invaluable as a fine double smut. Without any reason Mr. Boxer behaved insultingly to Phil. He refused to tell Bertha that a party, whose name didn't matter, wanted to say a word to her. He stared, and hummed (incorrectly) a popular air. Our lad understood that this rudeness was not intended for him personally, but merely because he was a friend of Bertha. To be revenged he criticized the footman's dirty chin, asking him innocently what he'd got there, and whether it was real, or only a wig for mornings? He also inquired if it hurt, and offered to buy it, if it wasn't too dear and could be done up in a small parcel. When the enraged footman seized a lump of coal to throw at his juvenile tormentor, the lad changed his tone, and expressed his astonishment that Mr. Boxer should so soon have forgotten his face after the merry night they spent together picnicking at Hampstead. He also inquired kindly after Mrs. Wortey and the girls. This caused a great alteration in Mr. B.'s manner. He was defeated, and acknowledged it by opening the street door.

Dressed in the neatest and crispest of cotton gowns, came Bertha, with a face as bright as the morning itself. She had made up her mind that Phil had got into trouble again, and was prepared to console him. But his eyes were laughing, and good news was written on every feature of his face. There was no trouble there. He took her hand, and, slipping the money into it, said, "There, Bertha, there's seventeen shillings, and all good ones, so you needn't bite 'em. Now we're quits as far as money goes, but if you think I'd ever forget what you've done, then you wrong me."

She was so startled she couldn't close her fingers on the money, but continued to look in wonder, first at it, then at him. Her large eyes opened more and more widely. He understood her thoughts and said, half reproachingly, "You never expected to see it again, did you? Well, it was natural. I don't blame you—not I; but upon my civy, sooner than rob you, Bertha, I'd steal halfpence from a blind man's tray—that's truth."

"It wouldn't have been robbery, you silly Phil, for I gave it you," was the answer.

But he would not let it be understood in that light. "No! what should you give your money to me for? I'm stronger than you a precious deal, for you're a girl, and I'm better able to work. No; if there's any giving to be done, it should be with me; and I will, too." And then, forgetting what trouble it had cost him to scrape together these savings, he, in the enthusiasm of the moment, promised that every month he would lay by a round sum; indeed, he pledged himself to the amount of ten shillings monthly, to be expended in bettering the condition of Nurse Hazlewood.

The sister, in her anxiety to learn if Phil's morals had improved, examined him at great length as to what he had been about, and how he had spent his time. Our young gentleman was sufficiently knowing to see the drift of this inquiry; and so well did he account for himself, that Bertha must, indeed, have been hard to please if she had not approved of the course of life he vowed he had led. When the time came to say good-bye, Bertha kissed him so affectionately, and expressed herself so gratefully for her foster-brother's reformation, that the boy, intoxicated with the sweets of praise, felt sorry he had partly imposed upon her belief. Knowing he had cheated her, he resolved that, for mere honesty's sake, he would make up the balance of virtue with which she had credited him.

It was but nine o'clock in the morning when this audience was over. With half-a-crown in his pocket, and the whole day before him, he determined to revel in a holiday of idleness. He visited all the old scenes of his crossing-sweeping adventures. He strolled about the Haymarket, and felt great enjoyment in calling to mind the different pranks he had played before this or that shop, and the narrow escapes of being locked up he had run in this or that street. Thinking that, perhaps, he might meet with some of his old friends he went towards St. Martin's Church, and strolled about the passage leading to the Lowther Arcade. He inquired tenderly after the rips of the old woman at the apple stall, and from her learned that Captain Drake had retired from the profession on account of his increased stature putting an end to his success as a caten-wheeler. Mr. Mike had got himself into trouble, and was then spending three weeks with the governor of Coldbath Fields, charged with highway robbery, he having forcibly taken a penny from a little girl who had been sent to fetch milk. This conversation with the apple-woman so affected Phil, that he determined to wait till his old companions should come to their crossings. He thought it would be ungrateful if he did not share his half-crown with them in beer and pudding. As these young sweepers seldom rose before twelve, he loitered about.

Now, there is no place in the world more dangerous to loiterers than London. Where everybody is so busy, for a boy to be seen standing idly is to invite mischief. Little did he think, when he made up his mind for a day's pleasure, how suddenly his amusement would be ended. He had twice witnessed the gratuitous performance of Punch, and had examined attentively every article of jewellery in a mosaic goldsmith's window, when just as he was wishing "those chaps" would make haste, somebody touched him on the back, and asked him if he wanted a job.

It was a gentleman with an enormous beard, who spoke with a slightly foreign accent. He seemed rather startled when Phil turned round to accept his offer. He drew back as if he knew the lad, who, on his part, appeared also to have some remembrance of the gentleman. If it had not been for the enormous beard, he might have passed for the French officer who had visited Hampstead with Helen Crosier's brother and father. The foreign gentleman at first repented of his offer, and said, "No, nevar mind, my boie." He was going away, when on second thoughts, he turned back, and once more opened negotiations, muttering, "Well, yas—very well, sen—you shall." Taking him up a deserted street, he placed a cheque in Phil's hands, and directed him to take it, together with a red linen bag which he gave him, to the banking-house of Messrs. Coutts and Co. "Sey will put someting in se bag, which you shall bring to me in five minutes here. Do sis, and I will give you ten shilling, my good boie." He patted Phil's head, and smiled till his teeth showed through his black beard white as linen through a hedge.

"Who shall I say I come from?" asked Phil, fancying himself the luckiest fellow in the world. The foreigner thought for a moment, and then handed a card on which was engraved, "Alphonse Lerouville et Cie., Lyons and London," once more patted the boy on the back, and dismissed him on his errand.

Innocent of what he was about to do, Phil entered the banking-house, and presented the cheque to the first person he saw, who happened to be the doorkeeper. He was directed to take his turn after some eight or nine others, standing in a line by the counter behind which was the pay-clerk.

What a land of dreams this banking-house seemed! The only sound was that of the ringing of gold or the rustling of silver paper. Money appeared to lose half its value by being seen in such vast quantities. The gentleman behind the counter absorbed all Phil's attention. He beheld him take out shovelfuls of gold and throw them about as if they had been lozenges instead of sovereigns. It was as if bins of coin were hidden behind the mahogany. He was delighted, too, at the rapidity with which the clerk counted the pieces, moving his fingers as quickly as the paws of a terrier scratching at a rat-hole. How carelessly, too, the bald-headed gentleman seemed to handle a quire of notes. If they had been curl-papers he could not have treated them with less concern. He wetted his finger, and turned them over most roughly, or held them up to the light, and jerked them about till they snapped like straps. The boy was in an agony lest he should tear them. There were huge scales, too, and curious diving-bell shaped weights, all of the brightest brass. Our lad stared again, as he saw the gold weighed out as coolly as if it had been coffee-berries. One thing that startled him was, why those clerks, seated each at a little desk, with a large green shade over the lamp above him, should be working so hard in a place where there was so much wealth.

What a crowd of people flocked to this bank! Some brought bags full of coin, and rolls of soiled, dirty notes, that looked smudged and creased as an old playbill. Phil thought he had suddenly discovered the currency laws. He imagined that the bank was a kind of wash-house, where dirty paper was brought in and exchanged for clean. He could not exactly understand why gold should be left there. The taking it away he could easily account for; but whatever theory he might have framed was suddenly interrupted by a gentleman attempting to edge in before him and take his place, a liberty that Phil would not allow. He called out so lustily for justice, and appealed so often to the "master" paying the money whether "he wasn't first," that he quite interrupted the silent business of the banking-house. To get rid of so noisy a visitor, the clerk asked what he wanted, and the cheque was handed over. Innocent Phil, with his elbow resting on the counter, and his legs paddling about, did not know how to answer when the clerk asked him how he would take it. He handed in the linen bag and said, "In this." The clerk began to explain, "I mean, will you have it in gold or in notes?"

"Well, he didn't say," answered Phil, "but he's waiting over the way. If you like, I'll go and ask him."

"But did not Lord Ascot give you any directions? You are his groom, ain't you?"

"His groom! no!" answered Phil, rather indignantly. "It's a foreigneering gent as sent me, and he said he'd give me half a sovereign."

A new light broke in upon the clerk. He examined the cheque attentively, and then, telling Phil to wait a moment, went towards a glass door at the back; but, before doing so, he gave a significant nod to the doorkeeper, and if Phil had looked round, he would have seen that portly personage take up his post directly in front of the exit.

Little suspecting any danger, the lad, when told to wait, said, "All right, master, don't keep a fellow long, please."

For the next ten minutes he could not make out why all the clerks, who had before been so busy with their heads down to their writing, should be now sitting upright on their stools, and staring at him. He was getting rather angry, and a strong inclination to make faces at them came over him, but he resisted it. His cool manner, and the indifferent way in which he took up a pen and began to clean his nails, seemed to astonish these gentlemen.

Instead of getting his money as he expected, Phil was asked, or rather ordered, to step into a back room, where he found the pay-clerk showing the cheque to a bald-headed gentleman with a big diamond in the middle of a spotless white cravat. The boy had so many questions put to him that he soon found out there was some-thing wrong. In rapid succession he had to explain how he came possessed of the cheque, and describe the person who gave it him. Then out came the fearful truth. The document was a forgery, but so cleverly executed, that had it not been for Phil's artless answers, the clerk would most certainly have cashed it. Whilst Phil had been kept waiting, a messenger was despatched to Lord Ascot's residence, and the answer returned to the inquiries corroborated the suspicions of the clerk. His lordship asserted he had never drawn a cheque for three hundred pounds, and further recognized the paper, by the number on it, as being that which had been stolen from him, together with his purse, some month or two ago. He had, he said, intended to have given notice to the bank of this theft, but the circumstance had slipped his memory.

When our unfortunate boy had somewhat recovered from his terror, he began to lament aloud his miserable position. "May I die like a dog," he cried, "if I knowed it was a forgery. 'Pon my word, I didn't. He said he'd give me half a sovereign. That's what made me come. I wish he'd been hung before I saw him, a dirty villain. I hope you won't think I did it, gentlemen. Mr. Sparkler, my master, will tell you I'm a very honest boy. I wouldn't rob the cheese from a mousetrap."

"That remains to be seen, boy," replied the bald-headed gentle-man. "Certainly your behaviour, here, has been in your favour; but I am sorry to tell you I shall have to hand you over to the police as soon as they arrive, in order that some inquiries may be made."

"Give me in charge!" stammered out Phil. "Then what are you going to do to the other fellow? It was him, not me. You ain't a-going to let him off? He's waiting for me over the way, I tell you. Oh! why don't you send somebody quick, or he'll be gone? Oh! do make haste, please!" He entreated and implored, though with little effect, for the bald gentleman did not even answer him. The boy was so wrapped up in his despair that he did not hear the door at the back open, or notice that two policemen had entered. Indeed, it was only when a voice said, "Come, my man, you must go along with us," that he knew he was in custody. "'Pon my word, I am innocent," said Phil, throwing his arms about in despair.

"Ay, of course you are. We shall soon see about that," was the officer's sarcastic remark. "Everyone on you's innocent. That's the old game. I never see such a lot of virtuous people as you young prigs. Here, come along."

He was led off between the two men, dragging them towards the meeting-place appointed by the foreigner. He pulled forward as a dog does at its chain, and was so earnest that one of the officers mistook his motives, and warned him it was no good trying that dodge, for he should not escape.

It is almost needless to say that the foreign gentleman was not at his post. The representative of " Alphonse Lerouville et Cie." was a very knowing fellow, and, judging by the time it took to get the cheque cashed, had sniffed danger afar off, and renounced all idea of plunder.

Nearly broken-hearted, Phil was led off towards the police station, the crowd at his heels increasing with every street they passed through. Many who saw his pale face, his staring eyes, and teeth clinched with fear, declared they had never beheld such a ruffianly countenance. Numerous were the inquiries made of what he had done, and very various were the answers. Some asserted positively he had been found in the strong room of a bank with his pockets stuffed with notes. Others were equally circumstantial in their account of how he attempted to snatch a bag of gold off the bank counter. But one old lady gave a more terrible version than any, and affirmed she had been told by someone who heard it from a party present, that the young villain had attempted to murder and rob the Governor of the Bank of England whilst the poor old gentleman was hard at work signing bank-notes.

And yet, as the reader knows, poor Phil was perfectly innocent, and the only guilty person was the representative of Messrs. Alphonse Lerouville et Cie., Lyons and London.

CHAPTER XVI.

IN WHICH THE CAPTAIN DOES NOT CONDUCT HIMSELF AS A GENTLEMAN.

NEVER for one moment did Captain Merton forget the bet he had made with Charley Sutton that he would, before six months were over, add the name of poor Bertha Hazlewood to the list of those victims who had been unable to resist the fascination of his person and the exquisite perfection of his manners. Even if he had not wagered this £50, the gallant captain would not have been less earnest in his pursuit of the poor little girl. For Bertha had such a pretty face, that, to possess it, any of the gentlemen on town would have put themselves to considerable exertion or expense. The captain had often given himself more trouble, and exercised all his abilities for a less comely object. He declared that the girl for whom he had nearly ruined himself whilst quartered at Canterbury was no more to be compared with Bertha than the painting on a snuff-box to

a Titian. But there was a strong protection about Bertha which, had she been left to herself, would have saved her from any evil. She was so perfectly innocent that she could not imagine any unworthy design in others. She had many a time seen Captain Crosier examining her through his opera-glass, but the severest term she applied to his actions was that of rudeness. In fact, she was not aware young gentlemen were capable of enticing poor girls away from their homes, and ruining their happiness. It was Miss Tomsey who first taught Bertha the real purpose of the young officer's attentions.

Every morning Mr. Crosier might be seen standing at his window, half hidden by a curtain, with his glasses as immovably fixed to his eyes as the telescope to the little wooden figure over the nautical instrument makers' shops. He daily examined Bertha's beauties. He had settled in his own mind that her forehead was white and round as the swelling sides of a marble vase. Through his excellent binoculars he could see the temples beat like the sides of a lizard. He preferred the shape of her nose to that of any Grecian Venus, giving as his reason that the nostrils were small as the inner leaf of a rosebud. If her upper lip was thin, he vowed her under one was full, round, and moist. It pouted out, as he told Fred Tattenham, like a velvet cushion to lay kisses on. With her head bent down at work, her chin formed a pretty double, and her hands—he was very particular about her hands—were so small, with fingers so tapering, that he would have wagered a sovereign Houbigant's "sixes" were too large for her. He made up his mind that she was the prettiest girl in the world, and declared it was a disgrace she should have to work so hard, thereby meaning that she was worthy to live in idle shame. Once he was heard to say that, if he could only be satisfied her parents were respectable, decent people, and pretty well off, he really believed he should feel half inclined to marry her.

Many a time had Miss Tomsey noticed the captain watching her house. At first she thought he was gazing at her, and, although she naturally felt indignant at such a liberty, somehow tolerated the impertinence. It was only when she discovered that the glasses dropped the moment Bertha retired, that she became keenly sensitive to the gentleman's rudeness.

"What on earth is that man looking at?" at last she exclaimed to the girl. "He's been bobbing behind that curtain for the last three hours. There he is again, the impertinent, low rascal!"

Of course Bertha said, "She didn't know what the gentleman meant," and in her curiosity turned to look at him, and nearly sent the captain into a fit of rapture by affording him an excellent view of her exquisitely oval countenance.

To put an end to this annoyance, Miss Tomsey sent to inquire the name of "the gentleman who occupied the first floor" at No. 89, and, within half an hour, Merton received a dignified note, in which

"Miss Tomsey presented her compliments to him, and hoped and trusted that he would cease a system of the most persecuting and annoying, not to say ungentlemanly, espionage, which could have no other result than to injure the welfare of the young woman who was its object."

Instead of feeling remorse at this most just reproof, the captain sought to turn it to his own advantage. He instantly dressed himself for going out. He was studiously careful at his toilette, putting on a waistcoat which he had only just that morning received from his tailor's (it opened very low in front and allowed the third stud to be visible). He hastened towards Miss Tomsey's residence, and, in the hope of seeing Bertha, requested an interview with her mistress.

Nothing could surpass the dignity of Miss Tomsey's behaviour on this trying occasion. So strongly did she express herself against the captain's conduct, that, but for the philosophy mixed up with her remarks, she might almost have been accused of violence. The young man seemed crushed by her reproofs, and kept his eyes turned to the carpet. His agitation was evinced by the restlessness with which he played with his hat.

"I appeal to you as an officer and a gentleman not to trifle with the repose of this young woman, for—you must forgive me for saying so—Captain Crosier can have no honest purpose in his attentions."

"I am surprised to hear a lady of Miss Tomsey's appearance," modestly muttered Merton, "denying to our sex the only privilege we have, that of admiring hers." He endeavoured by these words to persuade the old girl he had used his glasses for "her." He partly succeeded; for it is a law of human nature to feel kindly inclined towards those who admire us.

The many counsels with which Miss Tomsey now endeavoured to fortify Bertha against the captain's attacks first taught that young lady she had an admirer in the world. Very naturally she wished to know what her admirer was like, and many a time, whilst Crosier was intently watching the drawing-room, did Bertha take a sly peep at him from the second floor. She thought him a good-looking young fellow, and that his moustache, carefully pomaded into a ring at each end, became him. Owing to the effects of late hours, his waving light hair—as she looked down upon him—seemed thin on the top of his head, and dissipation had tacked on five years to his appearance. Altogether, Bertha had no fault to find with her admirer, and, now she had once seen him, did not care whether she ever again experienced that pleasure.

The young officer was too bold and knowing a campaigner to be frightened away by Miss Tomsey. He sternly blockaded his enemy's street door, and had his glasses constantly levelled at their camp, so that, should the pretty Bertha ever make a sortie, he might hasten after her, and attempt a conquest. Many a time, when Miss Tomsey went out for her evening walk, did he rush for his hat, mistaking her for someone else. As soon as he discovered his mistake he would return to No. 23, and employ every stratagem for entering that fortress. He would walk up and down the street, in the hopes of seeing the fair one, and, if ever she did approach the window, begin to make signs, entreating that she would come out and speak to him. But all in vain; for Bertha plunged him in despair by retiring into the dark recesses of the room. If she sometimes continued to watch him from her hiding-place, it was only because she was startled to think that anybody should take so much interest in her, and wondered what he could want to see her about. In his despair, the captain called in the assistance of his man, Teddy Cutler, judging, and rightly, that, where the lion cannot enter, the mouse may sometimes find admittance. If there was any virtuous hesitation on the part of Mr. Cutler to join in this scheme, the exact value of his scruples may be fixed at the sum of one guinea, for that was the amount for which he consented to abet and aid in the nefarious undertaking. The next day the ingenious groom, through the agency of Mary Anne, the maid, caused a letter to be placed on Bertha's dressing-table. It was a high-flown declaration of love, savouring rather of "The Complete Letter Writer." It had cost Merton nearly a quire of Bath post before he was satisfied with his performance. We will just give one extract from the sixth side to show that the captain was enthusiastic in the extreme :—" If the most patient admiration that man ever bore, if, despite difficulties almost insurmountable, obstacles truly formidable, oppositions bordering on insults, I still continue to seek for your affection, surely no one will deny the purity of my love, or dare to assert any other opinion of my constancy than that which would do honour to any gentleman, no matter how fastidious the age in which he lived."

The captain had intended this note to explode like a barrel of gunpowder in poor Bertha's bosom, and blow away any hesitation or timidity she might have. How great was his surprise when he received the following answer, worthy the virtue and innocence of her who sent it :—

"SIR,—You do not know me, or you would not have written me that long letter, which I do not understand. I am a poor, penniless girl, whose mother is in a workhouse, and am totally unworthy the attentions of so great a gentleman as yourself. I hope you will think so too, and allow me to live in peace."

Nobody must blame Bertha for sending this answer, for she did so by the advice of Miss Tomsey herself, to whom she very properly showed the fiery declaration of love, and the icy answer she endeavoured to cool it with. It was by Miss Tomsey's directions that the words "whose mother is in the workhouse" were inserted. Perhaps Miss Tomsey was to blame in this matter, and ought to have remembered that, however discouraging the reply might be, it was a sanction to the correspondence. But that excellent lady, although too

P

aged to hope for a taste of the joys of matrimony, was still not totally insensible to the influence of love, and took great delight in witnessing in others what she could have no chance of practising herself. In fact, she was a match-maker.

One evening Bertha went out alone, and, before she had turned the corner, the captain was by her side. He began to talk very rapidly, nearly thrusting his head into her bonnet. His conduct was so remarkable that everybody who passed turned round to look at him. She was hurrying on, and he was chasing her, treading on her dress, and almost forcing her into the road, in his endeavours to keep close to her side. The pace at which they were walking caused his voice to tremble as if from emotion. As she never answered him, he had all the talk to himself.

"How earnestly I have waited for this opportunity!—I have watched for days, for months.—How could you send me that cruel letter?—Why should I care if your mother is in the workhouse?—It is noble in you to tell me so; but I love you in spite of every consideration.—Have you a father?" By this ingenious question he hoped to make her speak, but she would not. Then he continued: "You will not answer me.—You despise me.—Yet all I am guilty of, is admiring you.—If I annoy you, tell me so.—You treat me with more contempt than I deserve.—They have warned you against me. They have told you infamous stories of me, have they not?" This second attempt, however, failed. She would not open her lips. "Your face is too good and beautiful, Bertha" (he had learnt her name), "for you to be so unkind, unless at another's instigation.— Why do you walk so fast?—Are you afraid of me?—You take me for a scoundrel, and fear me.—See, the people are turning round to look at us.—You are telling them I am a scoundrel.—Do speak, Bertha.— Say anything.—Tell me to go, and that you hate me." He was rather anxious to discover whether her voice was a sweet one or not. Bertha was this time caught in the trap. She stopped suddenly, and, after he had checked the impetus of his pace and turned round, said, in her own musical voice,—

"Do leave me, sir. Unless you do, I must go home."

But not he. It might be the only chance he should ever have of speaking to her, and he could not relinquish it. With great ingenuity he managed, by continually declaring he would leave that moment, since his presence was distasteful to her, to remain in her society. He tried to dazzle her by the magnificence of his offers. Nurse Hazlewood—whom he vowed he loved for her sake—was to be taken from the workhouse, and made the happiest of women. Bertha herself was to be rescued from the drudgery of servitude, and share with him—— But here she broke from him, and scampered home as fast as she could. As he never ran, there was no pursuit.

It soon became known to the ladies in Miss Tomsey's kitchen—for Teddy Cutler told them—that the captain "was sticking up to 'Miss.'" Mrs. Wortey was overpoweringly indignant against "the baggage" and her "fellow," and Mary Ann was seized with a fit of prophecy, and called upon Susan to mark her words, that no good would come of it. There was a sardonic smile upon Mr. Boxer's countenance whenever the subject was mentioned, but the only opinion he expressed was, that "no gal could withstand a red coat." The livery of Miss Tomsey—she being in no way related to the royal family—was sky-blue.

On the evening that the captain chased poor Bertha he met at the club Charley Sutton, who inquired of him, "How he was getting on with the little 'un?"

"She's shy—awfully shy," answered Merton, confidently; "but you know, old boy, I've got five months before that dinner comes off at Richmond. You'll have to hand over the fifty pounds, I can tell you. She's all right."

CHAPTER XVII.

THE DERBY DAY.

THAT great day of enjoyment for the would-be sporting men of London, "The Derby Day," had come round again. From the gentlemen in the Guards, who began to make up a book a year before, to the smallest beerhouse-keeper in Whitechapel, who betted his five shillings only a week previously, all the worthy children of modern Babylon were influenced by this exciting period. Every horse in Ted Argean's stable had been bespoken months ago, and there was not a coster who owned a donkey who had not made up his mind to drive down on his truck and see what horseflesh was like.

Our volatile but gallant captain has betted heavily on the great event of the day. He stands to win £15,000. With such tact has he made his arrangements, that, come what will, he says he must win. A friend of his, who is a trainer, and knows all the "dodges" of the race-course, has advised him to back Greased Lightning to the last penny in his pocket. She was thought nothing of then—a mere outsider at 70 to 1. She has since risen to be third favourite, and so cleverly has the captain hedged, that, whether she starts or not, he is sure to be in pocket some cool or hot hundreds. He has provided against every risk. Supposing it should be a wet day and the ground heavy, then Buttered Thunder, it is said, will be the winner, and the captain backs him, too. There are thousands of other men in London who say they are equally certain of success. They pretend that they have laid out their money as cleverly as Crosier. In fact, every gent with a fancy for the turf seems, according to his own account, to be a consummate genius, and to understand thoroughly what the knowing ones are about. The only wonder is why money should ever be lost at the business. They ought, all of them, to make spanking fortunes.

The Derby Day has dawned, and by six o'clock vans are waiting outside the greengrocers' shops and before coal and potato sheds. Barrels of beer have been stowed away by seven, and the passengers are to meet by half-past. With thirty persons to two horses they must take their time on the road. It is undecided as yet whether it is going to rain, or be fair; those who have paid for their seats suggest hopefully that the clouds indicate heat, and those who are to stop at home prophesy a very heavy fall of rain before twelve. But, however threatening the sky may be, vans and shay-carts are, by eight o'clock, rattling down every street, and cornopeans are playing on every side. The maid-servants who are beating their mats against the lamp-posts, or hearth-stoning the doorsteps, allow themselves to be abstracted from their work by watching the different vehicles. In Oxford and Regent Streets, the tailors and glove shops open earlier than usual. Lavender overcoats and grey wrappers ticketed " For the Races—30s.," adorn the windows. Gaudy cravats and gloves of light kid tempt, by their cheapness, youths to be fashionable. Cigar shops are preparing to sell any amount of the best Havannahs at seven for a shilling, and, at the linendrapers', the demand for veils is beyond belief.

Before the clock has struck nine, young gentlemen, got up in a slang style of costume, supposed to be suitable to the occasion, are hurrying, not to business, but to the rendezvous of their different parties. Suits of the loudest Tweed and fastest plaid ; neck-hand-kerchiefs of brilliant patterns, to possess which a simple negress would sell her first-born, are rushing about in all directions ; white hats, that will return brown ones, dart round every corner. Open carriages, with hampers lashed to the footboard, emerge from every turning, some with four horses and blue-jacketed postboys, others with steady-looking cobs and a careful driver on the box. Outside the hotels and club-houses more carriages are waiting, with more hampers, marked " Fortnum and Mason," tied and swung about them. Cases of cigars, branded " Regalia," rest on the folds of hoods. At the Regent Circus, omnibuses and stage-coaches, " Defiances " and " Resolutions," " Paddingtons " and " Royal Blues," have clapped on four horses, and tout for passengers ; men on the roofs play horns to attract notice, and make the turn-out look jolly and regularly first-rate.

Our gallant captain formed one of Viscount Ascot's party. They were to meet at the club. It took some time before they could start, for cabs had first to be dispatched to hunt up one Tom Garden, and another to carry off Charley Sutton ; then Fred Wigwam, at the last moment, sent word he could not come, and Ned Lombard promised to meet his friends opposite the grand stand. Twelve o'clock had

struck before everyone had taken his seat. The captain had volunteered to blow the post-horn. He took it from its long strawberry-
bottle of a case, and blew terrible notes that alarmed the grey tits.
The frightened bloods pranced and reared, little thinking what work
they had got before them, and how foolish it was to waste their
strength in ornamental display.

Now the stream of vehicles was rushing towards the bridges.
Every horse's head was turned in the same direction—open and
closed carriages with fours or a pair, cabs, gigs, and broughams,
dog-carts and vans. Many a horse whose usual daily labour was
to take out coals regretted that any change had occurred in his
avocation.

Down the Clapham Road the inhabitants of those respectably-
appointed and highly-painted family mansions were seated on the tidy
lawns, or leaning over the garden-walls, watching the mob of vehicles
dart past. In front of all these capitally-repaired dwellings were
seated mammas and daughters, and at the upper windows the servant-
girls were leaning over the sills instead of cleaning the rooms.
Though early in the day, winking and kissing of hands to domestics
had already begun. Declarations of love were made to the maidens
and all were called Mary. The dust was blowing about, as if the road
was brown paper smouldering. In every sunbeam the powder was
visibly curling.

On Lord Ascot's drag, the gentlemen who had "nipped" before
starting amused themselves by criticizing the vehicled multitude.
They cried out, "There's a pretty girl!" and pointed out little
"poppets" and pretty angels, dressed up in every kind of gauzy
protection against the dust.

About half-way to Epsom the vans that started in the morning
were discovered halting before public-houses, the horses streaked
with sweat, like hats through which the grease has penetrated.
Every gentleman had put on a green veil, and looked delicately lady-
like. The tender damsels had covered themselves up with net as
completely as the tarts at a pastrycook's. The brims and crowns
of hats were smothered with dust, as if nutmegs had been grated
over them. Hansom cabs had gauze curtains arranged in front,
imparting a highly furnished appearance to the conveyance. So
numerous were the carriages that the road was blocked up, the
vehicles shuffling along in a double line, one side now darting on,
then having to stop and allow the other to rattle ahead. Now
began the smashing of panels. Some prudent brougham people
had fixed stuffed sacks behind their turn-outs. Whenever a panel
was smashed there was a great bobbing out of heads and shaking of
fists, together with a taking down of addresses. The cosy couples
in gigs were often disturbed by finding a horse's head thrust between
man and wife, and the frothy-nosed animal turned the shawls and
coats into pocket-handkerchiefs to wipe its foaming mouth. The dust
had settled so thickly on Captain Crosier's coat that it presented a

moonlight effect of sudden lights and deep shades. He had imprudently oiled his whiskers, and the fine powder had combined with
the grease, and turned to a kind of paint. So handsome a man was
nervous about his personal appearance, especially as the drag was
just then alongside of an open britschka, in which reclined four
lovely Venuses with fawn-coloured hoods drawn over their bonnets.
The angelic maidens looked like fancy nuns who had taken green
veils. There was one with the most beautifully languid eyes, whose
half-closed lids seemed as if she were about to doze. There was
another with golden hair that waved like the grain of satin-wood. A
third had teeth so white that on each rounded surface of enamel a
little globe of light was focussed that made them sparkle like a string
of brilliants. The noble viscount on the box managed very cleverly
to keep the drag alongside this carriage. The beautiful young ladies
had the advantage of being stared at by twenty military pairs of
eyes. To increase the pleasure, a cab-horse in front was good
enough to fall down, and thus enable Tom Oxendon to make an offer
of marriage to her with the light hair, whilst Crosier, looking at the
one with the teeth, exclaimed, " Oh, you perfection ! " The gallant
Lord Oaks, wishing to inform the beauty with the languid eyes that
he considered her an angel, lisped out an inquiry as to " what time
she had promithed to return to Paradith that night ? "

Our noble party had been two hours on the road, and the race-
course was not far off. Already they were in the open country.
They were passing by farms, and had opportunities of remarking
that the young wheat looked well. Under the hedges, at the corners
of lanes, were ginger-beer stalls, or barrels covered with boughs.

The road had now become more free, and the dashing drag rattled
on, passing the omnibuses that started early. They soon distanced
the puffing, distressed nags. These omnibuses had nobody inside,
but carried such a cargo on the roof that they sank far into the
springs, and resembled barges deep in the water. Now horns begin
to play, and lend a romantic, Swiss-mountain effect to the day's
delights. The only turn-outs that passed our dashing trap were the
little perky gigs, that, in their hurry, took to the roadside turf, and
rattled ahead, the springs crackling as they jolted over the ruts and
mounds. There were plenty of beggar-women and mountebanks
hurrying along—poor, tired, thirsty mortals, with a rim of dust round
their dry mouths.

At length the grand stand was in view. A little longer and the
drag was bumping up and down over the turf. It passed the shay-
carts with the nose-bagged horses tied t'other way to the shafts. The
guinea to go on the hill was paid, and the rope lowered. A place was
soon found among the three lines of carriages. Our gentlemen
descended to shake the dust from their clothing, and restore their
fascinating exteriors. Men with brushes seized by main force upon
the captain, and began to rub him down as if he were a horse. For
the next ten minutes fifty stable-boys were, for many various reasons,

begging to be remembered—some for pushing the carriage to its
place and unharnessing the horses, and others for having supplied
clothes-brushes. The noble Ascot was often entreated not to be
hard-hearted, and reminded that the day was hot, and thirst painfully
prevalent.

And now our gallant company took a look at the course. Never
was there such a Derby Day, or so many people. Every carriage
roof was a crowded platform. Numberless parasols, of various
colours, seemed like painted lanterns at a Chinese feast, suspended
in the air. The grand stand, from its sloping top to the parterre in
front, was full of people. The roof was black with hats as a tray of
currants. In the balconies a streak of parasols gracefully revealed
the sex of the spectators. On each side stretched out the canvas
booths, mere trumpery concerns next to the giant building of brick
and stone. Whence could such numbers of carriages have been
raked together? The mob equalled in numbers (but in every other
respect surpassed) the population of a German duchy. There were
horses enough to mount twenty regiments. The poor brutes were
picketed under canvas, or stowed away as in a camp of cavalry.
They were stained with dust as a dirty skylight. There were kickers,
and jibbers, and bolters; some had sore shoulders, broken knees, and
sand-cracks; others had no tails, no eyes, or no wind; and a few ran
better at the nose than on their legs. The first race was on when
our dashing drag arrived, but nobody appeared to care much about
it. The captain took it as he would a glass of absinth before dinner,
to give him an appetite for the grand feast to come. He reserved
himself for the " second course."

There were many other drags besides Viscount Ascot's, very
dashing and highly polished turn-outs, like dandy stage-coaches,
only instead of " York ' or " Brighton " being painted on the doors
there were crests. Each gentleman on the roof of these drags had a
strap round his shoulder, to suspend the polished leather case of his
race-glasses. At first it was difficult to tell whether they had broken
their arms, or merely come armed with cartridge-boxes. Some
people fancied these exquisites had brought their morocco work-
boxes with them, and intended to embroider between the races.

As the time drew near for the Derby to be run, a strong wish to
win a bet animated each breast. Voices around were heard calling
out "Forty to ten against Queen Bee," or, " A hundred to five on
King Death." This desire to pocket somebody else's money gradually
increased up to the moment when the police began to clear the course
for the great race. Forming themselves into a line, this gallant
force was seen to march down the broad enclosure and sweep the
mob before them as dust with a broom. A bell rang out as if fifty
steamers, instead of horses, were about to start. The course was
soon clear as a river, the mob embanking its sides. The only living
thing that dared to defy the police and tread the turf was a white
dog. It walked along as coolly as when a cat, on its midnight

rambles, creeps down a garden walk. The multitude hooted the cur. It looked puzzled, tucked in his tail, and bolted.

Near the weighing-stand the betting men, holding little specks of books, were running about offering five to four, or taking a hundred to twenty. The crowd in the enclosure facing the grand stand was so closely packed that it moved like a basket of live crabs. Presently the horses were brought out, and the non-sporting public had its time occupied in consulting the correct card of the races to see which steed was Red Cap, and which Black Sleeves. It was at this period that young ladies consented to be helped up to perilous places on the roofs of carriages, and kindly allowed their natty little boots to become visible. Great insight into the powers of the horses was gained by closely watching the essay gallop. The animals, from the distance, looked no bigger than greyhounds. A youth, who knew no more of horseflesh than he did of roasted Phœnix, vowed that "he liked the look o' the chesnut." Another, who had never even ridden a rocking-horse, declared "the grey picked his legs up well." "The black one for my money," remarked a third, who, if the terms had been accepted, would have made a good bargain, for he only had three pounds in his pocket. One comic gentleman, noticing the red-coated clerk of the course trotting past, offered to back him against the field. The heavy swells on the drags were staring hard through their race-glasses, and watched the horses until they reached the paddock near the starting-post, when only the red, blue, green, and black jackets could be seen moving above the palings. The next half-hour elapsed and yet the horses did not start. It was said that Buttered Thunder had misconducted himself and tried to win by galloping off before his rivals were even placed. The hot sun soon tired everybody. Carriage-tops grew hot as hobs, and burned the feet. The glare of light was so great that, to relieve his sight, Captain Crosier watched a young lady with hazel eyes and a pink transparent muslin, whom a gentleman in the rumble was helping to what at first looked like champagne; but this mean fellow was only frothing up bitter ale, and when the gallants on the drag found out that so pretty a girl was condemned to sip such common tipple, they shouted, with one sympathizing voice, "Shame! shame!"

At length a cry rises from the grand stand, "They're off! they're off!" The shout passes along the mob like the rustling of a forest as a breeze sweeps over it. The roof of the monster building has changed from a black slope to a pink embankment, for every face is gazing towards the course. The progress of the horses can be traced by the excitement they raise. "Hats off!" is a favourite cry. "Where are they?" ask some who cannot see. "They've turned the corner," answer those who can. A few who have never been on a course before exclaim, "Beautiful! I never saw such a race."

The time was drawing near when a yard of ground would be more valuable than a whole estate. Fortunes were hanging on a neck, or a head, and thousands would be lost by a length. Many a man was

biting his lips as Pink Sleeves hung back, or Yellow Cap sprang
forward. The excitement was intense. Stable-helps and beggar-boys
climbed unrebuked up wheels and on springs, and attained high
places on carriage-tops and rumbles next to dashing blades and
fashionable dames. That knowing youth, Mr. Teddy Cutler, preferred creeping into a carriage full of ladies, who were chirping and
twittering like an aviary of singing-birds. These angels were betting
gloves.

Now began a mighty din of shouting. The horses parted. A few
more bounds and all would be decided. A thousand cries were
mingled together, of "Green Jacket wins!" "No! Red Jacket!"
"Pink's picking up!" "Blue Cap's first!" "No! Yellow Cap!"
"Blue Sleeves for a sovereign!" On came the closely-packed horses,
each with its neck stretched out straight as that of a swift-winged
bird. There were ten of them together as if they had been bound
side by side. The silken jackets of the jockeys rippled and crackled
like flags, with the wind of the pace. They bent forwards, and
threw their arms about them, as with desperation they lashed their
steeds. A swallow does not move so fast as they were moving. The
animals flung their legs from under them like hares, as they bounded
on. The mob shouted and pressed against the ropes, so that the
police had to beat them back, lest the cord should break. But none
cared for truncheons or threats, for the steeds were nearly home.
This was the moment for the clever jockey to show his art. The
close knot of horseflesh slowly separated and two or three steeds
darted from the rest. It was neck to neck between Yellow, Green,
and Pink. He who hit the hardest would win the race. People
screamed with ungovernable excitement. At last the fatal post was
passed. Two of the horses shot by as close together as if they were
running in harness. After all this enthusiasm and delight nobody
knew which was the winner.

There was one gallant youth dreadfully disappointed with the
race, for Greased Lightning made a bad twentieth and Buttered
Thunder did not start. To console himself, he devoted all his attention to luncheon, and determined to smother care in the salad-bowl.
The baskets from Fortnum and Mason were soon opened. The green
boxes from the pastrycooks had their lids taken off. The pigeon-pies
had come down safely, and only a little salt fallen into the jam tarts.
The blocks of ice, packed like grapes in sawdust, were taken from the
bags. The claret bottles were handed up with their coverings of
rushes, the Hockheimer, the Moussirender Moselle, and the Curacoa
sec, speedily produced, and the corkscrew screamed for. "This is
heaven!" cried one dashing blade, after a full tumbler. "For
Heaven's sake, more claret!" gasped in agony another tremendous
fellow. Soon the top of the drag was covered with silver dishes, and
everybody was eating ravenously. "I shall be human soon," said
Charley Sutton, taking the second half of a fowl. Champagne corks
flew about like tennis-balls, and the bubbling amber wine was poured

foaming into tumblers. With every empty bottle that was thrown down, the talk grew louder and the laughter more frequent. Friends came up to the drag, and, "How d'ye do, old boy?" "A glass of sherry?" "Where's Tom?" "Capital race!" was the short conversation mumbled through full mouths. Occasionally, a fellow in his drag would call out to another in his brougham, "Has Clara come?" or, "Have you brought Mary down? Where shall I find her?"—"Last brougham, second rank." One friend, ten carriages off, cried out, "I say, Ascot, and you fellows, I know where there's the prettiest girl on the course!" Twenty voices roared, "Where? Where?" A hand pointed to the carriage in which the nun-like beauties were seated. They had thrown off their hoods, and the excitement of the scene had coloured up their faces. It was dangerous for any but the strongest-brained to look at them.

After five minutes, Lord Oaks avowed a deadly hatred to a man with heavy whiskers, who was carving a chicken for the languid-eyed maiden. He inquired who that fellow was and vowed "he wath a thnob." All over the course eating was proceeding vigorously. Men were resting their plates on the boxes, springs, and steps of carriages, whilst the young ladies inside broughams and barouches were gobbling at their ease. Bits of bread, lobster-shells, and broken bottles, were lying on the grass around, and boys were hunting among the scraps to see if they could find anything eatable. Many were the requests to "Give us that bottle, your honour, when you're done with it," for there was a coster buying them up at a halfpenny each to sell again in London. Beggar-women, asking for a little penny, went among the carriages, and attracted the notice of gentlemen by pulling at their legs like bell-ropes. Frenchmen wearing earrings serenaded the feasters with guitars and accordions, and an Italian organ-boy executed several concerted pieces with a friend who whistled. There was no lack of gipsy-women, with hair as black as their satin dresses, and wearing their bonnets placed like flower-pots on their heads. "Shall I tell you your fortune, handsome gentleman?" they said, in a wheedling tone. At one carriage, a lovely girl, in a white cloud of muslin, covered over with blue butterfly bows, refused to have her destiny revealed, although the sun-stained Egyptian whined, "Faint heart never won a handsome gentleman. There's somebody coming nobody dreams of. It's all writ in your beautiful eyes. Try your little lucky sixpence, lady," &c. The most painful exhibition of the day was that of a poor wretch who tried to awe the carriage-folk into generosity by exhibiting a sore and leprous body. He stood with his ulcerous legs bared before those who were eating, until, out of mercy to themselves, they were obliged to purchase his absence by a donation.

To soothe his sorrows and forget Greased Lightning and Buttered Thunder, Captain Crosier devoted his energies to three-a-penny knock-'em-downs. He prided himself on being a "dab" at the game. He was soon in possession of a handkerchief full of humming-tops, shells stopped up with red daubs of pincushions, and wooden dolls. These he distributed among ladies of his acquaintance. He filled the lilac-silk lap of a Venus in ringlets, and on the strength of three lemons flirted for half an hour and drank a bottle of Moselle with two most lovely creatures in lace and cherry silk. When the postilions in plum satin and velvet jackets—when the postboys in blue spencers and white-cord thing-a-mees—had eaten their hunks of bread and meat, and half-fuddled themselves with champagne— when the grooms in natty frock-coats and plaster-of-Paris legs had packed up the silver dishes, and placed the spoons in security, then the horses were brought out, and preparations begun for returning home. Everybody was very merry, being full up to the neck with wine.

Whilst the carriages were waiting till it was possible to move, the time was passed in joking and laughter. If a gentleman with a lady on his arm happened to pass by, Viscount Ascot and his friends would instantly shout out, " Take her from him; take her from him !" The most complimentary speeches were addressed to the maidens in the neighbouring carriages, and they were entreated to leave their friends and return home on the drag. At last the way was clear, and the prancing greys had their heads "let go." Off they rattled past the line of booths where " Jones, from Reading," and "Smith, from Berks," had made such a good thing out of cold meat, bottled beer, and a slop-basinful of mustard. The dashing young blades were in ripe spirits for the fun of the road, as full of liquor as a fresh bottle, and as saucy as a Cheap Jack. The first gentleman they now saw on horseback was, as usual, requested " to get inside, and draw the blinds down." And the answer was the one common on such occasions, consisting of " I can't, for I promised to give your aunt a lift." Another horseman was informed that his fiery cob would " go, sir, if he only gave him a little hay sometimes." Directly a man was seen with a green veil on, he was termed " a ladylike young woman." Not being of a very witty temperament, Captain Crosier never made any observation more rude than "I see you," or " I'll tell your mother." When the drag stopped at Sutton, Tom Oxendon made an offer of marriage to a grey-haired and evidently married woman seated at the first floor. He stated that he had thirty thousand a year, but wasn't happy, for he loved her to distraction.

Although the noble viscount was rolling on his box under the influence of champagne, yet he managed his prancing greys most skilfully. He darted among the carts adorned with boughs like arbours, he grazed by the vans out of which twenty heads were thrust in alarm, and even the trotting ponies could not keep up with him. Hansom cabs, with rows of wooden dolls strung up before them, broughams, barouches, costers' trucks, everything was left behind, and all the time they galloped along, the gay young dogs sprinkled their insults plentifully on every side.

No sooner did they see on a stage-coach a man who was playing

the horn, than one of the wags cried out, " Would anyone oblige me
by cutting that fellow's throat ? " or begged as a favour that somebody would " hit the musician in the wind." Beautiful maidens
were accused of bad taste for remaining " with those ugly men ; "
and if any observations were made on the noble company's moustaches, the retort was sure to be, " They won't allow them at Swan
and Edgar's." But there is nothing so exhausting as wit, and at
last our gallant crew was tired out. The laughter and the
" chaffing " were followed by a dead silence. They passed the fair
on Clapham Common without insulting anybody ; they looked into
the parlours of the substantial Clapham mansions, and saw all the
family circles assembled round the windows without addressing one
rude word to them. And even when, on passing Kennington 'Pike,
the crowd criticized the greys by yelling " Cat's-meat, yah ! " the
jolly boys took no notice of the remark, for they were completely
fagged to death, and wishing they were at home.

As he drank his soda-water at the club, Captain Crosier felt quite
broken-spirited. There was a report among the members that poor
Charles Bouncey had blown out his brains through losing thirty
thousand. This reminded him of his own position, and he told Fred
Tattenham in confidence that if the men who were in his debt did
not come up to the scratch on settling day he should be regularly
" sewed up." Then he cursed Greased Lightning—denounced
Buttered Thunder—wished he'd never been born—and, on looking to
see what time it was, found his watch had been stolen.

CHAPTER XVIII.

LOCKED UP.

KNOWING that he was as innocent as a blind kitten of the crime
with which he was charged, it nearly drove Philip crazy to find himself treated like the most arrant young scamp that ever picked a
pocket at an execution. To be virtuous, and yet appear vicious, was
a harder state than he had strength of mind to endure. He more
than once muttered to himself, " I shouldn't have minded if I had
forged the beastly cheque, but to be hauled up in this way when I
knew no more about the robbery than the Bishop of London does of
the double-shuffle, is enough to make a fellow's heart go off like a
bottle of ginger-beer and choke him outright." Unfortunate Phil
did not belong to that class of high-minded mortals who find their
consolation in their approving conscience. He was not one of that
order of philosophers who walk singing to the stake ; but howled and

wept as loud as any baby teething. The policemen had almost to carry him along, so determinedly did he throw himself back, as if to resist their progress.

Now, when Inspector Darley requires the presence of Radcliffe Ned, that he may be allowed an opportunity of explaining away that little house-breaking affair at Notting Hill, the intelligent officer seeks for the daring thief among his haunts in the Mint. He enters the tap-room of the "Blue Cow," and seeing his man sipping gin, merely beckons to him, saying, "Here, Ned, you're wanted." Although the ruffian knows that this simple phrase means, perhaps, seven years "beyond the seas," yet he leaves the room as readily as if his sweetheart had sent for him, and walks off to the police-station without the least murmur. Radcliffe Ned has no doubt of his own guilt, and he yields himself into the hands of justice as meekly as a cab horse allows itself to be placed between the shafts. But our innocent boy could no more understand why he should be deprived of his liberty than a young colt out at grass, and he plunged and kicked, roared, and jibed, using every artifice in his power to break away from his captors. By the time he reached the station-house he was very hot and crumpled, and most certainly looked as if he was capable of any possible outrage on society.

The police-court in which the prisoner was to be examined had formerly been a private residence. It had been ingeniously converted into one of the most inconvenient tribunals it is possible to conceive. It was not a palace, but a kind of lodging-house of justice. The grand audience-chamber where the guilty were tried was situated on the drawing-room floor. To add a grandeur to the apartment the ceiling had been removed and the first and second stories knocked into one, whereby it was not only rendered lofty and airy, but it also enjoyed the advantage of having six windows. In the quondam coal-cellars, pantry, and sculleries the guilty males were locked up, whilst the criminal females were allowed the use of the butler's pantry and the front kitchen.

It was into the back parlour that Philip was first ushered, and the charge was taken down by a sergeant, whose plated buttons shone against his dark uniform bright as stars on a frosty night. Our silly youth, determined to let slip no opportunity of protesting his innocence, thought it a favourable moment for informing this official that he was entirely guiltless of the crime; but instead of being listened to, the stern order was given to "remove him." And the lad was whipped from the sergeant's presence as unceremoniously as an empty dish.

When the time came for his case to be heard, Philip, strongly guarded by four powerfully-built policemen, ascended in state the stairs leading to the drawing-room. He felt his valour evaporate rapidly as he stood before the judge who could as easily send him to prison as he could order a letter to be posted. There sat the stern magistrate, looking, despite his light summer waistcoat and blue coat with brass buttons, very awful and majestic. The delinquent muttered a short prayer that the gentleman's health might be singularly good that day and incline him to leniency, and then turned his eyes to the bald-headed clerk who sat at the lower desk, and instantaneously taking a dislike to that functionary, wondered to himself "what that yellow old buffer had to do with it." The mob of fifteen who crowded the public portion of the court became interested as they heard that Phil was charged with passing a forged cheque for three hundred pounds. The reporter, who, until then, had been trimming his nails, seized his pen to take down the interesting details, and even the magistrate and his clerk stared at the stripling as if wondering by what hydraulic pressure of circumstances so much vice had been squeezed into so small a body. "What's his name?" asked the magistrate. And as he did not distinctly catch the words "Philip Merton," his chief clerk was kind enough to assist him by saying it was "Philip Burton," a mistake which another official most courteously corrected by stating it to be "Philip Gurton," whilst one of the policemen endeavoured to prevent mistakes by asserting it to be "Philip Turpen."

One after another did the different witnesses give their evidence against Phil, and all the time the magistrate and his clerk were entering in their books every word that was spoken. To hear these accusations brought against him, and to see them all written down as gospel truth, so roused the indignant fire in Phil's bosom, that he boiled over with impatience to repel the charges, and exclamations such as, "If you please, sir," or "Upon my word, sir," bubbled up to his mouth. Even the magistrate's command to "Hold your tongue, boy," could not awe him into silence. When his turn at last came to tell his own version of the story, his tongue rattled along at such a pace that the chief clerk, although he scribbled down the statement with a speed that made the feather of his quill dance about like a thing of life, had to call out "not so fast" with every other word spoken.

This preliminary examination ended in Philip being remanded whilst the police were ordered to use every possible exertion in tracing out the foreigner who styled himself the representative of Messieurs "Alphonse Lerouville et Cie., Lyons and London." One portion of this examination pained Philip excessively. The magistrate inquired of the police whether any of them had previously known anything of the prisoner. An officer who was getting so stout in the service that if he remained much longer the witness-box would have to be enlarged to accommodate him, remarked that he thought he remembered having seen Philip's face somewhere that he couldn't call to mind—somewhere that he couldn't exactly remember. This random evidence made Phil give so big a sigh that it is wonderful how he could have heaved it.

On suspicion of being a vagabond, Philip was treated as one. The effect produced by this usage was to convince him that to respect the law was a waste of time. Although he had struggled bravely to keep out of harm's way, he was no better off in the end than if he had been the most arrant miscreant breathing.

It was perfectly just that Philip should have been detained, but it was also perfectly just that his imprisonment should not have been of the same severity as that allotted to a hardened malefactor. He was taken down to the back area of the building, and placed in a cell about as large as a coal cellar. So terrible did this wretched, dark dungeon of a place seem, that the boy drew back, saying beseechingly, " Oh! not in there." But a strong arm pushed him in, and the lock was turned. At first he lost all control over himself, and began kicking spitefully at the door until an officer came to the little iron grating—about as large as a brick—and threatened him with fetters if he did not keep quiet.

There were four others besides Phil in this dungeon. It was so hot that in a few seconds the perspiration burst from the boy. The stench which filled the place was so overpowering that the lad held his cap over his nose and mouth, so that he might filter the air through the cloth. The only means adopted to ventilate the dungeon was the small grating before mentioned, and although the crack under the door assisted in a small degree to moderate the poisonous effects of the atmosphere, still the position of the five prisoners resembled, to a painful degree, that of a mouse under the receiver of an air pump. It was only a question of time to produce the same deadly effect. Had a joint of mutton been hung up in that cell, it would in a few hours have been unfit for use.

People in misfortune soon become friendly. When Phil had told his companions his tale of distress, they also favoured him with their revelations. One was a youth dressed in a second-hand kind of fashion, whose misfortune had been to meet with a zealous detective in private clothes at the very moment when his hand had accidentally strayed into a lady's pocket. Another youth had been fined for assaulting a policeman whilst in a state of intoxication, and a third had by mistake passed off a bad half-crown, and four pounds' worth of the same pewter coin being found in his pockets, he had been most shamefully, he said, convicted as an experienced smasher. The fourth gentleman was a Mr. Mudgster, who had been taken up for obstructing the thoroughfare with " his little apperatus," by which term he designated a nut-board, at which ladies and gentlemen addicted to sport shot for Barcelonas. " That's why I was sent to this here Black Hole of Calcutter," cried Mr. M., " though it hadn't got nothin' at all to do with no obstructions of no sort, but only because I wouldn't square the policeman." By squaring, Mr. Mudgster meant bribing. This proprietor of the miniature shooting-gallery, perceiving that Phil was the most worthy of his companions, endeavoured to enter into conversation with him, by inquiring how long a term he expected to get for the forgery, and whether he would rather be transported, or only have three years of it at Coldbath

Fields. Worn out by the morning's excitement, Phil was almost heartbroken to find that even among all the prisoners his assertions of innocence were not believed. With tears in his eyes he endeavoured to convince the proprietor of the nut-board that he was the victim of cruel circumstances. He even related to that gentleman the greater portion of his persecutions through life, in the hope of impressing him in his favour. For two hours did Mr. Mudgster listen to the affecting biography, only interrupting the narrative occasionally by such exclamations as "That's a rum start!" or urging him on by inquiring, "What was the next move that he was up to?" The story was, unfortunately, interrupted at its most interesting period by the arrival of an officer, who informed Mr. Mudgster that his old woman (meaning that excellent lady, Mrs. Mudgster) had been selling her pots and pans, and raised the twenty shillings' fine for which he was detained. He did not leave, however, without saying farewell to Phil, adding, "If you get over this, and wants a job, come to me, which is Mudgster, Old Kent Road, and I'll see what ha'pence you're fit for."

For more than a week Philip was in custody. He was taken in the public van to the House of Detention and back again to the police-court twice before his innocence was admitted. It was principally through the evidence of Viscount Ascot that he escaped being tried at the Old Bailey. That nobleman spoke so decidedly of his suspicions of Colonel Rattaplan, and his evidence agreed so thoroughly with the boy's story, that the magistrate was forced to discharge the prisoner.

Another curious circumstance which had great weight on Philip's side of the scale was, that the dashing French officer, although carefully sought for and inquired after by many smart detectives, could nowhere be found in London, the only place where they could hear anything about him being a cigar shop in Oxford Street, where he owed a small account of three guineas.

Our friend Captain Crosier was so hurt at finding that he had been "taken in" by the foreigner, that he wrote no fewer than three letters on the subject to the French Government. In the answers which he received from the French Minister of War, he was assured that no such person as Victor Baudin Rattaplan had ever been colonel of the 11e Leger.

"I can't make it out," said the captain, when he was defending himself to his lordship, who rated him severely for having introduced such a rogue into his society—"I can't make it out. The man seemed to know all about our family. Besides, how could I doubt a man who brought such excellent letters of recommendation?"

CHAPTER XIX.

BERTHA IN DANGER.

IT is ten million pities that we cannot serve our dirty human nature the same as we do our dirty linen, so that by sending our impure thoughts and foul intentions to some moral wash, we might have them returned again milk-white and starched ready to make us respectable for at least a week. What a comfort it would be to clothe ourselves in unsullied goodness as easily as we slip on a clean shirt, or surround our bosoms with spotless innocence with no more exertion than is required to put on a white waistcoat!

If Virtue had turned washerwoman, she could not have had a more constant customer than Captain Crosier. Every week she would have taken away from his house a bundle of impurities and immoralities enough to break in the shoulders of a Covent Garden basketwoman. What we are going to relate of his wicked attempts upon defenceless Bertha would alone have been sufficient to make up a heavy washing bill. Among other items, there would have been at least 100 profligate ideas. 20 false oaths, 3 deliberate deceptions, 4 meannesses, and 6 seductive temptations.

It almost looked as if the captain was taking those vast pains simply for the amusement of his club friends. Whenever he met them, he had invariably some fresh incident to relate of how his deep-plotted schemes had been frustrated by the vigilant Miss Tomsey. "Begad, Tom," he would say to Mr. Oxendon, "I shall have to get you to buck up to the old girl, and carry her off. She spoils everything. I should have managed my little wench in half the time if it had not been for her." The joking that took place about the dinner that was to be forfeited was very offensive to the gallant Merton. Even whilst he was protesting that his success was inevitable, the wags would be selecting the dishes which they would prefer for the Richmond banquet; so that Bertha somehow got mixed up with "Mushrooms en surprise, with a purée of game," and Miss Tomsey was strangely confounded with "hare boned and stuffed, with cream sauce."

Very much puzzled was Bertha to imagine how the letters she so often found on her dressing-table when she went to bed could possibly have been smuggled into the house. She would take them unopened to Miss Tomsey, when her indignation would, even late as it was, have all the servants into the room, and questioned as to who dared to take such a liberty in her establishment. But if innocence consisted in protestations, never were domestics more wrongly

Q

accused. It was affecting to hear Mrs. Wortey wish that she might drop down dead if she knew anything about it, and the indignation of both Mary Anne and the scullery maid could only be equalled by the haughty denials of Mr. Boxer. One after another were these love letters flung into the fire without even being opened. For, although Miss Tomsey's fingers were itching to break the seal to see what " that fellow " had to write about, yet never once did she allow her curiosity to get the better of her.

Whoever the traitor in the house might have been, it is too late now to inquire; but that a secret correspondence was kept up between the captain and Miss Tomsey's servants was most certain. Indeed, the mistress, having one day occasion to travel as far as Clapham, she had not left the house ten minutes before Mr. Crosier knocked at the door. Unless he had received private intimation that the old lady would be absent for four hours he would never have dared to make the visit. The first intimation that Bertha had of her admirer's call was the tussle which took place between him and Mr. Boxer in the passage. "I have orders not to admit you, sir," shouted the footman. But the bold officer broke from the humble menial as easily as a wasp from a cobweb. Before the girl was aware of it, her admirer was in the room, bowing to her as humbly as a linen-draper to a duchess.

He told the trembling girl that in self-defence he had been forced to seek this interview. His letters, he complained, were not only unanswered, but he had reason to believe, even unread. "Was this just?" he asked; and meeting with no reply, he took upon himself to affirm that it was cruelly unfair. "The meanest culprit," he affirmed, "was at least tried before he was condemned." He would have continued speaking much longer had not Bertha, who had retreated to one of the windows, trembled so that he knew his speeches would be lost upon her. The hand with which she clutched the curtain shook as if palsied. He tried to advance towards her, but in a moment she had stepped on to the balcony, and looked so much as if she would jump into the street that he thought it prudent to draw back again. This great fear on her part was the result of the many warnings which Miss Tomsey had given. Bertha said she was fully impressed with the belief that if the captain could but once lay his hands upon her, he would carry her off as surely as the devil did Dr. Faustus.

One great evil resulted from the mistress's over-anxiety to protect her maiden, and that was that, in the course of half an hour, Bertha discovered the captain was not the dangerous and desperate man he had been described. He entreated her in the most pathetic manner to be seated and listen to him, and he even brought the chair to her with a grace that surpassed that of the stout Boxer as incomparably as do the elegant poses of Taglioni excel the attitudes of a 'bus conductor. The great importance which had been attached to all the captain's sayings and doings gave to his violent declarations of love a weight and consequence, and she listened withal to the bombast which at other times she would have laughed at.

At least half a dozen times did the amorous officer volunteer to leave the room if she desired it, but as she dared not trust herself to answer him, he concluded that she assented to the interview. Then did he begin to pour out a flood of vows and protestations such as would have carried away and dashed to pieces the strongest embankment of virtue. How many girls on ten pounds a year and a month's notice would have struggled against this torrent of praise ? The two big eyes of Bertha grew round as penny pieces with astonishment. At first she feared he had gone mad; then imagined he had learnt it from a book; and, at last, began to believe him.

" Do not fancy, beautiful Bertha," he said, in a low voice, for fear anybody should be listening at the door—" do not fancy that I would harm you. I come here to offer you my services—to benefit you, if I can. I would be your best friend. If any injury threatened you, I would break through walls, and peril my life to save you. I would ——" (Here followed five other examples of the great risks he should feel but too enchanted to run if he could possibly be of the slightest service to the maiden. Among the most significant of these were perils from fire and water, and the dangers of the battle-field. Indeed, he talked of pouring out his heart's blood as calmly as if he owned cisterns full of it.) "Then," continued the captain, " why have you taken so unconquerable a dislike to one who feels so ardent an affection for you ? It is because I am what is called a gentleman. If I came to you dressed in mean clothing—if I had to labour hard for my living—then my courtship would not be opposed. Simply because my coat is of cloth, the doors are barred against me. Because my income is large, admittance is refused. Yet you see I address you with respect, and there is nothing to be feared in my behaviour."

Her head was turning with wonder at what she heard, but she could not help confessing that there was a great deal of truth in what he said. Before he left her, he made her promise that not only she would not mention his visit to her lady, but that she would consent to read the next letter he wrote.

That night she lay awake many hours, thinking over the love phrases and their mysterious utterer. He swore so strongly to his affection for her that she could not help believing him a little. A judge of the land would have been influenced by one tithe of his oaths. Many a man has been hung on fewer. If Jove, as they say, laughs at lovers' perjuries, his heathen godship must have laughed heartily—that is to say, supposing that the captain was a false-hearted deceiver.

Next day Bertha found a letter on her table. She opened it, prepared to find at least four sides—crossed and recrossed—of most desperate protestations of love. To her utter astonishment there was but one line, informing her that on the morrow she would receive a visit from her mother. The proceedings of this unaccountable man puzzled her more and more. What could he have to say to a workhouse nurse? And the only reply that she could find was that he had gone there to beseech for her interference with her hard-hearted daughter.

For the next twelve hours Bertha's behaviour and manner were such as Miss Tomsey did not approve of. She was so absent that several times her mistress had to speak twice to her before she could get an answer. Her hands, instead of flying about her work, moved so slowly as to bring down the reprimand "that she had better go to bed if she was sleepy." Whilst reading the newspaper after dinner, she made many mistakes—talking of a bire in Fermondsey, and a dreadful surder in Boho; for, although Bertha saw the letters, she was paying no attention to their meaning, but putting the question to herself, why the captain had visited her mother? It is no wonder that Miss Tomsey lost her patience, and cried out, "Bertha! how can you be so absurd? You are thinking about that fellow, instead of paying attention to the newspaper. It is useless your entertaining any melodramatic notions, and fancying yourself the heroine of a domestic drama. I won't have any victims in my house, so pray don't think of the wretch."

"I was thinking of my mother," nervously stammered Bertha.

"Nonsense, child! go on with the murder," replied the mistress.

Presently, when Bertha and Mrs. Hazlewood were seated in the back library, chatting together, she learnt the motives which induced the fashionable officer to visit the workhouse nurse of St. Lazarus Without. Now, indeed, did she feel a great liking for the man.

"I couldn't for the life of me, Bertha, imagine what he wanted. He's a handsome fellow, and has the most remarkable eyes, I think, I ever saw. Says he, 'Mrs. Hazlewood, you have a daughter for whom I have the highest admiration and respect.' You should have heard him talk about you, Bertha, it quite brought tears to my eyes. 'For my sake, madam,' says he, 'I should like to be of some service to you,' and then he actually proposed taking me from the work-house, and setting me up in a lodging-house to let apartments. These were his very words: 'I can tell at once from your looks and bearing that you would be able to earn a comfortable living at it.' You may fancy how I stared—but I'm sure you can't—you never can. Then what did he do, but slip these five sovereigns into my hand, and, before I had time to thank him, he was off."

What could Bertha think of all this, but that Captain Crosier was, after all, a good and honourable gentleman? She might have been suspicious of his love for her, but his goodness to her mother in the workhouse admitted but of one interpretation. She felt so grateful to him that she almost hated Miss Tomsey for having ever mistaken his motives. In her turn Bertha told her mother all that had happened, and after mentioning her mistress's objection to her admirer's visits, concluded by asking the old nurse's opinion. She might just as well have sought advice from a lamp post, for the old lady could take but one view of the case. She thought her Bertha the most beautiful girl in the world, and after his conduct that morning, she could not help considering the captain as being the perfection of mankind. "Miss Tomsey may mean it very well," said the old lady, "but it strikes me she is crying 'wolf' before her lamb's in danger. There's no doubt about the matter. This gentleman's in love with you—he's violently in love with you."

The objection raised by Bertha was, "How could so rich and fine a gentleman think favourably of so poor a girl?" and this led to a long cross-examination, during which Bertha had to imitate as closely as possible the expression of the young man whilst speaking, so that the mother might judge whether he was in earnest in his courtship. The girl was asked whether he ever rolled his eyes, or put on a tender air. One question was, whether he was pale when first entering the room, and then gradually became flushed? whether his voice trembled and his knees shook? Great stress was laid upon whether he had ever been observed to gnaw his finger ends, tear at his gloves, or dash his hair off his forehead. The good old lady had once been to the theatre, and on that occasion the lover in the piece had during his interview with the fair one used most of these actions whilst revealing his passion. She therefore concluded that such was the usual pantomime employed during courtship. It was useless for Bertha to insist that she had never had sufficient courage to watch the captain's demeanour. The mother requested her so often to try and remember, and to think well, that at last the daughter was forced to make the required admissions. Then Bertha, blushing up to her eyes, repeated Miss Tomsey's warning that "the fellow" meant no good, and was only working her ruin. With an expression of horror Dame Hazlewood wondered how anybody could have "such uncharitable notions."

"She meant that I am merely a servant, and he is an officer, and very rich," stammered Bertha; "and it does seem strange that when he must know so many beautiful ladies he should choose to marry a girl like me."

"Lord bless me!" replied the mother, "when men are in love they do all sorts of strange things. Now look at that great Peter of Russia. He married a common girl that served behind the bar in the canteens. Then, again, many of the judges and the first lords in the land have married their cooks. And as for taking up with their housekeepers, that's quite a common custom with gentlefolks. Then why shouldn't he take a fancy to you?"

With such overpowering arguments against her, what could poor Bertha answer? She sighed, and said, "How happy it would make her to see her mother away from the workhouse, and earning an honest living. That was what she most thought of." Nor was the old nurse less delighted with the idea of living free of the parish, and being her own mistress again. The idea of having a house of her own had materially influenced her in framing her opinion of Captain Crosier's intentions, or she would never have told her daughter to countenance that gentleman's addresses, and not to judge too hastily until they had cause for suspicion.

As the old lady hurried back to the Union, the journey seemed short enough, so busy was she wondering where her house would be, and how much her drawing-rooms and parlours would let for. But Bertha remained for nearly an hour without changing her position, asking herself whether such a state of things was possible in a way that implied she was certain it was not. It was only when the candle was burnt down to the socket that she awoke from her trance.

CHAPTER XX.

OUT NUTTING.

IT so happened that Mr. Tobias Sparkler, when he was fatigued with his day's exertions, or in any way depressed in spirits, would retire to a beer-shop in his neighbourhood, and tried to forget his own troubles by reading in the daily paper the misfortunes that had befallen other people. Thus, "ANOTHER FATAL COLLISION.—FOUR LIVES LOST," would, even on his worst business days, make him exclaim, "Well, I ain't so bad off as those poor chaps;" and a "FRIGHTFUL SUICIDE" has been known—although one half of his donkeys had been idle all day long—to draw forth the remark that he "didn't feel inclined for that kind of lark yet awhile, thank God." On one of these occasions he was noticed by his friends to be seized with a sudden fit of what they, in their rude medical knowledge, termed the "staggers." He had been reading quietly enough, when in a moment he leaped from his seat, struck the newspaper violently, and then stamping with a force that made the spittoons jump like crickets, roared out, "Why, curse my hat and gaiters, if one o' my chaps ain't been hauled up for boning three hundred pounds!" There was no more newspaper reading that evening at the "Cat and Kitten," for Mr. Sparkler had too many questions put to him to be able to do anything else than answer them. "I'd ha' trusted that boy," he said, "with the national debt in ha'pence. I never see such a face. It smiled at you like an engraving, and every speck of it looked honesty. And here you see he's been boning three hundred pounds! I should as soon of thought of his going off with a donkey in his waistcoat pocket. Ah! human natur! human natur! who can be up to your dodges? I had made up my mind he had only bolted from me, whereas he has turned prig."

The worthy donkey-keeper's excited feelings were still prejudiced against Philip when, one afternoon, that young gentleman appeared before him to solicit a renewal of his employment. The master fell back in astonishment at the impudence of the request. He led the youth to a secluded corner, and thus addressed him, "If you'd asked me to lend you a twenty pound note, you'd ha' had more chance. Why, curse your young bones! what do you mean by it? Come back to me after that there three hundred pound affair? Just step it," and he indicated the road he was to take by pointing towards Hendon. Philip's prayers and entreaties, although they in some degree softened Mr. Sparkler's heart, only ended in a moral lecture. " You must say ' Ajew,' my lad, for its good-bye between us. Now, just ask yourself, do you think a chap as is game for such work as you've been up to is to be trusted with a weak infant or a shaky invalid? Why, I should expect to find the chairs and side saddles come home empty and find you'd ruined me by a highway robbery. No, no, young 'un, try Hounslow Heath, for Hampstead is barred and bolted agin you for the rest of your mortal life."

This advice Philip did not think it prudent to follow, for instead of trudging towards Hounslow, he made the best of his way to the Old Kent Road, and there he found Mr. Mudgster watching over his shooting-board, and calling out in a loud voice, "Try a shot, gentlemen! try a shot, ladies! Twenty in the bull's-eye! Plenty for your sport, and nuts for nothing!" After congratulating the lad upon his acquittal, Mr. Mudgster, guessing at the object of the visit, said, " I suppose it's all play-time with you, my boy, and you're cursed like a pig up a Jews' court? Well, you're come at the right time, for I and my missus are off on the circuit to work the country this day week, and I'll give you a job."

The remainder of that evening was passed in pleasant conversation, the principal topic of which was the beauty of Mr. Mudgster's shooting-board. "It's one of the handsomest in town," observed the proprietor, "and as I say, Kelly's masterpiece—for he's the chap that painted it—and there's nobody like him for showiness as a artist." (This board was a comic one.) " The sentimental ones ain't no good," he continued. There was painted on this screen the figure of a clown, and on his breast was a target at which the darts were aimed. The clown had his eyes and knees turned in, and was supposed to be saying, "I'm looking at you," for those words were written inside a bladder issuing from the mouth. On the wings on each side of the board were painted several scenes. One was of a Jack Tar slaying some twenty Chinese, and, by means of another bladder, crying, "Peace or war, you varmint, but none of your tricks." Another was an illustration of a soldier alarmed by a shower of cannon-balls, and exclaiming, " Oh! dear, I wish I was at home with mother." But Kelly's chef-d'œuvre, and the painting which the owner most frequently dusted with his cap, was a representation of a house on fire, with a fire-engine tearing along at full speed and

a policeman tumbling over a dog. "I've promised my missus to
have that there picture framed some of these days," said Mr.
Mudgster, admiring it with his head on one side. "It's a sweet
pretty thing, and as nat'ral as if it took place."

The nut vendor had certain prearranged jokes with which he
always entertained his customers. If a young woman took up the
rifle, he would say to her after each shot, "Well done, miss! If you
marries as well as you fires, you'll have an easy time of it." Or he
would cry, "You've a beautiful eye, mum, and as true as print, and
happy's the man you wink at." To the gentlemen he would remark,
"Try another shot, sir, and you'll be a man now before your mother."
When Philip heard these things said for the first time, he laughed
excessively, but owing to their being repeated some twenty times in
the course of an hour, the force of their humour was considerably
weakened.

The trip to the country was more a matter of necessity than choice
with Mr. Mudgster. Most of his pots and pans had gone to pay his
police fine and he proposed to refurnish his room with the profits
to arise from the visits to fairs and race-courses. "Battersea Fields,"
Mr. Mudgster would say, "was once tidy ground to me, but now no
good. I have taken 36s. of an afternoon in them there Fields, but
now that's all up."

The day before they started on their rounds, Philip accompanied
his new master to Duke's Place, in Houndsditch, the costermongers'
great market for nuts.

Duke's Place, as the costers have christened it, is a large square
yard, with a dead wall forming one entire side, and a gas lamp on a
circular pavement in the centre. Every householder in it is a Jew.
The place looks as if it were devoted to money-making, for it is quiet
and dirty. Over the shops are no names in gilt letters; there is no
display of plate glass, or glass mouldings, such as in the crowded
thoroughfares where the customer is to be caught by show. The
Israelite merchants know their trade to be so certain, they are content to let the London smoke do their painter's work. Never did
property in Chancery look more ruinous, for every house seems in the
last stage of dilapidation. The beams and ceilings are as black as if
a fire had raged in the dwelling—not a shop in the market but is
windowless and open as a coal-shed—and beyond the few baskets of
nuts exposed for sale, hey are empty, the walls within being
blackened with dirt, and the paint without blistered by the sun,
while the door-posts are worn round with the shoulders of the
customers, and blackened as if charred. A few dejected-looking hens
wander about, turning over the heaps of dried leaves that the
oranges have been packed in, or mope the time away roosting on
the rails and wheels of the nearest truck. Excepting on certain
market days, business is slack in Duke's Place, so that many of the
shops have one or two shutters up, as if a death had taken place, and
the large yard is as quiet as that of a quondam posting-house. At a

little distance, the warehouses with low ceilings, open fronts, and black sides, seem like dark holes. Were it not for the mahogany backs of chairs visible at the first floors, nobody would believe that the houses are inhabited; but in these drawing-rooms the floors are covered with thick Turkey carpets—old paintings in gorgeous frames hang against the walls, and the most comfortable easy-chairs stand on each side of the fireplace. There are not handsomer mahogany chairs, richer pier-glasses, or more elegant chandeliers to be found in a West End mansion than those with which these Jewish salons are furnished.

The appearance of a customer at such an unusual time caused some little excitement among the nut merchants. Very often was Mr. Mudgster beckoned by half a dozen rival vendors at once, but he paid no attention either to their signals, or the flattering words that accompanied them, and made his round of the warehouses in a calm, deliberate manner. At the door of one where they stopped sat an old woman with jet-black hair, and a face dried and wrinkled as a fig. She was nursing an infant, and watching over the mat-baskets of nuts ranged on a kind of carpenter's bench placed on the pavement. The interior of the shop was as empty as a loft, excepting a few bits of harness hanging against the wall, and an old salt-box nailed near the gas burner, in which sat a hen hatching. "'Ton't you like te looksh of tem?" muttered the woman, as Mr. Mudgster, after feeling the weight of the nuts, moved on. At another warehouse where they stopped, there was a stout, gaudy Israelite mother, with crisp negro's hair, her long gold earrings swinging to and fro as she rolled her child on the table used for salting the nuts. Here the black walls had been chalked over with scores, and every corner of the shop was filled up with sacks and orange cases. Before one warehouse was a family of six, all busy, from the father to the infant, washing walnuts in a huge tub, and around them were baskets of the wet fruit standing to drain. The Jewish women are known to make the fondest parents, and in Duke's Place there certainly was no lack of fondlings. Inside almost every shop a child was either being nursed or romped with. Some of the little things were being tossed nearly to the ceiling, and caught, screaming with enjoyment, in the jewelled hands of the delighted mother. At other warehouses were seated a family circle of five or six women—from the old grandmother down to the youngest unmarried grandchild—grouped admiringly round a fine-nosed infant, tickling it, and poking their ringed fingers into its plump little cheeks in a frenzy of affection.

The counters of these shops were generally placed, like stalls, in the open streets, and the shop itself only used as an empty store to keep the stock in. On these counters were ranged large baskets of different kinds of nuts, some piled up with dark brown polished chestnuts, shining like a racer's neck; others filled with wedge-shaped Brazil-nuts. There were heaps, too, of newly-washed walnuts, a few showing their crumpled kernels as a sample of their excellence. Before every doorway were cases of oranges, with the yellow fruit just seen through the bulging lathes on the top.

In front of one stall, the paving-stones were soft with the sawdust emptied from the grape-boxes. The Jewish merchant, in a gold-tasselled smoking cap, was puffing with his bellows at the blue bunches on a tray. About him were other grape-boxes, with the paper lids thrown back and the round sea-green berries just rising above the sawdust, as if floating in it. Close by was a group of dark-eyed women bending over an orange case, picking out the rotten from the good fruit, while a girl in black satin was busy with her knife scooping out the damaged parts. What with the sawdust and the orange-peel the air smelt like that of a circus on a summer's night.

Mr. Mudgster had brought a good sum of money with him, and his custom was so unexpected that the merchant of whom he made his purchase proposed a glass of ale at the "Jewellers' Arms," close by. Whilst they were enjoying their tipple, the nut-vendor informed them that if they wanted to see a sight they should come to that tavern on a Sunday morning, for very often the bar counter might be seen covered with golden ornaments, and sparkling with precious stones worth thousands and thousands of pounds. The jewellers came there to exchange their trinkets, and barter amongst themselves.

We do not intend following Mr. Mudgster through the whole of his provincial tour. As that gentleman travelled over some hundreds of miles, the exploit would be too fatiguing. We shall merely mention that he was accompanied on his journey by Mrs. Mudgster and the children, who, as they took with them a donkey and barrow, seldom over-fatigued themselves with walking. With a husband's tenderness, Mr. M. constructed a tilt out of an old blanket, so that the inclemencies of the weather might not affect the health of his family. Whenever they came to a hill, both master and man humanely pushed behind, and even in descending an acclivity, Philip invariably stayed the impetus of the vehicle by acting as a kind of skid. If business had always been prosperous, the happiness of this family would have been uninterrupted, but it sometimes happened that even when their appetites were keenest, they could not muster sufficient money to purchase a breakfast. In such cases, Mr. Mudgster did not think it beneath his dignity to borrow a swede turnip or two from a field on the way. If he saw his old woman—as he familiarly termed his wife—look discontented with the meal, he would try to flavour the vegetable with a little philosophy, telling her that it was a first-rate thing for sweetening the blood, and as good as medicine for the children. After all, it was a very up-and-down kind of existence, at one time making very large profits, and at another scarcely knowing what to do for want of a few pence. For instance, at Brighton races, the receipts amounted to £2 18s. in the three days, but at Reigate, business was so bad that, on leaving the town, our nutman was so inconvenienced for ready cash that he had to pay the toll of the next turnpike by leaving his pocket-knife. At Horsham, also, nothing being provided for the day's dinner, the family dined off a box of percussion caps—that is to say, that in exchange for it Mr. Mudgster obtained sufficient to purchase some meat and bread. Then, encamped on the grassy side of a country lane, did this roving family, having lighted a glorious fire, proceed to manufacture a magnificent stew, into which entered a considerable quantity of carrots, potatoes, and cabbages, which Mr. M. had taken the liberty of plucking from the garden of a gentleman who had forgotten to lock his gate.

For nearly two months did this little band travel about Sussex and Hampshire, and so great was their industry and perseverance, that, despite the heavy expenses of their establishment, the pocket of Mrs. Mudgster grew heavier and heavier with their earnings. It would seem that Mr. M. was an advocate for Sunday trading, experience teaching him that the receipts of that one day often surpassed those of all the remainder of the week. Being one day desired to deliver his opinion of the people with whom he mixed during his travels, he delivered this judgment: "Countrymen is, I find, very fond of shooting at the nut-board, and, generally, they are a good deal better shots than the Londoners. They are a thousand-and-one superior to the soldiers out and out. The girls and women, too, are, so to speak it, partial to the sport; more so perhaps at Chichester, where I took 28s. But females, as a rule, fires at random, anyhow, and don't often get into the bull's-eye, which wins twenty nuts invariable."

We next find this interesting family working their way along the southern coast towards Dover. Their prospects in life were so far improved that Mr. Mudgster had been enabled to exchange his donkey and truck for a horse and cart. He had taken such a fancy to Philip that he had made him a partner in the concern. In a letter to a friend in town, to whom he sent fifteen shillings to be laid out in nuts, Mr. M. makes use of these remarkable words: "Pitches is wery tidy, and business going ahead, and as prosperous as to be hoped. But roads are bad, and horses suffer amazen."

As some persons may imagine that there was a chance of the nut-man losing—supposing that all his customers were crack shots—we will, for the last time, quote from him, and use the very words he spoke on an occasion when this subject was under discussion. "When people are lucky, and gets in the bull's-eye, they'll have as many as sixpen'orth of goes right off. I like to see them get in the bull's-eye, because they're more like to stick to the sport, and, then, other people that are looking on come up, and has a fire too."

It is a pity that those who in adversity have been firm friends should, when their struggles are at last crowned with success, allow a few hasty words to sever an intimacy which formerly the most savage disputes could not even shake. Yet so it was. When in their donkey-and-truck days Mr. Mudgster and his assistant quarrelled at Reigate, and a blow was struck and a stone thrown, an hour afterwards they were drinking beer out of the same pot; but now, alas! in their horse-and-cart prosperity, a mere difference of opinion as to which turning of the road led to Margate laid the foundation of a feud which eventually led to a separation.

In these altercations Mrs. M. and her eldest daughter—who although not old enough to form an opinion, was sufficiently aged to express one—invariably sided with the head of their family. Perhaps the great wealth which lay concealed in the wife's pocket, and the continued success of the speculation, may have influenced to a slight degree the proprietor !in wishing to get rid of his junior partner. Whatever the reason might have been, all chances of future disagreement were at last removed by Philip's quitting the concern. After an unusually long dispute, in which the many harsh epithets made use of might have been heard at least half a mile off, the caravan drew up by the side of the road, and Philip's share of the profits having been agreed to at five pounds, he turned his back upon the Mudgster's family, and hurried away in one direction, whilst the nutman, smacking his whip, drove off in the other.

CHAPTER XXI.

WHICH WILL PROVE THAT A CERTAIN FRENCH GENTLEMAN WAS NOT ONLY ALIVE, BUT STIRRING.

It was about this time that the firm of Jonkopings, Tandstickor, and Co. opened an office in London. These gentlemen were, it appeared, Swedish merchants, largely engaged in the Russian, Prussian, Australian, American, and many other highly important trades. They had determined upon establishing an agency in England, the management of which they entrusted to a confidential clerk, Monsieur Chose, a gentleman of French extraction and great business energy.

The first thing that Monsieur Chose did was to take a back room on a second floor in Bread Street, Cheapside. The next was to order a brass-plate as big as the shield of St. George himself, and have it fastened up on the most conspicuous part of the door-post. All up the staircase—at every landing, in fact, was painted in large black letters, "JONKOPINGS, TANDSTICKOR, and Co." . Indeed, every provision was made for enabling the enormous mob of customers who were to have transactions with the Swedish firm to find out easily their way to Monsieur Chose in his little back office.

The clerks in the employment of Messrs. Finny, Haddy, and Co. (importers of Scotch goods on the first floor) were rather disgusted by the prominent manner in which Monsieur Chose had blazoned all over the house the name of his hitherto unknown firm. On one occasion their managing gentleman, Mr. Macpipes, meeting with the Frenchman on the stairs, could not help observing to him in his most sarcastic manner, that " if his business was as lairge as his brauss-plate, he'd soon raquiare a bigger apairtment than a wee bauck garrut." Such was the French gentleman's politeness that, instead of firing up at this taunt, he only laughed and shrugged his shoulders. The easy manner in which he talked of turning over a hundred thousand pounds, as calmly as if it had been a haycock, made a favourable impression upon the suspicious Macpipes.

The personal appearance of this French gentleman was simple and highly business-like. He evidently despised the foppishness peculiar to his countrymen. His bushy chestnut hair was seldom brushed, and the only golden ornament about him was his thin gold spectacles. His face was entirely shaved, and he walked with a stoop which half concealed the countenance. Every day as the clock struck five, the clerks of Messrs. Finny, Haddy, and Co. heard him rush downstairs, and whenever they chose to peep through the door, they saw him hurrying to the post with a big bundle of letters under his arm. Such a vast amount of correspondence was an excellent proof of the immense business Monsieur Chose carried on with Russia, Prussia, Australia, and America.

By degrees the business of the Swedish firm began to increase. Carriers' vans drew up before the door, and blocked up the narrow street whilst they delivered canvas-covered bales, belted in tightly with iron hooping. Even Mr. Macpipes entertained a higher opinion of Jonkopings and Co.'s commercial importance. Whenever Monsieur Chose went out, he never failed to stick upon his door a slip of paper to let his visitors know that he had gone " on 'Change," or to "the Bank of England," or " the Docks." He seemed perfectly over-whelmed with affairs.

The terms on which Monsieur Chose did business were half cash, and a bill at two months, and so exact was he in his payments that he won the confidence of Messrs. Crater, McRoney, and Co., the large factors of Bow Lane, and agents for several Irish linen bleachers at Belfast. His first transactions with this house might be called small ones. In the course of conversation with any of the Irish firm, the Monsieur never failed to boast of the extensive business he was doing in shipping goods to Texas, Sydney, Calcutta, or St. Peters-burg. He would also produce and read to the younger Mr. McRoney letters which he had received from Messrs. Jonkopings, Tandstickor, and Co., containing directions about the heavy purchases he was to make on their account. In this manner did Monsieur Chose slowly but surely earn for himself an excellent reputation amongst City men, and before two months had passed—the date of the bills he had given —he had grown to such intimacy with Mr. Crater, that that gentle-man would drink sherry with him in the counting-house, and with great playfulness solicit orders from the Swedish firm, and occasionally he endeavoured to tempt the Frenchman with samples of their linens.

One day Monsieur Chose rushed in a great hurry to the office in Bow Lane. He had that morning received a letter—which he showed—ordering an immense quantity of linens similar to those "as per former invoice," and these stuffs were to be shipped with the least delay possible direct to the Brazils. That business-pushing youth, McRoney, jun., undertook to conduct Monsieur Chose over the extensive warehouse, and to exhibit to him their large assortment of goods. If the Frenchman hesitated in his choice, the youth would descant on the excellence of the linens, and the smallness of the price. So irresistible was the junior partner's manner, that on almost every occasion the foreigner allowed himself to be convinced. By three o'clock, boxes of linen to the amount of £400 had already been selected. They only retired for a few moments to a private room upstairs, to partake of a little lunch of sherry and lobster. Business men like Monsieur Chose are never long at their meals, and in less than a quarter of an hour, he had dragged the young factor back again to the warehouse. When the knowing Mr. McRoney had pressed the foreigner to finish the bottle of sherry, the answer was that he never permitted himself to drink when on business. The young gentleman could not help informing Mr. Crater that he had never in all his life met with such a fellow for work as the Mounseer. It was past four o'clock before the Swedish agent had completed his purchases, and when we affirm that he had selected stuffs to the amount of £700, it will be easily understood that he had not wasted his time.

A van had been engaged, and, whilst the heavy bales were being carted, Monsieur Chose was settling about the payment of them. As usual, he gave a bill at two months for half the amount, and drew a cheque for the remaining £350. At ten minutes to five o'clock, the van with the goods drove off, and the agent took his leave.

It would seem that some doubts as to the solidity of the firm of Jonkopings, Tandstickor, and Co. oppressed the mind of Mr. Crater almost immediately after the agent had departed. At exactly four minutes before the closing of the bank, Mr. Crater in person presented the draft over the banking-house counter. He was seized with a weakness of the knees as the clerk returned the paper with the answer of, "Not effects to that amount." Overcome with despair, the unfortunate factor sought an interview with the bank-manager, and, after relating the story of the swindle, at last, by his agonizing entreaties, wrung from the official a confession that the account of the Swedish firm amounted to something over £100. To save himself from entire loss, Mr. Crater hit upon an expedient which might in similar cases prove useful to gentlemen in the City. He took out his cheque-book, and commenced paying in to the account of Monsieur Chose drafts to such an amount that at last on presenting the Frenchman's paper, it was duly honoured. By this clever scheme did the firm of Crater, McRoney, and Co. save £115 out of their £700.

It is but fair to assume that the French gentleman returned to Sweden, for he was never afterwards heard of in London. When the affair became known through the medium of the police reports, Mr. Macpipes was heard to say that he "allers sauspackted the fallow was an airant sweendler, and that he would na hae trusted him to cairy sop to a pairet, for he'd hae cheated the puir baird by devoorin' it his ainsel', the clarty vaigabond!"

CHAPTER XXII.

A HUNT AFTER PHILIP.

ALTHOUGH a great many years have passed since Katherine Merton died, yet Mr. Simcox, senior, the friend and solicitor of Nathaniel Crosier, Esquire, of Swanborough, is as well and hearty as when we last left him at the prison making inquiries after this most unfortunate lady. That ornament of his profession has grown grey and bald. He mumbles slightly when he talks, and is deaf; but his brain, he says, is as sound as ever, and many of his clients even now declare that they would rather have old Simcox's opinion than that of the first barrister in the land.

The long-headed solicitor could not imagine what sudden fancy had possessed his Swanborough client that he should take so great an interest in a lad named Philip Merton. Once a week did a letter come from the country banker—written in a most excited style—requesting that every possible search should be made after this boy, and that no expense should be spared in tracing out his whereabouts. When Mr. Simcox called in his clerk, of an afternoon, to take down in the attendance book the details of his day's work, there was usually some such entry as the following to be made: "To attending Mr. Tobias Sparkler, at his residence at Hampstead, when he, in harsh language, informed us that the lad Philip Merton had quitted his employment. On further pressing Mr. Sparkler for more minute particulars, both his conversation and behaviour became violent and illegal. Cab hire, there and back, 12s. Engaged three hours, £1 1s." Or, perhaps, the entry would be, "To attending at the workhouse of St. Lazarus Without, and requesting to see one Mary Hazlewood, the nurse, when we were informed that she was from home. Cab hire, 15s. Engaged four hours, £1 6s. 8d." Or the old lawyer might dictate as follows: "Attending at the police-office, when we saw the sergeant on duty, and requested to know whether he could afford us any information as to what had become of Philip Merton. He expressed it as his opinion that if we were patient and waited a year or

two longer, we should most possibly find him in Newgate. Engaged
two hours, 13s. 4d."

Ever since the day when Mr. Nathaniel Crosier had accompanied
his daughter Helen on her donkey-ride to Hampstead, he had
never ceased to think about the curious lad who had driven the animals, and called himself Philip Merton. It was so strange that his
mother's name should have been Katherine. She, too, had called
herself Katherine Merton. It struck him, too, the boy had a face
which had a genteel formation and good features, such as became the
offspring of gentlefolk. He would speculate to himself whether, by
any possibility, this corduroyed urchin could have been his grandson.
Nathaniel Crosier was a proud and wealthy man, and not from love
for the boy, but out of respect to himself, he was shocked at the idea
that a child of his should remain one of the world's outcasts. In
justice we must debit this gentleman with his good as well as his
bad qualities, and mention that there still remained in his heart a
tenderness towards his deceased daughter—very probably because she
was dead. We are too apt to weep for the corpse and neglect the
living. He would repeat to himself, "What a handsome girl she
was!" and remember how often he had been praised as the father of
so beautiful a child. He would call to mind how Sir Theophilus
Ermine had praised her at the county ball, vowing she was the handsomest girl in Hampshire. With a tightness of bosom he would
remember how young Lord Acres had danced with her the entire
evening, and called the next day on the pretence of inquiring after
her health. "She might have been 'My Lady,'" he would sigh, and
then fall to cursing that French scoundrel Vautrin.

It is true he never allowed anyone to mention her name before
him, but he would constantly commune with himself about the lost
girl, and often when his family thought he was taking his after-dinner
nap, he was in reality, with closed eyes, calling to mind by-past
scenes and events that had happened when poor Katherine lived at
home.

On the morning when he read in the newspapers the report of the
forged cheque case, he was in agony till he reached the line that stated
the prisoner was acquitted. He trembled at the bare idea that anybody bearing the name of Merton should be charged with a felony.
A dread, too, seized him, lest it should be suspected the culprit belonged to his family. "If I could only get him out of the country,"
was the thought that crossed his mind; and he once more sat down
and wrote to his lawyer. All that day he was very irritable. A man-
servant had notice to quit for not answering the bell the first time
it was rung, and Mr. Meekboy, his head cashier, received a severe
reprimand for having discounted at six per cent. some bills which any
other firm would have been glad to cash at five.

The last instructions given to Mr. Simcox were to pay a visit to
the prison in which Katherine Merton had died, and endeavour to
assure himself by undeniable proof, whether she really had been his

daughter, and, if so, by what name the boy she left had been christened. This kind of work was not, strictly speaking, such as Mr.
Simcox, senior, was accustomed to, yet out of consideration to his
friend, and the business he sent him, he paid a visit to Miss Perriman, the matron of the gaol. That lady had grown much stouter,
and had for the last three years worn a false front, but her memory
was so vigorous, that no sooner did the lawyer mention Katherine
Merton, than every little incident connected with the imprisonment
of that unfortunate lady rose up in the matron's mind. "Ah! I
remember the poor thing well," she said. "A most melancholy case!
A broken-hearted creature, who had no sooner brought her child into
the world than she went out of it. Wasn't she No. 43 ?" she added.
Then, hunting over one of the prison records, she continued, "Yes, I
thought so, No. 43—here it is, No. 43. 'Well-behaved, but refuses
to eat her food.' Poor soul! I always said she only got herself sent
to prison that her child might not be born in the streets. A lament-
able case!"

As a lawyer, Mr. Simcox, when he was engaged on business, never
allowed his sympathies to interfere with his judgment; so he answered
the matron with a dry cough, and then proceeded to ask whether the
unfortunate female prisoner had left any papers behind her by which
she might be identified. "I am acting, madam," he added, "for a
gentleman of great respectability, who, if he could be persuaded that
Katherine Merton really was connected with his family, would be
willing to use his influence on behalf of her wretched offspring."

"Are you one of the gentlemen," asked Miss Perriman, "who,
many years ago, made inquiries at this prison about this unhappy
lady, shortly after her death?" A formal affirmative bow was the
answer. "Then, sir," continued the lady, with great indignation,
"you may tell your respectable client that upon his soul will rest
whatever evil that deserted boy Philip may commit in this world. I
have nursed that infant in these arms, and you may tell your respectable gentleman that a sweeter babe never smiled. You see, sir, we
gaolers had more compassion for that unfortunate orphan than the
relations God had given it."

With great dignity, Mr. Simcox replied that he was a lawyer, and
had nothing to do with morals or moralists—that he had come there
as a professional man, and not from any mad, philanthropic idea—
that his business that day was to inquire after papers, and not to criticize his client's humanity. "And if you can produce any documents,"
he added, "they may be of more benefit to this orphan boy—in whom
you take such an extraordinary interest—than any expression of com-
miseration you may think fit to favour me with."

There was a small bundle of papers, which had long been kept in
the prison office, and, after an interview with the governor of the gaol,
they were produced. The lawyer was informed that these papers had
been found stitched inside the lining of Katherine Merton's tattered
gown. The old envelope in which these writings had been treasured

R

had become rotten as mummy-cloth, and, on opening it, the pieces separated as easily as the portions of a puzzle. Putting on his spectacles, the solicitor examined each document minutely, as a jeweller does diamonds, and with as keen an eye for flaws and impositions. He paid no attention to the remarks with which Miss Perriman chose to accompany the production of each morsel of paper.

"Six duplicates," said that lady. "They always have duplicates when they come here. First the pawn-shop, then the prison or the workhouse." Looking at one of the cardboard slips, she continued : "'White satin dress, with lace trimmings.' Poor soul! Perhaps she had danced in it when she lived with her respectable relations. It might have been her wedding-dress, for all we know. Here's another. 'Sable muff and cuffs.' Dear me! evidently well off at one time— sable! 'Three embroidered petticoats, gold earrings, and scent-bottle.' What a sad change from embroidery to prison clothes!" As all these articles had been pledged in the name of Mary Smith, the lawyer refused to admit them as evidence. One of these duplicates was for a pair of boots, and another for a wedding-ring. The matron, looking at the dates on the cards, remarked that the poor creature had walked barefoot before she parted with the ring.

There were three or four letters, in all of which the signatures had been heavily scratched out; but in one of them the words "Emile Vautrin" could—when the paper was held up towards the window— be imperfectly traced. Shortly before she died, the prisoner had asked for pen and paper, for the purpose, she said, of writing to her relations. This letter she had never completed, but the fragments, nevertheless, had been preserved. There was no direction to this letter, and it was headed, "From my prison." It was as follows :— " I thank my God that He will soon free me from this gaol, by taking from me the life which for this long time has been a heavy affliction and torment to me. By the weakness of my body, and the agony of my soul, what I now say to you is true; so pay attention to it as the last request I shall ever have need to make. Whilst I am penning these lines the pulse grows weaker and weaker, for death is on me. There is one—" By the indistinctness with which the last few words were penned, it was evident that the prisoner's strength had at this moment failed her. Most likely, too, that Miss Perriman's observation, that the unhappy woman was about to speak of her child, was correct. The tone of this unfinished letter had, as Mr. Simcox remarked, more the air of a threat than a supplication; but, as the governor observed, that was exactly in accordance with the prisoner's character. "She bore her sentence," he said, "with a proud resignation that would have convinced many people she had been unjustly condemned. Even to our chaplain she, although her minutes were numbered, refused to reveal her name and parentage."

The remarks of the lawyer were simply of a business character. "I see nothing in all these papers." he murmured, "to prove that this woman was legally married, and that was my chief object in coming

here. For, of course, if this boy is illegitimate, he can have no claim
to my client, however ingeniously the pretended relationship may be
argued."

Just as this interview was breaking up, who should enter the room
but Mr. Nathan, of Lyon's Inn. He was looking remarkably well.
He was as buckish as ever, and although he had grown unfashionably
stout, still, by wearing a cravat of unusual brilliancy, and ordering
his waistcoat of the showiest velvet, he had managed to defy the
ravages of time, and at ten paces off would have been taken for the
nattiest old sprig on town. No sooner did he see Mr. Simcox surrounded by strangers, than, to support the dignity of the profession,
he began to cannonade the old gentleman with compliments. Perhaps
he hoped that the favour might be returned.

"I am glad to meet you, Mr. Simcox," he said, "as I always am
any gentleman of talent." Then, turning to the governor, he added,
"If Mr. Simcox had gone to the bar he would have been Lord Chan-
cellor by this time."

The old attorney felt himself bound to respond handsomely. "I
have the highest opinion of Mr. Nathan's talents," he said, "not only
for his knowledge of the law, but also for his uprightness, candour,
and honesty as a MAN."

"If I were asked to-morrow," cried Mr. Nathan, "what gentleman
of the profession I should point to as being its greatest ornament, I
should say, ' Go to the Temple, and ask for the senior partner of Simcox and Nicholls.' I don't mind saying to his own face that to the
wisdom of a Solon he unites the charity of a Moore."

Nothing undaunted, Mr. Simcox replied, "Our firm has had many
dealings with Mr. Nathan, and I can only say I never met with a gentleman more thoroughly impressed with a notion of justice, and more
opposed to the trickery of the law than my friend beside me."

Presently the two solicitors proceeded to business, the Israelite
stating that his client, who was the husband of Katherine Merton,
was most desirous of obtaining any papers which might assist in
proving that the boy Philip Merton was his true son. He prudently
refused to divulge the name of his client unless there was anything
to be gained by the discovery. On hearing that Mr. Simcox had
possessed himself of the papers—the governor of the gaol had
handed them over to him—a discussion ensued which ended in the
two lawyers abusing each other with the same vigour as they had
before overwhelmed each other with compliments.

"If, Mr. Nathan, you expect that your pettifogging, threatening
ways will have any influence over me, you are much mistaken; I
know the law too well, sir."

"If you know it so well," retorted Mr. Nathan, "it is a pity you
don't make more use of it. I pity the client who falls into the hands
of Simcox, Son, and Nicholls, for your bill of costs is all the law he
will get for his money."

"When you are defending your Old Bailey thieves," retorted the angry Mr. Simcox, "or attempting to save some returned convict from some deserved punishment, this bullying might do, Mr. Nathan. You had better reserve this blackguardism till your next case, sir. It has no effect upon me."

"I have only one thing more to say," continued Mr. Nathan, "you know no more of law than you do of gentlemanly conduct."

To this Mr. Simcox replied, "You are as unfit to judge in one case as in the other, Mr. Nathan. Indeed, I cannot do better than term you a pettifogger and a bully." After which, both gentlemen seized their respective hats, and hurried off to their offices.

And now all Philip's chances of honourable progress in life were to be baulked by a lawyers' quarrel. That evening a letter was posted off to Swanborough, in which the confidential adviser informed his client that, although he had dived deep into this matter, he could trace no relationship between the Katherine Merton of the prison and the Nathaniel Crosier of the bank. The grandfather was counselled to set his heart at peace, and dismiss his fears. And such advice was but too thankfully received and acted on. But Mr. Nathan took an opposite view of the case. Enraged by the conduct of his professional brother, his advice was that not only was Philip Merton his client's son, but that an attempt was being made to take the child from its parent. And so the lawyer and the father redoubled their efforts to trace and claim the boy.

CHAPTER XXIII.

IN RE THE WINDING UP OF THE GRAND NATIONAL MARRIAGE INSURANCE AND UNIVERSAL MATRIMONIAL BENEFIT COMPANY, CAPITAL £700,000, WITH POWER TO INCREASE TO £7,000,000. A DEPOSIT OF 6d. PER SHARE TO BE PAID ON ALLOTMENT.

FOR two months the second column in the "Times" had been filled with the announcement of the above company. The advertisement had caused a great deal of excitement in the metropolis, not only from the singularity of the title, but also from the humanity of its objects and the greatness of the names with which it was associated. It would seem that the originator of this scheme was a Monsieur Coquardau, a gentleman—it was said—of a religious turn of mind, who was fast earning for himself the reputation of being the greatest philanthropist of the day. He had made it—according to his own account—his mission in life to alleviate the pecuniary sufferings of the female portion of the great human family. He called all women his sisters. He had travelled over the greater part of Europe, Asia, and America, gathering necessary statistics before he considered himself in a position to launch this great scheme before the public. He said it was the loving labour of his life.

The goodness of Monsieur Coquardau's character evinced itself even in his personal appearance. There was a solemn, pastoral air in his suit of black, relieved only by the exquisite whiteness of his neckcloth. He was of a bilious temperament, and at times the black ring round his eyes was of such depth of colour as to suggest the notion that he had received injuries in a personal encounter. His hair was black, and cut close to the head.

Such was the modesty of this good gentleman, that, even when he had matured his plans to ripeness, he would not allow his name to be made public as the originator of the scheme, contenting himself with the promise of a grant of £20,000 to be presented to him, in consideration of his services, out of the capital of the company. He made a present of the post of secretary to the company to a Mr. Horatio Bott, a highly deserving youth whose relatives had consented to embark £500 in the speculation. As a proof of Monsieur Coquardau's influence, it need only be stated that the chairman of the company was his All Serene Highness Prince Gloumpi, a Knight of the Neapolitan Order of Thunder and Blazes, of the Holy Poker, &c., &c. Among the illustrious directors might be found the name of his Royal Highness Prince d'Influenza, the extensive Italian landowner, and proprietor of nearly all the Pontine territory. The celebrated banker of Amsterdam, Herr Iceburger, also lent the powerful support of his name, whilst Mr. Sidney Tickell, a Fellow of the Institute of Actuaries, had joined the speculation, and Messrs. Okey, Pokey, and Winkey, of the Temple, were appointed solicitors.

No sooner had the first and explanatory meeting of the directors been held, than the moment it was advertised in the "Times" the shares rose to a premium. The philanthropic Monsieur Coquardau briefly detailed the objects of the company as follows :

" Out of the four-and-twenty millions of fellow Christians inhabiting Great Britain and Ireland, upwards of sixteen millions are females. Supposing, therefore, that every man in the country were to take to himself a wife, there would still remain upwards of four millions of poor women who could never hope to enter into the holy state of wedlock. Now, in order that I may check myself in my calculations," added Monsieur Coquardau, who was most nice and exact in his assertions, "I will set off the widows by the widowers, and allow fifty thousand for that most disgraceful of all crimes, wedlock with two women, commonly known as bigamy. If this calculation be admitted as fair, it follows that a grand total is left of three million nine hundred and fifty thousand spinsters.

" But here "—and by the mournful expression of Monsieur Coquardau's countenance it was evident that he was about to make a distressing revelation—" I must point out to you one most important fact. Many females are born afflicted with bodily deformities of so grievous a nature that even the most sanguine could not hope to see them enter the holy state of marriage. Some are sent into this world without arms, as in the heartrending case of the well-known Miss Biffin. Others grow to an unnatural size, as instanced by the celebrated Mrs. Armytage. History makes mention of females having for some wise and hidden purpose been created with the heads of animals. Need I refer to the pig-faced lady? Others, again, have, by an unnatural growth of their hair and moustache, lost those attractions of the female countenance which have an effect upon the heart of man. Many ladies either have no eyes at all, or have only one eye, or having the two eyes are afflicted with a squint. Some have little or no nose, or maybe an excess of that useful organ. I am happy to say that as yet we have had no instance of a female with two or more noses. Some have hump-backs. It would be foolish to express a hope that any of these unfortunate sisters should ever know a husband's tenderness. Let us put down these afflicted beings at a total of fifty thousand. You will find that this exactly balances my criminal double marriages. Now," continued Monsieur Coquardau, brightening up with philanthropic excitement, " it must be allowed that among the advantages accruing to the female from the marriage state, we may rank the cessation of toil on the part of the woman, and the obtaining a comfortable home. Then, how are those four millions of unhappy spinsters to reap such advantages? I will tell you : by means of our company.

"We bring down the payments to be made at our office to the smallest figure, so as to suit the means of even the poorest maid-servant in the realm—say, 10s. a year. What is 2½d. a week? A mournfully small sum; yet multiply that 2½d. a week by the four million women who have no chance of marrying, and what is the result? Why, a grand revenue to this company of two million pounds per annum."

When the excitement produced by the prospect of this enormous income had in some measure subsided, the good Monsieur Coquardau once more raised his voice : " Now, this company proposes to allow to every subscriber who attains the age of forty, and is unmarried, an income of £200 a year for the rest of her life. It may be objected that this sum is too generous. It may be stated that the necessities of women are few, and that they could live in comfort upon one quarter of such an annuity; but allow me to make one more state-ment. In fixing the age at forty years, I have been influenced by the opinion of one of the greatest actuaries living, Mr. Sydney Tickell, who has set down that period of time as being the average period of life permitted to unmarried females. So that you see that we should have but few calls upon our funds, and indeed I do not think I should be very wrong if I stated that ours would be a com-pany for receiving the immense sum of two millions of pounds annually and giving nothing at all in return for it. Under such cir-cumstances, even the most obstinate could not doubt the success of our undertaking."

So great was the success attending this announcement in the "Times," that the attorneys to the company thought themselves justified in advancing the money required for furnishing the offices. Chairs, tables, and desks, polished up until the flies could scarcely stand on them, soon decked the company's rooms, whilst wire blinds with a portrait of Hymen—in gold—flourishing his torch, adorned every window. Prospectuses of the company printed on thin paper were thrown down the areas of every square, place, and terrace in London, and in a short time the rush of servant girls desirous of becoming subscribers was so great that the presence of Inspector Beak and six men was requested to preserve order among the domestic crowd, with many of whom the officers appeared to be intimate.

Why this company should so soon have broken up will ever be a mystery. By some it was attributed to the over haste of the philanthropic Monsieur Coquardau, who, being anxious to realize whilst the shares were at a premium, swamped the market with five thousand which had been presented to him as originator of the scheme, and hastily departed for France, with a view, he said, of completing and carrying out another of his charitable schemes. When the aid of the Court of Bankruptcy was sought for in winding up the affairs of this company, it was discovered that the funds had entirely disappeared. Indeed, the only thing that there was any possibility of winding up was the clock in the back office—one of French's—which would seem to have stopped about the same time as the subscriptions. Although the Court of Bankruptcy despatched one of its messengers to Italy to make inquiries about His Royal Highness Prince d'Influenza, yet no satisfactory result was obtained, owing to the official being attacked by a severe fever shortly after his arrival at the Pontine territory.

Book the Third.

THE ROAD TO RUIN.

———◆———

CHAPTER I.

ON THE TRAMP.

AFTER parting with Mr. Mudgster and his family, Philip walked away rapidly for a mile or two, scarcely noticing the distance, so occupied was he in planning the vengeance that was to ruin and utterly destroy the nutman's future. At last his legs grew tired with his rapid pace, and, by the principle of counter-irritation, the aching of his knees drew away the pain at his heart. He sat down on a gate to think over what he had better " be up to " now. He had five pounds in his pocket, and plenty of time before him, and a desire seized him to see his native land, and become better acquainted with its beauties. If he had been possessed of a travelling-carriage this longing would have been patriotic and praiseworthy. But as his fortune could be counted at a glance, we are very happy to entertain the same opinion as our readers, and declare him to be reckless, and given to idleness.

For some weeks Philip journeyed alone, sleeping at lodging-houses and revelling in his liberty. He formed no acquaintances, for he was rather disgusted than otherwise with the coarse conversation and ill manners of those he encountered.

He was not, however, destined to remain long alone. At Birmingham, at a house for travellers, whom should he meet but two of his old schoolfellows—Billy Fortune and Ned Purchase. These lads were also on the tramp, Ned travelling as a tailor, trying for work occasionally, but oftener making use of his society's card to obtain a bed, breakfast, and pecuniary relief. The cripple had strangely altered since his schooldays, for his mind had now become as deformed as his body, and he traded on his afflictions to beg alms as he hobbled through the country. The other boy, Billy Fortune, had grown to be a tall, powerful youth, whom many a recruiting sergeant would have been glad to see enlist. His principal excuse for asking charity was, that he was a carpenter out of work. " I could as soon draw a tooth as plane a board," he told Phil, "but, by G—d, I make more money at carpentering than many a chap who works twelve hours a day at the trade."

It was resolved among these boys that they should "chum" together, beg together, and share together. They swore friendship over a pot of beer. A few taunts were made at Phil that he was a little bit green at the business. But when the sixpenny ale began to do its work young Merton swore so lustily, and showed so good a disposition to learn every kind of iniquity, that, in the end, his companions were induced to forgive his innocence.

Oh! these boys, these boys! They are soft as copper wire, and can be twisted into any shape. Give one of them the history of "Robinson Crusoe," and he will wish that he, too, were cast upon a desert island. Change the volume to "Captain Cook's Voyages," and he will vow to be a sailor. Once more alter the book to "Jack Sheppard," and a housebreaker becomes the hero of his dreams. This same Philip, if gentle-voiced Bertha had been talking simple moralities to him, would, with tears in his eyes, have promised to lead a saint's life. But because two rogues were pouring their villanies into his ear—that audience-chamber of the brain—he yielded himself to their noisome breath like a feather in the wind.

They tell him adventures of how they were nearly "lagged by the constables"; of the girls they had associated with, and then, when tired of them, "buried" them, as they termed the act of deserting them ; they relate laughable incidents of stealing linen off hedges— "snow-gathering,"—and "turning a white hedge green," as they phrase it. Then Philip, seeing how captivating roguery was, and what laughter came of it, felt for the moment as if he regretted not having shared in the perils.

The town of Stafford might, if it had chosen, have claimed the honour of being Billy Fortune's birthplace. It was to this town that he and Ned Purchase were tramping their way. They easily induced Phil to choose that road, for it was a matter of indifference to him which way he went. "I've been there three times already," said Billy Fortune, "and know every house where you can get 'scran' and 'rigging,' or food and clothes as you call it. I know every d—d 'trap '—that's a constable—in the place. And there's a first-rate 'diddle cove' (publican) keeps a gin-shop there. If you're fond of slush you may 'suck ' it without any danger of being 'hocussed,' or if you're hungry, you can be certain of not chewing 'bow-wow mutton' (dogs' meat)."

It was a fine summer's afternoon with a hot sun, making the earth steam like a dish of potatoes, when these boys drew near to Stafford. They had been four days on the road, and now had only a few more miles to tramp over. The country was so well known to Billy Fortune, that as they went along he pointed out to them everything that was worth seeing. When they came to the turnpike gate—all black and white like an Act of Parliament—Billy knew the keeper so intimately that he preferred going round by some fields to being seen by that person. They had had a quarrel about some gingerbread, which Fortune had purloined from a stall the man's wife kept. The apple-trees in this locality growing very kindly in the soil, they thought it a very good opportunity for tasting the fruit, and so much did they approve of it, that they even filled their pockets before leaving the orchard. They passed a turnip-field in which was a flock of sodden-looking sheep with ragged, matted wool, as if their hair wanted combing. The animals turned their black faces round, and stared at the three boys who were climbing the hedge, for Ned Purchase had suggested that, though the " bleaters had eaten down their swedes uncommon clean, yet a turnip often came in handy for supper." They could see Colwick village in the distance—a patch of new cottages and houses with slate roofs, and a white church standing up in the midst of them. The church was being repaired, and having its windows out, looked blind.

For the next half mile they did not enjoy their walk much, owing to the roads and meadows being flooded. The river rushed along as if it would tear away the bridge they had to cross over; the trees were standing in the wet half-way up their boughs, and only the top rails of hurdles could be seen above the water. As far as the eye could reach—right down to the line of poplars at the foot of the hill —the fields had big stains of water in them, almost as if covered with plates of metal. Some swans, taking advantage of the flood, were strolling over land they would never think of visiting in dry weather. When Mr. Billy Fortune saw these birds, he exclaimed, " If I could grab one of those ' biddies,' I'd have him boiled." They passed by the spot where Lord Southwark formerly kept his racers. It had gone to ruin, and the courtyard was filled up with rotting and rotted leaves. The thatch to the sheds had grown black, and looked as if water could be squeezed out of it. Intent upon plunder, the boys entered this yard, but there was nothing worth their taking. So when, for mischief's sake, they had pushed down a tottering wall and wrenched a few loose planks from the rusty nails that held them, they returned to the road, and continued their journey.

The estates on each side of the road were, according to Billy Fortune, strictly preserved. " In winter," he said, " it's covered with pheasants as thick as starlings." Suddenly the boy went all stiff like a pointer. " There's two or three on 'em now," he cried, growing excited. Despite his crutch, Ned Purchase whipped up a stone, and saying, " Here goes for luck !" threw it in the direction Billy was pointing. All that Phil could see were three brown dots, but they did not move, and looked like leaves. When the lads came to the grand entrance to Lord Southwark's park, and saw the richly-gilt iron gates stretching across the broad gravelled drive, and the handsome lodges with the coronet over each window, and the coat-of-arms in all its glory, Billy Fortune exclaimed in his admiration, " That's

your sort!" and then, having no respect for the aristocracy, wished he had "that old bloak's tin." They crept up Hurts Hill, watching in vain to see if they could discover any of the deer that abound in the thickly wooded grounds on the other side of the oak paling. Further on they halted at a farm-yard where there had been a sale recently, for the auction bills of the farming stock were posted on the big elm-trees around. This considerably annoyed Billy Fortune, for he said it was one of his places for getting "scran," and he was sorry to see it "coopered up."

There was a curious hollow in a field close by, known to the country people as the "Devil's Punch-bowl." Billy Fortune took his friends to see it, and told the story of a murder committed there. His Satanic Majesty's cup they found to be full of dried leaves, as if they were the dregs of his last draught. There being no chance of any halfpence to be picked up in the road, they continued their route by the fields. "It's a short cut to the Satnell Hills, and we can pad the hoof (walk) easier on the turf," said Billy.

These hills seemed to Phil as if they would never end. The long, round, bleak mounds rose up before and about him, bald as a Red Indian's head, with just a bunch of fir-trees like feathers on the top of the crown. At times he could almost imagine himself at the seaside, for the hill, as it slanted up, shut out the view, and gave him the idea of a cliff, with the sea lying beyond.

To vary the monotony of the walk, they tried to purloin some hens that were feeding in the road. There was a lodge close by, nearly hidden in the thick shrubberies, but Billy was a bold lad, and, despite the chances of detection, had nearly seized hold of a gallant cock who stood his ground, whilst his wives, with the wind blowing their tails open like fans, were scrambling through the palings. An old woman came out to see what the noise was about. But such rare talents did the would-be thief possess, that he turned her presence into an advantage, for he begged so hard for a trifle, and told such a mournful story of his not having tasted food that day, that at last she gave him a halfpenny.

When they reached the milestone on which was engraved "III. to Stafford," they rested awhile, and Master Fortune indulged his friends with an anecdote. "Do you see all this land?" said he, pointing to a large piece of undulating ground, dotted with big trees that cast a dark patch of shade under their branches—"well, the grandfather of this here Lord Southwark got it for 'nix.' He was the knowingest 'nob' that ever wagged the 'red rag' (tongue). He begged this land of King George for to make a kitchen-garden, as he said. The king didn't know there was so many thousand acres, and give 'em. That was a good day's work, wasn't it? He's turned some of the land into farms, and very nice ones they make. Now, if you or I was to do such a dodge as that, we should have the 'body-snatchers' (police-officers) after us, and get shoved in the blockhouse (gaol)." All criticism upon his lordship's actions was, however, stopped by the approach of a farmer on horseback, Ned Purchase suggesting that they might as well try and "kick him" for a few coppers. So when the yeoman drew near, the three boys, with their caps off, stood in the road, and under plea of asking for charity, impeded his progress, unless he had chosen to ride over the young rogues.

"Please, give a poor fellow a halfpenny, your honour. We've been walking all day, and had nothing but cold water." This was Billy Fortune's palaver.

"Help a poor cripple, your honour. I'm a tailor by trade, and here's my card, sir; I wasn't brought up to beg, I assure you." And Ned Purchase put on a broken-hearted look, and produced his society's card.

"And haven't you got anything to say?" asked the farmer, smiling good-naturedly at Phil.

Our boy was not yet thoroughly accustomed to begging. He had a feeling of degradation whenever, in imitation of his companions, he asked for charity.

"Well, sir," he said, "I haven't a penny in the world, but I'd sooner work for one than take it for nothing." He half meant what he said, though if the trial had been granted, perhaps he might have changed his opinion.

The farmer looked at him, and then said, "You're either an honest boy, or the worst scoundrel of the three," and gave him two-pence. Then, turning to Billy Fortune, he said, "Will you do a day's work if I give it to you? You look strong enough."

"Ay! and willing enough too, your honour," groaned the hypocrite. "And, Heaven knows, I should be grateful enough, if I could earn a few coppers. It's not what I've been accustomed to. I've had good parents, and now I knows what the loss of them is. I never thought I should have come to this here." To look at him, you would have thought he was going to burst with tears.

The farmer took from his pocket an envelope, on which was his address, and giving it to Billy, told him to come on the morrow; and when the request was made to him for the advance of a penny to get a "mossel" of bread, the honest victim gave sixpence to be shared among the lot, and then cantered off.

When he was out of hearing, Billy broke out with "We've 'bilked' (swindled) my nabs out of his 'pig' (sixpence). I thought he was a 'queer gill' (suspicious) at first, and smoked us, from what he palavered to Phil when he gave him his 'deux-wins' (twopence)." Somehow or other Phil did not join in his friends' laughter. What the farmer had said had made an impression on his mind. They had scarcely walked ten yards before Phil—though he seemed half ashamed of saying it—proposed that they should take the gentleman at his word, and do a few days' labour at his farm. The other two lads stared with wonder, and then burst into a laugh so loud that it frightened some crows slug-hunting in a field close by, and sent them flying away to a quieter spot.

If you don't like to go," said Phil, "give me his address and let me have a try."

"You want his address—do you?" sneered Billy. "Well, as I like to oblige a pal, here it is;" and he at once tore the envelope into a thousand pieces, and flung them in the air. This quarrel lasted for nearly a mile, although Master Fortune made many attempts at a reconciliation. In vain did he point to a hill covered with dry fern, and say, "Plenty of hares and rabbits there, Phil." He could get no answer. Nor did he succeed better when they passed a stubble-field that looked grey as an old man's three-days' beard; for though he remarked that it was the right sort of place for partridges, they answered not. So they walked on in silence, drawing nearer and nearer to the town.

Already they had reached the suburbs. All about the fields, and in strange corners, and on the roadside, were the quaint white cottages of labourers—small, two-roomed dwellings, with a heavy, natty-looking thatch that came down over the windows like hair over the eyes of a Methodist parson, and gave a frowning expression to the little buildings. Now they reached the parish church, with the ancient square tower that time and bad weather had robbed of its carved work, wearing it away like the crest on old family plate, and the ivy growing into the belfry windows, and half crowning the roof, as though the building—like a fiddle—were preserved in a green bag. Compared with this venerable edifice, the New Church further on seemed upstart and trumpery. There were no yew-trees, big as timber oaks, before its gothic porch, and its walls looked as drab as a pork-pie, from the damp stucco, whilst in the churchyard the evergreens were scarcely large enough for a Christmas-tree.

Presently Billy Fortune and Ned Purchase prepared for work, for they had arrived at a part of the road where there were many handsome mansions. They examined them one by one, undetermined which to visit first. Some of them were huge square-looking houses, proud buildings that have innumerable rooms and big dinner-bells, and turn their ugly backs to the road that they may keep their handsome faces for the lawn and park ground on the other side. Or they were large bricken palaces, with outbuildings, like a village, and surrounded by a long wall that must have made the fortune of some country bricklayer, and cost nobody knows how much a yard.

The boys did well at these mansions, and had so much broken victuals given to them that they were puzzled how to carry the load. "We can sell 'em to the 'mot' (landlady) of the 'libb-ken' (lodging-house) for a good deal, for it's first-rate 'scran.' There's that bit o' bacon the cook gave us that's worth at least a shilling, if we knew any 'bloak' who was fond of it."

They did not make so good a harvest when they came to the half-rustic, half-civic villas at the outskirts of the town. In vain did they ring at the doors of these handsome family residences, with their stucco-trimmed windows and porticos. Old ladies came to the

windows, and shook their fingers, or the servant-maids slammed the
doors in their faces, or the sash was thrown up, and a gentleman
threatened the vagrants with the beadle.

"Let's hook it," said Billy, at last, "and make for the 'padden-ken'
(lodging-house)."

As dusty as if they had been sprinkled with moist sugar, they
entered the town, and, hastily quitting the principal street, dived
into a labyrinth of back slums until they stopped before a dirty-
looking house, over the door of which was written "Accommodation
for Travellers."

"This is Mother Lully's," said Billy, before they entered. "There's
a very good back kitchen, and the beds is decent. But, mind you,
she's a rum 'un, and as fond of 'a line of the old author' (brandy),
or a drop of the 'South Sea Mountain' (gin), as any 'doxy' (woman)
in Stafford."

CHAPTER II.

CAPTAIN CROSIER NARROWLY ESCAPES BEING AN HONEST MAN.

It was nearly three o'clock in the day—the sun had been shining
with singular brilliance since six a.m.—when Captain Merton Crosier
thought he had better make an effort to rise and dress himself.
Seedy and dilapidated from a glorious overnight (the tumblers were
filled for the last time at four), he wrapped his dressing-gown around
him, and shuffled up to the windows of his sitting-room to have a
peep into the street and see what kind of day it was. The curtains
had been closed, and as he pulled them aside the bright daylight
made him draw back, as if a lantern had been flashed before his eyes.
He muttered to himself something about his being a fool to keep
such late hours, and, hurrying back again to his bedroom, rang the
bell for breakfast.

A man in the habit of stopping out until five in the morning
should never have a looking-glass in his room. It was a painful
thing to see the captain advance timidly to his toilet-table and gaze
upon himself. Despite the rose-coloured curtains, he looked as
yellow as mustard. He leaned forward to see if the wrinkles about
the eyes and forehead had deepened, and then sighed sadly, as if he
thought they had. He was looking far from well that morning.
The texture of his skin did not please him, the grain of it being
coarse as that of an ostrich's egg, and its colour that of cold size.
Even when he had pushed his hair off his forehead, coughed, struck
his chest, and vigorously thrown his shoulders back, there was
nothing prepossessing in his general appearance. In disgust he gave

up all attempts at personal embellishment, and returned to his bed.
As he lay there, he blessed his fate that he was not a married man ;
"for," thought he, "how disgusted my wife would be if she saw me
now."

He was very low-spirited—he had a slight headache—and fell into
a serious train of thought. As he tried to eat half a slice of dried
toast he accompanied each mouthful with a self-inflicted lecture upon
his dissolute mode of life, turning the bread over in his mouth as if
it had been embittered by his repentance. Not that his reflections
were the most moral ones, nor was the punishment which, according
to his ideas, his behaviour entailed, of the most distressing character.
"Another day gone!" he thought, fixing his eyes in melancholy
resignation upon the dirty boots he had forgotten to put outside the
door overnight. "Another day gone! This won't do! How can I
expect to feel well or look well leading such a life! It will be five
o'clock before I am ready to go out! What a fool, idiot, ass I am!
On such a day, too, when Regent Street will be crowded! Every
pretty face and every new bonnet in London will be there. It serves
me right—it serves me right! I must and will keep better hours!"
As if determined to lose no time in reforming, he leaped from his
bed and set about his toilet—the exquisite results of which, whilst
they roused the envy of Mincing Lane and the Stock Exchange, had
never failed to win the admiration of Piccadilly and the esteem of
Hyde Park.

Whenever the air was free from dampness and gave promise that
a curl was likely to retain its position for a few hours, the captain
took especial pains with his hair. He was of the same opinion as the
Messrs. Rowland—that a head of luxuriant locks was the greatest
ornament which nature had vouchsafed to the votaries of fashion.
How often would the captain comb forward his side hair until it had
assumed its proper grace. He was never tired of rounding the
rebellious mesh on his fingers, or fixing it with cosmetique. With
the greatest cunning the bushy portions at the back were made to
conceal the slightly bald spots in the front. He would brush and
brush till his arms ached and his scalp smarted, but he never
regretted either the time or the torment provided the Brutus stood
up boldly as a cock's comb above his classic brow. When the hair
was neatly grained with the comb, when the parting at the back was
as distinct as the centre bone of a fish, then he felt easy in his mind,
and smiled complacently as he twisted his head about before his
mirror.

As the toilet progressed, several philosophic reflections passed
through the captain's mind. As he saw his form gradually becoming
more and more attractive, he was led to ponder on the wonders of
art. Each time he dug his finger into his pomatum, and saw how it
turned the colour of his locks from a mild ginger to the rich tones of
a briskly-fried sole, he uttered a blessing on the great discoverer of
bear's-grease. After he had tied on his false collar, and seen how, by
concealing a portion of the fatigued face, it gave a brilliance to the

remaining features, he stood still to utter a benediction on the noble master-mind that first imagined " stick-ups." He inwardly rejoiced that he had been born in an age when all these great advances in civilization had been made, and asked himself " how the deuce the old fellows "—meaning the dead and gone of the Year One—" managed after they had been out boozing."

His hat was on—gently cocked on one side, so as not to crush the curls on the right temple. A petit verre had given a sparkle to his eyes, and a flush to his cheek. He was ready for Regent Street and conquest. But the servant entered and handed him a note. He looked at the address, and recognized Fred Tattenham's peculiar scrawl. " What the deuce can he want ?" he thought, as he broke the seal.

Fred Tattenham wanted fifty pounds, and he also wanted to know when that dinner at Richmond was to come off. " You know the bet we made together about that girl Bertha," ran the letter. " It is more than seven months ago, now, and I will trouble you for a cheque. I have spoken to the other fellows about the dinner, and we have agreed, as you will have to pay for it, you may order what you like—may I suggest Paradise soup and ortolans ? "

After he had bitten his lips for a minute or two, and twisted the letter about like a draper testing cloth, the captain whistled—a leetle too flatly—the first two bars of " Still so gently o'er me stealing." Then he took off his hat with a gesture as if he were about to dash it on the ground, but, suddenly remembering it was a new one, placed it carefully on the table. No word escaped him beyond " D—n it ! "

Everybody can understand that it is not always convenient to give a cheque for fifty pounds. It so chanced that the captain—it has also happened to many other brave officers—was particularly hard pushed for money. Even a demand for ten pounds would have distressed him. When his glover called for his little bill of five pounds he had been told the captain was in the country.

There was one thing to be said in Merton's favour—he did not abuse Bertha personally. It is true that, as he flung himself into his arm-chair, he muttered a wicked, unfeeling curse against the whole female sex, but did not particularize the little girl opposite. The best proof he was dreadfully upset was that he gulped down two more petits verres of brandy, jerking off the glasses as rapidly as if he had been taking pills. Then, with the fire of alcohol to inspire him, he threw himself on the sofa, and proceeded to make up his mind as to what was the best thing to be done.

It was a painful sight to see this comparatively young man engaged in the dreadful labour of " making up his mind." He could have packed up twenty portmanteaus in less time than it took him to arrange his thoughts. Whether his mind was of the diminutive order, and delicate as a bracelet watch, or whether it was vast and wild as a primitive forest, none but those who are acquainted with the secrets of nature can reveal. He frowned like a Newton at his calculations, and tossed about as uneasily as if reclining on a sack of potatoes, instead of a sofa stuffed with the best hair. Once he passed his hand through his locks, but the deranged curl aroused him to consciousness, and he quickly replaced it. He bit his lips till they were as red as if a whole hive of bees had newly stung them. But though the gilt shepherdess clock struck the quarters one after another, still the captain could not " make up his mind."

He had the greatest reverence for those debts which, however dishonourably they may have been contracted, are called debts of honour. If ever a friend of his was forced to take an invigorating walk through the Insolvent Court, the captain, however heavy the schedule might have been, had never refused to shake the freed man's hand, and pleasantly joke him upon the whitewashing performance. But should his most intimate acquaintance neglect to settle after a horse-race, he might as rationally expect to take tea with the Queen of Oude as obtain a nod from the indignant Merton. He admired the noble fellow who, to pay a gambling debt, did not hesitate to ruin his entire family. He despised the mean-hearted dog who preferred leaving his losses at blind hookey unsettled rather than reduce his father to beggary, or see his wife and family turned into the streets. Holding such opinions as these, the noble captain of course determined on sending Fred Tattenham his fifty pounds, even if he had to take to the Ratcliffe Highway, and garrote every sailor who was getting drunk on his voyage-money.

Now his thoughts were turned to Bertha, the pretty little witch who had brought upon him all this sorrow and tribulation. Fifty pounds for a pair of large eyes. It was dear. Confound her rich brown hair ! he might have bought a fine brown horse for the same money.

Now, what should he do with her ? Should he give her up and let her go her own way in life, or should he still pursue his plot against her virtue ? And now the captain's mind was wavering to and fro like a hair balance, the scale at one moment turning with an attempt at morality, while, at the next instant, as he thought over the girl's charms, his desires would weigh down every other consideration.

" I'll let the girl go," he undecidedly muttered to himself. " She will marry some journeyman carpenter, and have to get his one o'clock dinner ready. Fancy her pretty arms round the neck of a fellow in a flannel jacket ! Imagine those beautiful hands stroking a rough head full of sawdust ! That girl was born to sit in a mail phaeton." Then, striking his thigh, he added, " Hang me if I can give her up. Yet, suppose I should get tired of her, and, after a year or two, wish her at the devil ? If she was to marry one of her own class, most likely he would dote on her, as they do in the plays. I wish I had never seen those eyes of hers ! It is like hearing music to look at them ! Pretty little thing ! I know exactly the kind of bonnet that would make her look like an angel. A poor man could not give her such a bonnet. She would have to wear a common straw thing, with

8

her hair arranged like a workhouse girl's. I can't bear the idea of
Bertha down on her knees, scrubbing a miserable back-room. Now,
I should dress her out as showy as an album binding. Wouldn't the
fellows be astonished when they saw her in her silks, satins, and
laces, as beautiful as the queen of a harem!"

For some time he amused himself by picturing the envy which
Bertha's beauty would arouse in the bosoms of his intimate friends.
The glory of her loveliness would be reflected upon him. They would
be forced to avow that he was a better judge of beauty than any of
them. "Besides," he thought, "she is a kind of girl there would be
no fear of being jealous of; for, if once she gave her heart, there
would be no fear of anybody else carrying her off." Then, again, his
right to Bertha struck him in a new light. "I'm positively entitled
to her," he said. "I've bought her. I look upon this fifty pounds to
Fred Tattenham as a kind of purchase-money. What a fool I should
be to let her go, after investing such a sum! If I was to lay out
fifty pounds in a house, I should be called a madman if I gave up
the place without getting my money back. Then why should I give
up such a palace as Bertha?"

Whether it was that the captain could not make up his mind in less
than a day, or whether Fred Tattenham's letter had disgusted him
with the world, it is singular that for the first time in two years he
passed an evening at home. He sent downstairs to request that
Mrs. Bullunty would cook him two mutton chops. He drank a
bottle of sherry with them, and declared it was the filthiest dinner
he had ever eaten.

Try as he would, he could not determine how he should act towards
Bertha. To seek inspiration, he many times went to the window, in
the hopes of catching sight of that fair damsel, and, having a con-
tradictory mind, his disappointment only made him love her the
more. When eleven o'clock struck—that being the hour at which
Miss Tomsey's household invariably retired to rest—he lighted a
cigar, and went on to the balcony, whence he watched the window of
the room where Bertha slept. He saw a light come into it, and someone close the window, and then pull down the blind. The captain
felt his breath shorten as he looked upon this female form. "There
she is, pretty little creature!" he said, addressing the illumined casement. "You look more beautiful than ever! I cannot give you
up!" Perhaps if he had been aware it was Mrs. Wortey, the cook,
and not the lovely Bertha, whom he was thus apostrophizing, he
might have been induced to alter his opinion. But love is blind and
cannot see through a brick wall. In his agitated condition, the
captain tried to soothe himself with hot brandy-and-water. His
faculties became quickened with the stimulant, and before the third
glass was empty, he had "made up his mind" to one thing.

He vowed to himself that he would not go near any of his fellows,
or even walk down the Haymarket for a fortnight. "The fact is,"
he remarked mentally, "I go so little into decent society that I am

in an unnatural and demoralized state. The only women I talk to are those that disgust you before they have answered a dozen questions. The consequence is, that the first decent girl I see I fall in love with. Because she does not address me first, I consider her the most modest of her sex, and because she lowers her eyes when I stare at her, I persuade myself she is a paragon of innocence. But the truth is, I am not a fit person to judge."

So the captain promised himself that he would go into society. He had plenty of invitations—two, indeed, for the very next week. "You may depend upon it," he thought, "I shall find plenty of girls much prettier than Bertha, and, looking at them, shall forget all about the stupid little beauty. Why, it is evident enough that girls who have been well educated and brought up at home, and who are dressed in the most expensive manner, must be more captivating than my little witch. So, in this way I will save myself without destroying her. And, by Jove!" he added, "if I do meet with a girl who is prettier than my wench, hang me if I don't marry her."

By this last exclamation, some people might be led to imagine that a matrimonial alliance with Captain Merton Crosier was a most excellent and enviable position. But, knowing his character as well as we do, we very much doubt whether his society for life would be a fitting reward for superlative female excellence. The captain was selfish beyond the usual average. He had no taste more noble than sporting, was fond of change, and afflicted with a deranged liver, which at times made him irritable.

A man's true value is never known until he is missed. The first night that Crosier stopped away from his jolly companions they felt little or no anxiety about the absentee. But when a second and a third passed, and yet the captain withheld his society, then did those wild boys Tom Oxendon and Charley Sutton conclude that Merton's life must be in danger, and, with an impulse that did honour to their friendship, paid him a morning visit. Neither would Fred Tattenham have stopped away, but for fear that it would look, as he remarked, as if he had called for the fifty pounds. Many were the anxious inquiries which had been made down the Haymarket as to what had become of the captain. Mr. Alf Cox, of the "Jolly Trainer," had made tender inquiries after his "esteemed friend and noble patron," and had even volunteered to prescribe for him "in case he was attacked with these here brokelis as was about" (by which term he meant bronchitis), asserting that nothing was better for brokelis than a glass of the thick bottoms of a porter cask, took early on a hempty "stomick."

The two friends were astounded, and not a little disgusted, to discover that nothing ailed the captain. It was in vain he gave as his excuse that he was tired and knocked up, and wanted to be quiet for a while. They would not believe him, but, knowing him very intimately, swore there was some woman at the bottom of it. Before two bottles of bitter ale had been emptied, Crosier managed by his over-care to betray his own secret. That morning Bertha was working by the open window, and the extreme care Merton took to prevent either of his two friends having a peep at her raised their suspicions. On the excuse that the light was too strong, he drew down the blinds. If Tom, whilst wandering about the room, approached too near the casements, the captain would, upon some pretext or another, call him back again, either to show him some unimportant letter, which he pulled from his pocket, or to ask him what the exact time was by his watch. When Charley once rose to see if it were raining, Crosier rushed so precipitately to the window that both his visitors were startled by such unnatural politeness.

"What the deuce is the matter with you?" said Charley Sutton. "You have turned thundering civil all of a sudden. Are you going to turn counter-jumper?"

"I'll swear there's a woman somewhere," said Tom Oxendon. And although Merton tried to prevent him, and requested him not to make a fool of himself, that youth forced his way to the window and drew up the blind. No sooner did he see Bertha than he burst into a laugh and shouted out, "You scoundrel, Crosier! why, there's that little thing you lost the fifty pounds about. I should have thought you'd had enough of her by this time. You don't mean to say you are still bothering your head about her?"

If they had looked in his face, they would have noticed how angry he was that his secret should be discovered, and the best answer that could be made to the question was the anxious manner in which he endeavoured to get them back again to their seats. They began to banter him.

"Good Heavens!" said Sutton, "and you are really in love with this servant maid! Why, I call that wasting time."

"And money too," added Tom Oxendon, "for he won't get out of it under sixty pounds."

"Don't you know," continued Charley Sutton, "that it is no more trouble to make love to a duchess than to a serving wench? The same oaths and compliments have to be used, and, confound it, there's more glory in killing a peacock than bagging a sparrow."

"How can you like maid-servants?" thundered in Tom Oxendon, whilst the captain tried to look careless, as if the conversation did not pain him. "They are dirty creatures, and wear black petticoats. My dear boy, we must save you from this tomfoolery. Just imagine, now: these girls never wash their faces when they get up in the morning. They don't know what a toothbrush is, and they sift cinders. How should you like to kiss a girl's hand after she's been sifting cinders? Good gracious!"

"If you're seriously determined on laying your heart on the kitchen-dresser," sneered Charley Sutton, "what will you stand if I carry off the missus and secure you the key of the area gate?"

Stung to the quick by these rough criticisms on Bertha, the captain nevertheless pretended to be amused. He assumed a nonchalant manner, and said, "You've settled the matter very nicely between you, but I'll let you have your own way. Suppose I do like the girl, it's only a simplicity of taste, after all. It's about the same thing as if I chose to dine on bread and cheese. You wouldn't object to that ? "

" You may dine on acorns if you like," answered Sutton, " but you won't convince me there is any pleasure in simplicity that talks of ' h'ambition, 'h'oysters, 'atred, 'ouses, and that sort of thing. Why, the butcher's boy, or the baker's man would cut you out of the field in no time."

The conversation was becoming rather angry. The captain's face had grown red, and his mouth was stretched into a smile which was anything but amiable. So Tom Oxendon put an end to the discussion by saying, " Well, never mind. If Merton likes to hunt for his loves in the dusthole, let him. What the deuce does it matter to us if the adored of his bosom blackleads stoves and cleans knives ? It's a queer taste, and he'll soon get tired of it."

When the two friends rose to depart, they endeavoured to entrap the captain into a night on town, inviting him to supper, and promising him unheard-of fun at the rooms of one of their acquaintance—a certain Bob Tail—who was to give a kind of evening party, to which the guests were to come as soon as the Casino closed. But, with more determination than he had ever before displayed, Merton refused to join them, although he felt that to miss the enjoyment of Bob Tail's reunion was a cruel privation.

Instead of spending a night on town, the captain passed the evening at the sumptuous mansion of Gabael Golcondor, Esquire, the rich diamond merchant. He did not enjoy himself much, for there was only one young lady there whose personal attractions were of that kind which appealed to his tenderer feelings. And as she, when he asked her to dance, was engaged fifteen deep, he did not think it worth while waiting till four in the morning to be the sixteenth. The poor captain was what is called fast, and imagined, judging by himself, that whenever a gentleman danced with a lady he made the most violent love to her that his imagination could give words to. "By the time she has had her fifteen partners," he thought to himself, " she'll have had enough of flattery, and unless I call her a cat, or something of that kind, I don't see a possibility of startling her nerves."

The next party that Crosier went to, he danced with three young ladies, all of whom he criticized minutely before he hazarded his quadrille, waltz, or polka. The first, who was seventeen, and wore lank curls, which bobbed up and down like whalebone snakes at each step she took, discoursed with him on the merits of the different London preachers—a subject upon which, we are ashamed to say, the captain was profoundly ignorant. The second young lady, who had bushy eyebrows, and a fine promise of a moustache, annoyed him by making love to him instead of permitting him to attempt any advances towards her. She called him a wicked man, and a naughty man, almost before he had opened his mouth. The third young lady, he discovered, alas, too late! had a violent cast in her eye, and, from not knowing which one was looking at him, he made some deplorable mistakes, such as saying to her, when she was looking in his face, " I see you are noticing that painting against the wall. Are you fond of pictures ? "

The result of the captain's evening-party experience was that he made up his mind that Bertha was the loveliest and most charming girl he had ever met in the whole course of his life. As he lolled in his chair after his return home, and smoked the cigar he had been longing for all the evening, he could not refrain from bursting into a torrent of praise on Miss Tomsey's companion. " I've seen some two hundred of them," he said, " all got up like dolls, and in first-rate order. There is not one fit to drink tea with her out of the same pot. Her eyes are Argand lamps compared to their farthing rush-lights, and, though I have looked into every mouth I have seen, one of her teeth is worth a peck of theirs. It is no use! I must have Bertha, she's the prettiest girl I ever saw. If it ruins me, she shall be mine."

Now we would humbly submit that the captain was not a fit and proper person to form a correct opinion upon the merits of young ladies. In fixing upon a fair one, he did so as he would fix upon a horse, looking only to beauty and spirit, and taking only the warranty of the owner as to freedom from vice. He was so habituated to the rough license of the streets, so accustomed to the perfect liberty of the night-house, that he felt himself cramped and gene'd under the restrictions of respectable society. He lost his boldness and dash when he had to converse with a young lady whose mamma was present. To Bertha he could rattle out protestations and love speeches by the hour. To his partners in the dance he could only stammer a few commonplace replies. If he did not enjoy himself he accused them of being the cause, while the truth really was that when he was bold it was only because he felt a contempt for the woman to whom he was talking, and the moment respect was enforced from him he became stagnant and insipid. His was a vitiated taste. The man who drinks raw brandy has little relish for milk.

CHAPTER III.

"ACCOMMODATION FOR TRAVELLERS."

BEING both strong of body and proud of spirit, Billy Fortune sent the door of the "padding ken" flying back on its hinges with such a bang, that, for the moment, Mrs. Lully, who was smoking her pipe by the fireside, made sure the police were down upon her. There were four shillings in Billy Fortune's pocket, and the arrogance of wealth was strong upon him. He made the door do footman's work and announce his gentlemanly entrance.

"What! is that you, strapping Billy?" cried Mrs. Lully, who had started up from her chair in alarm. "Cuss your awkward limbs! how dare you frighten people? When was you made Emperor of China? You've done me worse harm than the west wind, and shook me like a bush. My fingers is really ready to drop off with trembling. I made sure you was the Peelers, hang 'em."

The old woman spoke so angrily that Ned Purchase and Phil were half afraid to enter. When they did so, they shut the door to again very gently, as a set-off to Billy's riot. Their confidence was a little restored by seeing Master Fortune advance to the old woman as dauntlessly as if she was a stuffed figure. "All right, mother!" said he. "You're as spreeish an old lass as ever sucked at a bottle, and I only did it that I might hear the squeak of your quail pipe, my jolly hen. I've brought a couple of bene coves, with lots of the queen's pictures in their sacks. Come, it's no good being chuff! Let's have a pot of that fourpenny English Burgundy of yours, and, whilst my mates are drinking the 'belch,' I want to talk business with you." He pointed to the bag he carried, and she, thinking he had brought with him stolen goods out of which a pound or two might be made, became civil enough, and asked him into her back room.

Few men who "stalled" at Mrs. Lully's hotel dared to be as free and easy with her as Master Billy. She was a woman of sixty, but those who had felt the weight of her arm declared "it hit remarkably young for its age," and "tasted very strong of the hammer." On her fifty-ninth birthday, one Nosey Sam, a pedler, who was fond of full glasses, forgot his good breeding and behaved rudely, whereupon the hostess, taking him up as easily as a cat does her kitten, carried him to the door and flung him into the street as she would have cast away a pan of ashes.

This woman stood straight and firm as the Farnese Hercules in petticoats. Beneath her short skirts were seen a pair of thick-soled highlows which would have pinched the toes of a railway navvy. Her grey hair hung about her forehead and temples long as the forelock of a horse. For fear she might, from her massive build, be mistaken for a man, she had labelled herself "woman" by means of a deep-frilled nightcap, over which she wore a plaid shawl arranged as a hood. Her thick eye-brows hung down in weeping-willow fashion and shaded a pair of black optics that sparkled like stars through a hedge. The first time Phil had occasion to speak to her, he, in his timidity, called her "ma'am," which annoyed her, for she exclaimed, "Cuss you for a lobb-mouth. Call me mother, you black spy."

When Mrs. Lully found that Billy—whom on seeing the bag, she had, with sudden affection, called her darling—had nothing but "scran" to dispose of, she swore at him, and called him a beast and a ken-cadger, and hoped he would end his life on the twister. She told him to take his broken victuals to some other pig's trough. This indignation was only assumed in order to obtain the food at a cheaper rate; and eventually—being short of provisions—she purchased the lot for a shilling and a gratuitous supper, the big piece of "sawney" (bacon) being thrown in for nothing.

The lame Ned and Phil much preferred remaining in the public room during Billy's interview. By industriously staring about them they managed to console themselves pending their companion's absence. The "travellers" who frequented the house were evidently of simple taste, and cared little for ornament or furniture. There were four whitewashed walls, which had become so dirty that it seemed as if no washing of any kind would ever make them white again, and at shoulder-height a dark panelling of grease had been formed by the friction of the customers' backs. The safety and privacy of her customers seemed to have been more attended to by the landlady than their comfort. The window had been boarded over up to the topmost panes, at least a foot higher than the tallest policeman in England could ever hope to peep over; but the tables and forms that stretched along each side of the apartment were outrageously narrow. For those who came in cold or wet there was a roaring fire, that would bake limbs or cloth into hot dryness in a very few minutes, and the sand on the floor had the double advantage of covering the nakedness of the boards and making them serve as a large spittoon.

Beyond a few inscriptions scratched on the stained whitewash, there was nothing to relieve the broad expanse of even wall. For fear the inmates should grow tired of gazing at the ceiling, and seeing nothing to amuse the eye, a gentleman, who signed himself "Yorkshire Jack," had, with the flame of a candle, written these words: "Just out of the 'blockhouse' (gaol), and never felt better."

When Phil became more at home in this lodging-house he got on the forms to read the writings on the wall. The desks at Eton, or the visitors' book at Shakspeare's house, are not more crowded with carved names and gratuitous remarks than was this whitewash. Tramps on their circuit seem to be of the same flesh and blood as gentlefolk on their travels, and to be bitten with a similar passion for leaving behind them a written trail of their progress. One of these inscriptions was, "Joe the Bouncer at his old game again!" Another related that "Blinky Sam" stopped there, and "found the fleas as hungry and saucy as ever." A third, who called himself "Mike Tedder, the Rat," stated that he "hated the police worse than years ago, but was otherwise hearty." There were rude drawings of profiles and men hanging from gibbets; indeed, no Government clerk's pad could be more covered with caricatures.

In front of the fire sat a woman bending over it so closely that her tattered gown smelt of scorching. Her feet were bare, and she held the soles as near the bars as if they had been toast, curling her toes about with the heat. She had caught an ague from "skippering it," that is, sleeping under haystacks, and was trying, she said, "to draw the cold out of her bones." The men seated at the tables were talking openly either of their day's adventures, or what they intended to do on the morrow. One, who hawked "kite" and "sticky" (paper and wax) as an excuse for begging, was telling another, who was a cadger, which were the best houses to go to. He seemed, to judge from his talk, perfectly acquainted, not only with every street, but with the dispositions of most of the inhabitants in the town. "The brick house agin the bridge is bene if you can catch the 'burerk' (mistress) at home, but the 'toff' is a mortal downy bird, and fly to everythink pretty night!"

"Have the scaldrum dodge been worked much?" asked the cadger, referring to the art of mutilating the body to make the limbs appear as if they had been injured by fire. "I'm thinking of working the 'glim,' and going on the dreadful conflagrashun lurk."

One of the men present had been drinking heavily, and, being half intoxicated, had lost all command over his tongue, and was complaining he had been out all day on the "monkry," and had only taken three "twelvers" and a "grunter."

"That won't keep me," he said. "It's scarcely wages for a 'knight of the rainbow' (footman). What's come to people I don't know. They don't seem to have no feelings nowadays. I'm sure I looked awful affecting, and shivered fit to come to bits. Ah! it's a rum world, and hearts is turned to paving-stones."

The three young tramps ate a hearty supper, composed of a stew made out of the broken victuals they had brought with them, and which, with the aid of onions, had been rendered highly odorous to the nose, and stinging to the palate. As the night drew on, the room gradually filled with the lodgers returning from their rascally work. In they came, one after another, some with success written in their knowing, brazen faces, others with a dull, dejected air, the best proof that the day had been a bad one for halfpence. The man with the full pocket entered in as if the house had been built for his sole accommodation. He stalked, whistling, to the fire, and stood before it as a screen. He laughed loudly, and called his pals by their nicknames, pelting them with slang witticisms. He was fearlessly impu-

dent, for he knew that if a quarrel ensued, he had the money in his
pocket to pay for the infallible ointment—a glass of liquor—for a
cadger's bruised pride. But the unsuccessful tramp sneaked into the
room as a dog does into a butcher's shop. He opened the door only
just wide enough to admit his body, as if he would not have his entry
observed. He ordered his pint of twopenny ale in a whispering
voice. He sat trembling lest the successful man should single him
out as a butt, and, if his cringing form had the misfortune to attract
notice, he had not the heart to resent the jest, but joined in the laugh
against himself, although inwardly vowing to have vengeance.

There were all kinds of men and women present, each representing
some special style of imposition. They were all boasting of the
dodges and tricks they had played to melt the hearts of the charitable. Many a kind-hearted townsman, who had listened to the tales
of distress, had gone to bed that night with a lighter heart, consoled
by the good aid he thought he had rendered. But here was the rogue
who had whined out his miseries now laughing until every tooth in
his head was visible.

There were men so ignorant that they could speak their thieves'
slang more easily than their native English, fellows whose signature
was a cross, whose knowledge of the beauties of the world began and
ended with eating and drinking. But there were others whose
tongues were glib as a barrister's—men whose memory retained a
sufficient remnant of their schooling to enable them to drag a Latin
quotation into their sentences. One coarse-featured fellow, who was
nearly " bung-eyed " over his beer (as they call being drunk), was a
stealer of boxes from the backs of carriages, a purloiner of pots from
public-houses, or even of bread from bakers' baskets. He could tell
tales of trunks knowingly cut away from their lashings to the hind
springs, or how he had " pricked for panam in the wicker," or
" sneaked a cat and kitten " from the tap-room. He sat beside a low-
browed, meek-faced villain, who called himself a " mumbler," and
passed off as a broken-down tradesman, ruined by his faith in a
friend. In the furthest corner of the room was a thin, active lad of
fourteen, who sat smoking so short a pipe that the bowl of it seemed
close to his nose. He had a face pale and tired-looking, as if he had
just risen from a fever, but his disease was only hard living—a bed
one night, and a hedge for the remainder of the week ; meat and beer
at one dinner, and turnips for the next. He was ready for anything,
either to sing ballads in the "paviors' workshop" (streets), or to
"sneak down an area " in the hopes of purloining a silver "pap
feeder" (spoon), or even a teapot, if it was at hand. The man in
decent black clothing, seated near the fire, and laughing and talking
as if he was the oracle of the room, would have nothing to say to such
low-class thieves as these. He never "chummed with ken-cadgers."
He was a " high-flier," a genteel beggar. When he worked, it was in
jewellers' shops, whipping up gold rings and chains as soon as the
tradesman's back was turned. Or he might fraudulently collect

subscriptions for charitable institutions. But as for a vulgar "lurk," that would bring in a few halfpence, he was above such dirty practices. The man he was talking to had studied medicine, but, after being ten years a student, and four times unable to pass his examination, he had gradually sunk lower and lower, until now he had become a tramping swindler, earning his living by passing himself off as a sea captain ruined by shipwreck; and excellently he seemed to live on the deception.

There were men and women from every part of the United Kingdom. Irishmen, who pretended to have been old soldiers, and had papers to prove the battles they had never fought, and medical certificates describing the wounds they had never received. There were Scotchmen, who for the last five years had been weavers out of work, and were begging for money to enable them to return to Glasgow, although they had that day tramped in an opposite direction. Some of the English passed themselves off as poor needle-makers, whose health had been destroyed at the business; others had sore legs and arms to exhibit, or for the last ten years had told, with tears in their eyes, distressing tales of a child that died overnight of the small-pox, and begged for a few shillings to purchase the coffin. There were women, too, whose living depended upon an imaginary daughter, whom they were taking to London to get cured of the king's evil; and others whose supposed husbands had fallen off scaffolds, or been injured in a railway accident. The writings, or "fakements," which testified to these mournful narratives were to be obtained for a few shillings at any of the principal towns, so that when one story grew stale, it could easily be changed for another. The man who carried on this trade at Stafford was well known by the frequenters of Mrs. Lully's house. His false petitions were highly esteemed, and he enjoyed the reputation of being a first-rate fist at "screeving a fakement," though, owing to his forged signatures having been too often detected, he was declared to be "a duffer at coopering a monekur."

Tramps are not regular in the hours they keep. They measure the length of the evening by the length of their purses. Plenty of money means four in the morning, and an empty pocket, to be in bed by nine. They paraphrase the French proverb, and hold that he who sleeps—drinks.

About twelve o'clock Master Billy, who was commissariat-general to his company, ordered a jug of what he termed "hot flannel" for three—a mixture of gin, beer, and eggs—which he declared wrapped round a fellow like wool, and made him sleep like opium. Then, their money being spent, they retired to rest.

The dormitory was a large, bare-walled room, with ten beds in it, each one intended to accommodate two, or, on a pressure, three sleepers. In winter, when the windows were kept closed, some of the lodgers complained in the morning of headaches, and asserted that thirty persons in one room "was a leetle crowded." But in summertime nothing could be more delightful, the company being usually gay and disposed to converse until daylight.

Before he went to sleep, Billy Fortune had some serious business conversation with the gentleman in the next bed. He was sorry to learn that there was just then little doing in Stafford.

" The town's been overworked," said the gentleman, " but I wouldn't give it up in despair. You say you've got a lame chap can play on the ' howling-stick ' ? " (flute).

" That he can," answered Billy, " beautiful! Anybody would give twopence to get rid of him. And I can make myself as humpbacked as a prawn, if I like."

" Can the other cove do anything ? " was the inquiry.

" Well, he ain't an out-and-outer," answered Billy, contemptuously ; " but he's a good-looking chap, and the servant-girls takes to him. He helps to bring in the ' belly timber' " (food).

The next day, the three vagrants, dressed as genteelly as they could manage it, were parading the back streets, Ned with his stump bandaged up, and limping as if each step caused him the greatest agony. Billy had crooked his back, till he was bent like a fish-hook, whilst Phil, with his face washed, and his hair neatly combed, was appointed to hand the cap round for pence. The "patter" Master Fortune undertook to deliver, his voice being very penetrating and powerful. The appeal, with |this affecting opening, "Leddies and gentlemen, and keyind Christian free-ends," he bawled out as they crept slowly along in the centre of the road; " we hare ashamed to appear thus before you and to soliceet your charitee. We hare without free-ends or the comman necessairees of lief, being crippels, and hunhable to procure hany keyind of hemployment." Each time he concluded this oration, the three boys joined in a verse of a hymn, which they sang with such vigour that it soon brought the women and children to the doors and windows.

But affairs did not prosper with them. They seldom took more than five shillings in a day, and, owing to Mrs. Lully's objecting to any of her lodgers living beyond their income, their enjoyments were limited. Ale and " hot flannel " became scarce, decreasing from pots to pints, and at last were highly prized when served up by the mugful.

Before leaving Stafford, Master Billy took advantage of an offer made him by a recruiting sergeant who was staying at the " Goose and Bottle " public-house purposely to receive all smart young men who fancied a military life. The brave Billy drank several pots of beer with his martial friend, took the shilling, borrowed half-a-crown, and then, relating his adventure to his pals, proved to them, in forcible language, that it was necessary to fly from Stafford. He justified his deceit upon the sergeant in these words : " I ain't going to fight their quarrels for 'em. When these big wigs chooses to have a row, they alwers tries to get us little wigs to do the fighting."

On leaving Stafford, it was determined by the lads to direct their steps towards the South of England. "Confound the north," cried Billy. "It's too cold for charity. I like the south, where it's hot. They gives a penny in half the time."

CHAPTER IV.

GREAT CARE IS TAKEN OF THE HAZLEWOOD FAMILY.

MISS TOMSEY had come down to breakfast feeling far from well, and in a decided ill-humour. She had supped rather late the night before on a crab salad. The consequence of this fish repast was an unpleasant dream, in which she imagined there was a Frenchman under the bed. "I never was so terrified in my life," she told Mary Anne when the latter brought the hot water up. "I imagined the bearded villain was pushing knives through the mattress and trying to stick me in the back."

Being in a bad temper, Miss Tomsey quarrelled, not only with her bread-and-butter, but also with her new-laid egg. She gave it so vigorous a tap that it broke as readily as a bubble. She found that the dried toast was as thick and limp as a new undersole, and declared the tea to be undrinkable. When Mr. Boxer heard the parlour bell ring as if a mad dog was biting at it, he knew there was something very wrong upstairs. "Either she's got fits or upset the tea-hurn," he thought, ascending the kitchen stairs at a pace that made his calves tremble as if they would drop off and roll down the stone steps like cocoa-nuts.

"Boxer, where did you procure this egg?" began the spinster; and, without giving the man more time than permitted him to exclaim, "That hegg, mum!" she continued, "I have told you thousands and thousands of times that I would not have any more eggs from the potato and coal man. How dare you buy my eggs from a man whose fowls roost in a coal-cellar? I have seen those hens with my own eyes lying in the gutter up to their necks in road scrapings. Then how dare you bring me one of their eggs?"

Once more Mr. Boxer, whose raised brows denoted his astonishment, was permitted to exclaim, "The hegg, mum!" when his mistress declared she would not be answered, and ordered him to keep a civil tongue in his head. Then, pointing at the teapot with tragic stiffness, she added, "And remove that! It would disgrace a Greenwich tea-room."

Although hurt, Boxer still remained respectful, merely hinting, in an injured tone, "Perhaps it hasn't drawed yet, mum." But so thoroughly was the lady under the influence of her ill-humour that, instead of listening to the suggestion, she became rude and vulgar, calling out, "Drawed! what does the man mean? How dare you talk of the best orange-flavoured Pekoe as if it were a blister?"

In this excited state of mind was Miss Tomsey when Bertha's mother called and requested a few minutes' conversation on important business. The notion of the workhouse nurse having important business so tickled the elderly maiden's fancy that she could not help saying, with a sneer, "Bless me! we shall have the London sparrows talking of important business next! How these poor mice do try to be elephants!"

All this was very unlike Miss Tomsey's usual manner of thinking, and the blame of it must be laid, not to her, but to the crab supper, which, according to the learned Buchan, when taken late, destroys the system by deranging the juices of the blood.

The old nurse was received with a frigidity of manner which was intended to show Miss Tomsey's disapproval of all airs and graces in poor people. Although the aged maiden was astonished to find the good woman dressed, not in her workhouse clothes, but in a gown of shining black silk, and with a shawl that never cost less than a sovereign upon her back, yet the influence of crab being strong, she would not permit herself to make any remarks that would betray her wonder.

Being in high spirits, Mrs. Hazlewood did not require to be told twice to say what she had come about. "I've taken the liberty to call, ma'am," she began, "for, since I last saw you, I've had the good fortune to meet with a kind friend, who, indeed, has been a friend to me. It's a gentleman I'm speaking of, ma'am." Judging from Miss Tomsey's looks, she seemed to disapprove of such connexions. "Thanks to this kind friend, ma'am—and I hope I am and ever shall be grateful—I am now in a comfortable house of my own, and furnished fit for the first in the land. May Heaven bless him!" Miss Tomsey's expression of countenance seemed to say that Heaven might bless him if it chose, but she would have nothing to do with the matter. "They tell me, ma'am," continued Mrs. Hazlewood, finding all the talk was left to her, "that my drawing-room is a certain pound a week, with attendance and boot-cleaning extra. I wish you could see the rooms, ma'am, you'd be surprised. There's an easy-chair as big as a gig, and so comfortable, it's worth while being tired only to sit in it. Flock and feathers on every bed, and the carpets as lovely as water-colour drawings. There's a three pair front, with a separate bell, and a turn-up chest of draws a member of Parliament might sleep on."

"And might I inquire into the important business upon which you wished to see me?" asked Miss Tomsey, in her coldest manner.

If a snowball had been sent into Dame Hazlewood's face, it could not have surprised her more than did this frigid question. In one moment her smiling face was turned into a countenance overflowing with indignation. The instant she had recovered her senses, she replied, " I wish to ask you, ma'am, if it would be convenient to you to spare Bertha to come and live with me, now my circumstances are so much improved, and her assistance would be almost indispensable."

So strong a hold had the demon crab on Miss Tomsey, that she pretended to burst into a laugh, though it was as shrill and forced a twitter as ever was uttered. "My good soul! you may have her altogether," she said, "for lately—I don't know what has come to the girl—she's not of the least use to me."

The mother looked daggers, but answered mildly, " Thank you, ma'am! I'm sure you're very obliging."

Determined not to be beaten, Miss Tomsey replied, " Not at all, Mrs. Hazlewood, I have to thank you for ridding me of her. You can go."

The indignant old nurse got up from her seat so suddenly that her silk sounded like the whir of a partridge rising. She had already grasped the handle of the door, and was about to leave Miss Tomsey for ever, when that maiden remembered suddenly she had forgotten to ask who the good friend was who had taken such a sudden interest in Bertha's mother. So she called out to the dame, saying,—

" Stop a minute! What's the name of this kind friend who seems to give away houses of furniture as if they were so much firewood ? "

In a tone of voice as sharp as if it had been ground on purpose to cut Miss Tomsey's ear off, Mrs. Hazlewood answered that " she was not at liberty to give any information on that subject."

The idea of being bearded in her own house by a pauper was more than Miss Tomsey's self-respect could put up with. Planting herself firmly upon her pride, she said, " That will do," and gracefully motioned to the door.

At heart Miss Tomsey was as good a woman as ever had her ears pierced, and, about one o'clock in the day, when her indignation had somewhat abated, she, little thinking Mrs. Hazlewood had taken in earnest the conversation which had been held about Bertha, rang the bell, and requested that the latter young lady should be sent to her. She fell back in her chair when Mr. Boxer replied that both mother and daughter had left the house some two hours. Now, Miss Tomsey had a real affection for her pretty companion, and was greatly hurt that, after the kindness shown her, the girl could depart with so little ceremony. Through force of habit, she made use of the simile about having nursed a serpent in her bosom, though, as Miss Tomsey laced very tightly, the cradle must have been a very uncomfortable one.

By-and-by she fell to thinking who this kind friend who had so suddenly turned up as a guardian to the Hazlewood family could possibly be. By degrees her curiosity grew so absorbing that she even allowed the hour at which she had the " Times " to read to glide by without even glancing at the paper. Had she known where the

Hazlewoods' new residence was, it is most likely she would have paid them a visit. She had to content herself with a useless cross-examination of Mary Anne, in which she endeavoured to worm from that young housemaid whether Bertha had ever spoken of any rich relative, or hinted there was any property coming to the family.

It was not till the next day that she was in any way enlightened on this subject, and then she learned the truth from the lips of Bertha herself, who, unable to endure the idea of parting from her former mistress without even saying good-bye, had returned to Harley Street to beg for a shake of the hand.

" They told me," said Bertha, " that you were very angry, and would not speak to me. And I thought it must be true, for I could not understand why you turned me away so suddenly. You have always been so kind to me. But I fancied I must have done some dreadful thing or other that was past forgiveness. Now that I hear you speak to me in your good, kind manner, I wish I had never left."

" I never turned you away at all, you silly child ! " answered the spinster, sharply. She was forced to appear cross to prevent the tears from coming into her eyes. " It was that foolish mother of yours. How could she be such a silly creature !—stupid enough to fancy that I was in earnest ! "

Very numerous were the entreaties made on the one hand for Bertha to return, and very timid were the refusals given on the other.

" I'll double your wages, Bertha," said the one. " You shall have twenty pounds a year."

" Mother says she cannot do without me," said the other. " If I am not with her she must give the house up."

" I shall be miserable without you," continued the lady.

" Mother says she will never part with me again," answered the girl.

Finding all entreaties useless, Miss Tomsey desisted, but, burning to discover the secret of the unknown friend, bluntly, and in as unconcerned a manner as she could assume, inquired his name.

Bertha's face turned as red as a signal-lamp, as she answered, " it was Captain Merton Crosier."

If Miss Tomsey's hair could have stood straight up on her head, up it would have flown, ringlets, back hair and all, so great was the horror she felt when she heard that name. Nothing but the force of strong-toothed combs held down her locks. She experienced a strange sensation pass over her scalp, and gradually descend with icy coldness down her back. She could not simply repeat the words " Captain Merton Crosier," but screamed them out, and threw them, as it were, hissing and red hot at the terrified maid.

" Bertha ! " she at last said, nervously flourishing her hands till they worked as the claws of a beetle on its back, " Bertha ! either your mother is a very bad woman or the greatest fool that walks the earth. I tell you this Captain Crosier is a worthless, low fellow. I have made inquiries about him, and find he seldom returns home before four in the morning. He is what they call a man on town, child, and is trying to act a villain's part to you. You shall not go back there, Bertha. I'll keep you under my own eye, and watch over you. If necessary, I will, out of my own pocket, pay for a servant for your mother; but you shall not return to her."

As she said this, the good little lady thumped a book with such force that a big rose in a vase in the centre of the table was instantly jolted to pieces.

How could Bertha believe her mother's benefactor was a villain? Was it the act of one to open a workhouse door and restore a broken-hearted pauper to the freedom of the working world? When she heard her former mistress call the generous friend such harsh names, she uttered almost unconsciously, "No! no!" Before long, both these women were shedding tears, one weeping over the victim that was to be, the other moved by gratitude for the interest felt in her welfare. But prayers and entreaties were only met with protestations and solemn promises, and in the end Bertha took her leave to return to her new home.

Miss Tomsey was standing at the window that she might see to the last the pretty girl who had so long been her companion, and whom she believed she was never to behold again. As Bertha turned up her pale face to the drawing-room window, the kind spinster shook with agitation.

"Poor lost thing!—poor lost thing!" was all she could say.

There was a regular shout of laughter when Crosier, for the first time, made his reappearance at the club. He had acknowledged his defeat by paying Fred Tattenham the fifty-pound bet. And now, as he told them, he had come down purposely to arrange about the dinner.

They were too hard upon him. They roasted him too severely. Lord Oaks said some deuced severe things about him, and Fred Tattenham was never so funny before in all his life.

"Well, and what do you intend to do with the girl now?" asked Tom Oxendon.

The cunning captain had long since determined upon the course of conduct he should pursue when he met his friends. He thought it better to appear to them as if he was disgusted with Bertha, and resolved to give her up. He rather dreaded being made the target for all their jokes should he persist in declaring his attachment to her.

"Do with the girl!" he said, laughing—"egad! I've had enough of her. If anybody likes to buy my share and interest, he shall have it for a pound of cigars."

When they asked him to give a history of his love, he did so in a

T

very honourable manner, as far as regarded Bertha. He called her a lump of ice, which would be invaluable to a confectioner, but was perfectly useless to a fellow in a hurry. He rattled off some of the impassioned declarations he had made, and appealed to his companions "whether that was not the genuine stuff." He confessed, with a hearty frankness, he had been sold, and gave them his word, as a gentleman, that the next time he went after a girl he would not interfere with the legitimate property of footmen and grooms.

When the dinner came off at Richmond, he was so determined to impress upon his companions that he had completely done with Bertha, that he kept continually talking of her during the entire entertainment. He made several comparisons between the dishes served and the peculiar beauties of the maiden, affirming that the truffles were the colour of her eyes, and a rich brown sauce the exact tint of her hair. During dessert, to such an extent did he carry his fanciful humour that, imitating the ways of an auctioneer, he put up Bertha as a lot to be bid for.

"A very beautiful and accomplished creature!" he cried, "and exactly suited for a gentleman of fortune. What shall we say for this little lot? Will anybody bid ten pounds? Her eyes are worth the money. Remember! she is under eighteen years of age, perfectly free from vice, has only an aged mother, and, I daresay, would have no objection to travel."

To keep up the fun, Charley Sutton bid a shilling, and the lot was knocked down to him.

"Now, mind, Crosier," said the purchaser, in a serious voice, "she's mine; and if I catch you following her up, it will be a d—d dishonourable thing."

The solemn, business-like tone in which this was said made the captain feel rather uncomfortable, and regret having carried the joke so far. But, remembering the girl had changed her abode, and was not likely to be traced, he picked up his courage again, and blustered out, "They don't allow any followers where she is, and her Sunday out is only once a month."

The house in which Mrs. Hazlewood had been installed by the captain was situate in Camberwell. It had long been to let furnished, and when the offer was made to take it for a year certain, paid in advance, there was no difficulty about handing over the keys.

"I don't mind risking another hundred pounds on the little witch," argued the captain. "I must have my revenge upon her before I let her go. Besides, I shall save the money before the year is out, for it will keep me away from night work."

He had calculated his game very deeply. The street in which the house stood was not a very excellent one for letting apartments, and he clearly foresaw that if the lodgers did not come without delay, the Hazlewood exchequer would soon be down to the last farthing. Then the women would have to borrow from him. By his lending them money, they would fall into his power, and the deuce was in it if he did not arrange matters in his own way.

So as to have the right of entering the house when he liked, he told Mrs. Hazlewood he would take the parlours at her own price, for at least a year.

"I shall very seldom be with you, madam," he said, in a mild voice. "You will not be put to much trouble on my account; only I think it would assist you a little at beginning, and might be the means of bringing you in a little ready money."

The poor old lady could have fallen down upon her knees and worshipped him as a miracle of goodness.

The first Sunday that was passed in the new house, Crosier dined with his protegees. He had in a playful manner asked the old nurse to invite him to their table. She, of course, was delighted. She told Bertha in the evening that she was the more pleased "because, don't you see, dear, we shall have an opportunity of observing how he behaves himself, and seeing whether there is any truth in those reports against him." Silly woman! As if she was any match for the cunning captain.

He was afraid lest they might "stick him down" to a leg of pork with onions, baked mutton and brown potatoes, or some other poor man's delicacy. To guard against such a catastrophe, he ordered a little bit of fish, a few birds, and some fruit to be sent in on the Saturday night, "with his compliments."

"He must be made of money, and as generous as a prince," said the mother.

"He has a good heart," added the daughter.

He was well aware that his success would, in a great measure, depend upon his behaviour at this dinner. He knew he must do everything in his power to gain the old mother's confidence. "It was deuced hard work," he grumbled, "to be obliged to win the mother first, before he could hope for the daughter;" but his honour was somewhat at stake, he thought, and he must not mind a little trouble. It would be such a rich thing to deceive those fellows, and show them that, whilst they imagined he had given up all notion of Bertha, he was actually working out a deeply-laid scheme.

If ever a man did reap golden opinions, Crosier certainly was that lucky harvest man. For on the Sunday in question his behaviour and conversation were so strict and guarded that even the clergyman could not have acquitted himself with greater propriety. He addressed very few of his remarks to Bertha, but occupied himself principally with the mother. "It won't do to make love to the little witch before the old one," he thought. "That would cause her to run cunning and spoil the match." So he was very attentive to Bertha, and very chatty with Mrs. Hazlewood. He opened the door, placed a chair, fetched a book, and handed the salt with exquisite politeness to the young girl, whilst to the old one he told amusing anecdotes about his noble friends, asked for her opinion upon the affairs of the

nation, and inquired whether she had been to hear this or that
preacher. In fact, he treated the dame as though she had been one
of the fashionables of London instead of having recently quitted the
workhouse. The old woman felt her vanity bubble and swell at the
respect shown her by so grand a gentleman. The only wish of her
heart was that the master and matron of "St. Lazarus Without"
could have seen her in her great glory. Though Bertha once or
twice thought he might address a few words to her, yet from the
ardent manner in which she, two or three times, surprised him
gazing in her face, she readily understood his admiration was none
the less because he was silent.

At dinner he insisted that Mrs. Hazlewood should take the head of
the table, "she being the mistress," as he said. He also, in a tone
full of religious earnestness, inquired of Miss Bertha if she would be
kind enough to ask a blessing before meat. On being requested to
take another glass of wine, he declined for the following reasons : " I
always limit myself, Mrs. Hazlewood, to two glasses, that quantity
being, in my opinion, perfectly sufficient for any man. Even then I
prefer taking it with water. I have so great a horror of drunkenness,
that I am most watchful over myself in case I might be insensibly
betrayed into that degrading vice."

He certainly had been betrayed into it the night before, for Fred
Tattenham had hoisted him into a cab, and on waking in the morning he discovered he had been sleeping with his hat on.

When this happy repast was finished, Mrs. Hazlewood, in a friendly
manner, inquired if he had enjoyed his dinner.

"That I have, indeed," answered the captain. " When I tell you,
madam, that I have dined at ministerial banquets, that I have frequently been at the tables of the first in the land, that I have three
times been present at a Lord Mayor's feast, you will easily understand my meaning when I tell you that, in spite of their delicious
viands, their delicious wines, their numberless servants, I never in
all my life so thoroughly enjoyed a repast as this one. I am a con-
firmed bachelor, you know, Mrs. Hazlewood "—and with a pleasant
smile he turned to Bertha—" but such a happy insight into the joys
of domestic bliss is almost enough to upset my prejudices against
matrimony. Indeed, although I have enjoyed excessively the good
things I have partaken of at your table, yet that which has been
most to my palate is the perfect fireside bliss of this little meeting."

This was what Charley Sutton would have called " drawing it
with a little too much froth on." But the mother had no suspicion
of her lodger's hypocrisy, and Bertha felt as if she could listen for an
hour if he only would have continued talking. The evening passed
away very slowly indeed, and the captain felt himself bored to death
with the quietude and monotony. He smoked, and tried to read the
weekly paper, but, though his eyes were on the print, his thoughts
were in Harley Street, wondering whether anybody had called upon
him that day. More than once he thought to himself, " I cannot

stand that old woman's twaddle much longer. If she does not go out of the room, and leave me with Bertha, I shall cut it."

At six o'clock he rose to take his departure, giving as his excuse that he had promised an aunt of his to accompany her to chapel. Before leaving he promised them, as a consolation for the grief they showed at parting with his company, that he would in the course of a week or two come and stop a few days. "Only I am afraid I may annoy you," he added, "for sometimes my friends will not let me leave them, and that would be keeping you up to a very late hour."

When he had gone, Mrs. Hazlewood told Bertha she was delighted with the captain's manner and ways. "I never saw so pleasant a young man, and such good company. To hear him talk, you would fancy he was in the Church. Now, our chaplain at St. Lazarus was not half so fluent as he is, and, as for choice of words, there is no comparison."

The reply Bertha made was, that she wondered anyone could be so wicked as to call Mr. Grosier a bad man, for that certainly both his words and his deeds were irreproachable.

Many persons proceeding quietly through the streets were surprised at seeing a dashing-looking gentleman, who had been walking at a great pace, stop suddenly, and, leaning against an area railing, burst into a tremendous laugh. For fear he should explode before he was beyond the reach of the Hazlewood ears, the captain "stepped it" with a vigour that almost put his boots out of shape, and just as he turned the corner his mirth grew restive and beyond his control. He laughed as if a thousand fingers were tickling him—not merely fit to split his sides, but his cheeks and waistcoat into the bargain. "What an enormous lark!" he thought to himself. "It's very jolly for once, but I should not like to do it again. I must never eat another Sunday dinner there, or I should let the cat out of the bag." The only regret he had was that he could not rush off to his companions and spend a jolly evening in laughing over the wonderful adventure.

CHAPTER V.

STONEHENGE.

NED leaned heavily on his crutch, and grumbled loudly at the speed of his companions, as they wound down a steep hill, from which a bank of fine grass, soft and short as velvet, shelved on one side ; while on the other hand palings stood primly up shoulder to shoulder —like a crack regiment—sturdily protecting the sacred plumage of game within. Here and there Billy paused to examine with his stick a hole in the fence, and speculate on the possibility of finding a rabbit in a snare. But his vigilance was not rewarded even with a mole's skin.

"Come along, Billy, no snailing," shouted Ned, who, poor tortoise as he was, had, by his persevering hobbling, got ahead of his companions. "Come on! you'll find nothin' in them holes. Here's Phil eatin' toadstools. That'll be a pretty go to-morrow; and there ain't ne'er a hatband among us."

Here Phil, spitting out the skin of a mushroom, joined his growl to Ned's, in the hopes of urging on the stubborn Billy. It was like coaxing a terrier out of a rat ditch this tearing away of Master Fortune from these hare runs.

"Come along—here's the 'pike!" shouted Phil, "and they said the town was close to it. Come away, Billy, or I'm jiggered if I don't toe-and-heel it. When three chaps are in the same swim, they ought to be accommodating."

These forcible remonstrances had their due effect, and the three young vagabonds, mending their pace, shuffled onwards. Having said something saucy to the "old doll" who was minding the turnpike, and eyed them as they passed through, they turned to the left, and saw the outskirts of Drudeshurst before them, although the town was so small that to say it had outskirts seemed as absurd as to say that a ballet dancer has petticoats. The cows were chewing the cud, the tips of their horns and the warm colour of their hides lighted by the setting sun. Near the banks of the river, that sparkled like a smile along the meadows, a tired angler was winding up his tackle. Whilst the boys stopped to witness this operation, three or four labourers, with spades and forks on their shoulders, passed and turned to look at the strangers rather too curiously to please Billy, who, with his head on one side, stared back again as impudently as he could.

"They look tired, poor chaps," said Phil. "They can hardly lift their feet."

"More fools they," responded Billy. "Got blisters on their hands, I'll warrant, the duffers; and all for a bob a day. That's wus than soldiers' wages. Why, we shall get more in an hour if we've any luck."

"I'll tell you what they've got, though, that we haven't," added Phil. "They've got a home to go to, and a wife to say ' welcome!' and a good bed to rest on. I think, as far as we are concerned, they've the best of it."

At times Phil was subject to these fits of melancholy. They attacked him whenever he had overwalked himself.

But Doctor Billy Fortune was at hand to prescribe for the patient. He administered stimulating jibes and taunts, and soon restored Phil to what he considered a healthy condition of scoundrelism.

"Listen to the preacher," he said to Ned Purchase; "what a rattling soul-driver he'd have made, wouldn't he? Give him a spouting-box and black togs and he'd send such chaps as you and me,

Ned, singing psalms before a week was gone. Wasn't it moving, that idea of his about the wife and home? He ought to have stuck in a few squeakers climbing up dad's knee whilst he's gorging his cat-lap and panam."

To show that he sided with Billy, the lame boy hopped into a puddle and sent the water splashing over Phil, perhaps in the hopes of putting out this spark of virtue.

"I hate a snivelling, water-headed chap," said Ned. "Just stow it till we're working the town, and let the women have it for their pence."

The town of Drudeshurst [1] had an amiable look. The parsonage-house, cloaked with fat-leaved ivy; the doctor's house, from the door of which the brass knocker glistened, as if it would burn the fingers of any one who raised it; the round, ruddy, yellow-haired children trotting about the road; the candles flickering from the darkness of the cottage parlours; the merry songs, heavily charged with local r's that swelled from under the vermilion paws of the Red Lion—all seemed amiable, and sinking happily to the coming night's rest. Here some labourers were piling spades and rakes in a tool-house; there a cottager, with his shoulder planted against his door, was sending grey wreaths of smoke into the air to get gilt edges from the sunset; and sometimes the shrill voice of a woman broke the silence, as she called her little ones from a neighbour's doorstep to bed.

" This looks queer," said Ned, as he hobbled heavily along. " Not much to be nabbed here. They'd offer you blessings and a farthing."

"Not a house good for a cold tater, that I can see," continued Billy Fortune, sullenly.

" It's the prettiest place we've passed through," said Phil.

Presently a turn in the street (it was a compromise between a street and a high road) brought them into a broad thoroughfare. But the houses were low, and the sagacious eye of Billy Fortune saw at a glance that there was little hope of picking up anything if they whined and moaned at every door in the row.

"It's the beastliest crib I ever come in," growled Ned. " Confound it! ain't there any nobs about—no slap-up gentry, nor nothing of that kind? It's a queer look-out—a regular bog-trotters' nest! I wish we'd gone to Salisbury; we should have done bene there."

" Let's have a try at that old gal," said Billy, pointing to an elderly woman taking the air on her door-step. " She looks nervous and old, and if we say something about giving to the poor being the short cut to heaven, perhaps she'll tip something through funk."

Phil and Ned paused in the middle of the road, while Billy advanced towards a cottage upon which the whitewash appeared fresher than that upon the habitations round about. Over the door was a long plank, announcing to the passing antiquarian the existence of a museum within. As he didn't understand what a museum meant,

---

[1] This name was formerly written Druidshurst.

Billy was in doubt whether it was the name of a public-house or of some charitable institution. If he had looked at the little window, he would have observed several pamphlets exposed for sale, in which the "History and wonders of Stonehenge" were fully related and described by "Charles Lorts, of Drudeshurst."

"Poor carpenter out o' work, please marm," whined Billy Fortune, "and would be very grateful for a trifle."

The person addressed shifted her position several times to try and avoid the beggar; but, as he still remained, she at length said in a shrill voice, "You carpenters are always out of work. There were two last week. Why don't you beg of carpenters that are in work, instead of me? I'm not a carpenter, boy. I'm afraid you're idle; and remember this, boy—it's the root of all evil."

"I know that too well, mum," sighed Billy; "and many's the time my mother's used them very words. But it ain't idleness I'm suffering from, but hard times and hard masters, and the uncommon price of wood. Deal's gone up frightful, mum."

The pals were watching Billy with all their eyes.

"He pitches it into her most uncommon powerful," observed Ned; "but she seems close and stubborn, and perfect fireproof."

It was to the sister of Mr. Charles Lorts that Billy Fortune was appealing. Though apparently not more than forty years of age, she wore spectacles with an exemplary daring which proved that if her eyes were weak her mind was strong. Her nose was what is termed "retrousse;" that term, however, but ill expressed the curious upturning of this singular feature. It curled as if it had become dog's-eared. It seemed to have quarrelled with the mouth, and to be attempting a separation for life, thereby greatly inconveniencing the nostrils, which were tightened to whiteness, and uncomfortably twisted. Her spectacles rode on this nose as securely as an Arab in his high-pommelled saddle, and could as easily have tumbled off a hook as slip from their place. Her eyes had a set expression of surprise, aroused evidently by a chronic admiration of her nasal organ.

Very often did Miss Lorts, in her permanent falsetto, assure Billy that she had nothing to give him. He still remained. A sudden idea crossed the lady's brain. She wouldn't part with a penny, because it was wrong to encourage beggars; but she might, without fear of any transgression, endeavour to improve his mind. She would show him the museum for nothing.

"Come in, young man," she said, leading the way. "I'll see what I can do for you."

"And I was going to give it up as a bad job," thought Bill.

He had only to cross the threshold to enter the museum. The front parlour had been set aside for scientific purposes. Wafered up against the walls, and covering them as completely as if they had been the eccentric pattern of the paper, were plans of Stonehenge, pictures cut from illustrated papers, and coloured charts of scriptural revelations. With an air of disgust Billy looked about him, first at the walls, and then at the woman. An idea crossed his mind that she was mad, and being at heart a coward, he grew frightened and watched anxiously for an opportunity to be off. But she was not mad; she was only a weak-minded, enthusiastic creature, with vanity enough for six women of her size. In the village she was considered a prodigy of learning. The rising generation of Drudeshurst were entrusted to her care, and every form in her infant schoolroom was crowded. As he stood in the museum, Billy could hear the little voices repeating their lessons, the twittering sounds forming a curious accompaniment to the solemn tone in which Miss Lorts—who, when inspired, always became gruff—began her lecture. She advanced to a table, on which a pile of something was covered by an oilcloth. With her eyes fixed on Billy, she said, "I am about, young man, to show you some pre-Adamite formations."

He felt inclined to reply, "Please don't," for fear was upon him. The slightest question on the part of Miss Lorts would have sent him flying for safety into the road.

The oilcloth covered a heap of twisted, gnarled flint-stones. The vagrant felt relieved when he saw them. The poor lady had, in her admiration for Stonehenge, framed a theory that it was built up by no less a person than Adam himself as an atonement for his great sin. She had written a book on the subject, and perfectly proved the matter. But, lest the vulgar should doubt her assertions, she had collected on the plain, in the neighbourhood of the Druids' temple, a vast number of curiously shaped flint-stones, which, from their bearing some rude resemblance to the forms of birds or the limbs of animals, she now exhibited in her museum as "petrifactions of pre-Adamite formations."

"I daresay, young man," she sternly asked Billy, "you wonder what all these mean?"

"Well, marm," replied Billy, nervously, "I should call it about a barrow load of stones."

"What painful ignorance!" exclaimed the "savante;" "they're fossils, and the finest you ever saw."

"They're very good uns," said Billy, though he felt convinced he had seen larger ones on the mounds for mending the roads.

"That," said Miss Lorts, pointing to a misshapen flint, "we take to be the thigh-bone of a child—and that" (pointing to a round stone) "is the head, as I and learned folk judge."

He couldn't help laughing. With a broad grin he answered, "If that's the head and thigh, I know where you may find the other bits of the body. Well, this is a start. If I'd ha' seen 'em in the road, I should have pitched 'em over the hedge."

"The world is still in darkness!" exclaimed Miss Lorts. "Pitch a fossil over a hedge!"

"If these was children," continued Billy; "I'm glad the breed is so werry much improved. I should say, mum, their parents must have been a queer sort."

He saw Miss Lorts was harmless, and was growing saucy.

"Young man," replied the lady, impressively, "you are not prepared for these revelations. You would no doubt deny that this is a fossil bird, and this a human hand." She drew out a drawer, and taking a clean pamphlet from it said, "Read this, young man, and when you thoroughly understand it, and are impressed with its truth, come to me. You may go."

Billy took the book, turned it over, but kept his temper. It was a copy of "Lorts on Stonehenge."

"Can't you give us a bit of bread to wrap in it?"

"There's not a morsel in the house, young man, so don't ask. I've my pupils to send home, so good night."

Billy saw there was nothing to be had. He glanced into the schoolroom beyond the museum, where rows of pinafored children were whispering and giggling; then, as he turned back into the road, he said, "Well, you've sold me most complete, old 'Bob-tail.' I axed you for bread, and you shove a lump of flint into my hand. Here, take back this 'fakement.'" He flung "Lorts on Stonehenge" on the floor. "If I'd known this was your little game, I'd have smashed the cussed head of that there stone child of yourn. If you could add your heart to the heap of flints, I should say the collecshun would be fust rate."

He found his pals at the corner of the road examining the lock-up house—it was not much larger than a London pork-pie, and they did not seem afraid of it. They could tell from Billy's face that he had brought nothing back with him.

"I never see such a woman," said Billy, as they stared inquiringly at him. "Jawed me for half an hour, and then asked me to read a cussed 'fakement.'"

They remained leaning against the lock-up house, discussing what had best be done. They had but little money, and were hungry and tired. They would have liked a bed and supper, if Drudeshurst had owned a padding ken for travellers. But at the White Hart and the Blue Pig beds cost more than threepence a night, and every supper served up came to a shilling, and something for the waiter.

It was unfortunate for them this discussion took so long, for it happened that Miss Lorts, to be revenged on Billy for his impertinence, had despatched one of her scholars to the constable, informing him that three suspicious vagabonds were loitering about the town. Delighted at an opportunity of exerting his authority, the official clapped on his hat, and hurried towards our young rogues.

The moment Billy Fortune saw the constable, he knew, from his angry expression and pompous walk, he was somebody in power. The first suggestion was, that they should "slope," and give the "trap" the slip. But Phil indignantly replied that they had done nothing, and insisted upon standing his ground. They were threatened with the lock-up house if they did not instantly leave the place. It was in vain they pleaded they were tired and hungry, and wanted a night's lodging. The man in power would not listen to them, but told them to move on—a request they eventually complied with, but not before the constable had been well soused with abuse. Indeed, he that night told the company at the Blue Pig that, if he had had anybody to help him, he would have nailed the varmints as sure as eggs was eggs.

"Confound you!" Ned Purchase had said to him, "why, it's me as pays you;" whilst Phil, in his indignation, had demanded to be taken before a magistrate; and Billy had threatened, not only to write to the public journals, but also to complain to the Secretary of State—threats which the official seemed to despise, as if he had been aware that Master Fortune had forgotten all about his "pothooks and hangers."

They moved on slowly by the same road they had come, the cripple complaining that the crutch was wearing his arm off, and that his poor leg ached, whilst Phil growled lustily at Billy, murmuring that he had led them out of their way, and that now they must either sleep with empty stomachs in the ditch, or trudge ten miles further to the nearest town.

In so painful a predicament, Billy's wits became unusually quickened. "I'll tell you what we'll do," he said. "There's no chance of 'nabbing any rust'" (taking any money), "so we must make up our minds to sleep on the daisies. It's as hot as ten blankets. I know a place not far from here where we shall be as jolly as birds in a thatch."

"Where?" asked both Ned and Phil, incredulously.

"Why, at that there Stonehenge, to be sure!" responded Billy, triumphantly. "There's stones there as big as houses, and corners where the wind can't come. It's only a mile or so off!"

"Well," retorted Ned, sarcastically, "having found such a pertickler soft bed, where's the 'scran'?"

"Leave that to me," was Billy's mysterious reply. "If there's a goose or a hen within ten miles of us, I'll wring his neck or be grabbed. Are you fond of birds?"

But Ned was not altogether satisfied with his pal's assurance, and as he turned with his companions down the road to Stonehenge, muttered and growled.

"Growlin' again!" said Billy Fortune. "Come, out with it! What's your lay? But no yelping."

"I wish you'd only one leg, you'd yelp then," was Ned's evasive answer.

The moon winked as she rose above a distant slope, and the wind sang sadly among the trees, or boomed like distant cannon over the vast plain of Salisbury, to which these young urchins were advancing. The shadows from the waving trees played along the pallid moonlit road a very mystic game. The boys, although they would not confess it, didn't half like the look-out before them, for the trees decreased in size, and appeared, in the distance, only at wide intervals.

More—they would take such unpleasant shapes! Now an abrupt scrap of hedge rose like a file of ghostly policemen, and now a willow, its silver underleaf turned to the moon by the wind, bowed to and fro—a white, nodding spectre.

Billy Fortune started, and caught Ned's arm.

"Don't be a fool—you're tugging me over. It's only a tree," replied the latter young gentleman, graciously.

"It's only a tree, of course," jerked out Phil, too, as he regained his breath.

"So it is," said Ned. "And here, my hearties, to show you that I ain't such a funky cove, I leave you."

And Billy Fortune, twirling his stick knowingly, leaned against a gate, from which a path that, to judge by its curves, must have been trodden out by an incessant file of drunken men, led along the jagged outskirts of a wood.

"But," asked Ned, "what game's up? Keep your teeth. Didn't I promise you supper? Now, sharp, and cut on to Stonehenge. Pick up any old wood you see—scrape something like a fire together; I'll be with you in less than no time. But no whistlin'. Keep them bag-pipes o' yourn quiet, just for an interval."

Having given these directions, Billy Fortune stole along the zig-zag path. His silent footsteps would not have scared a hare from his way.

Ned and Phil, having mutually agreed that their pal was "a born genius, only spoiled in the baking," turned from the gate behind which the young desperado had disappeared, and went on their way. The wind swept in gusts past them, and, as they left the shelter of the last hedge behind them, forced them to bow their heads and pull their caps firmly down.

A broad, vast, and gloomy expanse, unrelieved by tree or bush, lay in front, seeming mysterious in extent, as if a fog surrounded them. Here and there were mounds standing up, as Phil said, "like warts." The road dipped into a valley, then gently rose. Along the dark edges of the plain, here and there, lights of solitary cottages shone like glow-worms. The wind appeared to have the dark-green, broken plain to itself, and to shriek over it and moan over it as though it knew its ancient story, and was mourning for the fallen temple of the Druids, and the forgotten dust of ancient Britons buried deep under the tumuli. The moon, too, was provokingly playful. Now she hid her face behind a floating vapour, light and white as fretted silver; now she played hide-and-seek with a cloud of ebony blackness, which she fringed with white, making it look like a dead baby's pall. Then, lavish of her silver, she spread it upon the tops of the tumuli, dropped it magically about the edges of a milestone, turned the flints of the broken roads into so many nuggets; and now she tipped with milky light a dark, confused mass, that stood up, like Titans mourning, upon a rise on Phil's left. Were the sighing and moaning of the wind the great voices of these mourners?

Ned and Phil kept close together.

"I suppose that's Stonehenge, there?" said Phil, softly, to his cripple friend. "There—on the top of the hill. It don't look too comfortable."

"One of Billy's games again. There's an airy bedstead for you, with ghosts for blankets, and lizards, I know, for bedfellows."

Both the boys began to jeer and laugh at the distant ruins. As children in their impudent health and thoughtlessness will mock at helpless age, so these lads scoffed at the Druids' temple. They called it a seedy graveyard; one said he had seen better flagstones; and the other replied that the sooner the granite served to mend the roads the better.

But the huge monument soon avenged itself, and punished its insulters. The wind that had torn up trees and shaken houses had vainly raged around these massive columns and rushed against their broad sides, howling and shrieking as it tried to hurl them to the ground; the tempests of centuries had pelted them with rain, until the granite was scarred and wrinkled with hard wear and tear, and still one half the granite blocks remained firm and upright as ever, their companion pillars lying about them like slain giants. They soon avenged themselves upon the two puny, vagrant boys.

The lads, to make a short cut to the ruins, had left the high road, and were walking across the soft grass of the plain. Their footsteps fell soundless, as upon a cushion. The silence of the night became oppressive. A tinkling, rustling sound filled the ear, a sound that seemed to come from within themselves. They longed to be able to shuffle their feet along the road, and hear the pebbles crunch under their heels. When they spoke to each other, they still kept their eyes fixed upon the ruins before them, and gradually their questions and answers became shorter and less frequent. With each step the monster stones increased in size, rising from the ground as if issuing from it to welcome the young tramps. At last they appeared to hang above their heads, as though they would overwhelm them. Both the boys felt afraid, and thought inwardly how much better it would have been had they crept into some dry ditch to pass the night, instead of sleeping beside these stone monsters, with the black shadows stretching across their bodies.

Well might they feel alarmed. Such wonders as the giant stones on Salisbury Plain should be visited only in the daytime, when the sunshine drives from the mind all ghostly imaginings. Then how different do the monster blocks appear! The picnic parties who resort thither laugh and philosophize by turns as they gaze upon the ruins, and, whilst the hampers are being unpacked, wonder how such big stones could have been carried there. As each bottle is emptied, the useless glass may, without an after-thought, be flung against the massive pillars. Then, "Greaves, from Kent," and a thousand others, may scratch their names on the walls of the ancient temple, and spoil their penknives that they may leave behind an evidence of their callousness; or, "Hooper, of Manchester," and many more, lying at full length upon the grass, cut out their names in the smooth turf, and record their folly in the kindred dirt. But would they, do you think, find courage for such silly profanation in the dead of night? With the huge blocks frowning down upon them through the darkness, they would creep by reverently as through a churchyard, nor dare attempt such violation, lest the spirits of the Druid priests who sacrificed in that very temple should punish the insult.

The two tramps walked into the precincts of the ruins, and stood in the centre, gazing around. The stones, arranged in circles, enclosed a plot of ground in which the tent of a travelling circus might have been erected with ease. At first sight the boys could hardly comprehend the meaning of these stones, and the mystery awed them.

Some of the blocks—gnarled and moss-covered—had fallen from the perpendicular, and sunk into the earth, as a drunken man falls into the snow. About and around these downcast monuments grew a fringe of tall grass and nettles. Others still retained the position in which, more than eighteen hundred years ago, they had been placed by the hands of men, and stood lofty and massive as the entrance to an Egyptian tomb. Each block had the marks and signs of great age upon it. The edges were worn and rounded as thawing ice, and in some places had fallen in like the sunken features of an old man.

The Druids' temple is a wonderful chapter of the accidents of time. On one side the upright rocks still carry, though apparently ready to drop it at any minute, their enormous mass of horizontal granite. One pair of pillars appear to be balancing a rock, as an acrobat balances a pole. It is difficult to imagine how the rock keeps its position. Phil and Ned looked on so nervously at this conjuring of Time, that they determined to give the wonder a very wide berth.

"Why shouldn't the great stone fall that night as well as any other?" was Phil's philosophic suggestion.

"It must tumble down some time or other," added Ned.

Afterwards, at Salisbury, the boys were told that one hundred years ago two of the pillars actually did fall, casting the horizontal rock from their shoulders. The fall, too, made the noise of a park of artillery, and shook the earth like an earthquake. Without knowing it, the boys had seated themselves upon these identical fallen columns, rested their feet upon the enormous burden that, after untold centuries of patience, the columns had cast from them, and then lain themselves deep down in the earth to rest and crumble. There they were, with the grey lichen creeping over them, and wearing holes upon their rugged surface, freckled with the hardy growth which damp extracts from stone. Close to these fallen giants was the leaning stone, a slanting, coffin-shaped block, that seemed ready to fall upon any human being, or any score of human beings, who might be bold enough to venture under its shelter. Resting against a post in front, it looked to the lads like the inclined brick of a gigantic bird-trap, set to catch innocent youths such as themselves. Other huge blocks lay here and there in wild confusion, some massive as Roman baths, others seamed and wrinkled; others again had deep hollows into which a dog might have crept; others lay buried in the earth, year after year sinking lower and lower into their grave.

The boys—these thoughtless, daring young tramps—felt uneasy in this grand circus, every brick of which was "a ruin in itself." The moon shone upon their pale, serious faces as they gazed from the sanctum where sacrifice was once offered, and the deep voices of the Druids were heard upon the awful confusion. The moon had been provoking to Phil and Ned on the road, and the ghastly way in which she now threw her white light, like linen sheets, upon the great stones, or let it play wickedly through chinks, and in the depth of the awful shadows, frightened them more than they cared to confess.

Phil was the first to cast away his fear, and he did it by opening a game of leapfrog (in which poor Ned could not join him) over the smaller stones, while his companion faintly laughed at him. And then the young fellows determined to light their fire in a snug corner close to the leaning stone, or the "coffin-lid," as Ned called it. They were afraid Billy would be back before they had gathered even a few sticks. So they began to grope about the grass—taking care not to stray far from each other. They soon discovered they were not the only tramps who had taken shelter under the stones of the old Druids' place of worship, for here and there the grass was burnt by the camp fires into a round black patch. Ned was the first to call out that he had found something. "Here's a lot of paper! It's greasy, and smells of 'am. And here's corks and an empty bottle! Shall I bring 'em?" "Grab all you can find," was Phil's prudent suggestion. Presently he added, "They've been eating here to-day. Here's a heap of straw, and an old basket."

By-and-by Ned gave a low whistle, and on Phil creeping up to him, pointed to the road, and asked, "What's that?" Phil looked out beyond the stones. "Somebody with a light, coming along at a rattling pace."

"It can't be after Billy?" suggested Ned; "but he's such a des- perate cove!" As he said this, he looked searchingly towards the horizon, where the wood lay like a bushy black head upon the rotund bosom of the earth. A light was travelling rapidly along the road towards them, and the distant burr of wheels reached the lads' ears. After a few minutes of perfect silence and anxious watching, Ned exclaimed, "It's only a confounded gig!" and turned his attention once more to gathering fuel for the fire.

They were both so nervous and timid, that the least noise alarmed them. A dog barked in the distance, and Ned called out, " Do you hear that howling, Phil ? "

Phil had heard it, and was listening attentively. " It ain't Billy's voice ? " he suggested.

After a moment, the lame boy dispelled all fears for Fortune's safety by saying, " All right ! it's only a sheep dog. I hear the sheep-bell. But it did give a chap a twist, I can tell you ! " And then, remarking that it was " as cold as a lock-up," he proposed they should instantly prepare their fire.

The boys returned to the leaning stone, and, crouching into a corner sheltered by the granite blocks, lighted a fire. Soon the dry sticks were fairly crackling, and the smoke rose like a white scarf in the moonlight. The light and heat of the fire were both cheering, for the wind began to moan very sadly, and the white slips of moon-light between the great columns of the temple shifted and looked unearthly. The stones themselves took queer shapes as the flame of the burning wood illumined their edges. One seemed to resemble a large toad, and another appeared like a kneeling figure.

The quiet of their fireside was destined to be disturbed. No doubt the cripple was more nervous than Phil, for he was continually hear-ing suspicious noises. This time he declared "there was a rum row, like muffled drums a long way off. I don't like the look o' this here," he added; " I wish Billy was come, we'd be off."

This was apparently Phil's wish also, for he crawled from under the leaning stone, and climbed upon a block that commanded a view of the plain. He stretched out his neck and stared in every direction till his eyes ached. Then, urged on by Ned, he summoned up courage to break the dead silence of the night, and, putting his hands to his mouth, sent forth a shout that echoed among the ruins, and was carried by the wind across the gloomy waste. The sheep dogs round about were the only living things that answered to the cry.

CHAPTER VI.

BILLY FORTUNE PROVES THAT HE CANNOT BE TRUSTED ALONE.

TIRED out with having to wait for Billy's return, Phil and Ned Purchase took to the only consolation left them, that of abusing the cause of their trouble. They sat for a time one on each side the fire, as quiet as hobs. They saw the embers turn into white ashes, and neither had energy enough to throw on another piece of stick. Occasionally Phil would push the black wood closer together with his foot, but even that exertion disturbed the resigned feeling of

despair which was turning him as sour as a bill discounter's claret.
It shook up the vials of his wrath to move.

"I wish I'd got hold of Billy," he muttered at last. "Give me a
firm grip of his hair, and I would stain him plum coloured."

He looked remarkably savage, and frowned like the lion on a door-
knocker, but his body remained drawn up and motionless as that of
an Indian at a war council.

"His turn will come next," growled Ned. "Won't I keep him
waiting, that's all; the middle of next week shall be nothen to it."

"I wish he was hung, curse him!"

"Or roasted alive," added the cripple, who was thinking of the
dying fire.

The wind grew more violent as the morning approached. When
the east became streaked with the returning light, as if the day had
opened its Venetian blinds to let the bright dawn peep through, the
wind swept over the plain howling like a dog let loose to chase away
the ugly night. The beggars crouching beneath the big stones of the
Druids' temple cursed the wind as it circled around them and made
their teeth chatter. It got up the sleeves of their coats, swelling
them out, round and tight as drain-pipes; it tugged at their caps,
and blew their hair away as if to get at their ears and make them
ache. Sometimes it caused the dead black embers of their fire to
grow suddenly crimson. It blew away the ashes and the dust,
tidying up the hearth better than any spinster with a broom.
Strange sounds came with these sudden gusts. They heard the
clock of Drudeshurst strike, and both lads pricked up their ears to
learn the hour, but at the third stroke the breeze had passed and
taken the sound with it. The crushing, grating noise of heavy
wheels—perhaps miles off—would seem as close as if a waggon were
lumbering along the road across the plain, or the barking of dogs
would flit by them, the yelping becoming more and more distinct and
then gradually dying off as though the animals themselves were
racing through the air.

They listened with assumed courage to the screaming and moaning
of the hurricane rushing through the pine-trees on the distant hill.

"It's just like some one being murdered," said Phil.

"By jingo! I think it is," replied Ned, seizing his crutch.

He was told not to be a fool, but sit still. But for this, he would
have limped away.

Then came the same mysterious sound of muffled drums which
had before disturbed them—a rolling, deadened noise, that appeared
to come from every side. Was it thunder under ground, or an earthquake that would topple over the huge stones like so many skittles?
They held their breath and listened. It seemed as if daylight would
never come.

The cripple began to complain that the cold had taken hold of the
stump of his leg and made it ache as though it had been crushed.
He began to move it, rocking to and fro as if he had a child in his

U

arms. He would soon have fallen asleep with the rocking motion ;
his moans were gradually dying away, but, just as he was dozing off,
his arm was violently seized, and, starting from his nap, he saw Phil
white as moonlight, and looking intently into the black distance.

"Ned! Ned!" gasped the boy, "there's that cussed row again, and
awful. Get up—it's coming here."

Ned heard it too. The same muffled sound—the same dead noise.
It seemed to roll along, and the earth on which they were seated
appeared to jolt. The cripple tried to rise, but fell sprawling on the
ground, whilst Phil, seizing the crutch, stood valiantly on the
defence. They had given themselves up for lost, when, as if by
magic, the entire space of the temple became filled with countless
sheep, and as the animals stood still to stare at the boys, the noise
ceased. The stamping of their feet as they raced over the turf had
played this devil's tattoo.

There were hundreds of the yellow-woolled beasts. They drew
themselves up in a circle around the boys, and, with raised heads
stared their hardest. Presently a dog made its appearance, and
walked round the strangers with a crouching, wolfish step, growling
the while. He showed his teeth so spitefully, Ned was not sorry
when the shepherd stalked up to their side.

The man began to snigger as he approached the tramps, saying,
"Well, a bit of fire ain't a bad thing of cold nights ; " and, opening
his palms, held them to the smouldering embers. He was a familiar
sort of fellow, well accustomed to seeing encampments under the big
stones. When the lads related how they had been frightened, he
laughed, and told them "they was not the first by many a score,"
adding, "that the ground of the plain was, he believed, underminded,
and that gave it its sounds."

"Who underminded it ? " asked Ned.

"Ah, that was before we was thought of," answered the man, who
had seated himself, and was carefully arranging on the smouldering
embers the few sticks that remained. The dog approached and
crouched near its master, whilst the sheep commenced grazing and
nibbling the grass around.

Tired of their own society, the boys were not sorry to have a
companion.

"What did they undermind it for ? " asked Ned, thirsting for
knowledge.

"You'd better ax him as stuck up these here stones," the man
replied, pointing to the granite pillars.

No doubt it was in order that he'd find out the gentleman that
Ned inquired his name.

"Why, the devil, to be sure," was the answer. "Did you never
hear of how he built this here Stonehenge ? "

Unlike many educated persons, the lads were not ashamed to confess their ignorance, Ned observing that he thought "they growd
there promiscuous-like."

The shepherd had been by himself all the night, and was not sorry to have the chance of talking.

" What I'm going to tell you is as true as if it took place yesterday—leastways everybody in these parts believes so, and there's some thousands of us, so we can't all be wrong. A many years ago—some says such a long time ago, that hang me if I thinks there ever could have been such a time—there was a conjuring chap as was called Merlin by name, and says he to the devil (he knowed him very intimate), ' Go over to Ireland and bring me some stones as you'll find there '—these here very ones. So off goes the devil—for he was mortal afraid of this here conjuring chap—and, when he gets to Ireland, he dresses hisself up first-rate, and goes to the old woman as owned these stones—the same as you sees—and says he, ' You shall have as much money for these here stones,' says he, ' as you can count out,' says he, ' whilst I'm removing of them.' She was agreeable, and thinks she to herself, ' What a fool the devil must be, for,' says she, ' they ain't exactly the kind of things to be slipped into a coat-tail pocket,' says she. He claps down a bag of money, but just as she's going to count, he cries out, ' Hold hard ! old woman, the stones is gone ! ' She thought he was gammoning her, but she soon found out her mistake. They was gone, and she only got fourpence for them, though they're worth many a honest sovereign to the people about here, for they draws a world of people to Drudeshurst."

" That's a bouncer ! " exclaimed Phil, laughing.

The shepherd was hurt at the expression. He would have refused to continue the legend if Ned, on being appealed to, had not avowed the most implicit belief.

" When the devil brings these here very stones to this conjuring chap, says he, ' Where shall I put 'em ? ' so they was stuck up · here, as it's airy and open, and here they're likely to stick, at any rate for our time, thank God ! "

" Do you mean to say you believe that crammer ? " asked Phil.

" Believe it ? " replied the shepherd. " I tell you there's sulphur in every ounce of them. Why, go to Bulford, and you'll see one of these here blocks as the devil dropped in the river there, owing· to the lash round the bundle getting loose."

Phil indignantly cried out, " Go on with you—you won't goose me ! " A quarrel ensued, in which the shepherd called the young tramps " a couple of blackguard thieves," and, in return, was termed " a mutton-headed fool." Eventually the man whistled his dog after him, and walked off from such unbelieving company.

They laughed over the story of Stonehenge, and the stupid shepherd who had related it, little thinking it was not the simple rustic, but Jeffery of Monmouth (A.D. 1130), who was to blame for the strange history. Just as the excitement of the quarrel was wearing off, they heard a low, tremulous whistle, which they instantly recognized as the signal peculiar to, and much used by, William Fortune, Esq.

That youth, jolly and lively as if he had found a five pound note, advanced towards his friends as unconcernedly as if he had not been absent more than half an hour. "Here comes the supper-tray," he cried, "and the chap as supplied it."

They neither of them greeted him, but looked as sulky as if they sat in the stocks. The sensitive Billy was pained by so cold a reception. "Making faces!" he cried. "Hullo! why, what's all this here about? Whose cow has died, eh?"

"I'll soon tell yer what this here's about," retorted Ned. "What do you keep chaps waiting for like this here? Do you think we let ourselves out by the hour? It don't wash, I can tell yer."

"Who said it washed?" answered Billy. "Do you think I've been enjoying myself so werry comfortable, eh? You're good 'uns! Ain't we all in the same swim? Ain't I been near grabbed as touch and go?" He pulled up his trouser, and exhibited a wound in the leg. "What do yer think of this kind of amusement? Very nice, eh? Well, I prefers going in when half-price is begun—that's all!"

Naturally enough, they began to pity their wounded companion. A dozen questions were asked before he had time to answer one, as to how he had met with the misfortune.

"Wait till we're eating," was the victim's only reply. Whilst he was searching in his pockets, he asked them, "Now, what would you like pertic'lar luptious—fowls?"

"If they'd been dead a month I'd eat 'em," cried Phil.

"Or a rattling young chicken?" suggested Billy.

"Very sweet eating, and not to be by no means sneezed at," was Ned's rapid response.

"Well, then, here's some of the youngest chickens as is manufactured under the present process," continued Billy, producing from his tattered coat some dozen eggs—"chickens as will never live to see daylight in this here hard-hearted world of ourn." Without noticing their disappointed looks, he added, "Shove 'em in the fire and fry 'em. They're sweet as innocence, and the feathers won't choke yer."

To complete the repast, he had brought some apples and a few potatoes, with the wet earth still about them. The young fellows were soon eating as if he who swallowed fastest was to have the largest share. They began with the apples, then set to at the half-cooked eggs, and wound up with baked potatoes.

Billy's adventures were the salt which gave the meal its relish. He told them how a dog as big as a cow, with teeth like clothes-pegs, caught him in the hen-house, and kept him there. He related his fears on hearing the farm-house windows thrown open, and voices call out, "Who's there?" He tried to stuff a fowl into the dog's mouth and make his escape, but the brute was too knowing to allow itself to be gagged. Seven hens, with twisted necks, were ready for being carried off. The eggs were in his cap when the dog made his appearance. He took down the pole on which the birds were roosting to defend himself, but "the cussed birds made such a row" at being toppled from their perch, that they might be heard miles off. At last he heard men coming towards the hen-house. He heard them ask one another if the gun was loaded, and, as he preferred risking the dog's teeth to being riddled with shot, he determined to rush off. "I sent the pole slap into the dog's gullet, and cut; but the beggar was after me as soon as he'd emptied his mouth, and just filled it again with a bit of my leg. Now do you understand what all this here was about—eh?"

The apologies that ensued were most handsome, and Mr. Fortune listened to them with great meekness and gratification. He even borrowed Phil's neckerchief with which to bind up his wound, having first applied a poultice of bruised grass and yolk of egg to draw out the poison of the bite. Not that Mr. William was in any way versed in the use of medicines, but he was impressed with the belief that anything wet and unctuous was an excellent remedy for all kinds of sores.

The morning was coming. The east was pale, and the light rising like a mist from the horizon. It was only in the west that the stars were still visible. The clouds were floating along rapidly as weeds in a mill-stream, and the air tweaked the boys' noses as only the air of early day can. All three bent over the fire, and felt so cruelly cold they would have set fire to a cottage had they dared, for the sake of the heat it would give.

A dog barked—a loud, deep yell that came from jaws opening wide as garden shears—and Bill Fortune's head turned round suddenly, as if his name had been called. He knew the sound, and had felt the jaws. He leaped to his feet, and listened with his head towards the barking, his eyes straining the while with fear. There was no mistake. He recognized the clarion of the enemy who was rushing upon them.

"If you don't want to be lagged," he said, in a tone which was convincingly earnest, "we must look slippy. Come on, before that infernal dog sees us. They're down on us. Push forwards, Ned, and hop as if you was a frog in pumps. Our names must be Walker, and no catchee no havee the word."

A farmer close by had a field of promising corn, and through it the three boys bolted, doing ten pounds' worth of mischief in their course. They cared not if the farmer were ruined provided they got clear off. A field of beans lay before them, and into it they plunged like rabbits into underwood, levelling the thick, pulpy stalks as they waded along. The barking of the dog still followed behind, and once Billy thought he could distinguish the sound of horses' hoofs. On they rushed, the cripple working his crutch with desperate energy, and almost heading his companions by the immense leaps he took. They gained a plantation of firs, and darted into it by Billy's advice, to "take the shine out of the chaps on horseback," as he said.

It was slow work winding their way among the trunks, and the yelping seemed to be gaining upon the fugitives. Neither could Ned use his crutch so advantageously as on the road. They determined to remain concealed in this wood, and it was further agreed that Billy should venture on a reconnoitring expedition, to see if they were really being hunted. " For," said that bold young vagrant, " perhaps we're only funking ourselves useless, and it mayn't be the farm chaps at all. If anything happens, we meet at Salisbury." But Billy was a deep rogue. It was not for his friends' safety, but for his own, that he undertook this errand. He determined to be off. " I am the only chap they could prove against," he thought. " They could sessions me, but Ned and Phil are safe enough. Whilst they are being collared I shall slope away easy." From curiosity, he went to the edge of the wood and passed down the road. He saw a mob of men with pitchforks, led on by one mounted on horseback, while in front ran the terrible mastiff. Standing upon the highest of the hillocks, or barrows on the plain, was the figure of a shepherd directing the pursuers which way to take. It was the man who had related the legend of the Druids' temple.

Master Billy got safely off, and the other two were seized. The man on horseback was very wrath, and swore he would give them six months at the tread-wheel. He would drag them off then and there to the nearest magistrate, and have them committed.

That morning Sir William Hatcher was in deep consultation with his banker—Mr. Nathaniel Crosier—relative to certain moneys which he wished to raise on mortgage for immediate use. As the security was excellent, the business did not take long. They were chatting on other matters, when the baronet was called upon, as a magistrate, to commit our two young gentlemen to the county prison for robbery. As Sir William was much pleased with the banker's prompt manner of advancing money, he asked Crosier if he would like to hear the case. " Sometimes these examinations are very amusing," said Sir William.

The banker smiled in answer.

But the pleasant expression soon left Mr. Crosier's lips, and the case ceased to promise amusement when he caught sight of one of the culprits. He stumbled backwards as if some person had struck him. " Good Heavens!" he said to himself, "that boy must not go to prison whatever he may have done."

Despite the assurances of Mr. Simcox, sen., of the Temple, the banker felt that Philip Merton was his daughter's child. He heard the boy, when his name was asked, give it boldly, and, though he was a man of great nerve, he could not prevent his lip from twitching. He gained heart a little when he found that robbing a henroost was the only charge brought forward. " Twenty pounds will settle the matter," he thought. The determined denials of guilt made by Phil gave him great ease. " I shall not have to give the money after all," he said to himself.

The son of Katherine Merton saw the solemn, hard-featured banker, and in an instant recognized the father of the laughing school-girl whom he had known in his donkey-driving days. He fancied the old gentleman did not remember his face. "I shouldn't like her to know of this," thought Phil.

The farmer couldn't swear to the boys, but they swore lustily to their own innocence, so—aided by a few remarks from Nathaniel Crosier, Esq.—the case was dismissed. The banker drew a breath that made his neatly-plaited shirt-frill expand like an accordion.

"Boys!" exclaimed the magistrate, pompously, "let this be a warning to you. Return to your friends and be honest. Remember, many now rolling in wealth have begun life as poor as you. Have you any friends?" The baronet looked at Phil, and the banker closed his eyes with fear.

"Sir," answered the grandson, "I don't know a single person in the world who cares that for me," and he snapped his fingers.

The banker felt the lad spoke truthfully.

They were discharged, and set off walking as fast as if they feared the magistrate might alter his decision and send for them again. They asked their way to Salisbury, where they were to meet Billy. "How he would laugh over the adventure," they said, and "thank his stars he was not 'lagged.'"

They had gone some three miles, when they heard a gig, driven at a furious rate, following them. They stood on one side to let the vehicle pass. The horse, covered with sweat, seemed to be running away, but to their surprise its speed was checked as it neared them, and the gig stopped within a few yards of where they stood. It was the solemn, hard-featured banker who had been driving in this reckless manner. He descended, and beckoned Phil to him.

"You have had a narrow escape, young gentleman," he began, "and I'm glad you were able to acquit yourself. You say you have no friends. I feel interested in you, and should like to save you from ruin. Supposing I felt inclined to assist you—I say supposing —could you, do you think, lead an honourable life for the future?"

The protestations that followed sounded as if the boy spoke sincerely: "If he only had work," &c., &c.

"If, as you say, work is so scarce, why not go to other countries where it is plentiful? Would you emigrate, now, if the passage were paid for you?"

The anxiety with which Mr. Crosier waited for the reply was painfully evident. He flushed when Phil vowed he was ready to start on the morrow.

He gave the boy a hastily-scribbled note—on a leaf from his pocket-book—addressed to Simcox of the Temple, and—which pleased Phil more—a sovereign to take him up to town. Then he got into his gig again and drove away, but at a very gentle pace this time.

The story was soon told to Ned. "Shall you emigrate ? " asked the cripple.

" Not I," replied Phil.

They read the letter to Simcox of the Temple. Written in pencil were the words, " This is the boy."

" He knows you! " exclaimed Ned.

" It's rum, ain't it ? " answered Phil.

The next morning Mr. Simcox received a letter, announcing Phil's speedy visit to the Temple, and giving full directions about shipping him off to Australia. In Mr. Simcox's next bill of costs was this serious item : " Having received instructions from you relating to the boy Merton, waiting at home three days, but he never came, £9 9s."

CHAPTER VII.

IN WHICH WE BLUSH FOR THE CAPTAIN.

WHEN a man of thirty—Captain Crosier was thirty-one—falls in love, he is as thoroughly lost as if he had fallen over Shakespeare's cliff. The heart of a man of thirty is tough and solid. It has changed from clay to brick, hard-baked by experience. It chips, and the marks remain.

What a boy of eighteen calls a heart is a soft yielding mass, to be dented and impressed by the merest squeeze of the hand, or slightest pressure of the foot. Youthfulness wraps it up, and !keeps it ever plastic, as the wet cloths about a sculptor's model. A little water—a few tears—just to soften the clay, and the last image may be obliterated, and the clay ready for a new face.

A boy's love is as the flame of a spirit lamp—lighted in a moment, blown out in a moment; giving little light, and burnt out quickly. A man's love is a house on fire, difficult to kindle—but, when it does rage, not all the fire-engines of philosophy, nor all the mains and plugs of resolution, can conquer the blaze. It will roar and crackle until the house gives way, and dust is returned to dust, and ashes to ashes.

That Captain Crosier was in love was as certain as that London is in Middlesex, and that his love was dishonourable and mean is as positive as that the aforesaid London was not built in a day. He was almost ashamed that Bertha should have obtained such power over him. Not an hour passed without his asking himself, some twenty times, whether he really loved the girl. He endeavoured to persuade himself that his affection was a mere caprice, a stupid whim, which, if he chose, he could get rid of as easily as he jerked off a slipper. If he found himself growing too sentimental, he summoned to his aid his stronger and coarser nature, and, to conquer his weakness, would abuse the girl, calling her a housemaid and a drudge at ten pounds a year. He found great temporary relief in assuming a disgust towards himself for not "flying at higher game." He liked to persuade himself he was making a great sacrifice in loving Bertha. He could mention thirty young ladies who would be only too glad to change places with this hesitating housemaid. Some of these young ladies could sing, play the piano, speak French, and that sort of thing. All Bertha could do was to look pretty, and mend linen. Besides, she wasn't grateful.

How do we know that Captain Crosier was in love? Did he, like Sir Proteus, go ungartered? No! he wore socks, and required no garters. Did he wreathe his arms like a malcontent? No! they usually hung down straight and limp as bell-ropes, for he was an idle man, and of little energy. Did he relish a love song? If an organ played "Still so gently" beneath his windows, he swore at it. Did he sigh frequently? Only after long draughts from the tankard of bitter ale. He was beyond all poetic tests, for he was of a gross nature, and, unless moved by drink, but little addicted to sentiment. In describing his sufferings—for he did suffer—it would be absurd to waste any flowers of speech. Most decidedly this long-legged officer could not be likened to a captive bird struggling for liberty, and beating its pretty bosom against its cruel cage, as Bertha might fantastically be styled. We would not even typify the moustachoed swain as a wretched dog whining to be free of its chain, and vainly trying to force its head through its relentless collar—another allusion to the cruel maid. We much prefer, in matter of fact parlance, to state that, since his mind had been spurred into briskness by Bertha's piercing eyes, and whipped into gentle exercise by her long lashes, ever since he had had something to think about besides prize-fights, horse races, and rat-killing, his body had become more and more listless and torpid, as if his organization did not contain energy enough to keep both muscle and brain working. He lay from morning till night upon the sofa, motionless as a bundle. His cigar went out twenty times before he had finished smoking it. He looked more as if he were thinking of suicide than love, as though he were reflecting on razors and prussic acid instead of on Bertha and a cottage near a wood.

Sometimes his reflections became so painful that he was forced to relieve himself with a whistling accompaniment. Whenever he despaired of success, he whistled. Whenever it struck him the girl might in time become a nuisance, and he wish to get rid of her, he whistled. If he pondered over the guilt and wickedness of such an abandonment, and reflected on the harsh view the world would take of his dishonourable conduct, he whistled. The sadder the thought, the lower the whistle. Sometimes it was not louder than the wind rushing through a keyhole.

This seductive young officer had all the inclination to become a villain, but he lacked the courage, and perhaps the ability. He was very much afraid of the world. To make a good rogue, a man should be nine-tenths a genius. He must be a skilful diplomatist, know how to plot, and dare to execute, not caring the value of a bad egg what his neighbours may say. Could Crosier read thoughts in the glance of an eye? He could scarcely read them when in good bold print. Had he strength of mind? Weak as bonnet-wire. Could he adhere steadfastly to one purpose? He was blown away as easily as flue from polished marble. As for the world's opinion, the criticism of a street boy distressed him. He discontinued wearing a white hat in consequence of a rude observation delivered by a vulgar lad of twelve.

This seductive young officer was a weak, timid man, who if he did an evil action one moment, repented of it the next. Although he had animal courage enough to stand all the warlike tests of an active military life, he was not bold enough to resist the temptations which beset the idle life of a soldier in time of peace. His great ambition was to render himself worthy by different excesses of the friendship of such dashing blades as Tom Oxendon or Charley Sutton. Had he stopped at home instead of entering the army, Crosier would most probably have taken to gentler pleasures, and felt delight in the pleasant pastimes of Sunday School teaching, and keeping tame rabbits. He would have turned religious, not from any inward conviction, but to gain the esteem of the old ladies in the neighbourhood.

He had a half suspicion that his noble brother officers looked down upon him for being the son of a banker. It was excessively mortifying to his pride to hear a banker called a tradesman. To counteract these annoying prejudices, he did all he could to convince his gallant friends that he was a reckless, clever dog, ever ready for any roguery, however desperate and dangerous it might be. To earn their good opinion, he drank two glasses for their one; and, although his income was infinitely less, he spent as much money as they did. It was to gain their esteem more than to satisfy his own desires that he first laid siege to Bertha. If Lord Oakes or Viscount Ascot had, when he entered on this amatory campaign, spoken one disparaging word, Bertha would have been left in peace. To oblige a nobleman, Crosier would make any sacrifice. He always considered that England's hope was its aristocracy.

There are some men who only admire a woman because others are captivated by her. On the day when Bertha was seen stitching at her window, the captain was rather astonished that his friends should have thought her so beautiful. He had seen her many times before, and looked upon her as a pretty, badly-dressed thing; but it was not until his fashionable companions dilated upon her beauties that he felt any violent affection for her. Their praises had served to trim the wick and turn up the cotton of his flame. His love began with envy. Because she lived in a house facing his apartments, he considered her as his property, and it delighted him to think that anything he possessed should be envied by his set.

There was a time, as we have said, when one drop of cold water applied by the noble lord or viscount, would have completely extinguished the little love-spark that ran about the tinder of Crosier's bosom. But now that time was gone by. It was too late. His heart, like a hayrick stacked when damp, was heated and smouldering; and if the entire "Blue Book" had cast their buckets full of freezing reproofs at the ardent swain, it would not have cooled his love.

He thought of Bertha at all times and all places; whilst shaving or pulling on his boots; when in cabs or taverns. Even whilst his hair was being cut, the soothing sensation of having his locks played with called up especially tender thoughts. He entered jewellers' shops to ask the price of brooches, bracelets, and earrings, thinking only of Bertha. If his love was not equal to the sacrifice of the ten or twenty guineas asked, it was only because his success was as yet doubtful, and the speculation too heavy. Because he saw some resemblance to Bertha's eyes in a thirty-shilling print, he bought it, and ordered a costly frame. It was a foreign production, with the title in three languages, the English one being "The Return of the Dances." It represented a well-proportioned young lady, risking a severe cold by reposing herself, en deshabille, after the fatigues of an evening party. Do not imagine that it was on account of the value of this print, or because it was an elegant piece of furniture, that the captain had it so expensively framed, for he treated with equal honour a common shilling lithograph, entitled, "A Glass of Gin, young man?" and that solely because the mouth and chin of the barmaid represented were of a similar shape to those in the possession of his beloved Bertha. When, in answer to his question, the stationer who sold this shilling lithograph told him it had been much admired, and uncommonly successful, he felt a thrill of delight play about the third button of his waistcoat that the entire British public should have the same taste as himself, and patronize a face bearing such a resemblance to his adored one.

Occasionally of an afternoon, when he felt very lonely, and yet not inclined to sleep, Crosier would take up a book and stumble through a page or two. He would mark in pencil any sentimental passage that struck him as being particularly tender. Formerly, he used to skip what he called "twaddle." Now, he felt great relief in reading the amiable sufferings so like what he experienced. He entered with a sympathizing spirit into the descriptions of the lover's trials, and would even utter a pitying "poor devil!" if the agony was very great. Whilst reading in this way he would long for Bertha to be by his side, that her sighs might mingle with his own over the harrowing portions, or her prima donna laugh be joined to his basso profundo chuckle at the comic passages. "When she is melancholy," he would mutter, "she does look so thundering handsome, though she's just as rattling when she laughs." He often said she had a prettier smile than any woman he ever knew, and his acquaintance was very extensive. It did him good to catch sight of those fault-less white teeth, with a little dot of light sparkling on the bright enamel. At such times he felt a weight in his chest from excess of admiration, similar to that caused by a slight indigestion, but more gratifying.

The most peculiar effect produced upon the captain by his loving condition was that it was gradually purifying his mind, and cleansing it from its thick outer crust of grossness. The midnight haunts began to disgust him, late hours made him feel sleepy, and even drink lost many of its charms for him—for at a second glass he would feel slightly intoxicated. He no longer cared to stare at women, his ogle lost all its winning piquancy, and he could no longer smile as he was wont to smile. If an elegantly-dressed lady passed, he might look at her dress, but he cared nothing for her face. Where could he see any one lovelier than Bertha? After he had examined her toilet, he invariably thought what an assistance silks and ribands were to the female form, and how overpoweringly resplendent his Bertha would be if she had such advantages to assist her. Once—it was in Curzon Street—he stood still for ten minutes, gazing after a well-arranged shawl, and, all the time he was admiring the neatly adjusted folds on the shoulder, and the admirable manner in which the Cashmere was pulled in at the waist to make it fit smoothly on the back, and give it a bell-like sweep as it rose over the skirts, he was saying to himself, "That's art, not nature; that woman has been, I know, hours arranging her shawl. But with Bertha it would have been the work of a minute. If she were to fling a shawl on her, it would look fifty times better. She has the most exquisitely-proportioned figure, the roundest, best modelled, prettiest formed," &c., &c., &c., for, were we to give at full length all the captain's praises, we should require at least one entire page.

It would have been a great relief to this loving man if he had been blessed with an intimate friend to whom he could have confided the emotions which filled his mind. No doubt this intimate friend would have been bored to death, and have many times wished that either the lover or the loved one would depart this world. You can under-stand that after having publicly announced he was tired of the girl, and even offering to sell his share and interest in her for a pound of cigars, he could not with decency pour his love-wailings into the ears of Tom Oxendon, or any of that set. It was a relief to him when alone in his room to address even the chairs or tables, and declare to these chattels how great was his affection for the incomparable Bertha. Frequently whilst dressing of a morning he would rehearse to himself all the speeches he would make to the little girl the next time he saw her, and, carried away by his fancy, would utter them aloud, giving the words with great feeling and action, flourishing his razor about whilst his chin was covered with a smooth coating of suds, most unromantic to behold. If any one, during these monologues, happened to knock at the door, the captain's reason returned in an instant, and, half-ashamed of such childish conduct, he would endeavour to turn the vehement declaration of love into a badly-hummed opera air, in the hopes of impressing the intruder with the belief that he was not half crazed with love, but only very fond of music. Then, again, how many witty things did Bertha utter during his interviews with her, all of which—spoken, dear girl, as if she were quite unconscious of their merit—were lost to the world, because he knew nobody to whom he dare repeat them. There was that observation of hers on tea, made by her the last time she presided at the tray. How clever it was!—how true! What a knowledge of human nature it evinced! He had asked her, in a pleasant joking manner, why ladies whilst drinking tea talked so wickedly of one another? She had answered, laughing most divinely, "Because ladies seldom drank tea till dusk, and that was scandal (candle) time." He swore she meant it. He called it true wit. He sent it to a comic paper of the day arranged as a conundrum. But he knew no one to whom he could rush off in a cab and relate the wonderful mot. He felt as if he were being cheated out of the praises to which he was entitled for giving his affection to a lady of such wit and perception. Our opinion is that Bertha did not mean to be funny, and did not even attempt it. It was the captain who made the pun, not she, poor innocent girl!

Despite an excellent education, the captain found great difficulty in writing even a letter. He disguised a great quantity of bad spelling under a scrawling style of penmanship, so that a dash in the middle of a word would pass for one or more m's or n's, as the necessities of the English language might require. He, however—so potent is love—purchased an elegant memorandum-book, in which he penned down the excellent things wherewith Bertha at different times favoured him. His desk contained this precious volume. Every maxim and sentence in it he declared to be excellent, saying, "If they arn't witty—which I think they are—they are sure to be d—d sensible, and that's something." The first entry was to this effect: "How wretched it must be to be without a friend! It is the heart's exile." To the end of this apothegm the adoring Crosier had added the words: "True, by Jove! and poetical, too.—M. C." Another line ran as follows: "Soldiers and sailors are never friendly, because fire and water cannot agree." This time the captain's remark was more vigorous. He wrote: "Thundering hard; but by blazes she's right!—M. C." The forcible language used by the military annotator may be accounted for by stating that the gallant gentleman usually entered his souvenirs of the evening's conversation on his return home, an event for which there was no fixed hour. The later the return, the greater strength he threw into his commentary.

CHAPTER VIII.

THE CAPTAIN'S PLOT.

OF his own love for Bertha the captain felt perfectly assured, but he was not quite so positive about the return she made to his tenderness. He would have given a good deal—say five pounds—to have been acquainted with the real state of her feelings. He felt his affection hampered by not knowing whether it was reciprocated, for he did not like to pour out the entire flood of his passion until he was certain the wells and cisterns of her heart were prepared to receive the sudden flood. He felt it would be a degrading waste of tenderness, and too humiliating an experiment, should she, after the display, still hold her head up, keeping it high and dry above the loving deluge. Could he have been sure of swamping her, he would have given flow to his words.

Many persons will say, " Why, if the captain was so desperately in love with Bertha, did he not propose to marry her ? " We will tell them. This thought had once or twice entered his brain, as a last expedient in case every other failed, but the gallant gentleman had rapidly chased away the idea, hunting it out with the same angry hurry as he would have pursued a strange cat from his bedroom. You see Mrs. Hazlewood had been a workhouse nurse, and Bertha herself only a superior kind of servant. Gentlemen born of respectable parents do not like workhouse people. They pity them, perhaps, but seldom regard them in a matrimonial light. It is a prejudice, and a strong one. The captain saw no objection to passing many years of his life in Bertha's society; he would allow her to carry his name, and have felt much offended if his friends had treated her with disrespect; but he could not for one moment think of making her his wife. That would disgrace him; the other position disgraced only her. He could put up with the latter indignity much more cheerfully than the former. Besides, he was never able to overcome the obstacle he saw in the person of Bertha's mother. "Fancy calling her mother-in-law," he said, making a wry face, and then laughing at the absurdity. "I could sooner swallow a quart of her own confounded workhouse gruel." In his more pathetic moments—for instance, after he had spent the evening with his beloved, and had returned home perfectly enchanted—Crosier would combat any idea of making Bertha his wife by the ordinary argument, "that he was not a marrying man." He did not see the stupidity of such reasoning. He generously pleaded he should only make her miserable, leaving it to be implied that the fact of not having the service read over their union would ensure her happiness. He was not a very bright genius, as we have before hinted. Bertha had no friends beyond her mother and the boy she termed her foster-brother. There was nobody to demand explanations, and with clenched fists and scowling brows talk of vengeance· He was very glad the Hazlewood family was so limited. He had no relish for brothers in the carpenter's business or the blacksmith's line of life, who, though they speak curious English, are powerful of arm and spiteful.

Another objection to the marriage was that he was as yet not positively sure the girl loved him, and he considered that nothing under an attack of madness, brought on from adoration for him, would justify such an absurd step.

The great difficulty was to devise some plan by which he might discover the real state of Bertha's feeling towards him. He was, although a soldier, not quick at strategy, and had no idea how to proceed in the matter. He cunningly sought the assistance of his friends. He met Tom Garden airing himself in Regent Street, and presently inquired of him the best method by which a man could discover whether a woman loved a man. This Tom Garden was a coarse-minded fellow, and the only suggestion he could make was to ask the woman to lend the man a good round sum of money, "and if she lends it," he added, "you may be sure she's spoony." The idea of asking Bertha to lend him money so tickled the captain that he laughed himself into a headache. On another occasion, he made a similar inquiry of Fred Tattenham. This time the reply had more wisdom in it, but not more consolation. "Ask her to bolt with you,'· answered Mr. F. T., "and, if she will trust herself to your honour, be certain she loves you." That was precisely what Crosier did want Bertha to do, but he scarcely thought she was in a proper state to accede to such a request.

After deliberating for a week—during which he did not once pay a visit to Camberwell—the captain hit upon the following scheme. The Hazlewoods he knew had no money. The pound or two he had presented to them could not, if they were ever so careful, last out more than a fortnight. He would let them feel what the want of money was like. The most savage animals, he argued, were to be tamed by hunger. Perhaps Bertha was to be conquered by the same method.

To a certain extent this experiment succeeded. The mother and daughter saw their little stock of money grow gradually less and less, and became more and more frightened. They prayed every night Providence would sent them single gentlemen to take their first and second floors and pay a week's rent in advance, but still no lodgers arrived. At last it became positively necessary that the experiment should be made of obtaining credit of the baker and the butcher. Those tradesmen knew very well the house had been let furnished, and, not liking the personal security of the would-be customers, declined all further favours. Things were at this dreadful pass, when the mother determined to pay a visit to the captain. He was in arrear for his parlours, and it was necessary something should be done. She started early in the morning and returned at dusk. It was easy for Bertha to see that her mother had tired herself to no purpose. The captain had gone into the country and would not return for a week. They dined on tea that day and the next as well. It is useless to add that they generally rose from table with an excellent appetite.

But the captain was not in the country. He heard with great delight of Mrs. Hazlewood's visit. He felt very much inclined to rush off in a cab and relieve her distress, for a fearful picture rose to his mind of Bertha grown very thin from starvation, and gradually turning to a skeleton. For two days he resisted this impulse, but on the third his good-nature obtained the mastery.

As he stood at his window he noticed, crouched up in a corner of the area beneath, a wretched cat, that was slowly dying of want. It looked dusty, solemn, and hopelessly weak. A trussed fowl did not show its formation more perfectly. The skin hung about the body in loose folds. It seemed to Crosier as if the spirit of the starving Bertha had come there to rebuke him. He would fly to his beautiful one, and console her with food. He pulled on his boots with despairing haste; he rang the bell so violently that at first Mr. Cutler imagined some muffin-boy had dared to enter the house. Mr. Cutler was ordered first to fetch a cab, and then give some food to the cat in the area. The former of these commissions Mr. Cutler executed, the latter he neglected. He was not going—to use his own words—to turn cat's-meat man to please anybody.

How glad they were to see him! How their eyes sparkled as they ran to greet him at the door! They knew his knock in a moment. The captain was quite overcome by his reception. But a sudden thought crossed his brain, and soured his milky joy. Was he welcome for himself alone, or only because he typified, as it were, so much food? Was it the quartern loaf, was it the leg of mutton, or was it Crosier, that rejoiced Bertha's eyes, and made them sparkle? Did she smile on him, or was it on the vision of hot meat for dinner? Terrible misgiving!

In the most delicate manner, he gave Mrs. Hazlewood the amount of rent due. In his best style, he apologized for his remissness in neglecting an earlier settlement. He was rather pleased to find that Bertha, far from resembling the cat he discovered crouching in the area, was looking remarkably pretty. The prolonged fast had made her appear fascinatingly delicate, and imparted a peculiar blueness to the under portions of the eyes, which was exceedingly becoming.

"That man is our guardian angel," cried Mrs. Hazlewood, when the captain took his leave.

"Who could help loving him?" added Bertha.

The starvation experiment was, the captain considered, a failure.

Being a man much given to extremes, he now resolved to see what a sudden rush of plenty would do towards softening Bertha's heart. He would send them wine, and every luxury—things they could never hope to enjoy—and feast them into a voluptuous laziness. Then, if necessary, he would starve them again. They would feel it even more after the excessive profusion.

The area bell never ceased to ring, and single knocks made the hall resound, like a shooting-gallery, with sudden noises. No sooner was Mrs. Hazlewood at the top of the house than she had to run down stairs. One man, with a yellow flannel apron, left a turbot—a thick, white fish, and so fresh that the cord which lashed its tail and head together was as tight as a fiddle-string, on which Paganini could have played. Then came a game-pie, as big as an oyster-tub, and Fortnum's man said there was nothing to pay. Before night a pheasant was hanging from a hook in the pantry, and a hamper of wine was standing in the back kitchen.

Perhaps it was that Crosier, who was fond of good living, thought he might as well partake of the sumptuous fare he would have to pay for, or perhaps his affection for Bertha became ungovernable ; but for an entire week he dined at Camberwell. He tried to make himself very entertaining and amiable. Towards the mother he adopted a behaviour which was distantly respectful, and excessively flattering to that lady's self-esteem. To Bertha he endeavoured to convey the idea that he was her slave, her victim. He wished to impress her with the belief that his constitution was being slowly destroyed by love. His sighs were powerful enough to blow out a gas lamp.

One evening, he brought with him a paper parcel of considerable dimensions. It seemed, from the careful manner in which he handled it, to contain something of great value. This parcel he would allow no one to touch, but with his own hands carried it into the parlours —his own rooms—where they usually dined. During the repast he was excessively attentive to the mother, and made her take wine so often that she was at last obliged to remark that her poor head was becoming affected. She laughed immoderately, and upset a water-bottle.

Both the ladies were very anxious to know what the paper parcel contained. Their curiosity did not escape his notice. Whenever there was a pause in the conversation their eyes turned to the mysterious bundle. They had to wait till the cloth was cleared. Then up rose the captain, and, with a trembling voice, stammered out a statement, to the effect that as he was passing down Regent Street he had noticed a remarkably elegant dress. As if afraid his next sentence would give offence, he, with great agitation of manner, requested the mother's permission to present this robe to the daughter. Blushes rose to Bertha's temples, and her eyelids closed in modesty over her eyes. Of course, Mrs. Hazlewood could not object. She was even foolish enough to hint that the gift was

x

excessively acceptable. The blushing girl only raised her head to thank the generous captain, and then resigned herself to her crimson confusion.

A most magnificent dress. A skirt with three flounces that pouted out like enormous pen-wipers. Silk as thick as leather—that whistled like wind through rigging when the hand swept down it. It was a robe to make the eyes start from the head with surprise. For five minutes the only words Mrs. Hazlewood could make use of were, "How beautiful!" and she touched it nervously, as if she expected it to move. Poor Bertha was bewitched, and ready either to cry or laugh. In a glance the captain saw the sensation he had created, and proceeded to take advantage of the situation.

He took Bertha's hand, and, looking at the mother, said, with a sweet smile, he should insist upon being paid for the dress—that he was a very stingy man, and never gave anything for nothing. Whilst the mother was tittering at this foolish speech, he took Bertha's head between his hands and kissed her on the forehead. It was done in so brotherly a manner that it would have been absurd to make any objection. It was a poetic salutation. He appeared so much affected that instead of blame he seemed more to deserve consolation.

When he left—he always asked for his hat at ten—the mother and daughter began to chat. They had another look at the dress, and a conversation ensued as to how the body was to be fashioned. The length of the skirt was also tested to see if it suited Bertha's height. With a mean knowingness the captain had left in the parcel the mercer's bill, and with unpardonable baseness altered the amount from £4 5s. to £4 15s. He argued that persons in the Hazlewood walk of life only judged of a present by the amount paid for it.

Mrs. Hazlewood began to have ambitious visions. "I never saw a man so completely in love as that dear captain," she said to Bertha. "Something—I can't tell what it is—but something always convinced me you were destined to be lucky. You have a mole on your left cheek, my dear, and that's considered a sign of luck. Your poor father used to say you were born to be a lady, and, upon my word, I think his words will come true."

She was inconsiderate in saying this, for Bertha's ideas were galloping along quite rapidly enough without additional spurring. She was beginning to worship the dear captain.

"Poor fellow!" continued the mother, "I wish you could have seen his beautiful look when he kissed you. On the forehead, too. Well, if my time was to come over again, he is just the kind of man I should dream about."

The captain's reflections were more manly and less virtuous. He was muttering to himself, "Thank Heaven, I've introduced kissing! It was expensive, but by-and-by I shall get as many as I want—ah! more than I want—for nothing. I dare say a thirty-shilling affair would have answered just as well; but I always overdo a thing like a fool."

The next time the captain visited Camberwell he took with him a bonnet, fresh from the Burlington Arcade. A simple straw, bound with velvet, and adorned with violets. The strings were broad and long. It was a kind of bonnet a princess might have worn, it was so quiet and good. When this new bonnet was tried on, after dinner, Merton became once more to feel like a brother, and demanded payment in kisses. He chose on this occasion to salute the cheek.

"Get gradually down to the lips," was his thought.

He determined that, the next time he offered up sacrifices of clothing to his idol, he would make the grand experiment. He objected to foreheads and cheeks. "What the deuce were the lips made for?" he asked himself. "Come what will, I'll risk the trial. If she takes it quietly, well and good; if she makes a row, I'll cut the business."

What should he take her? Gloves? That didn't seem enough. A shawl? That was too much. The foolish man had an idea that Bertha's embrace was to be bought, and he was prudent enough to wish to get them at the cheapest price. He fixed upon a velvet mantle with a quilted satin lining and a silk fringe as deep as a horse's mane. It looked fearfully expensive, and, as he paid for it, he thought it was so, too.

He did kiss her. The girl with the mantle on her shoulder allowed him to touch her lips. He felt, or fancied he felt, her tremble. He would have promised her twenty mantles for another embrace, but the mother—deuce take her—was standing by, and he dared not.

This old Nurse Hazlewood was a simple-hearted creature who had been so little in the world that she had forgotten all about its deceits. She only remembered that, when her husband courted her, he used to kiss her whenever he brought her any simple present. She looked upon Crosier as the noblest and best man living, and regarded the fact of his embracing Bertha—in her presence, too—as a proof he wished to make her his wife. The old nurse had grown as childish as the infants she looked to in the workhouse nursery. She was without suspicion. The only marvel to her was that so great a gentleman should condescend to notice so humble a girl as her Bertha.

The sofa in Harley Street was once more covered during the day by the bulky form of the long-legged officer. He had again fallen into his habit of letting his cigar go out, whilst he dreamed, with his eyes open, of Bertha, and the next steps to be taken. "Dash my wigs," he thought, "I can't afford any more kisses. I felt the little witch tremble. She must love me, and she ought, too, after ten pounds' worth of presents. How the deuce can I make her worship me. I want her to leave off eating and go nearly mad for my sake. It's so cursed difficult, and takes such a time. It's no use asking her to bolt yet, confound it! I wish she'd grow romantic and follow me all over the world as some of them do."

It had long been a matter of deliberation with this gentleman whether he should pack up his trunk and occupy, for a week or so, his parlours at Camberwell. It was the idea of being "bored by the old mother" that restrained him. There were many advantages, such as being constantly near the daughter and having her to wait upon him. But the family dinner frightened him. Mrs. Hazlewood would insist on changing the plates, and he couldn't bear the muddle and mess; it gave him the idea he was dining in the kitchen. She was so confoundedly civil, too, and talked such twaddle. These things were what he called the drawbacks to his happiness. He often wished the old nurse would be obliging enough to die and leave Bertha, alone and friendless, to be cared for and tended by him.

Now the unhappy youth was a victim of ungovernable passion. His love had, like a cucumber in a bottle, swollen to such a size that he often wondered how it could have entered his bosom. He was drunk with parfait amour. His thoughts ran zigzag, and tumbled about in tipsy helplessness. What could he do?

For four years the captain had never passed more than an hour at once over a book. That was, perhaps, twice a week. He looked upon reading as a pleasant manner of taking opium. Following the lines made him feel sleepy. Now he was seized with a sudden desire for literature. He sent Mr. Cutler to the nearest circulating library, and, the subscription paid, an astounding number of three-volume novels were carried backwards and forwards. He could finish off an entire romance in a morning, reading perhaps a line here and there, but always following the story. He skated through the books.

Being entirely devoid of imagination, he was taking advantage of the brains of others. He was anxious for a lesson or two in love-making; and, above all, he was desirous of learning how those heroes, whose trials were invariably so severe, whose affections were so constantly blighted in the bud, always managed to win their fair ones, and end the story happily. "These novels," thought the captain, "are supposed to be based upon incidents in real life; perhaps they may put me up to a wrinkle or two about Bertha."

In the greater number of the romances Crosier found the fair lady was never moved to forget her maidenly reserve and confess her love until some serious danger threatened her admirer. For instance, in " LUCY D'EGBERT, OR A LIFE," she (Lucy) treats Henry Sinclair with positive disdain up to the time that he is wounded in the duel with Alfred Holbrook. " When on the third day consciousness returned "—we are quoting from the novel—" a cloud seemed to obscure his brain and veil his vision. In the midst of this confused shadow, he beheld a gentle face and two pitying eyes, moist with sympathy, like two stars half hidden by a moonlit cloud, which appeared to beckon him back to life. Did he dream, or was it reality? Little by little, the feverish mist cleared away, the features became more distinct, and he recognized the angelic countenance of the once proud, but now humbled Lucy D'Egbert. With all the strength he was master of he called aloud, 'Lucy, my beloved! can this be true?' 'It is time to take your cooling powders,' she answered, in a voice of superlative tenderness. She loved him."

After reading such a passage, the captain would give himself to thought. "That's all very fine," he would argue, "but I'll see Bertha further, before I get myself shot in a duel merely to find out if she loves me. That's a little too strong, hang it!"

That book would be laid aside and another taken up. He was particularly struck with an incident in "JOY AND SORROW, OR SHINE AND SHADE." In that popular romance, Sir Herbert Brompton is thrown from his horse, and is found by Ellen Trevor perfectly senseless, with one leg dangling over a precipice. She has him conveyed to Trevor Castle, where his fractured arm is set, and she nurses him all through his dangerous illness. It is whilst she is shifting the bandages from his arm that he proposes and is accepted. "Despite the agony he suffered," writes the author, "despite the torture that racked his frame, despite the worse than torment of his mind, Sir Herbert could not regard without feelings of the liveliest pleasure the lovely countenance of his tender nurse. How carefully did she handle the fractured limb. He scarcely felt the taper fingers that played about the now useless member." Then he feels a tear drop on his wrist, and that convinces him he is beloved.

Neither did Crosier care much to undergo such a trial as Sir Herbert. He didn't like the idea of being thrown from a horse and breaking an arm. "Begad," he thought, "it might break my head, and then where should I be? No, no, I'm very fond of Bertha, but I don't think my love goes to the length of a broken arm. Besides, a fellow looks such a fool rolling about in a dusty road with perhaps his trousers split."

He read and he read, and he liked none of the incidents. Those which pleased him most were when the heroine was in great danger and the lover rescued her from peril. But even then, there was either a burning house, or a boat upset, or an enraged bull to be risked, and he had no fancy either for being singed, ducked, or gored. So, when he had waded through some dozen of these novels, he vowed they were all romance, and not worth the trouble of opening. He found he must trust to his own wits after all, and felt the true awkwardness of the position.

He was determined to be ill somehow or other, and then to hurry over to Camberwell and ask Bertha to nurse him. He would take something to make himself look pale and interesting, and sham the remainder of the sickness.

He remembered once buying some ipecacuanha lozenges to ease a troublesome cough, and the young man at the chemist's had strongly cautioned him not to take more than one at a time, as they produced a sensation of sickness. To this vendor of medicines did the gallant captain despatch his man, who presently returned with two shilling boxes. The next day the captain packed up his portmanteau, and then, everything being ready for his departure, drew forth his lozenges and commenced to eat. They tasted very pleasantly, and six were rapidly disposed of. He began to consider the chemist a swindler. He vowed he would send a letter to the "Lancet" exposing the infamous imposition. Before he was half-way through his seventh lozenge he had excellent proof that no more veracious man existed in this world than the druggist who had warned him not to take more than one.

The emetic asserted itself. With his forehead bathed in cold perspiration, and with a face as white as a clown's, the captain threw himself on the sofa and began to pant. A dreadful idea seized him, that he might have poisoned himself. He almost wished he had never seen Bertha. Oh! how ill he felt. He ran to look at himself in the glass, and the vision shocked him. One or two pimples glowed on his pallid countenance as the strawberries do on the top of a blancmange. He could never dare to show himself to Bertha with such a face—she would be disgusted.

About three o'clock he had a little recovered, but he had undergone a severe time of it, and was positively unwell. He had only sufficient energy to arrange his curls in the looking-glass, and then get into a cab.

CHAPTER IX.

HOW THE BEST YEARS OF PHIL'S LIFE WERE WASTED.

SOME few years ago, the masters of the Unions throughout England became aware that a gang of vagrants was travelling through the land—an organized band under the command of a captain, who directed their actions and ruled supreme, appointing the workhouses where they were to meet, and the towns they were to work. The police were on the alert to lay hold of this band, but, though some few of them were seized, the majority escaped. These captures did not decrease the numbers, for recruits were more numerous than the captain chose to accept.

The name of this captain was Philip Merton. This is how he attained to the honour. He was nearly eighteen years of age when he, Fortune, and Purchase were on the tramp. Passing through the different towns they found acquaintances. Four other wanderers joined the schoolfellows. Being a silent, thoughtful youth, Phil was slightly feared and greatly disliked by his companions. They often reproached him that he never stole or worked as they did. If, when they begged at a cottage door, they saw even a scrubbing brush or a morsel of soap, it was pocketed. But Merton never "boned," and was half suspected of being a sneak. In vain Phil pleaded that this

The Fight in the Vagrant Ward

morality was owing to no virtuous scruples, but he thought it mean
to carry off such useless "penny lots." They considered—and right
they were—that the youth, though he dare not confess it to them,
objected to theft on principle, and he was nicknamed the "Amen
bawler" (parson), and recommended to take to the "hum box'
(pulpit) as better suited to him than cadging. Stung to the quick by
these taunts, Phil—poor weak fellow—at length gave way. They
were working Preston at the time. "I'll show you whether I'm
afraid," he cried, leaving them. Presently he returned with a huge
basket of clean linen. He had seen a man leave it at a house close
by, and knocking at the door had stated that by mistake the wrong
basket had been given. The foolish servant had handed back the
clothes. "Now," cried Phil, " do you believe I'm a croaker?" They
answered with cheers, for the linen was worth at least five pounds
" And now," added Phil, " I will do another thing which none of you
would have courage even to think of." He walked off again, carrying
the basket, and his pals saw him return it to the rightful owners.
This action, and a severe drubbing administered to Billy Fortune,
caused Phil to be regarded as an astounding mortal. His companions
grew afraid of him. He could read, write, rob, and be honest. He
could sing, recite, tell wonderful stories, and bamboozle old women
with his glib tongue and handsome face, better than any of the
ragged crew. They elected him captain.

He proved himself a wonderful commander. He learned by heart
the long list of Unions from Land's End to the Scottish borders, and
could tell what rations of food were served at each—where cheese
was allowed, or the bread either sour or short weight. He could inform you which vagrant wards contained beds, where the rugs were
warm, or where only straw was served out. To prevent confusion
when working a town, he caused certain signs to be used by his
gang. A chalk mark on a doorpost was sufficient to indicate whether
it was worth the next comer's while to beg at that house, or to warn
him if it was dangerous to make the experiment. Even for the
corners of roads, or milestones, or guide-posts, he had different marks,
so that if the band was by any misfortune broken up, the members
were soon enabled to meet together again.

Very strange were the nights passed in the casual-wards. Outside
the town the gang would separate. One by one they asked for admission at the workhouse-gate. To avoid being traced in their
wanderings, they seldom gave their correct names on entering "the
house." On different occasions Phil had christened himself Joseph
Hume, Arthur Wellington, and Richard Turpin. If any workhouse
master offended this gang they would, after a time, revisit the union,
and in revenge break the windows, burn the rugs, and destroy whatever was destructible. They carried lucifer-matches with them, concealed in their clothes, and, not unfrequently, short, stout sticks.

Against the Irish tramps this band waged continual warfare. A
law was passed that no lad from the sister isle should be admitted

into their troop. They even went out of their road sometimes to visit a workhouse where they knew they should find Irish tramps, merely to fight and drive them out of the union. Then the most dreadful battles would ensue. In the depth of the night Phil and his crew would rise silently from their beds. Armed with sticks, they would set upon the unoffending Irish, belabouring them cruelly. It was useless to shout for help; no master would have dared to interfere during such engagements. The only hope was to strike in return. Occasionally the band got the worst of the encounter—and serve them right. Another infamous practice of these young ruffians was to seize upon a sleeping man, and, whilst some held him, others rifled him of any money he might, before entering, have secreted about his clothing. There was no redress for the sufferer, for at the union-gate he had confessed himself a pauper without a penny in the world. Sometimes these banditti would prowl about in the neighbourhood of a workhouse, waiting for the Irish tramps to come up. The un-suspecting wanderer, if he had any money in his possession, would usually seek for some hidden corner in which to stow away for the night what he had earned during the day. Under waterspouts, in the hedge-bank, or in the hollows between bricks, the few shillings would be carefully deposited, to be soon taken out again by the rogues who were upon the watch.

If these young vagabonds could secure a ward to themselves, the night passed merrily, and very little sleep did the crew indulge in. Sometimes stories would be told of the doings of famous robbers, or the contents of a novel would be condensed into a twenty minutes' tale. If any one was called upon for a yarn, he was forced by the laws of the band to invent one, if he could not remember any he had read. The set style of beginning these narratives was in these words: "Once upon a time, mates, but not in your time or in my time, but in the time gone by, when it was a good time," &c., &c. If they grew tired of stories, they would sing or give recitations. "The Drunkard's Soliloquy" was an especial favourite. There was a great deal of what actors call "business" in it. It began in this way: "Well, here I am, just come out of the public—public (hiccup) house; I've only drunk fourteen glasses of brandy-and-water (staggers about), and I'm as drunk as a p-p-parson! (hiccup)· Talking of the parson, reminds me of the devil, and talking of the devil, reminds me of my wife (hiccup)," &c., &c. The songs Phil was especially celebrated for were "The Slave's Dream," "O what a sight for a mother," and "Dearest, touch the castanet." The only subject Billy Fortune could talk about was penny theatres. He was a constant frequenter of gaffs, and had a peculiar knowledge of the performers at them, being able to tell when those gentlemen made their first appearance, and in what "line" they were famous. "Any of you chaps seen Madame Mossi in her tablow vyevant? Ain't she first-rate as Wenus attended by the syrins—stunning!" Or he would inform the company that Jimmy Byson, "the original monkey," was to be at Oxford in three weeks' time, and proposed directing their steps in that direction to have the pleasure of witnessing his curious antics. "To see him go up a pole is a regular knock-me-down!" he would add.

In this manner did Phil allow his youth to pass away. He grew to be a man, and the only advantages age brought him were greater strength of body, and greater cunning of brain. He could imagine bolder schemes than in his boyhood, and his limbs were strong enough to face any danger his reckless life might entail. Some fifty tramps were ready to sing his praises and call him Captain, but to the remainder of the world he was a rogue and a vagabond.

CHAPTER X.

BERTHA BEHAVES LIKE A WOMAN.

KIND-HEARTED Mrs. Hazlewood nearly fainted on the cocoa-nut fibre doormat when the ghost of Captain Crosier first met her gaze. She screamed out for Bertha, and then exclaimed, "Good Heavens! what has happened?" The captain, who had arranged in his own mind the story he was to tell, and the way in which he was to act, clutched for support at the old lady's shoulder, and in a weak voice murmured "Let me sit down . . . . parlours . . . . sofa."

Both the women stood over him in the greatest anxiety, as with closed eyes he lay upon the couch and panted. He heard Bertha sob, and, as if with an effort that cost him much agony, turned his head towards her, took her hand, and murmured, "Do not weep . . . I shall . . . soon . . . be . . . well." Presently he appeared to recover his strength, for he was—though with difficulty—able to express a wish to retire to bed. Away flew Mrs. Hazlewood to prepare her dear, good friend's four-poster. Alone with Bertha, he again began to pant, and had the satisfaction of once more hearing her sob. It was very pathetic to see this poor invalid, now gasping like a trout on the grass, now moving his lips about feverishly, and begging for water. He was put to bed, and the bell-pull fastened to a chair by his side, that he might ring the moment he required anything.

He recovered mightily when left alone; indeed, he began, for the hundredth time, to curse the chemist who sold him the lozenges. He remained in bed for about an hour, staring at every piece of furniture in the room, wondering where the deuce the wash-hand stand was picked up, or whose portrait it was hanging over the drawers. About ten o'clock, the Hazlewoods heard the bell tinkle, and upstairs they raced to wait on the patient. He had risen—very imprudently they said—and, wrapped in an elegant dressing-gown, with his shirt-collar a la Byron, was seated in a roomy arm-chair before the fire. "He was better, yes . . . much . . . better," he said, in a voice that sounded as if he was worse, much worse. He was implored to relate the cause of his indisposition, that was, if he had strength enough to do so. In a few words he told his story:

"Returning home from a friend's house," so he spoke, "he had the misfortune to hire a drunken cabman. The fellow drove, he thought, very recklessly. Just as the vehicle was turning the corner of Oxford Street, it came in contact with a heavy market-cart, and he was pitched out of the hansom on to the horse's back." Now his voice became fainter, as he added, "The animal kicked me in the side," he panted for a moment and looked wildly, but presently added, when the women had finished hiding their faces in their aprons, and drawing in their breath with horror, "thank God, no . . . bones . . . were broken . . . but . . . the internal injuries . . . they tell me . . . are . . . se . . . vere." Then he fell back in the chair exhausted. He was hypocrite enough to ask Bertha to feel the place on his ribs where the cruel steed had struck him with its iron hoof, and, with fear and trembling, she allowed her hand to be guided to the wound. She declared it was dreadfully swollen, and felt as if there was a deep hole.

"I thought I would come here," said the captain, with a languid air, as he by-and-by drank some tea, and tried to eat some dry toast. "I have no right to inflict you with my sufferings and make nurses of you, but I am a poor, lonely bachelor, Mrs. Hazlewood, and I thought you would in mercy not refuse to assist my recovery."

The mother replied, "Oh! sir, we are grateful you should think us worthy of such a task;" and the daughter, though she did not speak, looked as if she would willingly have taken all his sufferings from him, and endured them herself, if it had been possible.

The next day, and the next, the captain grew better. The pretty Bertha waited on him, bringing him his breakfast, his lunch, his dinner, or anything he required. He was ringing the bell for her every ten minutes. The mother was very much pleased to remark the great modesty of his behaviour. He locked his bedroom door as regularly as if he had been afraid of thieves. If, before he rose, he required anything, he had it sat down outside the door, and presently a white hand, with a gold signet-ring on the third finger, would issue from the slight opening of the door, and take in the thing asked for. If he had been a young girl of sixteen he could not have been more modest and decorous.

When he had been in the house a couple of days, he got to learn the hours at which Mrs. Hazlewood usually went out on her household errands. If she had no occasion to leave the house, he was clever enough to find one. Either he required jellies, which he insisted should be fetched from Gunter's, or he would touch no fish but that

vended by Groves, of Bond Street. A cab was ordered to carry the
mother on her errand, and Bertha was asked to keep the sick man
company until she returned.

He saw plainly enough the little girl was in love with him. He
caught her looking at him with the tenderest expression in her large
eyes. She answered his bell when he rang as rapidly as if she slept
on the mat outside. The first time he slept in his rooms she had, in
the middle of the night, fancied she heard him moaning, and,
slipping on her dress, had descended to assure herself whether the
sound was fancied or real. He never knew that—but we do.

Ask yourselves whether it was not natural she should adore this
man. You have been shown all the falsity and trickery of this
captain's character and behaviour. She believed that everything he
said or did was true and honest. He, a gentleman in the army,
with noble friends, rich and generous as the prince of a fairy tale,
she, a poor sewing-girl, with a pauper mother! Remember, too,
that this Crosier, in all he did, never transgressed any one of the
rules laid down by society, but made love to her as respectfully as
if she had been a little Russell Square miss. The companions
pointed out to her as fitting her station in life were the servants of
the house, yet she had received education, and was by nature gifted
enough to feel she was their superior. She preferred the well-expressed
conversation of one who was called a gentleman to the tittle-tattle
of a kitchen, and felt grateful he should consider her worthy of his
notice.

They had some curious conversation together, whenever the mother
was despatched on these jelly and fish errands. The captain was
very desirous of forcing from Bertha a confession that she loved him.

"You have a dear, good heart, Bertha," he said, on one occasion,
in a voice still weak from the effects of his severe kicking. "I shall
never forget your sweet look of pity on the day when I came here so
ill. You have cured me now, pretty Bertha. I shall soon be able to
leave you, and cease to trouble you."

"You should not call it trouble, captain," was the inevitable
answer.

"Dear, good girl! Bless you for those sweet words!" he continued. "I might have died without your care, Bertha. I shall
always think of you, Bertha. Do you know that, when I lay under
that plunging horse, and saw his iron hoofs gleam in the moonlight,
I thought of you. Why did I not think of my father or my sister?
I ought to have done so. Why did I think of you, sweet Bertha?"

Of course she could not in decency inform him.

He took her hand, and she did not resist.

"Bertha, tell me!" he said, speaking excitedly, "is it because I love
you? You know how I have always admired you—how for your dear
sake I have braved insults and denials. Yes, I do love you dearly—
more dearly than I dare to tell you, for it passes belief, and you might
refuse me yours."

At this moment the mother returned, and the captain, cursing his luck that he had not begun the conversation sooner, was obliged to release his trembling angel.

Once, to ensure a lengthy absence, Crosier despatched the mother to his apartments in Harley Street to fetch something he didn't want, and neglected to give the old lady the money for a cab. He knew she would never ask for it.

As soon as he was alone, he requested the pleasure of Miss Bertha's society to cheer his solitude, and, before a quarter of an hour had passed, was making love more desperately than ever. He was determined that this time she should make a confession one way or the other.

Ever since the world was an educated world, the same method, manner, and almost phrases of love have been employed. They seem to succeed so well, that swains do not think it worth while inventing fresh ones. The captain once more told Bertha he worshipped her, and, by repeating the same sentiment in fifty different ways, impressed her with a belief that each declaration was a new one. She sat still and listened, staring at the fire. He saw the reflection of the flickering flame in her eyes. Her hand was raised to her lips as if she was in deep thought. Never had she looked prettier. The heat of the coals had flushed her cheeks, and the captain's declaration had turned every other portion of her countenance to an ashy whiteness.

As she did not willingly answer him, he determined to wrench a reply from her somehow or other. He became silent for a few seconds, and then letting go her hand, placed his own against his bosom as if in pain. For a few minutes he was plunged in thought, frowning and breathing loudly down his nose. When at last he did speak, it was in a timid, hesitating voice, as if his life depended on the reply. "Bertha! tell me truly, do not deceive me—that would be too cruel!—Do you love another?" She turned round and stared at him with her big eyes, but said nothing. "You do," he cried, starting forward. "Now I can understand why you reject me. Why have you trifled with me." As if exhausted, he fell back in his chair and panted. He was perfectly well aware the poor girl knew no one, and cared for no one, but himself. Excepting the portrait of George III. in the drawing-room, she never saw anything resembling a man from one week's end to another.

She had taken her eyes from the fire and was looking at him. He didn't move. For nearly a quarter of an hour he never stirred a muscle, and he felt a cramp was coming on. A hand was placed on his shoulder. It was a mute confession, the only one she dared to make. He started round, and, with a smile of consummate beatitude, cried, as he seized her head between his palms, "Then you do love me! Oh! let me hear those words. Whisper them to me, dearest." Instead of speaking, the tears came welling up to her eyes. "Now," he cried, "I am ready to die for you! Now, I am certain of happiness. Tell me, dear one, have you loved me long, and how have I gained your affection?" He wanted to learn all the particulars of the case as minutely as a physician.

It was evening, and the room was in half obscurity, the flickering of the coal fire only lighting up, every now and then, the objects around. Mothers of families take this advice, never leave your daughters alone with captains in the dusk of evening. The mysterious dimness gives an air of privacy, and many a confession of love has been made under its dreamy influence which the lips would have been ashamed to utter if a couple of candles had been burning on the table. A lamp in a bedroom will frighten away a thief. A gaslight is said to be worth three policemen. There are other thieves besides those who break into houses, and they are equally afraid of being viewed distinctly. The flame of the smallest taper would have been sufficient to prevent Bertha from answering as she did, with downcast eyes and a trembling of the lips, "Yes, I do love you, I have for a long time. I was afraid you knew it, and that made me very unhappy. I don't know why, but I was ashamed of—liking you." She spoke so much because she was crying. A very little would have brought on a fit of hysterics.

Instead of falling into an ecstacy of rapture, the captain began calmly to contemplate his happiness. The confession that she had for a long time loved him, annoyed him considerably. He considered he had been wasting a vast deal of money and many valuable weeks. "What a timid fool I am," he thought. "I am so disgustingly delicate. If I had only had sense enough to make these inquiries before, what trouble and expense I might have saved myself."

After Bertha had confessed her love for him, he saw no harm in indulging in lovers' ways. He placed his arm round her waist and often kissed her temples or smoothed her hair. They did not talk much. A half grunt of delight frequently came from the captain, but the girl remained motionless and thoughtful. Perhaps she already regretted she had spoken so much. She had parted with her liberty, and placed a master over herself; even now the new master was taking advantage of his authority, indulging himself in affectionate caresses. Two hours previously he was as respectful as a linendraper; now he was as saucy as a Jack in office.

At the end of the first week the captain, instead of leaving Camberwell, inquired—with a pleasing humility—of Mrs. Hazlewood whether he might be permitted to lengthen his stay to a fortnight. His side, he complained, was still painful, especially when he coughed. "He felt," he said, "as if living at his own home, and the tranquil happiness did him more good than all the medicine in the world." How different was his behaviour to Bertha to what it had been on his first coming. He became epithetic and called her "his life," his "beauty," and many other sweet endearing terms. Frequently he pressed her against his bosom, more particularly when she held the breakfast-tray in her hands and could not resist.

Towards the mother he adopted a severely moral deportment.

"She is always bothering me with her company, poor soul!" he silently complained, and, to drive her off, he sermonized to his utmost during her visits. He usually chose the horrors of intemperance as his theme, that being the subject he was best acquainted with. Sometimes he would say to her, "When will the English be a sober nation, Mrs. Hazlewood? I have often been struck by a peculiar expression used by the vulgar; they call it—I think—'treating one another to drink.' Now, how much more appropriate would it be if they said ill-treating one another to drink, since the morrow's headache, the burning brow, the hard, dry tongue, the deranged stomach deserve this expression." The old lady—who was seriously inclined—felt as if she could listen to him by the hour. He shared with the workhouse chaplain her humble admiration. At another time he would say, "Drink, Mrs. Hazlewood, is a cruelty imposed on us by custom. If I were to raise a pistol to my friend's head and blow away his brains, society would call me a heartless murderer, but if I raise a brimming glass to his lips and blow away his brains with the fumes of alcohol, society smiles and terms me a loving companion. Yet the insensibility of drunkenness is to me as terrible as the stillness of death." Little did the admiring old lady imagine that this preacher had brought to her house, concealed in his portmanteau, four bottles of overproof brandy which were rapidly being emptied of their contents.

In his love-makings with Bertha he was extremely cautious in avoiding all reference to marriage. He fancied that if he did not mention the fact of making her his wife he should not be bound in honour to wed her. The only time he ventured on this subject was done solely to sound her notions on the subject, and, if possible, to convince her that the ceremony at the altar was an unphilosophical and useless rite. Like other innocent girls, Bertha believed that love and the church were synonymous.

For fear she might relate to her mother the incidents of their love scenes, he bound her over to silence by solemn promises and threats of the serious injuries that would befall him if his family should hear of his affection for one so lowly conditioned as herself.

"This absurd—this foolish world!" he cried in disgust, "it insists that we should do not as we like, but as it chooses. Now what can be more absurd than marriage? A man loves a woman so fondly that he finds he cannot even exist out of her presence. To have her near him is his dearest wish. She must be by his side within reach of his hand, as it were. Is it natural that a man in such a state of feeling would ever dream of quitting this woman? No; it would be death. I should die if you, dear Bertha, were taken from me. But what says this stupid world? You must go to church, a priest must read from a certain book certain passages to which you are too excited to pay attention. You must ride home in a carriage, and eat a peculiar kind of cake, and then you may live together as man and wife. Absurd! absurd!"

Whilst he was laughing derisively, the girl was wondering why he should think the ceremony so ridiculous. She had always considered it as the most solemn event in a maiden's life. She felt particularly hurt to hear the cake abused.

"How much more honourable," continued the captain, "is that union which without the fetters of the law, remains constant."

Because he was looking at her, she replied that it was so; but she added, "I have been told they sometimes leave one another, and then the poor woman—— There was one my mother knew who was deserted—her character was lost—and he was a gentleman's son and very well off."

The conversation ended. For fear she might imagine he entertained any such designs against her, he ceased talking, and began to fondle her, patting her hands and praising her eyes—asking her to g ve them to him to be made into shirt studs.

" She's not quite ready yet," thought the captain, as in the evening he sat before the fire plotting how he was to carry off the girl, "Not quite ready, but rapidly coming round. I could no more get her to cut away just now than if she was of the blood royal. I must give her time, and she'll come round. Never whip a jibbing horse—you may break your whip to atoms, and yet not advance a step. Patience, patience, that's the virtue for me!"

CHAPTER XI.

THE TRAVELLING CIRCUS.

THE town of Elbury is a quiet place, with some two thousand inhabitants, and it struck Monsieur Le Cobbe, the celebrated equestrian performer, and the boldest somersault thrower in the world, that it would be worth his while to pitch his tent in the neighbourhood for one night only. He waited upon Sir Frederick Wigwam to seek his patronage. He obtained an indirect promise from Dr. Pinnock, of Milton House Academy, that his forty scholars would be present, and altogether the speculation looked, as Monsieur Le Cobbe said, "healthy."

The bills appeared. Long blue ones at the pastrycook's; long pink ones at the circulating library. Labouring men were to be admitted at half the price demanded of the gentry. The inhabitants of Elbury became excited, and the butchers', the bakers', and the doctors' boys began to practise standing on their heads.

To increase the enthusiasm, Monsieur Le Cobbe and his talented troupe entered Elbury in grand procession. The gentlemen riders with their thick necks exposed, and their long hair tucked behind their ears, wore romantic costumes, while the lady riders looked lovely in their velvet habits and gold lace. The band in the ornamented car played with such spirit that the spotted and cream-coloured steeds became inspired, and danced like Christians. Not the least wonderful part of the sight was the dexterity with which Monsieur Le Cobbe drove ten-in-hand. He turned the corner of the market-place as easily as if he had been pushing a wheelbarrow.

Orders had long since been given to Mr. Barton, the carpenter, to have so many sacks of sawdust ready by a certain day. Four cart-loads of fine garden-mould had been bespoken at Daddy's nursery-ground. The erecting of the handsome and commodious tent attracted hundreds of lookers-on—indeed the beer-boy from the "Pink Sow" was constantly running backwards and forwards with gallon-cans of ale. In the course of the day, Sir Frederick Wigwam and the ladies honoured the stables of Monsieur Le Cobbe with a visit, and expressed themselves much pleased with the beauty and condition of the numerous stud.

There was, that evening, such a rush that it was a mercy the tent did not get turned over, or collapse like an umbrella. The shilling places were packed in half an hour. The youngest child of Mr. Waters, the greengrocer, had to be sent home to be washed, having been rolled into a mud-heap, where it lay like a pigeon in a pie, with only its little hands showing above the crust.

What business Philip Merton had at Elbury does not signify just now. Perhaps it is better not to inquire too closely into the matter. There he was, and well dressed too. How he paid for, or otherwise obtained, these excellent clothes, we had rather not be forced to explain.

The inside of the tent was worthy of being painted in a picture. The oil-lamps cast a mellow-light, and the striped bunting decorations were draped with exceeding taste. There was a mixed smell of horses, sawdust, oil, and oranges, which was far from unpleasant. In the centre of the tent was the ring, resembling an enormous snuff-box filled with rappee, and in a stand—raised like a railway cistern—over the door at which the horses would enter, were placed the band.

As soon as the noble patron had arrived, the performances commenced. First there was an equestrian drama, entitled "The Fair Maid of Sahara, or the Arab Steed and the Lover's Vow."

Seated next to Philip was a young lady—evidently under the protection of her maid-servant, a savage, elderly female, who, whenever she caught the youth peeping at her mistress, looked murder, and clenched the handle of her big basket tightly as if it were a stick. But the face was so pretty that all the servants in the world could not force Phil's eyes away from it. A round forehead, on which a little

Phil watches the others dispersing

globe of light was focussed just above the temple, of such whiteness that pearl powder would have soiled it. The lashes to the eyes were so long that they sheltered them like a screen, and, casting a shadow, gave a velvet softness to the pupils. The strings to her bonnet tightened when she laughed, for she had the smallest taste in life of a double chin, which plumped out on such occasions and looked remarkably lovely.

She listened very attentively to the drama, apparently believing every word of it to be true. The hero always came in on horseback, and never once was he permitted to mount or dismount his steed without slow music. He often addressed the animal, calling it " his beautiful bright-eyed charger." He would tell the passive-looking cream, " that right well had it carried him on its lightning feet amid the battle fray." These praises caused the young lady next Phil to exclaim, over and over again, "Pretty creature!" She trembled in horror when the villain of the drama, making his horse prance, roared out, "If she reject me, my revenge shall, indeed, be fearfool and ter-reebel." How she rejoiced when the bold lover, raising himself in the stirrups, shouted, " If we meet, his blood be upon his own sohole." Phil, who was watching her, felt quite jealous of the actor who played the part. There was no scenery to this piece, which was performed in the circus, but it gave great satisfaction, and the horses and actors went out amid immense applause.

During the scenes in the circle, Phil gazed so intently at the young lady that the maid-servant once proposed to change places with her mistress. The entrance of Madlle. Vanille, in that graceful scene d'equitation called the " Flower-girl of Florence," saved Phil from this misfortune. Every eye in the circus followed the flower-girl as she moved round the ring. It was a prettily-conceived scene. First she had a spade handed her, and began to dig at the saddle as if it were a garden bed. Then a groom ran after her, and exchanged the spade for a rake, with which she proceeded to level the imaginary earth about the saddle. Every time the ring-master smacked his long whip, the fair one of Elbury trembled lest the flower-girl of Florence should tumble to the real soil. The saddle with the embroidered covering was as broad as a tea-tray, but what is that when a jolting horse in underneath? Towards the close of this graceful performance, when " Hi, hi!" was shouted to make the horse gallop faster and faster, when the rider was being carried round at a speed that nearly tore away her satin skirts, the velvet-eyed beauty seemed in great fear lest the Florentine damsel should break her neck on English ground.

There was a capital clown, who first did his gymnastic exercises, and then made the audience shout at his wit.

" How do you do, sir?" asked the ring-master. "Very poorly, thank you, sir," answered the clown, forcing down the corners of his mouth. " How is that, sir?"—" Why I've had the hen-flew-in-at-the-window, sir." " What is that, sir?"—" It's a kind of severe guitar, with head-rakes and roomy attics, sir." " You mean the influenza,

Y

with a catarrh, head-aches, and rheumatics, I suppose, sir ?"—"Yes, sir; but I take my medicine regular—a wine-glass of mustard poultice three times a day, and my feet in cough-mixture before going to bed." When the pretty young lady laughed at this, Phil laughed too, and then their eyes met. They then laughed more violently than before.

There were some acrobats in spangled tights, who glittered like fresh herrings. These men had legs flexible as riding-whips, and lifted each other in every possible manner; there was a young lady who executed the rapid and brilliant act of leaping over banners and through paper hoops; there was another maiden (with weak knees that bent each time the horse moved), who performed most elegantly with a scarf. Whenever the audience applauded, Phil and the young lady looked at each other, as though comparing notes, and exchanging opinions about the merit of the entertainment.

The eccentricities of the clown amused the old maid-servant, and she forgot to watch her young mistress.

Mr. Merryman told the ring-master that provisions were very dear —"Sorry to hear it, sir," answered the gentleman. "Yes, sir," continued the clown, "milk has gone up so high, the cream can't get to the top of it." When Mr. Merryman was asked if he was afraid of a horse, he said, "No, it was himself he was afraid of." There seemed no end to his humour. He remarked that one of the steeds was a thorough-bred and a penny loaf a top of that. He even invited the ring-master to come and spend a week at his house. "I shall be delighted, Mr. Merryman," answered that gentleman. "Where do you live, sir ?"—"In the same place, sir, before I removed to where I used to live now." "That's a rather strange address, sir!"—"I've gone up and down on the other side facing." "I am not much wiser, sir."—"You can't mistake the house, sir, because the door opens just as you go in." Whilst everybody was roaring with delight, Philip most impudently whispered in the young lady's ear, "He is very good, don't you think so ?" and she, laughing, answered aloud, "Oh, very amusing, indeed!"

Presently the ring-master advised Mr. Merryman not to walk before him, adding, "I never follow fools;" upon which the clown fell into the rear, and, making a face, said, "I do." This gave Phil an excuse for again speaking to the young lady.

"Have you never been to a circus before ?" he asked.

She answered so loudly that the maid-servant heard her, "No; this is the first time I ever saw anything of the kind;" and then fell to laughing again.

But, alas! for Phil, all further chance of renewing the conversation was put an end to by the maid-servant, who, crimson with indignation, threw herself between him and the fair one.

"For shame, Miss Lucy!" cried the faithful domestic, "to talk with a strange gentleman. Well, I never did before!"

When he heard that her name was Lucy, Phil opened his eyes with delight. He did nothing but repeat the name to himself during the remainder of the performance. It was in vain he endeavoured to catch another glance at the pretty face—the eye of the servant maid was watching him with threatening activity.

At last the audience rose to depart, and Phil, although the domestic did all she could to get rid of him, followed closely at the heels of the beauty. He had resolved to find out where she lived, though, as he said to himself, " It's only waste of time. They wouldn't let a chap like me marry her."

CHAPTER XII.

THE CAPTAIN IS GUILTY OF WHAT HE CONSIDERS A GREAT WASTE OF MONEY.

OUT of respect to its age, we were about to make use of an old saying, but most fortunately we are, without departing from the truth, enabled to vary it a little. The course of Captain Crosier's base love did not run smooth. It was full of hard, flinty obstructions, that made it foam and bubble ; it had to rush by difficult points, and overcome a variety of disagreeable stoppages. This course was a muddy stream, such as a lover would prefer drinking, in a poetic manner, with his eyes.

He might just as well have given up his rooms in Harley Street for the use he made of them. From one week's end to another he never showed his face there ; in fact, more than once, Mrs. Bullanty (he owed her, as she said, "a pretty penny") became seriously alarmed at the prolonged absence of her first-floor lodger, and had even gone to the extreme length of using her duplicate keys, to see if the effects in the locked-up drawers were equal to the value of her debt. The vast amount of time left on Mr. Teddy Cutler's hands enabled him to add to his varied accomplishments by learning several new songs from "The Little Warbler." He could also make his appointments for the evening with greater certainty of not breaking them. Had he dared to grow a moustache, his worldly happiness would have been complete.

They lived well and looked well at Camberwell. The captain became so curiously domesticated, that it almost seemed like a wager between himself and the cat, as to which of them should remain indoors for the greater length of time. The only journey of any consequence that he undertook was to the chambers of Mr. Edward Dancer, in Holborn, to request him to let some little matter or other stand over for a few weeks. When he returned, he told Bertha it seemed to him as if he had been absent for hours. He also made this journey an excuse for embracing his beloved as fondly as if he had been to India and back.

The gallant captain, in the full bloom of his happiness, felt a worm in the bud gnawing at the tenderest leaves of his love. He was disappointed with himself. He had come, he had seen, but instead of his conquering, there had been a very hard battle for the victory. The other chaps—his dashing friends—would cut him if they knew what a mess he had made of the business. With them, carrying off a girl was either the affair of a week or a fortnight, or she might stop where she was. Charley Sutton had bolted with a baker's daughter from Cheltenham before he had wasted ten pounds in the courtship. Fred Tattenham could tell twenty highly amusing stories of his loves (one was with a lawyer's wife), and in no instance had he devoted more than two months to even the most troublesome case. The captain felt the awkwardness of his position. Even after he carried off Bertha, he scarcely knew what he should do with her. It was his dream to give pleasant little dinners at her villa in St. John's Wood. He wanted to make the fellows envious of his good fortune. But then, with these delicious morsels of swagger, the truth would peep out that it had taken him ages of the most assiduous attention to captivate a servant-girl. He felt ashamed of himself, and would often examine his countenance in the chimney-glass to try and discover some reason for the tardiness of the result.

If we were called upon to give any explanation of the captain's fear of the world, and a dread of the exposure which might follow his dilatory method of proceeding, we should impute it to an excessive adventure. This gentleman was, even then, in great trepidation lest any rumour of what he was plotting should reach the ears of certain parties at Swanborough. He more particularly dreaded the remarks his mother might make on such a theme. She was very much opposed to these amiable indiscretions. Even if his father, who was an easy-going man upon all human frailties but those of robbery and dishonouring a bill, were to remark that young men would be young men, the strict mamma would most likely add something about it not being necessary for them to be rogues as well. "That woman," thought the captain, " is actually capable of insisting on a genuine marriage."

The occurrences of daily life reported in our morning newspapers had also a checking influence on the captain's boldness. He never opened the "Times" without fear and trembling. His eye fell down the columns with the rapidity of a stone. If he saw anything about "Heartless Seduction by a Gentleman of Fortune," it brought on an attack of frowning and biting the lips. He was pained to see that, in such reported cases, it was usually the mother of the girl who applied to the magistrate for advice under the distressing circumstances. One of these reports would run thus : " A respectably-dressed female, who appeared greatly excited, entered the court as it was about to rise, and appealed, &c., &c." Then the bold captain would mutter to himself, "D—n that Mother Hazlewood! that's exactly the little game she'd be after. The woman would cry her eyes out to make a case of it." Sometimes the report was slightly varied: "A woman who was humbly but cleanly attired, and who, though overcome by her feelings, refused to give her name—" This he could read with a more full breath. The refusal to give her name had great hope in it. With his eyes slantways through intensity of thought, he would wonder to himself "whether the old woman would have decency enough to keep her daughter's shame secret." But by the way in which he would immediately afterwards term the poor old nurse "an old jade and a whining hypocrite," he showed he had not much reliance on the family pride of the Hazlewoods. "All done to extort money," was his usual criticism upon such police cases.

Yet to see how pleasantly the days skipped, and hopped, and danced along over the heads of these happy sojourners in Camberwell, who could have suspected that even one bosom had a thorn in it? As for that house having a skeleton in it, the very mice and black-beetles were fat jovial Daniel Lamberts in their small way. The happy mother might wake up in the morning dreaming either that Bertha's wedding-dress had come home too late to be worn at the bridal, or that the hooks-and-eyes wouldn't meet! but even a pork-supper could not trouble her with any misgivings more terrible. The intended bride seldom dreamed at all. She usually fell to sleep towards three in the morning, being by that time thoroughly tired out with thinking about her prince, her king, her demi-god—the lanky Merton, snoring in the back parlour. If there was any uneasy conscience in this humble residence, it was in the bosom of the wicked soldier. He might, perhaps, kick about his blankets, and moan, as he writhed and plunged his head into his pillow, perhaps, to find a comfortable place. But even he had no night or morning visions. He usually dreamed with the candle burning, and his eyes fixed on the curtain-rings, whilst he smoked his last cigar in bed. He was troubled with dreadful imaginings of the scene that would take place on the day when Bertha discovered that she had been tricked into being his mistress. The perspiration would make his forelocks cling, curling like feathers, to his forehead as he sketched to himself the tragedy that might follow.

He fancied he saw her seated in a corner of the room—a pose plastique of bitter sorrow—her eyes fixed with a terrible stare that looked through the walls in front, and far beyond the houses on the other side of the way. He might call to her, and she wouldn't hear him. If he touched her, she would turn round, like one just awakened, and then, her chin crumpling up and her lip quivering with anguish, gaze at him for a moment or two as if she had never before seen his face. He would suppose himself standing over her, telling her to bear her trial with fortitude and resignation, but, however eloquently he

besought her to "Never mind, love," or to "Be a woman, dear," no
answer was returned. He fancied he could hear the big tears fall
heavily on the little silk apron that fitted so jauntily round her slender
waist. If he went out, and returned ever so late at night, he would
find her—not in bed, but still in the same attitude. The servant
who followed him into the room would, as she sobbed, tell him how
her mistress had eaten nothing, and wouldn't have the candles, but
hid her head when lights were brought. Or may be he would have to
listen to some miserable tale of how a cup of tea had been placed near
her lips, and she never even tasted it, and although some was, with
the spoon, forced into her mouth, she wouldn't swallow it, but
allowed it to trickle on to her bosom. Then the captain, with a
sigh that blew away the tobacco fumes curling and twirling, would
utter, "It would drive me mad, unless I bolted away and left her.
Confound it! that tragic humbuggery wouldn't do with me, I can
tell her."

The convulsive manner in which he unlocked a private drawer and
took out a bottle of brandy; the peculiar shaking of the hand as he
poured out the stimulant; and the reckless manner in which he drank
off the raw spirit, were proof sufficient that he was terribly disturbed
by these forewarning phantasms. Brandy ever stood his friend in
these attacks. As the spirit worked, his pluck returned, and he
would fall asleep, calling himself an idiot and a weak fool, to suffer
mere mental hobgoblins to make a child of such a strong man as he
was.

It had been the captain's wish that, during his sojourn at Camberwell, he should remain hidden from the eyes of the world. In all he
did, he kept in view the chances of an action at law, and so conducted himself as to favour his own case, should any proceedings
follow his flight with Bertha. The captain liked the mystery of the
business. It made him fancy himself a grand personage. He noticed
that he grew fat for want of exercise, but yet he remained indoors.
How disgusted, then, he must have felt when, despite all his precau-
tions, he found himself one of the most talked about and closely
watched personages in the neighbourhood. He was enraged to find
that, whenever he ventured into the street, he became an object of
great interest to the neighbours. As he slammed the street door
after him, the servants at No. 6, next door, would either rush to the
windows, or race to the parlours and throw up the sash to stare after
him. At the butcher's, the young man and the young lady would
trip out into the street and gaze most impertinently. Women in shops
left their customers to catch a peep, and the lovely apprentices in
the millinery establishment nearly upset the bonnets exposed for sale
in their hurry to see the "capting at No. 5." Several times Crosier
felt his face become hot and red as these rude people whispered to
each other, "That's him!" and even if the criticism was favourable,
and consisted of "He's a niceish sort of chap," or (as at the bonnet
shop) of, "He's just my style of feller," it did not compensate for the

indignation caused by his notoriety. He was not long in accounting for these annoying impertinences. "Confound that Mother Hazlewood!" he growled—"confound the cunning old fox! She wants to force me into a marriage, does she? She thinks that by spreading about a report that I am courting Bertha, I shall be afraid to bolt with her. We shall see, old gal. It's a fight between us." He even distilled a few drops of consolation from these troubles, assuring himself that, for the future, he need feel no delicacy towards the poor mother, for it was clear she knew what his intentions were, and was speculating on his modesty and fear of public opinion. Now, the Lord Mayor of London was not more innocent of these attacks upon the parlour lodger than unfortunate Mrs. Hazlewood. Poor creature, she was ready to sink to the ground when, one day, Mrs. Gosport (where she dealt for the captain's sausages, bacon, &c.) wished her joy on the excellent match her daughter had made. She tried to deny it, but her nervousness so twisted her words, that her answer more than admitted the fact, and even led the garrulous shopkeeper to infer that the day had been fixed, and the cake ordered.

If the captain had calmly considered the matter, he would have soon discovered why the neighbours busied themselves so unceremoniously with his affairs. He had four or five times (but not until the new dresses had been made up) taken Bertha for a walk. As she leaned on his arm, his head was bent down to enable him to peep under her bonnet. He walked with his body twisted on one side. He spoke to her in rapid whispers, she having her eyes directed to the pavement, and never raising them but to look up in his face and smile, when he was lucky enough to utter something particularly delicious. Everybody who saw this couple concluded they were in love. It is much to the credit of everybody that they also concluded this couple were to be married.

How lovely did the maiden appear in her silken robe, velvet mantle, and dainty little bonnet! The enamoured officer felt giddy with rapture as with the gentlest pressure her arm rested on his. The gown rustling with each step affected his nerves worse than the scratching of slate-pencil. He watched her little feet bob in and out from under the waving flounces until he felt giddy. He took her small hand—made smaller by the tight kid glove—and said innumerable playful things as he laid it on his own big palm, that held it easily as a dish does a chop. He called it "an ugly little paw," "a stupid, useless little daddle," and, with a miraculous softness about the eyes, would inquire "when that silly little hand was to be his?" How happy these walks made him. He watched the reflection of Bertha's figure in the shop-windows as they passed. He saw fellows lean from their cabs, and turn round in their saddles to stare at his little beauty. Some impudent scoundrels would walk in front of this couple, looking round at every other step at the abashed angel. He heard many of them cry out, "By Jove! what a pretty girl!" And although the rage of the bold captain was such that his fists rolled up tight as hedgehogs, yet he was secretly pleased that the world should so unmistakably approve of and envy his choice. On one occasion, Charley Sutton passed the couple as they were sauntering down Regent Street. Crosier shook his hand, and said, languidly, " How-dedoo ? " a recognition which Sutton acknowledged by raising his eye-glass, and staring his hardest at Bertha. He did not recognize the little servant-girl. In a letter he sent Crosier a few days afterwards, he asked him bluntly " where the devil he picked up the little blood he was trotting out ? " adding, in his strange style, that she was " a regular petrifier, very choice and becoming, and, indeed, he might add, the slap-up perfect ginger." The captain smiled as he read these lines. He felt as if he had been avenged. " They pretended to laugh at me, the fools ! " he cried ; " they dared to sneer at my judgment, the donkeys ! Wait till they see her at the Opera, in a low-necked dress, with a wreath round her head, and just one diamond bracelet. The idiots, I'll pay them out ! "

The captain, whenever he was alone with Bertha, never chatted about any other subject than their approaching wedding. He would ask her in the merriest manner not to weep at the altar, and entreat her to give out the awful " Yes " in a bold, joyful tone. He even made her rehearse to him her conduct before the priest, uttering in a ludicrously gruff voice the question of " Will you, Bertha Hazlewood, accept this horribly spooney wretch to be ? " &c., &c. ; and insist upon her replying, " Yes, if you please," or " I should think so," or some other absurdity, which made the supposed bride blush and titter. But if ever the unfortunate Mrs. Hazlewood dared to indulge in any of her maternal jokes upon the forthcoming event, her wit was speedily checked by the son-in-law's frigid replies. If, as she left the room, she threw out hints about their preferring to be alone, and bobbed her head, or looked sly, the captain would coldly answer that he saw no reason why " Mrs. Hazlewood should deprive him of her delight-ful company." Once the mamma caught Bertha reading the advertisements of marriages in the " Times," and playfully quizzed the girl about the delight somebody would feel when a certain announcement appeared in the paper. The captain gave her such a haughty look, that in her alarm the poor creature, who was making tea, poured the whole of the fragrant decoction into the slop-basin, mistaking it for a cup. That evening he told Bertha he considered her mother's jests " highly indecent and vulgar." Not that he was really disgusted, but he was determined in no way to admit to any-body, who could be brought forward as a witness, that he had either by word or gesture given any promise of marriage.

" No, no, not a bit of it," thought he ; " not so green as that."

It cut Bertha to the heart to hear this king of hers speak in ungenerous, not to say rude, terms of her poor mother. He was con-stantly reminding the girl that she was never to repeat to mamma any of the fond conversations they held together. " It isn't her fault, poor creature, but her ignorance and stupidity are most offensive to me," he would give as his reason for desiring this secrecy, whilst the daughter stared at him in wonder, almost doubting her own ears. By-and-by he would compensate the outraged child by informing her of the provision he intended to make for the mother, fixing her mainten-ance at sixty pounds per annum and a comfortable cottage. The captain, seeing that no great opposition was offered to his plans upon Bertha, grew bolder in his behaviour to the parent. He several times hinted to his angel that it was high time she should give up any share in the household management. He told her that the heat of the kitchen fire was deleterious to the skin of the face, and requested her to leave all the cooking to the old lady. He occasion-ally examined her hands, saying he would not permit her to spoil their whiteness by housemaid's work. He even lectured the damsel on her want of "proper spirit" in rendering any assistance whatever to her mother. "You should remember, dearest," he said, chiding her, "that you will shortly bear my name, and this hand" (looking at it closely) "should come to me unsullied by the most vulgar of labour. If your mother had any sense or delicacy she would under-stand these things, without my being forced to speak on what is, naturally, a painful subject. Pray speak to Mrs. Hazlewood, and inform her of my wishes." If he thought Bertha cruel enough to do this he was mistaken. She would have preferred deposing "her king" to deserting her doting, gentle parent. After hearing such unkind words, she would wonder "why Merton was so altered of late," and what her mother could have done to offend him; but she never shocked the old nurse by repeating her lodger's injunctions.

Despair had the effect of brightening the captain's wits, giving to his leaden intellect a silvery polish. He laid him down on the sofa and invented fresh snares for the unprotected maiden. In the present emergency he resolved on writing letters to himself, in a dis-guised hand, which—telling her they were received from his home—he would read to her, to prove that his parents were violently opposed to their son's union with one so lowly born, and that the only chance of his being united to her was by a clandestine marriage. One great advantage of this forged-letter process was—according to this base man—that he could puff and glorify both himself and the worshipped one of his wickedness.

Each epistle took him many hours to perfect. The handwriting was carefully disguised. The thick down-strokes of his ordinary caligraphy became thin ones in the counterfeit, "t" and "l" were decreased in size, and every other letter of the alphabet artfully altered. On the day the first of these deceits arrived per post, Crosier did all he could to force Bertha into the trap. He first rang the bell for the girl, and when she entered the room she found him sighing and slapping his forehead with good hard knocks. When asked if he was ill, he rolled his eyes, and replied, "Yes, ill indeed—sick at heart!" From bashfulness, most likely, Bertha, instead of putting any more questions, merely stared with her large eyes stretched to twice their size with sympathy. As this silence did not suit the captain's plot, he murmured forth, "Why did they send that letter—that cruel letter!" On this Bertha was forced to ask, "What letter?" The question did not clear the mystery much, for Crosier replied, "That cruel letter which has cut me to the very soul!" Then, fearing lest she might leave the room, and so spoil the affair, he drew the girl close to him, and, swearing no one should ever part them as long as he had health and strength to resist, told her, with an effort, that he had written to a dear friend, imploring him to sound his mother and father on the subject of his marriage with one far beneath him in fortune, birth, and position. "I told him, beloved one," added the captain, gazing on the girl with a fond, sickly expression of eye, "that you were an angel on earth; that your beautiful face was a greater treasure than mere worldly riches; and I added that the noblest born could not be more virtuous than my Bertha" (and, thought he to himself, "That is painfully true at any rate"). To see him fall-to again banging his poor forehead and casting up his eyeballs as if he were trying to look backwards, prepared the girl for the most terrible news, and made her tremble pitifully. As he read aloud extracts from this dreadful letter, every word seemed to hit her. The cunning fellow pretended to make mistakes whilst hunting after the particular paragraph, and so managed to introduce several passages highly com plimentary to the maiden, and which, having the appearance of being the confession of a secret correspondence, did not fail to move her heart with excessive love and gratitude.

He standing by the window, she trembling by the door; the reading commenced: "'You do, indeed, speak in glowing terms,'" mumbled the captain, "'of the lovely being who has inspired in you so honourable a love—' No, that is not the passage," he muttered, turning the leaf; "ah, here it is: 'You describe her as the most fair and perfect of her sex, and your manly views on marriage—' No, that isn't the place; ah, here it is: 'Your mother, when I spoke to her on the subject, became excessively indignant, and declared that, if a son of hers dared to bring a kitchen-wench into the family, he must do so at his peril; and, perhaps, when starving in a garret, he would regret having sought in the arms of a serving-maid the love a mother would henceforth refuse.'" Not daring to turn his head to see what the effect of this letter had been, the captain assumed a fit of rage and threw the epistle into the fire, calling it an inhuman and wicked performance. He waited some time for Bertha either to faint or burst into tears, but as she remained silent, he was forced to turn towards her. Her face was crimson with indignant blushes, but she seemed collected, and firm of limb.

"Your mother is right," she said, as he stared inquiringly at her, "I am punished for my presumption." He tried to prevent her leaving the room, but, although he upset two chairs, she was gone before he could seize her arm.

The girl went upstairs to weep, and he plumped into his arm-chair to think. He admitted the attempt had failed. The wording was too strong. He banged the fire-irons about with vexation. She would be afraid to come near him. Of course, she didn't like such name-calling—who would? The only good thing was, he had burnt the letter. That couldn't tell tales, or bear witness. "Always burn your letters," murmured the captain.

He set to work writing another letter. It was a milder style of authorship. On the second day it was delivered at Camberwell, and, as Crosier had not seen Bertha for two days, he sent to her, request-ing an interview. She came, but so pale in face, and so dejected in manner, that he was really shocked and pained. Her eyes were crimson with weeping, and by the hurried manner in which the hair was tucked behind her ears, he saw she had been thinking of nothing but her sorrow. Being fond of stimulants, he insisted upon her instantly taking a "restorative of sherry," and, though the glass rattled against her teeth as she raised her trembling hand to her lips, he begged that its contents should be swallowed, even if it choked her. But what did her more good than his wine was the happy expression of his face. "We shall have no more saucy letters, dear Bertha," he said, kneeling by her side, and as he wrote them himself he was well enabled to make good the promise. "I warrant they will be civil enough now. My little queen shall not be made to cry for nothing. Every tear shall be avenged with a shower." As she tried to smile, he continued: "Cheer up, my pretty May-queen! laugh again, darling flower! there is good news this time!" And producing his forgery he opened it. "Read this, dear, with your own pretty eyes. See what Alfred writes me: 'If, as you say, you cannot live without your beloved Bertha, take my advice and get married privately. Your mother has already greatly changed her tone. She loves you dearly, and would soon pardon any act you might commit.' Do you hear that, dearest? Yes, yes! that is what we will do. I will buy the license, and we will be married at once. When they see my sweet wife's pretty face, I am sure to be forgiven for loving you, for they will all love you as fondly as I do." But Bertha shook her head. She began to sob again, and, though he wiped up the tears as they trickled down her cheeks, she would not be consoled.

Whilst matters were at this crisis, a real letter arrived for Captain Merton Crosier, whilst he was waiting for the post to bring him another of his fictitious ones. He had resolved to expedite matters by a line or two from his mother herself, half-assenting to the match, and had passed the day before in forging as well as he could that lady's handwriting. Anxiously was he looking out of the window to catch sight of the ten o'clock postman, when to his astonishment he beheld Mr. Edward Cutler, his man, hurrying at the top of his speed towards No. 5. "Now, how the devil did that fellow discover my hiding-place?" thought the captain, ducking his head. On came the valet with rapid strides. The master, through the wire blind, saw him unhesitatingly ascend the steps, and heard him knock as rapidly and violently as if a steam-gun were being exhibited. "That fellow is sacked to-morrow!" vowed the master, boiling over with passion.

All his rage, all thoughts about his hiding-place, all his vows of vengeance were forgotten when Mr. Cutler entered the parlour and handed him two letters; one with "Immediate" on the outside, and the other with a deep black border round the envelope. After he had opened the first he scarcely needed to break the seal of the second—the black edging told the news. In the one, he was besought, if he wished to see his mother alive, to start instantly for Swanborough. In the other, his father informed him, with stinging coldness, that the mother had expired asking for her absent son. Scarcely had he recovered from the terrible surprise of this news than the postman delivered the letter he had forged in his dead mother's handwriting. Without even opening it, to the astonishment of Mr. Cutler, he flung the epistle into the fire.

"How long have those letters been delivered?" asked Crosier, but in a mournful voice, as if all his manhood had left him.

"Four days, sir," replied the man, frightened by the ghastly face of the questioner. "I sought for you everywhere—in the Haymarket and at the clubs—for I knew Mr. Nathaniel's writing; but you were nowhere to be heard of. At last Miss Tommy thought you was here, and—"

"Go home and prepare my trunks. I must leave town instantly."

Standing in the hall, Mrs. Hazlewood heard this conversation. She hurried off to tell Bertha that something dreadful had happened to the captain. Shortly afterwards, when the bell rang, both these women, as if they did not dare to be alone, entered the parlour together. He had been weeping bitterly, and, although he had bathed his face in water to remove all traces of his grief, his eyes were swollen and inflamed. Then did these women, sympathizing with the trouble of their dear friend, begin also to shed tears. He told them as well as he could speak, the terrible news he had received. His voice was strangely altered, and had become hoarse and short-breathed. The women were fearfully frightened, and stood close together, as if they expected the sad tale was not half finished.

The mother, wiping her eyes on her apron, was despatched for a cab. The daughter, left alone with Crosier, advanced to his side, and laying her hand on his arm, said, in a tone of great agony, "It was I who caused your mother's death! This marriage broke her heart. God forgive me! I wish I had died in her stead!"

Whether it was that grief for his loss had crushed every other feeling in his heart, or whether he had not courage to enter into the details of the deceit he had practised, most certain is it that he had the cruelty to leave the house without making even an attempt to undeceive the poor girl. She construed his silence into a tacit acknowledgment that her self-accusings were just. For days and nights did she pine and mourn over the life she imagined she had destroyed, She began to hate herself, and curse her pretty face for the evil it had wrought. Her poor mother would miss her in the day-time, and hunt through room after room, calling aloud for Bertha, to find her at last huddled up in some corner, with her head resting upon her knees, dreaming with open, straining eyes of the loss she had brought upon her dear Merton. Sometimes, at night, the mother would wake, and discover the girl had risen. But she knew where to find her, for Bertha had crept downstairs to fling herself upon the bed in which he had slept, and pray there that he might forgive her the misery she had caused. The house No. 5 became a miserable habitation, such as neither first, second, nor ground-floor lodger would have stopped a day in, and all because Captain Crosier had not courage enough to speak some half-dozen words of truth.

By the death of his mother, Crosier became a gentleman of inde-pendent fortune. The deceased lady's jointure of £400 a year descended to himself and his sister Helen, but by her will he inherited the sum of nearly £5000, moneys which had at different times been bequeathed her by her relations. The sorrow of the son became more intense when he discovered to what an "amount" his departed parent had loved him. He spoke feelingly of the loss he had suffered, and, even when he was calculating mentally what the total of his debts might be, his grief seemed uncontrollable. Simple Helen forgot to cry when brother Merton began to groan and sob. She said pretty, tender consolations about the miseries of this life and the blessings beyond the grave, and used her utmost to check the bitter wailings of the soldier brother. But he was touched to the quick with the loving kindness of the special bequest, and his spirit refused all comfort. Nathaniel Crosier, banker, argued with his broken-hearted son, but to no avail, so he drank his port wine after dinner in solitude, and never bothered his head about where Merton had gone. Yet of the two, Nathaniel Crosier was the more stricken down by the blow. The old man spoke little, but he pined sorely for the lost wife. He grew day by day more and more morose and taciturn, whilst Merton gradually recovered his health and spirits, and was, before a month had passed, in a fit state to write several letters to town, one of which made Mr. Dancer of Holborn very lively, whilst · another did more good to the conscience-tormented Bertha than if fifty physicians had held a mighty consultation in her case. It was a short, rapidly scrawled note, but it contained a wonderful prescrip-tion in these words : "I find my poor mother was not, after all, so much opposed as we imagined to our marriage. Her death was caused by the rupture of a blood-vessel. I enclose you a remittance. She lingered for only two days. Be kind enough to see that my room is prepared, for I shall be in town shortly. I now, alas! know how heavy is the loss of a fond parent. What can replace a mother's love ? Send your answer by Cutler, who brings this."

It seemed as if the best response the captain could find to his ques-tion of "What can replace a mother's love ?" was to fall in love with

somebody else. After a month's absence he returned to London, and
drove direct to Camberwell. Here he passed his time in listening as
patiently as he could to Mrs. Hazlewood's solemn consolations, and
in endeavouring to persuade the dejected Bertha that she was in no way
accountable for the family bereavement. He was delighted to find
that sorrow had had a softening influence over the maiden's heart.
Out of respect to the memory of his mother, he thought it would
seem heartless, if he commenced his love-making until the edges of
his mourning suit evinced something like wear and tear. He even
suited his voice to his sable garments, imparting a mournful tone to
his sentences, which convinced all hearers that grief was in his heart.
It was not until some three months had crept past, that he allowed
his lips to utter fond expressions. Even then he pressed his suit in
doleful accents, making his affectionate requests in a melodious
cadence of sad suffering such as no tender-hearted maiden would wish
by cruel refusals to increase or aggravate. He was enchanted at his
success, and persuaded himself that, provided he allowed some six
months or so to elapse before he pressed the girl to elope with him,
there would be no impropriety in the act as far as mourning a mother's
loss was concerned.

Six months are a long period of time. For fear the girl should grow
nervous and withdraw her consent, he endeavoured to secure her
affections by divers little acts of great kindness and generosity. He
caused his will to be drawn up, and, when everything was prepared,
read it over to Bertha. He bequeathed all he possessed to her, and
named her as his sole executrix and legatee. He signed the deed
in her presence, and had the signature properly witnessed, by a
policeman, who charged one shilling as his fee, and the old nurse,
who shed tears of gratitude. There was no great importance to be
attached to this act, for, as he very well knew, a will is destroyed in
much less time than it is prepared. Nevertheless, he made a great
fuss about this ceremony, and assured Bertha—who, from a childish
idea that men never make their wills until on the point of death,
imagined her Merton intended to quit this life—that as she was to
replace a mother's love, so she ought to receive a mother's legacy. He
talked too much about his mother to please honest, sensible persons.
But Bertha and her mother were both under the influence of a sentimental fit, and considered these allusions to his parent as beautifully
filial, and extremely affecting. We know the captain better than they
did, simple creatures.

He was for ever impressing on the girl, by making her presents
necessary to her future state, that it was now too late to break off the
match. He talked with her about the printing of her wedding-cards
and the ordering of the cake, although, as their match was to be a
stolen one, he never intended to be at the expense of either. His
object was to be continually talking about the marriage, and allow
her no time for thought or repentance. He had plotted with her
how they were to leave the house. He was to send her wardrobe to

Harley Street in his boxes. The shopkeepers where extensive purchases were made had instructions to leave their bulky parcels at the
same address. The mother would suspect nothing if she saw no pre-
paration for the wedding. He was to leave the house the day before
on some important business or other, and she was to join him early
the next morning. Then to the Registrar's, and afterwards to the
north to enjoy the honeymoon. "But," added the captain, "we
will not break poor mamma's heart by keeping her in suspense; you
shall send her one of your sweet little letters, telling her that you
are right and happy, and that sort of thing, and entreating her to·
keep the business secret." How kind and considerate he was; he
thought of everybody but himself, dear man.

We consider it to be the duty of a young gentleman, even if he
does not very deeply mourn the loss of his mother, at any rate to
assume a certain show of grief for the bereavement. The captain
had fixed six months as the period his affliction was to last. By that
time he calculated all his tears would be expended. But before half
that time had expired his lachrymal ducts were as dry as gas-pipes.
He could hardly persuade himself he had not been an orphan for
years. He could not understand why the crape on his hat should
wear so well and remain so stiff and black. Every day he referred to
his almanac to see how long he must yet wait before Bertha should
deliver herself into his loving custody. He was as impatient for this
great holiday as an Indian boy who has been at school all his life.
He prepared everything. He remained patiently for an entire hour
in a cab at the door of an outfitting establishment whilst she was
inside selecting the trousseau. On another occasion—the evening was
very dark and looked like rain, so that few people were abroad—he
escorted Bertha to an eminent jeweller's in Regent Street, to purchase the wedding-ring. He did not tell the girl the purport of their
walk until he was close to the shop. Then, in a husky voice, he tried
to be poetically affecting on the subject of the "link that was to bind
them together for life." He never was much of a hand at sentiment,
and any other girl but Bertha would have laughed in his face as he
stammered out, "As that ring, my sweetest, is to typify, as it were,
our loves, I should like you to select a good, solid, strong one; and
also, my beauty, when once I have placed it on your finger, never on
any account take it off again; even wash your hands with it on. Do
you understand, my dearest treasure?" Bertha listened to all this
twaddle with as solemn a countenance as if it had been spoken from
a pulpit. She was, indeed, rather affected by the sentiment.

Outside the jeweller's shop, the captain felt very nervous and
uneasy. He was nearly on the point of asking Bertha to make the
purchase alone. A man, he thought, looks such a fool buying a
wedding-ring, and everybody grins at him. He darted in, dragging
"his sweetest" after him in a manner that would have made many
believe that this goldsmith and jeweller advanced money on certain
securities besides vending precious ornaments. As the nervous

couple stood before the counter, they had to undergo another distressing trial. The captain tried to assume an air as if he had only come there for the fun of the thing, and expected Bertha to reply to the man's question of " What can I show you ? " whilst she, unfortunate child, was so overwhelmed by her bashfulness, that she left it to her dashing lover to give the necessary orders. The captain scowled and coloured, fiddled with his eye-glass, and bit his moustache, but eventually had to gasp out the words, " Rings—wedding ones." This was spoken in an undertone, as if he were confiding a secret.

Unfortunately, the tray in which these plain gold ornaments were kept was exhibited in the window, adorned with white satin bows and other chaste decorations. Some dirty little boys were idling their time, discussing, in vulgar language, which trinket they would most prefer as a present, when the tray of wedding-rings was lifted away from under their small noses, which they had flattened into whiteheart cherries by pressing against the glass. These dirty children also saw a lady and gentleman inside, and quickly guessed what they had come about. Their laughter and rude remarks attracted several other persons to the window, and a complete audience was formed to witness the conduct of the lovers. All this the captain witnessed. He heard the children outside prattling about " That's him who's to have her," and knew it was to him the infants referred. He understood that the playful remark of " Her hand's skinnier than my sister's," was meant for Bertha. He didn't like it, and asked Bertha to make haste. In vain did the jeweller observe " that the lady had such a remarkably small finger ; " it was no consolation, for the glass window seemed nebulous with eyes, all staring at him with impudent expressions. The language of those eyes was rude and personal. Every ring that was tried on Crosier declared would do very well, and, had not the shopman objected to the fit, he would have accepted a golden circle that dangled as loosely on the girl's finger as a hoop on its stick. At last the exact size was found ; it was weighed and paid for; and the captain, at a brisk trot, left the shop.

Dreadfully annoyed by this humiliating trial, the captain could scarcely speak civilly to her whom, but a few minutes before, he had styled " his treasure." He walked along sulking. " I was a fool ever to mention anything about the ring," he soliloquized. " What the deuce does she want with a ring ? I hate such tomfoolery. Throwing sixteen shillings away—for what?—a thing she will never be entitled to wear. Much better have bought herself a pair of boots." Yet, despite these extraordinary remarks, when Bertha, that very evening, whilst making his strong coffee, asked him (mother was downstairs) if he liked this much-abused ring, he tried it on her finger, and, then kissing her hand, exclaimed with rapture, " Bertha, I worship it, as an emblem of yourself, for its purity and simplicity. On such a hand, it does indeed appear lovely." And he fell to kissing her fingers as if he could have eaten them, the ring included.

CHAPTER XIII.

SOME OF THE ADVENTURES WHICH BEFELL MONSIEUR EMILE
VAUTRIN DURING TEN YEARS OF HIS LIFE.

THE heading to this chapter is so startling that, without explanation, the reader might feel inclined to treat it like a dirty puddle, and just skip over it. The idea of having to devour ten years of adventure at one sitting is depressing and unnatural. The dish is so enormous that it sickens the appetite, and even curiosity's capacious stomach feels overladen before a single sentence has been tasted. But we intend to grind down and knead this long period of time, so that these ten years shall make as thin a slice in the loaf of this story as if they had been so many ears of corn.

Emile Vautrin was a reckless, unprincipled man. He might have carried his virtues in his snuff-box, and there would have been plenty of room left for the rappee. He thought no more of taking a new name when his old one was worn out than he did of taking a newer hat or a fresher umbrella whenever a favourable opportunity presented itself. On one occasion, as we have seen, he had, in a free and easy manner, unauthorized by any government, joined the army as Colonel of the 11ᵉ Léger; on another he had entered into commerce as one Coquardeau, a clerk; and, as a crowning touch, he had turned philanthropist, calling himself Chose. Whenever one cognomen was a little out at elbows, or spoken of too familiarly by the police, it was changed for a better, fresher, and less celebrated appellation. No godfathers were troubled to attend such christenings; nobody became security for future sins; and a petit verre was the baptismal font.

Usually Emile Vautrin led an ignoble and vicious life, caring no more for the eye of the law than he did for the eye of a potato. If that coach and four which can be driven through every Act of Parliament had been in want of a coachman, this desperado was the man of men to handle the reins. He was what the Americans call "a bad egg."

Yet there were moments when Vautrin complained bitterly of the ill-treatment he had suffered in the world. This unjust man, who had wronged so many, had an idea that he had been driven into his reckless course of vice by the wrongs heaped upon him by his enemies. When in the fourth stage of drunkenness, or depressed by ill luck, he would talk by the hour, and grind his teeth, over the injuries that had crushed him. He once informed an eminent advocate, who undertook some little law business, "that his natural was good," but, added the client, "I have been made what I am. My guilt be on

z

their shoulders. They massacred the wife I adored, they robbed me of her fortune, and they stole from me my beloved child. They left me the miserable being you behold." At the door of Nathaniel Crosier of Swanborough did Vautrin deposit the big bundle of his crimes, trusting that it would trip up that respectable gentleman whenever he might set out on his way to heaven.

There was some little truth, and a great deal of imagination, in the Frenchman's complainings. His sentimental raving about his wife and child was mere bombast, but the lost fortune he wailed over was as true as arithmetic. Bitterly did he regret it. Nathaniel Crosier had married a Miss Merton, and father-in-law, not liking son-in-law, had insisted that the bride's fortune—a pretty little income of about four hundred pounds—should be settled on her as tight as lawyer's pens and red tape could bind it. After the mother's death, the children—if any—were to inherit this jointure. If the children died, leaving husbands or (legitimate) issue, these were again to become possessed. So it stands to reason that Vautrin had a distinct and perfect claim to one-third of these yearly four hundred pounds. Boldly and with much noise would he have demanded justice in the English law courts, but that the little affair of impersonating the Colonel of the 11ᵉ Léger rendered such an experiment hazardous and unprofitable. He had peculiar notions about the value of liberty. Besides, gruel was his aversion.

We have often heard it asserted that thieves are thieves because they delight in their daring life. Many are of opinion that a pickpocket, earning thirty shillings weekly at his illegal craft, would, if his honesty were better paid, refuse to quit his wickedness. This is mere ill-natured talk. Nobody would have been more delighted than our Frenchman to become respectable, had his virtue been priced at even the value of a cigar above the returns of his roguery. We do not mean to say that he would have worked more laboriously, or risen one hour earlier, or toiled one hour later, for the advantage of being considered an honourable man. But, provided the exertion imposed and the earnings were to be in both cases similar, Vautrin would have embraced the respectable in preference to the disreputable life. He had made many attempts to steady himself in society. With the plunder obtained from his "Colonel du 11ᵉ Léger" performance he vowed to reform, and, if it answered, repent. On his return to Paris he had speculated in an eating-house, spending his capital of about three thousand francs in fitting up a cheap restaurant in the Quartier Latin. He announced dinner, consisting of four plats and a dessert, at one franc ahead. The carte du jour always contained "filet de bœuf" and "gibelotte de lapin." The salle à manger was not a sumptuously-furnished apartment, but it served. The rush-covered stools were comfortable enough, and the deal tables looked neat, and occasionally, when hidden under the cotton napkins, clean. A row of hat-pegs, a crockeryware stove, and a few looking-glasses were even more than the one-franc customers expected or needed.

They cared little about ornamentation provided the portions were large. The establishment of Monsieur Tinton (he had again changed his name) soon won the esteem of the students. His "bif-teks" were tres solides, and gifted with the distinguishing characteristics of caoutchouc, being both indigestible and elastic. The medical or legal student who ate one of those steaks might possibly suffer from indigestion, but certainly hunger would not for that day again trouble him. The gibelottes de lapin were also favourably received by the customers, and the absence of more than one head in each portion termed honourable treatment. But, despite the twopence-halfpenny charged for wine (when required), despite the weakness of the Julienne soup, the scantiness of the salad, and the one apple for dessert, the restaurant, to Vautrin's sincere regret, was a failure. He again vowed it was useless trying to be honest, and, secretly selling off his stools, tables, and stewpans, decamped before the landlord had time to ask for the rent.

Then he came to England—the richest country in the world, as he called it. Once more he succeeded in filling his pockets, his commercial speculation, as agent for the firm of Jonkopings, Tandstickor and Co., being eminently prosperous. He made Irish linens refund what he had lost by beef-steaks. Had the climate of Great Britain been more genial, and the amusements of the metropolis more various, or its Sabbath more gay, Monsieur Vautrin asserted that he would have permanently settled in our monster city. He liked the business methods and the great facilities "paper" offered an ingenious merchant. But his health suffering, and Inspector Gyves becoming alarmingly alert, he once more asked for a passport, and departed.

Again he determined on giving honesty a fair chance. People spoke so loudly about the better policy of integrity that he could not imagine it was done expressly to deceive him. He had about £800 to speculate with, and if plain dealing would give him cent. per cent., it was, he considered, as good an investment as any other. This time he opened a café estaminet. It was richly decorated with pier-glasses and marble-topped tables. The velvet couches were as broad as beds. The comptoir was fanciful and elegant, with its gilding and inlaid woods. The two plated urns in which the sous given to the garcons were deposited shone like lamps. A mountain of portions of sugar sparkled in crystalline purity at each extremity. The young lady who presided on this throne was fascinatingly attired, and her beauty soon made an impression upon the hearts of the coffee, beer, and eau-sucree drinkers. In addition to this, Monsieur Everard (Vautrin thought his new name had an innocent and poetic sound) mounted "trois billards"—noble tables, nearly ten feet in length, with ormolu lions' heads instead of pockets, and highly-carved legs. Before the garcons were engaged, express stipulations were made as to the number of clean aprons they were to wear weekly.

Soon the Cafe Mirabeau began to be talked of. The lumps of

sugar were reported to be sublimely generous in their dimensions; the coffee was declared to be "du veritable moka;" and the cognac spoken of as being soft as satin. The two garcons in their jackets and pumps found the sous given them mounting up. The cry of "Ver-r-r-sez" might have been heard on the other side of the street. The customers for du noir, choppes, and canettes increased daily. The bains de pied—as the overflowings of the cup into the saucer are called—were overwhelmingly liberal. The Cafe du Roi, higher up, had to retain its customers by lowering the price of the demi-tasse one sou, and the Cafe de la Reine, lower down, tried to avoid insolvency by turning its petits verres into large ones.

Presently the Cafe Mirabeau had its habitues who came there night after night, wet or fine. A pipe-rack was mounted to hold the "clays" these constant customers were colouring. Now men began to make appointments "chez Everard," and spend the evening together emptying choppes of beer and playing at billiards "who should pay." The rattle of the dominoes on the marble tops of the tables was like the clatter of plates in a scullery. There were little square boards covered with green baize for card-players, and many whist parties passed the entire day over the fascinating game, wearing out a pack of the flimsy paper cards by the constant wetting of the thumb whilst dealing. Every paper published in Paris was taken in, and fastened to the razor-strop-looking holder—excellent preservers of the journal, but rather too much like perusing a flag, to be pleasant to the reader.

In a short time, Monsieur Everard became a great man in the "quartier." He had always longed to be respected in some "quartier" or other. The boulanger, who kept the iron-railed bread shop next door, the epicier in his grocer's shop opposite, the marchand de nouveautes, the marchand de vins, all the neighbours, in fact, spoke of him as a "good child" and "a very amiable boy." He never refused to give a customer, who had even twice left his purse at home, credit till better times. He never ceased to smile unless it was to restrain the love-making of some impertinent student whispering at the "comptoir" to Mademoiselle Constance. Even then he spoke mildly and frankly. "Let us see," he would say; "let us finish these follies. Her father is one of the old of the old who followed Napoleon. Let us respect the only child of a brave." When he joined in a game of billiards with his more cherished customers, he would delight all with the quaint phrases he used. A ball under the cushion was said to "manger du merinos." He would with each stroke request his ball to go "vigoureusement, ma belle," or to "lever ses pattes." When the stakes played for were trivial, he managed after a desperately close game to lose, but on other occasions he was wonderfully fortunate. "A-t-il de la chance, ce diable d'Everard!" his opponents would cry out when he made eight or nine cannons running.

He might have done well at this estaminet, but his gipsy nature would not allow him to remain long at any quiet occupation. It was at this time that he had written to Mr. Nathan, of Lyon's Inn, to find out his son Philip and send him over to France. If the boy could have been discovered, perhaps the father would have remained steady at his coffee-selling, but, annoyed at the failure of Mr. Nathan's search, Everard, alias Vautrin, took a dislike to the jog-trot estaminet, and disposed of the business.

He had always complained that his life had been a failure simply for the want of a little ready money to go to work with. He would talk of the "voleurs" on the Bourse, and with bitter scorn taunt them that, with their chances, they did not do more. It really seemed as if there were some truth in his boastings. A week after he had sold his cafe, Everard had started "the Grand National Marriage Insurance Company." What he made by it, he never confessed. He was, how-ever, sufficiently enriched to become a large speculator on the Bourse and one of the little kings of the Passage de l'Opera. A few more lucky hits, and his vagrant boy, Phil, might have been a dandy, a "rentier." But it was the old story. He realized a fortune in four transactions, and lost it by the fifth. In his mad endeavour to re-establish himself, he parted with every sixpence, and eventually did something or other which was considered, even by the frequenters of that national gambling-house, to be swindling, and the gates of this paradise of fools were closed on the "coquin."

Without even a bad shilling in his pocket, Everard changed his name to Boustache, and began the world afresh. His old friends, the wine sellers of the Temple, received him again to their hearts and back parlours, upbraiding him slightly for his two years' absence, and perhaps delighted that, after all his grand doings, he was no better off than themselves. This was the bitter winter and discontent of Vau-trin's life. He remembered to his dying hour the hardships he was forced to endure. His brain was so fogged, and his heart so dejected with his failure, that he could devise no scheme to raise himself above the vulgar pickpocketing herd. To prevent himself from starving, he turned vendor of tooth-powder and square tablets for removing grease from cloth. Those who bought the powder had the tablet given them for nothing.

For the entire summer, with his tray of merchandise before him, he took up his post on the Boulevard du Temple. He had composed an address to the people, which collected a vast mob, and always delighted his audience. He prefaced the exhibition of the marvellous effects of the tooth-powder in these words :—

"This specific, being both odontalgic and balsamic, is a sovereign remedy for the caries, canker, and corrosion of the teeth. It was presented to a gentleman of distinguished character in the highest circles by his Excellency the Ambassador of Persia. Its virtues shall be proved by public experiment. . . . Come here, ignoble boy ! Behold the teeth of this infant are of the most perfect black. You place a little of the specific on a brush in this manner—you humect with water. Do not imagine that the water is prepared; water, the first that comes to hand, water hard or soft, from the cistern or the barrel, or, as in this instance, water from the gutter. You rub the teeth and thus render them whiter than enamel, strengthening the gums and soothing the nerves." Then he would scrub at the unfortunate boy's mouth, and, as the powder would have served equally well for cleaning knives, it did certainly in a remarkably short time grind away some of the dark stains from the teeth. Whilst this operation was proceeding, Monsieur Vautrin would exclaim, partially to drown the cries of the suffering lad, " The price of my specific is only five sous the box! dedicated to the Peuple Fr-r-r-rancais, at five sous the box ! "

He was a patient, much-enduring man, this Vautrin, gifted with the indomitable perseverance of a caterpillar, which, however often it is knocked down from the stem of a tree, will again and again commence to climb upwards. When at the bottom of the ladder, Vautrin was always thinking of the topmost round. When he had picked up enough money with his tooth-powder to enable him to travel to England, he gave up dentistry, and, with a forged passport, left Paris. He had no definite object in coming to London beyond that of plundering whomever and wherever he could. The first day he arrived, he experimented on the memory of the police, by entering the Bow Street Court as a spectator. He was delighted to find that neither inspectors nor men had the least suspicion of him. He had left the metropolis in a black wig and heavy whiskers, and he returned with flaxen locks and an elegant moustache.

It was shortly after Vautrin's return that a great many letters were sent to the "Times," complaining of the darkness of the metropolitan roads. Applications were constantly being made to the Hammersmith magistrate by gentlemen and ladies who had been followed and robbed by a tall, powerful man, who wore a comforter so arranged that it masked his face. His method was to creep after a foot passenger until he or she had reached a portion of the road where, in consequence of the discontinuance of the gas-lamps, the darkness favoured the robbery ; and then, having pinioned the arms of the victim, a pocket-handkerchief was thrust into the mouth, and the pockets rifled without dread of any interference. One of these complainants had lost thirteen sovereigns, another his gold watch and a pocket-book of bank-notes. In all these robberies the tall man was assisted by a shorter and apparently younger companion. In one evening it was calculated that they became unlawfully possessed of some fifty pounds' worth of property. The Hammersmith police, the moment the robberies were committed, became very active. But the man and his associate had left the neighbourhood before the constables attempted to seize them. They were next heard of at Brixton, after that at Hackney, and subsequently at Peckham. They always seemed to post themselves at a short distance from the tavern where the omnibuses stopped, and, having then fixed upon the victim to be plucked, to follow him until he reached some secluded, dark spot favourable to the plucking.

This tall man was Vautrin. Who do you think the associate was? No other than Jack Drake, the quondam captain of the Crossing Sweepers' gang. The Frenchman had picked him up at a low twopenny lodging-house in Gun Yard, Whitechapel, and tempted him into joining his foot-padding expeditions. The Duck was in a terrible state of destitution, and the prospect of being clothed and fed soon placed him in Vautrin's power. Up to that time he had been a mere prig, purloining bacon, and wrenching off brass bell-pulls to sell as old metal. The idea of being a highwayman had something grand in it. Purses were better plunder than the scraps on a butcher's stall. It was like a militiaman entering a Queen's regiment.

Vautrin had promised to make a fine fellow of the Duck, and, as far as clothing was concerned, kept his word. After the exploits in the dark London roads, the pair journeyed into the country. They had plenty of money, and travelled like gentlemen. Not a town they passed through but they left it with greater wealth than when they entered. Their plan was for Vautrin to enter an hotel and engage the best suite of apartments to be had. He drove up to the house with heavy trunks on the cab. Whilst choosing his bedroom, he would give great trouble to the housekeeper, asking why he could not have such and such a chamber, until he learned pretty nearly which rooms were occupied. After an excellent supper he would ring the bell for his candle and proceed to his bedroom to arrange his hair, having previously inquired of the waiter whether there was any place of amusement open in the town. As he went upstairs, a glance at the candlesticks ranged on the side-table at each landing told him whether many of the travellers were in their rooms or downstairs. All he wanted was half an hour to himself, for by that time he had made the round of the bed-chambers, ripping open trunks and boxes with his chisel and short crowbar. If he found any money or jewellery they were crammed into his coat pocket. He never meddled with bulky plunder. He could rifle a trunk in one minute and a half.

Then, with the greatest sangfroid, would this extraordinary man descend the staircase, and, telling the waiters that he should not return before twelve, hurry off to the rendezvous he had made with Jack Drake. It was the Duck's business to carry about his person, and dispose of, the stolen effects. The descriptions that were, instantly after their exploits, published of Monsieur Vautrin's person and costume rendered it highly dangerous for that eminent leader to risk too great an exposure of his manly form in the public streets.

CHAPTER XIV.

CONTAINING MANY INCIDENTS WHICH OUGHT TO HAVE BEEN TOLD
PAGES AGO, RELATING, AMONG OTHER CIRCUMSTANCES, HOW
FATHER AND SON MET, THE CONVERSATION THAT ENSUED,
AND IN WHAT MANNER PHIL FOLLOWED HIS PARENT'S
ADVICE.

As chance would have it, Philip Merton was wandering about the
streets of Derby on the very same day that Monsieur Vautrin and
his friend, the Duck, arrived by the express from Nottingham, to see
if there were anything to be done in their little line of business.
The vagrant in his black, mangy rags, with his shoulders up to his
ears, was paddling with his naked feet along the muddy road, wishing
that somebody would try and hit him in the eye with a sixpence,
when the Duck, attired so fashionably that even the Governor of
Coldbath Fields would not have recognized him, sauntered past, his
ever active mind endeavouring to recall the words of a song he had
joined chorus to overnight :

> " It's all for that ale, that confounded ale,
>   That confounded ale and tobaccy."

was all he could remember of the poem, and it annoyed him considerably. When, therefore, Phil—little dreaming that the Duck
stood before him—commenced in his cringing voice to petition " his
honour to spare a copper," Jack Drake, who was up to cadging in all
its branches, having professed the calling, assumed a pompous
demeanour, and asked the beggar why he did not work, and if he
wasn't ashamed of himself for leading such an idle, disgraceful life.
It was pleasant to the Duck to be able to repeat the rebukes he had
himself so frequently met with. Whilst explaining the reason of his
distress, Phil addressed the buckish prig so respectfully, and made
use of so many flattering expressions, that, pleased with this evidence
of his prosperous appearance, the Duck gave alms. More, he
endeavoured to read the vagrant a moral lesson.

" Sich a reg'lar strong-made chap as you, as has the wear of cast-
iron in yer, to be cadging about, is rather too stiffish for my swallow.
Why, you could carry a load o' bricks on them shoulders, and feel
'em no more than a coat collar."

Philip was startled to hear such a fashionable person talk such
very rickety British. He gave the usual excusing answers almost
mechanically, whilst his mind was busy wondering whether the dandy
was a genuine or forged article.

" Now, how do you think I should perwide for myself if I didn't
work ? " continued the moralizing Duck. " Do you think I likes

work? Not me. It's too rich for my stomick; idleness is my drink, only it pays you out so tremendous the next day."

The vagrant considered that, after this charity sermon, a collection would follow, so he listened humbly. The ex-captain grew more and more virtuous.

"Do you think sich as me don't know the value of pence, but must be continual getting change for sich as you? We earns our money too severe for sich extravagance. Sooner than be a lumping about the streets, I'd take a broom, and start a crossing. I never see finer mud or likelier pitches," he added, his great experience in these matters making him for a moment forget himself.

A little learning proved a very dangerous thing for Master Drake. The ragged beggar had often looked up slily in the lecturer's face. He had noticed that two of the big front teeth were missing. If ever the fashionable gentleman smiled, his face, which before had been blank and smooth as a table-cloth, crumpled up like a collapsed balloon and became a mass of wrinkles and dimples. Had Jack kept his knowledge about crossings and mud locked up in the dark cellar of his brain, he would have escaped detection. As one who has forgotten a certain tune requires but to have the few first notes hummed in order to start off in full voice with the remainder of the melody, so Phil, the moment he heard the words "take a broom," was, as it were, carried back to the days of his dirty childhood, when "caten-wheeling" was his trade, and the Haymarket his workshop. The first idea that crossed his brain was, "What a tip-topper the Duck has turned out." That gentleman was expecting a cringing, supplicating reply, and his knees almost bent under him as Phil, in a moment brightening up and looking sharp as a terrier at a rat-hole, cried out, "You cussed Jack Drake, shut up that patter; I'm Phil Merton!"

We will say this for the Duck: he had great presence of mind. He never attempted to deny his identity, but assumed a pleased air, as if the sight of an old comrade cheered him. He expressed his delight by exclaiming, "Here's a start! a reg'lar twicer!" He admitted that he was in Phil's power by saying, in a low voice, "Don't blow the gaff—follow me." Thus, by a few simple words, did Jack, without insulting his friend by objecting to the neglige of his costume, avoid being seen walking with rags and tatters. Further, the dilapidated friend felt his heart kindle towards his old pal, even though he followed like a dog at his heels.

For fear Phil might burn with rage after the moral lecture, the Duck poured beer down his throat sufficient to have extinguished a smouldering chimney. He also presented his old mate with five shillings. His manner was most affectionate and affecting. The wretched Phil, despite the drink, felt sad and embittered as he listened to the Duck's history. "I'm on the square now," boasted that wonderful youth; "regular straight and open. I'm a wallet to a French gent, a good 'un to pay, and remarkable civil-tempered."

This was wormwood to the listener. He was jealous of the luck the ignorant, coarse Master Drake had met with. When the Duck rose to depart, it was as much as Phil could do to assume a straight-lipped smile, and allow his black hand to be shaken. He even regretted that he had given the direction of the travellers' padding-ken where he was lodging. "I'd as soon drown as see him again," thought Phil. "It's like taking poison to hear him talk of his luck."

Had it depended upon Master Drake, a second meeting would never have taken place. Like a good and faithful servant, he rushed home at a speed which crimsoned his face, and gave warning to the French gent that they must slope from Derby with the greatest activity.

"If we ain't minus in less than no time, we're blowed upon," the excited Duck said, in a confidential murmur, which no one, however close his ear might have been to the keyhole, could have overheard. "I've just met a chap as knowed me, and, from the looks of him, he'd peach for the vally of a pipe of baccer."

Men of nerve never allow themselves to feel alarmed. Although Monsieur Vautrin was trying to remember when the next train started, he replied, "We shall have done our business by to-morrow. To-day, I am too tired to travel any further. Who is this friend, and why the devil do you go exhibiting yourself in the street?"

The Duck, who feared his master to such an extent that at times he felt inclined to betray him, took no notice of the rebuke, but continued:—"I tell you this chap is dead on us. We shall be coopered if we don't pad the hoof, and that rapid. He's a chap of the name of Phil Merton, who—"

What else he was going to say was interrupted by the peculiar behaviour of the Frenchman. Master Drake's sentence ended in a moan similar to that dismal sound produced when the music of a barrel-organ is suddenly cut short. Monsieur Vautrin had jerked his body most strangely to one side as he heard this name, almost as though a stone had been thrown at him, and he had drawn back to avoid it. He had also dropped his cigar, and, although he turned his back to the window, and tried to conceal his countenance, Jack noticed it had turned to a corpse-like hue. His voice had a dry, hoarse sound as he asked: "Do you know where this boy is to be found?" Because Jack stammered a little as he replied, "How should I know?" Emile Vautrin twirled round on his heel, and scowled as if he was about to fly at the youth's throat. "Because he told you. Go and fetch him. I must see him. Do you hear me? Bring him here."

"Bring him here!" cried the Duck. "Well, you do talk. Why, he's as ragged as an old kite in a tree. They'd want to carry him upstairs in a dustpan."

"Buy him clothes, then," roared Vautrin. "Have you no sense, blockhead? Or, stay; your things will fit him—let him wear them."

"And what am I to do?" inquired Jack, saucily. He had a suspicion that the Frenchman wanted to get rid of him, and that was a
thing be would not stand. There had been a misunderstanding the
day before at Nottingham. He could see through "the dodge" well
enough.

"What are you to do?" answered the master; "why, wear his
rags, if you like, or get others, if you choose. Understand me, Jack
—that boy must be here in an hour, or I shall hunt him up myself."
In a mild, sneaking tone, he added, "If you put me to that trouble,
I shall not consider you my friend, nor feel the same affection for
you that I do now, my good Jack. So go along at once, and here is
money for you to buy the clothes—mind, good clothes, such as I
wear."

The good Jack looked about as amiable as a baited bull, and on
taking the proffered note, crushed it up savagely, as if it had been
the giver's neck. But he did not dare to be disobedient, and
shuffled to the door. The Frenchman, with his bright eye, grey and
round as a new bullet, called to Jack as he was about to turn the
handle, and said in his mild, patronizing manner,—

"My poor Jack, you are angry, and hate me, because you are
jealous. That is wrong, my boy. I am your friend, and would not
desert you for any one. Now you can go, and, to please me, do not
be long."

As he descended the stairs, the Duck remarked to himself, "How
did that chap know why I was riled? He's up to everything.
There never was such a dodger. Wouldn't he make a spanking
Peeler!" The prospect of gaining a few shillings, by overcharging
for the purchase of the clothes, helped to smooth the Duck's
ruffled feathers.

How different was his manner to Phil, when he sought out that
wandering youth at the padding-ken. He shook his old companion's
hand with a brave, hearty manner, and thus addressed him :—

"I never see a old pal in the suds but my spirit's willing to give
him a hist up'ards. I've stood your friend, Phil, and put in a good
word for yer in the right quarter—the same as is meat, drink, and
toggery to me." He then related to Merton an affecting history of
how his heart grieved to see the friend of his youth in so sad a
plight. He had interceded with the French gent, and ultimately
prevailed on him to take an additional servant into his employ. "I
can tell you, it was touch-and-go work; but I was so precious hard
down on him, says he, at last, 'By Gosh, Jack! you'd talk a milestone over to the t'other side of the road.' And there he give in, and
took it quite sweet and nat'ral."

No one would imagine that Phil could see anything to object to in
such a brilliant future as Jack had sketched out for him. Warm
clothes, warm dinners, and warm beds, have their attractions. Good
money paid quarterly, a new suit per annum, and little or no work to
do, sounds temptingly. Perhaps Phil objected to have Jack as a

benefactor. Perhaps he—as many persons do—felt hurt that an ignorant, coarse fellow should have it in his power to render a service far above any he could realize for himself. Much to the Duck's delight, Merton did not jump so eagerly at the offer. He asked how much tin was given? and when the knowing Jack purposely understated the sum, he remarked, "That's short earnings." Many other business inquiries were made, to all of which the most unfavourable replies were readily given. The Duck was already congratulating himself upon having choked off his rival.

"I do pretty well at cadging," said Phil. "Of course I don't wear these rags you see when I knock off work. I live pretty well, and it's middling jolly."

"And you're your own master," suggested Jack. "Nobody to swear at you but the Peelers, and they comes under the head of destiny, and don't rile a chap no more than thunder or rain."

But, too knowing to let the chance of a new suit of clothes slip by, Phil, after all, determined to see the Frenchman. The Duck had felt so certain of a refusal, that he had arranged in his own mind a clever anecdote to enable him to keep the five-pound note. He had determined on soiling his coat with mud, and then telling the Frenchman that Phil, suspecting foul play, had pushed him, and bolted off just as they were within five minutes' walk of the hotel. His disgust, therefore, when Merton took up his hat, and said, " There is no harm in seeing what this rich chap is made of," was so great, that he tried to pick a quarrel, saying he would hear the gent spoke of in that manner by no one, nowhere—no, not if they was as big as a house, and forty-horse power."

The tailor makes the man. Always wear a good coat. It is almost as serviceable as a good character. Many persons who in the morning had threatened Phil as a vagabond would, had they met him adorned with his excellent suit, have styled him a very gentlemanly, well-behaved young man. A barber had cut his hair and pomatumed it with a highly-scented grease. His boots, his clothes, and his hat were lustrous with the varnish of newness. Waiters drew back, and made way for the well-dressed gentleman. The chambermaid gazed on him, and felt how easy it would be to love such a man. And this miracle was produced by a good coat. Ten years of a rogue's life atoned for and forgiven through a thirty-shilling paletot.

As they ascended the stairs, the man waiting for them heard their footfalls, and, tossing off a glass of brandy, tried to be calm. For the last half-hour he had stood at the window, gazing right and left to catch the first sight of Philip Merton. He dare not trust himself to speak when the lads entered. He knew the words would stick in his throat and betray him. So he motioned Phil to a chair, and, leaning against the mantelpiece, stared at him. For more than ten minutes he did not utter a word. The Duck was wondering to himself "what the doose had come to the governor." The Duck would have made great allowances for human nature had he been aware that only once before the father had seen his son, and then under painful circumstances. Now Vautrin could examine the latter without fear or interruption. He could trace a resemblance to himself in the long-missing son, and that pleased him, for Phil was a better looking man than the father had ever been. The shoulders were broad, the strong arms filled up the coat sleeve with the bulging muscles, and he had the slimness and the strength of a greyhound. Vautrin looked at the handsome face, and half laughed as he wondered if in his youth he had been such a "joli garcon." He also thought of the mother, who had died giving life to this fine youth; but he did not dwell at length on this subject. He had become entitled to property through his wife's death—he had ceased to deplore her loss. He rejoiced in the son as a means of claiming the inheritance and baffling Crosier.

Those who believe in the voice of nature will be surprised to hear that on this occasion Philip felt no thrill in his bosom as he beheld his father. He was, instead of being overcome by the parental gaze, considerably annoyed at it. He moved uneasily in his chair, brushed his hat with his hand, and finally occupied himself with the improvement of his nails. "When he's done staring, perhaps he'll say so," thought Phil.

When Vautrin felt the muscles in his throat relax, he began to speak. He ordered up wine. He laughed, and joked, and talked on every subject but the one Phil considered the most important. They dined together. "This is a strange kind of gent," the son could not help thinking, "to dine with his valets. There's something very deranged in these clock-works." When the hour grew late, Vautrin rang the bell, and ordered a bed to be prepared for his young friend. They shook hands and retired to rest excellent friends. Determined to make some inquiries into the mystery, Phil followed the Duck into that bold outlaw's chamber, and, shutting the door, inquired, "Jack, who the devil is this chap?"

"He's allers like you see him," replied Mr. Drake; "remarkable haffable and free."

"What does he want with me?" inquired Phil.

"You might as well ax me which side of his starchers has the most hairs," answered Jack.

"He's a rum 'un," added Phil.

"Uncommon so," responded the Duck, "and very good company, leastways when so inclined."

In the morning, before Phil was awake, Vautrin entered his room, bringing him clean linen and shaving tackle. He could scarcely bear the boy to be out of his sight. It seemed as if he feared Phil should run away. They went out walking together, and he was kind to an astonishing degree. He insisted that Phil wished to smoke, and purchased cigars. He joked him about some ladies that passed by. He asked him constantly to enter taverns and call for what he liked.

"This is very jolly," thought Phil, "only very difficult to come at."

In the evening the explanation ensued. Master Drake was, in very polite but very unmistakable language, desired to make himself scarce. He grumbled, and asked for the loan of half a sovereign, as if those were his terms for absenting himself. To Phil's surprise the French gent lent his valet the required sum. When father and son were alone, the following conversation took place over some cigars and brandy-and-water:—

"Come closer to the fire, I want to talk with you on business. You have, Drake tells me, led a miserable life. Is that true?"

"I have lived as well as I could," said Phil doggedly.

"I know the life—the same rags from the first week of the year to the last—a twopenny bed at a lodging-house, or a turn-in under a hay-stack. Food when the begging has been lucky, and none, or a bone snatched from a dog, or a root torn up from a field, when half-pence are scarce. I know."

"And, if you do know, what comes of it?"

"Why, it's a low game, and the only thing that comes of it is what it gets—rags and starvation. You must leave this life and follow mine."

"What is yours?"

"Plenty and good covering. Do I live well? I have only to ring this bell to order what I require. I have money enough to give orders to half the shops in the town. Yet I only work one hour where you toil an entire day. Will you join me?"

"What is your business?"

"The same as yours—to get money. You, for a few pence, risk a prison and the treadwheel. I, for the same punishment, speculate for hundreds of pounds. You are forced to work under the very eyes of the police, therefore, the chances of escape are slight. I choose my own time, and plan my labours so as to render them secure. After ten years' toil, you have perhaps five shillings in your pocket; I, after a few weeks, have as many hundred pounds. Why do you hesitate to join me?"

"I thought you were up to some such game as this. But don't you see where your calling is worse than mine? I'm not worth the nabbing; whilst at this very moment the police are after you. I belong to the small fry, and swim through the meshes of the net; you are the large fish, and worth being hauled up. You're always being hunted; I'm not worth the taking. It's very good of you to make the offer, but I'll keep myself to myself."

"You refuse. Very well; you have a right to your own opinion. But there is another circumstance that I will mention, and which I hope will alter your determination."

"What is that? Out with it, I want to be off."

"You are my son."

"Gammon! What was my mother's name?"

Vautrin was annoyed that the revelation had not produced more effect. I tell you I am your father. Your mother, calling herself Katherine Merton, died in prison whilst I was in France. We were married."

" Who drove my mother to prison ? ` You deserted her. You left me to die in prison, too, if the parish had not had more pity than a parent. There was a time when I wished to see you. Now I would sooner be alone. Let me go."

"I did not desert you, Philip. I can refer you to my lawyer to convince you of the many attempts I have made to discover my child. You shall see his bills some day. I was driven from you. A man with a heart of stone has separated father from child. It is he that drove me to my desperate life. The fortune we are entitled to is withheld from us, and, sooner than starve and rot, I—I—I—do anything."

" Who is this man who separated us ? "

" Nathaniel Crosier, the father of your murdered mother."

Phil suddenly remembered the offer that had been made him to emigrate. " That sounds true. I know Crosier—an old man, yellow and wrinkled, with a bald head and fluffy hair like a young bird. Why don't you go to law ? "

" He knows I dare not. But you can, and you shall. Now will you join me ? Will you allow the wretch who destroyed your mother, who has made us both outcasts, to enjoy the property his roguery has wrested from us ? "

"I'll tell you in two days. But wait ! What name am I to call you by ? "

" My real name is Emile Vautrin. At present call me Monsieur Boustache."

When three days had passed, Vautrin paid the hotel bill, and, celebrating his reunion with his son by respecting the property in the house, he journeyed to London accompanied by the Duck and Philip.

CHAPTER XV.

LOVE AND VENGEANCE.

PHILIP MERTON wore excellent clothes and had plenty of money in his pocket on the night he patronized the travelling circus. He had still better apparel in his trunks at the hotel where he was staying. Polished-leather boots, velvet waistcoats, shirts with delicate fronts, formed portions of his wardrobe. We have before objected to reveal how he employed his leisure and earned the money that made his waistcoat pocket bulge out. There were notes and golden pieces in that same trunk at the hotel. His father, Vautrin, had taught his son many things since they met. But we reserve these disclosures for another chapter, for fear our readers should in disgust refuse to have anything more to do with so depraved a young man.

He had followed the beautiful Miss Lucy and her savage maid-servant after they left the circus, resolved to keep close at her heels if she wandered about for a month. The young lady had mingled with the crowd returning to Elbury, but he never missed her once. He saw her moving down the dark lane that leads to the market-place; watched her raise her dress, and pick her way on tip-toes through the mud, and presently beheld her ring the ostler's bell at the Royal George, the very hotel at which he was staying. Once he thought she was gazing about, as if to see if he had pursued her. He hid himself under a doorway, and presently from the stableyard issued a jolting chaise, drawn by a grey ball of a pony that appeared as broad as it was long. Both the female forms took their places, and the animal did its best to trot off. For that night Phil thought it better to give up the chase and go to bed.

The next morning the ostler had a shilling placed in his big hand. The man had to earn it by answering these questions: " Does Miss Lucy—what the deuce is her other name?—you know—keep the grey pony that was put up here last night?"—" Green chaise?—pony, swelled hock?—one ear cut?" inquired the ostler. And when Phil on speculation replied, " Ay, that's it!" the fellow continued. " That's Mr. Crow the pork-butcher's, of Hillocks."

The smitten youth, not liking such parentage for the beautiful Lucy—he had grown proud since he had been told he was of gentle birth—refused to accept this evidence. " No, no," he cried, in disgust; " a young lady and her maid who went to the circus last night; Miss Lucy—what is her name?" A new light illumined the ostler's dim brain. " You mean Miss Lucy Grant—of course you do. Why, their pony ain't got no swelled hock. As sound as a onion, ear and all."—"Ah! Miss Lucy Grant—that's it!" exclaimed Phil. Then he inquired if the family were still living in the same place, and was told "it hadn't shifted as was known on." He next tried whether any information could be gleaned by requesting to be shown the nearest route to Miss Grant's residence, and was directed to keep straight on down the Swanborough Road till he came to it. At last he produced half a crown, and, to obtain the coin, the ostler told all he knew, describing as well as he could the character and appearance of Lieutenant Grant, R.N., and the outward signs by which his residence might be distinguished.

Before any clock of regular habits had struck twelve, Phil had breakfasted, walked three miles, and was inspecting the building for the rent and taxes of which the old sailor was quarterly answerable. He thought the shutters of a pleasant lively green; he approved of the careful manner in which the climbing roses had been trained about the casements, with the branches bent as regularly as if they had been raked into their places, and the whiteness of the blinds and curtains at the different windows met with his entire approbation. The garden, too (for he passed through the swing iron gate set in a holly-hedge a cannon-ball could not have penetrated), was prettily arranged, and the show of flowers satisfactory. He very soon guessed to whom the little lace collars bleaching on the rose-bushes belonged, and he felt sure the big straw hat on one of the rustic chairs on the lawn was the property of the same young lady.

A lane ran down one side of the impregnable holly-hedge. There he had a view of the back premises. The savage servant who lived in the room with a bird-cage and a Dutch-clock, was seen through the window. She had been washing something in the tub on the stone steps. A petticoat, with a delicately-shaped body, was hanging from a line, and, though it was dripping wet from its final rinse, he would have kissed its embroidered hem if he had dared.

He watched for two days, and only lost his time. He caught sight of the lieutenant's tarpaulin hat, creeping along just above the hedge-top, and in an instant Phil had disappeared in a ditch. He heard a youthful but shrill voice call out "Mary!" and heard a discontented answer of—"What's gone wrong now?" In the dusk of evening he had entered by a back gate, and, making as little noise as he could on the gravel walk, crept round to the parlour windows, but he gained little by peeping, excepting a foreshortened view of the lieutenant sleeping on the sofa. There was the model of a ship on a side-table, and a spaniel on the rug that barked violently, but no Miss Lucy. "Where the deuce can she be gone to?" thought Phil; "she never walks out, or goes into the garden. What a rum girl!" Determined not to be beaten, he devoted yet another day to this search after the Beautiful, but though he twice narrowly escaped falling counter of the vixenish servant, his eyes were never refreshed by the sight of the R.N.'s pretty daughter. The spaniel had become his bitterest enemy. It stood watch at the gate and tried to get at him between the narrow rails. It barked as if trying to blow itself to pieces. If he moved along the edge it followed him, yelping and dancing about, as if determined on having his life. Lieutenant Grant, R.N., was so astonished at the dog's vivacity, that he on one occasion went to the gate and looked into the road. He only saw a very respectable young gentleman walking rapidly in the direction of Swanborough. So he chided the spaniel, saying, "What's the matter with you, you little fool! don't you know a gentleman when you see him?" About five o'clock that evening, patience met with its reward. Phil was thinking seriously of the delicious flavour of well-cooked animal food, when he beheld—and trembled as he beheld —a large straw hat moving among the trees in the orchard. He bounded down the lane, and, in less than a moment, was stretching his neck and jumping his highest to see over the edge. The face, shaded by the large hat, did certainly look very lovely.

She was reading, holding the book in a blue-veined hand, with a turquoise ring on the second finger. As the hedge became less and less dense, he saw her red lips move and her round chin work up and down as she repeated to herself the words of the author. He felt he must speak to her if he were killed for it. "How do you do, Miss Lucy?" he gasped out.

She looked up, and answered, "How do you do? Won't you step in and see papa?"

He thought this was odd, and, objecting to the invitation, replied, "I have not seen you since we met at the circus; have you been ill?"

Then she seemed to be aware that the voice was that of a stranger, for she advanced to the hedge and looked through. "I don't know you—go away!" was the only answer he obtained to his kind inquiries.

The spaniel, as his mistress retired, took up the quarrel, and, forcing itself through the stumps of the hedge trees, flew round and round Phil's legs, as if it was examining them to discover the best place for biting. "Love me, love my dog," muttered Phil; "but until then, hang me if I stand this cur's nonsense." He first took off his hat and flung it at the animal. The dog seized it in a moment, and began to shake and batter it on the ground. But suddenly a coat was thrown over the little thing, and, before it could squeak out for help, Phil was running as fast as he could across the fields. A few knocks on the head and the spaniel was frightened into subjection, and even began to lick the hand of its new proprietor.

"There may be advantages to be gained with this yelping pet. To-morrow," thought Phil, "bills will be out offering a reward. I'll keep it for a week, and then enter the house in triumph with the little brute in my arms." A man on whom Phil could depend (he knew many curious characters whom nobody but himself dared trust) undertook to keep the spaniel in a safe place, away from eye and ear. In a back cellar of the "Gun and Crow" did the faithful animal throughout the night lift up its head and whine without ever disturbing the repose of any living creatures except the rats that dwelt among the beer-barrels.

When Phil returned to his hotel, he was told a friend of his, in the coffee-room, had been making inquiries after him. He was completely "taken aback" when he beheld his father seated near the fire with a decanter of sherry by his side. The son had grown to love his sire, so their meeting was affectionate. Unless he had received a look, Phil would have addressed him as "Father," but Vautrin's quick eye stopped the word. When they were presently in a private room, dining together, the Frenchman cautioned his son on the subject, saying, "Everybody is aware it is a wise father that knows his own child, but remember, too, it is a confoundedly clever child that at times doesn't know its own father. Your name is Merton, mine is Boustache."

Vautrin had come down more for pleasure than business. Ever since Mrs. Crosier's death, the family had been away from the house at Swanborough. As Elbury was only some six miles distant from the banker's residence, Vautrin—to amuse himself, he said—had determined on visiting the birthplace of his " dear wife, to see if it was the same old rickety pile as when he knew it." The strangest fancy he expressed in connection with this trip was, that they should visit the place by night. "The building is highly picturesque," said Vautrin, " and in a strong moonlight really a pretty sight. I should like you to see it, Phil."

Father and son stayed together, passing the time very agreeably for three days, when a letter arrived for "Mr. Boustache," and after reading it, Vautrin said he must return to London on the morrow, so they would go to Swanborough that night. They left the hotel after an early dinner, resolved on walking the distance. But, before they had gone two miles, Vautrin was fortunate enough to meet—quite accidentally, as he remarked—at a roadside beerhouse, two friends of his, who promised, if he would drink away an hour or so, to drive him over to Swanborough in their own trap, and even back again if his time were precious. "It's better than walking," answered Phil. "Much," added Vautrin; "and infinitely preferable to being thirsty."

Although a common beershop, the people sold excellent spirits, and were excessively friendly and attentive. Phil had smoked innumerable pipes and emptied more glasses than he could count, when (about eleven o'clock) the horse was ordered to be put to. Off they drove, not at a rapid pace, for the beast appeared worn out and stiff, as if it had been that day overdriven, but with whipping and pulling at the reins they made it hobble along.

If Crosier had been a nobleman instead of a banker he could not have lived in better style or in a better mansion. The party in the chaise with the hobbling horse saw the building half a mile off from the road, a grey, solemn pile, surrounded by black trees. Well did Vautrin know the property and the grounds. He told the driver which turning to take so as not to arouse the man who slept in the lodge; he guided them up lanes with deep ruts, in which the chaise bumped till the springs were nearly broken; and eventually they stopped at a field gate which, he told them, led to the back premises of the mansion.

Here they alighted, and, tying the horse to a tree, onward they went, Vautrin leading the way through orchards, down dark filbert-walks, round by reed-covered ponds, across rustic bridges, past greenhouses and cucumber-frames, till they arrived at an iron gate which, after a vigorous kick on the rusty lock, opened. Now they were in the garden, standing in front of the building with its big stone bay-windows, peaked roofs, and tall Elizabethan chimneys.

"That's where your poor mother was born," said Vautrin, with pride. Then he added, savagely, "By G—d, it shall be ours some day, if we have any chance."

Next they visited the outbuildings, Vautrin still acting as leader.

They heard the horses stamping in the stables, and one of the friends
remarked, "Lots of prads, Frenchy, if we want them." A big dog,
which had been barking violently, dashed to the full length of its
chain at the trespassers; but Vautrin advanced to it fearlessly, and
threw it something which had the effect of instantly quieting its
anger and rendering it harmless as a kitten. Every door in the
building Vautrin knew as thoroughly as his alphabet. That one led
to the sculleries; that one to the kitchen, another to the wood-house.
"Where's the winder you spoke of?" inquired one of the friends.
Then their cicerone conducted them to a casement, shuttered and
barred, but only a few feet from the ground. "It used to be a
servant's bedroom," said he, "but there's nobody sleeps there
now."

"Shall we star the glaze and see what the inside's like?" asked
one of the friends.

"Well, there's no harm in it, is there, Phil?" answered Vautrin,
turning to his son, who was puzzling his brains to discover the intention of these men. However, no time was given to any of them
to discuss the question, for a scream, which made them fall back in
alarm, gave proof sufficient that the room was tenanted by some one
who, even if unarmed, carried a well-charged throat about her
person.

That morning Helen Crosier and two of the servants had returned
to Swanborough to prepare the house for her father, who was to
follow them in a few days. She had felt alarmed at being left alone
in so large a dwelling with only one man and a woman for its protection, and had persuaded the maid to occupy this chamber, which,
from its proximity to the ground, was the only one through which an
entrance could easily be effected. When she heard the scream,
Helen Crosier, instead of fainting, proceeded to ring vigorously at
her bell to rouse the man sleeping above, and, then rushing into her
father's room, took down a gun which was always kept loaded above
the mantelpiece. Like a brave Amazon she flung open the window,
and, seeing a man standing on the grass-plot before the principal
entrance, fired.

Of course she did not hit him, but if, instead of falling backwards in
an almost senseless condition, she had stretched forth her neck and
listened, she still would have heard one voice cry out, "Here! help
me! I'm in for it!" and another instantly rejoin, "By G—d, boy,
don't say that!—mind, catch him, or he'll fall!"

The old jaded horse was made to gallop as fast as if he had not
trotted a mile that day, for Vautrin, holding the butt end of the
whip, beat its loins each time its pace flagged. And between the
blows he turned to look at Phil, and tell him to hold up, for "he
should have some brandy soon, and be all right again."

CHAPTER XVI.

VAUTRIN GIVES HIS SON PHYSIC AND ADVICE.

VAUTRIN was one of those iron-hearted, far-seeing rogues, who, even in the most desperate reverses, never permit themselves to lose courage until the chances of escape have been carefully weighed against those of capture. Fortune had so often broken him on her wheel that he had grown accustomed to the persecution. He seemed to know the exact point where danger began and security ended. His pulse did not beat a throb the faster when he heard his son call out for help. Until the wound could be examined, he considered it childish to give way to fear.

His friends, less self-possessed than their leader, had, when they saw Philip totter and nearly fall to the ground, rushed to the youth with the view of carrying him off as rapidly as possible. Vautrin calmly checked their haste. "Curse you, where's your hurry?" he said, pushing them back. "It will be at least twenty minutes before the neighbours are aroused. Don't let us fly off like a lot of crows because a gun is fired."

He took from his neck a thick woollen comforter, and bound it around Philip's bleeding shoulder; then he placed a heavy rough great-coat about the shivering body. "Now," he said, turning to his nervous companions—"now you may take him. Follow me as fast as you can. No blood can trickle through all those coverings. They will have to guess at the path we have chosen, and not be able to track us at once, as you seemed by your confounded haste to prefer."

Instead of returning by the route they had come, Vautrin ordered the horse's head to be turned in an opposite direction. Wherever the sides of the road were covered with turf, the chaise was guided into it, so that the wheel-marks might be lost.

At first the two friends imagined, from finding themselves in a different part of the country, that Vautrin had mistaken his way. Yet the influence the Frenchman possessed over his assistants was so great that some time elapsed before either of them dared to suggest he was in error. Vautrin gave his directions in so positive a manner that his friends could hardly imagine he was straying. At last one of them found courage enough to say, " What's your game, Frenchy? Here's the boy pretty near a croaker, and the prad will be bow-wow's meat if he has to hoof it much further, and yet, instead of getting to some libb-ken, on the main-toper, where a drop of lap could be had, you're sticking to the back drums as if we was come out to see how the crops was getting on. What's your lurk?" No answer was given, but it seemed as if Vautrin heard the question, for he fell to beating the horse savagely. The two men, annoyed at being treated with such evident contempt, grumbled together threateningly.

"D—n it, he seems to think I was a dog barking," said the last speaker; to which the other added, " When chaps come out with chaps, I'm for haffability. We're all eggs in the same nest, and should be treated likeways."

Presently Vautrin, who had taken the reins, drove down a lane just wide enough to allow the chaise to pass through. The brambles on each side scratched against the panels and had to be thrust aside to protect the faces of the occupants. At the end of this narrow way was a dismal-looking cottage, before the door of which the vehicle drew up so closely to the wall that Vautrin, by standing on the driving-box, was enabled to tap at a window, about the size of a school slate, in the thatch. " Come down, Tom, and bring a lantern," he said to a rough head, which was, after a little squeezing, thrust from the casement.

Now the two men were in ecstasies of delight with the deep cunning of their foreign friend. They felt that pursuit was out of the question. If any search were made after them it would be on the highway, between Swanborough and Elbury. It astonished them, too, that Vautrin should not only know of this humble hiding-place, but have sufficient power over the owner to wake him out of his sleep and order him about like a servant.

The simple fact was that the Frenchman, accustomed whenever he visited England to run down to Swanborough and have a look at the banker's premises, felt a savage pleasure in walking about his father-in-law's grounds, and growling out curses against the old man. He laboured under the idea that he was himself entitled to that rich domain. When those visits took place he usually put up—not wishing that his presence should be known—at the humble abode owned by the rough-headed Tom. The man was a gardener by trade, and, as he expressed it, kept himself to himself.

The horse was stabled, and corn enough heaped up in the manger to have stocked a baker's shop. A bottle of spirits was placed on the table, the men lighted their pipes, and Tom was requested to retire to his bed. They were afraid to examine Phil's wound in the gardener's presence for fear it might furnish some clue to their detection. Phil's pale face and looks of agony were accounted for by "a fall from the chaise."

When the confederates were alone, Philip's clothes were removed and his shoulder examined. They felt about the wound, and pressed it in every direction, endeavouring to discover where the bullet had lodged. This rough surgical treatment caused much agony, but Phil never once uttered a sound of pain. His father was constantly reminding him " not to howl out and wake the fellow upstairs."

The gardener in his bed heard many strange sounds as he tried to get to sleep again. Men went into the garden and fetched water from the pump. There was a noise of tearing linen, and a bucket was emptied into the manure heap, near the pigsty. He wondered what all the stir was about, and inwardly wished folk would wash their hands at proper times and places.

All the three men agreed that Phil's wound was nothing. The youth was the only person who differed from this opinion. He went so far as to tell them that if they "had it," they would think it something and a good deal to spare. The injury was pronounced a flesh wound, which would heal up as tight as wax and be better than new in less than a week.

When the gardener rose at five o'clock in the morning, he was astonished to find the gentlemen seated round the fire and deep in conversation. He saw by the manner in which the voices ceased as he entered the room that his absence was desired, so, casting a look at the young gentleman who had "fallen from the chaise," he left the room, wondering why they hadn't put the youth to bed instead of giving him three hard wooden chairs to sleep upon.

Vautrin, alias Boustacke, had been consulting with his friends about what they had better do on the morrow. They had come to the conclusion that the father and son should remain at the cottage, whilst the other two returned to town with the chaise. In this peculiar instance the two friends felt convinced that the longest way round was, if not the shortest way home, at least the safest. A journey of considerable length had been mapped out, so that they might avoid passing near Swanborough or Elbury. At mid-day the stiff-legged horse was brought out and harnessed to the clean-washed chaise, and, a mug of strong beer having been poured down the animal's throat, the friends drove away.

For a fortnight the Frenchman remained at the gardener's cottage, watching over Phil. He dressed the wound himself, and did all he could to heal it without the necessity of calling in a doctor. Herbs, poultices, and cold bathings were applied in rapid succession. Gradually the maimed limb grew to be sound. It was tedious work for a man of such active life as Vautrin to have to watch by a sick-bed, but he never appeared restless or tired. Whilst the fever was on, he seldom quitted the youth for a second. He made for him various infusions of different plants, similar to those given in such cases in France. He never even seemed to sleep, for if ever Phil awoke in the night the first thing he saw was his father sitting at the foot of the bedstead, watching him with a solemn, anxious face. Their eyes would sometimes meet, and remain staring at each other, but very little was spoken on either side.

One day, when Phil was nearly well enough to rise, he asked Vautrin what he had been thinking about so intently these many days past.

"How I can pay off the long score I owe these Crosiers!" answered the man.

"Let 'em alone," suggested Phil, too exhausted to feel much animosity. "They're not worth the bother."

"Let 'em alone!" roared Vautrin, hitting the bedclothes with his fists. "Let 'em alone! I tell you, I'll never leave them until I have that old man on his knees, begging for his life. I will make him disgorge the money he has robbed us of, whilst I hold him tightly at the throat, with my fingers biting into his flesh like hooks." Suiting his action to his words, he seized Philip's ankle, and squeezed it so hard that the youth gasped out,—

"Do what you like to Crosier, but don't break my bones!"

When Phil was nearly well enough to venture once more into the wide world, his father, as they were at dinner, asked him, "Who that girl was he raved about in his fever?"

"Did I talk about a girl?" answered Phil, evasively.

"Yes, a girl of the name of Lucy," coolly replied the parent. "Who is she, and where did you pick her up?"

For some time the youth endeavoured to avoid the desired explanation, but Vautrin pressed his examination as roughly and closely as an Old Bailey barrister, and nothing short of a direct refusal could have put an end to the inquiry. At last, the son gave a modified account of his adventure at the circus, and his subsequent and most unsatisfactory interview with the hard-hearted maiden herself.

"Does the father look as if he had any cash?" asked Vautrin, when the love tale was ended.

Phil gave a favourable description of the cottage, and further added that, at Elbury, the old lieutenant was considered to be well-to-do, and of easy circumstances.

"Why don't you marry the girl?" said Vautrin.

Philip laughed. "That's very easy to say," he answered; "but how am I to keep a wife?"

"Didn't you say her father was well off?" asked Vautrin, with a look of astonishment, as if he considered the question one of extreme simplicity. "What more do you want? I'll lend you enough to go on with at first. In about six months you can make the old fellow stump up."

"I tell you I don't know the family. I've only seen the girl at a circus and over a hedge," expostulated Phil. "I've never once been inside the house. How can I ask her to marry me? She'd laugh in my face!"

This was spoken in the hopes of putting an end to the conversation, for Phil had already planned and arranged how he was to obtain a footing among the Grant household.

"It's a good chance for you," continued the obstinate parent, "and you are a fool if you let it slip by. If they want to know who you are, tell them plainly you are Merton Vautrin, Crosier's grandchild. He's known all about here, and that alone will make a swell of you. They'll fancy you're full of money, and take to you directly. I'll send you down a copy of your mother's marriage certificate, in case there should be any dispute. At any rate, stop a month in Elbury, and see how matters go on. With that damaged shoulder, you're not fit for town work yet. Keep your pluck up, and go in and win."

This was consoling to Phil, and set his brain to work thinking over the feasibility of the plan. It was true he was the rich banker's grandchild, but he knew it was a deceit to make use of the relationship, where the education, respectability, and honesty which such a statement implied were wanting. Boasting is a leaky saucepan, and sooner or later the truth drips out. If at any time it should be whispered that, besides being a banker's grandchild, he had been a workhouse bird, a tramp, and a street beggar, he considered the blood of the Crosiers, however good it might be, would fail to give a healthy complexion to such blackness.

Vautrin almost forgot all about his sworn vengeance against the banker in the interest he took in the new scheme of his son's marriage. As they sat one on each side of the gardener's bricken hearth, their thoughts were continually occupied by this one subject. Sometimes, after more than an hour's long silence, the father would look up and say, "If they were to ask old Crosier any questions he would be afraid to tell the truth."

To this Phil would reply, after about half an hour's consideration, "Suppose they did, and the old man was to split on me, what then?" Instead of giving a speedy reply, Vautrin would stare at the wood fire, and long afterwards, as if he had looked deeply into the matter, answer, "He'll keep his mouth shut for his own sake. Besides, he'd be glad to get you respectably settled. Go in and win. The world lies before you as smooth as a garden-walk."

"Suppose they found out I had been smashing?"[1] Phil whispered, after carefully looking around the apartment.

"If that were possible," retorted the parent, "the police would have made the discovery long since. Don't be afraid of that. You are a timid blade."

"Well, but suppose they did?" urged the son.

"And what harm could it do you, if you are married to her?" retorted the father. "Do you fancy the girl's father would call in a constable and give you up? Why, he'd be the very first to use all his endeavours to keep the matter dark. Don't be such a fool. Marry the girl and your future is an easy one."

When the wounded shoulder was healed, when Phil was strong enough to bear the weight of his coat sleeve, and carry his arm without a support, Vautrin spoke of returning to London. "The Duck, as you call Drake, will be turning traitor, and offering to become Queen's evidence against me," he said, laughing, "unless I'm there to keep his cowardly heart in subjection." There was also a very urgent reason why Phil should speedily make his appearance at the hotel in Elbury.

"Suppose they should think I have bolted, and break open my

---

[1] Passing counterfeit money.

trunks?" he faltered out. "That would about cook me up. They'd find enough there to put an end to my hopes of marriage."

He knew that the false bottom to his portmanteau contained more than sufficient to ensure at least seven years of punishment.

On the day that father and son parted, Vautrin, as he affectionately squeezed the youth's hand, said, "Send me a letter as soon as you can, Phil, telling me how you get on with this girl."

"Suppose I don't get on?" faltered the son.

"Confound you, boy! You have always got some 'suppose' or other to fling in my face," replied Vautrin, passionately. "You talk as if you didn't want to win the wench. Make up your mind to get hold of her, and you're sure to do it. You haven't one half my spirit, rot you, or you wouldn't talk in that faint way. Now look at me. I have sworn to have old Crosier down on his knees cringing at my feet, and begging for his very life. That's a harder task than yours. I doubt if the old man kneels even when he says his prayers, such is his cursed pride. Now you've got a girl to deal with. You ought to be married and have a child on your knee by this time next year, if you keep your wits about you. Come, Phil, try and cram a little more devil into your pasty head, and go to work as if you had some of your father's pluck in your body."

So they parted: the father mourning, as he went his way, that his boy took too much after his mother in disposition; and Phil determined, "if he swung for it," to make Lucy Grant change her name to Lucy Vautrin before she was a month older.

CHAPTER XVII.

SHOWING HOW PHILIP MADE VAST SUMS OF MONEY.

WHEN a youth, whose father is not in flourishing circumstances, is found to be in the possession of round sums of money; when he has no evident occupation, yet wears such clothes as become a Regent Street dandy; when his linen is of fine texture and frequently washed; when he can sport his bottle of wine with the best of the company, it is not an infrequent thing to inquire how that youth manages to live in such good style, and who suffers for the expenditure. If Philip had been bothered by such an awkward question he would have avoided all chances of committing himself by giving the most impudent reply he could, in the hurry of the moment, invent. When he liked he could be very abusive. If, in his milder moments, he had chosen to enter into any explanation of the singular phenomenon, he might have hinted that a lady of fortune had fallen in love with him, and placed her bulky purse at his disposal, or, giving Nathaniel

Crosier, Esq., credit for more charity than his whole life could afford evidence of, he might have asserted he was indebted to the old banker for his plentiful income. But, alas! it was neither the grandfather nor the lady of fortune who had to suffer for Philip's extravagance of living. It was from the tradesmen of Great Britain that the youth drew his large resources. They were the victims that furnished him with the luxuries and means he sported to such advantage. In a few words, Philip had turned passer of bad money, or, to use the slang of his class, "smasher."

A very terrible scene had taken place between the young man and his father shortly after their meeting at Derby. The old offender against society had laboured hard to drag his offspring down to his own level—to rub and daub him with the same vicious filth which debased his own nature. It was fearful, indeed, to see this Vautrin tempting his child to adopt a craft which was to be his soul's ruin. It is true this man laughed at the world, and called honesty undetected fraud; it is true he considered robbery as only an unrecognized profession; yet in his heart he had an impulsive knowledge of right and wrong, which made him easily distinguish between crime and virtue.

The only being he loved in the world was Philip. Every day he grew more and more delighted with his boy. He gloried in the strength of his child's stout arm, and would make him double it up that the muscles might be more visible. He would look in Phil's face and criticize the features, until he felt proud of having so comely a son.

He considered it as a personal compliment if, as arm-in-arm they walked the streets, anybody looked at the handsome countenance. He could almost laugh with pride that such notice should be taken of his offspring, and unconsciously repeated to him such phrases as, "I made him—he's mine," or, "You had better look again, sir; it will be a long time before you see such another." Then why did Vautrin design such evil against the youth?

The truth was, Vautrin feared his son. He had taken a sudden affection to him, and with men of his stamp such affections are violent and uncontrollable. With his love was mingled a jealous feeling lest any circumstance should separate him from his son. Up to that time, he knew that, of the two, the youth's life had, although less lucrative, been immeasurably the more honourable and upright. It is not, therefore, very difficult to understand how depraved and vicious must have been Vautrin's existence. It was a constant dread lest Phil should by any means become acquainted with his parent's evil courses, and turn from him in horror, that harassed and annoyed Vautrin. In their daily converse, the youth would occasionally speak boldly upon certain immoralities of the world, and seemed to possess a strong consciousness of honesty. Vautrin trembled whenever Phil moralized. The rudely-conceived and badly-expressed notions of virtue had more effect upon his mind than the best-worded sermon ever preached from a pulpit. A savage resolve entered the man's breast, that, if his boy should attempt to turn from him, he would, "if he swung for it," take back the life he had begotten, rather than be deserted and despised.

This Vautrin conceived that the only effectual method of binding his son tightly to himself was to make him as wicked as his sire. He would make him a bird of his feather, and ensure their flocking together. When he had rendered the boy as base as himself, then a sympathy would spring up between them. It was a work of time, thought Vautrin, but a sure policy. So this fellow calmly prepared himself to demoralize his child. He, as it were, held the ladder to steady it, lest his son, in climbing up to the gallows, should fall and escape his doom.

He seized every opportunity of instilling his own doctrines into Phil's mind. If he took up a copy of a newspaper, he had several remarks, all relating to his dishonest philosophy, to make upon the events. "A good list of bankrupts," he would mutter, as his eye glanced down the column; "one for £60,000, another for £30,000. Go on, noble British merchants, that's the way to rob!" Then he would turn to the police reports, and, finding an account of a man who, for stealing a piece of cloth, was sent to prison for three months, grow purple with indignation, and exclaim, "That's justice, is it! Here is one scoundrel steals goods to the amount of £30,000, and another who pilfers a mere remnant valued at four shillings. The one is sent back to his home cleared of his debt, and placed in a position which enables him to rob again on the morrow. The other, who turned thief to get food, perhaps, is packed off to a prison to come out, after three months, a branded reprobate. Which of the two, now, do you call the rogue, eh, Phil?"

The boy, of course, agreed with his father that the prig, compared to the bankrupt, was an angel of purity. He gave no credit to the charity of the law, which can only judge of men's actions by the intentions that prompted them, but, as loudly as his father, denounced the justice dealt out in these two reported cases as being a scandal and disgrace to the land.

"Never rob trifles, my boy," Vautrin would say to his child. "I always attack the world with its own wisdom, and act according to its wise maxims. Now they tell you that it is equally criminal whether you steal a brass farthing or a thousand golden sovereigns. My common sense therefore tells me that, although it may be the same thing to my soul, it isn't to my pocket, so I aim at the thousands."

To laugh at evil is to sanction it; Phil now certainly adopted that of his father, for he roared at the cunning of the argument, until his jaw felt cramped.

Another of Vautrin's methods of argument was this. He would stop his boy in the street, and, pointing first to some warmly-clad and evidently prosperous man, riding comfortably in his carriage, say,

"Do you see that rich-looking old rogue, lolling in his confounded equipage?" Then he would point to some ragged, half-starved bone-grubber, and add, "And do you see that poor, crushed, dirt-stained fellow?" Of course, Phil duly acknowledged that both his eyes were in due working order. "And now," Vautrin would ask, as he frowned, "will you tell me what right that old overfed rogue has to be pulled about by a couple of horses, when that miserable mortal has not perhaps breakfasted?" If Phil did not make any attempts to solve this problem, Vautrin would add, "That fat citizen has his hot joints and full decanters, and, eat and drink as he will, he can empty neither dish nor bottle; and, if he did, he would have but to sign his name to a slip of paper, and at the first flourish of the cheque up would come carts laden with provisions for his use. By what right has he such plenty and that street worm so little? Do you consider, now, that there is any crime in the starving brother putting his hand into the pocket of the glutton brother, and helping himself to food for at least one day's eating?" This sounded very noble and philosophic, and Phil considered there would be no great evil in such an act. He was deceived by the glitter of his parent's logic. It was the first time he had heard such arguments, and they over-powered his reason. Yet, although he had many silver coins in his pocket, he never for once thought of parting with one of them to the bone-grubber.

As father and son were constantly together, and every day at least one of these devil's sermons was delivered, the youth's immoral train-ing progressed rapidly. From being repeatedly told that robbery was the great principle of life, and that it was no sin for the needy to take from the rich, Phil became firmly impressed with the truthfulness of the doctrine. It was a kind of philosophy which a lazy youth was likely to take to kindly. The drudgery of a desk, the slavery of from nine till eight, seemed very distressing, when placed alongside of one brilliant exploit per diem, and a full pocket.

When the boy had become thoroughly accustomed to good feeding, good lodging, and good clothing, Vautrin turned upon him suddenly, and, stating that his resources were at an end, asked what he intended to do for his future living. This staggered the youth. "You have several careers in the world open before you. You may go back to cadging, if you like, or I'll try and get you a post as a porter, or perhaps as junior clerk, where you may earn your honest £30 annually. What do you think of doing? I must myself set about something, for I'm cleared out."

"What are you going to do?" ventured the boy.

"What I do does not concern you," answered Vautrin, whilst his heart was beating with fear lest the boy should be of the same opinion. "I earn a good living in a very curious manner. I hold peculiar tenets of my own which I don't wish you to adopt. I cannot live on bread-and-cheese dinners, or wear only one shirt a month. You must take your chance in the world away from me."

"Why ? " returned Phil, in a miserable tone. "Why cannot I be at the same business as you ? "

"Because," said Vautrin, "you are made of different stuff to me. I see no crime in helping myself to the necessities the world would, if I begged for them till my tongue withered, refuse me."

Then followed a long speech, in which the wily tempter made use of his favourite illustrations of the rights and wrongs of property. He launched out into a splendid description of the happy life he led, of the luxuries he indulged in, and the slight risk he ran. As Phil heard all this his interest grew intense, and, although he half guessed the solution of the riddle, he was greatly anxious to be thoroughly assured of the peculiar character of the business so profitable to his parent.

And when at last Vautrin, in a frank voice, confessed openly that he was a malefactor and systematic outrager of the laws of the land; that he robbed and plundered for his existence; when he added, in a bold tone, that "he was not ashamed to confess it," styling himself, in a grandiloquent manner, " one of the captains of the standing army of poverty, who fought the everlasting war of want with their enemies, the rich "—when he did this, Phil, instead of drawing back in fear, only looked on his parent with wonder, in which there was a strong admixture of admiration. In the end, Phil enlisted under this pauper captain, and was told that with a little drilling he would rise rapidly in the service.

Now that no disguises of speech were necessary, Vautrin spoke openly. He felt he loved his son more dearly than ever for sharing with him the wickednesses of the world. He vowed to protect him, and save him from all danger of detection. He would in the hour of peril snatch him from the very grasp of the policeman, if necessary. Philip was to thrive and be merry. "By-and-by," added Vautrin, "when the pile of wealth is tall enough to satisfy us, we will retire from work and mix with the world. It will receive us, my boy, with open arms, as soon as we can rattle our money-box in its face. We will sing out "honesty" to the jingle of our purse, and that's the only music to which the world's song should be sung. When people find we are rich enough to be worthy of being robbed, they will ask us to come over to their side and scowl at the thieves. As soon as we convince our neighbours that we have no desire to plunder them they will dub us honest. How I do enjoy the virtue of this world. Answer me this, Phil: if cheating left its mark on the face, as the small-pox does, how many men would pass you in the day with an unscarred countenance ? Ha, ha ! it's the greatest swindle ever started."

Terrible and depressing as this may sound, Phil saw no horror in it, but lifted up his voice and laughed note for note with his parent.

Before many days had passed, the son had to take his first lesson in roguery. Vautrin told him the largest profits were to be made by passing off bad money. "Smashing is easy work, and pays well," said the parent. "I couldn't do it, I am too old. My face has a peculiar hard expression in it, which alarms people. They would never forget me. But with you, your features are changing every day; even a week alters your looks. It's your first appearance in London, too, and the police do not know you. You have a safe two years' work before you, without creating the slightest suspicion. I shall take you off then, and put you to something else. You have a genteel manner, and a voice that has a hearty upright ring in it. Yes, for at least two years, you are as safe as London Bridge."

To initiate the novice in his new calling, Vautrin accompanied him on his first swindling expedition. They entered a public-house and called for two glasses of hot brandy-and-water. Asking "How much?" Vautrin flung down a good sovereign, making it rebound high into the air from the metal counter, and send forth the peculiar sound of genuine golden coin. The barman took the sovereign, examined it, and was on the point of giving the proper change, when Phil, turning to his father, said, "Where is the use of your changing a sovereign to pay for eightpence? Let me stand the drink." The barman, hearing this, returned the golden piece to Vautrin. On hunting in his pockets, however, Philip discovers that "after all he has not enough silver," so Vautrin once more tenders the sovereign; but this time it is not the genuine, but a counterfeit piece—one that has been dexterously concealed up the sleeve. The serving-man, angry at having his time wasted, and having no suspicion of his customers, snatches at the gold, and, without considering it worthy of a second examination, rapidly counts out the necessary silver. Not until the till is emptied, before the landlord goes to bed, is the fraud discovered. In performing this act, Vautrin pointed out to his boy that a little legerdemain was required, and with great good-humour favoured his pupil with the instruction necessary to perfect the performer.

For an entire week did the father and son work together, and the profits were enormous. In one evening they practised this same cheat at eight taverns. As Phil was, being a beginner, nervous, and showed his fright in his countenance, Vautrin, before they left home, rouged with a light delicate hand the youth's cheeks, so that their pallor might not excite attention. "Now," said the parent, as he returned the carmine to the drawer—"now you may go as white as an egg, but you can't frighten the colour out of 'slap.' That's the stuff. Just enough to cover your finger-tip, and you look as bold as a Bank of England beadle."

It was Vautrin's practice never to remain long in any neighbourhood when he had been successful. He hailed a cab as he left the public-house, and invariably placed a mile between himself and his victims. When engaged at this rogue's work, Vautrin made a purse of his mouth, and carried the illegal coin tucked in the hollow of his cheek. Long practice enabled him to speak with great distinctness even though half a dozen of these worthless pieces were resting against his tongue. The speech was not thickened, nor did the metal jingle.

The care this parent took of his child, whilst he taught him his evil courses, was pathetic to witness. He never trusted him alone at the work. No bird teaching its young one to use its inexperienced wings could be more beautifully careful than Vautrin as he instructed his first-born to be "fly." He almost made a science of his wickedness. "There are some fools, Phil," he would say to the attentive youth, "who go out in gangs to do this work. They employ as many hands to palm off a sovereign as the perfecting of a pin is said to require. Now, the only safe plan is ' straight pitching ' —always be alone at your work. The ignorant are destroyed by their numbers. There is one who swags—that is, carries the coin; there is another who pitches or passes it; there is a third who watches the police. This is vulgar ignorance, for it requires three tongues to keep the secret. Always be above such brutish conduct, and depend only on yourself."

The school was a good one and the pupil progressed rapidly. He soon found he could dispense with the use of rouge to prevent the cheek blanching with fear as he handed over his spurious metal. The breathing became neither quicker nor shorter as the man behind the counter took the coin. There was no spasm of joy when the change was given and the shop quitted. Philip had become an experienced smasher—one that even Vautrin ceased to be nervous about. If of an evening the father reached home first, he felt no uneasiness at the absence of his son, but knew full well that in an hour or so the youth would present himself. Such delays in the meeting by the fireside only augured great success in the daily transactions.

Then what joy did they feel as they reckoned up the gains of the day. How they amused each other with the racy account of the dangers they had run; how this man had looked twice at the money, and even then changed it; how this young girl behind the counter had taken the bad coin, and, blushing at the compliment intended to throw her off her guard, given the silver in return without even a suspicion of the cheat. The firm of Vautrin and Son did well, and put by money. A St. Swithin of rainy days was provided for.

When the warm weather set in and the country was worth visiting; when London was hot and dusty and the lanes and fields fresh and cool, the junior member of this iniquitous firm was despatched into the provinces to try his hand on the " clodhoppers and johnny-raws," as Monsieur Vautrin nicknamed every individual not born within ten miles of the metropolis. Then the correspondence that passed between the father and son was very singular. The most active inspector of police might have been as full of suspicion as a Dutch doll of sawdust, and yet been able to detect nothing from the most indefatigable perusal of the letters. The business tone employed by traders when giving their orders to their town agents was adopted by Philip in these epistles. He usually wrote to his parent in this style :—

"SIR,—I have to acknowledge the receipt of yours bearing date the —— instant. The five score of best gilt tacks, as per invoice, came safely to hand. Pray forward, without delay, ¼ gross gilt nails according to sample received per last. We are also in want of plated waistcoat buttons, and strong monkey jacket ditto. Awaiting your speedy reply, I have the honour to be, sir,

"Yours, &c.,

"PHILIP MERTON."

When Vautrin read such a charming document, he felt his heart rejoice that the fates had blessed him with so sweet a child. He was puzzled to know how one so young became possessed of such great business energies. He would instantly comply with the request in the letter. The five score "best gilt tacks" was a figure of speech intended to represent that number of counterfeit half-sovereigns. As the parent read the order for "¼ gross gilt nails," he knew that sovereigns were wanted. "Plated waistcoat buttons" was but a term for bad shillings, and "monkey jacket ditto" referred to half-crowns.

We have merely given this letter as a sample of the correspondence that passed between father and son; but it must be understood that Vautrin never permitted his child to endanger his liberty by touching bad coin of such little value as shillings and half-crowns. The "gilt tacks" and "gilt nails" were the only commodities he dealt in. He would say, "It takes the same time and peril to pass a shilling as to get rid of a sovereign. The good business man economizes time to the utmost; do thou likewise, O my son. The hand of the policeman does not hold less tightly, whether the theft is for a penny loaf or a cash-box."

Such men as Vautrin would not thrive so well on their iniquity unless there were other rogues to help them in their undertakings. The Frenchman was acquainted with the addresses of some ten Birmingham firms, all of whom were proud to own such a customer. At the head of these illicit mints are men of great intellect and attainment, well versed in metallurgy and the alloying of metals. They have studied hard to discover the peculiar admixture of copper, tin, and iron, which shall have the feel and ring of gold and silver. They have their galvanic batteries to throw down the thin coating of the precious metal which is to deceive the eye. They understand the nice arts of die-sinking and stamping. In fact, they are so extremely clever, that, if their ingenuity and great attainments were but properly directed, it is to be doubted whether the profits of these firms would decrease in amount. Some men are of magpie organization, and look upon thieving as the spice that flavours the monotony of life.

B b

Monsieur Emile Vautrin dealt exclusively with Birmingham. His invoices amounted to a very considerable sum total. The firm that received most of his "favours" was in the habit of pricing its "half-James" and "James" (i.e. half and whole sovereigns) at 2s. 10d. and 7s. But then the customer had a very superior article. It was hard, and well cased in gold. To the eye it had a lovely appearance. No ingenious apparatus for bending illicit coin was of avail, and if thrown on the counter it rang as merrily as the purest Bank property. In weight alone it was deficient. Nature has most cruelly put this check upon the smashing community—they cannot get any cheap metal of the same weight as gold.

A man of enlarged notions dislikes a confined sphere of action. He wants elbow room and leg-room for his genius. Thus it happened to Vautrin that at last he grew discontented with the small profits arising from the thirteen shillings out of the seven-shilling sovereign, and began to turn his attention seriously to forged notes. "To pass a note," he argued, "requires an elegant exterior and a pleasing manner. My boy possesses both these great qualifications. It seems like wickedness to waste such valuable gifts. He shall dabble in paper money."

A letter recalled Phil to town. He was hard at profitable work, but he obeyed the parental summons. The project was mentioned to him, and, from the enormity of the undertaking, rather staggered even his notions of audacity. But, if his spirit grew faint, the lion-hearted Vautrin was at his elbow to use his glib tongue and prove that the danger was fancied, and that, in fact, fictitious five or ten-pound notes were the easiest things in the world to get palmed away. "I am sorry," the smiling Vautrin murmured, "that you—you, Phil —should have such little judgment. You see I call it judgment because I know that nobody could, or dare"—he said this last word defiantly—"accuse you of wanting pluck. Your fault lies the other way. But I reverence everybody's opinion, so let us examine into your objection. The amount of the gains frightens you. Surely it is foolish to debate this stupid point. You mean: the extent of the fraud will, you imagine, arouse the indignation of the victims, and make them spitefully alert to catch the offender. Nonsense, sheer nonsense! The men who are in a position to change five-pound notes are just those who are more annoyed at the success of the trick than the amount lost. They are just as angry at taking a bad sovereign. You shall see me go to work a bit, and that will restore your confidence. Really and truly, it is a much safer game than smashing. I'll tell a most singular circumstance to prove this to you."

Vautrin stirred the fire, and with the most cheerful of faces related as follows: "The notes I use are so excessively well made, that but for the private marks of the Bank authorities it would be impossible to detect them as forgeries. I obtain them from a first-rate Birmingham house, and when I tell you that a ten-pound note costs me two pounds, and even a fiver, one sovereign, you will understand they are masterpieces of imitation."

" Go on," muttered Phil.

" In the olden time, when men had bread poultices in their heads instead of brains, they used to do the water-marks with a kind of varnish which made the silver paper transparent. Holding a note to the fire, when the heat melted this varnish, was a sure test. Now we manage matters better. My man in Birmingham assures me he uses the Bank paper, and I can answer for his water-marks, however he does them."

" How can he get hold of Bank paper ? " muttered Phil. " That sounds like a very strong cram."

" My dear boy," exclaimed Vautrin, sorrowfully, " you speak without judgment the dictates of your noble heart. Answer me this. A few years ago the Bank of France made a fresh issue of notes. How was it that on the day before those new notes appeared we were all of us supplied with excellently executed forgeries, so that we might go to work with them on the very morning of the issue ? To be able to forge you must have an original to copy from. People high in authority at the Bank itself had never seen the notes, and knew no more what they were like than you do of what the King of the Cannibal Islands is to have for dinner to-day. Yet we had the forgeries—astoundingly perfect forgeries—ready to pass off as the genuine notes. Why, my boy, bribery did it. Workmen, watch them as you will, can perform as wonderful feats of dexterous legerdemain as the best conjurors going. A note was placed in an oil-silk bag and swallowed. An emetic earned the man a thousand francs. Do you see ? "

" What about the singular circumstance you mentioned ? " asked Phil, when his smiles of wonder had passed off.

" I'll tell you—not that I want to bias your opinion, but as a curious instance of the very little risk a clever person need run if he has his wits about him. A man I knew passed off a note, was detected and tried. He pleaded he did not know the note was a forgery. When the case came on for trial the Bank solicitor had to swear to the illegality of the document. He admitted it was so excellent an imitation that but for the private Bank mark he himself should have thought it a genuine article. A juryman heard this, and says he, ' Then I might have taken it.' Of course he might. The private mark at that time was a pin hole over the ' B ' in ' Bearer.' The jury of course discharged the prisoner. ' We might be standing in the dock ourselves,' they argued, ' and yet be as innocent as turtle doves of an intentional crime.' Do you see, if you deal with well got-up notes such as I use, there is very little danger."

As Phil still hesitated, his father considered that his remaining objections must be on the score of morality. He set his ingenuity to work to demolish the broken reeds to which his boy was trusting. " You will hear a lot of nonsense," he cried, energetically, " about the wickedness and such stuff of passing away these notes. Who raised this moral hue and cry? A parcel of City men, who are themselves at the very same game. They want to keep it all to themselves—the rogues. Now if I, not being worth ten sovereigns, put my name to a bill for two hundred, isn't that passing off a fictitious document? There are hundreds of men in the City now, men who keep their carriages and their hunters, who never sit down to dinner without three differently coloured wine-glasses by their side, who, if their bills were all to be returned the same day, would go smash as sure as your name is—no, I mean as sure as your name isn't Merton, but Vautrin. Don't be humbugged by these scamps. They are only afraid we should spoil their market.

"Now look here, Phil, my boy," continued Vautrin, "if we were to remain at this work all our lives, of course we should in the end be nabbed. I don't intend that, be certain. I shall give the plan full scope for two years. Then we shall have enough. We shall retire from business and become genteel. Our money will not be taken less freely because we got it in a peculiar style. We will be gentlemen, live like and look like gentlemen. Are you game?"

The firm in Birmingham received twenty pounds in good notes, and by return of post came one hundred pounds' worth of bad ones. In less than a fortnight these had been passed off by Phil, who travelled through the land like a dashing young blood of fortune, and dropped his silver paper usually at jewellers'. His stock of jewellery became extensive. He preferred investing in trinkets of solid gold, that metal being always of value, and readily disposed of. Some of these Birmingham imitations were paid into provincial banks, and so excellent was the forgery, that it was only when they eventually reached the establishment in the City that the cheat was detected. Others remained for a long time in circulation, until the backs of them became as crowded with signatures as a subscription list. It was Mr. Philip's peculiar care never to sign the same name on two notes when offering them for payment. He usually selected his cognomen from the County Directory. He also was very attentive that his address should frequently differ.

And this was the reason why Philip had so much money in his pocket, and such excellent clothes on his back, when Monsieur Le Cobbe's Circus visited Elbury.

CHAPTER XVIII.

IN WHICH A FATHER DRINKS AWAY HIS DAUGHTER.

THE broken-hearted spaniel was left for nearly three weeks to weep and howl among the beer barrels of the " Gun and Crow." It stared and winked at a ray of light that came in like a big paint-brush through a broken pane of the dirty cellar window. It seemed to think its beautiful mistress would appear at this broken pane, and, walking down the ray of light, free it of its fetters of old rope. But, though the tears guttered down the corners of its eyes in big stains, no living creature visited the captive, unless it was a bold rat or two, who crept out occasionally as if to learn when the dog would allow itself to be eaten. In vain did the fond creature whisk its tail to the gaoler that brought the daily heap of bones and crusts. The only response to the affectionate motion was a " Lie down, will yer! " The whites of the spaniel's coat became black, and its long glossy hair clotted and hung in lumps like icicles. Poor dog !

With a face of interesting paleness, and a nervous twitching of the face, Philip presented himself at his hotel. The waiter was glad to see him, and curious to know where he had been. With the charac-teristic presumption of people who wish to deceive, Phil volunteered his lie even before it was asked for. " Been shooting with a friend of mine," he said, with more truthfulness than he intended ; and, when the waiter inquired whether the sport had been good, he thought of his shoulder, and answered, "Not very." He did not feel easy until he learned that his room had been locked up and kept for him. Before ten minutes had passed he had examined the false bottom of his trunk, and assured himself that no inquiry into the extent or value of his wardrobe had yet been instituted.

The next day saw Philip dressed like an emperor's valet. His hair smelt of sweet pomatum—a shining, greasy nosegay. He purchased a pair of tight white gloves, and brushed his hat till it seemed French polished. Altogether there was about him a wild, rakish look, with an attempt at foppery which was attractively vulgar.

A policeman of great experience, if he had seen the youth, would have been puzzled to tell whether he was a midshipman on the loose, a young nobleman given to sporting, or a prig. His head was as much on one side as a boat on the beach, his necktie looked as gaudy as a flag, and he carried his big arms and hands as if he was prepared to fight at a moment's notice. The peculiar method of arranging his hair so that two big curls fell from each temple, was eccentric and suspicious. But, despite all, there was many a maiden in the market-place of Elbury who felt the pressure of her stays greatly increased as she saw the swaggering gentleman stroll past her shop. The butcher's daughter raised her blue eyes from the rumpsteaks she was weighing, to sigh. The barber's eldest girl shook her curls and stared her hardest.

With the dirty, clotted spaniel under his arm, Philip walked over the mile of dusty road that led to the R.N.'s dwelling. He rang boldly at the bell, employing the time until the savage maid-servant made her appearance. in dusting his boots with his pocket-handker-chief. The little dog, when the faithful domestic drew near, began to squeak and wag its pretty tail as if wishing to wear it off at the joint. The savage attendant was no less moved at the sight of the animal. She spoke to it, and called it through the iron grate " dear Silky," she bungled over the lock, and eventually started off at full speed, calling out at the top of her voice for Miss Lucy to come.

"This looks well," thought Phil. "At any rate they are glad to see me this time." He was shown into the room with the model of a ship on a side-table, and told to wait a minute. He had time to glance over the names on the cards in a china basket in the centre of the table. Almost the first one he took up had a black border round it, and "Miss Helen Crosier" engraved in the centre. "That's odd," he muttered; "does that mean bad luck or the other thing?" He believed greatly in luck.

Miss Lucy and the lieutenant entered the room together. They bowed, and she blushed. Perhaps she recognized him, for she instantly began to caress her long-absent favourite, calling it so many endearing names that it made a Christian feel jealous to hear them. The old gentleman was—as they say—made of rougher and coarser stuff; indeed, so rough and coarse, that he stared at Philip as if he had been a picture instead of a dashing young fellow, while the first words he uttered were, " I suppose you saw the bills, and have come for the reward?"

Any other man but Lucy's father would—Philip afterwards said —have received " something hot and strong." His pride was hurt. He might pass off forged notes, but he felt that, hang it, " he had not come down to dog-stealing yet." He stared back at the R.N., and smiled an insult.

The beautiful Lucy's papa was fat and slovenly. He had a Chinese-pig appearance. By what peculiar good luck he contrived to own such a lovely child was a startling enigma. His legs filled his trousers so completely, that what would have been as loose as a fiddle bag on any ordinary man became his tights. Even his coat-sleeves seemed rammed down with flesh. He startled Philip by his voice, which was a full octave lower than that of the hoarsest mortal that ever shouted fresh herrings in London streets. It sounded as if he had swallowed an ophicleide.

As Philip only smiled, the R.N. construed that silent movement of the lips into a consent, and turning to the captivating Lucy desired her to fetch ten shillings from the purse she would find on the study table. Then out spake Philip,—

"I purchased that dog from a gipsy boy, about six miles away. When I returned to Elbury, I was told it was your dog, so I brought it to you. You needn't trouble the young lady to go to the study ; I decline to receive the reward." This was spoken in a troubled voice, as if his feelings had been wounded—and so, indeed, they had been, for, excepting in the matter of forged notes, he hated meanness.

The effect of this speech was electrical. Miss Lucy said, "Oh, papa, dear, you shouldn't ! " and the R.N., who wore neither braces nor waistcoat, began to rub his chest uneasily, as if he felt cold. "Won't you sit down ? " he asked, trying to make friends with the youth who had a soul above ten-shilling rewards.

Then followed a rather tame, but, to Philip, a delightful conversation about the dog Silky and the robber gipsy boy. It was remarked that Silky was thin and dirty. Miss Lucy admitted he must be washed. The R.N. vowed he would have the gipsy boy caught and transported for life. The opinion of the company was taken as to whether the dog Silky had been fed once during the three weeks of his absence, and then whether the meal consisted of meat. Lieutenant Grant inquired whether Philip should know the robber boy again if he saw him, and swore to prosecute him if it cost a fortune.

After the dirty, clotted Silky had been fondled until each hair must have received a kiss, a decanter of wine was produced, and the conversation took a pleasanter turn. Remembering the advice Vautrin had given him, Philip, after a time, said,—

"I was looking at the cards on your table. I see you are acquainted with a relation of mine." Naturally enough came an exclamation of " Indeed ! " and then an inquiry was made as to which was the particular piece of pasteboard referred to. When Lucy took up Helen Crosier's card, a glance of singular expression passed between herself and her papa, in which he was evidently rebuked for having insulted one so highly connected by the offer of a trumpery reward, and he endeavoured, as forcibly as " a look " could speak, to say, " How the devil was I to know who his relations were ? "

Rapidly was Philip asked whether he thought Helen Crosier pretty and a very nice girl. " There's something so very striking about her," cried Lucy.

Philip felt inclined to add, " Particularly when she has a gun up to her shoulder ! " but he knew better than to say so.

The lieutenant almost cross-questioned Phil as to his degree of relationship with the family. Had he considered Phil's statement in the light of a misrepresentation he could not have been more exacting in his inquiries.

At last Philip avowed he was the rich banker's grandson. A dead silence followed this revelation. The R.N. asked him whether he wouldn't take another glass of wine, and inquired whether he was engaged to dine anywhere that day.

" You mustn't think I meant to offend you about that ten-shilling affair," stammered the old sailor. " How the devil was I to know who you were till you told me ? Now it's all right, you know; but it looked queer. Our girl, Mary, said you were the same person that spoke to my Lucy at the circus, and I felt deucedly inclined to break your head, I can tell you. In fact, to speak the plain truth, I believed you had yourself stolen the dog."

There was a burst of laughter as the R.N. said this. It was such a ludicrous idea.

The knowledge of human nature possessed by Vautrin had made him prophesy most correctly. The Grant family were quite enchanted to number the banker's grandson among their friends. Even the savage maid-servant, on hearing of the relationship, regretted she had, when at the circus, spoken so harshly to the young gentleman. " Now, I dare say," suggested Mary, " he meant no offence, but merely did it for company. Neither was he free-spoken, but chose his words most genteel and choice."

There was a mystery in the Grant family. Every family has some disgrace or other in it, which takes up half its time to keep secret. The peculiar misfortune of the R.N.'s household was that the lieutenant was uncontrollably in love with liquor. It was a constant fight between Lucy and her father to keep him away from drinking. She never dared leave him by himself, for if she quitted the house but for an hour, she was sure, on her return, to find him out. She knew where he was. About a quarter of a mile down the lane was a low public-house, and Mary was certain to discover her master sotting in the bar-parlour. Once in that establishment, the R.N., as long as consciousness remained, continued to drink. The pony-chaise had to be sent for him, and shillings paid to men called in from the road to help carry the incapacitated gentleman to his bedroom.

Perhaps the lieutenant might remain sober for three months at a stretch. After such a long duration of abstinence the drunken fit would seize him, and for at least a month he was like a wild beast with drink.

Lucy had many trials to undergo. If a bricklayer, dustman, butcher's boy, or intimate friend came to the house, the first thing the R.N. called for was the bottle. A dram of old whisky, or a glass of wine, was, he considered, the proper welcome to be given to anybody. He had found out that this was his only chance of getting one himself. Naturally his daughter did not like to confess that her father was a drunkard, so with a heavy heart she obeyed his commands.

She had found bottles of whisky, to be emptied during the night, concealed under the mattress. He had bribed men to run over to taverns by giving them the boots off his feet. He drank the scent off his daughter's dressing-table. He indulged in bottled beer for breakfast. After every meal he swore he was dying of an indigestion which strong brandy alone could relieve. During the cholera season his specific was raw spirit. Three times a day he would be attacked with the epidemic and rear for alcohol.

The great object of the daughter's life was to keep her father sober; that of the father's to get tipsy. She was too weak to rule him by any other means than tears and entreaties; he had the cunning of strong desire, and cared not what artifice he employed, so long as it gained him the reward of liquor.

The day Philip dined at the R.N.'s, he noticed how lovingly the old man stuck to the wine. The daughter had put on the table but one very small decanter of sherry. Before the fish was removed the wine had disappeared. It pained Phil to witness the reluctance with which Lucy brought in a fresh supply. He thought she had no more, and did not like to confess the barrenness of the cellar; he fancied the family was short of money and couldn't afford the luxury. He quite won the girl's gratitude by his continued refusals to take more wine. It would have been better if he had swallowed his share; there would have been less for the lieutenant.

After dinner, when the gentlemen were to be left alone, Miss Lucy placed a bottle of port on the table, and whispered something in her father's ear. " She's telling him not to be extravagant," thought Phil. He determined on sending in from his hotel a dozen as a present at the first opportunity. The lieutenant attacked the port with thirsty desperation. Every glassful went down at a gulp. In vain did the savage Mary come in some six times to announce that tea was ready.

To make matters worse, Philip, out of kindness—to save the wine, in fact—declared he would sooner have a glass of grog than all the port in the universe. With intense delight the R.N. sent for Lucy, and that unfortunate young lady had to produce the keys of the spirit chest. She looked at Phil with a resigned expression, as much as to say, " I have done all I can to keep my father's infirmity secret, but, since you are both against me, I must submit to the disgrace."

When the port was gone, the whisky was attacked. The old sailor began to tell stories of about the time when he was an officer on board H.M.'s ship " Bullyrag." He inquired into Phil's history. Men who drink are much given to rudeness. The guest was obliged to tell many violent falsehoods. He stated the income allowed him by Vautrin, his father, to be £400 a year. He spoke of the fortune he was entitled to by his grandmother's death. To counterbalance anything the Crosiers might say against him, he fudged a romantic account of the great quarrel existing between Vautrin and the banker. The lieutenant went so far as to call Nathaniel Crosier, Esq., a miserly vagabond. He also expressed his astonishment that any man of even decent feelings should behave in so rascally a manner towards his own grandchild.

To prevent the servant, Mary, from entering the room every five minutes to announce in tones of increasing pathos that the tea was getting cold, the door was locked. Uselessly did Phil entreat that they should join the lady. He didn't want to sit drinking hot grog with the old boy. He infinitely preferred cold Twankay with the young damsel. But the R.N. struck the table with his fist, and swore they would empty the bottles like men. "D—n tea!" he cried, "it's only child's wash at the best. It drowns a man's nature. My heart can't swim in hot tea like a confounded duck. Cold grog is the stuff to wash your soul in. Try this whisky; it is as soft as a baby's neck; bottled joy and laughter!"

After the fifth tumbler, the R.N.'s speech thickened. He pretended at first that he spoke badly on purpose. He grew sentimental, and talked about his daughter, asking Phil if she was not a beautiful girl. At least twenty times he repeated this question, until Phil, ardent admirer as he was, could find no new terms to express his great admiration of Miss Lucy's beauty. He felt bored, and wished the old R.N. would fall under the table and hold his tongue. Suddenly the lieutenant was seized with a new idea. The youth seated before him had so openly expressed his devotion for the lovely Lucy, that the stupid drunkard grew jealous and distrustful. His fuddled brain was labouring with the notion that he must check and intimidate the young gentleman. He began to throw out hints that if any man dared to trifle with his daughter's affections, he would kill the base scoundrel.

"I'd kill him!" he screamed, after he had been silently frowning for some ten minutes. "I'd seize him by the neck"—he took hold of the bottle—"and pour out his life's best blood"—he filled up a tumbler and drank it off. "That girl is a beautiful girl," he continued, "a lovely girl, with every accomplishment. The school bills are upstairs if you don't believe me. If any man dare"—he commenced to weep. "If any scoundrel attempts—I'd tear his heart out—I would, by Heavens! I'm serious. Don't fancy I say it because I am drunk. Yes, I admit I am drunk, but that's my own business, not yours." Then he ceased to shout and began to blow hard down his nostrils, pout his lips, and frown. Occasionally, without speaking, he would strike the table violently, and then pluck at his shirt front. It is probable that the unfortunate young lady who formed the subject of this indecent conversation overheard every word spoken, for a gentle tap at the door was given at very short intervals. Terribly bored with his tipsy companion, Phil at length rose to reply to the tapping; but the R.N., drunk as he seemed, had his wits about him. He knew Lucy was there. "Sit down, sir," he howled at Phil—"sit down, sir. Is this my house, or yours? I order you to sit down, sir, and fill your glass." The young gentleman, who understood very well that if he offended the old one the house would be forbidden him, complied with the order, though his heart bled for the little lady trembling and weeping in the hall.

It was nearly two o'clock before the lieutenant was dead drunk. His head had fallen on his bosom, and he breathed heavily, giving occasionally a choking, guttural sound, as if his windpipe were closed. Then Phil, having made sure his host was insensible, by calling to him several times in a loud voice, unlocked the door.

The daughter was seated in the hall chair with her handkerchief before her eyes. She couldn't speak, neither could Phil. He felt as if he, also, were to blame for that night's misery. At last he stammered out, "If you will permit me I will assist the servant to carry your papa upstairs," and, no reply being given, summoned the harsh-visaged domestic. He was a strong man, and the R.N. was a heavy one. He weighed about three sacks of potatoes, according to Phil's reckoning. It was tough work to climb the stairs with the load. He did it though, and afterwards undressed the sot, and hoisted him on to his bed.

When he came down again, Miss Lucy was seated before the dining-room grate, still in tears. He felt he could not leave the house without saying a few words to her. His voice nearly failed him as he remarked, "You must not accuse me, Miss Grant, with being the cause of what occurred to-night. It is a most painful thing—I trust—indeed—it would be extremely unjust to condemn me—" When a beautiful young lady is sobbing, what can a man do? At any rate, the lovely Lucy could see he was sober enough. That was his great consolation.

After three or four efforts to swallow, Miss Lucy looked up and spoke. "I hope, sir, you will have sufficient respect for our unfortunate family not to mention to any one the scene that— My poor father has but this one fault."

"And a pretty good allowance too," thought Phil.

He tried to persuade her that if a pistol were presented at him; if he felt the cold tip of the barrel touch his ear; if the sharp point of a sharp knife were pricking his bosom, not one word would his tongue utter to cause one moment's sorrow to one so amiable as Miss Grant. He rattled on for a long time, and every word betrayed that he was a devoted admirer of the R.N.'s daughter.

The parent's drunkenness caused this evil—Phil was, by one night's exhibition, placed on a familiar footing with the household. He held their reputation, as it were, in his power. He was intimate. The daughter was grateful to him for carrying the father up to bed; the servant liked him because he took to the job with good-humour and never uttered even one reproach against the sot, but tried to find excuses for the failing, such as, "All nautical men love a glass," or, "All men who are free with the bottle are generous with everything else." The savage-visaged maid had been ten years in the family, and was pleased to hear her master so pleasantly spoken of.

The youth and the damsel remained for one hour chatting over the evening's misfortune. Her tears were dried up by Phil's pleasant voice. He promised to call on the morrow and see the R.N. He also promised never again to dine at the house, and never to accept any invitation unless it was to tea. The maid-servant, when three o'clock struck, helped him on with his coat, and the beautiful damsel accompanied him to the gate. Then, as it was pitch-dark, he was many times requested to pass the night at the cottage. "We can easily make up a bed on the sofa," offered the maiden. She even hinted that he might be attacked on the road. Phil laughed at that. "Hang it," he thought, "that's my own line of work."

CHAPTER XIX.

PHILIP "GOES IN AND WINS."

WHEN Lieutenant Grant was sober, his brain was singularly clear and active. He could shake off his gin-and-water as a dog, after bathing, shakes off the moisture from its coat. Two hours after rising, he was coaxing his child to forgive him, not in direct appeals, but by various acts of kindness of which she very well understood the meaning. His brain, after the most violent boozing, would, with a few hours' sleep, right itself, and, as everybody allowed, a pleasanter man did not breathe than the R.N. when sober.

Philip made his appearance at the cottage about three o'clock. He found the lieutenant in the garden. "Begad!" said the sailor, "we had a jolly time of it last night. Any headache this morning?" he inquired, knowingly. By-and-by he added, "Are you aware we emptied two bottles of wine and all the spirit decanters? We must have kept hard at it." Of course, Philip allowed the old fellow to include him in this vast exploit. He knew exactly how much stimulant he had taken, and humoured the toper by sharing, without a dissenting murmur, the disgrace of the excess.

Every day Philip, on some excuse or other, visited the Grants. The cottage in which the family resided was known to polite people as Prospect Lodge, but the coarse multitude had christened it the "Green Shutters." Thus, at Elbury, the ostlers at the hotel would wink to each other and say, "There goes the swell to the Green Shutters." Well educated folk, however, preferred expressing the same thought in genteeler words—for instance, the butcher's daughter would exclaim, "The gent from the hotel is off again to Prospict 'Ouse."

Such a young fellow as Phil was just the sort of person to win the sailor's esteem. He was lithe, active, and given to nick-nacking. He often assisted Miss Lucy in her garden, digging, raking, and sweeping with violent enthusiasm. When the lieutenant watered his rose-trees, young Vautrin would bring him pail after pail of water, and wet his trousers and boots till they were drenched, yet declare he enjoyed the sport amazingly. If the lock of a door did not act, Phil had it

off, and on again, in a perfect condition, in no time. He turned out
a huge dog as big as a calf that had entered Miss Lucy's poultry-
yard with the evident intention of seeing how chicken tasted. On
the occasion of the pony falling down during an afternoon's drive,
he lifted it up again by sheer strength of muscle, without a buckle
being unfastened. He jumped and moved about with the elasticity
of a harlequin. If a rose-tree wanted training, Phil had the tall
ladder out and turned gardener. The laughter and joking which,
whenever he was present, made the time pass like sleeping, impressed
everybody with the belief that there did not exist in the whole world
another young man worthy to hold a candle to Phil's sunny qualities.
He sang, too, quaint character songs. He had learnt them in the
days of his wandering. The old lieutenant laughed till his eyes disappeared behind his fat cheeks whenever he heard the famous love
song of "I'll feed thee as fat as my feyther's old seow." In such
pleasant society the old man could manage to live on a half allowance
of grog. Then did Lucy say to the hard-favoured Mary, he would
be cured of his weakness if Mr. Vautrin were to stay a year with us."
To which the domestic would reply, "That he would. I'm sure it's
as good as raw spirits to listen to him." Even the savage attendant
had been won over to Phil's side. Phil joked the stern-visaged maid
about her sweethearts, and, although she had given over even praying
for a husband, the mention of one was to her sweet as the droppings
of fresh honey. Many a shilling was placed in her hand, hardened
with washing-days and strong soda. She at last grew so fond of
the handsome young visitor that when he came she would whisper
to him, "Master's in the garden, but she is in the parlour." Poor
thing! she meant it kindly enough, but as Phil, whenever he found
Lucy alone, always made love to her, the hard-favoured housemaid
was, in reality, guilty of a great cruelty in thus encouraging their
secret interviews. A marked change came over Philip when he was
near the lovely Lucy. The voice became gruff and pathetic : he
seemed almost afraid to move about; and, if she shook hands with
him, he kept hold of her fingers long after there was any occasion to
do so.

Whether it was that from the length of his abstinence from liquor
the lieutenant's intellect had brightened, or whether anybody had
whispered in his ear that it was improper to allow a handsome
young gentleman to make open love to a lovely young lady without
having first asked that young gentleman what his intentions might
be—whether it was from the first or last of these reasons we cannot
say, but, after Philip had been an almost daily visitor at Prospect
House for more than two months, the R.N. became suddenly savage
and uncivil to the amiable youth. He refused to allow him to sit in
their pew at church. He said he would have no more reading from
the same prayer-book, or walking home across the fields. He put a
stop to the drives in the country, and for a week the pony did nothing
but eat until it grew too fat for its leather clothes, and had to suffer

the horrors of tight lacing when at last the harness was put on.
The same adviser, whoever she or he was, caused the lieutenant to
pay a visit to the princely mansion of the rich banker of Swanborough. The R.N. insisted on seeing that sallow millionaire.
Then, in bold words, he inquired if he was willing to do anything for
the advancement in life of Philip Vautrin, his grandson, in case that
young gentleman led the beautiful Lucy Grant to the altar.

Bankers, it would seem, have a respect for great speculators.
Nathaniel Crosier thought the better of Philip that he had raised
himself into a position to marry into Her Majesty's navy. The
banker was a man who wore a face as if it had been a mask to hide
his emotions. By long practice, he had paralyzed the muscles of his
countenance. Although he was greatly startled by the question, his
face remained a perfect blank. He urged the lieutenant to speak as
much as he could, before he delivered himself of any opinion on the
subject.

Now Mr. Nathaniel Crosier was well pleased with the lieutenant's
visit, for this reason. He thought to himself, " If Philip can establish
himself respectably in the world, it relieves me of a great weight of
care. He is evidently a clever little fellow, and I must not quarrel
with him. Since this stupid old sailor chooses to give the boy ' a
back' to leap over his evil courses, it is not for me to grumble. Let
the consequences be on his own idiotic head."

Hence it was that Philip received such a character from his grandfather as amounted to no character at all. The banker admitted that
there was a certain income, which, if certain other matters could be
found, would be coming to Philip's father. Then was the R.N.
advised to ask Philip for his mother's marriage certificate. "That
would greatly expedite business," observed Crosier, "and I could
advise you with more certainty."

How ably did Vautrin foresee what would occur when he had
promised to forward the marriage document to assist his son in his
courtship. He seemed to know it would be wanted. Why didn't
Vautrin turn lawyer, instead of openly styling himself scamp? He
would have been the leading member of his profession.

It made Phil stare when the R.N. asked him for his mother's
certificate. The R.N. said he must have it, or the lover must never
show his face at Prospect House again. " It's for your good I'm
working, my boy," added the sailor. " Do you fancy it's any pleasure
for me to go to Swanborough and be shut up with that yellow
banker?" He also hinted that a handsome income would follow the
exhibition of the official paper.

What took place at the second interview between the R.N. and
the rich grandfather need not be stated. The lieutenant returned to
dinner a smiling man, with a strong inclination to get drunk. He
asked Phil to favour him with an interview. The request was
granted. Then did Vautrin, junior, speak as he had never spoken
before. He trembled like a parrot in a thorough draught. His voice

grew full and impressive as he begged for Lucy as a wife. A thousand times he swore genteelly to love her to her dying hour. He would work, slave, perish for her happiness. The excellent old R.N. was affected to tears, and would have given his little finger for a sip of rum. "Take her, my boy, take her," he moaned forth; "only, confound you! always live with me, or else I shall be ruined by the bargain. She is an angel, sir, and I am a beast. Live with us. God bless you! Go and ask her for the sideboard key, or I shall be making a fool of myself. Make haste!"

So Philip became engaged to Lucy Grant. On that very night, before he went to bed, and with tears in his eyes, he wrote to Emile Vautrin, his father. He told his parent that henceforth his life should differ from his past existence. "I will be honest, despite all temptations. She shall never risk disgrace. Our children must not run the peril of dishonour. I thank my God that I am allowed to repent." Curious enough, there was a postscript to this letter requesting the loan of £50, though Philip must have known that every farthing of the money he demanded had been won by dishonour and roguery. In that letter did the son enclose every forged bank-note he possessed. He posted the packet himself. Then he felt as if he had a thousand lungs in his body, so freely did he breathe.

An answer—a polite, friendly answer—arrived in due time. The father congratulated the son on his marriage, and was sorry he could not be present. He applauded the virtuous resolves of his child. As to the matter of the £50, he regretted he was out of cash, for, after reading the letter, he had thrown it to the other end of the room with rage. "He wishes to reform and be virtuous. Let him try, poor fool! Wait till every shilling is spent. The last farthing and his morality will go together."

CHAPTER XX.

A MARRIAGE WHICH WAS NOT EVIDENTLY MADE IN HEAVEN.

THE wedding took place. Mr. and Mrs. Vautrin returned to Prospect House at twelve o'clock on a certain day to eat a magnificent breakfast. If it had not been for a present of some fifty pounds to Mr. and Mrs. Vautrin by the delighted lieutenant, the happy couple would most likely have been greatly inconvenienced for ready money during their honeymoon trip. The painful fact was, that Mr. Philip was really distressed for want of that extraordinary article, a five-pound note.

He felt a happy man. He had given up his wickedness; he had taken to his arms a wife whom it pained him to leave for even five minutes. If Lucy went into the garden to see if it rained, Philip followed her. They walked about with their arms round each other's waists. If Philip went upstairs to change his coat, Lucy, when he returned, would say, "Where have you ,been all this long time, my dearest ? " They were more in love with each other than before they were married.

Oh, that happy, happy time, when he and she are "lambs" and "angels," "pretties" and "dearests!"—when they cannot look at each other without a sickly smile and a peculiar softness of eye— when they would sooner sit by each other's side than visit theatre, opera, or ball! Why do ye last so short a time, ye fleeting months? How pathetic it is to stand by and watch those fond loves! How their bitterest quarrel consists only of an injured tone of voice—how Lucy weeps if Phil but looks unkind, while he falls on his knees, as the first tear trickles, to beg forgiveness. If she but say it is a cold night, he will fly up a Jacob's ladder of steps to fetch a shawl for her white shoulders. She is sleepy, and rests her lovely head for a moment on the sofa cushion. Then fiercely does he mount guard to prevent any noise from opening those angelic eyes. If a footstep creaks in the passage, he is after it, ready to fight or chastise the heavy-booted individual. Oh, ye first ¡six months after marriage! Why cannot ye last for sixty years! Why should men get tired of these sweetmeats of life, or women cease to be as attractive after fifty years of wedlock!

It was a fine tale Philip had told his father-in-law of the amount of his income. The R.N. considered he had made an excellent match of it. He told his friends that "his son-in-law had a very pretty little annual sum, which would enable him to live like a gentleman, sir." A nice rumpus it would make when the truth came out!

Yet Phil had sworn to himself not to pass another false note. Perhaps as his money became more and more easy to count, he regretted this promise. But he was just then sentimentally inclined, and looked upon the vow as one made to his Lucy. The thought sometimes came uppermost that he could in one day at any country town pick up enough to keep beautiful Lucy in plenty for a month at least, but he was faithful to his resolves, and upbraided himself for even allowing his fancy to turn traitor against his virtue. No! no! Lucy should never be disgraced. Poor, dear, sweet, gentle girl, her heart should never be broken!

He borrowed first one fifty pounds and then another of dear father-in-law. The fat R.N. began to look glum. He began to dislike Phil, and, when he saw his son-in-law coming one way, trotted off in the opposite direction, for fear Phil should want any more fifties " for a day or two."

At last Philip thought he would run up to London and see papa Vautrin. He would punish his father by nature for the next loan.

The lovely Lucy pouted, but yielded to the distressing absence of three days, on condition that darling Phil wrote by every night's post, and promised to take great care of himself.

Week after week did Emile Vautrin, when he reached home at night, ask if any letter had arrived for him. He opened many with a hasty hand, but not one was from Philip. "Confound him!" growled Vautrin, "where does he get his money from? How does he manage to hold out so long?"

Then it struck him that most likely his son, instead of writing, would pay him a visit. For two months he never left his home of an evening. "He must come," argued the man; "the fool sent his false notes back." If a cab stopped in the street, this anxious watcher thrust his head and shoulders from the window, in his impatience to see if the expected son had arrived. He bought time-tables, and learned the arrivals of the trains from Swanborough. He even burned night-lights, and piled up coals on the fire before going to bed, that he might be prepared to welcome the penniless Philip back to crime and his father.

At length the son came. He walked into the parental presence with a bashful, ashamed mien. He was received in an open, loving manner. Chops were cooked, and tumblers filled. "I knew it, I knew it!" joyfully thought the father. "I am a lost man," moaned the son.

The poor bridegroom was in the unfortunate position of being thought well off, without having a penny in his pocket. He was in the still more unfortunate position of requiring large sums of money without seeing any possibility of obtaining them honestly. Gambling or robbery are the only resources in such cases.

Philip asked his dad to lend him £200. The dad opened his eyes, stared, and then laughed. "My poor boy! are you mad?" he cried. "£200! where do you imagine I am to get them from? You might as well ask me for two hundred real flesh-and-blood sovereigns with their royal crowns on!"

The son sighed, and looked sadly put out. He muttered something about "he must get the money somehow." The old rogue's heart leaped like a trout in a clear stream. "I shall get back my son again; I shall have my boy—ha! ha!" he chuckled to himself.

Lucy received a long letter from "her pet Phil," telling her he should be away for three weeks. She was not to fret. There was some bother about his drawing his income as usual, and a friend who had promised to advance him some money refused to do so unless Phil stayed for a few weeks' shooting at his place. "I shall dream of you every night, love," wrote Phil. The darling Lucy wept till her eyelids were as pink as rose-leaves, and wished in her heart her beautiful boy knew nobody in the world but herself, and that money and shooting had never been invented.

After arguing for an entire night and day, the papa Vautrin had convinced the son Vautrin that the only known means of getting together £300 in three weeks was to commit a burglary. He had also clearly demonstrated that there was no danger in such a proceeding. "I love you too dearly, my boy, to let you risk your life," said the affectionate parent. "I'll show you the way. Leave it to me." The unhappy boy consented. He swore, looking up at the ceiling, "This shall, at any rate, be my last crime!"

Canterbury was fixed upon for the exploits of Vautrin's gang. "It's a good ecclesiastical town," said that unworthy man, "and there is no place like a dean's house for solid silver spoons." A list was obtained of the good houses in the suburbs of the town. One Tater-trap Sam, a big-mouthed burglar, joined the venture when Canterbury was mentioned. "There hasn't been a crib cracked there these four 'ear," he said. "It's uncommon adwantageous ground."

Philip, as we know, was a very good-looking fellow, of that powerful build and impudent expression of face, and with those charmingly free-and-easy manners which maid-servants find it so difficult to resist. He had a delightfully roguish trick of tickling, flirting, flattering, and promising marriage. To Canterbury was he despatched, armed with full instructions, in order to find out which of the inhabitants "was worth most sugar."

He made most of his inquiries at public-houses. Dressed like a respectable tradesman, he went up to the bar and ordered a glass of ale. The drinking of this refreshment took a long time. He "tried all he knew" to get into conversation with the landlady, calling into play his softest tones of voice, using his prettiest speeches, and generally displaying those blandishments which are supposed to win the roughest heart. When the road was properly prepared he would commence operations. "I came down from London this morning," he would begin, "on very important business. You can do me a kindness if you will, but I shouldn't like you to mention it to anybody. Mr. So-and-So, who lives in such and such a house close by, has given our firm a very heavy order—and, indeed, it's as good as five hundred pounds to us. We are rather nervous about taking the work without making inquiries. Are they respectable people? Do they live in style?" The landlady, taken off her guard, would—fancying she was doing good service to her neighbour—answer any questions put to her about the wealth of the gentleman in question.

The safest plan was to get hold of a man-servant, and learn from him the necessary particulars. For this purpose Phil would dress up as a groom, and frequent taprooms where coachmen, and occasionally footmen, passed their evenings. He would run his eye round the room and pick out the handsomest livery. It was not difficult to get into conversation with these men. A glass of grog soon made a friend of the most diffident. On such occasions, Phil pretended that he was looking out for a "place," and inquired whether his companion could "put him up to" a comfortable berth.

If any situations were mentioned, one of Phil's questions was whether "there was much plate to clean."

Or else Philip, when he had nearly decided on the establishment to be attacked, would inquire in the neighbourhood the name of the coachman "who served the family." Then he walked boldly up to the house, rang the stable-bell, and asked to see Mr. Smith, the coachman, for a few minutes. As soon as the domestic appeared, Phil began, in a confidential whisper, " I understand you're going to leave." This led to a lengthy conversation, in which Mr. Smith denied the fact, and became anxious to know how such a report could have got about. Then Phil inquired whether Mr. Smith couldn't slip out for a few minutes to have a glass of ale. If the stupid man consented, Phil reckoned his job nearly completed. The ale led to pipes, and the pipes to grog. The talk was all about their relative places. "Mine was a very good place, and very good money, but I couldn't put up with their temper. It was a good place if you'd got the temper to stand their temper." Growing more and more condential, he would describe the wealth of this supposed master. He would brag of the family plate and the young ladies' jewels. Generally it set Mr. Smith bragging too, and out came the required information. "Rum old fellow, my governor," Phil would next begin; " every night the plate was carried up to his room. We kept it in the footman's pantry in the daytime, but sometimes he'd be that suspicious he'd actually come down in the daytime and count it over. He would, by gum!" Thus was Mr. Smith gradually wheedled into confessing the secret arrangements of Mr. So-and-So's establishment.

Another of Philip's tricks was to call at one of the rich-looking mansions with a letter addressed to anybody he first thought of—say Jones—with these words underneath, " Care of Mr. ——" whatever the name of the wealthy owner might be. This letter did the footman carry into the parlour, where the wealthy owner was seated, and announced that a groom was waiting for an answer. This caused much commotion. The wealthy owner swore he didn't know who Jones was. The mistress of the house was consulted, as were also the young ladies and gentlemen, to learn if they knew anything of the mysterious Jones. This took time, and permitted Phil, at his leisure, to examine the bolts, bars, and street-door key.

Every morning at seven o'clock did Philip rise, and, after dressing in his natty groom's costume, sally forth into the streets to transact his evil business. At that hour the servant-maids were cleaning the doorsteps, and, knowing the family were in bed, not averse to a flirtation before breakfast. The natty groom did not pick his maidens according to their looks, but the houses in which they dwelt. On one of these excursions he fixed upon an unfortunately plain female hearth-stoning the entrance to a noble establishment. The open street door revealed a hall as long as a shooting-gallery. The youth began proceedings by carrying away the maid's pail. She pursued him, calling him "Mr. Impudence." He swore he would only surrender the pail on receiving a kiss. She, noticing that nobody was about, recovered her master's property on the terms mentioned. After she had returned to her hearth-stoning, Phil stood by and tempted her: "You'd make a nice little wife to take care of a fellow's home, and keep it clean, for you're a tidy little body, I can see, and a mortal foe to dirt."

"That I just am—you're right there," the girl replied, although there was round her unwashed neck a rim of black like a leathern strap.

In these dialogues the young rogue always mentioned marriage at the first set-off. He found the damsels looked more kindly on him. They did not object to the abruptness of the proposal.

"It would save me a deal of money, keeping me out of public-houses, for I make a goodish sum of money, and easy come, easy go," continued Phil. "Hang it! I've half a mind to make a rush of it, and get spliced. What do you say, Mary? Are you agreeable?"

"Go along with you—you don't mean it," the girl replied. "You're only making a fool of me. If I was to say: Yes, you'd think: No. Besides, my name ain't Mary, but Emmerly."

"Thank Heaven for all its blessings!" continued the wooer, "for Mary's a name very much against my grain. I can tell you one thing, Emily, my dear—we shouldn't want any candle to go to bed by so long as you have those bright eyes of yours. That's a saving, ain't it?"

His playfulness during these walks was pleasant to behold. If a servant was sweeping, he took hold of her broom and insisted upon helping her. If she was beating a mat he relieved her of her duty. After rendering these services, the handsome groom invariably told all of them he was looking out for a pretty little wife, and requested them, if they wouldn't have him, to speak to their sisters, "for he liked the pattern much, and must have one of the family." It followed that Phil's evenings were taken up with keeping appointments with the different servant-girls of Canterbury. He was frequently invited, on the sly, into the kitchen. That was the end and aim of his gallant attentions.

The sturdy vagabond Vautrin was highly pleased when he and three others joined the youth at Canterbury. Even Tater-trap Sam, that "righteous man," [1] complimented Phil on the completeness with which he had done his work. They determined on going to business at once. With consummate ability, Phil had even persuaded a policeman "to stand in for a share" of one of the undertakings. The constable had evidently suspected that something "was up," and, to keep his mouth quiet, Vautrin, junior, had proposed to fill it with one-fifth of the plunder.

They were very fortunate in their work. On the Sunday afternoon, they rifled three houses. At one of them, Philip had made an

---

[1] The slang term for a regular cracksman.

appointment with Emily to meet him in the summer-house at the end of the garden, whilst the family were at church. Whilst the love-making was proceeding, Vautrin and his men packed up the plate and emptied one or two desks of their contents.

In the evening Phil took another servant-girl out for a stroll, whilst her mistress was at chapel. The gang, after knocking twice at the street-door to assure themselves that the house was deserted, picked the lock and entered. The forks and spoons were soon collected and carried away.

One evening they broke into an extensive mansion about a mile from the town. Their friend, the policeman, arranged matters very prettily for them, and even consented, in case any danger threatened, to give them "the office," that is, warn them. He was to shout out "Bill Thomson!" at the top of his voice, and, if that failed, to spring his rattle.

At two in the morning, the gang entered the grounds of the doomed house. They met the policeman at the gates, and satisfactorily answered his inquiry of "will it be all right?" It took about two minutes to "star the glaze." A bradawl was inserted through the putty of the window-pane, and a handkerchief placed against the glass to deaden the sound. With one turn of the awl the brittle glass splintered. A wet thumb was rubbed backwards (as on a tambourine) against the pane, and one of the rays of the "star" followed the jarring finger. The piece was taken out, and, the catch being unfastened, the window opened. The "james"—a short crow-bar—and the centrebit soon cleared away the obstruction of the shutter.

The darkie—a lantern—was little used. The men were silent as ghosts. They expressed themselves by pantomime. They "muffled the hoof" with list slippers. One thing they noticed especially. As they threaded the passages, they were particular about the way they entered, that there might be no bungling if a hurried escape became necessary.

The household slept in peace. The maids above and the men at the back might have occasionally heard a suspicious sound, but, after listening for a second, cursed the cat, and turned over to sleep. The thieves were practised at their work, and the clock in the hall made more riot than they.

Whenever they came to a landing with two doors, they tried them, and, if both were open, locked one. The keys were taken from the inside and placed on the outside. They even entered bedrooms and locked the sleeping inmates in their apartments. A key was turned with less noise than the chirp of a cricket.

They visited the drawing-room. A silent match was struck and a wax taper lighted. Be sure they cared nothing about spilling the grease on the thick-piled carpet as they hunted about. Five minutes sufficed to pillage the room. The silver inkstand, the watch left by mistake on the mantelpiece, the notes in the desks, were all they took.

They were so careful not to burden themselves with plated goods, that, if no hall-mark could be discovered, pieces were cut off the suspicious article to see if any copper could be detected. Every time they entered a room, Vautrin waved his arm to set the searchers to work, and they, creeping, like snakes, up to the chiffonniers and cupboards, pocketed anything they imagined of value, whilst the leader, with a life-preserver in his hand, guarded the entrance.

Once they heard a voice ask "Who's there?" They couched and held their breath till a snore gave them liberty to move. In one bedroom, two young ladies were sleeping. The wax taper was flashed before their eyes to test the soundness of their repose, because forcing drawers occasions a little noise. If these young ladies had opened their eyes at that instant, they would have seen these rough men with craped faces standing around the bed, and, by their dumb show, expressing great admiration for the nightcapped faces on the pillow. It was Vautrin who always kept guard over the sleepers. His "neddy," or life-preserver, was held above their heads, ready to strike if necessary. The men hunted for and pocketed the trinkets. Diamonds, emeralds, and pearls were thrust into the capacious pockets. It was a good "find," and made one fellow so jocose that he took up a little boot belonging to one of the sleeping beauties, and lifted his hands in wonder at its smallness.

The proprietor of this establishment had to be aroused from his sound repose to say where he concealed his treasures. At first he rubbed his eyes and stared in wonder. He was beginning to call out, when Vautrin struck him on the shoulder with the life-preserver, and swore to murder him if he made the slightest noise. The gentleman's wife entreated him to be peaceful. In a wonderfully short time the treasures that it had taken the owner years of prudence to amass were handed over to the robbers. Silver tea and coffee services, numberless spoons and forks, a silver tea-urn, candlesticks, bank-notes, watches, and jewels, were delivered up, and the lives of the plucked ones spared. The policeman who "stood in" for this robbery saw the rogues depart with their plunder. He asked them, as they passed him, "if it was all correct?" An appointment was made with this guardian of the public safety, according to which he was to meet the thieves on a certain day, and receive his share of the booty. Housebreakers never break faith with the police. The officer knew this, and trusted them like gentlemen. He was wondering how much his share would come to, when the alarm of the burglary was first given.

The division of the spoil took place in a back room in Houndsditch. Vautrin knew the value of diamonds as well as any merchant. The plate was tested with aquafortis and weighed. The gold settings of the trinkets were equally divided. Philip and his father claimed two shares each; the others were well contented with what they got. It was the best prize they had ever had. The Jew who came

to buy the silver at 4s. the ounce complimented the robbers on their adroitness, as he crammed the metal into his "old clo'" bag. He was obliged to make three journeys to carry away his purchase.

Both of Phil's pockets were crammed with notes when he returned to his darling Lucy. His heart smote him as she caressed and scolded her naughty husband, kissing him for coming back, and rebuking him for being away so long. She threatened to make him account for every moment of his time. He turned pale and tried to smile, but his lips felt stiff and his heart heavy. At night he prayed by his bed so long that his wife was frightened. She asked him why he was sobbing, but, when he replied, "With joy at returning to his beloved Lucy," she thought it very natural, and wished she knew how she could express the great love she felt for her "darling boy."

Once more Phil swore he would never again trespass. He would change his life. For the sake of her he loved, he would be honest. But Phil was not his own master. His soul was not his own. Did he think Vautrin had forgotten the vow he had made to have his hand about the banker's throat? That man never broke his oaths, if Philip did.

When Vautrin came down to Swanborough, he did not inform Phil he was so near Prospect House. He lived and slept at the cottage of rough-headed Tom, the gardener. He never cared to witness the domestic felicity of his first-born.

The Frenchman took to exercise, unless it was towards dusk. Then he would wrap himself up in his thick coat, and, concealing his face behind the upturned collar, stroll across the fields. As he neared a tumble-down cart-shed, he would give a shrill whistle, and, if the signal was answered, his pace was increased. Then two men would step forth from the dark shadow of the shed. They never greeted each other with any terms of friendship. It was a business meeting. The shafts of an old cart were their seats. Pipes were lighted, and liquor produced and shared, the drinker placing his lips to the neck of the bottle. The men spoke in whispers. The important business on which they met was kept very secret. If the discussion became animated, it was only by their gestures being more frequent and sudden that the confederates betrayed their excitement. There was evidently more roguery afoot, and that of a dangerous kind.

Vautrin had determined on letting Phil enjoy his home for a time. "He shall have no share in this spec," he said to himself. "His brain is not strong enough to bear much of this sort of thing. Besides, he lives too near to that cursed scoundrel. It might ruin the boy, and break his pretty wife's heart, if we failed. He is better at home, drinking tea and staring into her eyes. This time I'll go alone."

CHAPTER XXI.

CASSANDRA II.

ONE of the disadvantages of Truth is the difficulty of getting people to believe in it. Men who will take pleasantly to a brisk falsehood shake their heads dubiously at a ponderous truth. There are thousands of truths scattered about the world, lying idle as a miser's hoard, but it is such break-neck business to meddle with them, that prudent people prefer closing their eyes and passing them by unheeded. The work is too dangerous. A line in an almanack is poor compensation for poverty and persecution. The discoverer of gunpowder most likely blew himself to atoms.

How many victims have there been to unrecognized truths! There was poor Socrates. He might have conducted his academy prosperously, and died comfortably between the sheets, but truth drove him to poison. Diogenes might have rolled in his carriage instead of his tub. In his sixty-fourth year, Cicero was assassinated, that being exactly the period of life when easy-going gentlemen, who care no more for truths than cows do for roast beef, retire from business to enjoy ease and plenty. The usual way in which truth confers immortality upon the discoverer is by causing his death.

Among the sufferers from truth must be enumerated Miss Helen Crosier. The mighty Columbus himself, wandering over Europe seeking for some prince to put faith in his dreams of continents beyond the seas, was not more laughed at than the above-mentioned young lady, whenever she insisted that on a certain moonlight night she had beheld suspicious-looking men prowling about the grounds at Swanborough. Her heroic behaviour in firing the gun caused innumerable allusions to be made to her great capacity for shooting with the long bow. She flew into passions which made her eyes appear most becomingly bright; she stamped with her little foot until her heel ached; she slapped her pretty hands until the palms tingled, but to no effect. She frequently inquired whether she ought to believe what she had seen with her own eyes, and was by way of answer favoured with several interesting instances of curious optical delusions. It became a custom among her jocose acquaintance, whenever they met, to inquire whether her repose had lately been disturbed by any more robbers. Very intimate friends, who dared to take liberties with the young lady, hinted that probably the robber had been some love-sick youth, about to commence a serenade beneath her lattice. Whenever the captain wrote to his sister, he never missed inquiring whether "she had shot any more ghosts." These constant doubtings and contradictions began to affect the unfortunate damsel's health. She grew nervous and snappish. Her own maid, Harriet, who had been six years in the family, was so frequently ordered to "leave the house that very instant" that she grew quite accustomed to the command, and refused to pay it the slightest attention.

The spot where Helen had seen Vautrin standing had the next morning been carefully examined by the police and neighbours. No traces of footsteps could be discovered. In vain did Miss Crosier affirm that she wounded some one, and uselessly did she give imitations of the cry of pain that followed her shot: not a drop of blood could be found, and her exertions went for nothing. The constables, not liking to contradict her, said the whole affair was very curious; her father desired her not to be so sentimental and absurd; her brother suggested (per post) "nightmare," and inquired carefully into what she had that night eaten for supper, and everybody laughed at the miserable Helen, who, after all, was correct in everything she had said.

No watch-dog ever guarded a house more carefully than did this unhappy young lady ever since that eventful night. Her nerves were completely shattered. For nights she could not sleep a wink. The window near the ground was grated with thick iron bars, but even that did not dispel her fears. She bought a most villainous cur from a boy in the village, a restless, discontented beast, that barked itself into a sore throat even if a cricket began to chirp. Every night did this sour-hearted dog sleep in Miss Helen's bedchamber, and, by the great number of its false alarms, caused its amiable owner to pass the greater portion of her bedtime either peeping into the garden from behind the blind, or listening with the most acute interest to detect the sound of the supposed robbers ascending the stairs. Now she could distinctly hear the gravel of the walks crunching beneath a heavy boot, now it was the crack of a lucifer struck in the hall. More than once the old banker caught her wandering about the house at three in the morning, to make sure that the servants had bolted some particular door or other she had been dreaming about.

She became the Cassandra of the household, always predicting the fall of the Swanborough Troy, and always being laughed at for her warnings. When her father was away of an evening, she was too timid to sit alone, and insisted upon one of the maids keeping her company. Every female in the house dreaded her society on these occasions, for at least once an hour something occurred to make them both tremble and turn pale with fear. It was one constant inquiry of "What was that, Harriet?" or, "Did you hear anything, Harriet?" A rose-branch scratching against the window would make their eyes open to the size of soap bubbles. A shouting in the road would make them jump as if a blackbeetle had nipped their ankles. So nervous was the unhappy young lady that she dared not even look at the portrait of her poor buried mother when once the lamp had been lighted, for the eyes seemed to have life in them and to be staring at her as she sat still, or to follow her about the room whenever she stirred. Another constant cause of alarm were the window curtains. Every night, after the shutters had been closed, these long curtains were drawn closely together. On stormy nights, the wind found its way through the cracks of the woodwork and caused the drapery to bulge out, somewhat as if someone were concealed behind the cloth. Instantly the little mistress would direct the attention of the maid to the suspicious-looking appearance of the curtain. In a half-joking tone—for she was ashamed of being thought a coward—Helen would ask whether anybody wouldn't swear a man was hidden behind the hangings? The servant acquiescing, and the cloth continuing to swell out and move, the two girls would at last grow so alarmed that neither of them had the power to move. In vain would Helen call out in a commanding voice, "If there is a man behind that curtain, I order him to come out." In vain were books thrown at the supposed housebreaker. The usual end to the scene of terror was to ring the bell for the footman, and on the pretence that the shutter was not properly fastened, ensnare that unsuspecting menial into risking his liveried form in an encounter with the imaginary assassin.

One night, the vigilant cur was so restless and savage that it became a question with its mistress whether it was going mad or really heard thieves. It sniffed at the crack under the parlour door, and barked with remarkable strength of lungs. Even pats on the head and gruff orders to "Be quiet, sir," failed to have any other effect than to change its noisy bursts into continuous growling. The old gentleman, writing in the library, rang the bell twice to desire that the animal should either be turned into the yard or kept quiet. It continued to creep cautiously about the room, with its tail tucked tightly between its legs, and its ears pricked up as stiff as fir-cones, snarling and yelping most perseveringly. Even in the bedroom the rebellious little imp refused to be comforted. It kept its eyes fixed on the window, and grumbled sternly. Its unfortunate mistress felt certain that some evil threatened the family. She lay trembling in her bed, expecting every moment to hear the front door forced in with a crash. She endured this torment of mind for more than an hour, but, at last, summoned up sufficient courage to creep to the window and very slightly draw aside the blind and look into the garden.

She nearly fell forward with fear, and clutched at a chair by her side with such force that her finger-nails were bent backwards like the nibs of quill pens. Standing on the lawn, almost on the same spot she had fired at, was a tall figure. He was staring up at the house, as if studying every window in its walls. When he saw the reflection of Miss Helen's head and shoulders cast by the night-light upon the white blind, his form retired slowly to the thick shrubs, and disappeared behind them.

As soon as he was out of sight, the young lady recovered strength

mails of Nathaniel Crasier Craft: rom: vill by an altern: A: 56.74

enough to commence screaming. Followed by the barking dog, she
flew to her father's room, and between her gasps announced to the
alarmed gentleman that robbers were about to break into the
premises. One by one the servants, in their nightgowns, with shawls
thrown hastily over their shoulders, came creeping downstairs.
Windows were thrown open, and a dozen heads thrust forth to look
after the marauders. The night air was cold, and the inmates
quickly came to the conclusion that it was a false alarm.

Mr. Nathaniel Crosier grew angry. He frowned, and, despite his
tall nightcap, looked terrible with rage. Two of the maids were
desired to take their beds down into Miss Helen's room, and pass the
night there. "If she has any more of these hysterical attacks," said
the banker, "let the groom saddle the pony, and gallop over to the
doctor's. I'll put an end to these midnight disturbances."

It was useless for poor Helen to vow and protest she had seen some
one staring up at the house. Her father would not even answer her,
but closed his door and locked it whilst she was in the middle of her
statement.

The next morning a severe "talking to" awaited the daughter when
she descended to breakfast. She was told she must submit to
medical treatment, and have a little courage poured down her throat
from physic bottles. Her parent professed himself shocked that a
daughter of his should be so childish. "Even if you did see some
one in the garden, is it so difficult to enter from the road?" argued
Mr. Nathaniel. "What is there so dreadful in it that you must rush
up and down the house like a banshee, frightening everybody out of
their night's repose? How are the servants to do their work? I
should not wonder if some report were spread about that the house
is haunted, or something of the kind, and not only will the domestics
refuse to stop with us, but the value of the property will be
considerably depreciated; and for this loss of domestic peace and
money invested, I shall have to thank a young school-girl's romantic
stupidities."

The unhappy lady, although spiteful at being styled a school-girl,
began to weep. In her most beseeching voice, she implored her
father to believe her. Again she prophesied that great evil was
threatening the family of the Crosiers. She even went so far as to
mention the word "death." If her father had seen the fellow's face
staring up, with the full moonlight on it, he would, she was certain,
think as she did. But papas are very slow to listen to the wisdom of
their children. Her stern parent hinted unmistakably that if she
persevered in her absurdity he should lose patience, and bade her
attend to the teapot, and leave robbers and such stuff to him. The
wretched Cassandra moistened her dry toast with her tears, and
munched solemnly.

Yet this unfortunate young lady had been most truthful in her
warnings. It was Vautrin whom she had seen, and there was evil in
his eye as he scowled upon the building.

But the earnestness of his daughter's manner had, despite himself, impressed the old banker. Whilst the daylight lasted, he treated her cautionings with apparent indifference. The darkness of night is the time for fear. As the gloom of evening set in, he grew nervous. The head groom was sent for and orders given that the big house-dog should be unchained and allowed to roam about the grounds till morning. The old man was ashamed to betray his fears before his servant, and, assuming a laugh, stated that his daughter had teased him into these foolish measures. Before proceeding to bed, he saw to the fastenings of the door, trying the bolts with his own hands. A staircase window over the portico attracted his notice from the facilities it offered to any speculative burglar. It struck him that a few iron bars might not be misplaced. Then he retired to rest, thinking to himself what steps he should take supposing an attack were made upon the premises. As he could not sleep, he left the candle burning, a thing he had not done for years. Yes, the banker was afraid.

There was only one man in the world whom he really dreaded. He hated Vautrin and feared him. "It is an unequal match between us," he argued; "that rogue doesn't care a curse what he does. He has no property to lose; no reputation to risk. I wish the scoundrel would die and leave me at peace."

Curiously enough, the thoughts of the very man the banker was cursing were bent upon the same subject. He was leaning over the fireplace in rough-headed Tom's kitchen, and, as he watched the wood smouldering, said to himself, "It's a hard fight. The old rogue has money and the law on his side. He has only to raise his voice, and the police are at his elbow. But, hang him, or hang me, I'll be even with him. It shall be a clean slate between us before I have ended the business."

As the banker could not sleep, he rose, and, slipping on his dressing-gown, passed the time in letter-writing. A hurried note was scrawled to the village smith, giving directions about the bars for the staircase window. Then he began a note to his brave soldier-boy Merton.

"Your sister," ran part of the letter, "has gone crazy lately, and will insist that the house is to be attacked by thieves, or some such stupidity. I fear the girl will be ill, unless something is done to quiet her alarm. I am very angry, but at the same time I cannot help pitying her, her terror is so sincere. I am sorry to interfere with you, my dear Merton, but I should be pleased if you would run down to Swanborough and pass a week with us. Indeed, I insist on this, so do not disappoint me. I have ordered the footman to sleep with loaded pistols by his bedside. You are a soldier, and your presence would have a very excellent effect upon poor Helen, who is really suffering. I shall expect you by the day after to-morrow, at the latest."

CHAPTER XXII.

A WEDDING TRIP.

To console the unfortunate of this world, some humane philosopher started a theory that more men were ruined by success than by failures. A gentleman who has just passed the Insolvent Court, and finds himself at two o'clock on a wet morning without twopence to pay for a night's shake-down, may feel a glow of satisfaction from this paralogism, but, until Whitecross Street is crowded with prisoners possessed of five thousand a year, or the House of Correction be crammed with vagabonds who keep their carriages, we cannot place perfect confidence in this curious speculation in morals. There was Captain Crosier. Was he a ruin? If it be insisted that he was, then we must add, that never was a ruin in a more perfect state of repair. His ivy of remorse was neatly clipped and trained; the weeds of repentance were most carefully kept under. He ate and drank with a heartiness pleasant to behold, and, altogether, was healthy and amiable.

Unfortunately for his victim, the only chance he ran of being ruined was from his indecision of mind. He never once lost sight of the object he had in view, but he loitered on the way, and rested often on the road. Yet he was successful. Bertha was most decidedly his. He had only to call a cab, and order her to step into it, and she would have obeyed.

He was like a timid man at a gambling-table. He longed to join in the game, and win as his noble friends had done, but yet he held back, nervously calculating the chances of losing. Whilst the ball was moving, he felt undecided, and it was not until it stopped that he determined on making the venture. Thus it was only when adverse circumstances dimmed his hopes of making the delightful Bertha his, that he felt the gratification of his desires was necessary to his happiness, but the moment the path appeared easy, and conquest seemed certain, he drew back to think the matter over and repent. His mind was a miserable coasting-vessel, that could only steer its course so long as the rocks were in view.

The pretty Bertha pined and thought. At times, her dear Merton treated her most coldly, ordering her about in a commanding tone, as if he wished purposely to remind her that, after all, she was only a maid-servant. Then the poor girl would regret the days when she lived so peaceably under Miss Tomsey's roof, and, restored to reason by her sorrowful thoughts, allow her brain to rebel against her heart, until she was thoroughly convinced of the impossibility of ever being Mrs. Captain Crosier. How charmingly, when he again evinced symptoms of wishing to renew their love, she would warn him to leave her in peace, and permit her to try and forget they had ever met. "You are ashamed of me now," she would say, very sorrowfully, in a clear voice, without a sob in it, although the tears ran down her cheeks. "Of course you will deny it, but I can tell from your ways that you are. It is much better that we should part; better for you, and a thousand times better for me. It would kill me— don't laugh, I am speaking seriously—it would kill me if you should ever consider that I disgraced you. When they asked what I had been—when they inquired who my mother was—I know you would feel terribly sorry that we ever met. Do go away. I think I could bear it now—at least, I can promise you shall never know if the separation is more than I can endure."

As, when a lusty poker, wielded by a broad-palmed hand, is driven among the dull, red embers, the flame with each thrust springs upwards to the chimney, so did these iron words arouse the dormant affection in the grates of the captain's bosom, and send his hot love leaping to his throat. He swore and vowed, he knelt and pressed, and gradually the glow of his love imparted its warmth to the chilled heart of the fair one. In a book of domestic economy there is an excellent receipt for making a good, cheap fire. The author says, "Damp the cinders with a little water, and they will burn exceedingly well." The tears from Bertha's eyes had this effect on the dull black dust of Merton's burnt-out nature.

It was after such a scene as the one above described that the captain, in the full heat of his affection, had gone out to cool his ardent love and commune with himself in the seclusion of the back streets of Camberwell. "Poor little thing!" he thought to himself, "I can't bear to see her cry. Her sorrow is so confoundedly calm, it frightens me. I know she'd kill herself somehow or other if I left her, and, although I don't believe in ghosts, yet I should be always thinking of her, and that's as bad. There are all those things I bought for her lying at my place in Harley Street. What the deuce could I do with them? They are too large for Helen, so I couldn't give them to her—besides, it looks so odd making presents of linen to one's sister. Hang me, if I know what to do! I love her better than she thinks—confound her!"

In the midst of his reflections, he felt some one touch him on the shoulder. He instantly recognized the countenance of Jack Towser, formerly of his regiment. But Jack Towser had very materially altered since they had last met. Formerly Jack Towser had been a great dandy; now he was most undoubtedly ragged. His hat was dented and coppery; his coat was as patched as a barge sail, and his boots opened and gaped like the shells of a dead oyster. The dashing Merton hunted with his eyes for Jack's shirt, but, even if he had drawn the cover of the closely-pinned waistcoat, it was doubtful whether any linen lay concealed beneath.

"Good Heaven, Jack!" cried Merton, "what is the matter?"

Jack had been a great fellow in his time. He drove a spanking curricle, and never wore a coat more than a fortnight. His tailors worked for him night and day. Jack used to worry cats to death with bull-dogs in his drawing-room and play blind-hookey for three days and nights at a time. Now his money was gone, his wits had returned, and he admitted he had been a great fool.

He told a mournful story about no dinners and no baccy. His former companion in arms understood the meaning of the complaint, and when they reached a deserted street took money from his purse. In the evening, Merton weeded his wardrobe, and carried round to Jack's garret a bundle of clothes that any dealer of cast-off apparel would have been happy to purchase for ten sovereigns.

This Jack Towser, in the days of his magnificence, had been a desperate admirer of the female sex. The captain could remember several wonderful stories that had been told at the mess-table of his extraordinary impudence and success. "He is the very man I have been wanting," thought Merton. "He knows nothing about Bertha, Mother Hazlewood, or her workhouse, neither need I mention how long I have been after her. By Jove! it seems like a providence, my meeting him."

Of an evening the captain would slip a bottle of brandy into his pocket and go round to Jack's, and smoke, drink, and chat. The quondam buck had descended from the roof to the ground-floor. After the third visit, Merton took Jack into his confidence. He told a long story about his meeting with Bertha in Kensington Gardens, some few weeks since, and detailed the conversation they had whilst he was following her home. He took great credit to himself for his tact in engaging rooms in her mother's house. He related many other imaginary incidents with such excessive minuteness, that Jack knew he was lying, although he was too clever to say as much, but only laughed, and vowed it did him good to hear such jolly stories. "She's a respectable girl, and deuced well educated, and that sort of thing," continued Merton, not so much on Bertha's account as his own. "I never saw any one so head over ears in love with a fellow as she is with me. Of course, it's her game to hook me into a marriage, and mine to fight shy of the business. And yet the rum thing is, she's ready to bolt with me whenever I like. What would you advise me to do?"

Such gentlemen as Jack Towser are not long in framing schemes, for their ideas are not governed by any delicacy of feeling, or the slightest respect for the person to be deceived. The night's conversation appeared to have led to a highly satisfactory result, for, on leaving, Merton squeezed his friend's hand warmly, and said, "I'm confoundedly obliged to you, old boy. Not a word to any one—keep it dark. And mind, it's a bargain. You help me in this little affair, and I'll stand a fifty."

All the captain's affection for Bertha now returned. He began once more to look in her face, and make strange noises in his throat. He asked her fifty times a day if she really loved him, and poured blessings on her head as she modestly blushed in reply. Then he inquired if she had carefully hidden away her wedding ring, and looked pleasantly sly as she assured him it was not lost. The love-sick maiden felt so light-hearted with joy that she seemed to walk on clouds. Her darling Merton was himself again. His beautiful smiles had returned to his handsome face. He was all goodness and truth.

Now the fond lover began to press his beloved with great importunity to name the day. He pretended to be seriously offended when she implored him to allow her to consult her mother. "What!" he cried, "this from you, Bertha, when you know, as well as I do, how important it is that our union should be kept secret? Would you ruin me, dearest angel? Surely it cannot make much difference whether your mother hears of our marriage a day sooner or later. Beautiful but imprudent girl, you wrong me, for this looks like suspicion."

But he teased her and allowed her no rest until the wedding day was fixed. All his arrangements were laid before her with an appearance of the greatest candour. They were to be united at the Registrar's Office. It was, he said, a much quieter and more sensible method than at the church. So as not to arouse the mother's suspicions, he was to quit Camberwell the day before. The next morning they were to meet. Her clothing was already at the lodgings in Harley Street. He would have everything ready for leaving London the moment after the ceremony. Then for years of happiness and delight—"eh, Bertha?"

Three days before the eventful morning, Merton received his father's letter, summoning him to Swanborough to protect the house and its inmates. He couldn't help laughing when he read the epistle. "Just the thing!" he thought. "I'll make it our wedding trip. Couldn't have happened better. There's a capital hotel at Elbury. I can leave her at the Royal George, and gallop over to the governor's, blow him up, and rush back again to Bertha."

Time flew on. Portmanteaus were packed, locked, and strapped, and Mr. Cutler was informed that for three weeks at least he might consider himself his own master. The cab was called, and off rattled the bridegroom.

He was the first at the rendezvous. With his watch in his hand, he waited impatiently for the fair one. He thrust his head frequently from the window, and cursed and swore as he looked anxiously up and down the road. At last she came, with tears in her eyes and with a face full of wretchedness, to implore of him to let her remain with her mother. He drew her into the cab, and, whispering an address to the cabman, ordered him to drive rapidly. The man saw that something "was up," and, dreaming of a little bit of gold, lashed his horse into full speed.

Presently the captain told Bertha they had reached the Registrar's Office. He alighted first, and inquired if Mr. Towser was at home.

She hesitated to leave the cab, but in a snappish voice he bade her make haste, saying that these public officials did not like to be kept waiting. So she was introduced to Mr. Towser, the Registrar, a thin gentleman with a dissipated face, but solemnly clothed in black. He also wore a white neckcloth and steel spectacles.

"Crosier! Crosier!" repeated the Registrar, as if the name was familiar to him, and at the same time hunting over his books. "Perfectly correct, sir. The notice was left with me three weeks since," he added, as if reading an entry. "Is this the lady?" he asked, raising his solemn face. When Bertha had faintly smiled in answer, he continued, "Then we had better commence the ceremony at once. Step this way."

For fear Bertha should refuse to put faith in the excessively short ceremonial known as a marriage before the Registrar, the captain had cunningly purchased a law-book on the subject, and, to prepare her mind, had not only shown her the printed description of the rite, but even made her read the words out loud. The couple were ushered into a front drawing-room, in one corner of which was a desk. Then, looking fearfully solemn, Jack Towser proceeded to business. First, the captain had to declare that he, Merton Crosier, was anxious to make her, Bertha Hazlewood, his wedded wife, and also to declare that he knew of no just cause or impediment why he, Merton Crosier, should be thwarted in his desires. The poor girl, who felt as if her tongue was withered, was made to repeat that she, Bertha Hazlewood, was equally anxious to be united to him, Merton Crosier. Finally, Mr. Jack Towser, turning up his eyes from excess of zeal, solemnly declared that the two were tightly joined together; and, with the signing of names in a big book with a red cover, the ceremony was declared to be at an end. It made Bertha start when Mr. Jack Towser. in his gruff voice, addressed her as Mrs. Crosier. She also noticed that when Merton paid the Registrar his fees, it was with a note for £50, and she could not help thinking how much more expensive it was to be married in that quiet manner than at the church by the regular process. It did both their hearts good to hear the Registrar wish them a pleasant honeymoon. He spoke in such an affectionate manner, hoping that their lives would be one long sunny holiday, undisturbed by the slightest conceivable cloud, and praying that their family would grow up around them, a blessing to their parents and a glory to the nation. He was only checked in his benedictions by the captain inquiring when the marriage certificates would be made out and ready for him. "How very considerate of dear Merton," thought Bertha, who was extremely desirous of possessing documentary evidence of her lawful union. The papers were to be prepared and waiting by the time they returned from their wedding trip.

They drove down to the railway station. She was so flurried and so supremely happy, that it seemed as if the hobbling old cab-horse flew over the ground with lightning speed, so rapidly did the time pass. They held each other by the hand, and, whenever her companion muttered "darling Bertha," she sighed "dearest Merton."

Seated in the railway carriage, this scoundrel felt his soul shrink up within him as he calmly contemplated his villainy. She, poor unhappy victim, was unconsciously smiling on him, worshipping with her eyes the generous man who, forgetting her humbleness and his own grandeur, could raise her to the dignity of his wife. He could not for some time talk to her. If it had been possible, he would, at that moment, have let her go unharmed, but by some curious fatality it would seem as if these virtuous impulses only enter the heart at the exact time when it is impossible to comply with them.

Encouraging himself with the consoling thought that it was now too late to back out of the business, and that he must go through with it as best he could, he placed his arm round her waist and began to chat most amiably. He warned her, in a tender voice which seemed to deny his words, that occasionally, perhaps twice or thrice a year, they might have quarrels and disputes. He tried to convince her that he was now and then irritable. He went so far as to confess that he was at times overbearing and exacting. "But, my dearest angel," he continued, " you will soon teach me to be a better man. When you see that I am inclined to quarrel, you will conquer me by your amiability. We shall live so happily that all the world will be envious of our great joy. My pretty little wife shall be the envy of the men, and all the women shall bite their nails with vexation that they have not married such a constant, doting husband, as I shall prove—eh, Bertha ? "

Then the silly girl began to chatter about the future. "Never, dear Merton," she said, "let us have any secrets away from each other. Whatever you may do, I will forgive you, if you will confide in me. It would break my heart, dear, if I thought you considered me unworthy to be trusted, because it would seem as if you had withdrawn your love from me."

"Blessed angel ! " exclaimed Crosier, in a rapture, "how can you suspect me of ever deceiving you ? I promise you that you shall share every thought. I will take no important step in life without previously consulting you. Your advice shall have more influence over me than even my own judgment. Does that calm your fears, my beautiful little wife ? " They smiled with superlative fondness, and gazed on each other's eyes for an unusually long time.

"I shall be so jealous of you, Bertha," sighed Crosier, as he felt his sight grow misty. "Already I hate men, because I know they will admire you. I was foolish to marry such a pretty wife."

Is it to be wondered at if the poor child had no suspicion of the infamous cheat that had been plotted against her honour ?

When the journey was about half over, it suddenly struck the captain that the name of Crosier was one very well known to the inhabitants of Elbury. It would never do, he considered, to take Bertha to the first hotel in the town and style her Mrs. Crosier. The old man would be sure to hear of it, or some busybody would certainly carry to his sister Helen the news that her brother was married. That would about blow up the whole business. If his name had not been painted in huge white letters on the waterproof coverings of his portmanteaus, he would have assumed a false one. It was very awkward, indeed.

In the first place, there is a certain delight and importance in being able to talk of "my wife," which he was sorry to miss. It seemed like talking of his property. It was a hundredfold better than speaking of "my groom" or "my horses." He was fond of that. He longed to be able to ask waiters and chambermaids "whether Mrs. Crosier had ordered dinner?" or if "Mrs. Crosier had arranged about the apartments?" But, hard as it was to forego this self-glorification, he felt he must defer the enjoyment until they left Elbury.

He showed Bertha the letter he had received from his father, and told her that, as they would pass within a few miles of Swanborough, he would leave her at an hotel whilst he paid a visit to his parent and laughed him out of his fears. It wouldn't take long, he promised, for the old gentleman was as sensible as a bench of bishops put together, and would soon listen to reason. "In the meantime, dearest," he continued, nervously, "I think it would be better—not that I care much—although, until the proper time arrives for declaring ourselves, it is a highly prudent measure—it would be better, my love, for you to go by an assumed name. I can say you are a Mrs. Tattenham, whom I am escorting to Southampton. It will only be for a short time. I shall only be away for about three hours, and then we can take a post-chaise and hurry on to the next town. Do you object to this, my darling?"

She did object, and felt hurt at the proposition. It struck her as being odd that within so short a date of their union it should be necessary for her to forego her husband's name. But then she suddenly remembered that this was not the first time he had warned her it was necessary the marriage should be kept secret, and with as much good nature as she could summon, she consented to his wishes.

The waiters at the Royal George danced about with remarkable activity when Captain Crosier's trunks were handed down from the railway fly. Mine host turned out to attend to the rich banker's son. A handsome sitting-room was ordered for Mrs. Tattenham, and a decanter of sherry and some biscuits were placed before the travellers. The landlord seemed quite wounded in his feelings when he heard the captain only intended remaining in Elbury for a few hours. He said he would have exerted himself to the utmost to make his stay agreeable. "Why, you silly fellow," replied the captain, "if I went anywhere I should put up at Swanborough. There's plenty of room there. I'm escorting Mrs. Tattenham to Southampton, or you wouldn't have seen me. As it is, I've only just time to eat a hurried dinner, so pray consult with Mrs. Tattenham about what there is in the house fit to be eaten."

"I wish he wouldn't call me Mrs. Tattenham," thought Bertha. "It makes me feel cold all over, as if something were going to happen. I shall be glad when we leave the place."

They dined at three o'clock, to allow Crosier plenty of time to make his visit to his father. It was a pleasant repast, not so much on account of the viands the host provided as for the loving conversation which they held. Had any inquisitive waiter been listening at the keyhole, the secret of the supposed marriage would soon have been discovered. The captain invariably addressed the imaginary Mrs. Tattenham by such endearing terms as "my life," "my love," or "my sweetest pet." The matter under discussion was of a monetary character. The gallant officer hinted that possibly Mrs. Crosier would occasionally find that a little cash was useful, and informed her that she was to consider his purse as her own. "I would not hurt your feelings, my darling, by doing as most men do, for I consider it a most blackguardly and impertinent thing to allowance your wife so much weekly. It seems to me like paying wages. No, my sweet lamb, remember that whatever I have is yours." This singular gentleman felt a great delight in mimicking the ways of a lawful husband. With a delicacy that pierced clean through Bertha's heart, he took from his pocket his own purse, and handed it over to her, crammed as it was with notes, saying, "That for the future she should be the banker." But he could not help the thought crossing his mind that it would be excessively easy to check this unbounded trust at any moment he liked. "Does good now, and soon stopped by-and-by, when we are more intimate, and she grows extravagant," he repeated to himself.

A horse was ordered, and the captain rode away, his fine military figure looking most imposing, as he turned round in his saddle to wave his hand to his beautiful Bertha. The three hours he was to have been absent passed. Then she went to the window again to watch for his return, and stood there, poor little thing, for another three hours, until it was so dark she could not see ten yards down the road; but she listened very industriously. In vain did the waiter enter the room to know if "Mrs. Tattenham" would have tea served. The same answer was constantly given, "No, I thank you. Captain Crosier intends leaving Elbury the moment he returns." Nine o'clock struck, and her nervousness was such that the slamming of a door was enough to make her burst into tears. At last, the waiter again entered, with a letter and bunch of keys on the silver salver. She almost guessed what the note was about, even before she read it. "My pretty darling," it began, "the people here are mad, and the old man worse than any one. He swore at me, and commanded me not to leave the house. I was obliged to obey him, for not only is he my father, but worth at least a couple of hundred thousand. Queer way of beginning our honeymoon, isn't it? Never mind, sweetest. I send the keys. Go to bed, and have breakfast ready by eight, for I shall have my arm round your waist by that hour."

By eleven o'clock, a pair of interesting small bottines were placed outside Mrs. Tattenham's bedroom door. The "Boots" could only just find room enough on the soles to chalk the number of the chamber.

CHAPTER XXIII.

MR. VAUTRIN, JUN., VISITS THE CONTINENT.

To a gentleman with nothing to do but to try and make the time between breakfast and dinner pass as rapidly as possible, a daily newspaper is invaluable assistance. He feels as if the doings of the entire globe were put in evidence before him. His arm-chair becomes a judgment-seat, and he frowns with sternness over the tripping and backsliding of his brother and sister millions. For fourpence daily he shares with cats the privilege of looking kings in the face. Ministers and members of Parliament are as fearlessly criticized as dinner, port, and sherry.

In this innocent manner did Lieutenant Grant, R.N., indulge himself. Now he was a police magistrate, a Jardine or an Elliott, seated in the judgment arm-chair of Bow Street or Lambeth. Wives stabbed by husbands, scandalous cases of fraud, etc., etc., were brought before him. As he read the reports, he felt as if the fines and committals were his doing. Or, if he took pleasure in continental news, he could, with the turn of an eye, enter the Tuileries as easily as if he were the Emperor himself, or attend a meeting of ministers in the Queen of Spain's audience-chamber. "Bless my heart," the R.N. would sometimes exclaim, "another change of ministry in Greece. Confound the fellows! they are always changing." And yet the lieutenant cared no more for Greece and its rulers than you do for the sea-slug soup of the Chinese, but he paid fourpence daily for his newspaper, and felt bound to offer his opinion on the events of the day.

"Enjoying your paper, papa?" the mild-voiced Lucy would ask, as her parent finished the last column in the last page.

"Nothing in it—positively nothing," would be the answer, although the journal invariably contained some twenty yards of closely-printed matter.

The brave R.N. was also a constant subscriber to the local newspaper. It gave him pleasure to support a journal printed, as it were, under his very nose. He had a confused notion that he was assisting a neighbour and encouraging his own speculation. Frequently, after reading the leading articles of the Elbury newspaper, he would burst into a fit of swearing, and strike the table till it hopped, declaring, between his oaths and blows, that "the fellows on the little journal wrote infinitely better than the chaps in the 'Times.'" To such an extent did his enthusiasm carry him, that on one occasion he insisted on reading aloud to Phil the remarks made by the editor upon the discovery just then made, that an alarming quantity of forged notes had within the last year been circulated in the country.

"By jingo! if the rogues see this, it ought to make them tremble in their confounded boots," roared the R.N., as he began to spout the leader. "'The audacity with which this gang has proceeded in its infamous work, the nicety with which the spurious notes have been passed away, the curious completeness of the imitation, all prove that the villain who has organized this cruel robbery is a man of vast attainments—one who has degraded the blessings of education by converting them into the means of base and cowardly plunder.' What do you think of that, Phil? That's good outspeaking, eh?"

The young rogue who heard these words did tremble, if not in his boots, at least in his slippers. He felt his nerves and courage give way as he further heard that a local committee of inquiry had been instituted, at the head of which was Mr. Nathaniel Crosier, the respected banker.

"We'll soon have the ruffian," roared the lieutenant with glee.

The route which the utterer had taken was ingeniously traced. The towns through which he had passed were known by the victims he had left behind. He had advanced to within a few miles of Elbury, but as yet that town had not been visited with any calamity. Even the house of Crosier and Company had been deceived and accepted the notes as genuine, so excellently had the Bank of England paper been imitated.

No one was louder in his denunciation of the culprit than the culprit himself. By shouting with the mob he hoped to escape its notice. The more alarmed he became the more lustily he inveighed against the forgers. He even delivered his opinion as to the punishment he should like to inflict upon the rascals. Little did the tippling father-in-law think, as he applauded Phil's assumed virtuous indignation, that the real culprit sat scarcely the length of a policeman's arm from his side.

Unfortunate Lucy often told Phil in the morning that he had been throwing his arms about in his sleep, and tossing in the bed like a man with a fever. Then he would inquire anxiously if he had talked any nonsense in his dreams. "I should think you did," the unsuspecting wife would reply; "but you mumbled and jumbled your words up so that I could not understand a syllable. But I'll have a good laugh at you some of these fine mornings and discover all your secrets."

Under these distressing circumstances, it seemed to Phil that the wisest thing he could do would be to retire from Elbury for a short time. The police, with Nathaniel Crosier at their back, were almost at the threshold of his hiding-place, and he had lost all power over himself, so that even the gabblings of his waking moments might convict him. But he was not so foolish as to decamp and arouse suspicion by his flight. He waited three or four anxious days, pondering over a sensible excuse for packing up his trunks. At last, he saw advertised in the "Times" an announcement of some cheap excursion to Paris to view some fete or other. The subscribers were to be carried, housed, and fed, for something less than the ordinary railway fare. Instantly Philip began to talk with Lucy about Paris. He dilated on its pleasures; reminded her that all the fashions came from there; asked her if she liked French cooking, or preferred French boots and gloves; and hinted at Lyons velvet and cheap clocks, until at last he imbued her with so strong a desire to visit the capital of the polite, that she began to calculate the expense of the trip, and to prove that the cost would be a mere nothing.

Like a good-natured, kind-hearted husband, Phil first laughed at his little wife's entreaties, and gradually acceded to them. "She has set her heart upon this excursion, sir," he remarked to the not over-pleased lieutenant, "and I suppose I must let her have her own way. See what we poor husbands have to suffer. I shall just let her have a wine-glass of claret and a sniff at a French kitchen, and then bring her back again with a whole nosegay of roses on her pretty cheeks."

With sorrow in his heart, the lieutenant, having written to a maiden sister to come and keep him company in his solitude, saw the young couple depart. He grew more and more depressed when the pony-chaise, with the trunks behind, turned the corner of the road and disappeared. Nothing but the knowledge that he had the key of the sideboard in his pocket supported his drooping heart. The only consolation he felt was in following the route of his children almost step by step, on their way to the French capital. "Now," he thought, "they are in London. I wonder at which hotel they are staying? I wish I had told them to go to the Chesterfield, in Bruton Street. They might have tasted the '34 port." The next morning, he considerably annoyed his spinster relation by arousing her from a steady doze, to ask her opinion as to whether the sea was likely to be rough across the Channel? "I should enjoy a good toss, you know," he shouted, through the half-opened door, "but I'm afraid poor Lucy will be half killed."

By the time Phil and his wife reached Paris, the old lieutenant wished sincerely in his heart that his daughter were back home again. But not so the young husband. He drew forth his purse, and, showing Lucy the sixty sovereigns that constituted his fortune, informed her she must manage somehow or other to make them last for at least six months. She stared with wonder, for the poor thing thought they had journeyed for pleasure. He mumbled out some excuse about being in debt, and wishing to economize by living cheaply in France. He had not courage enough to tell her he had fled to escape shame and punishment.

CHAPTER XXIV.

A BED OF THORNS.

THE house was well protected when Nathaniel Crosier retired to rest. The men-servants had pistols within arms' reach; the big dogs were wandering about the gardens; and, above all, the brave soldier-son was to sleep in the spare bed. He would be a determined thief, indeed, that dared to face the gallant captain on the second-floor front.

He would have given a hat full of sovereigns, that loving, martial youth, if he could have escaped from the parental roof, and flown on the swift wings of love to the side of the adored Bertha. But he was a captive. Iron bars do not make a prison, but a stern father's iron will grate up every door and window. He had struggled hard for his liberty, sifting his miserable pate for the merest attempt at an excuse to be freed from his dungeon. The old gentleman had been forced to frown and talk loudly; he had been obliged to say cutting things about the ingratitude of sons; and eventually, when all entreaties had failed, to shout out imperative commands that his first-born should remain beneath his roof. There had been quite a scene. When at length the unhappy son yielded, he did so with a heart-broken air, which the papa was quite unable to account for. It almost seemed to him as if Merton wished the house to be broken into and pillaged.

About eleven o'clock, the old gentleman jumped into his bed, and, feeling secure under the protection of one of Her Majesty's officers, made up for previous nights of restlessness by falling to sleep with wondrous rapidity.

The unhappy Merton stayed up until two in the morning, gazing at the moon, and mourning over his miseries, until sighing changed to yawning, and he determined on burying his grief between the blankets. A snore of rich tone and volume soon gave proof that the blotting-paper of oblivion had dried up his tears of anguish.

The banker dreamed. He was seated in his office, and a man, who years ago had failed, owing him a large sum of money, entered the room, carrying a heavy box. He had a confused idea that this man had long since died and had no right to be walking the earth, but he was not frightened by the visit. The debtor told him he had at last come to clear off his liabilities, and pointed to the ponderous chest. They had a long chat about bygone times, and then the lid of the box was raised. There was gold enough to fill a wheelbarrow. In the handsomest manner, the man begged of the banker to accept it all. Together they tried to move the treasure, but it seemed fixed as to the ground by its weight. Yet the man had before carried it easily as a bandbox. It seemed to old Crosier that he pushed and

pushed at this chest until his hands bled, but it was only inch by
inch that it yielded to his exertions. He called for his clerks to help
him, but no one came. Then, without any cause or reason, it seemed
to him that he was no longer in his office, but standing with the heavy
chest on a hill not far from Swanborough. The treasure slipped
from him and fell rolling down the declivity. With each revolution
the money rattled as if it would burst asunder the wooden sides of
the chest. It bumped over ditches and dashed against stones with
an explosive noise. As he stood wringing his hands in despair, some
one touched him on the shoulder, and——he awoke.

At first, in the confusion of drowsiness, he knew that a human
being was standing by the bedside, but he never for one second
thought of robbers. Gradually as his brain settled itself and his
eyes opened, he became aware that no one had authority at such
an hour, in the dead of night, to shake him from his slumbers. He
half raised himself from his pillow, and mumbled out, "What is it?
Who are you?"

The answer made his eyes start open with sudden terror. "If you
dare to move or call for assistance I will dash your brains out." The
banker stared, and thought it prudent to obey, for a heavy life-preserver, that carried an ugly conviction of danger in its manufacture,
was placed within six inches of his skull. A twist of the wrist and
he was a dead man.

The robber threw the light of a dark lantern full upon old Crosier's
face, and seemed to be examining his features. The banker submitted
to all this passively, his mind busy in thinking whether the burglars
would be able to find out the strong-room where the plate was kept.
He felt resigned to the loss of such stray silver as was in daily use.
He knew exactly the value of everything on the premises. In an
iron chest let into the wall of his dressing-room there was a bundle
of notes, for which he trembled. A table stood before the metal door
of this chest, and sincerely did the old man pray that it might escape
detection.

The strong light of the lantern was removed, and the banker, as he
lay, looked round him. The drawers had been forced, and his clothing
scattered about. "It was the noise of bursting the locks that made
me dream," thought the old man, as calmly as if he were in a police-
court. Somebody, who knew the premises well, formed one of the
robber band, for a secret drawer in which the old man kept his dear
wife's jewels had been opened, and the red morocco caskets were evidently ransacked. He saw all this, yet there he lay helpless, fearing
even to breathe too loudly, lest the bludgeon above him should
descend upon his grey head with a deadly stroke.

The minutes fled slowly. His watch beneath his pillow throbbed,
and appeared almost to shake his head with its vibrating. He was
gaining courage in the silence, and meditating upon the policy of
leaping suddenly from the bed and alarming the house. The only
thing which restrained him was the idea that possibly Merton was as

strongly guarded as himself. Much as he loved money, he loved his life better.

The man by the bedside moved. He drew the heavy curtains back, and leaned over the bed until his crape-covered face was so close to that of the banker, that the latter could distinguish the glowing eyes beneath the heavy mask, and see the beads of condensed breath on the fibres. The robber gazed at him attentively, and then, more as if speaking to himself, said, "The same as ever. I should have known him anywhere. You wear well, old man. Yours must have been an easy battle with the world if wrinkles are to be counted as scars."

"Thank God! I shall be able to swear to his voice," thought Crosier.

"Do you know me P" asked the robber.

The banker tried to say "No," but his throat and lips were dry with fear, yet the man understood by the mere movement of the mouth what was meant.

"Have you no enemy in the world who would like to play you such a trick as this P Come, think!" continued the ruffian. "Try and call to mind the name of someone who hates you; of one who would work his fingers down to the knuckles to ruin you; who would pray or curse if his breath could blight you."

The banker shook his head.

"Turn back that memory of yours," snarled the ruffian. "Think of olden times. Have you wronged no one P Is there no blood on your hands P Do you expect no vengeance P"

The old man thought of the daughter that had died in prison, but he grew dogged at being so roughly questioned, and still shook his head.

The ruffian began to lose his temper. He breathed quickly with rage, and leaned closer and closer over the bedside. "By G—!" he cried, "I could tear that strong heart of yours from your withered bosom, since it feels so little, and knows no repentance. Look at me, man! Now do you know me P" As he said this, he lifted up his mask of crape, and scowled upon his prostrate victim.

"Vautrin," murmured Crosier, in a tone so devoid of astonishment that it was evident he had long ago recognized his tormentor.

"It is some time since we last met," Vautrin said, in a calm tone. "Perhaps you never reckoned on seeing me again. I dare say you have often prayed I might leave the earth and make more room for you. Foolish old man. Many a night have I stood before this house, and, whilst you slept comfortably, sworn to have this meeting. You were the master then. I was not prepared. Now I am the better man." Each of these short sentences was accompanied by a different gesture, quickly changed, but all energetic and threatening.

The man's vehemence prevented the banker from collecting his thoughts. The finger pointed close to his face, the fist shaken before his eyes frightened away his ideas. He could plan no means to escape punishment, and felt he was in the Frenchman's power.

"I have come to settle our long accounts," continued Vautrin. "I will begin with system. First, where is my wife—your daughter?"

No answer was given.

"Where is her child—my son?" hissed Vautrin, bringing his mouth so close to the banker's face that the breath made the grey hairs flutter. "Where are they? Answer me, or, by the Heavens above! it is your last chance of ever speaking again."

"She died," was all the old man had strength to reply.

"You killed her," quickly retorted Vautrin. "She was your daughter. The life in her came from you, and you murdered her. If I offended you by making her my wife, was she the less your child? I was honest then! If she preferred my chances in the world to your wealth and power, did that rid you of a parent's duties? You beast, it was your hand that slew her. Shall I tell you how and where she died?"

The old man was wondering to himself how this Vautrin, after his cruel desertion of his wife, had the boldness to refer so calmly to her death. As he did not reply to the question, the other continued :—

"She died in prison, of a broken heart, praying God to forgive you that most wicked murder."

The words sounded harshly in the old man's ear, and he shuddered. There was biting truth in them, and it gnawed at his heart. "I tried to save her," he gasped.

"Old man," snarled Vautrin, "as you hope for heaven, do not bar its entrance with lies. If the daughter was beyond your aid, why was the child cast aside? You have your excuse! I know it. You fudged up a report that your daughter was a mother, but not a wife. Not contented with her life, you took away her honour as well. You defiled her grave with your unjust wickedness. Where is that boy —my son?" As he asked this, Vautrin ground his teeth and shook his open hands over Crosier's face.

"That boy was turned loose upon the world. Your flesh and blood, sir, has been within a finger's length of the hangman's grip. Now I come to you for justice. Years ago you knew that boy was lawfully begotten. He has told me of your offers to ship him away from England, and, like so much rubbish, shoot him into the waste ground of Australia."

"What do you want?" asked Crosier. "Is it money?"

The son-in-law looked at the old man with contempt. Then, with an assumed nobleness of manner, he said, "How you have loved this money. For it you sent a daughter to a felon's prison; to save your gold, a grandson was apprenticed to roguery and crime. Even now, when your life is mine, you call your money to the rescue, and think to escape."

Despite this virtuous harangue, the banker knew well enough the object of Vautrin's visit.

"I have come, sir," said the man, "for my money, and not for yours. I am not the robber—I am the victim seeking justice against the thief. This is my law court. Six months ago your wife died. You knew my son was lawfully begotten. Even the marriage certificate was shown you. Why was he defrauded of his inheritance? Answer me that." The threatening manner in which the thick fingers closed around the bludgeon made Crosier tremble. He saw the hand grow white as the violent straining of the grip forced the blood away.

Hurriedly he replied, "Yes, I was wrong. I admit it. He shall be righted. I swear it."

"I give you three weeks," added Vautrin, "and, if by then you do not fulfil your word, you die. That is my oath."

"Be it so. I agree," the banker cried, eagerly.

"Now give me the key of your iron chest," Vautrin continued. "You forgot to present your daughter with a marriage portion, when I took her as my wife. You used to keep your money in that safe. Whatever it contains I will accept as the forgotten dower."

A hope crossed the banker's mind. He would arise, and, whilst appearing to comply with Vautrin's order, make so much noise that he should alarm the house, and bring the servants to his aid. First, he began to cough, pretending that the cold, after he left the warm bed, affected his lungs. Then, as he went shivering to the. dressing-room, where the iron safe stood, he upset a chair and knocked against a table. An old hand like Vautrin was not to be easily deceived. He observed mildly to the banker, "You had better transact this business quietly. I have friends downstairs. If any one attempted to enter this room, do you know what I should do?—kill you!" The hand of the banker shook, as he tried to place the big key in the lock of his chest. The heavy door, as it opened, did not groan more than did the unfortunate victim's spirit. The robber stood over him, and ordered him to pull out paper after paper. "Make haste, sir," growled Vautrin. "You have notes here. I advise you to find them rapidly."

It was a heavy bundle, thick as a roll of ribbons. It made Vautrin's waistcoat pocket bulge out as if he carried his handkerchief there. He knew by the banker's face that the amount was heavy. His good humour returned. He remarked in a pleasant tone, "We have not finished yet, but in a few minutes you shall be rid of me. You must sign this paper." He drew forth a stamped document. "A little legal affair," explained the rogue, "stating that, in consideration of your affection for me, you have, of your own free will, presented me with the amount of these notes. I will fill in the amount to-morrow, when I have reckoned it up. I thought it would prevent any after unpleasantness. Now to bed again. Fulfil your oath, and I'll promise never to trouble you again." He blew out the night-light, placed his lantern in his pocket, and withdrew, locking the door after him.

Very quietly did Crosier remain in his bed, listening to catch some sound indicating the departure of the robbers. He struck his repeater frequently, to learn how the time passed. He was perfectly astonished to find that what he considered at least half an hour was only a few minutes. The house was so silent, that he had misgivings whether he might not be the only living man in it.

At last, he found courage to ring the bell. He pulled at it until the wire stretched and looped from the ceiling. Then came a quick footstep, and a voice asked if master wanted anything. "Unlock the door," was the hasty command. The footman, with his coat slipped over his night-dress, stared in wonder, as the excited Crosier told him that thieves had broken into the house and stripped the place. The servant looked in amazement on the disordered room and forced drawers, and believing after he had seen, set up a shout for help that caused the bedroom doors to open and inquiries to be made with marvellous rapidity.

Where was the gallant soldier that should have guarded the citadel? The father flew upstairs to seek the bold son, calling out passionately for the sluggard to arise. But his angry voice ceased suddenly. He saw a form lying full length across the passage, and in an instant felt that it was his child.

The servants heard the old man whine and sob, and hurried to his help. The lifeless body of the first-born was raised and carried to the bed. Whilst father and sister mourned over the corpse, men were galloping on swift horses to summon doctors from far and near, and other half-dressed domestics ran through the village, shouting for help and the police.

Soon the house was crowded with constables and surgeons. The pulse was felt; eyes exchanged sad glances; and the lancet-cases were returned to the pocket. The men of science retired and left the case to the men of the law. There was no hope, unless it was for vengeance on the slayer.

CHAPTER XXV.

ACCOUNTS ARE SETTLED.

THERE was one poor creature connected with that unhappy family who, all unconscious of evil, rose cheerfully from her bed, thankful that the daylight had returned again to send her dear Merton to her side. He would be there at eight, she thought. Two hours more of patient waiting, and his arm would be round her waist, and his lips on her cheek. He had promised it.

The sad news came harshly upon her. Had the people of the hotel known how dearly she loved that wretched man, they would have dribbled out the miserable tidings so that she might have guessed at her sorrow. But to them she was merely Mrs. Tattenham, a friend of the dead captain.

The landlord undertook to carry up the intelligence. He rather liked the office. He gave strict orders to the waiters not to speak a word. He would manage the business.

Whilst the breakfast-cloth was being laid, Bertha stood watching at the window. She desired the waiters "not to bring up the eggs" until Captain Crosier arrived. They answered, "Yes, mum," in their usual tone, but could not help strange thoughts passing through their minds.

The landlord made his appearance. Bertha wondered what he could have to say to her, and listened coldly to the remarks he passed upon the weather. At length he coughed and commenced the speech he had prepared. "Sad affair that, last night, ma'am, at Swanborough. They say Mr. Nathaniel Crosier is nearly out of his mind." She listened inquiringly. "You have not heard of the robbery, then, ma'am? They broke in about two this morning, and, I am told, carried off an amazing quantity of things." Having reached this climax of his news, the landlord coughed again, and hesitatingly said, " I hope you will not give way, ma'am—or allow your feelings to —overcome you, but no hopes are entertained of Captain Crosier's recovery—in fact, he is no more."

Poor Bertha!

They put her to bed, and the same doctors who in the morning had stood around the dead body of Merton Crosier were now consulting over the almost lifeless form of the girl he would have ruined. She lay without consciousness for two days. The women of the house came often to the bed and spoke to her, but not a limb was moved in answer. The doctors sighed when they felt her pulse, and then said such things as: " Life is trembling in the scale," and " We must

trust to Nature; that is our only chance." The nurse had
stringent orders to force open the lips, and drop ether into the
mouth. "Miss one half-hour," said the medical gentleman, "and she
dies."

The inquest on Merton Crosier's body took place. The surgeons
who performed the post-mortem examination gave it as their opinion
that the deceased had died from disease of the heart, accelerated
by excitement. One man, when he read this verdict of the jury, drew
a deep sigh, as if a heavy load were taken off his shoulders. The
fellow called Tater-trap Sam knew more than the doctors. He
remembered very well the struggle that had taken place on the
landing, and how he held a thick cloth to the dead man's
mouth to smother his cries. It is possible that the captain died of
a diseased heart, but Tater-trap Sam was certainly the accelerating
cause.

Three days after the funeral, a lady in deep mourning insisted upon
seeing Mr. Nathaniel Crosier. He repeatedly sent word he wished
to be private, and could not be disturbed in his affliction: but the
visitor was stubborn. Finding that her entreaties were of no avail,
she called for pen and paper, and on the hall-table wrote a letter,
which she signed "Your daughter—Bertha Crosier." She was
admitted.

He pitied her because she wept so bitterly, and therefore listened
patiently to her story. His quick brain soon understood the part
his son had acted. The private marriage at the Registrar's, and
Merton's disinclination to introduce his bride into his father's family,
were sufficient for the banker to guess the remainder of the romance.
But he was softened by the loss of his well-beloved son. He had the
mercy not to undeceive the poor girl. "She is virtuous, and, Heaven
be praised, unharmed," he thought. "Why sully the memory of my
unfortunate boy?"

"Did dear Merton leave any will?" he inquired, in the gentlest
tone he could utter.

When he heard of the will drawn up whilst the knowing soldier was
courting her at her mother's house, and in which Bertha Hazlewood
was left sole possessor of whatever her lover might at his death
possess, the father rejoiced greatly, for now he foresaw there would
be no occasion to disturb the secrecy of the deceit.

. . . .

The banker kept the promise he made Vautrin. He summoned
up all his courage, and, although he cursed and swore as he made
over the moneys to his grandson, managed to sign the deed. His
hatred to Vautrin extended to the man's offspring; indeed, it was
only when he learned that at the time of the burglary Philip was in
Paris, and could not, therefore, be inculpated in the robbery, that he
considered himself justified in fulfilling his oath.

The news of this inheritance had already been communicated to the young man by his own father, whom he had met lounging on the Boulevards, dressed in a style of fashion which, as a man of fortune, he was entitled to assume. The roll of notes had done what nothing else, in the opinion of the world, could have done—made a gentleman of a scoundrel.

THE END.

GILBERT & RIVINGTON, LD., ST. JOHN'S HOUSE, CLERKENWELL, E.C.

www.ingramcontent.com/pod-product-compliance
Lightning Source LLC
Chambersburg PA
CBHW031817270326
41932CB00008B/459